HORROR!

THIS IS A CARLTON BOOK

This edition published in 2013
by Carlton Books Limited
20 Mortimer Street
London W1T 3JW

10 9 8 7 6 5 4 3 2 1

First published in 2006

Text © Carlton Books Ltd 2006, 2010, 2013
Design © Carlton Books Ltd 2010, 2013

A CIP catalogue record for this book is available from
the British Library.

ISBN 978 1 78097 391 3

Editors: Lorna Russell, Penny Craig, Alice Payne
Designers: Gulen Shevki-Taylor and Anna Pow
Picture Research: Paul Langan and Steve Behan
Production: Dawn Cameron

Printed in Dubai

HORROR!

THE DEFINITIVE COMPANION TO THE MOST TERRIFYING MOVIES EVER MADE

KIM NEWMAN & JAMES MARRIOTT

CARLTON
BOOKS

CONTENTS

CONTRIBUTORS

[JC] John Coulthart's work as an artist, illustrator and designer has appeared on record sleeves, CD and DVD packages for Hawkwind, Cradle of Filth, Alan Moore & Tim Perkins, Steven Severin and Fourth World music pioneer Jon Hassell. His work in the publishing world has included book designs and cover illustrations for Savoy Books, Pan Macmillan, Granta and Random House. As a comic artist he produced the notorious Lord Horror series Reverbstorm with David Britton for Savoy Books, and his collection of Lovecraft adaptations and illustrations, *The Haunter of the Dark and other Grotesque Visions*, was republished by Creation Books in 2006. He lives and works in Manchester, England.

[SJ] Stephen Jones is the winner of three World Fantasy Awards, three Horror Writers Association Bram Stoker Awards and three International Horror Guild Awards, as well as being a Hugo Award nominee and a 16-times recipient of the British Fantasy Award. One of Britain's most acclaimed anthologists of horror and dark fantasy, he has written more than eighty books including *The Hellraiser Chronicles, Clive Barker's A-Z of*

Horror and *The Essential Monster Movie Guide*. A contributor to *The Encyclopedia of Fantasy, The BFI Companion to Horror and Supernatural Literature of the World: An Encyclopedia*, you can visit his web site at www.herebedragons.co.uk/jones

[RL] Rebecca Levene has been a writer and editor for 15 years. In that time she has storylined *Emmerdale*, written a children's book about Captain Cook, a science-fiction novel and the *Beginner's Guide to Poker* as well as editing a range of media tie-in books. She was associate producer on the ITV1 drama *Wild at Heart*, story consultant on the Chinese soap opera *Joy Luck Street*, scriptwriter on *Family Affairs* and *Is Harry on the Boat?* and was part of the writing team for Channel 5's *Swinging*. She has reviewed numerous films for a number of magazines and is the author of a horror novel based on the *Final Destination* films.

[KS] Kerri Sharp is a London-born film school graduate with a particular interest in art, writing and cinema that explores the unconscious, confronts the lunatic gloom of patriarchal religion and disrupts the bourgeois order. Buñuel, Lynch and Clouzot are her cinematic heroes, and dark, disquieting fairy tales her inspiration. She is co-editor of *Inappropriate Behaviour* (Serpent's Tail, 2002) and the author of *The Black Lace Book of Women's Sexual Fantasies*.

[ST] Stephen Thrower is the author of *Beyond Terror: The Films of Lucio Fulci* and editor of *The Eyeball Compendium*. His *Nightmare USA: The Untold Story of the Exploitation Independents* delves into the hinterlands of American exploitation. As a musician, he works with Cyclobe, Nurse with Wound, The Amal Gamal Ensemble and Matmos. He has also written for the following books: *Shock Xpress Vol.1* (ed. Stefan Jaworzyn); *The BFI Companion to Horror* (ed. Kim Newman); *Art of Darkness: the Cinema of Dario Argento* (ed. Chris Gallant, 2001); *The Flesh & Blood Compendium* (ed. Harvey Fenton); *Ten Years of Terror* (ed. Harvey Fenton); and the forthcoming *No Focus* (eds, Chris Barber & Jack Sargeant). As a long-term fan of Italian cinema, he bitterly envies anyone who discovers giallo films for the first time on crystal-clear, uncut DVD ...

[PT] Pete Tombs was born and grew up in London. His life was changed forever by a chance encounter with a werewolf called Waldemar Daninsky in a Dalston cinema. He later confessed all in the book *Immoral Tales* (with Cathal Tohill, 1995) and went on to compound the felony with *Mondo Macabro* (1998). He founded the video labels Pagan, Eurotika! and Mondo Macabro and now runs (together with Andy Starke) the production company Boum. He has co-written/directed/produced two series for Channel 4.

'Beginnings' and the introduction to each chapter are by Co-author Kim Newman.

All other unsigned contributions are by General Editor and Co-author James Marriott.

EDITOR'S NOTE

This book contains 333 film reviews, listed in chronological order. Each decade is prefaced by an introductory chapter putting the films in context, and the review sections also contain features that either explore the ideas behind horror's favourite monsters (**Ghosts**, **Vampires**) or introduce related fields of interest for the horror fan (**Giallo**, **Serial Killers**), alongside box entries on everything from **Dr Jekyll & Mr Hyde** to **H.P. Lovecraft**. The entries are designed to complement each other rather than duplicate information, and have been cross-referenced where necessary.

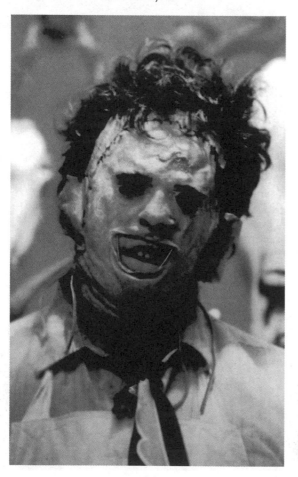

Films are listed by their original title in their country of origin, with a full list of alternate titles in the index. While this may prove confusing for English-language viewers more familiar with *The Bird with the Crystal Plumage* than **L'Uccello dalle Piume di Cristallo**, it seems the best way to handle films that, like Jorge Grau's Peak District zombie epic **No Profanar el Sueño de los Muertos**, boast five alternate titles.

Choosing which films to review here has not been an easy task. Horror is at once the most creative and most formulaic of genres, and I've used a milestones and mavericks policy of covering the key titles alongside entries that bring something new to the genre: innovations rather than sequels and remakes, with a few notable exceptions. While the emphasis is on feature films, relevant shorts and television films and series have been included, and the book also has an international scope: at least one film from every country with anything approaching a horror-film industry is covered, so you'll find little-seen gems from India and the Philippines nestling among better-known offerings from Japan and Italy.

Horror is, it seems to me, better defined by its effects – fear, shock, revulsion – than its iconography, effects often better served by films that sit on the edge of the genre or which are not generally considered genre items at all. This applies particularly to post-'80s cinema, and while the global horror renaissance has thrown up some indisputable modern classics, elsewhere the conventional trappings of genre – gothic castle, straight razor, shambling zombie – have proved less fruitful than prison bars (**Ghosts ... of the Civil Dead**) and SM clubs (**Irreversible**) in providing the true descendents of **Night of the Living Dead** and **The Texas Chain Saw Massacre**.

Horror criticism has often been bogged down by an over-reliance on factual detail or a dry academicism that rarely conveys the sheer enjoyment of watching many of the films listed here. With film facts available to anyone with Internet access at the click of a button, we've favoured opinion over technical details, and hope that enough of our enthusiasm for the genre has infected the reviews for you too to want to track down some of the scariest, strangest and most imaginative films cinema has to offer.

CHAPTER

1

BEGINNINGS

Horror Cinema. Where to start?

The movies perhaps began in 1891. Celluloid roll film, introduced by the manufacturer George Eastman, enabled the American inventor Thomas Edison, assisted by William Dickson, to devise the Kinetograph, a camera capable of exposing images in rapid succession. Developed in a strip and viewed inside a turn-the-crank device called the Kinetoscope, this ribbon of pictures gave the illusion of movement. The Kinetoscope, a coin-in-the-slot fairground novelty, was designed for a rapid turnover of single spectators. Though slide-shows, magic lanterns, praxinoscopes and other pre-cinema spectacles had been popular attractions for decades, the idea of showing movies to an audience gathered as if for a lecture or a play did not immediately appeal to Edison.

In 1895, the Frenchmen Auguste and Louis Lumière developed the Cinématographe. This could take moving pictures (like the Kinetograph) and also project them on a screen. On December 28th, the brothers held the first film show for a paying audience. In the basement of the Grand Café in Paris, they screened brief snippets taken during the year: workers leaving the Lumière factory (*La Sortie des Usines Lumière*) and men playing a hand of cards (*Partie d'Écarte*). *L'Arroseur Arrosé* (*The Sprinkler Sprinkled*), a staged gag in which a boy plays a trick on a gardener, might claim to be the first fiction film – and the first act of movie violence. The hit of the evening, and the first true sensation of the cinema, was *L'Arrivée d'un Train à La Ciotat* (*The Arrival of a Train at La Ciotat*). Having never seen a motion picture before, Parisian patrons could not quite tell the difference between a silent, black-and-white image of a locomotive steaming towards the camera and a real train crashing through the basement wall and threatening to plough them under.

For a decade or so, Kinetoscope and Cinématographe co-existed, apparently not even in competition. However, the Lumière vision of cinema as a theatrical attraction caught on around the world, drawing huge audiences and inspiring many other film pioneers, while Edison's gadget was primarily used for "what the butler saw"-style peepshows. By the early years of the 20th century, Edison had moved to the projected-on-a-

screen variety of cinema – among his best-known productions was the first film of *Frankenstein* (1910). Ironically, by then, the Lumières were out of the business and Edison was getting richer thanks to a near-stranglehold on American film production – he had patented sprocket holes, the perforations that allowed film to run through a projector. This hold would only be broken by mountebanks who fled the Edison-dominated New York film scene to found a new movie capital in California – Hollywood.

So much for cinema; what about horror?

Formats that would become movie genres were mostly well-defined in other media before Edison and the Lumières came along. Adventure and detective stories were developed in prose, the musical was a staple of the theatre, Westerns proliferated in cheap novels, the love story informed every form of narrative art, the conventions of the religious spectacular were familiar through painting, the great epic had been with us since antiquity and, in the late 19th century (thanks to Jules Verne and H.G. Wells), even science fiction was coalescing into something recognizable as a distinct branch of narrative.

But in 1890, if you called something a horror story, no one would have known what you meant. Which isn't to say they didn't exist. Just as cinema was coming together through the efforts of a disparate bunch of creative minds, so was horror.

Of course, the genre had been a long time coming. There are gruesome, fantastical elements in the earliest-known narrative, *The Epic of Gilgamesh*. Heroes who fight monsters are commonplace in Graeco-Roman and Norse mythology, reaching a peak in the eighth-century Old English epic poem *Beowulf*. In a typical horror scenario, something is raiding King Hrothgar's hall every night, leaving dead and mutilated corpses. The hero traces the trouble to the monster Grendel, whom he kills in battle. This story even contains its own sequel, as Beowulf then has to confront Grendel's vengeful mother.

Many other myths, stories, epics or cycles conform to the structure of the horror story. If given a certain slant, they could be made or remade as horror films. In the Bible, we find the plagues of Egypt (later inspiration for Dr Phibes), the tribulations of Job (perhaps the first great *conte cruel* or cruel tale) and the apocalyptic vision of the Revelation the source for **Rosemary's Baby**, (1968) **The Omen**, (1976) and sundry "Christian" horror tales.

Classical drama is full of bloody business, from Oedipus blinding himself when he realizes how dreadfully he has transgressed to the cycle of hate, murder and revenge in the *Oresteia*.

There were bursts of activity on the horrific front, giving rise to self-contained sub-genres. Elizabethan and Jacobean theatre audiences thronged to "revenge tragedies", which drew on classical models but played up ghosts and gore. *Hamlet* has its vengeful spectre, exhumed skull, multiple stabbings and poisonings and Ophelia's mad scene, while the doom-haunted tone of *Macbeth* is set by the witches on the blasted heath. William Shakespeare *really* went all-out for the kind of shock which '70s Italian filmmakers would relish in *Titus Andronicus* – source for the sequence in **Theater of Blood** (1974) where Robert Morley chokes on his beloved poodles and in which rape victim Lavinia has her hands cut off and her tongue cut out so she can't identify her abusers,

BELOW: Rackham's suitably gothic cover to a 1935 edition of Poe.

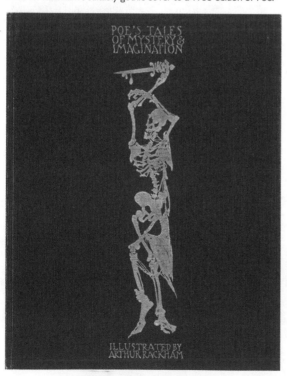

but foils them by writing down the guilty names with her bloody stumps. And *Titus* is tame next to Christopher Marlowe's *Tragicall History of Dr Faustus* (the archetypal deal-with-the-Devil story), Cyril Tourneur's (or Thomas Middleton's – no one is sure) *The Revenger's Tragedy* (which opens with the stage direction "Enter Vindice, holding a skull") or John Webster's *The White Devil* and *The Duchess of Malfi*. These plays demanded increasingly elaborate stage effects – hidden bladders of pig's blood pricked by daggers, fake heads brandished after offstage decapitations, Gloucester's bloodied eye-sockets in *King Lear* – which would remain in the stage repertoire, being taken to greater extremes in the French *Grand Guignol* of the 19th century, and eventually forming the basis of the movies' discipline of special make-up effects.

In 1764, the English novelist Horace Walpole published *The Castle of Otranto*, which he claimed to be a rediscovered mediaeval Italian manuscript. This saga of ghostly and criminal doings in an old Italian castle was the first of a cycle of increasingly lurid "gothic" novels. The most commercially successful of the gothic novelists was Mrs Ann Radcliffe, whose many works (*The Mysteries of Udolpho*, *The Italian,* etc.) deal with imperilled heroines, magnetic yet repulsive villains, more old Italian castles, contested inheritances, secret passages and the like. Any supernatural business is explained away Scooby-Doo-style as ghost riders turn out to be bandits in disguise. By the time Jane Austen paid homage to, while parodying, Radcliffe and her many, many imitators in *Northanger Abbey*, the form was an established strand of what passed for popular culture. Parents worried that their daughters (the gothic audience was predominantly female) got strange ideas from over-consumption of gothic novels. Frivolous mock-mediaeval fashions in architecture (Walpole spent his earnings on a new-built ruin) and clothing showed how pervasive the influence was.

Parents didn't really have much to worry about in the genteel works of Mrs Radcliffe, but might well have been given pause by Matthew Gregory Lewis, whose 1796 best-seller *The Monk* unashamedly plunges into the supernatural, along with an enthusiastic catalogue of wild depravity (and a virulent anti-Catholicism typical of the British gothic novel). Another variant on the Faustus story, *The Monk* follows the eponymous, saintly Ambrosio, who is visited by the demonic in the form of a youth who turns out to be a girl and tempts him into a succession of fleshly pleasures and crimes — including matricide, incestuous rape and worse — that lead to his being torn apart by the Devil. The only contemporary writer more extreme than Lewis was the Marquis de Sade, who wrote in 1800 that the gothic novel was "the necessary fruit of the revolutionary tremors felt by the whole of Europe" — making him among the first critics to perceive a connection between upheavals in society (which he knew a lot about) and apparently fantastical fiction. The later gothic period produced masterpieces like Charles Maturin's 1820 *Melmoth the Wanderer*, and the style lasted into the 19th century, perhaps petering out with J. Sheridan LeFanu's longer novels like *Uncle Silas* or *The House by the Churchyard* (LeFanu is best remembered for short stories or novella-length work, like the much-filmed vampire tale *Carmilla*) or evolving into the serialized "penny-dreadfuls" following the exploits of Dick Turpin, Varney the Vampyre or Sweeney Todd.

The most famous and lasting horror novel of the gothic period is *Frankenstein, or The Modern Prometheus*, published anonymously in 1818. The author was not then the respectable Mrs Shelley, but the scandalous Mary Godwin — teenage runaway adultress (Lewis wrote his masterpiece in his teens too) and, essentially, romantic poetry groupie. Purportedly the fruit of a tale-telling contest involving Percy Shelley and Lord Byron, as seen in the prologue of **Bride of Frankenstein** (1935) and several full-length fancies like *Gothic* (1986) and *Haunted Summer* (1988), *Frankenstein* owes its convoluted structure (tales within tales) to the gothics, but breaks new ground in its story of the callous scientist Victor Frankenstein and the tragic yet malign Monster he creates. The book is a cornerstone not only of horror, but science fiction. Despite the frequent use of the Frankenstein name as a stick to beat science (as in scares about genetically modified "Frankenfood"), it should be remembered that Victor's crime is not making a monster, but being a *bad parent* — everything would have been all right if he'd taken care of his creature rather than rejecting it simply because it looked hideous.

Before the supposed contest, the Shelley-Byron ménage — which included Dr John Polidori, author of a scurrilous but influential bit of bitchery called "The Vampyre" (a caricature of Byron, and the first vampire story in English) — had been poring over volumes of folk and horror tales translated from the German. They might have looked at the works of E.T.A.

ABOVE: The beast in the bedroom. A 1939 engraving by Abot for Poe's "Murders in the Rue Morgue".

Hoffman — his doll-come-to-life Olimpia in "The Sand-Man" is a Frankensteinian precedent — but there were many others to choose from. The American Edgar Allan Poe acknowledged the influence of the Germanic gothic when he began to write his own distinctive horror tales in the 1830s and '40s. After dashing off the archetypal "Metzengerstein", he broke away from this tradition by claiming that his terror "was not of Germany, but the soul". By this, he meant that he dropped the mechanical plot elements of the genre to creep into the minds of deranged protagonists, presenting torments at once more physical and more spiritual than those of the typical gothic protagonist.

Poe was too prodigious to limit himself to one form – besides his horror, he practically invented the detective story and wrote important early science fiction, bizarre humour, journalistic hoaxes, puzzles, alternately vicious or toadying reviews and begging letters. However, he left a core of tales of mystery and imagination that would be adapted over and over – "The Black Cat", "Murders in the Rue Morgue", "The Pit and the Pendulum", "The Fall of the House of Usher", "A Cask of Amontillado", "The Tell-Tale Heart" and "The Masque of the Red Death". While the gothics tended to revolve around a virtuous but imperilled heroine who would be saved at the end, Poe's tales present women who were dead, dying or spectral and concentrate on the kinks of their male protagonists – on the verge of either madness or transcendent wisdom, obsessive on details to the exclusion of all else, and thinking in frenzied, dash-ridden sentences that spill from the author's pen like the compulsive ramblings of a drunk or a lunatic. It's too easy to write Poe off as a neurotic who put his own failings into his tales: just as his poetry uses complex metre and rhyme schemes, his prose is finely wrought to seem like madness while the author is in complete control of his effects.

By the late 19th century, the gothics seemed quaint and comical (Gilbert and Sullivan had a bash at sending them up in *Ruddigore, or The Witch's Curse*), though trace elements lingered in the more labyrinthine constructions of Charles Dickens (*Bleak House*) or Wilkie Collins (*The Woman in White*). Poe was remembered as much for his messy life as his work, which was more popular in translation in France than in England or America. However, in the decades immediately before and after the birth of the movies, there was an unparalleled burst of activity. More key horror texts were produced in a comparatively brief time than in all the centuries preceding and, arguably, all the years since.

Consider this parade – 1886: *The Strange Case of Dr Jekyll and Mr Hyde*, by Robert Louis Stevenson; 1887: *She*, by Sir H. Rider Haggard; 1891: *The Picture of Dorian Gray*, by Oscar Wilde; 1894: *Trilby*, by George du Maurier; 1895: *The King in Yellow*, by Robert Chambers; *The Time Machine*, by H.G. Wells; 1896: *The Island of Dr Moreau*, by H.G. Wells; 1897: *Dracula*, by Bram Stoker; *The Invisible Man*, by H.G. Wells; 1898: *The Turn of the Screw*, by Henry James; *The War of the Worlds*, by H.G. Wells; 1902: *The Hound of the Baskervilles*, by Sir Arthur Conan Doyle; *Heart of Darkness*, by Joseph Conrad; 1903: *The Jewel of the Seven Stars*, by Bram Stoker; 1904: *Ghost Stories of an Antiquary*, by M.R. James; *The Empty House, and Other Ghost Stories*, by Algernon Blackwood; 1906: *House of Souls*, by Arthur Machen; 1908: *The House on the Borderland*, by William Hope Hodgson; 1911: *The Phantom of the Opera*, by Gaston Leroux; *Alraune*, by H.H. Ewers.

And that's only the books that have lasted. If there had been awards for genre fiction in this period, readers would probably have voted for Marie Corelli, author of *The Sorrows of Satan* and *The Mighty Atom*, who once outsold all of the great writers listed above and is now entirely forgotten.

While these books were coming out – along with a torrent of short stories, many by the same authors – the cinema was advancing from flickering experiments that were basically moving snapshots to feature-length stories that could compete with the

BELOW: Griffin on the run. Illustration by Louis Strimpl to the 1912 French edition of The Invisible Man.

grandest stage productions. A few of these works have surprisingly resisted adaptation – we still await the great Arthur Machen or William Hope Hodgson movies (Ishiro Honda's *Matango*, 1963 – an unauthorized version of Hodgson's "A Voice in the Night" – honourably excepted). However, most of this batch have been filmed over and over again, and spun off so many sequels, imitations, homages, revisions, reworkings and other variants that it's possible a full half of the horror films ever made are, in some way or another, drawn from this brief two-and-a-half decades of literary production. Toss in *Frankenstein* and Poe, and you can make that a full three-quarters.

Though M.R. James and Algernon Blackwood wrote only ghost stories, the other writers in this group had varied careers as popular novelists, playwrights and tale-tellers. Stoker might be as eternally associated with his vampire Count as Doyle is with his Great Detective, but they covered a wide range in other works. Stevenson, whose "fine bogey tale" of Jekyll and Hyde seems to have kicked off this remarkable run, was hailed for his stories of adventure, and – like Wilde, Conrad, Henry James and Wells – contributed lasting masterpieces to several genres. It may be that this outpouring of what would soon be horror was linked to the contemporary rapid development of cinema and other technology, from the telephone to the automobile to the aeroplane. When the world changes rapidly, people are scared and excited at the same time. That *zeitgeist* encourages storytellers to play on those emotions, which underlie much horror fiction and throb dangerously throughout this shelfload of masterpieces.

With all this activity, some people started making connections – in a letter congratulating her son on the good reviews for *Dracula*, Bram Stoker's mother said there was "nothing like it since *Frankenstein*" ("Poe is nowhere," she snipes with maternal short-sightedness). The gothic novels all looked back, with settings either in the past or a fantasized foreign country. Even if we now view them through a London fog of gaslight nostalgia, the late-19th-century horror cornerstones tend to be up-to-the-moment. Stevenson, Stoker and Leroux include newspaper clippings to add weight to their fantastical tales, Wells and Haggard traipse off to far corners of the globe (or the universe) only to bring stories home to oak-panelled clubland, while Hodgson, the Jameses and Blackwood find ancient ghosts, curses and sorceries nestling in an uncertain modern world.

In some of these stories, the horrific elements aren't even primary: *Jekyll and Hyde* is a twist-at-the-end crime thriller (in 1886, the last chapters must have been a jaw-dropper which made Mr Hyde the Kaiser Sose or Tyler Durden of his day); *Dorian Gray* is a black (or at least very dark mauve) satire; and Wells's novels are considered to be scientific romances (though he wrote better monsters than anyone else – cannibal morlocks, beast-people, invisible maniacs, vampires from Mars). *Heart of Darkness* is "serious literature" (albeit with severed heads stuck on poles) and *Hound of the Baskervilles* is a whodunit of the rationalized supernatural. Yet what we remember, what lingers in pop culture, of these tales are the set-pieces that have made them cinema staples: Dorian's portrait and Ayesha in the blue flame, ageing (or de-evolving) to withered corpses; Jekyll taking the potion and transforming into the "somehow deformed" Hyde; the Martians devastating the Home Counties; the creepily angelic kids under malign, perhaps spectral influence; M.R. James's nastily physical little ghosts (whoever tagged him a master of "subtle" horror missed the face sucked off the bone in "Count Magnus"); and, most of all, the vampire Dracula in his Transylvanian castle, climbing down the walls, creeping into English ladies' bedrooms, drinking blood, defying an array of heroes and decaying to nothing when his heart is pierced.

If modern horror starts somewhere, *Dracula* is as good a place as any. It deploys exactly the strategies, learned from Collins and Stevenson, that still serve for Stephen King and almost every horror film, yet has a plot which isn't far removed from *Beowulf*. A credible, "realistic" setting – unlike those of the gothic novels or, say, *Dorian Gray* – is established, allowing for suspension of disbelief when the monster intrudes. There is a mystery element as normal characters, aided by a scholarly type (here, Dr Van Helsing) puzzle over strange phenomena (those two holes in the neck) and work out who and what the villain is, discovering the monster's powers and limitations and weaknesses. In the climax, the hero (and, often, a heroine) overcomes the monster through applied knowledge and moral superiority, and destroys it – though usually not without cost (Quincy dies).

However, a full year before Dracula came to the printed page, the Devil made his movie debut.

CHAPTER

2

1896–1929

In *Le Manoir du Diable* (*The Devil's Castle*, 1896), a bat flies into a haunted castle and transforms into the Devil, represented, as often on stage, in the person of a nattily dressed gent with a beard. From a cauldron, this Mephistopheles conjures up and dispels imps, demons, ghosts, witches and a skeleton. A cavalier brandishes a crucifix and the Devil vanishes in a puff of smoke. All in two minutes.

This is officially the first horror film. It derives its imagery from centuries of books, legends and stage plays – among those conjured up by the Devil is an old man with a *grimoire* (a manual of magic), presumably Faustus himself. Much has been made of the bat transformation and the power of the crucifix, which means the vignette tends to be further listed as the first vampire movie – though these tropes wouldn't be exclusively associated with vampires until Stoker's book became well-known.

The director and star of *Le Manoir du Diable* was Georges Méliès, father of the cinema of the fantastic. The Lumières, fathers of the cinema of documentary realism, came to the movies through technical interest in photography and, incidentally, saw little future in them beyond a passing fad. But Méliès was a showman, a conjurer in an era when illusionists were top-of-the-bill attractions, who saw trick photography first as an aid to magic. In films, Méliès used multiple exposures, dissolves, perspective tricks, elaborate props and stage make-up to accomplish what were basically vaudeville acts on film. *Le Manoir du Diable* has no "story", just a parade of tricks, with a flourish for an exit.

Between 1896 and 1914, Méliès directed over five hundred movies. He did not confine himself to fantasy, making early stabs at animated "French postcard" (*Après le Bal/After the Ball*, 1897), historical re-creation (*Jeanne d'Arc/Joan of Arc*, 1899), religious spectacle (*Christ Marchant sur les Flots/Christ Walking on Water*, 1899), topical drama (*L'Affaire Dreyfus/The Dreyfus Affair*, 1899), literary adaptation (*Les Mousquetaires de la Reine/The Queen's Musketeers*, 1903) and a bogus newsreel about the coronation of Edward VII that the King himself thought genuine. Before his own distinct style caught on, he was among the cinema's first rip-off artists, capitalizing on the Lumières' *La Ciotat* by filming trains at other stations, *L'Arrivée d'un Train – Gare de Joinville* (1896) and *L'Arrivée d'un Train – Gare de Vincennes* (1896).

But it is for magic that we remember Méliès.

After *Le Manoir du Diable*, he delivered many films along the same lines, often in the same genially demonic persona, sometimes building whole movies around a single illusion: in *L'homme à la Tête de Caoutchouc* (*The Man with the Indiarubber Head*, 1902), he inflates his own head to giant size until it bursts like a balloon. Taking his act from stage to screen, Méliès lived up to the title of one of his 1899 films, *A Turn-of-the-Century Illusionist*.

Eventually, Méliès's films grew longer and more ambitious. Among his literary adaptations – highlights rather than the whole story – were the screen debuts of Rider Haggard's Ayesha (*La Danse du Feu/Haggard's She: The Pillar of Fire*, 1899), the charlatan Cagliostro (*Le Miroir de Cagliostro/Cagliostro's Mirror*, 1899), E.T.A. Hoffman's living doll (*Coppélia: La Poupée Animée*, 1900), Little Red Riding Hood and the Wolf (*Le Petit Chaperon Rouge*, 1901), Bluebeard (*Barbe-Bleue*, 1901) and the Wandering Jew (*Le Juif Errant*, 1904), while he returned often to Faust and Mephistopheles. His filmography is littered with titles that suggest sub-genres in the

OPPOSITE: Lon Chaney shows off his dentures in the lost film *London After Midnight* (1927).

BELOW: One in the eye for the man in the moon. *Voyage dans la Lune* (1901).

ABOVE: Jazz Age icon Louise Brooks in *Die Büchse der Pandora* (1928).

making: *L'Auberge Ensorcelé* (*The Bewitched Inn*, 1897), *La Caverne Maudite* (*Cave of Demons*, 1898), *Le Spectre* (*Murder Will Out*, 1899), *Cléopâtre* (*Robbing Cleopatra's Tomb*, 1899), *Le Savant et le Chimpanzee* (*The Doctor and the Monkey*, 1900), *Le Fou Assassin* (*The Dangerous Lunatic*, 1900), *Les Filles du Diable* (*Beelzebub's Daughters*,

1903) and *La Fée Carabosse et le Poignard Fatal* (*The Witch*, 1906).

His biggest success, and most-often-seen work, was *Voyage dans la Lune* (*A Trip to the Moon*, 1901), which almost has a plot in combining bits from lunar trips made in books by Verne and Wells. This encouraged him to make more "impossible voyages", to the sun, under the sea or to the North Pole. Méliès set out to amaze and obviously chuckled when nervous patrons were terrified by phantoms, skeletons or the Devil – but he was not truly in the horror business, nor even really interested in cinema as a medium for telling stories. Nevertheless, he invented the tricks and first put on moving film the images that would recur.

In the early years of the 20th century, the movies took hold around the world – and there was already competition between nations. In America, pioneers like Edwin S. Porter paved the way for geniuses like D.W. Griffith; in Italy, there were feature-length epic spectaculars in the second decade (Maciste, the ancient muscle hero, made his debut in *Cabiria* in 1914); in Germany, the heirs of E.T.A. Hoffman began to play with shadows, and in Britain one- and two-reel melodramas began to proliferate (a typical British film title of 1902 was *A Fight With Sledge-Hammers*).

Activity was so hectic that oft-told tales made their debuts and were done over again within months. William Selig's *Dr Jekyll and Mr Hyde* (1908), a film of the stage play that had been touring since Stevenson's day, might be the first American horror movie. It was rapidly followed by a British remake (*The Duality of Man*, 1910), a Danish effort starring Alwin Neuss (*Den Skaebnesvangre Opfindelse*, 1910) and another American version (1912) with James Cruze and Harry Benham sharing the title roles (an interesting approach rarely reused). In 1913, a German *Der Anderer* vied with two American films called *Dr Jekyll and Mr Hyde*, one starring King Baggot and produced by Carl Laemmle (later patriarch of Universal Pictures, where the horror movie *really* began), the other in a primitive colour process. Then things went quiet until 1920, when three versions arrived simultaneously: John S. Robertson's lavish star vehicle for John Barrymore (whose steeple-headed, spider-fingered Hyde pre-empts Max Schreck's similar-looking vampire by two years), a quickie imitation with Sheldon Lewis (famed as "The Clutching Hand" in serials) and F.W. Murnau's *Der Januskopf*, a tragically lost adaptation with Conrad Veidt as the transforming doctor (metamorphosing under the magical influence of a two-faced bust rather than mad science) and Bela Lugosi as his butler. The first parody was *Horrible Hyde* (1915) but Stan Laurel got in on the act in *Dr Pickle and Mr Pride* (1925).

Though Jekyll and Hyde was the most-adapted horror story of the silent era, other famous monsters made their debuts. Edison's *Frankenstein* (1910), with Charles Ogle as the wild-haired creature whipped up in a vat like instant soup, was followed by *Life Without Soul* (1915), in which Dr Frankenstein becomes "William Frawley" (William A. Cohill) and the Monster is "the Brute Man" (Percy Darrell Standing), and perhaps the first Italian horror movie, *Il Mostro di Frankenstein* (1920). *The Picture of Dorian Gray* was first filmed in Denmark (*Dorian Gray's Portraet*, 1910), but there were soon versions from Russia (*Portret Doryana Greya*, 1915), America (1916, starring Henry Victor – the strongman of **Freaks** – as the beautiful youth), Germany (*Das Bildnis des Dorian Gray*, 1917) and Hungary (*Az Élet Királya*, 1918 – with Lugosi as Dorian's mentor Sir Henry). Sherlock Holmes made his debut as early as 1900 in *Sherlock Holmes Baffled*, featuring an (or possibly the) Invisible Man, while *Sherlock Holmes in the Great Murder Mystery* (1908) was another crossover: here, Holmes solves Poe's "Murders in the Rue Morgue", feeling the collar of the killer gorilla. The sleuth's creepiest adventure was first filmed in Denmark (source of a surprising number of early gothics) as *Den Graa Dame* (*The Grey Lady*, 1903), with a spectral lady instead of a Hound of Hell. Germany not only turned out a faithful *Die Hund von Baskerville* (1914) but followed it with six sequels in which Holmes pursues the novel's dog-training villain. There were also multiple early versions of staples like *She*, *Trilby*, *Notre Dame de Paris*, *Sweeney Todd*, *Maria Marten*, Faust or *Dr Faustus*, "The Monkey's Paw" and Fu-Manchu.

Poe was often adapted, in France (*Le Puits et le Pendule*, 1909, *Le Système du Docteur Goudron et du Professeur Plume*, 1913) and America (*The Sealed Room*, 1909, *The Raven*, 1912, *The Pit and the Pendulum*, 1913). D.W. Griffith first took a frequently reused tack by combining several Poe stories into one episodic narrative for *The Avenging Conscience* (1914). *The Avenging Hand* (1915), the first feature-length British horror film, sounds like an unauthorized adaptation of Stoker's *Jewel of Seven Stars*, with a revived ancient Egyptian princess and a severed hand. It was among a run of mummy-themed films: *The Mummy* (1911), *The Dust of Egypt* (1915), *Die Augen der Mumie Ma* (*The Eyes of the Mummy*, 1919). *The Vampire* (1913) was an East Indian snake lady, whereas *The Werewolf* (1913) was an American Indian shapeshifter. A cycle of films about monkey-gland transplants (a medical fad of the day) and Darwinian theory stretched to a French 1913 adaptation of Gaston Leroux's novel about a humanized gorilla, *Balaoo* (remade as *The Wizard*, 1927, and *Dr Renault's Secret*, 1942).

Already, some filmmakers were specializing in the macabre, and a few actors were building reputations on the strength of horror roles. The German Paul Wegener, a director-star, cut a hefty figure as Balduin in *Der Student von Prag* (1913), adapted from H.H. Ewers's Poe-like novel of a deal with the Devil and a deadly doppelgänger, but achieved fame under a clay wig and built-up costume in and as *Der Golem* (1915), the legendary living statue of the Prague ghetto, revived to rampage in modern times. This was such a success that Wegener delivered a parodic sequel, *Der Golem und die Tanzerin* (*The Golem and the Dancing Girl*, 1917) and a more elaborate prequel, **Der Golem, wie er in der Welt Kam** (*The Golem*, 1920). Wegener also took bizarre roles in *Der Yoghi* (1916), *Der Rattenfänger von Hameln* (*The Pied Piper of Hamelin*, 1918), as a warlock modelled on the then-scandalous Aleister Crowley in Rex Ingram's French-shot American film *The Magician* (1926), the title part in *Svengali* (1927) and a mad scientist in another Ewers adaptation, *Alraune* (1928). Wegener's last bow in horror was in the multi-episode *Unheimliche Geschichten* (*The Living Dead*, 1932), written and directed by his rival Richard Oswald, who had come into the genre with a couple of the *Hund von Baskerville* sequels and stuck around to deliver adaptations of Hoffman (*Shlemihl*, 1915, *Hoffmanns Erzählungen*, 1916), *Das Bildnis des Dorian Gray* (1917), a first *Unheimliche Geschichten* (including tales from Poe and Stevenson, 1919), *Cagliostro* (1929), an elaborate remake of *Die Hund von Baskerville* (1929) and a talkie *Alraune* (1930) with Brigitte Helm re-creating her silent role as the artificially created *femme fatale*.

Wegener and Oswald were principally adaptors of others' work – their films have pictorial virtues and an obvious feel for the material, but little sense of the developing potential of cinema. Others came at horror from a different direction, not just hoping to trade on well-known material but seeing ways to expand the boundaries of film art. The key title here is **Das Kabinett des Doktor Caligari** (*The Cabinet of Dr Caligari*, 1920), directed by Robert Weine, but as importantly the work of scenarists Carl Mayer and Hans Janowitz, art directors Walter Röhrig and Hermann Warm (who devised the stylized sets, painted shadows and other visual trickery of "Caligarism") and even Fritz Lang, who was signed up to direct but moved on to something else after devising the frame story that reveals the whole action to be taking place in the mind of a lunatic. Lang's bookends turned what might have been a confounding art movie into a gimmick picture. The revelation meant patrons disturbed by the imagery could leave the theatre thinking they now "understood" what they had seen, the visualized ravings of a disordered mind. Mayer and Janowitz despised this angle, having intended to depict a world that was cruel and insane rather than simply a protagonist who was having bad dreams. The breakout performers were Werner Krauss, as the top-hatted mountebank and mesmerist Caligari, and Conrad Veidt, as the leotard-clad, hollow-cheeked somnambulist/ murderer Cesare. Both would join Wegener among the elect group of proto-horror stars: Veidt, whom Universal considered casting as Dracula in 1930 (arguably he would have been a better choice than Lugosi), played *Der Graf von Cagliostro* (1921), the rumoured diabolist-violinist *Paganini* (1923), the pianist with a murderer's hands (Robert Weine's *Orlac's Hände/Hands of Orlac*, 1924), Ivan the Terrible (*Das Wachsfigurenkabinett*, 1924), Balduin in a remake of *Der Student von Prag* (1926), *Rasputin* (1930) and *The Wandering Jew* (1933); Krauss played Iago (*Othello*, 1922), Jack the Ripper (*Das Wachsfigurenkabinett*, 1924) and the Devil in *Der Student von Prag* (1926).

F.W. Murnau cast Veidt in *Der Januskopf*, scripted by *Caligari*'s Janowitz. Having got away with this full-length Stevenson adaptation by making name changes (this is the strange case of "Dr Warren and Mr O'Connor") and plot alterations, he made the mistake of assuming that Bram Stoker's widow would be as negligent as the Stevenson estate (who, one suspects, had earned little from the many Jekyll and Hyde movies) and turned Count Dracula into Graf von Orlok for **Nosferatu, eine Symphonie des Grauens** (*Nosferatu*, 1922). Whereas **Caligari**'s "Expressionist" style was created entirely in the studio, Murnau took his vampire out on location, filming in Slovakian mountains and ruins. **Nosferatu** still stands as the only screen adaptation of *Dracula* to be primarily interested in terror. Max Schreck's rat-featured, corseted stick insect of a monster has no undead glamour, nor even the melancholy that Klaus Kinski and Willem Dafoe bring to variations in **Nosferatu, Phantom der Nacht** (*Nosferatu the Vampyre*, 1979) and *Shadow of the Vampire* (2000). Just as *Dracula* can serve as a template for the horror novel, **Nosferatu** (far more than **Caligari**) serves as a template for the horror film. Murnau added wrinkles to Stoker that have persisted, notably the vampire vanquished by the first light of day.

Caligari and **Nosferatu** aren't the whole Expressionist story. Throughout the '20s, as German society spiralled out of control, German cinema was shadowed by figures as sinister as Caligari, Cesare and Orlok. Fritz Lang turned out the epic *Dr Mabuse, der Spieler* (1922), in which Rudolf Klein-Rogge (a bit-player in **Caligari**) incarnates superhuman evil as a master criminal in the tradition of Fu-Manchu and Professor Moriarty. Mabuse is a founding text for all manner of far-fetched thrillers, including the Hitchcock japes of the '30s, the *films noirs* of the '40s, the super-spy pictures of the '60s and the paranoid conspiracy dramas of the '70s. Lang brought Mabuse back, extending malign influence from an asylum cell and beyond the grave in *Das Testament des Dr Mabuse* (1933), but his most influential early talkie is **M** (1931), the first great serial-murder film, with Peter Lorre as the paedophile killer stalked by cops (including Mabuse's nemesis, Inspector Lohmann) and criminals. Paul Leni, another interesting German director of the '20s, put Jack the Ripper on screen in *Das Wachsfigurenkabinett* (1924) before decamping for America. The missing link between Werner Krauss's tubby, trench-coated Ripper and Lorre's whistling, whining Franz Beckert is the mild-mannered, pathetic Jack the Ripper (Gustav Diessl) of G.W. Pabst's masterly *Die Büchse der Pandora* (*Pandora's Box*, 1928), killing the innocently fatal heroine Lulu (Louise Brooks) in a clinch under the mistletoe. Alfred Hitchcock had already taken note of what was going on in Germany, where he served an apprenticeship, and essayed his own Ripper story, the British Expressionist classic *The Lodger* (1927).

ABOVE: John Barrymore's Hyde looks for love, *Dr Jekyll & Mr Hyde* (1920).

Hollywood didn't yet have horror films, but had a horror star in Lon Chaney, master character actor and make-up artist. Chaney plays full-on monster roles as the ape-man in *A Blind Bargain* (1922), Quasimodo in *The Hunchback of Notre Dame* (1923) and the skull-faced Erik in **The Phantom of the Opera** (1925), plus a (very funny) parodic mad scientist in *The Monster* (1925) and a (fake) vampire in *London After Midnight* (1927), but his most distinctive work comes in melodramas, usually directed by Tod Browning. Their masterpiece is **The Unknown** (1927), in which Chaney plays a murderer hiding his giveaway double-thumbs by binding his arms and posing as an amputee, performing a knife-throwing act with his feet. The heroine (a young Joan Crawford) affects to abhor a man's embrace, so "Alonzo the Armless" has his arms surgically removed to become her ideal lover – only to learn she's changed her position on hugging and is canoodling with the circus strong-man, whereupon Alonzo plots a revenge nasty enough for the EC Comics of the '50s. The difference between Chaney's grotesques and the creatures of German Expressionism

is that most of Chaney's brilliantly mimed, remarkably made-up freaks are just grumpy guys who don't get the girl (a theme Chaney raised to obsessive levels), rather than incarnations of evil or insanity in semi-human form. Perhaps this is why his most horrific films, though illuminated by moments of masterly acting, wear less well. Chaney's best work – in Browning's *The Unholy Three* (1925) and Victor Sjöström's *He Who Gets Slapped* (1924) – falls on the outskirts of genre.

When Universal Pictures, who backed *Hunchback* and **Phantom**, lost Chaney to MGM, they replaced him with Conrad Veidt as the Joker-grinning freak of *The Man Who Laughs* (1928). That was directed by Paul Leni, who had made the most important American horror film of the decade, **The Cat and the Canary** (1927). John Willard's 1922 Broadway play was a semi-spoof of the already-established genre of Old Dark House mystery, in which a group of people gather for a reading of a will in an isolated, spooky locale and are menaced by a monstrous figure who turns out to be the most cheerful, helpful suspect. Leni got the most out of clutching hands, secret passageways and bodies tumbling from wardrobes. There were many similar efforts: *The Monster* (1925) and *The Bat* (1926), directed by the talented Roland West, who remade the latter as a widescreen talkie, *The Bat Whispers* (1929); *Seven Footprints to Satan*, directed by Benjamin Christensen, who had handled the striking Danish semi-documentary **Häxan** (*Witchcraft Through the Ages*, 1921); multiple versions of *Seven Keys to Baldpate* (1917, 1925, 1929), a property thought worth rehashing as late as *House of the Long Shadows* (1983); *The Ghost Breaker* (1922), *The Gorilla* (1927), *The Thirteenth Hour* (1927), *The Haunted House* (1928) and the first all-talkie, *The Terror* (1928). Leni even got to do it again, in the Old Dark Theatre tale *The Last Warning* (1929).

As talking pictures caught on, Murnau and Leni were in Hollywood, perfectly positioned to direct horror films. *Dracula* had been running on stage in Britain and America since the mid-'20s, and the rights had legitimately been bought by Universal Pictures in the hope that Chaney would star. However, within a few years, Murnau, Leni and Chaney were all dead through freak accidents or illnesses. The future of *Dracula*, and hence the genre, was up for grabs.

DER GOLEM: WIE ER
IN DIE WELT KAM
AKA THE GOLEM:
HOW HE CAME INTO THE WORLD

1920, Ger, co-dir/co-scr Paul Wegener, co-dir Carl Boese,
co-scr Henrik Galeen, starring Paul Wegener, Albert Steinrueck,
Ernst Deutsch, Lyda Salmnonova

The Jews of Prague are exiled in an edict from the Emperor. Rabbi Loew summons a demon to animate his golem and protect his community. The golem saves the Emperor's life when his palace crumbles, and the edict is removed. However, when Loew's assistant directs the golem to attack a rival suitor for Loew's daughter's charms, it goes on the rampage. Wegener's magnificent prequel to the Henrik Galeen-directed 1913 version is the most successful take on the golem legend, showcasing amazing set designs, from the imaginative inventiveness of the Prague ghetto, all misshapen roofs and warren-like homes, to the asymmetrical, organic interiors, seeming as animate and made from the same clay as the golem himself. Loew's house is a particularly remarkable design: the principal room appears to be modelled on an inner ear, with the smallest features, down to the hinges on the doors, ornately detailed. It's never quite clear how Loew believes the golem will protect the ghetto: his imagination doesn't extend far beyond sending it out with a shopping list, and his magic is to blame for the palace's ruin. In fact, the principal

BELOW: A psychodrama nightmare played out in a damaged brain, **Das Kabinett des Dr Caligari**.

factors behind the edict – that the Jews "practise black magic" and "endanger the lives and property of their fellow men" – are borne out by events, highlighting a vein of anti-Semitism running throughout the film: the Jews' cramped, close confines and shabby dress are contrasted with the finery and open spaces of the court; a Jewish warden is seen in close-up counting a bribe; and it takes a child outside the ghetto (and thus, implicitly, non-Jewish) to stop the golem. A clear influence on **Frankenstein**, particularly Wegener's trajectory of bewilderment to rage as the titular creature, it entirely lacks the later film's piety: Loew encounters problems simply because he hasn't read far enough ahead in his and the invocation of the demon, one of the film's most startling sequences, invites us to marvel at his control of the elements.

DAS KABINETT DES
DOKTOR CALIGARI
AKA THE CABINET OF DR CALIGARI

1920, Ger, dir Robert Weine, scr Hans Janowitz, Carl Mayer, starring
Werner Krauss, Conrad Veidt, Friedrich Feher, Lil Dagover

Caligari's story is a simple Hoffmannesque tale of a sinister doctor with a somnambulist patient, "asleep for 23 years", whom he parades at town fairs then wakes at night to murder people in their beds. The undistinguished Robert Weine was second choice for director after Fritz Lang. The producers were luckier with the production design when Hermann Warm asked two painter friends to help with the sets. It was Fritz Lang who suggested that the central story of a man trying to expose the evil doctor's crimes be framed by a prologue and epilogue, thus revealing the somnambulist tale to be the delusion of a man in an asylum who believes his doctor is Caligari.

The film's extraordinary visual appearance has far exceeded its qualities as a piece of cinema, making it the Expressionist movie par excellence. The shots of tilted walls, angled windows and doors, and canvas painted with black and white rhomboids for light and shade was immediately imitated in other European films. This influence later crossed the Atlantic with German filmmakers heading to Hollywood, surfacing in diluted form in horror films such as **The Black Cat** and **Son of Frankenstein**, in numerous dream sequences, and (much later) in the films of Tim Burton.

Weine's direction is static and uninspired yet the film remains compelling through the carefully structured chaos of its design and an eerie performance by Conrad Veidt as the somnambulist, Cesare. The Expressionist theme bleeds from the sets into the characters. Cesare is a sharp and angular silhouette, with waxen

sections, the woodcuts come to life, Christensen mounting convincingly detailed re-creations of Middle Ages witchery ranging from the uses of magical potions to the tortures meted out by the Inquisition. The film's approach is intelligent, informed and resolutely non-exploitative, although it acknowledges the scatological grotesquery of witch confessions in scenes of sorceresses kissing demons' bottoms, flinging the contents of chamberpots over their enemies' doors and stripping naked to meet their horned lord. The Devil (impiously portrayed by Christensen himself) is a gleeful personification of lust, an ecstatic trickster figure in sharp contrast to the cruelly repressive Church, attacked with Buñuelian vigour as yet another innocent is sent to the stake "for the benefit of mankind and the pleasant smell in God's honour". As an exploration of the social and psychological roots of witch hysteria **Häxan** is peerless, but Christensen is too much the showman to stop there, his superlative collection of hags, crones and torture implements topped only by such startling animation sequences as a Méliès-style conjuring trick of coins flying through a door, nightshade visions of witches birthing Satanic horrors and flying to the Sabbat, broomsticks aloft, and infernal debauches resembling Bosch's nightmare visions brought to life. The film was re-released in the '60s, with William Burroughs's laconic Midwestern drawl replacing the intertitles to the delight of freaks and the horror of silent-cinema purists.

pallor and glassy stare, stalking into rooms with a long blade in his hand. Jane, the woman he abducts, is a deliberate contrast in white fabrics, her room all rounded shapes and vertical lines. The controversial framing scenes may unnecessarily distance the central narrative and prevent the film from achieving the density of, say, **Eraserhead**, but they help turn the story into an extended dream sequence, a psychodrama nightmare played out in a damaged brain. [JC]

HÄXAN
AKA WITCHCRAFT THROUGH THE AGES

1921, Swe, dir/scr Benjamin Christensen, starring Maren Pedersen, Oscar Stribolt, Clara Pontoppidan, Benjamin Christensen

Christensen's "history of mysticism" starts unpromisingly enough, with a parade of woodcuts whose features, described in the intertitles, are pointed out with a pencil: the director's delivery of "a lecture within the framework of the history of civilization" appears initially to be just that. But, with the second of its seven

NOSFERATU, EINE SYMPHONIE DES GRAUENS

1922, Ger, dir F.W. Murnau, scr Henrik Galeen, starring Max Schreck, Gustav von Wangenheim, Greta Schröder, Alexander Granach

Murnau's silent masterpiece is something of a revenant film. Henrik Galeen had radically slimmed the plot and changed character names but the unauthorized adaptation was still nearly destroyed by a lawsuit from Bram Stoker's widow. Prints survived, however, and with Galeen's script and some extraordinary designs from occultist Albin Grau, Murnau produced one of the classic works of early German cinema.

Although primitive by contemporary standards, it has the distinction of being the first truly successful horror film, as well as a considerable influence on later vampire movies: Max Schreck's iconic figure — hairless head, flared ears and elongated fingers — has become a secondary archetype for screen vampires after Bela

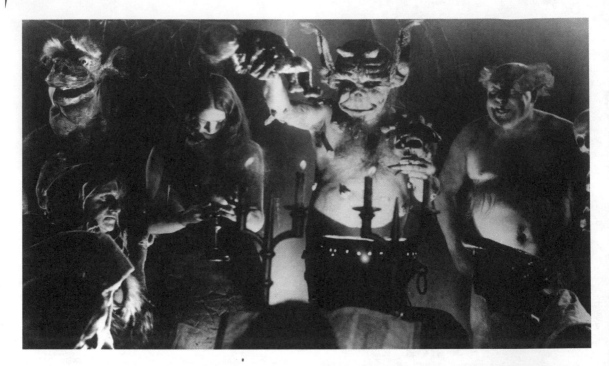

ABOVE: Scatological grotesquery at the Sabbat in **Häxan**.

Lugosi's Romanian lounge lizard. Galeen's story takes estate agent Hutter to Count Orlok's castle in the Carpathians. When Orlok sees a picture of Hutter's wife, he attacks him and leaves him locked in a room, then journeys to Bremen to pursue the woman and bring plague upon the town. Murnau and his crew saved money by shooting on location, which gives the film a freshness that studio-bound productions of the period lack, especially in the mountain scenes. Nothing is accidental for Murnau: each shot is as carefully framed and precisely intended as in a Kubrick film, with Schreck's vampire shown continually emerging from areas of darkness, often within an arched frame. Murnau provides a host of very memorable images, ranging from the eerie negative shot of the coach flying through the trees, and the striking image of the vampire rising bolt upright from his coffin then stalking across the open deck of the ship, to a thoroughly chilling montage of Orlok's shadow purposefully stalking its way upstairs towards Ellen Hutter's room.

Other films of the period such as **The Phantom of the Opera** had equally memorable characters and performances but only Murnau created a work that combines character and scenario to such powerful effect. The film survives in prints of varying quality; the tinted BFI restoration with an excellent score by Hammer composer James Bernard is highly recommended. [JC]

THE PHANTOM OF THE OPERA

1925, US, dir Rupert Julian, scr Frank M. McCormack (uncredited), starring Lon Chaney, Mary Philbin, Norman Kerry, Arthur Edmund

The new owners of the Paris Opera House ignore the Phantom's warning to replace Prima Donna Carlotta with her understudy Christine in a performance of *Marguerite*. Carlotta is crushed by a chandelier and the Phantom abducts Christine, who is intrigued by his attentions until she sees his horribly scarred face. Universal's lavish production remains the finest and most faithful adaptation of Gaston Leroux's novel; in its original conception (with the Phantom discovered lying dead on his organ by the mob) it was still closer to Leroux, but producer Carl Laemmle, unhappy with Julian's work after previews, ordered reshoots. Julian, a temperamental and dictatorial director, refused to comply, and Edward Sedgwick was recruited to shoot new scenes. This version also previewed badly, and the film was re-edited, with additional scenes shot featuring comedian Charles Conklin. These were in turn removed by Laemmle, but the re-edit was used for the original release. Muddying the film's history still further, Universal re-released it in 1929 as a sound film with additional scenes featuring Carlotta's mother and a new soundtrack; this edit is the version most commonly seen today. Chaney's performance as the Phantom is justly celebrated, his marvellously expressive eyes and theatrical

DRACULA

Dracula's cinematic life began with **Nosferatu, eine Symphonie des Grauens**, the first and unauthorized screen adaptation by F.W. Murnau. Albin Grau's vampire design re-imagined the Count as an alien presence a world away from Stoker's deathless aristocrat, creating an icon powerful enough to be resurrected in later works such as Tobe Hooper's *Salem's Lot* (1979). Official imprimatur came in 1931 with Tod Browning's film of the Hamilton Deane stage adaptation. Bela Lugosi's vampire has since become a universal signifier for the Count (much to Lugosi's dismay, since it typecast him for life), but the film is meagre fare next to other horror movies of the period. Lugosi's performance is static and the whole production betrays its stage origin with a singular lack of drama despite some wonderful scenes in the ruined castle. George Melford's Spanish-language version, made alongside the American film with the same sets but different crew and actors (Carlos Villarías was the vampire), used the same resources but managed everything better.

Hammer did everything better still when Christopher Lee blazed onto the screen in 1958, seething with diabolic energy. Stoker's story was mutilated even further, leaving only bare bones, but this hardly mattered with Lee and Peter Cushing's Van Helsing confronting each other for the first time. While Lugosi's Dracula has devolved to the level of Halloween masks, Lee's rampaging performance is the one future actors still have to beat. The film made him an international name but he despaired of the sequels, preferring to point people to his role in Jesus Franco's 1970 version, with Herbert Lom as Van Helsing and Klaus Kinski (later to play Nosferatu) as a typically manic Renfield. Franco's story followed the book with greater care than previously attempted but the film is still hostage to its low budget.

The late '70s saw several Draculas arrive at once, with the BBC's faithful TV adaptation starring Louis Jordan, Werner Herzog's remake of **Nosferatu** and an expensive Hollywood production by John Badham based on a Broadway revival of the stage play. Frank Langella played the Count on stage and screen and was popularly considered "the sexiest Dracula of all", a rather confused emphasis given that Stoker's vampire was a shape-shifting monster. Badham's production has great sets and some impressive scenes but the story was as mangled as ever, with Dracula even staking Laurence Olivier's Van Helsing at the end.

Francis Coppola's equally lavish **Bram Stoker's Dracula**

ABOVE: Max Schreck emerges from the shadows, **Nosferatu, eine Symphonie des Grauens**.

(1992) took the usual liberties but managed to create something quite unique, a sumptuous film that carves out its own identity (Gary Oldman's powerful Dracula has a different guise in nearly every scene) while acknowledging its predecessors. Coppola pulled off a difficult balancing act, mixing outright horror with rich aesthetics to create something as heady and delirious as the absinthe that Dracula drinks with Mina. Dracula's character has become an archetype that each generation seems compelled to reinvent. With screen vampires as active as they ever were, we're probably due a 21st-century version any time now. [JC]

opulent sets – the Piranesi-like chambers of the underworld are particularly memorable – and inspired art direction, the film is let down only by overwrought acting from Philbin, some ludicrously purple prose for the intertitles – "No longer like a toad in these foul cellars will I secrete the venom of hatred!" – and the hackneyed image of a mob armed with torches that ends the film.

THE UNKNOWN
1927, US, dir Tod Browning, scr Waldemar Young, starring Lon Chaney, Joan Crawford, Norman Kerry, Nick de Ruiz

Browning drew on his carnival background and obsession with sexual pathology for this astonishingly perverse *conte cruel*, the most concise expression of castration anxiety in the director's *oeuvre* of truncated torsos (for synopsis see p.21). Alonzo is an entirely unsympathetic character, a murderer and thief who tries to use Nanon's phobic fear of men's hands to his own ends: Malabar the Mighty saves him from a beating, but Alonzo encourages him to take Nanon in his arms – "Let her listen to the song of your blood!" – while knowing full well what her response will be. Alonzo's love for Nanon is selfish and possessive, however insane the sacrifice he makes; Malabar, by contrast, is willing to help cure her of her phobia. Browning uses Chaney as a sideshow display, showcasing him drinking wine, smoking cigarettes and playing a guitar with his feet, as well as shooting a rifle and throwing knives at Nanon in his show itself. However, Chaney brings a tragic intensity to the role that makes him a powerful identification figure, expressing everything from tortured pathos through fidgety uncertainty to delirious happiness using just his marvellously expressive eyes and feet, all underscored with the blackly comic tone that sees a post-operation Alonzo, on being told by Nanon that he looks thinner, admitting that "I have lost some flesh". **Freaks** remains Browning's masterpiece, but Sidney Hayers's *Circus of Horrors* (1960) maintained his sexual perversity in a similar tale of a criminal hiding out in a circus, while Jodorowsky's **Santa Sangre** is a fittingly lurid tribute to the director's work.

THE CAT AND THE CANARY
1927, US, dir Paul Leni, scr Walter Anthony, Alfred A. Cohn, Robert F. Hill, starring Laura La Plante, Creighton Hale, Forrest Stanley, Tully Marshall

Eccentric millionaire Cyrus West's relatives gather 20 years after his death to hear the reading of his will. He has left his money to his most distant relative, Annabelle West, but only on condition that

ABOVE: The Phantom unmasked. Lon Chaney, **The Phantom of the Opera**.

gestures anticipating Karloff's Frankenstein creature in its balance of pathos and monstrosity. The actor also designed his own make-up, luridly impressive even today, and the character remains one of the most compelling explorations of the silent cinema's obsession with romantic disfigurement. The Phantom's lair is an infernal underworld five floors beneath the opera house, itself built over a network of mediaeval torture chambers. The secret passages are reached by passing through a mirror and crossing a Stygian lake, lending the story the quality of Classical myth. The Phantom represents the necessary inverse to the witless merriment of the opera house, a reminder of ugliness, pain and mortality distilled in his appearance as the Red Death during a masked ball, a spectacular sequence shot in early two-strip Technicolor. But he is still a sympathetic character, his achievements as a showman (engineering the crushing of the leading lady under a chandelier is an operatic coup) and his romantic conviction easily outshining the deceitful, fame-obsessed Christine, unable to look past the Phantom's surface ugliness, and her dull lover Raoul. Aided by

she be proved sane. The housekeeper is convinced that West's ghost roams the house and an escaped lunatic is on the prowl: will Annabelle last the night? John Willard's 1922 play, a haunted-house spoof, proved durable enough to spawn a 1930 Spanish-language film, a 1939 Bob Hope vehicle and a 1979 misfire by softcore auteur Radley Metzger, but Leni's version is the classic, its iconography of fake walls, hidden passages and ghostly corridors providing the visual inspiration for everything from **The Old Dark House** (Whale openly acknowledged Leni's influence) to **The Raven**, Corman's Poe films and the Italian gothics of the '60s. While it lacks the broad palette and rictus grin of (1928), a historical melodrama that is probably Leni's finest American film, *The Cat* is packed with the visual flourishes Hollywood studios expected from their German émigrés, from double and triple superimpositions to distorted reflections, shadow play, restless POV (point-of-view) meanderings and outlandishly animated intertitles. Yet for all its visual innovations, the source material ensures the film remains light-hearted, stagy and less sophisticated than its Continental peers, its chills mostly relying on "Behind you!" pantomime frights as Leni's Teutonic gloom evaporates in the Hollywood sunshine. Martha Mattox's marvellously grim housekeeper – "I don't need the living ones" – and Lucien Littlefield's fearsome doctor aside, the cast do little but cringe and run in comic cowardice, with Hale particularly grating as the craven, owl-faced Paul Jones, as terrified of physical contact as he is of ghosts, making Annabelle's evident fondness proof of such unaccountably perverse taste that she probably was insane after all.

BELOW: Roderick Usher paints his wife, **La Chute de la Maison Usher**.

LA CHUTE DE LA MAISON USHER
AKA THE FALL OF THE HOUSE OF USHER

1928, Fr, dir/scr Jean Epstein, starring Margaret Gance, Jean Debucourt, Charles Lamy, Abel Gance

A friend visits Roderick Usher and his ill wife Madeleine. Usher is painting a portrait of Madeleine that seems to sap her strength. When it is completed she appears to die, but his conviction that she has been buried alive is justified when she returns from the grave. One of the milestones of the French avant-garde, Epstein's sumptuous visual feast, "based on themes by E.A. Poe", betrays Poe's original conception in its shift of Madeleine from Roderick's sister to his wife but still achieves an atmosphere of cloying morbidity of which the writer would doubtless have approved. Epstein's other key change is to situate Usher in the world of natural phenomena, extended shots of the misty marshland and bare trees surrounding his house giving the film an acute air of wintry despair; lighting and wind take on supernatural dimensions, with shots of horned owls and mating frogs spliced in to express ideas of death and resurrection, while Epstein contrasts the film's roots in the natural world with the artifice of triple superimpositions, slow motion and negative photography, showcased most spectacularly in the funeral march to the crypt. These visually stunning sequences partly redeem the dull creakiness of many of the scenes in Usher's house, although they were not enough for assistant director Luis Buñuel, who was presumably dismayed by the humourless piety of the resurrection sequence and made this his final collaboration with Epstein.

CHAPTER

3

1930s

Again, it starts with **Dracula**.

When interviewing Bela Lugosi about his stage performance as the Count, journalists lumped **Dracula** in with **The Cat and the Canary**, *The Gorilla* and *Seven Keys to Baldpate*, and asked him if he was worried about being typecast in "mystery plays".

After Lugosi had starred in Tod Browning's 1931 film, with **Frankenstein** in pre-production at Universal as a follow-up and competing studios rooting about for similar properties to chase the **Dracula** dollars, the term "horror film" slipped into general usage.

When the British Board of Film Censors instituted a special rating for these distasteful items, they labelled them "H" for "Horrific" – which seems to have sealed the deal in so far as naming the genre went. It wasn't a linguistic inevitability: terms like "macabre", "gothic", "weird" (as in the pulp *Weird Tales*), "terror", "monster" and "shudder" were also available.

Though **Dracula** founded a genre, there's a feeling that neither the studio nor the director really had their heart in the film. Both were involved with the project because of Lon Chaney. With his death, it may have seemed like a contractual obligation. Universal faffed about with casting choices before resorting, essentially because he was cheap, to Lugosi. It may be they didn't go with Conrad Veidt because they didn't see **Dracula** as a super-spectacular like **The Phantom of the Opera**, which was in re-release in a part-talkie version, or *The Man Who Laughs*. Browning hardly gave **Dracula** his best shot – though stunningly designed and photographed by the German Karl Freund (who had done **Der Golem**, 1920, and *Metropolis*, 1926), the picture is basic filmmaking, certainly not on a par with **The Unknown** or other surviving Chaney-Browning films. Some have argued that the simultaneous Spanish version shot on the same sets (from a translation of the John L. Balderston script) is more excitingly directed (by George Melford). It should be noted that it's far less excitingly script-edited – Browning tore out redundant pages which Melford faithfully plods through. The English-language **Dracula** has pace to recommend it above its Spanish shadow, not to mention Lugosi's iconic performance in a role Carlos Villarías cannot claim to own in the way the Hungarian did (and does). Browning's film also has a definitive fly-eating Renfield from

---

OPPOSITE: Bela Lugosi fakes his fangs, Mark of the Vampire (1935).

Dwight Frye, whose cracked laugh is almost as imitable as Lugosi's lububrious "I … am … Dracula" accent.

There was enthusiasm for **Dracula** on the part of studio head Carl Laemmle Jr, just promoted by a doting father. But no one seems to have considered how radical the material was. To the Laemmles, **Dracula** was a solid, proven property – a book everyone knew and a play that was still running. The studio that had coined it in with **The Phantom of the Opera** and **The Cat and the Canary** thought they knew what they were getting. **Dracula** was even a remake: **Nosferatu** might be officially suppressed, but certainly wasn't forgotten – clips turn up in a Universal short *Boo!* (1932), so there must even have been a print on the lot for easy reference – and Murnau was well-known around town as an Oscar winner for *Sunrise* (1928).

The difference between what had come before in Hollywood and **Dracula** was underlined by the play's epilogue, in which Dr Van Helsing (Edward Van Sloan in the film) comes out from behind the curtain to assure the audience that "there *are* such things". The Phantom was malformed at birth, the Cat just the secondary heir in a fright mask and Chaney's pointy-fanged *London After Midnight* vampire turned out to be a sleuth playing dressing up to catch a killer. Lugosi's Dracula is a real-life, honest-to-Bram Stoker bloodsucking reanimated corpse. Previously, Hollywood had been leery of "such things" and practical Yankee reviewers were a touch sneery about their appearance in high-falutin' European pictures which might do for the carriage trade but wouldn't pack 'em into the stalls. Browning didn't care either way. He remade *London After Midnight* as *Mark of the Vampire* (1935), with Lugosi in the cloak again, and tried to get away with a Scooby-Doo ending as if he *hadn't* founded a whole new genre with **Dracula**.

Junior Laemmle took note of the unexpected box-office bonanza of **Dracula**, which hit theatres in February 1931, and immediately began to develop **Frankenstein**, getting it out before the end of the year, despite a change of director and star midway through pre-production. Originally, the project was set for Lugosi and Robert Florey, but the Englishman James Whale, whom Laemmle valued as a Universal asset, was given the pick of all the studio's properties and plumped for Mary Shelley's "Man Who Made a Monster". Lugosi (who, forever after, claimed to have turned down the Monster role rather than being unceremoniously dumped by a Brit who didn't take him seriously) and Florey were shunted off into *Murders in the Rue Morgue* (1932), a Poe adaptation which is also a lightly disguised remake of **Caligari**. Whale cast his London stage associate Colin Clive as Dr Frankenstein, bumping out a possibly interesting Leslie Howard, and scuppered Lugosi's future career by selecting Anglo-Indian bit player Boris Karloff (born William Pratt) to wear Jack P. Pierce's make-up as the Monster.

In the opening credits of **Frankenstein**, Karloff is billed as "?" – his name, not familiar to the public despite decades' worth of secondary villains and one-scene psychotics, was not revealed until the "a good cast is worth repeating" closing crawl. If **Dracula** is a thrown-together piece that somehow works, **Frankenstein** is the result of considered thought by the director, make-up man (a great deal of the film's lasting strength is in that unbeatable, copyrighted Monster) and cast. The script is even more makeshift than that of **Dracula**, with too many irreconcilable ideas thrown in. A great deal of fuss is made of the plot point that the hunchbacked minion Fritz (Dwight Frye, whom Whale *did* hold over from **Dracula**) has snatched an "abnormal brain" for use in the Monster's skull, but this "explanation" for why the experiment turns out badly is at odds with Whale's (and Shelley's) depiction of the creature as an innocent who only reacts viciously when abused or rejected, and whose worst crime (drowning a little girl) is simply a sad misunderstanding.

The early stirrings of censorious grumblers (especially in Britain, the spiritual home of **Dracula** and **Frankenstein**) did more to excite than depress box-office figures. With *two* proven hits, Universal realized they had a new-made genre on their hands – complete with iconic stars, supporting actors, standing sets, behind-the-camera talent like Whale, Pierce and Freund, and a shelfload of suitable source material – and that their horror monopoly would not last long. Lugosi, though he quickly signed for a Poverty Row quickie (shot on the Universal lot), **White Zombie** (1932), retained some of the **Dracula** magic in the troubled *Murders in the Rue Morgue*, and would remain (resentfully) the studio's number-two bet for any horror role. But Whale and Karloff were treasured and were cannier and more ambitious than the Hungarian in parlaying their break-out success into

whole careers. The duo reunited for **The Old Dark House** (1932), adapted from a J.B. Priestley novel, which summed up the entire genre of pre-**Dracula** "old dark house" horror comedies – Whale even re-creates some of Paul Leni's **Cat and the Canary** compositions. The gloomy drawing room is filled with clipped, to-be-familiar British players (Raymond Massey, Ernest Thesiger, Charles Laughton) who spout sardonic dialogue, and Karloff is cast as a grunting "below-stairs" brute – Morgan, the drunken Welsh butler. Whale was a working-class lad who reinvented himself as an "officer material" gent and West End wit, whereas Karloff was the public school-educated black sheep of a distinguished diplomatic family who'd oddly served decades as a manual labourer before becoming an actor (Whale disparagingly referred to his discovery as "the truck driver").

Perhaps sensing that he was being kept in his place, Karloff passed on Whale's offer of **The Invisible Man** (1933), in which his voice would finally be heard but only on the condition that his face was kept off screen. Claude Rains, another well-spoken Englishman of humble origins, landed that plum, and his silky voice established him as a character star. Lugosi moaned that if only he had played the Monster, he would have got all the career breaks which came to Karloff; Karloff never suggested that, if he had played the Invisible Man, he would have landed Rains's stand-out roles in *The Adventures of Robin Hood* (1938), *Casablanca* (1943) and *Notorious* (1945).

Karloff was at last allowed to talk, revealing an educated lisp in **The Mummy** (1932), a swift rewrite of **Dracula** mingled with *She* and tabloid stories about the "Curse of King Tut". With Karl Freund promoted to director and a script that is streamlined rather than eccentric, **The Mummy** is Hollywood's first conveyor-belt horror film – commissioned by a studio that knew what they were getting, patterned closely on what had worked before, and showcasing a star who was not only a proven talent but a box-office draw in this type of picture. Withal, along with the snatch of *Swan Lake* over the credits (as in **Dracula** and several other Universals of the period) and another memorable Jack Pierce make-up job, a whiff of graveyard poetry informs the film.

By now, the competition was on the scent. Every studio in Hollywood had their own would-be **Dracula** or **Frankenstein** on the starting blocks. Paramount, the most elegant and sophisticated of

ABOVE: Henry Hull snarls, *The WereWolf of London* (1935).

the majors, looked to classic novels which nevertheless offered an opportunity for lurid, sexualized violence. First, they greenlit Rouben Mamoulian's **Dr Jekyll and Mr Hyde** (1931), with Fredric March trumping John Barrymore's silent performance by doing the handsome doctor as a parody of matinee idol Barrymore and the ape-like mister as a shaggy thug in evening dress with a nasty streak of sadistic humour. Paramount's second-string monster was Erle C. Kenton's **Island of Lost Souls** (1933), with Charles Laughton as a flabby, whip-wielding incarnation of Wells's Dr Moreau. An unrecognizable Lugosi hides under face-fur as a beast man added in post-production to beef up the film's horror status. March won a Best Actor Academy Award, which went some way towards silencing prudes who thought the film entirely too explicit about the double man's relationship with Soho tart Ivy (Miriam Hopkins), while **Lost Souls** was banned in England for its vivisection and implied bestiality. Paramount's **Murders in the Zoo** (1933) is just as nasty, if nowhere near as respectable.

Warner Brothers, who specialized in rattling, contemporary, torn-from-the-headlines dramas (even their musicals are realistic) had Michael Curtiz direct a pair of twisted whodunits in lovely Technicolor, *Doctor X* (1932) and *Mystery of the Wax Museum* (1933). These introduce Lionel Atwill as another British horror face, voice and leer (Paramount would snap him up for **Murders in the Zoo** and he would inevitably gravitate to Universal's stock company), employ Fay Wray as a leggy beauty (though she's upstaged by Glenda Farrell's wisecracking proto-Lois Lane in *Mystery*) and mix disfigured fiends, mad geniuses, "moon murders"

and "synthetic flesh" with snappy reporters doing self-aware gags ("he makes Frankenstein look like a lily") and complaining about Prohibition. Warner never really committed to horror, but Curtiz landed Karloff for *The Walking Dead* (1935), which has gangsters stalked by a vengeful zombie (it's one of the first "body count" movies), and the studio put contract player Humphrey Bogart in an unlikely "scientific vampire" role for *The Return of Dr X* (1939).

RKO had their own monster in the works, though **King Kong** (1933) doesn't seem to have been an attempt to get in on the **Dracula-Frankenstein** business and probably owes its inspiration to the 1926 film of Arthur Conan Doyle's *The Lost World*, which had proved that Willis H. O'Brien's hand-animated prehistoric creatures could carry a picture. While producer-directors Ernest B. Schoedsack and Merian C. Cooper were toiling over **Kong**, they had time to use the same sets and Fay Wray in a quickie classic, **The Most Dangerous Game** (1932). Here, Leslie Banks is cast in the Karloff-Atwill-Rains mould as Count Zaroff, a Russian huntsman with perfect Shaftesbury Avenue tones and a distinctive way of holding a cigarette. Zaroff's passion is for stalking "the most dangerous game", man. The Richard Connell story would be often remade and Zaroff is an archetype of the sadistic mad genius who would feature in many horror melodramas before mutating into the role model for all Bond villains (Christopher Lee's *Man With the Golden Gun* has many Zaroff traits). After Zaroff and the awe-inspiring **Kong**, RKO rushed out *Son of Kong* (1933), the genre's first disappointing sequel, and quit the horror business until the '40s.

MGM, which liked to think themselves the most prestigious studio on the row, obviously had to make horror movies. Chaney and

Browning had worked there through the '20s, under the aegis of the supposed genius Irving Thalberg – who had a strange streak that responded to stories like **The Unknown**. Browning was back with **Freaks** (1932) and Chaney replaced by real sideshow oddities – the result is Browning's masterpiece, though it's wildly inconsistent in tone. It was hastily sold off by the studio to grindhouse exhibitors who touted it as a roadshow shocker alongside Dwain Esper's astounding Poe-derived *Maniac* (1934). Since **Freaks** didn't work, the studio played safe by hiring Karloff and adapting a proven property in *The Mask of Fu Manchu* (1932): again, MGM vacillated, switching directors and never settling on a tone. However, this is the film where Karloff really breaks out and shows he can be more than a dutiful studio employee, relishing sadistic camp in a manner even Whale would never dare and hissing polite hatred as he plans to lead his Asian hordes in an apocalyptic conflict to kill all white men and mate with their women. Myrna Loy is fun as the devil doctor's "sadistic nymphomaniac" daughter too – and puritanical, moralistic studio boss Louis B. Mayer, in a perpetual power struggle with Thalberg, was duly horrified. Browning, though reckoned a burn-out, was still welcome on the lot; besides *Mark of the Vampire* (1935), he managed one other quirky effort, the grotesque science-fiction tale of miniaturized assassins *The Devil-Doll* (1936). Perhaps MGM's best horror was another attempt to fit Universal's template, **Mad Love** (1935), which hired Freund to direct, used source material (Maurice Renard's novel *The Hands of Orlac*) which had worked in a German silent film and teamed established second-rank horror player Colin Clive with Peter Lorre, whose performance in **M** impressed all those Hollywood executives who would never have greenlit a film about child-murder and who was well on his way to joining the elect company of horror stars.

The independent Halperin organization gave Lugosi one of his better roles in **White Zombie** (1932), drawing on the then-hot new topic of Caribbean voodoo. This introduced the apparatus of wax dolls and walking corpses, and exploited the sub-genre's simultaneous fascination with and denial of ethnic cultures: the implication of the title is that *Black Zombie* wouldn't be news. Never a force, even on Poverty Row, the Halperins managed a semi-sophisticated tale of possession, *Supernatural* (1933), and a near-unwatchable follow-up, *Revolt of the Zombies* (1936). Other quickie outfits were ready to sign Lugosi or Atwill and borrow Universal sets: Majestic made *The Vampire Bat* (1933), with Atwill and Fay Wray, and *Condemned to Live* (1935); and the success of **White Zombie** inspired *Drums o' Voodoo* (1934), *Black Moon* (1934) and *Ouanga* (1935). If things dried up in Hollywood, there were even jobs abroad – Karloff returned home in triumph for the rickety but wonderful *The Ghoul* (1933) and the calmer *The Man Who Changed His Mind* (1936), while Lugosi was made welcome in England for *Mystery of the Marie Celeste* (*The Phantom Ship*, 1935), from the newly founded studio Hammer Films, and the Edgar Wallace-derived shocker *The Dark Eyes of London* (*The Human Monster*, 1939). However, if horror had a home, it was still surely on the Universal lot.

Junior Laemmle's big idea for 1934 was to team Karloff and Lugosi and throw in a big horror name he didn't have to pay for, Edgar Allan Poe. **The Black Cat**, directed by the ambitious Edgar G. Ulmer, owes more to *The Magician* and **The Most Dangerous Game** than the Poe story, but nevertheless gives the stars material worth chewing over. Karloff is a perverted diabolist who lives in a modern castle built over the battlefield where all the men he betrayed in the war were killed, and Lugosi is a vengeance-seeking obsessive who plans on skinning him alive. It worked so well that the gang was back together, with Ulmer replaced by the less arty Louis Friedlander for **The Raven** (1935), in which Lugosi's Poe-obsessed mad plastic surgeon gives Karloff's gangster a new, hideous face. In this pair of films, the stars are evenly matched, alternating lead villain and vengeful stooge. By *The Invisible Ray* (1936) Karloff was the undisputed lead as a glowing mutant and Lugosi is just along for the name-value. Meanwhile, Universal – wary of Whale's increasing demands – tried to boost other directors as horror men. Stuart Walker handled a couple of gothic Dickens films, getting good mad work from Claude Rains in *The Mystery of Edwin Drood* (1935), and was given *The WereWolf of London* (1935), in which Henry Hull subs for Karloff as a botanist infected with lycanthropy by Warner Oland in the Himalayas. The first talkie werewolf movie, this still wound up being a rough draft for a sub-genre that didn't come together until **The Wolf Man** (1941).

What Universal really wanted weren't just follow-ups, but *sequels*: James Whale was given carte blanche – along with

ABOVE: Boris Karloff flees his Universal contract to star in *The Ghoul* (1933).

a dream cast, including Ernest Thesiger and Elsa Lanchester – to make **Bride of Frankenstein** (1935), which is at once a genuine expansion of his original and a deconstructive parody of it. Waspish, sly, charming, perverse and emotionally devastating, **Bride** shows how far Hollywood had come in only four years: already, the 1931 film, with its lack of music and dull, drawing-room chats, seemed antique, while **Bride** has a full score by Franz Waxman, no patience at all with boring characters (Valerie Hobson barely gets a look-in, though she officially has the title role) and enormous visual sophistication to go with its bare-faced, blasphemous cheek. If it had been up to Whale, the horror cycle would have ended with **Bride** – he certainly had no more to say on the subject (like Browning, he didn't really work after the mid-'30s). Universal, of course, saw things differently. They had *Dracula's Daughter* (1936) in production – albeit without Lugosi (Gloria Holden is luminously odd in the title role) and with a new, efficient briskness that makes for rattling entertainment and gothic charm but sadly few real chills.

Around the time of these sequels, the horror film fell off Hollywood's production schedules. Pressure from British censors and moralists brought about this hiatus – bizarrely, since the voice of Hollywood horror had a distinctly British accent, much of the subject matter came from British authors and the remarkable Tod Slaughter was in constant employment in tiny studios around London outdoing any depravity Karloff or Lugosi could imagine in the likes of *Sweeney Todd, or the Demon Barber of Fleet Street* (1936) and *The Crimes of Stephen Hawke* (1936). Still, Karloff was reduced to playing a Charlie Chan knock-off Chinese sleuth for the low-grade Monogram studio and Lugosi was on welfare – until the end of the decade, when the horror express was back on the rails.

Hailed as "the movies' greatest year", 1939 was big on super-productions: besides *Gone with the Wind*, that mammoth women's picture, and *The Wizard of Oz*, the ultimate children's film, there were several epic-scale, all-star, A-picture revivals of genres that had fallen to programmer status, notably the Western *Stagecoach* and the gangster picture *The Roaring Twenties*.

The usual account of the 1939 return of the horror film suggests that a successful double-bill re-release of **Dracula** and **Frankenstein** prompted Universal to produce **Son of Frankenstein** – inevitably casting Karloff (in his final go-round as the Monster) and Lugosi (in arguably his finest screen role as the broken-necked Ygor), with incisive Basil Rathbone and clipped Lionel Atwill aboard to make up for the absence of the dry, British Whale (replaced by the underrated Rowland V. Lee). However, *Son* wasn't the only horror restart project that year: Rathbone donned the deerstalker for the first time in Fox's *Hound of the Baskervilles*, Paramount polished off an old Universal property and put Bob Hope and Paulette Goddard in *The Cat and the Canary* (with perennial supporting suspects George Zucco and Gale Sondergaard) and RKO mounted a lavish version of *another* silent Universal hit with Charles Laughton as *The Hunchback of Notre Dame*. There was even time enough for follow-ups: Universal had Lee, Karloff and Rathbone do a historical horror (*Tower of London*), Fox got Rathbone back for a macabre duel with Moriarty (Zucco) in *The Adventures of Sherlock Holmes* and RKO got another Broadway mystery remake in the can in *The Gorilla* (with the Ritz Brothers, Atwill and Lugosi). Horror was back.

DR JEKYLL AND MR HYDE

1931, US, dir Rouben Mamoulian, scr Samuel Hoffenstein, Percy Heath, starring Fredric March, Miriam Hopkins, Rose Hobart, Holmes Herbert

Dr Jekyll, frustrated by Brigadier-General Carew's refusal to approve Jekyll's marriage to his daughter Muriel, tests a theory about the separation of the personality by experimenting with a serum. He becomes Hyde and does everything that Jekyll as a gentleman cannot; but soon Jekyll can no longer control the transformations.

Jekyll is a selfless idealist who will perform free surgery rather than attend society dinners, but Carew's obstinate denial of sexual access to his daughter proves too much for his reserve; rather than deny his instincts, like his colleague Lanyon, he proposes to divorce them into another body. Ivy, a prostitute Jekyll rescues from a beating, is an easy target for Hyde's lust, but ironically Hyde becomes jealous of Jekyll when Ivy shrinks from his advances. Far from embodying sexual freedom, Hyde is merely coldly sadistic, and is thus a product of Jekyll's repression rather than liberation. Hyde envies not only Jekyll's good looks but also his gentleman status: the doctor is a prig whose money allows him to escape responsibility for his actions, whether attempting to buy Ivy off or employing Hyde to do his dirty work. Hyde's resentment notes the hypocrisy of Jekyll's class, in which social convention is paramount, expressions of emotion vulgar and sexual desire denied: Muriel is lifeless and bland compared (as she is explicitly through diagonal split-screens) to the vivacious, sexually open Ivy and Carew's primness fully deserves a bestial incursion through the French windows. March shines in both roles, the pompous, formal Jekyll contrasting with Hyde's twitchy mannerisms and athletic prowess, even if the latter's make-up is faintly ludicrous: giving in to one's instincts clearly means poor dentistry and terrible haircare. Still, this is the best of the early versions of Stevenson's story, due to March's superlative performance, a compelling portrait of Victorian London and Mamoulian's inspired direction, showcasing extended POV shots, superimpositions and innovative editing techniques.

DRACULA

1931, US, dir Tod Browning, scr Garrett Fort, Dudley Murphy, starring Bela Lugosi, Edward Van Sloan, Dwight Frye, Helen Chandler

Universal's first horror "talkie" may have ushered in the first golden age of American horror films and saved the studio from financial troubles, but it remains an artistic failure on almost every level. Browning's direction is leaden and uninspired, favouring static camera set-ups and a doggedly unimaginative interpretation of the material – there is none of the obsessive perversity of the director's **The Unknown** or **Freaks** here and the latter's carefully structured compositions are entirely absent. After the opening sequence of Renfield's visit to Transylvania, showcasing the Count's magnificently oversized

LEFT: The beast within. Fredric March as **Dr Jekyll and Mr Hyde**.

ABOVE: "There are far worse things awaiting man than death." Lugosi takes a guest on a tour of the vaults of Castle **Dracula** (1931).

castle and a bizarre display of armadillos, the pace is sluggish and the extended sequences of characters talking are less cinematic than theatrical, recalling the Horace Liveright stage production that gave Lugosi his most famous role. One sub-plot – the destruction of the vampiric Lucy – is simply abandoned and there is no sense of a struggle with Dracula at all: Van Helsing (whose presence is never adequately explained) and Harker simply find his coffin and stake him, off screen, in the most perfunctory manner imaginable. Although Lugosi's performance is iconic enough to have inspired a *Sesame Street* character, it involves little more than a cocked eyebrow and an ability not to blink as a light is shone in his eyes; and other cast members fare little better – David Manners's Harker is given little to do but stride around in plus-fours whinging. The only defence of the film's uncertain, faltering tone is that many other early talkies feel similar and the studio's financial problems prevented it from being budgeted nearly as highly as other "super productions". However, **Frankenstein** succeeded in amply demonstrating the potential of the new talking medium.

FRANKENSTEIN

1931, US, dir James Whale, scr Garrett Fort, Robert Florey, Francis Edward Faragoh, starring Boris Karloff, Colin Clive, Mae Clarke, Frederick Kerr

The first great American horror film, a seminal release that earned twice the gross of **Dracula** and saw the naming of a genre, with Universal dubbing the film "a horror picture". Whale's later horror films would display a surer touch, but his stylistic flourishes take *Frankenstein* far from **Dracula**'s staginess, whether in the anchoring of the wild story in mundane details such as Fritz pulling up his socks or the theatricality of the animation sequence, Frankenstein announcing "One man crazy – three very sane spectators" to his audience. The relatively static set-ups are also interspersed with startlingly fluid outdoor shots, from the first display of the villagers' revels to the creature lumbering through the woods. But the credit is far from Whale's alone: the sets, particularly the watchtower, are marvellously stylized mixtures of Expressionist detail and Teutonic solidity and Pierce's make-up for the monster is both iconic and convincingly corpselike. Clive's neurotic Frankenstein is a far more compelling figure than his bland fiancée Elizabeth and bovine friend Victor; Frye is credible as the hunchbacked Fritz, delighted to torment a creature even more disfigured than himself. But it is Karloff's performance that carries the film, conveying childlike innocence, despair and rage through beautifully judged physical theatre and eyes weighed down by mortician's wax. Some scenes are missing from many prints: Clive's exultant "now I know what it feels like to be God" was originally left intact but removed for the film's re-release and the happy ending of the baron toasting his son's recovery was excised by the studio to make way for the sequel. Others were cut altogether,

such as the Monster's murder of Fritz by hanging him on a hook. Although the film is far from flawless – Frankenstein's remorse is particularly unconvincing, lowering him to the petty moralizing of Victor, Elizabeth and the baron – it is shot through with a mythic sensibility that makes it perhaps the most iconic Universal horror.

BELOW: Tod Browning demonstrates his affection for the cast of **Freaks**.

M

1931, Ger, dir/co-scr Fritz Lang, co-scr Thea von Harbou, starring Peter Lorre, Ellen Widmann, Inge Landgut, Gustaf Gründgens

Crime encapsulates culture, fixing historical details that might otherwise be lost forever. Everyday street life in Victorian London is far better described in accounts of Jack the Ripper than those relating to Queen Victoria; similarly, Lang's account of a child killer in Weimar Berlin provides not only the first great serial-killer film

but a convincing dissection of an entire society. The response to the murders is invariably one of self-interest: police and politicians are concerned by their effect on public opinion; the criminal underworld is alarmed by the increased police presence but also the threat to their own public image; the public are drawn to posters describing the killer's activities by the 10,000-mark reward; and the murders feed a growing trade in newspapers and pulpy serial adventures. Lang employs a semi-documentary style to depict the mobilization and militarization of an entire city in search of the killer, describing the film as a "documentary" although it is entirely studio-bound. Beckert's activities were actually informed by Weimar serial killers Fritz Haarmann and Peter Kürten, both in the case details and shots of sausages that inevitably recall Haarmann's Sweeney Todd-style disposal of corpses. Yet Lang mixes documentary realism with a highly sophisticated, Expressionistic use of sound (Beckert hears the *Peer Gynt* melody even with his hands clamped over his ears) and an ironic counterpointing of dialogue and imagery – we hear that the police are tired and overworked, but see them sitting at a table eating and drinking – that recalls the use of intertitles in silent film. Lang was in fact the last major German director to adopt sound, and *M* has been accurately described as a silent film with sound.

Entirely modern in its refusal to provide simple explanations for Beckert's killings, *M* also showcases an astonishing debut performance from Lorre, honing the alternation between slack-jawed imbecility and infantile fury that would become his trademark in later Hollywood horrors and reaching a climax in his impassioned defence during the trial sequence. *M* is widely considered a broadside against capital punishment today, but many contemporary viewers thought it ambivalent, and Goebbels thought it argued *for* the death penalty. The film was remade by Joseph Losey in 1951.

FREAKS
AKA FORBIDDEN LOVE; NATURE'S MISTRESS; THE MONSTER SHOW

1932, US, dir Tod Browning, scr Willis Goldbeck, Leon Gordon, Edgar Allan Woolf, Al Boasberg, starring Wallace Ford, Olga Baclanova, Harry Earles, Daisy Earles

Circus performer Hans, a midget, falls in love with Cleopatra, the trapeze artist, ignoring his former lover's warnings that she is only interested in his money. Following their wedding Cleopatra is seen poisoning Hans, and the freaks decide to make her "one of us".

Our first sight of the freaks is presented without any of the exhibitionist zeal of the framing device's carnival barker: we simply see bizarre forms lolling in a woodland idyll. The landowner is brought over by an employee complaining of "horrible twisted things" and they witness a group of pinheads (microcephalics) and other freaks dancing around in what looks like a demented sabbat, until the freaks run, frightened by the employee's oaths, to the arms of their keeper, who explains that they are like "children" and the scene is one of innocent play. Our sympathy switches from the employee to the more understanding landowner, even as he looks at Prince Zandia (a human torso) and Johnny Eck (a man with no legs) and repeats "Children?" For these are adults, with adult needs, and the film's concentration on sexual attraction, whether between "normals" and freaks or the freaks themselves, provides much of its power to shock. Strongman Hercules stares, intrigued, at the half-man/half-woman, then punches her when she witnesses his tryst with Cleopatra, resenting the affront her temptations represent to his masculinity. Siamese twins Daisy and Violet both marry and the practical problems of relations between Hans and Cleopatra are implicit in Hans's ridicule from the carny folk. Betrayal and exploitation are expected in the normals' world – Hercules uses Venus, the seal-tamer, for her money – but when betrayal enters the freaks' atmosphere of trust and mutual support, it is unexpected and intolerable. Although Browning usually presents domestic situations, a few displays have a carny show feel – Prince Zandia rolls and lights a cigarette using just his lips – and the use of real freaks will offend many modern sensibilities. However, their untutored acting lends raw immediacy and Browning finds a peculiar but genuine beauty in their community: the film is as much a celebration of difference as a plea for tolerance. It's by far Browning's most accomplished film, filled with astonishing compositions, and the climactic scenes of the freaks advancing through the storm to exact a hideous revenge are among the most powerful the genre has to offer.

ISLAND OF LOST SOULS

1933, US, dir Erle C. Kenton, scr Waldemar Young, Philip Wylie, starring Charles Laughton, Richard Arlen, Leila Hyams, Kathleen Burke

Edward Parker is rescued from a shipwreck only to be dumped on a tiny island belonging to Dr Moreau after a disagreement with the captain. Moreau's experiments with plants and animals have resulted in an island full of half-men and the doctor plans to breed Parker with his panther woman, Lota, until Parker's fiancée Ruth tracks him down. H.G. Wells was reportedly unhappy with this adaptation of his novel, although he had little cause for concern: the film is an exquisitely realized marriage of

surgical unease and Darwinian panic, two key horror themes of the period. Laughton's marvellously refined Moreau, drinking endless cups of tea as he fields Parker's shocked questions with lines like "You're an amazingly *unscientific* young man", has set himself up as a god, a point he makes explicitly: he creates his subjects, sets up laws (and a call-and-response ritual reinforcing them) and punishes infractions through visits to his House of Pain. But his subjects are, finally, offended by a god who does not obey his own laws and they subject him to his own torments, in a stunning shot of bestial hands reaching for scalpels. Far from demanding a Christian mortification of the flesh, Moreau is clearly interested in cross-breeding his human visitors with his subjects, first Parker and the scantily clad Lota, then Ruth and Ouran, an ape-like creature, the film depicting sexual attraction between the humans and beast people. The revolt of the downtrodden masses and the post-war sexual allure of South Seas exoticism, referenced as Parker asks Lota, "What island are you from? Tahiti? Samoa?", would both have struck a chord with Depression-era audiences but it was the film's implicit condemnation of vivisection, rather than the sexual or religious taboos, that led to its banning in the UK until 1958.

THE MOST DANGEROUS GAME
AKA THE HOUNDS OF ZAROFF

1932, US, dir Ernest B. Schoedsack, Irving Pichel, scr James A Creelman, starring Joel McCrea, Fay Wray, Leslie Banks, Robert Armstrong

When his boat crashes and sinks, big-game hunter Robert Rainsford swims to a nearby island owned by Count Zaroff. Zaroff, who has two other shipwrecked guests staying, is also a hunter and invites Rainsford to join him in hunting the ultimate game. When the hunter refuses, he finds that he will become the hunted. RKO's adaptation of Richard Connell's short story presented a cheap companion piece to **King Kong**, recycling sets, cast and creatives to offset the cost of the bigger film's giant ape effects. The story has been retold several times but never bettered in its mixture of grisly detail – we see Zaroff's trophy room, with heads mounted on walls and floating in jars – and sexual tension. Zaroff's hunting serves an explicitly sexual function as the "whip for the other passions" ("Kill, then love!") and there is no doubt that the prize is Wray's Eve Trowbridge, whose heaving bosom and heavy-lidded eyes make it easier for Rainsford to forget the fate of his friends, "the swellest crowd". Madly staring eyes aside, Zaroff is the picture of refinement, his cut-glass accent belying his Russian origins. His superior intellect and impeccable manners mark him out as a rarefied spirit compared to his Karloff-like manservant, the girl's drunken boor of a brother and Rainsford, whose stolidity allows him to resist Zaroff's Mephistophelean advances with a blandly unimaginative "What do you think I am?" But even the square-jawed adventurer finds the temptation of power heightened by the sight of Eve's clothes growing progressively skimpier and wetter as the film draws to a close.

BELOW: Joel McCrea resists temptation … just. **The Most Dangerous Game**.

THE MUMMY

1932, US, dir Karl Freund, scr John L. Balderston, starring Boris Karloff, Zita Johann, David Manners, Arthur Byron

Sir Joseph Whemple's Egyptian expedition unearths a mummy and a treasure box containing the Scroll of Thoth, detailing the secret of raising the dead. An archaeologist reads from the scroll and animates the mummy. Ten years later, Whemple's son Frank unearths a princess's tomb with the help of Ardeth Bey, the reanimated mummy who has taken a more human appearance. Bey discovers that Helen Grosvenor, an acquaintance of the expedition team, is the reincarnation of his lover and plans to murder then reanimate her to join him in eternity. Universal's attempt to tap into the public obsession with all things Egyptian (Tutankhamun's tomb had been unearthed 10 years before, and the "curse" had been closely followed by a sensationalist media)

MAD SCIENCE

The mad scientist is one of horror's most popular figures, predating the birth of the genre with key appearances in Mary Shelley's *Frankenstein*, H.G. Wells's *The Island of Dr Moreau* and R.L. Stevenson's *The Strange Case of Dr Jekyll and Mr Hyde*. Frankenstein, Moreau and Jekyll cast long shadows over the 20th century, each representing a different seam of mad science that imitators would mine over the years – Moreau experiments with the body and man's place in the animal kingdom; Jekyll experiments with the mind; and Frankenstein attempts to create life from death. If on their original publication the novels were routinely dismissed as potboiler trash, age has lent them the patina of respectability; modern mad scientists fare less well, marginal figures shunted to the side of popular discourse, their appearances restricted to psychotics like Lionel Atwill (*Man-Made Monster*, 1941), Bela Lugosi (*The Ape Man*, 1943) and Boris Karloff (*Before I Hang*, 1940). In their gleeful portrayals, the figure is essentially conservative, drawing on a puritan distrust of prideful knowledge that still feeds a current of anti-intellectualism, particularly in the US, and deflecting justified anxieties about the role of technology in the modern world by presenting characters as laughably histrionic – this is "mad" science, surely a world away from the technology we rely on in everyday life.

The science-fiction writer Arthur C. Clarke famously once remarked that any technology, sufficiently advanced, would resemble magic. The mad scientist bridges the gap between magic and science both by putting a human face on impersonal science, adding drama and passion to the dull routine of the lab, and through his resemblance to the dark magi of former times, particularly in his embodiment of the Faust theme. Many mad scientists' activities – notably Frankenstein's necromancy – have occult leanings, and the presence of other, benevolent scientists who warn them not to meddle in things man was not meant to know quickly became a horror staple.

Science is related to magic in other ways too, the mad scientist tapping into the quasi-religious, irrational confidence in the possibilities of science, or "scientism", but the other concerns and hopes he represents are far more rational. Darwin's toppling of Creationism provided the engine for the evolutionary anxieties that drive Moreau, who engineers his animals to be closer to humans; Jekyll, whose alter-ego is an evolutionary throwback,

smaller (in Stevenson's novel, at least) and more bestial than the doctor; and Frankenstein, who scavenges for materials in the abattoir as well as the charnel house, combining human and animal elements in his creation. The Scopes monkey trial of 1925, in which a Tennessee schoolteacher was prosecuted for teaching evolution, reminded the American public of Darwin's dethroning of humans and spurred a cinematic rash of brain transplants from ape to man and back again.

But it took the mechanized slaughter of the First World War to foster a more widespread discontent with the role technology had to play in civilization, and the Great Depression to provide a categorical illustration of the chasm between the optimistic rhetoric of technological advancement and the grim street-level reality, as many people were "mechanized" out of work. The Bomb also infused old myths – the fall of man, Pandora's Box – with new energy, the mystical language adopted by bomb scientists (Oppenheimer quoted the *Upanishad*: "I am become death, shatterer of worlds" after the first test detonation) doing little to allay widespread anxiety, and countries as far apart as the UK (*Fiend Without a Face*, 1957) and Japan (*Gojira*, 1954) spawning new radioactive-creature features. Modern scientific anxieties tend to revolve around environmental issues, particularly those related to genetic engineering – it's rare to find an eco-disaster film without some lab-coated lunatic lurking in the wings – and reproductive technologies, but they also draw on a general lack of understanding of science as its complexity increases, fed by half-understood, overblown newspaper headlines of the latest scientific discoveries.

It should come as no surprise that Moreau's most important creation in **Island of Lost Souls** is Lota, the panther woman. If men largely identify more closely with machines and rigidly ordered systems than women, it is the soft, mysterious female body that drives mad scientists to distraction and most often ends up on the operating table. The women may be subjected to torturous medical tests (**The Exorcist**), drained of blood, vitality and youth (**I Vampiri, Il Mulino delle Donne di Pietra**), have their faces removed (**Les Yeux Sans Visage**, **Gritos en la Noche**) or used to test radical surgery techniques (**Rabid**), but it is always men who loom over their prone bodies, scalpels at the ready. As the popularity of cosmetic surgery and eating disorders implies, many women too view their bodies as something that must be altered, but the image of male control has a broader resonance, encompassing reproductive technology from the development of the pill to abortion clinics. There is also a specific relationship between cinema and cosmetic surgery, recalling the queues of hopeful young starlets going under the surgeon's knife in the hope of fitting standardized models of glamour.

Even in mad science lacking a female body on which to operate, women are conspicuous by their absence: Frankenstein seeks to usurp women's reproductive function, persistently ignoring his lover's pleas for attention in favour of toying with dead meat. Seth Brundle in Cronenberg's **The Fly** may be both the instigator and the subject of his corrosive experiments, but he is finally motivated by a desire to control his girlfriend's womb. At least Brundle recognizes female bodies as having useful qualities – Frankenstein's construction in **Bride of Frankenstein** is more typical of a mad scientist's objectification of women.

Crucially, Moreau, Jekyll and Frankenstein are also surgeons: medicine, the science that relates most directly to people's lives, has a privileged position in mad science. Fears of vulnerability at the hands of doctors who may have financial or more sinister interests in the patient's body – or may simply be grotesquely incompetent, unworthy recipients of a patient's trust – reached fever pitch in the 20th century, an era ushered in by the shadowy figure of Jack the Ripper, whose surgical precision led many to assume the killer had a medical background. Medical paranoia drew fresh blood from Josef Mengele's notorious experiments during the Second World War, which cast Hollywood mad scientists in a more sinister light and had their Allied equivalents in wide-ranging medical experiments on unwitting subjects. The war fostered a bureaucratized distance between doctor and patient, a depersonalization that grew towards the end of the 20th century, along with doctors' salaries and a sense of technical showmanship and wizardry that objectified patients' bodies still further.

Given how easily horror lends itself to psychoanalytic interpretation – a trend feeding back into many filmmakers' conscious use of Freudian imagery – psychiatrists and psychologists come in for a particularly rocky ride, depicted variously as hapless (**Frightmare**), corrupt (*Frankenstein and the Monster from Hell*, 1974) and plain murderous (The **Silence of the Lambs**, **Dressed to Kill**). **Psycho**'s ending points to the glib futility of psychiatric explanations and, in the many films in which the inmates have taken over the asylum (*Asylum*, 1972, **La Mansion de la Locura**), it never seems such a terrible loss.

In the West, the novelists Robin Cook and Michael Crichton have mined surgical horror for a series of popular novels, drawing together the mad science strands from medical melodrama and horror for a blend of corporate distrust and corporeal anxiety that has proved remarkably resilient both in print and on film. But none of their creations approach the extravagance of David Cronenberg, filmmaker as mad scientist, who allows his virulent experiments on the weak spots of the Cartesian split to run unchecked, presenting viscerally disgusting images of bodily revolt with the cold, dispassionate gaze of the scientific observer.

BELOW: Plastic surgery disasters. **Les Yeux Sans Visage**.

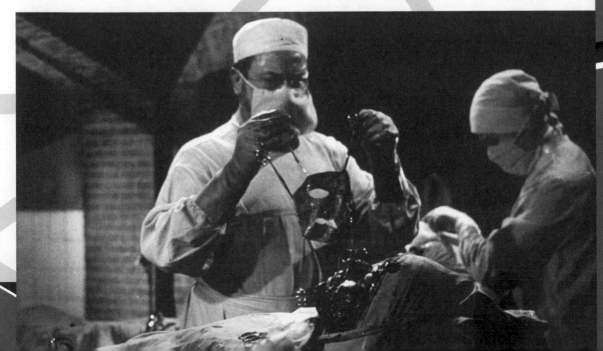

also marked Freund's directing debut and another showcase for Karloff, here in star billing. The opening sequence of the mummy's animation is exquisite, but the film then retreads **Dracula** territory – Bey's eyes command Helen in sexual thrall; the only defence against the occult power of the undead is a protective amulet; Edward Van Sloan (**Dracula**'s Van Helsing) plays another savant with esoteric knowledge – without once returning to the mummy's iconic image. While Karloff manages to distil a weary melancholy and the film is peppered with imaginative images – Bey's sunken yet glowing eyes and the scrying pool that lends him power over his environment – and superlative camerawork, by the end it descends into farce, with Johann entirely unable to save the role of the reincarnated princess from the script's absurdities: "I'm a priestess of Isis! Save me from the mummy – it's dead!"

THE OLD DARK HOUSE

1932, US, dir James Whale, scr Ben Levy, R.C. Sherriff, starring Boris Karloff, Charles Laughton, Raymond Massey, Melvyn Douglas

Five tourists take refuge from a storm in an old Welsh house. The owners reluctantly agree to put them up, but the tourists regret their decision when Morgan, the mute manservant, gets drunk and frees the occupant of the top room. Whale's second Universal horror, adapted from J.B. Priestley's novel *Benighted*, lacks the visual flair of his other work – the camera is relatively static, with none of the director's trademark tilts, and the high-contrast visuals resemble the silent pictures of a decade earlier, the montage of eerily reflected faces a rare directorial flourish – but compensates by having a deliciously fruity script and the most colourful batch of British eccentrics this side of *Sir Henry at Rawlinson End* (1980). Thesiger's Horace Femm seems to have walked out of a Ronald Searle cartoon, all quivering nostrils and waspish disdain, while his deaf sister Rebecca rants, Mrs Bates-style, about "the joys of fleshly love", sneering at the young, attractive female guests. Their father, Sir William, is a cackling, bedridden hag (played by an old woman); Karloff's Morgan, the manservant, is a scarred, dumb brute resembling one of the degenerates from **The Hills Have Eyes**; and then there's Saul, the dangerous one. Saul's appearance is built up to so well that when he finally emerges, a confused, little old man, lacking the physical eccentricities of the other inhabitants, we believe his story that he has been locked up for no reason – until the twitchy grin appears and he picks up a knife. Saul's dialogue and unpredictable mood swings are far more chilling than anything Morgan has to offer and Whale's depiction of the house's inhabitants judges the balance of humour and horror perfectly. The

guests are another matter: Laughton's comedy Yorkshireman soon grates and the romantic interlude between Penderell and Gladys makes the middle of the film drag. The ending is also unsatisfying, although the reappearance of Femm, breezily saluting everyone as though nothing had happened during the night, ends the film on a high note. The film was remade, badly, by Hammer in 1963.

VAMPYR, DER TRAUM DES ALLAN GREY
AKA VAMPYR

1932, Fr/Ger, dir/co-scr Carl Theodor Dreyer, co-scr Christen Jul, starring Julian West, Maurice Schutz, Rena Mandel, Sybille Schmitz

Dreyer's curious excursion into horror has often been overshadowed by his more serious works such as *La Passion de Jeanne d'Arc/The Passion of Joan of Arc* (1928) and his deserved reputation as one of Denmark's greatest filmmakers. *Vampyr* is subtitled "The Dream of Allan Gray" and it's as a dream that the film has to be considered, given that the narrative is frequently as elusive as that of **Eraserhead** or Cocteau's *Le Sang d'un Poète* (1930). The Allan Gray in question is a tall aristocrat in a double-breasted suit who arrives at a country inn where strange events are afoot. An elderly man appears and informs him that his daughter is ill then leaves a parcel "to be opened when I die". The next day Gray witnesses a peg-legged workman whose shadow has detached itself from his body and more disembodied shadows cavorting in the fields. When the old man is killed by the workman's shadow, Gray learns from a book in the parcel that a vampire is abroad and leeching blood from the dead man's daughter.

Despite being made with a rudimentary sound process, *Vampyr* is subtitled like a silent film and most prints have suffered considerable neglect during the passing decades. But as with Murnau's **Nosferatu** and **White Zombie**, this deteriorated quality often adds to its hazy, shadow-haunted atmosphere, giving many of the scenes an extra layer of mystery. Dreyer's direction is masterly and often extraordinary. Unlike most films of the period, the camera moves constantly, prowling around rooms or following characters, and Dreyer, like Cocteau, makes expert use of simple camera tricks such as double-exposure and reverse motion. The whole cast often seems to be sleepwalking or performing underwater, with an equally languid vampire, resembling Franz Lizst in a bishop's cassock, being controlled by a sinister, Einstein-headed doctor with a room full of human skulls. *Vampyr* avoids any final **Caligari**-like "explanation"; Dreyer ensures that Allan Gray's disturbing dream remains a dream for his audience as well. [JC]

WHITE ZOMBIE

1932, US, dir Victor Halperin, scr Garnett Weston, starring
Bela Lugosi, Madge Bellamy, John Harron, Joseph Cawthorn

Neil and Madeleine's Haitian wedding is hosted by Beaumont, a rich American who has designs on the bride. He enlists the services of plantation owner Murder Legendre, who has Madeleine poisoned and turned into a zombie for Beaumont's use. The Halperins' poverty-row classic capitalized on the American fascination with Haiti, initiated by William Seabrook's bestselling 1929 travelogue *The Magic Island*, for an enormously successful film that cost only $62,500 and grossed $8 million. The film tapped into several contemporary concerns: its sexual subtext, glossing necrophilia and sex slavery, sees Madeleine literally objectified as a tool for men's pleasure, commenting on the contemporary debate about women's autonomy. The sight of zombified workers exploited by ruthless employers would also have struck a nerve with the Depression era's dispossessed; the American military occupation of Haiti was being clumsily justified at the time through portrayals of the island as an anarchic hotbed of superstition, witchcraft and savagery – when Neil is told that Madeleine may still be alive, he protests, "In the hands of natives? Oh no, better dead than that"; and the American heroes, presented wearing white and riding white horses, must fight against the corrupting influence of Europe, embodied in the voodoo practitioner Legendre, reflecting fears of European involvement in Haitian affairs. Subtexts aside, the film is marvellously evocative, a morbid sense of decay informing images of the grave-covered hills and Legendre's coastal retreat, the "land of the dead". Halperin also uses superimpositions and diagonal wipes to give this fever dream of tropical lassitude a weird poetry, punctuated by repeated images of Lugosi's hands and eyes, his gaze staring out of the screen to hypnotize the viewer. A semi-official sequel, 1936's *Revolt of the Zombies*, was a disappointing misfire.

THE INVISIBLE MAN

1933, US, dir James Whale, scr R.C. Sherriff, Philip Wylie, starring
Claude Rains, Gloria Stewart, Henry Travers, William Harrigan

Jack Griffin takes refuge in an alpine inn to attempt to cure himself of his invisibility. When the innkeepers try to throw him out, he stays at the house of a former colleague, Kemp, and reveals his plans for world domination as the police hatch schemes to catch him. Whale's Wells adaptation, the director's personal favourite of his films, is a perfectly judged marriage of menace and comedy,

anchored by superlative special effects and a bravura performance from Rains. Returning the cinema to the Méliès era of camera trickery in which objects appear to move of their own accord, Whale sticks close to Wells's novel, glossing over the obvious erotic potential of Griffin's condition for an exploration of the impracticalities of being invisible. The film takes place in winter and Griffin catches a cold from running around naked outside; he must hide for an hour after eating, as his half-digested food is otherwise visible; he can only go out in fine weather, as mist and rain define his outline, and must avoid sooty cities, for the same reason. For all his megalomaniac conviction that "An invisible

---

BELOW: "They're not afraid of long hours." A zombie at work, **White Zombie**.

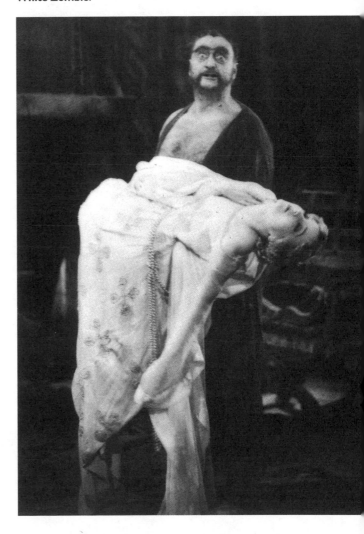

man can rule the world!", Griffin is limited to anarchic stone-throwing without a helper, but his glee in running rings around his would-be captors makes him a sympathetic character, up to a point. We may cheer when he throws a bottle of ink in the police inspector's face, but he then throttles the man to death. Yet he is exonerated by circumstance of much of the blame for his actions: he may have "meddled with things that man must leave alone", but he has been unwittingly driven insane by drugs and only experimented to prove himself a worthy suitor for his employer's daughter. Whale's eye for faces extends to the supporting cast, from Una O'Connor's shrieking landlady to the marvellous array of villagers and policemen, but Rains steals the show, by turns effete, sardonic and quivering with a demented passion that crowns him the greatest mad scientist of all. The film was followed by a predictable run of sequels and the inevitable encounter with Abbott and Costello.

KING KONG

1933, US, dir Merian C. Cooper, Ernest B Schoedsack,
scr James Creelman, Ruth Rose, Edgar Wallace, starring Fay Wray,
Robert Armstrong, Bruce Cabot, Frank Reicher

Carl Denham, a wildlife-documentary maker, recruits destitute Ann Darrow for a mysterious voyage to the South Pacific. Denham has heard the legend of a giant ape, Kong, on an uncharted island. On arrival they find the natives preparing a sacrifice to Kong; Ann is later kidnapped and offered to the ape. She is rescued and Kong is sent to New York City, but he escapes, to crush Manhattan. While *Kong* suffers from wooden acting, a bland script, peppered with "Say, boys" and endless reiterations of the "Beauty and the Beast" theme, and a breathtaking arrogance in Denham's thoughtless engineering of the natives' devastation, it is still a remarkable film. The parallels with "Beauty and the Beast" are redundant because *Kong* achieves its own mythic status, partly through the ape's sympathetic animation and the overwrought beauty of the jungle setting, but also through the fairy-tale simplicity of its plot. If Kong represents untamed desire, broken free from its bonds through explicitly sexual excitement – Kong undresses Ann at one point, although clearly he's too large to do much except eat her – intriguingly it takes a film crew to tame him, presenting him as a controlled spectacle, a commercialized dream sold back to a passive Depression-era audience. *Kong* has other spectacles on display too, from the presentation of the native

RIGHT: Love at first sight, **King Kong**.

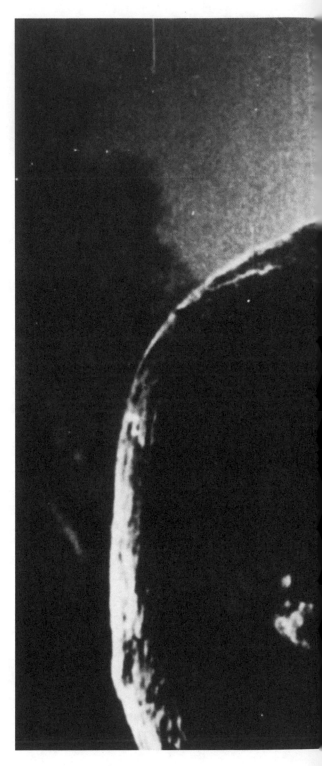

dance to the Lost World dinosaurs and biplane footage, all of which recall Cooper's background as a documentary filmmaker. A more explicitly reflexive strain runs through the character of Denham, who screen-tests Ann screaming, reminding the audience that Wray would have done just that, and presents Kong to his New York audience in the manner of a movie premiere. RKO offset *Kong*'s considerable costs by producing another film (**The Most Dangerous Game**) using the same sets and cast, and *Kong*'s enormous success helped the studio escape financial disaster. It was followed by a sequel, *Son of Kong* (1933) and two bloated remakes (1976, 2005), none of which achieved the mythic resonance of the original.

MURDERS IN THE ZOO

1933, US, dir Edward Sutherland, scr Philip Wylie, Seton I. Miller, starring Charlie Ruggles, Lionel Atwill, Kathleen Burke, Randolph Scott

"Millionaire sportsman" Eric Gorman, on a trip to Indo-China to collect animals for a zoo, sews together the lips of a man who tries to kiss his wife Evelyn, according to "symbolic Oriental custom". The incorrigible Evelyn meets another man on the boat back to the US, who also falls victim to Gorman's terrible jealousy. When Evelyn suspects foul play, Gorman turns his murderous attentions closer to home. This underrated gem shares a nexus of bestial exoticism with **King Kong**, **The Most Dangerous Game** and **Island of Lost Souls**, with which it also shares a writing credit (Wylie co-scripted the earlier film) and cast member (Burke, who plays Evelyn, was Moreau's panther-woman). Atwill is magnificent as Gorman, corrupted Conrad-style by protracted visits to the Orient and close proximity to the animals whose savagery he imitates. Like Zaroff, his lust is fuelled by murder, even though his unfaithful wife resists his advances, and for half of the film we share his viewpoint and alarm as his schemes spiral out of control. Surprisingly violent for its day, with a graphic image of sewn lips and one particularly grisly zoo death, the film also makes a virtue of its novelty setting by staging an astonishing fight between the big cats towards the end. The cast is efficient if, Atwill aside, unmemorable, the pace brisk and, if the comic relief from top-billed Charlie Ruggles as the animal-phobic zoo publicist quickly irritates, the gleeful sadism of both Atwill's performance and some unexpected plot turns make this required viewing.

OPPOSITE: "We know too much of life." Lugoshi and Karloff's finest pairing, **The Black Cat**.

THE BLACK CAT
AKA HOUSE OF DOOM; THE VANISHING BODY

1934, US, dir/co-scr Edgar G. Ulmer, co-scr Peter Ruic, starring Boris Karloff, Bela Lugosi, David Manners, Jacqueline Wells (Julie Bishop)

Joan and Peter Allison, an American couple honeymooning in Austria, are befriended by the psychiatrist Dr Werdegast. The three take refuge in Werdegast's friend Poelzig's house when their bus comes off the road. Werdegast had been in prison since Poelzig betrayed him and thousands of others during the war and he has returned to take revenge, convinced that Poelzig has also stolen his wife and daughter. Ulmer's film, "suggested" by the Poe story, actually bears almost no relation to it, although a black cat does appear several times, but the claustrophobic atmosphere and themes of necrophilia, incest and sadistic torture gives the film an authentic Poe feeling. Ulmer rejected a direct adaptation in favour of a tale inspired by Aleister Crowley, then very much in the public consciousness – Poelzig is a Satanist and plans to sacrifice Joan – but the film plays more like an elegy for Europe in the wake of the First World War, faced with the uncaring incomprehension of the New World. The honeymooners are out of their depth here; with no idea of the labyrinthine complexities of the plot unfolding around them, all they can do is mock European names like "Poelzig", and Peter eventually even kills a character who is trying to help him. The inanity of their lovebird banter is contrasted with the dialogue between Werdegast and Poelzig (both played by European émigrés), whether the former's grief when shown the body of his wife, preserved in a glass case, or the latter's astonishing monologue describing them both as "the living dead … we know too much of life". Poelzig's morbid weariness even extends to his house, a Bauhaus-inspired masterwork built on the site of his betrayal and primed with explosives: "You see? Even the phone is dead." Bewildering and hypnotic by turns and benefiting greatly from the disembodied POV of John Mescall's restless camera, *The Black Cat* is easily the best of Universal's three Karloff/Lugosi pairings.

BRIDE OF FRANKENSTEIN

1935, US, dir James Whale, scr William Hurlbut, starring Boris Karloff, Colin Clive, Valerie Hobson, Ernest Thesiger, Elsa Lanchester

The Monster has survived the windmill fire of the first film. Dr Pretorius visits the convalescing Frankenstein and blackmails him into helping with his experiments. Pretorius finds the Monster hiding in a crypt and offers to make him a female friend; Frankenstein is

FRANKENSTEIN

The dominant creation myth of the modern era suffers from a bad case of brand confusion. The **Son of Frankenstein** complains that the names of his father and the Monster have become inextricably muddled, yet has the temerity to add a "von" to the name for extra Teutonic weight; the Baron's first name bounces back and forth between Henry and Victor in the many adaptations; and is the **Bride of Frankenstein** meant to be Elsa Lanchester or Valerie Hobson?

That the tale remains potent despite such tinkering points to the reasons for its success: Karloff's heavy-lidded Monster may be a long way from Mary Shelley's tortured, self-educated creation, but the legend's patchwork-style growth, picking up a disfigured assistant here, a criminal brain there, is testament to its ability to tap into contemporary cultural fears and a symbolic flexibility that incorporates everything from the act of artistic creation to the themes of rejection and abandonment.

James Whale's Frankenstein films remain among the most impressive Universal horrors, although the studio cheapened the property through lacklustre sequels – **Son of Frankenstein**, *Ghost of Frankenstein* (1942) – that finally descended into the monster-mash mire. Hammer's cycle moved away from such infantile confections, **Curse of Frankenstein** taking things about as far as possible from its contemporary *I Was a Teenage Frankenstein*. While Bray's finest are more often associated with vampires, the studios Frankenstein cycle represents its best series, some of the sequels even improving on an impressive original in a way their Dracula films never managed. Shifting the focus from the Monster (which changes with each subsequent instalment) to Frankenstein himself, Hammer gave Peter Cushing his finest role as the ruthless, amoral ladies' man whose commitment to science makes him rise above his hypocritical, priggish peers even as he is repeatedly foiled by terrible luck and worse judgement. If Universal's Frankenstein films retain the iconic edge, Hammer gave the underlying themes of medical ethics and metaphysics their first proper outing, culminating in the astonishing isolation of the soul in **Frankenstein Created Woman**.

Terence Fisher, perhaps Hammer's most accomplished director, was taken off the Dracula series early on but stayed with Frankenstein for the duration, the only misfires (*The Evil of Frankenstein*, 1964, *Horror of Frankenstein*, 1970) notably missing his touch and his final entry, *Frankenstein and the Monster from Hell* (1973), representing a swansong for the glory days of British gothic, fast losing ground against the hipper, darker tone of Pete Walker and the grisly US imports.

The Monster has fared less well since Hammer's demise, his only notable appearances being in spoofs like **Flesh for Frankenstein**, *Young Frankenstein* (1974) and *The Rocky Horror Picture Show* (1975); Kenneth Branagh's modern retelling of *Mary Shelley's Frankenstein* (1994) proved an embarrassingly overwrought failure, leaving it to the James Whale biopic *Gods and Monsters* (1998) to shock the Monster into new life. Elsewhere, the legend has become more diffuse, bleeding into the related sub-genres of the medical thriller and the zombie film, whose most impressive '80s entries (**Re-Animator**, **Day of the Dead**) returned to Whale as their source of inspiration.

BELOW: Edward Van Sloan tests for signs of life, **Frankenstein**.

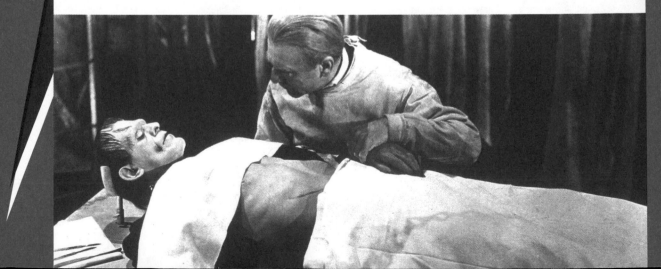

forced to help after the Monster kidnaps his wife Elizabeth.

Whale, initially reluctant to helm a sequel, insisted on a framing device that clearly marked the film out as a fantasy, narrated by its author, and allowed him to dispense with the bleak realism of the first film in favour of a peculiarly sophisticated mixture of acid satire, tenderness and horror. **Frankenstein**'s conservatism is turned on its head: its bland representatives, the Baron and Henry's friend Victor, are replaced by the deliciously camp Ernest Thesiger and Una O'Connor, while Elizabeth's hysterical arguments are uninspiring against Henry's fiery rhetoric. Heterosexual relationships are ridiculed throughout: Elizabeth is consistently sidelined, the happy ending that sees her reunited with Henry filmed at the studio's insistence (Henry can actually be seen being crushed by falling masonry, as in Whale's original conception); the only successful relationship is between the Monster and the blind violinist, society's rejects, and many have interpreted the film as a subversive celebration of Whale's own homosexuality. Christianity is also mocked by Pretorius, who exhorts Henry to "follow the lead of nature … or of God, if you like your Bible stories", and parallels are drawn between the Monster and Christ: he is put on a cross and stoned by villagers and shares a meal of bread and wine with the violinist. When he sheds a tear, cheesy organ music accompanies a cross lighting up in the background. Franz Waxman's influential score follows the quicksilver changes in mood from comedy to horror, culminating in a deranged wedding bell sequence to mark the Bride's animation, a tour-de-force montage of crazily tilted angles and delirious anticipation, and Whale manages to walk a tightrope between poetic intensity and parody that finally succeeds magnificently.

MAD LOVE
AKA THE HANDS OF ORLAC

1935, US, dir Karl Freund, scr P.J. Wolfson, Guy Endore, John L. Balderston, starring Peter Lorre, Frances Drake, Colin Clive, Ted Healy

When pianist Steven Orlac's hands are wrecked in a train crash, his wife Yvonne begs Dr Gogol, a celebrated surgeon who is obsessively in love with her, to heal him. Gogol grafts the hands of Rollo, a guillotined murderer, onto Orlac, then, when the hands take on a life of their own, sees a way to improve his chances with Yvonne. This gloriously demented masterpiece is the best adaptation of Maurice Renard's novel *Les Mains d' Orlac*. Lorre, in his first American appearance, gives the most florid performance of his career as the baby-faced surgeon who returns night after night to the Theatre of Horrors to watch

Yvonne being tortured, then buys her waxwork when the show has closed and serenades it with his organ, already the *de rigueur* accessory of the insane. Yet while Gogol is clearly sadistic – as well as Yvonne's show, he also attends executions out of morbid interest – he is also selfless, refusing to accept money for surgery,

BELOW: "I hope her bones are firm." Elsa Lanchester in **Bride of Frankenstein**.

at least until Yvonne's rejections drive him to madness, and he is finally convinced, on finding her in his apartment, that his waxwork has come to life. From the outset the film is peppered with imaginatively macabre touches – the headless cloakroom girl and demon-masked attendants at the theatre – and uncanny imagery, from Yvonne's waxwork to the cast of Orlac's hands that sits on his piano, taunting his inability to play. The pitch only becomes wilder as the film progresses, peaking when Gogol, seeking to snap Orlac's already unhinged mind, masquerades as Rollo, dressed in a set of metal hands with a large neck brace and dark glasses. It's a difficult scene to top and the ending, Orlac finally finding a use for his new talents, is vaguely unsatisfying. Yet even without Lorre the film is perfectly cast, from Clive's jittery, anxious Orlac to Rollo, the archetypal American hoodlum; only Gogol's alcoholic housekeeper and the wisecracking American reporter detract from the delirious atmosphere.

THE RAVEN

1935, US, dir Lew Landers, scr David Boehm, starring Boris Karloff, Bela Lugosi, Lester Matthews, Irene Ware

Retired surgeon Vollin reluctantly operates on Jean Thatcher after a car crash which almost kills her. After her recovery he is smitten, but Jean is engaged to another man. However, when escaped convict Bateman seeks Vollin's help in changing his appearance, the surgeon sees his chance to take revenge. The second of Universal's Karloff/Lugosi pairings comes closer to Poe in its quoting of "The Raven" and in Vollin's Poe mania, which extends to him constructing several of the author's ingenious torture instruments, including a pit and pendulum. The film hinges on two theories: Bateman's "maybe if a man looks ugly he does ugly things", which inspires Vollin to disfigure him and generate "monstrous hate", and Vollin's conceit that he will become "the sanest man alive" by torturing his guests. Both theories are disproved, of course: the suavely villainous Vollin commits far uglier acts than Bateman and grows progressively more maniacal throughout the film despite his guests' pain. Although the film is not one of Universal's best, Vollin's megalomania – he describes himself as "a god with the taint of human emotions" – is a fine showcase for Lugosi's hammy insanity, especially rich against the insipid supporting cast. Karloff's hoodlum is less convincing and, post-surgery, his grunting shambler simply rehashes his performances in Whale's films. The film is also notable for its ambiguous attitude towards surgery – Vollin's knife saves Jean but destroys Bateman – and the outlandish design of its house, featuring a mobile bedroom among other architectural oddities.

SON OF FRANKENSTEIN

1939, US, dir Rowland V. Lee, scr Willis Cooper, starring Basil Rathbone, Boris Karloff, Bela Lugosi, Lionel Atwill

A quarter-century after the events of **Frankenstein**, the Baron's son Wolf travels to Germany from the US with his wife and child to take possession of his rightful inheritance, but finds his enthusiasm for vindicating his father's work perverted by Ygor's thirst for revenge. *Son* marked the second wave of Universal horrors by playing fast and loose with its heritage: gone are the vulval fissure and gregariousness of **Bride of Frankenstein**'s Monster, whose huge size is now blamed on an abnormal pituitary gland rather than the usual surgical bombast, while the original Baron is renamed Heinrich von Frankenstein. The plot is wildly uneven: Ygor, a broken-necked Bela Lugosi who looks, down to the slightly fanged overbite, like a half-shaved Sayer of the Law from **Island of Lost Souls**, tries to kill Wolf then immediately trusts him enough to show him the Monster. Wolf shows no compunction in attempting to resurrect the Monster and is finally applauded when he leaves town, the villagers having apparently forgotten his hand in the carnage; and the Monster, unnaturally nimble due to a bad-backed Karloff's refusal to wear heavy boots, is alternately brain-damaged and confused and canny enough to disguise one of his murders as a travelling accident. Karloff effectively sleepwalks through his performance (his last as the Monster), leaving Lugosi to outshine him for once by displaying surprising skill as a character actor, while Atwill brings a remarkable dignity to the semi-comic character of Krogh, a police inspector who lost an arm to the Monster as a child; but the whole affair is nearly sunk by Donnie Dunagan's appallingly cute and barely coherent Peter, over whom the characters fawn as though he were the latest addition to the Laemmle clan – the film's final blow is that the Monster *doesn't* throw him into the pit of boiling sulphur. The real stars of *Son*, then, are the set designs, from the crazed Expressionist angles of the castle interiors, recalling the gothic futurism of **The Black Cat** to the **Der Golem**-style misshapen towers of the village itself, while the derelict laboratory resembles a fragment from some ruined Lovecraftian city, all nestling in the craggy landscape of blasted trees that reflected the popular contemporary American conception of war-torn Europe.

OPPOSITE: "I want you to change my face." Boris Karloff in **The Raven**.

CHAPTER

4

1940s

Son of Frankenstein retains much of the eccentricity of Whale but is concerned with delivering what an audience lured in by the title and the star names *expected* of a horror film. In the '40s, Universal had fewer visionaries behind the cameras, but a new studio regime knew how to crank out a double-feature horror bill just as it was expert in Deanna Durbin musicals or Abbott and Costello comedies.

After **Son of Frankenstein**, Universal looked to their backlist for properties that could have sequels, and 1940 found Vincent Price disappearing in *The Invisible Man Returns* and Tom Tyler bandaged in *The Mummy's Hand*. In 1941, with the ageing Karloff and Lugosi a little iffy about monster make-ups, the studio developed a new horror star in Creighton Chaney, son of their silent Quasimodo, who'd been working under the name Lon Chaney Jr and scored a critical success as the child-man Lenny in *Of Mice and Men* (1939). Universal had a leftover, unfilmed Karloff-Lugosi script which was retooled for Chaney Jr (and Lionel Atwill) and shot as *Man-Made Monster*. That turned out efficiently and Chaney was burly enough to be a physical threat in the way the bow-legged Karloff and the double-jointed Lugosi weren't, so director George Waggner was given a more elaborate project to build up the "screen's master character creator".

The Wolf Man (1941) casts Chaney Jr as Larry Talbot, an American schlub (only a few IQ points smarter than Lenny) in Wales who is bitten by a gypsy in wolf form (Lugosi, passing on the "curse" and the horror star status) and eventually battered to death with a silver cane by his father (top-billed Claude Rains). Well-mounted, with an ambitious script by Curt Siodmak (about to be a genre regular) and perhaps the last truly classic Jack P. Pierce monster make-up, **The Wolf Man** proved that Universal could still found horror franchises. Chaney quickly got to play the Monster (*Ghost of Frankenstein*, 1942), the Mummy (four times, from *The Mummy's Tomb*, 1942) and a Count Dracula (*Son of Dracula*, 1943). It must have burned Junior when Waggner was promoted to producing a lavish, Technicolor *Phantom of the Opera* (1943); his father's old role was deemed too important for him and went instead to his **Wolf Man** father-figure Rains.

Phantom, as much musical melodrama as horror picture and decidedly mild stuff next to the silent version, was unusually large-scale for Universal in the '40s. For the most part, they continued to make series horror the way other studios made series Westerns. Besides the ongoing Invisible and Mummy sagas, there was a three-picture run for Paula the Ape Woman, first played by Acquanetta in *Captive Wild Woman* (1943). Basil Rathbone and Nigel Bruce, signed from Fox, played Holmes and Watson in 12 modern-day mysteries, almost all directed by Roy William Neill, often with horror elements (notably *The Scarlet Claw*, 1944, and *The House of Fear*, 1945). In turn, the Holmes films spun off their own monster stars. Real-life acromegalic Rondo Hatton, the "Creeper" of *Pearl of Death* (1944), became a regular mad lab assistant in an Ape Woman sequel and got vehicles in *House of Horrors* (1946) and *The Brute Man* (1946). Gale Sondergaard, the black widow of *The Spider Woman* (1944), returned as a similar villainess (with Hatton as a minion) in *The Spider Woman Strikes Back* (1945). Chaney Jr starred in six sprightly *Inner Sanctum* mysteries, often in unsuitably intellectual roles (he's a college professor in *Weird Woman*, 1944). *Black Friday* (1940), *Night Monster* (1942), *The Mad Ghoul* (1943) and *She-Wolf of London* (1946) are Universal "stand-alones", but the familiar sets, players (Karloff, Atwill, Lugosi, Zucco) and storylines mean they might as well be series efforts.

The most significant Universal horror in franchise terms was Neill's *Frankenstein Meets the Wolf Man* (1943), a dual sequel to *Ghost of Frankenstein* and **The Wolf Man**, in which Lugosi (whose brain was put in Chaney's skull at the end of *Ghost*) plays the Monster and Chaney returns as the cursed Talbot. In *House of Frankenstein* (1944), Dracula (John Carradine) joined up, Lugosi was ditched in favour of bulky Glenn Strange and Karloff returned to play a distinguished mad scientist. *House of Dracula* (1945) lost Karloff, but is otherwise the same deal. These monster rallies remain endearing, not least for the strange twists of plotting that get round monsters' seemingly-permanent deaths and contrive to bring them together for yet another rumble, but they don't even try to be terrifying, and seem pitched entirely at children's matinees. The end result was *Abbott and Costello Meet Frankenstein* (1948) – or *Bud Abbott Lou Costello Meet Frankenstein* or simply *Meet Frankenstein* depending on how you read the credits – in which Universal's premier vaudeville comics run into Chaney's Wolf Man, Strange's monster and, in what amounts to a last hurrah, Lugosi's Dracula. If we love the earlier team-ups despite their lack of scares, we probably like the A&C film – and their later run-ins

---

OPPOSITE: Dorothy McGuire descends *The Spiral Staircase* (1946).

with the Mummy, the Invisible Man and Jekyll and Hyde – even though it's not as funny as it should be. The comics were better in haunted-house mode in *Hold That Ghost* (1941), and *Meet Frankenstein* sometimes goes out of its way to *avoid* funny ideas: the plot revolves around a scheme to put Lou's brain in the monster's skull, but this doesn't happen so we never get Strange's flatheaded, Karloff-look creature doing a panicky Lou Costello act or a doubletalk routine with Bud. This would be partially remedied in *Master Minds*, 1949, where a shaggy-faced Strange played a monster who got Bowery Boy Huntz Hall's brain and did do a silly Hall impersonation.

The B studios got in on Universal's act again with lookalike efforts. Columbia signed Karloff to a run of "mad doctor" movies from *The Man They Could Not Hang* (1939) before landing Lugosi and his werewolf minion (Matt Willis) in their own monster team-up picture *Return of the Vampire* (1943). Fox and Paramount felt obliged to produce a white slavery/gorilla brain transplant story (*The Monster and the Girl*, 1941) and a foggy werewolf whodunit (*The Undying Monster*, 1942). Down on Poverty Row, Monogram were delighted to keep Lugosi on retainer for nine lurid little efforts (*The Invisible Ghost*, 1941, etc.) and played the race card with pictures (*King of the Zombies*, 1941, *Revenge of the Zombies*, 1943) sold as mad-scientist melodramas toplining Henry Victor and John Carradine in white neighbourhoods and comedy vehicles for Mantan Moreland in black theatres. If PRC, even further down in the dumps than Monogram, couldn't always get Lugosi (as for *The Devil Bat*, 1941) there was always Zucco (*The Mad Monster*, 1942). Even before Abbott and Costello, every studio had their comedians mix it with fake spooks, old dark houses, Lugosi as a butler and secret passageways in the like of *You'll Find Out* (1940), *Whistling in the Dark* (1941), *The Smiling Ghost* (1941), *Topper Returns* (1941), *One Body Too Many* (1944), *Ghost Catchers* (1944), *Genius at Work* (1946), etc.

Counterprogramming for all this bustle came from RKO, which hired Val Lewton to produce their own small-scale horror pictures and got a clutch of polished, doom-haunted, poetic little masterpieces in **Cat People** (1942), **I Walked With a Zombie** (1943), *The Leopard Man* (1943), **The Seventh Victim** (1943), *The Ghost Ship* (1943), *The Curse of the Cat People* (1944), *Isle of the Dead* (1945), **The Body Snatcher** (1945) and *Bedlam* (1946). Directed by Jacques Tourneur, Mark Robson or Robert Wise – with the horror-icon presence of Karloff for the last three films set in

the past (and even Lugosi in **The Body Snatcher**) – the Lewton films are literate, adult and sophisticated, especially when set beside the competition. But the reason they worked for '40s audiences is that they are also serious about being scary in a way Universal had given up on. The stalking scenes in Central Park and a basement swimming pool in **Cat People** are models of a style of horror cinema Lewton would perfect, which would become the basis of the stalk-and-slash pictures of the '70s and beyond. In a typical Lewton suspense sequence, a woman alone in the dark becomes conscious of a menace hunting her down – paying off as often with a jump (a "bus") that startles the character but isn't a real threat, as it does with an actual attack. For all the John Donne quotes and visual cues from Arnold Böcklin, the Lewton films also spill more gore than the average Monogram – the trickle under the door in *The Leopard Man* is an especial shock – and emphasize extreme emotional states, like the neglected daughter driven nearly to child murder in *Curse of the Cat People*, and actual gruesome violence, like the man crushed by a heavy chain in *The Ghost Ship*. That Lewton had hit on a style (even a formula) that worked is proved by the way others tried to imitate it. After **Cat People**, Columbia managed its own effects-free, "subtle" horror *Cry of the Werewolf* (1943) and there was a trickle of Lewton-light from other studios that had been paying attention, *The Soul of a Monster* (1944) and *The Woman Who Came Back* (1945).

As far as intelligent, well-produced, carriage-trade horror goes, Lewton wasn't quite the whole act in the '40s. MGM had Victor Fleming, a hero on the strength of his credited direction of *Gone With the Wind* and *The Wizard of Oz*, mount a big-budget remake of *Dr Jekyll and Mr Hyde* (1941) as a showcase for Spencer Tracy's dual performance, with the full Metro glamour treatment for his co-stars, Ingrid Bergman as the abused Soho waitress and Lana Turner as Jekyll's society fiancée. This was followed by other fogbound literary properties, with bravura acting and careful production values: *The Lodger* (1944), with Laird Cregar as Jack the Ripper, *Gaslight* (1944), with Bergman persecuted again, and *The Picture of Dorian Gray* (1945). During the war and in its aftermath, there was a run of near-benevolent supernatural pictures, like *A Guy Named Joe* (1943), the British *A Matter of Life and Death* (1946) and *The Ghost and Mrs Muir* (1947). This trend took in a few scarier items: **The Uninvited** (1944) feels like a Lewton homage, to the extent of casting Lewton's favourite Elizabeth Russell as the wispily malevolent spectre (a nasty lesbian to boot), and stands as the model for many, many tales in which nice folks (here Ray Milland and Ruth Hussey) buy a picturesque, remote house and are pestered by spooks, which prompts an investigation into the cause of the haunting (allowing for a mystery angle) and a climactic exorcism. From Britain, neglectful of horror while fighting the war, came Ealing's multi-directed **Dead of Night** (1945), best-remembered for its haunted mirror and mad ventriloquist sequences, but highly influential in its use of a frame story with a twist and mix of moods from supernatural anecdote through clubroom comedy to all-out psychological terror.

Perhaps the greatest mystery in the genre is that in the later '40s, just as in the later '30s, the horror film completely died out. In the '30s, the phenomenon is almost entirely down to the unique circumstance of the British horror ban – but in the '40s, it just seems to happen. Some have suggested that, after Abbott and Costello, it was impossible to take monsters seriously – but they didn't meet Frankenstein until 1948, when the genre was already withering away, and it could equally be argued that it was impossible to take monsters seriously after, say, the third or fourth mummy sequel in which victims have to manoeuvre themselves into a corner so that the limping, pot-bellied, not-terribly-fearsome, bandaged bully can get his single functional hand around their throats. Between 1947 and 1951, Hollywood made almost no horror pictures – The Creeper (1948), Jean Yarbrough's weird mélange of Lewton shadows and Monogram mad science, is a lone exception. It could be that overproduction had killed off the genre, but programmer Westerns had been churned out in even greater numbers without slaking the appetites of cowboy fans (a statistic: there are five films in Universal's Kharis the Mummy series, which most fans rate as repetitive and formulaic; there are 51 interchangeable Three Mesquiteers pictures). It could be that, after the Second World War, gothic horror was upstaged by real-life genocides – but the First World War had proved a potent inspiration for the Expressionist horrors of the '20s and '30s, lingering subliminally in the films of Murnau (a fighter pilot) and Whale (a POW).

The irony is that, in the later '40s, American screens were as shadowed and haunted as they had ever been, but not in actual horror films. *Film noir* is a genre that was diagnosed rather than invented. French critics looked at a stream of American films (mostly thrillers and melodramas) and labelled them *noir*, in homage to their overwhelming darkness in imagery and subject matter. Lewton's

horror films are also important early *noirs*, and Jacques Tourneur proceeded from cat people and zombies to the *noir* masterpiece, *Out of the Past* (1948). Other personnel made similar shifts: Robert Siodmak, Curt's brother, helmed the gloomy, unusual *Son of Dracula* – the film in which the girl *wants* to be bitten by Dracula – and the early psycho-horror suspense *The Spiral Staircase* (1946), but also many outstanding *noir* films, *Phantom Lady* (1943), *The Killers* (1946), *The Dark Mirror* (1946), etc. When Edward Dmytryk moved from *Captive Wild Woman* to *Murder, My Sweet* (1944), the first major adaptation of Raymond Chandler's work, he pitted Dick Powell's Philip Marlowe against the sometime mad scientist Otto Kruger, playing a "psychic consultant", and Mike Mazurki's Moose Malloy, a cross between Lenny and Rondo Hatton. Karloff and Lugosi were too tied to castles and laboratories, but Peter Lorre segued easily from horror to *noir* roles – reprising his **M** act as a sorrowful psycho killer in what might be the first proper *noir*, *Stranger on the Third Floor* (1940).

Though even *noirs* in which the threat comes from gangsters tend to present implacable, monstrous forces closing in on a neurotic protagonist, several films in the genre seem to be working hard to do horror's job while the traditional fright film is on hiatus. John Farrow's *Night Has a Thousand Eyes* (1948), from a novel by Cornell Woolrich (source of major works from Lewton, Siodmak and Hitchcock), is about a fake psychic (Edward G. Robinson) who seems to discover real precognitive powers and is drawn towards a predestined fate. Edmond Goulding's *Nightmare Alley* (1948) has a similar milieu, with Tyrone Power as a carny (carnival) hustler who develops a psychic scam, and an even more downbeat, Browning-ish finish with Power reduced to working as a sideshow "geek" (biting the heads off chickens). Anatole Litvak's *Sorry, Wrong Number* (1948), from a radio play, is an early lady-in-peril suspense with Barbara Stanwyck trapped in her own home, driven to hysteria by a crossed wire which leads her to believe contract killers are after her – this type of story would become more common in horror or semi-horror decades later. And Jules Dassin's *Brute Force* (1948) is a prison melodrama in *Grand Guignol* mode, complete with sadistic guards inflicting beatings while playing Wagner and squealers are driven to fall into industrial machinery by cons with blowtorches – almost on a level with Tod Slaughter's wilder cruelties while sketching in the strategies of splatter movies to come by having not so much a plot as a series of compounded atrocities.

THE WOLF MAN

1941, US, dir George Waggner, scr Curt Siodmak, starring Claude Rains, Lon Chaney Jr, Ralph Bellamy, Evelyn Ankers

Larry Talbot returns from the US to take over his father's Welsh estate after the death of his brother. On a date with Gwen, a local woman, he attempts to defend another woman against a wolf and is bitten. He is later accused of murder: a man's body has been found instead of a wolf. Larry becomes convinced he is a werewolf, but nobody will believe him. Universal's moneyspinner, the jewel in the crown of their second wave of

horror films, ironically inspired RKO's string of Lewton chillers (see **Cat People**), although *The Wolf Man* couldn't be further from Lewton's suggestive approach. Having no original legend to work with, unlike Universal's previous monsters, Siodmak's much-praised script succeeds in achieving a mythic quality through its focus on destiny, allusions to fairy tales and the tight family dynamic at the core of the film. The repetitions of werewolf doggerel may be irritatingly heavy-handed coming from Gwen, Jenny and Larry's father, but the gypsy woman Maleva's lines have a genuinely eerie quality. Larry's transformation has sexual parallels: the first wolf attack comes when he learns that Gwen is engaged, although the film's psychosexual underpinning doesn't stop it from having a distrust of psychiatry typical of the genre. The film looks sumptuous, belying its relatively modest budget, and is well-cast, Lugosi's cameo as a gypsy werewolf is for once entirely credible, although none of the cast speaks with the Welsh accent fitting to its arbitrary setting. But Chaney Jr, an unlikely horror star who seems to have walked in from some buffoonish comedy, is unable to carry either the pathos required or the sexual attraction Gwen evidently feels for him – surely his jowly advances are eminently resistible. Rather than any lupine qualities, he most resembles an overfriendly dog; Jack Pierce's make-up is similarly unconvincing, although mercifully the actor is unrecognizable underneath.

CAT PEOPLE

1942, US, dir Jacques Tourneur, scr DeWitt Bodeen, starring Simone Simon, Kent Smith, Tom Conway, Jane Randolph

Oliver meets Irena in a zoo. They fall in love and marry, although Irena rejects physical contact, fearing that she will transform into a cat if kissed. Oliver sends her to psychiatrist Dr Judd and grows closer to his co-worker Alice. Irena becomes jealous, and Alice is stalked by an unseen menace. Oliver decides to have Irena committed, but Judd decides to prove her fears unfounded.

Orson Welles's extravagant productions had left RKO financially crippled in the early '40s and the studio decided to ape Universal's success with **The Wolf Man** by producing a series of low-budget horror B pictures with audience-tested titles, to be overseen by producer Val Lewton. Lewton's conviction that suggestion was more chilling than explicit display was not initially shared by studio bosses, but after a mixed critical reception, *Cat*

LEFT: Lon Chaney Jr drools over Evelyn Ankers. **The Wolf Man.**

People, the first in this new line, was resoundingly successful, its international gross exceeding $4,000,000.

Irena's fear of transformation is couched explicitly as sexual repression: she even has a dream in which animated cats, keys and swords loom before her and she cherishes her statue of King John, who has speared a cat on his sword, a potent sexual image. Although she is the "monster", our sympathies rest with her efforts to resist transformation: Oliver is a square-jawed hunk whose admission that "I've never been unhappy before" reveals a blustery immaturity; Alice accelerates the demise of her friend's marriage, provoking Irena through deliberate slips; and Judd, alternately bombastic and lecherous, undermines the credibility of both psychiatry and the voice of reason he represents. To modern audiences the film may appear closer to melodrama than horror, its innovative techniques over-familiar through imitation, and only a handful of scenes pack a genuine chill. It is moreover not without flaws: shots of a panther during the office scene undermine Lewton's carefully crafted ambiguity over Irena's condition and were presumably shot to appease studio bosses; Judd surreptitiously leaves Irena's door on the latch so he can return and seduce her, but Alice shows no surprise when he picks up the phone in Irena's apartment; and paw prints are shown transforming into high-heel prints, suggesting that somehow Irena's clothes change with her. Nonetheless, the film's psychological depth, sophisticated sound design and insistence on the power of suggestion marked a new and influential strand in horror cinema.

I WALKED WITH A ZOMBIE

1943, US, dir Jacques Tourneur, scr Curt Siodmak, Ardel Wray, starring James Ellison, Frances Dee, Tom Conway, Edith Barrett

Betsy, a Canadian nurse, is recruited to look after Mrs Holland, the wife of a plantation owner, in the Caribbean island of San Sebastian. Confused by Mrs Holland's apparently incurable condition, Betsy follows a local's advice and takes her to a voodoo ceremony, triggering a conflict between the locals and the plantation owners. When producer Val Lewton was given the second title for his run of RKO chillers and told to employ the scriptwriter for Universal's *Frankenstein Meets the Wolfman* (1943),

Curt Siodmak, he responded in characteristically high-minded fashion by ditching much of Siodmak's conception and relocating the plot of *Jane Eyre* to the West Indies. What resulted is probably the best of Lewton's RKO chillers, although it has even less overt horror content than **Cat People**: the scare scenes here (including the famous walk through the cane field) are almost all pieces of misdirection, in which nothing actually happens; even the film's "monster", Carrefour, does little but advance with his hands and eyes outstretched. But the film succeeds in creating a bewitchingly ambiguous atmosphere in which nothing is quite what it seems and what appear at first to be binary oppositions (voodoo/Christian, dead/alive, magic/science, black/white) become inextricably blurred. None of the characters' motives are at all clear, even the apparently innocent Betsy, whose potentially fatal insulin shock treatment of Mrs Holland might be motivated simply by her desire to remove an obstacle to her love for Mr Holland. Like their voodoo-practising counterparts, the white characters use indirect means to manipulate others but, unlike them, they are unable to express their emotions directly, repressing them until they boil over into fits of rage (Mr Holland) or jealousy (Mrs Rand). Lewton's characteristically meticulous research ensures the film's non-exploitative and well-informed approach to voodoo, even while it is careful to retain only hints of its viability, and Tourneur's handling of the cane walk sequence and the magnificently resonant ending remains memorable long after the subtleties of the plot have faded. However, although the film improves with repeat viewings, its chief drawback, as with **Cat People**, is a stiflingly mannered literacy that, while it provides a welcome alternative to the decade's infantile Universal horrors, ensures that the film never approaches the delirious vitality of the genre's best offerings.

THE SEVENTH VICTIM

1943, US, dir Mark Robson, scr Charles O'Neal, DeWitt Bodeen, starring Tom Conway, Jean Brooks, Isabel Jewell, Kim Hunter

On learning that her sister Jacqueline has gone missing, schoolgirl Mary Gibson searches for her. A private investigator, a poet and Jacqueline's lover all offer to help her and they learn through Jacqueline's psychiatrist Dr Judd that she is hiding from a group of Satanists intent on eliminating her. The incoherence of Lewton's fourth RKO chiller comes partly from its being scripted as an A film then cut to fit B running time: RKO refused to have Robson, an experienced editor, debut as director on an A film while Lewton insisted on Robson as a replacement for Tourneur, who had been promoted away from Lewton's ménage. Yet

although the plot doesn't quite add up – Judd's relationship to the Satanists is particularly confusing – the unremitting morbidity of its atmosphere has rarely been matched and the *noir* inflections of many key scenes make this compulsive viewing. Anticipating **Rosemary's Baby**, the Satanists are friendly and apparently benign tea addicts, who want Jacqueline dead but can't initially bring themselves to do any more than persuade her to commit suicide, their cowardly encouragement more ghastly than the assassin they later dispatch. Each of the characters is compromised in some way: **Cat People**'s Dr Judd reprises a role of sleazy pomposity that the film tries unsuccessfully to invert to heroics at the end; the blandly wholesome Mary cajoles the private investigator into meeting his death; and the heroes' sole defence against the Satanists' question "What proof can you bring that good is superior to evil?" is a rather limp quotation from the Lord's Prayer. Only Jacqueline carries the audience's sympathy, for all her grim obsession with death, her iconic, moon-pale face and straight black hair lighting up the screen.

THE UNINVITED

1944, US, dir Lewis Allen, scr Dodie Smith, starring Ray Milland, Ruth Hussey, Gail Russell, Donald Crisp

Roderick Fitzgerald and his sister Pamela move from London to Cornwall, but find their dream home haunted by a ghost none of the locals wants to acknowledge. *The Uninvited* may be the first serious ghost film, but its original poster – "From the most popular mystery romance since *Rebecca*!" – illustrates its proximity to Du Maurier's melodramatics rather than **Dead of Night**'s yawning terrors. Insensitive clot that he is, Roderick sets up his studio in the dark, cold heart of the haunting and Milland plays the part of the boorishly rational man troubled by the supernatural for laughs, always ready with an inane quip or fawning seduction, lending credibility to his paramour Stella's attempts at suicide but making the viewer yearn to see him ravaged by the titular amphibians of *Frogs* (1972). Roderick is exactly the type favoured by classic ghost-story writers for night terrors and, as such, deserves less to vanquish the supernatural than to be crushed by some thing with a face of crumpled linen. The jaunty orchestral score punctuates the action for irritatingly comic effect, the only credible note of local colour comes when a character complains of the slow Cornish trains and the dialogue is so mannered – from "Great Scott!" and "Is that she?" to up-to-the-minute slang like "a bit of a bad hat" – that the film seems far more dated than, say, Universal's gothics. The visuals occasionally achieve an effective eeriness – the wilting flowers, Stella's gaze at the sea by moonlight and the wraith itself (an apparition forced on Allen by Paramount, to make the supernatural element clear) – but are otherwise flat and uninteresting. Although the plot reveals intriguing intricacies, it finally puts the supernatural to the service of the established order: the villains of the piece are women without men, women whose reluctance to bear children codes them as lesbian. Such women, the film suggests, will either end as malign revenants or howling lunatics – the only "guest" of the Mary Meredith Retreat we see is clearly a batty spinster – and Commander Beech's attempts to keep Stella from Roderick's insipid clutches may condemn her to just such a fate. Predictably the film ends with two (heterosexual) pairings.

BELOW: Boris Karloff kills off rival star Bela Lugosi in **The Body Snatcher**.

THE BODY SNATCHER

1945, US, dir Robert Wise, scr Philip MacDonald, Carlos Keith (Val Lewton), starring Boris Karloff, Bela Lugosi, Henry Daniell, Edith Atwater

When Fettes, a medical student, takes a job as the celebrated Dr MacFarlane's assistant, he learns that the bodies his employer uses as teaching aids are stolen from graves by a coachman, Gray. Gray's relationship with MacFarlane is closer than the doctor will admit and Fettes soon becomes embroiled in their crimes. RKO responded to the contemporary popularity of period thrillers like *Gaslight* and *The Lodger* (both 1944) by making Lewton's eighth RKO horror production a version of R.L. Stevenson's story, itself inspired by the "resurrectionists" Burke and Hare. The film was a critical and commercial success, Lewton's second-most-lucrative after **Cat People**, and it's easy to see why. Karloff's performance as Gray is one of his best, his verbal duels with Daniell's MacFarlane making the most of the script's unusually rich characterizations and

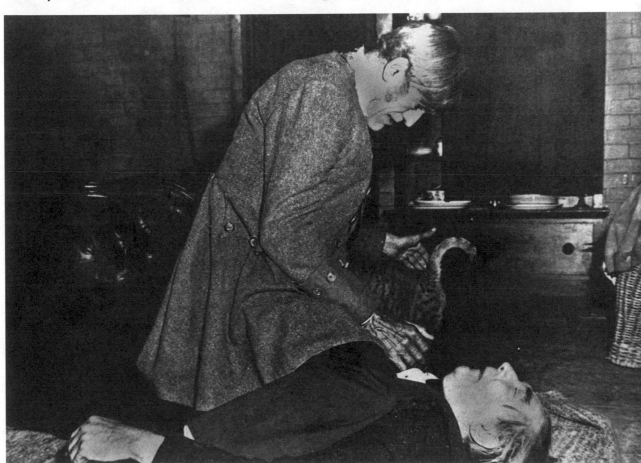

extended riffs on class and friendship. Fettes, MacFarlane and Gray are inextricably linked, inseparable enough to be different facets of one person: Fettes the young idealist, MacFarlane the established success, obsessed with appearance, and Gray the cynical shadow, transporting bodies, both living and dead, to make ends meet. Gray's poverty doesn't excuse his murders, but at least he is honest, unlike MacFarlane, the true villain of the piece, whose money keeps Gray robbing and killing and who pretends not to understand where his bodies are coming from, or Fettes, whose compassion for a crippled girl is little more than a ruse to curry favour with her mother and whose moral indignation doesn't stop him robbing graves as readily as the others. Wise's direction uses the chiaroscuro lighting and beautifully designed sets to paint a convincing picture of early 19th-century Edinburgh, even if none of the characters can muster a credible Scottish accent. The film's only real flaws are the contrived and saccharine story of Georgina, the crippled

BELOW: Peter Lorre ponders the secrets of the universe, **The Beast with Five Fingers**.

girl, and Lugosi's cameo, a gratuitous appearance which adds nothing to the film.

DEAD OF NIGHT

1945, UK, dir Alberto Cavalcanti, Charles Crichton, Basil Dearden, Robert Hamer, scr John V. Barnes, Angus MacPhail, T.E.B. Clarke, starring Mervyn Johns, Frederick Valk, Michael Redgrave, Googie Withers

Architect Walter Craig visits Pilgrim's Farm. He has never been there before, but recognizes the five guests and predicts the ensuing events accurately: he has dreamt this before. His story prompts the others, including a psychiatrist, to recount their own encounters with the unexplained. **Dead of Night** was among the first full-blooded English horror films, conceived as a showcase for Ealing's creative talent, and the first portmanteau horror film, a form not imitated until Amicus's run three decades later. Like those, it is uneven – all the more so because its segments are helmed by different directors – with two weak, disposable episodes, although their inclusion is understandable in the structure as a whole. The first tale presents supernatural presentiments as potentially benevolent; the second, a ghost story hobbled by an unconvincing teenage girl, carries in theory at least a faint chill; and the third, the story of a haunted mirror, is a genuinely disturbing portrait of repressed, unconscious desires "possessing" a bland accountant. A barely watchable comic episode involving two golfers leavens the tension, only to be followed by the film's terrifying showcase, the tale of Hugo the ventriloquist's dummy. Finally the film's oneiric qualities come to the fore as Craig falls through a riot of tilted angles and reality slips, revisiting each episode until he wakes up at home, only to take the call inviting him to Pilgrim's Farm – a call we see, for the first time in the film, coming from outside Craig's viewpoint, thus confirming his dream as an authentic premonition. The film's power rests on the dynamic between stolid English reserve and borderline madness: Craig's rudeness to the other guests is blithely ignored by his hostess until his non-compliance with the inevitable tea-drinking ritual, while Hugo's chief tactic concerning Redgrave's superlative ventriloquist Maxwell Frere is to embarrass him in public. We are embarrassed by, and for, both, cringing at the transgressing of social convention. For a purported ghost film, its explicit spectres are its weakest point, its terror deriving more from its vivid re-creation of a nightmare atmosphere and from inanimate objects – a mirror, a dummy – given uncanny powers of animation. Ventriloquists have been possessed by their dummies since then (*Magic*, 1978), but none has quite matched Frere's fall from grace.

THE BEAST WITH FIVE FINGERS

1946, US, dir Robert Florey, scr Curt Siodmak, starring Peter Lorre, Robert Alda, Andrea King, Victor Francen

When Mr Ingram, a tyrannical crippled pianist, dies, few mourn his passing but, when his relatives begin to squabble over his will, his hand takes on a homicidal life of its own. This lavish Warners production resembles an Agatha Christie murder mystery until the appearance of the crawling hand, which spurs Lorre's descent into a madness bouncing between somnolence and murderous rage. Along with **Mad Love**, this is the best showcase for Lorre's heavy-lidded dementia, as he alternately pets the hand, hammers it to a block and menaces the other guests. The uncanny hand effects still hold up today, even if modern audiences won't need the Italian inspector's joky epilogue reassuring viewers that "it's-a my hand!". Does the hand signify Ingram's revenge from beyond the grave, Bruce Conrad's artistic frustrations, nurse Julie's guilt over Ingram's death or Hilary's thwarted desire to learn the secrets of the universe through astrology? As a floating symbol it's effective enough, although the ending, Scooby-Doo by way of R.D. Laing, tidies everything up a little too neatly.

STRANGLER OF THE SWAMP

1946, US, dir/co-scr Frank Wisbar, co-scr Harold Erickson, starring Rosemary LaPlanche, Robert Barrat, Blake Edwards, Charles Middleton

Ever since an innocent man was hanged by a mob for murder, the men of his swamp town have died from a series of accidental stranglings. When the ferryman dies, his confession to having wrongfully accused the hanged man is found. His granddaughter Maria returns from the city to take over his job and falls in love with Christian Sanders, whose father refuses to bless their union because of her grandfather's actions. This simple morality tale is a retelling of the director's earlier *Faehrmann Maria* (1936), a German version of the legend of Death and the Maiden. Maria says that "the swamp makes me think of fairy tales", and a fairy-tale romance ensues. But the swamp's atmosphere is also one of grim foreboding, concentrated in the figure of the ghostly strangler. His look is genuinely eerie, his sunken eyes and blurred face anticipating the look of modern Eastern hauntings, while Maria's willingness to sacrifice herself to lift the curse also recalls the Oriental tradition. If some of the acting is wooden (notably Joseph, the ferryman), the principals are engaging – Edwards, here in his only horror role, would later become a successful director – and the romantic interest is less distracting than usual, while the film's piety can be overlooked in its wonderfully atmospheric setting (provided by one studio set) and flashes of poetic intensity.

GHOSTS

Ghosts may be the least tangible of all supernatural presences, but they draw the largest audiences, both at the contemporary box office and in the wider world: a recent poll showed that more British people born in the '70s believe in ghosts than in God. Part of the reason for their enduring popularity is that ghosts are paradoxically as reassuring as they are disquieting (witness the popularity of spiritualism after the First World War) – there is another world beyond ours. The content and function of this world may be obscure, but it is precisely this lack of clear definition and explanation that defines the spectral, offering a different world view from the rigid materialism of science or the fundamentalist certainties and bland reassurances of religion, both of which seek to explain and reduce to comprehensible cause and effect. The best ghost stories, by contrast, intimate an unknown and unknowable world; they trade on what the Germans term *Ehrfurcht*, or reverence for things one cannot understand.

Other manifestations of the supernatural rely on systems – werewolves will transform at the full moon and can be killed with silver bullets; vampires sleep by day, must drink blood to survive and can be despatched with a stake through the heart; magic and witchcraft rely on a series of correspondences (as above, so below) for effect; and even zombies have a clearer ontological status, as reanimated corpse, whether they have a taste for human flesh or not. Ghosts, however, range from voluptuous revenants demanding physical love (**La Danza Macabra**, **Ugetsu Monogatari**) to ethereal spectres able to manifest themselves only as a suggestion on wallpaper (**The Haunting**). They've proved so difficult to pin down that cinema didn't even know quite what to do with them before the release in the mid-'40s of **The Uninvited** and **Dead of Night**, whose ghosts were at least *meant* to be scary. Before then they were relegated to the role of light entertainment, explained away Scooby-Doo-style in *The Ghost Breaker* (1922) or used for comic relief in *Topper* (1937).

The Uninvited and **Dead of Night** also wore their literary credentials on their sleeve – the latter adapts stories by E.F. Benson and H.G. Wells – reminding viewers that ghosts have traditionally best been served in print. If ghost stories represent the acceptable face of horror literature, attracting literary luminaries from Dickens and Henry James to Kingsley Amis and Susan

Hill, then ghost films, often relying for their effect on restraint rather than the genre's more characteristic excess, represent the acceptable face of horror cinema, and are occasionally considered too genteel to fall under the parameters of the genre: some notable entries (*Queen of Spades*, 1948, **Ugetsu Monogatari**) are routinely skipped in otherwise exhaustive histories of the horror film. Restraint and respectability have also drawn the more staid forms of radio and TV to the ghost story, the latter's budget-conscious reliance on the unseen resulting in some of this book's most terrifying entries, with adaptations of classic (M.R. James's **Whistle and I'll Come to You**) and modern (Susan Hill's period **The Woman in Black**) ghost stories. Yet respectability doesn't always work in the sub-genre's favour: films like *The Changeling* (1980) and *Ghost Story* (1981) are stifled by their obstinate, mannered adherence to literary models.

Most filmmakers have tended to focus on ghosts for which some kind of explanation exists, however flimsy. Poltergeists, for instance, are reputed to be manifestations of pubescent energy, lending them a physicality – levitating beds, dishes flying across rooms – and simple structure attractive to studio executives. **Poltergeist**, an enormously successful effects extravaganza, glossed over director Tobe Hooper's grit with Spielberg's hygienic cosiness for a family-friendly haunting that presents its wraiths in **Close Encounters** terms and anticipates the CGI spectres clanking their way through multiplexes at the end of the millennium, while **The Exorcist**, evading the implications of its title, suggests early on that a poltergeist may be responsible for Linda Blair's rocky nights. Although vampires have vampire-hunting savants to bridge the human and supernatural realms, ghosts have mediums and spiritualists, although apart from genuinely chilling encounters in **Don't Look Now** and **The Others**, the most characteristic portrayal is as charlatans (*The Amazing Mr X*, 1948, *The Medium*, 1951, *Séance on a Wet Afternoon*, 1964). The boundary between the spectral and scientific provides the subgenre's only genuinely fruitful structural underpinning, the parapsychologists manning this liminal zone in **The Haunting**, **The Stone Tape** and *The Legend of Hell House* (1973) providing some of horror's most chilling moments.

Other ghost films tend to fall back on the popular conception of vengeful spirits seeking to expose a wrong done to them when alive, an idea long since discarded by most ghost literature. The theme is particularly prevalent in Japan, where the motif of the avenging female spirit, with wide staring eyes and long black hair, draws on plot devices and imagery from traditional literature and theatre, including Noh's *shura-* (ghost) and *shunen-mono* (revenge plays). Given the traditionally subordinate role of women in patriarchal Japanese society, it doesn't take too much imagination to see these enraged wraiths as expressions of sublimated guilt over the mistreatment of women. Using a similar strategy of displacement to the portrayal of hillbillies in US urbanoia films, the men may be guilty of adultery and murder, but the women's monstrosity, whether figured as "unnatural" supernatural powers (**Ringu**) or facial disfigurement (**Tokaido Yotsuya Kaidan**) goes some way towards retrospectively justifying the men's actions.

Most Japanese ghosts nowadays don't even care who they take revenge on, as long as blood is spilled. While modern American ghost films looked back at the end of the millennium, with flashy, redundant remakes of William Castle ghost trains such as *The House on Haunted Hill* (1999) and *Thirteen Ghosts* (2001), Japanese ghosts bridged the gap between ancient and modern by haunting videotapes (**Ringu**), phones (*Chakushin Ari/One Missed Call*, 2003) and, perhaps most impressively, an apocalyptic vision of modern Tokyo (**Kairo**). The cycle has played itself out domestically, with even the more interesting recent entries failing to find an audience in a Japan sick of etiolated long-hairs emerging from unlikely places. However, their international importance is enormous, many original Japanese hauntings (**Ringu**, **Honogurai Mizu no Soko Kara**, **Ju-On**) being retooled as US teen-friendly box-office bonanzas like *The Ring* (2002), *Dark Water* (2005) and *The Grudge* (2004), which often import the originals' directors in a bid to soften the blow of such naked cultural appropriation.

Yet, while the best of these films still tend to rely on attempts to explain their hauntings, a hangover from the reductive mentality that plagued the early Hollywood ghosts and coarsens the gossamer spectrality of **The Others**, **The Sixth Sense** and even **The Innocents**, the scariest ghost films shy away from such easy explanations. If the horror genre draws much of its energy from collapsed boundaries, ghost films worry the boundary between our own private universe and the objectively "real" world of consensus reality. To wonder whether the events in **The Haunting** are caused by a haunted house or Eleanor herself misses the point: the film blurs the line between internal and external, making the ghost film in its more impressive manifestations – **The Haunting**; **The Shining**; **Jangwha, Hongryeon** – as much about the farther reaches of the psyche

ABOVE: Claire Bloom clutches Julie Harris in a terrifying scene from **The Haunting**.

as the supernatural. These films do not suggest reductive, **Repulsion**-style readings, trading haunting for hallucination, but rather demonstrate a refined strategy for the spectral, hinting that its source may as easily be internal as external. Even the better ghost films that lack the broader psychological dimension – **The Blair Witch Project**, **The Woman in Black** – rely on *not* providing definitive explanations for their hauntings and draw on an economy of sound and vision that has a devastating impact missed by Hollywood's CGI clunkers of the same period. Here, like the hapless protagonists of **Blair Witch**, we have lost the map, the forest is closing in and so is the dark.

CHAPTER

5

1950s

If the cinema of the late '40s was typified by the high-contrast black-and-white of *film noir*, with shadows like pools of ink and protagonists slipping into near-insanity, the dominant tone of the early '50s was semi-documentary grey, with heroes so relentlessly everyday and average that latterday audiences take them for seed-pods from outer space even before the films started revealing that some of them were.

The '50s presented an image of back-to-business normality, with finned cars in every suburban garage and labour-saving devices in every gleaming home, but it was the decade of the Cold War, McCarthyism, fears of atomic warfare, juvenile delinquency, Suez and rock 'n' roll. As the decade began, horror was out of fashion – after the Nazis and the Reds, a lone Count from Transylvania didn't seem much of a threat and Dr Frankenstein's rampaging monster appeared less disastrous than the possible side-effects of atomic testing. However, monsters would soon be back, in force, dressed to suit the new era.

You can gauge how influential **The Thing From Another World** (1951), directed by Christian Nyby and produced by Howard Hawks, was on subsequent science-fiction monster movies by looking at Edgar G. Ulmer's *The Man From Planet X* (1951), produced as a "spoiler" for the higher-profile film and rushed to beat it into the cinemas. This means that, uniquely, Ulmer's movie is a '50s alien invader film *not* made in imitation of **The Thing**. Without any pre-existing model for a tale of a helmeted dwarf from outer space, Ulmer's film opts to look like an old Universal horror film. The setting is an isolated, fogbound island – as credibly Scots as **The Wolf Man** is Welsh – and the weird-looking scientist (William Schallert) who makes first contact with the imp-like alien works in the sort of ruined ancient pile Karloff and Lugosi were familiar with. When things get out of hand, villagers pick up their agricultural implements and flaming torches – "angry mob supplies" as Wallace and Gromit have it – and harry the monster in exactly the same way earlier mobs had pursued the Frankenstein Monster, the Wolf Man and the Mummy (often in footage recycled from **Frankenstein**, 1931).

Ulmer, veteran of **The Black Cat** (1934), is a Poverty Row Expressionist: his film looks like something from decades earlier.

The Thing knows it's in the line of descent from Universal's monster: its alien vegetable biped (James Arness) looks like a bald Frankenstein Monster in a boiler suit and has the Dracula-like habit of drinking human blood – but the film follows Sam Goldwyn's dictate by inventing a lot of new clichés. The shadows of the menaced Arctic base may be deep, but in place of the angry mob we have a coalition of quick-thinking, good-humoured, professional men (and a token spunky woman with a man's name – Margaret Sheridan as Nikki) who show only sensible fear and treat the monster like a problem to be solved. As in *The Man From Planet X*, a weirdo scientist with a beard (Robert Carrington) wants to communicate with the implacable enemy rather than exterminate it – but even he isn't a madman, just a

OPPOSITE: The Metaluna Mutant, *This Island Earth* (1955)
RIGHT: An imp-like alien, *The Man From Planet X* (1951).

ABOVE: Wait till you see what happened to *The Fly* (1958).

"fellow traveller". For five years after **The Thing**, almost every alien, dinosaur or radioactive mutant on the rampage would be dealt with by the kind of straight-arrow characters found in **The Thing** (Kenneth Tobey, the star, joined the exclusive ranks of '50s monster fighters with John Agar, Richard Carlson and very few others) and the matter-of-fact semi-documentary tone of the film would be copied (less eptly) by many, many B quickies.

Rockets alone were most often not enough to carry '50s science-fiction films (*Destination Moon*, 1950, is a rare case). Almost every major SF picture takes care to include a monster to qualify at least as a semi-horror movie: the elegant, intelligent *The Day the Earth Stood Still* (1951) has its tall, enormously powerful robot Gort; the lusty, adventurous *20,000 Leagues Under the Sea* (1954) has its tussle with a giant squid; the lively space opera *This Island Earth* (1955) has the bug-eyed, insect-limbed, exposed-brain Metaluna Mutant; the philosophical *Forbidden Planet* (1956) has the roaring, invisible Monster From the Id; and *The Incredible Shrinking Man* (1957) doesn't forget to have its miniature hero menaced by a relatively gigantic cat and spider. And that's only SF films that *aren't* primarily monster movies. Even if many '50s mutants turned out to

be old fiends in atomic clothing – witness *The Werewolf* (1956), *The Vampire* (1957) and *Frankenstein 1970* (1958) – this was still an era of great innovation and imagination in monster-creation.

The Beast From 20,000 Fathoms (1953), animated by the newcomer Ray Harryhausen, is a radioactive dinosaur thawed out by a bomb test at the North Pole, while in *Them!* (1954) giant ants are descended from insects irradiated by the first atomic explosion in 1945. Both had many imitators and descendants: Ishiro Honda's *Gojira* (1954), a Japanese semi-remake of *Beast*, founded an entire genre of *daikaiju* (giant monster) pictures, even making an impression in America when released, with the addition of Raymond Burr, as *Godzilla, King of Monsters* (1956). H.G. Wells's Martians arrive in sleek, aerodynamic murder machines with tri-lobed, snake-necked probes to terrorize the heroine in *The War of the Worlds* (1953), one of relatively few mass alien invasions. For budgetary reasons, lone troublemakers like the Thing were more commonplace, as in *Phantom From Space* (1953) or *Devil Girl From Mars* (1955). Soon, in the spirit of Jekyll and Hyde, human mutations were resulting from atomic-era mad science – *The Neanderthal Man* (1953), *The Fly* (1958), *Monster on the Campus* (1958), *The Hideous Sun Demon* (1959). At least the mask-makers and stuntmen were back in business – dear old Lon Chaney Jr, flabbier than in his Wolf Man days, went on the rampage again as *The Indestructible Man* (1956).

Universal, now Universal-International (U-I), were again at the forefront, in films produced by William Alland, mostly directed by Jack Arnold. They made an alien-visitor picture (*It Came From Outer Space*, 1953) and a giant-bug movie (*Tarantula*, 1955). Alland produced Jack Sherwood's *The Monolith Monsters* (1957), one of several disaster-type efforts (see *The Magnetic Monster*, 1953) that inflate natural phenomena (mysteriously growing elements) into threats worthy of the "monster" tag. The Alland-Arnold team's most significant creation was **The Creature From the Black Lagoon** (1954), which features a fish-human hybrid described as a "living fossil" and an evolutionary by-blow. The odd Metaluna Mutant or Mole Man model kit aside, the Gill Man was the final addition to Universal's pantheon of copyrighted, franchised and memorabilized monsters. The Creature returned in two sequels, Arnold's *Revenge of the Creature* (1955) and Sherwood's *The Creature Walks Among Us* (1956), and its gill-frilled visage is on merchandise to this day.

Arnold's best films show a tension between the clipped, grey-flannel, matter-of-fact style of SF and the poetic, lurid, sexualized, perverse feel of the classic monster movie – epitomized best in the masterly sequence in which the sinuous Creature swims just underneath the curvy heroine (Julia Adams) as she does the backstroke on the surface of the Black Lagoon, whose depths represent the Unconscious as much as they do prehistory.

In the mid-'50s, the science-fiction cycle changed in several significant ways. The major studios found they had competition from upstart grindhouse outfits like James H. Nicholson and Samuel Z. Arkoff's AIP, who had less money to spend on big effects (though they could usually stretch to one Paul Blaisdell monster outfit per picture) and were more directly focused on a mostly teenage, drive-in audience. To the kids, heroes in uniform like Kenneth Tobey seemed square: hence, *Invasion of the Saucer Men* (1958) and *The Blob* (1958), in which grown-ups are useless

and only misunderstood teenagers know how to combat the menace of archetypal bug-eyed monsters or an all-consuming red jelly. While even fag-end Universal efforts like the dreary *The Deadly Mantis* (1957) are concerned with some sort of plausibility, AIP unleashed imaginations like those of young producer-director Roger Corman and turned out unabashedly lurid, unashamedly entertaining and surprisingly quick-witted efforts like *It Conquered the World* (1956), *Not of This Earth* (1957) and *Attack of the Crab Monsters* (1957). It would be wrong to suggest that Corman's films are better than their titles sound or even that they live up to their amazing posters, but they all have terrific pace set next to the trudging of much of their AIP stablemates (see, for example Bert I. Gordon's *The Amazing Colossal Man*, 1957) and bristle with a sense that even something called *The Wasp Woman* (1959) doesn't *have* to be bad.

This shift of the front line, from prepared military men and scientific experts to the home front, also made room for Don Siegel's **Invasion of the Body Snatchers** (1956), from Jack

---

BELOW: A tense moment from *The Black Castle* (1951).

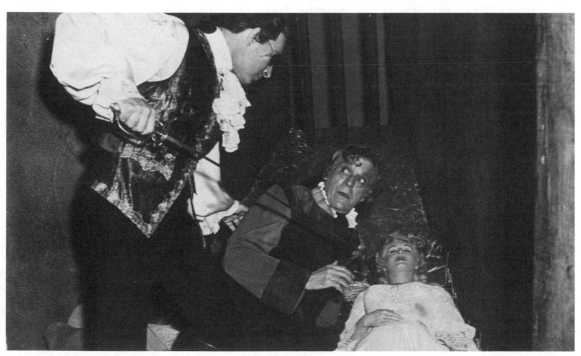

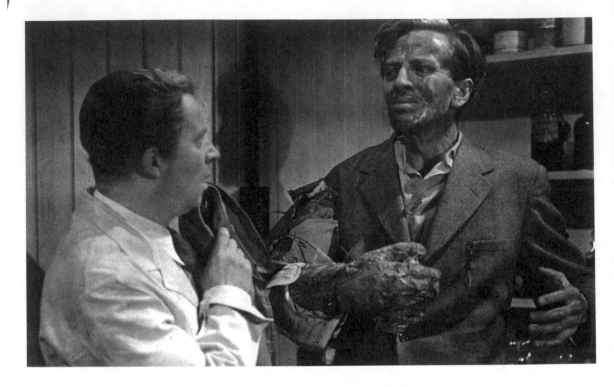

Finney's novel, one of the key films of the era. *Invaders From Mars* (1953) and *It Came From Outer Space* (1953) had played with the nightmare potential of parents and authority figures mind-controlled by Martians or replaced by malign xenomorphs, but it took **Body Snatchers** to lift this concept to the status of a sub-genre. Set in a small town where people come down with an epidemic of an unusual delusion – that their friends and relations have somehow "changed" – the film has been read as both a vision of Senator McCarthy's nightmare of Communist infiltration into the heartland and an allegory of the way witch-hunting Red-baiters turned America against itself. Either seems valid, but there are also psychological readings that make sense. The Body Snatchers, grown from seed, owe a little to stories of doppelgängers (all the way back to Poe's "William Wilson" and *The Student of Prague*), vampirism or demon possession, but Finney set out a modern myth, which has proved useful ever since. Even more lasting in the genre is Finney's and Siegel's depiction of an American small town, suitable for a real-estate ad, that harbours nasty secrets, and is at once penetrated from without and eaten away from within by the monstrous. Santa Mira, California, home to the Body Snatchers, has twin towns all over the map, from Jerusalem's Lot, Maine, to Twin Peaks, Washington.

Many studies imply that gothic horror was completely out

ABOVE: Half man, half cactus-tripe-squid creature,
The Quatermass Xperiment (1955).

of fashion between *House of Dracula* (1945) and **The Curse of Frankenstein** (1957), obliterated first by Abbott and Costello and then by the '50s science-fiction creature feature, but this isn't strictly true. A tentative return came as early as *Son of Dr Jekyll* (1951), while Universal signed Karloff back for minion roles in *The Strange Door* (1951), an R.L. Stevenson story toplining Charles Laughton, and *The Black Castle* (1951), another rerun of **The Most Dangerous Game**. These are tentative costume films, but André de Toth's **House of Wax** (1953), a remake of *Mystery of the Wax Museum* (1933), is more confident in setting a new style, not only in full colour but eye-popping 3D (and stereophonic sound). The contemporary setting of the original was shifted back to the 1890s, complete with can-can girls and starched collars, and plummy Vincent Price – who had flirted with horror as early as *The Invisible Man Returns* (1940) – was elevated to full genre stardom as the mad sculptor. Price seems benign and charming in his wheelchair (handing out smelling salts to a fainting patron he has just terrified), adding slightly more deliberate self-mocking comedy than Karloff or Lugosi would have liked, but he also nips about nimbly in cloak, slouch hat and fright-face while

ABOVE: *Fiend Without a Face* (1958), or a leg, or an arm....

stealing corpses and attempting to dunk Phyllis Kirk in wax.

There were other 3-D horrors – Price returned as *The Mad Magician* (1954), another old warhorse was trotted out in *Phantom of the Rue Morgue* (1954) and William Cameron Menzies's *The Maze* (1953) is remarkable by any standard – but that craze came and went. A prod for specifically supernatural horror was prompted by the nine-days-wonder of the Bridey Murphy case, in which a hypnotist claimed to regress a modern housewife to a previous life as an Irish servant girl. This was filmed as *The Search for Bridey Murphy* (1956), but also prompted pulpier efforts like *The She-Creature* (1957), Corman's *The Undead* (1956) and *The Bride and the Beast* (1958). U-I started to add a few old-style monsters to their roster: the snake-woman picture *Cult of the Cobra* (1955) reminded audiences that a creature didn't have to be atomic to be worth making a movie about. Faith Domergue's avenging Cobra Woman pioneered a minor trend for pin-up mutants, followed by Marla English as the modern incarnation of the She-Creature and middle-aged matrons desperate for a return to youth (and damn the side-effects) in *The Leech Woman* (1958) and *The Wasp Woman*. Relics of earlier decades still needed work, as Edward D. Wood found when he signed Bela Lugosi for his own odd SF/

horror/melodrama/autobiography films. The last gasp of a gothic style which was about to get a shot in the arm from England came in a clutch of quickies built around old stars (Lugosi, Chaney Jr, Carradine, Karloff) or ideas (19th-century mad science, voodoo, mummies), either directed by Reginald LeBorg (who had done *Inner Sanctum* films) or produced by Howard W. Koch – *The Black Sleep* (1956), *Voodoo Island* (1957), *Frankenstein 1970* (1958) and *Pharaoh's Curse* (1958).

Britain's small-scale Hammer Films had made forays into semi-horror as early as the Lugosi vehicle *Mystery of the Marie Celeste* (1936) and the Jack the Ripper drama *Room to Let* (1949). Hammer were the first British studio to essay American-style science fiction in Terence Fisher's *Spaceways* (1953) and *Four-Sided Triangle* (1953). Their break-out genre hit was Val Guest's *The Quatermass Xperiment* (*The Creeping Unknown*, 1955), adapted from Nigel Kneale's BBC TV series, with Brian Donlevy as a stolid boffin and Richard Wordsworth dragging himself over London wastegrounds as an astronaut painfully transforming into a cactus-tripe-squid creature which threatens to absorb all life on Earth. The film was successful enough to prompt Hammer to produce sequels (**Quatermass 2**/ *Enemy From Space*, 1957), imitations (*X – the Unknown*, 1958) and other Kneale properties (*The Abominable Snowman*, 1959). Other UK producers got in on the act by adapting ITV serials made in

ABOVE: "The ghosts are moving tonight – restless, hungry."
House on Haunted Hill (1958).

competition with the BBC's Quatermass franchise: *The Trollenberg Terror* (*The Crawling Eye*, 1958) and *Strange World of Planet X* (*The Cosmic Monsters*, 1958).

The American producer and monster fan Milton Subotsky pitched Hammer the idea of remaking **Frankenstein** in colour, preferably with Boris Karloff in the lead. Hammer paid him off and took the project in another direction. Terence Fisher's **The Curse of Frankenstein** (1957), scripted by Jimmy Sangster, seems to have been constructed, probably on legal advice, to be as little like Universal's 1931 film as possible, which meant it was free to establish its own approach to familiar material and devise a look and a feel which would soon become a style of its own. At the time, most attention was paid to the colourful gore which was a new ingredient of the genre – we'd seen severed limbs and brains in tanks before, but the blood spurts had not looked as red or the "grey matter" quite so pink. However, **Curse** also stressed quality in art direction (compare the under-designed laboratory

of *The Black Sleep* with Frankenstein's array of period scientific equipment), costume, cinematography, supporting cast and music (James Bernard's blaring follow-the-title themes). Perhaps most importantly, **Curse** made two new horror stars: Peter Cushing carries the film with his incisive, amoral, chilly-charming performance as Victor Frankenstein, an aristocratic bastard who lets nothing get in his way; Christopher Lee, cast as the Monster mainly because Bernard Bresslaw's agent wanted more money, gets less to work with, but has a remarkable, wounded animal presence. Both men would come to be indispensable in Transylvania-on-Thames.

With **Frankenstein** coining money, **Dracula** (*Horror of Dracula*, 1958) was inevitable. All the key creatives were back. Again, Cushing has the lead, as a businesslike Van Helsing, and Lee barely gets a look-in (eight minutes of screen time, no dialogue after his first scene), but in his black cloak and hissing through bloody fangs Lee redefines Dracula as a far more dynamic, sexual being than the stolid Lugosi. Plunging necklines and women awaiting the Count with open negligées up the skin quotient, at least as important as gore in Hammer's appeal. Bosomy Continental starlets dubbed by British stage-school graduates (Yvonne Monlaur, Yvonne Romain) or well-bred ex-models polished by a few seasons in rep (Hazel Court, Barbara Shelley) recur in British horror, competing with the tight-sweatered rock 'n' rollers, white-swimsuited lady scientists and 50-foot women of American double features. After **Frankenstein** and **Dracula**, Hammer went on a remake jag: *The Hound of the Baskervilles* (1959), *The Man Who Could Cheat Death* (1959, from *The Man in Half Moon Street*), **The Mummy** (1959), *The Two Faces of Dr Jekyll* (1960) and *The Phantom of the Opera* (1962). **The Curse of the Werewolf** (1960) is adapted from Guy Endore's novel *The Werewolf of Paris* rather than any previous film version, but stands as Hammer's take on **The Wolf Man** (1941). Even the "original" *Kiss of the Vampire* (1964) is a rewrite of **The Black Cat** (1934) with vampires instead of Satanists.

Hammer's gothic revival was soon imitated, often by folks who hadn't yet had time to study the style and so fell back on earlier models or their own instincts. Hammer screenwriter Jimmy Sangster dashed off *Blood of the Vampire* (1958) and *Jack the Ripper* (1959) for the producers Monty Baker and Robert Berman, but these blood-bolstered, theatrical melodramatics evoke Tod Slaughter rather than Peter Cushing. When Baker and Berman signed Cushing for John Gilling's *The Flesh and the Fiends* (1958), about Burke and Hare, Gilling simply remade a script he had written for a Slaughter movie, *The Greed of William Hart* (1948). The producer Richard Gordon, in Britain to make mock-American SF films (the astonishing *Fiend Without a Face*, 1958, and the Quatermass knock-off *The First Man in Space*, 1959) also looked to the Slaughter style, leavened with a little Universal, and signed Boris Karloff to a couple of Victorian melodramas, *Grip of the Strangler* (*The Haunted Strangler*, 1958) and *Corridors of Blood* (1958); he even found room for the rising horror star Christopher Lee as a body snatcher in the latter. Jacques Tourneur, in the UK after the fizzle of his post-Lewton career, directed **Night of the Demon** (*Curse of the Demon*, 1957), a busily influential film.

Producer Herman Cohen arrived on the monster scene at AIP, and started a minor craze for mixing juvenile delinquency with atomic-age takes on old horror tales with *I Was a Teenage Werewolf* (1957) and *I Was a Teenage Frankenstein* (1958). Cohen came to Britain and hooked up with Anglo-Amalgamated, an outfit that wanted to get in on the horror action. Cohen hired Michael Gough, a dreary hero in Hammer's **Dracula**, and cast him in *Horrors of the Black Museum* (1959), as a limping, impotent, misogynist, slightly gay, sadistic megalomaniac crime writer (who happens to have Dr Jekyll's old potion lying about the house). *Black Museum* really is as extreme as critics said the Hammer films were: it's the one which opens with the girl receiving the trick binoculars that sprout eye-gouging spikes when the focus is adjusted. Cohen and Gough continued their depradations in *Konga* (1961) and *Black Zoo* (1963), while Anglo delivered more mutilation, with Anton Diffring wielding the scalpel, in *Circus of Horrors* (1960) and backed Michael Powell's still-jolting essay in Eastmancolor psychosis **Peeping Tom** (1960).

Back in America, the teenage-monster boom continued: Edgar G. Ulmer made *Daughter of Dr Jekyll* (1957), Richard Cuhna contributed *Frankenstein's Daughter* (1958), Herman Cohen bowed to the inevitable and did a teenage vampire in *Blood of Dracula* (1958) and the low-rent Jerry Warren threw out *Teenage Zombies* (1960). Universal noticed their properties were back in business and made the low-key, contemporary-set *Return of Dracula* (1958), with Francis Lederer as a vampire with a cloak-like coat thrown over his shoulders. This disguised remake of Hitchcock's *Shadow of a Doubt* (1943) was the first film to bring Transylvania to small-town USA, but certainly not the last. The studio even tried a vampire Western, *Curse of the Undead* (1958). Much more distinctive were the films of the producer-director William Castle, famed for promotional gimmicks like "Percepto" and "Emergo" but also of note for cementing Vincent Price's genre star status and catching the cynical, blackly comic tone of the EC horror comics in *House on Haunted Hill* (1958) and **The Tingler** (1959). Castle would stick with the genre, but arguably never trumped the centipede creature, generated at the base of the spine by fear and prevented from killing the host by a scream, found in **The Tingler** – this stands as the single strangest premise ever put forward by an American horror film.

The return of Dracula & Co was noted farther afield than Shepperton and Hollywood. After the '20s, "foreign" horror had been a matter of occasional one-offs like the Dane Carl Dreyer's arty **Vampyr** (1932) or the Frenchman Henri-Georges Clouzot's thriller **Les Diaboliques** (1955); now horror truly became an international field. In Mexico, Germán Robles played a Dracula lookalike in **El Vampiro** (*The Vampire*, 1957), which seemed a south-of-the-border *Son of Dracula* (1943) in its monochrome Universal style, but led to far wilder Mexican efforts, featuring Aztec mummies, brain-sucking alchemists and masked, monster-fighting wrestlers like El Santo and Blue Demon. In Italy, Riccardo Freda directed **I Vampiri** (1956), which features another matron who kills to enjoy renewed youth, and *Caltiki, il Mostro Immortale* (*Caltiki, the Immortal Monster*, 1959), in which an all-consuming blob crawls out of a Mayan temple. In France, Georges Franju – perhaps influenced by the Paris-set **I Vampiri** – directed **Les Yeux Sans Visage** (*Eyes Without a Face*, 1959), a mix of pulp and poetry featuring a mad plastic surgeon trying to give his daughter (a masked, elegant Edith Scob) a new face. In the Philippines, Wells's Dr Moreau inspired Gerardo de Leon's **Terror is a Man** (1959), which would trigger the "Blood Island" cycle a decade on. In Germany, mad science and cheesecake met in *Die Nackte und der Satan* (*The Head*, 1959) and *Ein Toter Hing im Netz* (*Horrors of Spider Island*, 1960) and Dr Mabuse was about to make a comeback.

At the end of the '50s, horror was everywhere.

THE THING
AKA THE THING (FROM ANOTHER WORLD)

1951, US, dir Christian Nyby, scr Charles Lederer, starring Kenneth Tobey, Margaret Sheridan, Robert Cornthwaite, Douglas Spencer

The producer Howard Hawks had bought the rights to John W. Campbell's short story "Who Goes There?" in the '40s, and closely supervised Nyby, who had edited several Hawks films, in his direction – the overlapping dialogue, which adds to the realism and builds tension, is indelibly Hawks's property. For all its resolutely modern approach, the film also bears **Frankenstein**'s fingerprints, from the appearance of James Arness's monster, giant, lumbering and enraged, to the conception of Dr Carrington, the inevitable mad scientist whose misty-eyed paean to the "neat and unconfused reproductive technique of vegetation" recalls his Teutonic forebear's distaste for standard human reproduction. The convincingly hostile polar setting works both to isolate the group (which can survive only if it works *as* a group: there is no room for mavericks on the base) and as an analogy for Carrington's emotionless, cold science, which sees "emotional or sexual factors" as a "handicap". The creature is also a vegetable – "an intellectual carrot, the mind boggles!" – albeit a vampiric one, moving away from the Darwinian evolutionary fears that had characterized mad science in the '30s and '40s into an entirely new realm of species anxiety. That **Invasion of the Body Snatchers** shared its fears of vegetable consciousness suggests that the idea was informed by anti-Communist hysteria or the subtler fears of conformity exercising '50s America, but it is Nikki's conformity to gender

BELOW: A young Charles Bronson waits to pounce in **House of Wax**.

expectations – "Boil it!" she suggests brightly when a character wonders "What do you do with a vegetable?" – that finally saves the day. Fast-paced and tightly plotted, *The Thing*'s magnificent action sequences and iconic imagery have provided a touchstone for horror and SF films ever since, from explicit remakes (John Carpenter, 1982) to magpie tributes (**Alien**'s motion detector even apes *The Thing*'s Geiger counter).

HOUSE OF WAX

1953, US, dir André de Toth, scr Crane Wilbur, starring Vincent Price, Frank Lovejoy, Phyllis Kirk, Carolyn Jones

The sculptor Henri Jarrod survives a fire at his waxworks display and opens another, a chamber of horrors. He will stop at nothing to achieve the verisimilitude he seeks, but the model he wants for his Marie Antoinette, Sue Allen, is convinced that he is using real corpses for his dummies. Warner's remake of *Mystery of the Wax Museum* (1933) was the first major-studio release in 3D and used the effect for an unusually recursive exploration of cinema's relationship to carnival sideshows. The film foregrounds elements of display throughout, whether in the 3D effects themselves (at one point a carny barker addresses the audience as he bats a ping-pong ball at them), Jarrod's dry commentary as he leads his customers – and the audience – around the chamber of horrors, or the film's key oppositions, art versus commerce, reality versus representation and human flesh versus sculpted wax. The film's play with the uncanny properties of waxworks, a genre staple since Paul Leni's *Das Wachsfigurenkabinett* (1924), is mixed with a perverse eroticism only partially obscured by the flat, *Mary Poppins* creakiness of the script and period detail. Jarrod's necrophiliac obsession with parts of women, most clearly visible in his preoccupation with the inner workings of his dummies – he apologises to Marie Antoinette for "discussing your intimate secrets" – is only the most glaring display of wayward sexuality in a film driven by the literal objectification of women and liberally decorated with isolated body parts. Sue's boyfriend takes her to a can-can show to cheer her up; the displays in the chamber of horrors are all eroticized, one customer leaning over a bath for a glimpse of Marat's wax penis; and Sue moans and writhes as she is strapped to a table, Jarrod spurting a hypodermic needle in the air as his obscenely smooth pink face leers over her naked body. Contemporary critics criticized the film for its eroticized violence, but such dismissals encouraged a curious public to make the film a major success and establish Price as an exploitation star. It was remade as a forgettable Paris Hilton vehicle in 2005.

UGETSU MONOGATARI

1953, Jap, dir Kenji Mizoguchi, scr Yoshikata Yoda, starring Masayuki Mori, Machiko Kyô, Kinuyo Tanaka, Eitarô Ozawa

In 16th-century Japan, during the throes of civil war, Tobei and Genjuro dream of leaving their farming lives behind, Tobei to become a samurai and Genjuro to grow rich as a potter. Their dreams come true, but at what cost to their families? Conflating stories by Akinari Ueda and Guy de Maupassant, Mizoguchi's film, perhaps the most lyrical ghost story ever told, was the first Japanese ghost film to be distributed in the West, winning the Silver Lion at the Venice Film Festival and demonstrating both that Japanese ghosts were far more corporeal than their Western counterparts and that the supernatural could be the province of major, respected filmmakers. Widely interpreted as an allegory for Japan's involvement in the Second World War, the film tempers its conservatism – its peasant farmers appear to be punished in part for seeking to better their social standing – with a humanism that leaves superficially similar offerings (such as two episodes of **Kwaidan**) in the shade. Mizoguchi achieves an unearthly, spectral beauty that tops anything in Kobayashi's film while retaining an acute emotional sensitivity that makes scenes such as the ending (showcasing one of the director's signature pans) almost unbearably poignant. *Ugetsu*'s respect for tradition – its underlying theme is less regret for Japan's martial ambitions than its modernization, explored with a resonant sense of loss – is also notable in its delicate, non-exploitative treatment of the supernatural, its phantoms less simple avatars of paranormal menace than rounded characters with a broad emotional range, although their fury is still chilling to behold. A masterpiece.

THE CREATURE FROM THE BLACK LAGOON

1954, US, dir Jack Arnold, scr Harry Essex, Arthur Ross, starring Richard Carlson, Julie Adams, Richard Denning, Antonio Moreno

A team of ichthyologists travel up the Amazon in search of fossils, but find instead a living gill-man. David wants to study and learn from the find, but his boss Mark wants to kill it as a trophy, while the Creature's main interest is Kay, David's girlfriend. Most accounts of *Creature*, after the obligatory mentions of the gimmicky 3D effects and the Creature's superlative design, see the gill-man as representing primal male sexual desire, but the film's sexual dynamics are more interesting and complex than that. While the Creature is certainly the focal point for the sexual

ABOVE: Vera Clouzot and Simone Signoret poison monsieur's whisky in **Les Diaboliques**.

OPPOSITE: **The Creature from the Black Lagoon** makes a play for Julie Adams.

tensions of the expedition, embodying Mark's displaced hostility towards David as they compete for Kay's attentions, along with David's own immaturity (the other characters wonder out loud why he has not yet married Kay), it is less sexual than romantic in its approach to Kay, shyly reaching up a claw to touch her as she swims rather than presenting a credible threat of rape. In fact, in its mixture of male and female characteristics, equally at ease in water and on land, it represents an evolutionary nostalgia for an archaic, pre-gender age, resisting Mark's attempts to bring it from its womblike lagoon into the modern world. The oceanic security of the lagoon is explored through the photography, underwater sequences shot with a languid beauty that contrasts with the flatness of the world above the surface: Kay is at home here, swimming for pleasure, while the men only approach the water

armed with cameras or harpoons, seeking to exploit its uncharted environment. Responses to the Creature also represent different approaches to science: Mark wants to bask in the glory of the Creature's corpse, while David wants to learn from it as a living creature. Only Kay, objecting to the men's competitiveness while relishing the attention to her bathing suit and skimpy tops, wants to leave it alone. This was followed by two lesser sequels, *Revenge of the Creature* (1955) and *The Creature Walks Among Us* (1956).

LES DIABOLIQUES
AKA DIABOLIQUE
1955, Fr, dir/co-scr Henri-Georges Clouzot, co-scr Jérôme Géromini, Frédéric Grendel, René Masson, starring Simone Signoret, Vera Clouzot, Paul Meurisse, Charles Vanel

The headmistress of a Parisian school, Vera Delasalle, tires of her husband Michel's brutish behaviour and teams up with his lover Nicole to kill him. They think they have committed the perfect crime, only for the body to disappear. Has Michel returned

ABOVE: "You're next!" Kevin McCarthy and Dana Wynter flee the **Invasion of the Body Snatchers**.

from his watery grave? Clouzot secured the rights to Boileau and Narcejac's source novel *Celle qui n'Était Plus* a month before Hitchcock attempted to do the same. Its international success triggered Hitchcock's desire to make **Psycho**, although he first adapted the authors' *D'Entre les Morts* as *Vertigo* (1958). But, for all the similarities between Hitchcock and Clouzot's most famous films, where **Psycho** loses momentum after the murder of Marion Crane, *Les Diaboliques* cranks up the tension to a near-unbearable pitch by the end and relies solely on judicious editing and a superb cast for its effects – there are no shrieking strings here, indeed no conventional score at all. The minute attention to physical detail – a van springs up when the weight

of a wicker box is removed and a tap drips on the waterproof tablecloth covering Michel's body – roots the film in a grubby authenticity that makes its horrors still more shocking. Clouzot also expertly manipulates the viewer's sympathies by presenting Michel's murder as justifiable: he rapes his wife, beats his lover and routinely feeds the schoolboys rotting food. Our sympathies are with his murderers – the remorseful, weak-hearted Vera and the icily brusque Nicole – as they narrowly avoid discovery of their crime, especially when contrasted with the other pompous, petty-minded characters. But, as the plot unfolds, the cold sadism of Nicole, not a bleached hair out of place as she casually drowns her lover, becomes more apparent, her mental cruelty topping even that of Michel and crowning Signoret, all dark glasses, high heels and immaculately belted raincoats, queen of the phallic women. The film was remade in 1996.

INVASION OF THE BODY SNATCHERS

1956, US, dir Don Siegel, scr Daniel Mainwaring, starring Kevin McCarthy, Dana Wynter, King Donovan, Caroline Jones

Doctor Miles Bennell returns to Santa Mira after a trip, to find many of the town's occupants claiming that their friends and family have been replaced by impostors. His scepticism is tempered when his friends find an unformed body and soon he and Becky, an old flame, realize that nobody can be trusted. The Cold War context of this SF/horror classic has led to interpretations of the film as embodying both anti-Communist and its opposite, anti-McCarthyite hysteria. **Invasion** supports both readings, principally because it taps into the anxieties that underpin each: fears of conformity and depersonalization. Advertising, psychiatry and rationalized work practices in '50s America were ringing warning bells for many social commentators: in its search for prosperity the country was sliding too close to its totalitarian mirror image of Red Russia. **Invasion**'s characters don't trust their instincts and emotions, relying instead on "experts" to interpret experience for them – Kaufman the psychiatrist becomes the spokesman for the pod people, reflecting a widespread distrust of pharmaceutical social engineering – and the characters who first notice that something's wrong, a child, a woman and a writer, are traditionally aligned with the intuitive and irrational. Yet Kaufman's pitch is not unattractive and the protagonists are hardly non-conformist, compared to the freaks of the 1978 remake: the film's doppelgänger theme suggests finally that the pods represent the characters' fears of their own desires to merge with the crowd. Jack Finney's original conception (the screenplay adapted his serial) had no overt socio-political concerns; he was simply intrigued by the notion of people becoming convinced that their friends have been replaced by sinister doubles, aligning the film with the psychological condition Capgras Syndrome. The framing device, insisted upon by the studio, unwittingly offers another explanation, as it presents the entire story from Bennell's viewpoint alone – perhaps his pill-popping has led to a psychotic episode, his pod story being nothing but a florid paranoid fantasy. Siegel's tone of taut, suspenseful documentary realism ensures that the film's essentially ludicrous premise remains credible and disturbing, with Bennell's panic palpable as the familiar faces and surroundings of Santa Mira grow ever more alien and menacing. The film was remade, superbly, in 1978, and less successfully in 1993.

I VAMPIRI
AKA LUST OF THE VAMPIRE; THE DEVIL'S COMMANDMENT; THE VAMPIRES

1956, It, dir/co-scr Riccardo Freda, co-scr Pierre Regnoli, starring Gianna Maria Canale, Antoine Balpêtré, Paul Muller, Carlo d'Angelo

A murderer, dubbed "the vampire" by the press, stalks the streets of Paris draining women of their blood. Journalist Pierre Lantin is desperate to solve the mystery, resenting the distractions of society hostess Giselle du Grand, but when his photographer disappears he realizes that the du Grand castle may hold the key. Freda's updating of the Countess Báthory legend is the first Italian horror film of the sound era, spearheading the global horror renaissance despite its poor performance at the box office. Mario Bava, the leading light of Italy's gothic revival, worked as cinematographer on the film, shot in beautifully crisp black-and-white Cinemascope, and took the helm for two days after Freda walked off the set 10 days into the shoot. While much of the running time is padded out with static accounts of police and journalist investigations, contrasting with a frenetic soundtrack that seems to have been lifted wholesale from some old women-in-peril serial, Bava's roving camera comes alive in the gothic trappings of the du Grand castle and grounds. The film's juxtaposition of gothic and modern anticipates **Psycho**: the vampirism of the title is entirely modern, featuring blood transfusions carried out in antiseptic clinics, but the lab in which the villainous doctor carries out his sub-Frankenstein experiments is located in a cavern beneath the castle, accessible through the du Grand crypt and equipped with flashing alarm lights that recall some supervillain's lair. The film's theme of an elderly aristocratic woman so desperate to retain her beauty that she is prepared to slaughter the young also has a peculiarly modern resonance, its treatment here inviting parallels with **Les Yeux Sans Visage**.

QUATERMASS 2
AKA ENEMY FROM SPACE

1957, UK, dir/co-scr Val Guest, co-scr Nigel Kneale, starring Brian Donlevy, John Longden, Bryan Forbes, William Franklyn

After a chance encounter with a couple injured while picnicking at Wynerton Flats, Quatermass discovers that the area houses a top-secret military installation and that the meteorites that have been falling there show signs of intelligent design. The best of both Hammer's Quatermass films and their pre-gothic horror output,

Quatermass 2 is an underrated paranoid masterpiece on a par with **Invasion of the Body Snatchers**. But Kneale's vision of alien invasion is more pessimistic than the competition – here the highest echelons of government have already been infiltrated – and more concerned with technology than **Invasion**'s simple metaphor for conformity, even if the aliens are "a multiple organism ... with a single consciousness", turning their human subjects into antlike drones. The sleek, featureless helmets of the guards recall not only the huge domes of the plant, a soured vision of the optimistic bubble cities of '30s utopianism, but also the smooth lines of Quatermass's car, implicitly suggesting that whatever the aliens represent is here already. The sense of mounting panic comes less from an understanding of the scale of the infiltration than the juxtaposition of uneven, soft human lines and smooth, clean technological surfaces, and a growing conviction that the former cannot survive the clash. The film also draws on an acute sense of place: here rural England is a kind of desolate scrubland, part building site, part lunar landscape, the twilight greys – virtually

all of the exteriors appear to have been shot at dusk – leaching the environment of any emotional associations. The plant, by contrast, is an astonishing confection of concrete and steel that simultaneously evokes Paolozzi sculptures and some arcane temple to technology, explored in a series of static long shots, Gerald Gibbs's exquisite cinematography ramping up the unseen menace. The villagers' bunting-draped dance hall belongs to a bygone era, their initial optimism at the extra work of building the plant quickly fading as they are replaced by drones: the political inference is clear, but secondary to a pervasive, near-psychotic machine fear. The film is not flawless – Donlevy is too brusque to play the boffin, his two-fisted American drawl closer to a hardboiled private eye than a rocket scientist, while Sid James as an alcoholic reporter and the predictable happy ending pull their punches – but as a chilling expression of technological paranoia it has few peers.

BELOW: Christopher Lee's wounded animal presence in **The Curse of Frankenstein**.

THE CURSE OF FRANKENSTEIN

*1957, UK, dir Terence Fisher, scr Jimmy Sangster, starring
Peter Cushing, Christopher Lee, Hazel Court, Robert Urquhart*

Hammer's first full-blown horror film not only revived gothic horror but also kicked off the British horror boom, drawing the genre away from the atomic monsters and wisecracking teens of the US SF/horror cycle and into far darker territory. The studio might not have been able to use the trademarked Karloff make-up, but other changes from Universal's conception are more telling: Cushing's Frankenstein is a womanizer who lacks any of Colin Clive's tortured self-doubt, a brilliant scientist whose ruthlessly amoral experiments are hampered not by God but by his doggedly small-minded assistant, Paul, who has his own reasons for standing in the Baron's way. What is most remarkable about *Curse* is the confidence and verve with which it is executed, especially given that there was no known audience for gothic horror at the time. The film's humour is sophisticated rather than camp, coming from the Baron's bone-dry wit and the edits that follow – his trip to "get materials for my work" is followed by a shot of the municipal charnel house – and both Cushing and Lee make the key roles their own, displaying remarkable self-assurance given their relative lack of experience, Lee even managing to invest his horribly disfigured creature with a degree of poignancy. The film's gallows humour extends to the scenes of surgery and body parts – the Baron delights over fresh eyes, hands and a brain – which also, critically, acknowledge the goriness of surgery, a horror milestone in lurid Eastmancolor, even if it involves little more than the Baron wiping a bloody hand on his top. The Baron's chief ideological adversary is not Paul but Professor Bernstein, whose speech – "The trouble with us scientists is, we quickly tire of our discoveries, and pass them over to people who are not ready for them" – joins the dots between the gothic setting and contemporary nuclear paranoia. The Baron's treatment of him is perhaps his least forgivable act.

NIGHT OF THE DEMON
AKA CURSE OF THE DEMON

1957, UK, dir Jacques Tourneur, scr Charles Bennett, Hal E. Chester, starring Dana Andrews, Peggy Cummins, Niall MacGinnis, Maurice Denham

"Casting the Runes" by M.R. James features one of the many fictional manifestations of the occultist Aleister Crowley, here named Karswell, a man with a foul temper, sinister abbey and

ABOVE: "It's easy to see a demon in every dark corner."
Night of the Demon.

band of fearful acolytes. *Night of the Demon* updates the story, with the core narrative – a runic curse on a piece of paper must be returned to its owner before death results – being expanded by the Hitchcock screenwriter Charles Bennett into a thrilling metaphysical detective tale.

Dana Andrews made his name in the *noir* films of the '40s and there's much *noir* ambience in Jacques Tourneur's direction as Andrews's psychic investigator, Holden, finds his scepticism about the supernatural overturned on a visit to England to expose Karswell's devil cult. Tourneur directed **Cat People** and **I Walked with a Zombie** for Val Lewton at RKO and his skill at conjuring tense and oppressive atmospheres from arrangements of light and shadow is put to brilliant use here, together with smoke and mists that conceal or augur supernatural terror. The use of genuine English locations is refreshing, with Stonehenge appearing in the prologue and the scene where Holden journeys to the stones to confirm the antiquity of the runes of the curse

VAMPIRES

Vampires are everywhere. From Sesame Street and Count Duckula to adverts for mouthwash and cat food, the vampire remains a potent cultural icon worldwide. Fittingly for this most corporeal of supernatural beings, his primacy is most evident in cinema, the dominant art form of the 20th century. Bram Stoker's *Dracula* has been adapted for the screen more often than any other novel, only Sherlock Holmes appearing as a fictional character on film more often than Stoker's Count, while in terms of sheer volume vampires vastly outweigh other horror monsters.

The term "vampire" derives from the German *vampyr* and the Hungarian *vampir*, but similar legends are found worldwide, all – from the Greek *bourkabakos* to the Malayans' *hantu penyardin* – sharing the same crucial features: a dead person has returned from beyond the grave to feed on the lifeblood of the living. Some legends reach back into antiquity – Lilith, described in the Talmud and other Semitic writings as Adam's first wife, set the template for the sexual politics of Victorian vampirism by refusing to subject herself to her husband's will, leaving her damned to walk the Earth forever in search of human blood. But others were based on historical personages, the term also being used for bloodthirsty, tyrannical rulers such as Elizabeth Báthory, reputed to have bathed in the blood of virgins to maintain her youth; or Vlad IV, a 15th-century Transylvanian ruler and source of the Dracula name, whose taste for torturing and impaling his enemies led to rumours of the impalement of over 30,000 victims.

But the popular Western conception of the vampire has its roots less in ancient myth or secular mayhem than Eastern European folklore. Rural 18th-century communities from Russia to Turkey bristled with tales of rough farmhands as ready to gnaw on a neighbour's neck as on a sheep, condemned to vampirism after dying in a state of sin. One such legend, that of the Romanian *nosferatu*, came to exert an astonishing influence over Western culture for the next two centuries: a living corpse whose victims became vampires when their blood was sucked, the *nosferatu* could only be vanquished by an eclectic mixture of Christian and pagan defences, many of which filtered down into vampire lore as it is known today.

The notorious weekend at the Villa Deodati that gave birth to Mary Shelley's brainchild Frankenstein is also associated with the Monster's dark twin. Byron's entry in the ghost story contest, a fragment about an aristocrat named Darvell, was reworked by his physician, John Polidori, in *The Vampyre*, published in 1819. Widely credited as Byron's work, *The Vampyre* transformed Darvell into Lord Ruthven, a Byronic aristocrat who travels from Turkey to London to nibble his way through London society, indelibly associating vampirism with the Byronic image of sexually irresistible, decadent aristocracy rather than the earthy rustics of Romanian legend.

The vampire's entry into mass culture followed, with the 1847 publication of the 220-chapter penny-dreadful *Varney the Vampyre*, but the subsequent flowering of female vampires, particularly in France, proved far more influential and the simultaneously seductive, tragic and monstrous presentation of the titular vampire of J. Sheridan le Fanu's novella *Carmilla*, an overheated fable of lesbian desire, provided a key influence on Stoker's *Dracula*.

Stoker's novel, rather than inaugurating the genre, came at the culmination of a century of vampire fiction and presented a thoroughly modern conflation of the vampire imagery that had preceded it: Dracula is at once aristocratic and bestial, tapping into the late Victorian preoccupation with the struggle between evolutionary progress and bestial degeneration – a degeneration notably coded as feminine. It's no exaggeration to state that Victorian vampire fiction is obsessed with the "evil" of female sexuality – and the male struggle to control it – although Stoker betrays a characteristic ambivalence in his tone: his women are far more sexually attractive once they have been bitten. This mixture of desire and disgust became one of the defining tropes of the vampire legend and Stoker's related oppositions – sun/moon, day/night, rational/supernatural, intellect/intuition – provided the dynamic around which virtually all subsequent vampire narratives revolved.

Bizarrely, given *Dracula*'s runaway success, few literary copycats followed and even many of the films inspired by Stoker explained their vampires away through non-supernatural means. Many of the different strands of vampire cinema were visible even in the '30s, but they wouldn't coalesce until the '50s, the release of Hammer's **Dracula** providing fresh impetus through its use of colour – which made the film both more realistic and more oneirically intense than its monochrome forebears – and its explicit foregrounding of the sexual tensions at the heart of the legend.

The vampire's principal appeal, at least since Polidori, has been its embodiment of the sexual hostility that is an innate part of human sexual relations, tapping into a primal relationship between the sexual and supernatural. The 20th-century screen interpretations have capitalized on this, from Hammer's riot of heaving cleavages to Jean Rollin's idiosyncratic fetish visions.

Hammer's vampire films are routinely accused of being sexually reactionary – the vampire's female victims (men are bitten too, but rarely in such lingering detail) are despatched in gruellingly brutal punishments like the quasi-rape staking of **Dracula**, **Prince of Darkness** – but the criticism often misses the feel of the films which, while they may condemn vampirism in principle, allow the viewer to enjoy its sexual licence in practice. Hammer's **Dracula**, for instance, can equally well be seen as critical of stuffy sexual repression as liberation, an exploration of male weakness and fear in the face of powerful female sexuality as much as an assertion of patriarchal power. Later Hammer vampire films (**Taste the Blood of Dracula**, *Twins of Evil*, 1971) explicitly distrusted patriarchal authority altogether.

Sex has been both a boon and a curse for vampire cinema. The relaxation of censorship in the '60s that gave horror a greater freedom to explore sexuality – particularly sexual sadism – had given way by the mid-'70s to the popularity of softcore and hardcore pornography, and the vampire film (in its period setting, at least) went into commercial decline. Yet the figure unexpectedly not only survived but flourished, its sexual redundancy perversely fuelling a focus on other, subtler aspects of the legend. The vampire's survival is due in part to its symbolic flexibility, incorporating invasion, disease, colonialism, teenage angst, drug addiction, the dangers of foreign property ownership and exploitation, financial or otherwise, and most of the revisionist vampire films that proudly presented their bloodsuckers to the modern world have tapped into one of these strands.

It's easy to forget with explicitly modern takes on the legend like *Count Yorga, Vampire* (1970) that the 1931 **Dracula** had a contemporary setting, as did its children *Dracula's Daughter* (1936) and *Son of Dracula* (1942), the Count's widespread

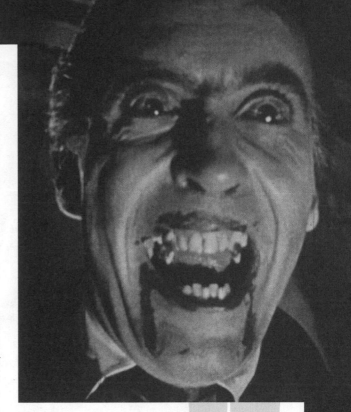

ABOVE: Christopher Lee seethes with diabolic energy, **Dracula** (1958).

association with period settings a testament to Hammer's cultural importance. While Romero's **Martin** may stand as the final word on contemporary vampirism, that hasn't stopped the theme from enjoying outings ranging from the trashy (*Subspecies*, 1991) to the impenetrable (*Trouble Every Day*, 2001). One of the more bizarre but fruitful flowerings has been the New York indie vampire, notably the blood junkies of Abel Ferrara's *The Addiction* (1995), Michael Almereyda's whimsical *Nadja* (1995) and Larry Fessenden's accomplished debut *Habit* (1997).

Today no other supernatural being enjoys such a dedicated subculture, the mid-70s explosion of hardcore giving rise, not coincidentally, to a legion of black-fingernailed goths devouring Anne Rice's Vampire Lestat books along with each others' carefully screened bodily fluids: as always implicit in the vampire's Byronic roots, the figure has finally become explicitly aspirational. As immortal, powerful beings who have dared to reject God's salvation and take what they want without remorse, the figure is enticing. Add a sense of romantic tragedy in the pining for death's release, and the archaic nostalgia of a pre-industrial figure surviving in the harsh neon of modern urban life, and the appeal is clear.

that Karswell has given him. Dana Andrews is rather lacklustre in many of his scenes but Niall MacGinniss's Karswell is one of horror cinema's great villains, a subtle and intelligent performance, by turns genial, knowingly amused and dangerously Mephistophelean. Tourneur apparently approved the inclusion of shots of the demon but hoped the results might be less obvious than they eventually were. Whatever the objections, there's nothing cuddly about the monstrous creature that comes rampaging out of billowing mist and flame to tear its victims to shreds. The climax of the film is brilliantly staged with the nightmarish creature manifesting amid the thundering steam and smoke of passing trains. One can only wonder how Tourneur might have enlivened Hammer's productions had he remained in England. [JC]

EL VAMPIRO
AKA THE VAMPIRE

1957, Mex, dir Fernando Mendez, scr Ramón Obon, starring
Germán Robles, Abel Salazar, Ariadna Welter, Carmen Montego

Duval, a vampiric foreigner, has arrived in Tierra Negra to resurrect his brother, killed there over a hundred years earlier. But his efforts to buy the Los Sicomoros *hacienda* are thwarted by the owner's niece, Marta, while Enrique, a doctor, grows increasingly suspicious of Duval's designs. The producer and co-star Salazar took inspiration from Universal's **Dracula** for a film that started the first substantial wave of Mexican horror but added little in the way of specific local flavour to the bloodsucking legend. The plot and setting are actually closer to *Son of Dracula* (1943), a rundown *hacienda* surrounded by mist-wreathed jungle standing in for Siodmak's southern gothic, and Mendez milks the environment's faded grandeur and the Catholic iconography of death for impressive atmospherics, while the Spanish émigré Robles anticipates Christopher Lee's Count in his convincingly aristocratic mien as Duval. But Salazar's background in light comedies is regrettably visible in his portrayal of Enrique, a Mexican Bob Hope running in mock terror from ghosts and vampires while hoping to seduce Marta with a winningly cheesy grin. Obon inverts what would become standard Hammer practice by giving his servants – visibly less European than their masters – privileged information, and replaces the standard savant with diffuse rural folklore that the urbane Enrique, who wears his city suit as a badge of sophistication and proudly proclaims his hatred of the countryside, must believe to survive. The sight of

OPPOSITE: Christopher Lee embodies the superhuman power of Stoker's vampire in **Dracula** (1958).

Duval attacking a young peasant boy further suggests a theme of foreign exploitation of rural Mexico blithely ignored by city people intent on emulating their foreign neighbours, but Mendez finally glosses over any potentially interesting ideas in favour of more creaky bats on strings.

DRACULA
AKA HORROR OF DRACULA

1958, UK, dir Terence Fisher, scr Jimmy Sangster, starring
Peter Cushing, Christopher Lee, Michael Gough, Melissa Stribling

The film in which Hammer revitalized horror cinema by looking backwards, making an international star of Christopher Lee. While American films were throwing a menagerie of radioactive monsters across the screen, Hammer had quietly bought the rights to **Dracula** and **Frankenstein** from Universal, determined to treat gothic drama seriously again after Universal's monsters had perished at the hands of Abbot and Costello. Jimmy Sangster's script mangles Stoker's story even more than the 1931 version but this hardly matters considering the liberties taken in the later films. Jonathan Harker in this version is a vampire-hunter masquerading as the new librarian for Dracula's castle. When he falls prey to the Count's brides, Van Helsing comes in pursuit, setting up the Lee/Cushing opposition that would continue to the end of the series. The Hammer films had an edge over Hollywood B movies with their colour photography, lavish (for the genre) period detail, a stock cast of decent British acting talent and a potent combination of sex and blood that pushed vampire cinema into previously unexplored areas. Christopher Lee's appearance as Dracula immediately swept away memories of Bela Lugosi's wooden posturings, establishing a new archetype, aristocratic yet ferocious, and radiating an erotic intensity that made his power over women seem thoroughly believable. The revelation of the Count's vampiric nature here is terrifying after early scenes of him talking with Harker. Lee's Dracula fully embodies the superhuman power and bloodshot fury of Stoker's vampire more than any actor before or since.

The Hammer horrors are sometimes flawed in their lack of sustained mood, oscillating between scenes of tremendous drama, powered by James Bernard's terrific scores, and drab chunks of exposition leading to the next scare. Yet Terence Fisher brought an energy to the screen lacking in other British films of the period. Van Helsing's pursuit of the Count back to his castle is a marvellous climax to the best of the Hammer Draculas, still in many ways the best Dracula film of all. [JC]

THE REVENGE OF FRANKENSTEIN

1958, UK, dir Terence Fisher, scr Jimmy Sangster, H. Hurford Janes, starring Peter Cushing, Michael Gwynn, Francis Matthews, Eunice Gayson

ABOVE: A new body for Karl, **The Revenge of Frankenstein**.

Having escaped the executioners of **The Curse of Frankenstein**, the Baron has moved to a new town under a new name, under which he becomes a popular society doctor, as well as volunteering in a hospital for the poor. His crippled assistant Karl volunteers to have his brain put in a new body for a chance of a new life. The operation is a success, but when Karl discovers that he is to be paraded as a medical curiosity, he escapes and seeks revenge. Hammer's sequel to **Curse** improves on the first film in almost every respect, being more confident, radical and altogether pacier. The Baron is a sympathetic and dashing figure, rebuffing society ladies' attempts to marry him off with their daughters. His talent, generosity and popularity with women

make him unpopular with the other doctors, who consequently seek to discredit him. Their petty hypocrisy contrasts with his genuine desire to advance the cause of science and his sole crimes here are ruthlessness towards his patients (although he helps many of society's rejects) and a desire to glory in the fruits of his labours: Fisher's sympathy for him is evident in the audacious ending. As elsewhere with Fisher, the film hinges on the dynamic between a series of oppositions – beauty/ugliness, exemplified in Karl's feelings for the minister's daughter; rich/ poor, as the society ladies vie for Frankenstein's attentions while the destitute shrink from his knife; and order/chaos, as a disfigured Karl breaks through the windows of a society party. The Technicolor saturation of the film is astonishing, lurid green and red lighting anticipating Mario Bava's work and setting an

LEFT: "It's hideous – but it's eloquent." Dick Miller finds his muse in **A Bucket of Blood**.

Maxwell, a bearded, sandal-wearing giant, chants lines like "Life is an obscure hobo, bumming a ride on the omnibus of art", which Walter memorizes and repeats to himself, whether justifying his killings (which move swiftly from the accidental to the murderous) or courting Carla, a fellow employee. When Maxwell accepts him as an artist the beatniks take him as one of their own, although he's still naïve enough, when cornered by an undercover narcotics agent, to ask "Wasn't that nice of Nioli to give me that expensive horse?" When Walter sells his first artwork (the Yellow Door is full of straights looking for the next big beatnik thing) he swaggers to the coffee shop dressed in a beret, smoking a long cigarette and demanding cappuccinos and Yugoslavian wine, but a model tells him, "You're just a stupid little farmboy and the rest of us are sophisticated beatniks," and it's clear that inspiration will soon strike again. Miller is perfect as the lonely halfwit Walter, hungry for acceptance, and the rest of the cast excel with their fruity beat gibberish, from Nioli's wayward flirtations – "Walter, you've done something to me! Something deep inside my *prana*!" – to Maxwell's poem in Walter's honour – "Necrophiles may dance on the place mats in an orgy of togetherness". Boasting a great, bongo-heavy jazz score and more wheatgerm bagels than you can wave a zen stick at, this was quickly followed by the better-known but less effective *Little Shop of Horrors* (1960).

THE MUMMY

1959, UK, dir Terence Fisher, scr Jimmy Sangster, starring Peter Cushing, Christopher Lee, Yvonne Furneaux, Eddie Byrne

1895, Egypt. Stephen Banning opens the tomb of Ananka, ignoring local warnings and fulfilling a 20-year quest. What he sees drives him insane and three years later, back in England, he and the other members of the expedition are menaced by a mysterious assassin. Fisher's reworking of Universal's 1932 film adds little thematically, save for a greater awareness of cultural relativity, but by making the titular creature the focus of the film it is visually far richer. Lee's size has rarely been used to better effect, and his lumbering walk and the excellent make-up, decaying grey-green bandages offset by the muted Eastmancolor backgrounds, make this one of Hammer's most memorable monsters. The art design elsewhere is also extravagant, if not always entirely convincing, and the film's sedate pace is enlivened by some of Fisher's most breathtaking images, particularly the mummy's animation from,

impressively hallucinatory tone. The film's only drawback is Gwynn as Karl, whose hammily mad overplaying belongs to a '30s film, as do the parallels drawn between his disfigurement and his propensity for evil.

A BUCKET OF BLOOD

1959, US, dir Roger Corman, scr Charles B. Griffith, starring Dick Miller, Barboura Morris, Anthony Carbone, Julian Burton

Walter Paisley, the naïve and put-upon waiter of the Yellow Door coffee shop, worships Maxwell, the resident poet, and dreams of becoming an artist himself. When he accidentally kills his landlady's cat, he covers it in clay and his dreams come true. But where will he turn next for models? Shot in five days for $50,000, Corman's hilarious cheapie is *the* beatnik horror comedy.

and return to, the swamp, and kinetic action sequences such as Cushing's hero blasting holes in the mummy with a shotgun. The studio's future attempts to tackle Egyptian curses (*The Curse of the Mummy's Tomb*, 1964; *The Mummy's Shroud*, 1966; *Blood from the Mummy's Tomb*, 1971) were less successful.

TERROR IS A MAN

1959, US/Philippines, dir Gerardo de Leon, scr Harry Paul Harber, starring Francis Lederer, Greta Thyssen, Richard Derr, Oscar Keesee Jr

An American sailor is shipwrecked on a remote tropical island. He finds that the native population have fled in terror leaving behind Dr Girard, a former Park Avenue plastic surgeon, his wife and his drunken assistant, Perrera. The exodus was caused

ABOVE: **The Mummy** rises from the swamp.

by the escape of Dr Girard's experimentally altered panther. Following the doctor's surgical work, the creature is now more man than animal but has been driven mad by pain and the cruelty of Perrera.

This variant on H.G. Wells's *The Island of Dr Moreau* was one of the first successes of local producer Eddie Romero, who was a pioneer in US-Philippines co-productions. Although he directed many of his subsequent productions himself, this one was helmed by the older and more experienced Gerry de Leon. A widely respected artist in the local film community, de Leon gave the modestly budgeted production a gloss and emotional impact that lift it well above the norm for what became known as the "Blood Island" series. Making the most of his small cast

HORROR COMICS

Horror comics in the West have their roots in the pulp magazine boom of the '40s that produced landmark publications like *Weird Tales* and *Strange Tales*, and radio series such as *Lights Out* and *The Witch's Tale* (probable source of the EC framing device of a witch-like narrator).

Early comics had dabbled in the supernatural, with occult investigators like Dr Occult and Zatara taking on everything from wereleopards to zombies, but things only really took off with the '50s. Between 1951 and 1954 more Americans read horror comics than *Reader's Digest*, an average of over 50 horror titles hitting the newsstands each month, the cover of *Weird Terror #6* spelling out the characteristic appeal – "Shrunken skulls – Decapitations – Cemeteries – Murders" – as publishers pillaged Poe, Lovecraft and the simmering dementia of freelance hacks for grisly tales of vengeance.

EC is the best-remembered name from this period, specializing in alliterative, pun- and exclamation-heavy text to flesh out ghoulish morality tales in comics like *Tales from the Crypt* and *The Vault of Horror* (both of which lent name and stories to '70s Amicus films, the former also rattling TV viewers as an HBO series, while Romero's *Creepshow* (1982) is an explicit EC tribute). But they were hardly the only publishers in the field, titles from ACG, Ace, Harvey and Atlas (later to become Marvel Comics) jockeying for position as purveyor of the nastiest flaying, the most spectacularly decayed corpse, each outdoing the last in a bid to pop those teens' eyeballs just that little bit more.

Such a good thing could never last: concerned parents bought into Frederic Wertham's specious thesis in the bestselling *Seduction of the Innocent* that horror comics were a root cause of juvenile delinquency, and in 1954 the Comics Code Authority was formed, ensuring that by 1955 only one or two defanged, bloodless horror titles were still in circulation.

The monster craze of the early '60s brought horror comics back into business with titles like *Creepy* and *Eerie*, and the late '60s and early '70s saw the genre thriving in both the undergrounds (especially S. Clay Wilson's nauseating work in *Zap!*) and the majors, Marvel and DC, introducing a darker tone to their superhero comics while publishing a range of explicit horror titles (*Chamber of Chills*, *Dead of Night*, *Vault of Evil*, etc.).

Alan Moore's award-winning '80s run on DC's *Swamp Thing*

(disastrously filmed by Wes Craven in 1982) cemented the Northampton magus's reputation as the most innovative creator in the comics mainstream, but Moore's finest work in the genre came in *From Hell*, a monumental study of Jack the Ripper that owes as much to Iain Sinclair's fevered psychogeography as Ripperology but which made for an execrable 2001 film.

Yet while horror comics have flourished everywhere from Italy (the fumetti Dylan Dog was filmed as **Dellamorte Dellamore**) to Brazil (where José Mojica Marins aka Coffin Joe has his own comic book), the key player on the international stage today is Japan, whose **horror manga** and anime (or animation) are major influences on modern genre cinema.

BELOW: Comics to corrupt children. Primetime EC fun with Tales of the Crypt

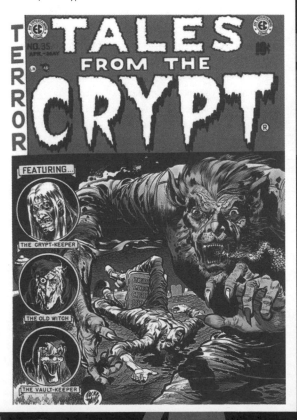

and limited locations, de Leon uses shadows and angles to keep the frame fresh and always full of menace. While not shying away from the creature's dangerous brutality, he still manages to make us empathize with its pain and sympathize with its "neither-man-nor-beast" plight. An ambiguous ending suggests that the creature may have escaped from the island on a fisherman's boat. Although this set up the possibility of a sequel, it was nearly 15 years before Romero returned to the Moreau theme with *The Twilight People* (1973).

Subsequent Blood Island films (all in lurid colour) were far more schlocky but built up a steady following in US drive-ins via their use of fun promotional gimmicks (a Blood Island ring, a phial of green blood, etc). The gimmick here is limited to a "fright bell" that was sounded as advance warning before one of the surgery scenes. [PT]

THE TINGLER

1959, US, dir William Castle, scr Robb White, starring Vincent Price, Judith Evelyn, Darryl Hickman, Patricia Cutts

Dr Warren Chapin's research into the nature of fear is on the verge of a breakthrough: he has almost managed to isolate the Tingler, a centipede-like manifestation of fear, but his screams invariably kill it off. Mrs Higgins, a mute acquaintance, offers one avenue of research, as does Chapin's philandering wife, but Mr Higgins has his own plans. Castle, the ultimate carny showman of the cinema, relied on a variety of in-cinema effects to bolster his takings: his two haunted-house movies, *House on Haunted Hill* (1958) and *Thirteen Ghosts* (1960), used "Emergo", featuring a luminous skeleton sailing over the audience's heads on a pulley, and "Illusion-O", customized 3-D glasses allowing viewers to switch between "ghost viewers" and "ghost removers", respectively. But Castle reserved his most infamous gimmick for *The Tingler*: "Percepto" had small electric vibrators attached to certain cinema seats, designed to buzz in scenes where the Tingler is loose in a cinema, and audiences were encouraged to scream and kill the creature. Even without a tingling rear the film is enjoyably bizarre, a mishmash of creature feature, *film noir* and cautionary drug tale (characters variously dose themselves or each other with LSD, with disastrous results), garnished with Castle's love of **Les Diaboliques** and silent film. The latter – much of the film is set in a cinema screening silent films – gives the film a cut-price reflexive quality, as we are repeatedly reminded of the mechanics of film screening and cinema maintenance: the Tingler even unspools the film and climbs across the screen at one point. The **Diaboliques**-inspired "haunting" of Mrs Higgins also sees her husband using the kinds of gimmicks that would make Castle proud, although it would be a mistake to view the film as having serious aspirations to cinema commentary. Price does his sissified best with an inconsistent character, but it's the supporting cast that shines here, Lucy and David's dull love affair aside. The fate-ravaged Mr and Mrs Higgins could have stepped out of any classic *noir*, Warren's scheming wife is perfectly poisonous and the rubbery titular creature endearingly shoddy.

TOKAIDO YOTSUYA KAIDAN
AKA THE GHOST OF YOTSUYA; GHOST STORY OF YOTSUYA IN TOKAIDO

1959, Jap, dir Nobuo Nakagawa, scr Masayoshi Onuki, Yoshihiro Ishikawa, starring Shigeru Amachi, Noriko Kitazawa, Katsuko Wakasuki, Shintaro Emi

When a samurai laughs at Iemon Tamiya's request for his daughter Iwa's hand in marriage, Iemon kills him, blames the murder on a rival and vows to Iwa to avenge his death. But life with Iwa soon descends into grinding poverty and, at his friend Naosuke's prompting, he plans to murder her and marry into a rich family, only to be haunted by her vengeful spirit. *Yotsuya Kaidan*, written in 1824 by Tsuruya Nanboku, is the paradigmatic *kabuki* ghost play and has been frequently adapted for the cinema: 11 versions were made between 1928 and 1994, with three in 1959 alone. Nakagawa's is the classic, anticipating his **Jigoku** in its conception of karma and Buddhist insistence that yearning can never be satisfied: desire is always stronger than its fulfilment. The film pays tribute to its theatrical origins over the stage-set opening titles, but feels far more cinematic than stagy. Nakagawa mixes languid pans with abrupt montages, balancing the lushness of his scope compositions with an admirable economy of camera movement. After the death of Iwa the visuals take on a hallucinatory quality, whether beautiful (the wonderfully atmospheric swamp) or horrific (the ghastly pallor of the corpses haunting the villains; a surprisingly gory limb-lopping), and eventually shift into a **Jigoku**-style wildness for Iemon's final hallucinations. But even earlier there's a sense of solipsism to the film, Naosuke representing Iemon's baser instincts and the ghosts his conscience. With a protagonist so hopelessly compromised, our sympathies are finally with the film's women, treated as property throughout.

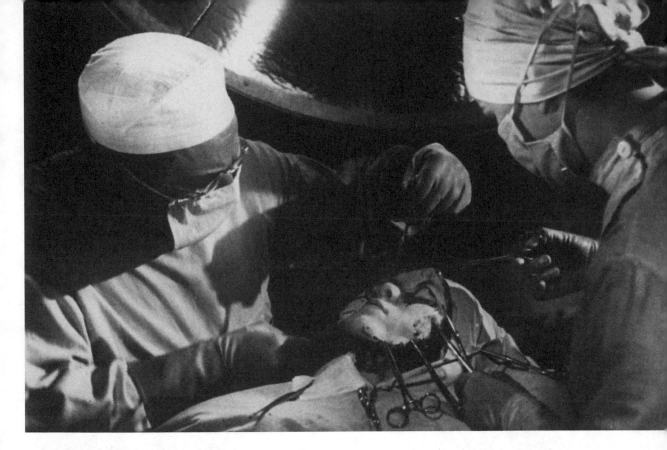

LES YEUX SANS VISAGE
AKA EYES WITHOUT A FACE; THE HORROR CHAMBER OF DR FAUSTUS

1959, Fr/It, dir Georges Franju, scr Jean Redon, starring Pierre Brasseur, Alida Valli, Edith Scob, François Guerin

Eminent Parisian plastic surgeon Professor Genessier uses his secretary Louise to lure young women to his house so that he can perform facelifts on them to reconstruct his daughter Christiane's features, disfigured in a car crash. Franju's film is a horror milestone less as an originator of Euro-horror, providing an influential template of sex and surgery, than as the first thoroughly modern, adult horror film, dispensing with the gothic trappings that had kept other modern genre films, from **The Curse of Frankenstein** to the purportedly contemporary **I Vampiri**, mired in the past. Although Franju's film was, like **Psycho**, made partly in response to the international success of **Les Diaboliques**, its privileging of imagery over plot (the story of *Les Yeux* is absurdly hackneyed) aligns it more closely with '60s Italian genre cinema, particularly Bava's work, than Clouzot's meticulous plotting. But, while Bava's visuals draw on a phantasmagoria unmoored from realistic concerns, Franju's are anchored in a coldly dispassionate realism that perversely

ABOVE: Facelift, Franju-style, **Les Yeux Sans Visage**.

renders them more effective. The key to the film is its title: "Les Yeux" points to its central theme of looking, from Christiane's haunted, isolated eyes to the film's structure, which presents its shocks in a series of carefully staged displays and crucially refuses to cut away as a victim's face is removed, raising the bar for cinema gore. The camera also lingers obsessively on surfaces, from Christiane's fibrous bandages to Louise's shiny black raincoat, bringing an unusually tactile, fetishistic quality to the film. "Sans Visage" hints in turn at the related theme of vanity, the film opening with Genessier claiming to a group of elderly women that "man's greatest new hope is the recapture of physical youth". He is more interested in surgical success, whatever the cost, than Christiane's happiness, while one of his victims, Edna, would rather die than live without a face. The spectre of plastic surgery slicing through the young hopefuls of the Hollywood dream factory underpins the film, in part an exploration of the ugly exploitation and fakery underlying the screen's obsession with female beauty. But Franju leavens the tone with deliciously black wit and moments of astonishing visual beauty that remain with the viewer when the story is long forgotten.

CHAPTER

6

1960s

The '60s were years of change, of revolt, of upheaval.

Among the first young folk to make their voices heard was Roger Corman, who talked Arkoff and Nicholson into giving him a budget he could have used for two black-and-white creature quickies and spent it all on **House of Usher** (1960). This Edgar Allan Poe adaptation was in colour like the Hammer horrors, but also (significantly) in windshield-shaped widescreen for optimum drive-in viewing. With a careful, imaginative script from novelist Richard Matheson and enough acting from Vincent Price to make up for the woodenness of the other three-quarters of the tiny cast, **House of Usher** kicked off its own cycle of Corman-Poe-Price-AIP pictures (*Pit and the Pendulum*, 1961, *Tales of Terror*, 1962, *The Raven*, 1963). AIP proceeded to find work for more mature horror stars like Ray Milland (a Price substitute in *The Premature Burial*, 1963), Lorre, Rathbone, Karloff and Chaney Jr (Lugosi, unfortunately, was dead) alongside youth-appeal faces like Frankie Avalon, Jack Nicholson, Barbara Steele and Hazel Court. Originally made in answer to British horror films, Corman's Poe parade eventually crossed the Atlantic for the director's last, comparatively lavish entries, **The Masque of the Red Death** (1964) and **The Tomb of Ligeia** (1964). AIP and Price stuck around in the UK as things changed, most notably for Michael Reeves's historical horror **Matthew Hopkins: Witchfinder General** (1968) – sold in the US as a Poe picture, *The Conqueror Worm*.

Hammer stayed in the game, with Fisher and Cushing delivering outstanding Frankenstein sequels from 1958 to 1973 and fine work from Don Sharp (*Kiss of the Vampire*, 1964) and John Gilling (**The Reptile**, 1966, **Plague of the Zombies,** 1966). Christopher Lee returned to the cloak in Fisher's **Dracula – Prince of Darkness** (1966), then strode through sequels which see-saw from excellent (Peter Sasdy's **Taste the Blood of Dracula**, 1970) to dire (Roy Ward Baker's *Scars of Dracula*, 1970). By the mid-'60s, Milton Subotsky, who had started Hammer's ball rolling, was offering serious competition with his Amicus outfit, known for omnibus horrors on the **Dead of Night** pattern like *Dr Terror's House of Horrors* (1964). Amicus used Cushing and Lee, and other Hammer types like Michael Gough

(not to mention the director Freddie Francis), but Subotsky was more prone to draw on contemporary sources like the stories of Robert Bloch (*The Skull*, 1965, *Torture Garden*, 1967) or EC horror comics (**Tales From the Crypt**, 1972). Hammer answered by adapting novels by the stuffy British Dennis Wheatley, which gives **The Devil Rides Out** (1968) and *Lost Continent* (1968) an almost nostalgic edge, though they aren't free of the rumbles of dissent felt throughout the genre in the later '60s. The ambitious, tragically short-lived Michael Reeves directed a quickie with Barbara Steele in Italy (*La Sorella di Satana/Revenge of the Blood Beast*, 1965) and returned to the UK to make two outstanding movies: **The Sorcerers** (1967), a science-fiction/generation-gap picture in which Boris Karloff and Catherine Lacey mind-meld with Ian Ogilvy for kicks, and **Matthew Hopkins: Witchfinder General** (1968), an English historical *Grand Guignol* with Vincent Price. *The Oblong Box* (1969), a Reeves/Price project intended to slot into AIP's Poe series, was passed on to Gordon Hessler, who brought in Christopher Wicking for rewrites: Hessler and Wicking followed up with several interesting pictures, notably the kinetic, complex, clever, exciting **Scream and Scream Again** (1969). If Hammer's horrors were in the Gainsborough-period bodice-ripper tradition, then Reeves and his contemporaries looked to other models – American thrillers and Westerns, mod TV shows like *The Avengers* – and expressed something of the vibe of Swinging London.

In 1960, horror changed radically – not in the old house on the hill, despite what could be found shrivelled in the fruit cellar, but in the pristine, tiled bathroom of a cabin at the Bates Motel. Alfred Hitchcock's **Psycho**, adapted from Bloch's novel, was the director's attempt at getting his Master of Suspense crown back from Henri-Georges Clouzot, who had staged his own bathroom atrocity in **Les Diaboliques** (1955). A sustained exercise in misdirection, the film elevated the multiple-personality serial killer – hitherto found in foggy melodramas like *Hangover Square* (1945) and a few *films noirs* like *While the City Sleeps* (1955) – into a major figure in the horror film. Hitch, it should be remembered, had been intrigued by Jack the Ripper as early as *The Lodger* (1928), and gave American cinema its first great serial killer in Uncle Charlie (Joseph Cotten) in *Shadow of a Doubt* (1943). Anthony Perkins's performance as mama's boy Norman

---

Bates, who dresses up as his murdered mother to slaughter Marion Crane (Janet Leigh), set the tone for many madmen to come. Hitchcock followed up with **The Birds** (1963), a more apocalyptic horror, which also proved influential on the siege set-up of **Night of the Living Dead** (1968) and more broadly on many '70s films in which hitherto-subservient animals decide to predate on human beings.

But **Psycho** made a bigger splash and is directly or indirectly responsible for a great deal of activity. Robert Aldrich directed *What Ever Happened to Baby Jane?* (1962), a melodramatic tale of psychosis in which another close family relationship festers into insanity inside a decaying California mansion. Aldrich added faded icons Bette Davis and Joan Crawford – evoking the Gloria Swanson of *Sunset Blvd.* (1950) – to the recipe. Considering that Mrs Bates seems to be a real character until the very end of **Psycho**, this identification of axe-wielding madness with ageing holdovers from Hollywood's golden days isn't such a stretch. Crawford swept into a Bloch-scripted *film à clef* about Lizzie Borden, *Strait-Jacket* (1964) – produced by William Castle, who had managed the first **Psycho** imitation, the gender-bending *Homicidal* (1961) – while Davis reteamed with Aldrich (and Olivia de Havilland) for a Southern gothic tribute to **Les Diaboliques**, *Hush … Hush, Sweet Charlotte* (1964). Hammer took note of **Psycho** and ran up a series of "mini-Hitchcock" efforts that also seemed to owe more to the twisted who's-killing-who of Clouzot: Seth Holt's *Taste of Fear* (*Scream of Fear*, 1961) and *The Nanny* (1964, with a subdued and scary Davis), Freddie Francis's *Paranoiac* (1962) and *Nightmare* (1963). The **Psycho** cycle continued well into the '70s, and is arguably still running; an interesting late '60s attempt at changing the focus is Noel Black's *Pretty Poison* (1968), in which Perkins again plays an unstable, perhaps-homicidal young fellow, but it turns out that the blonde, all-American teenage cheerleader (Tuesday Weld) he draws into his mad fantasies is a far more dangerous character.

In Italy, Hammer and **Psycho** influences percolated. Freda, in the suggestively titled **L'Orribile Segreto del Dr Hichcock** (*The Horrible Dr Hichcock*, 1962), pitched a horror as British-accented as Hammer or Hitchcock, with Robert Flemyng as an obsessive necrophile in the 1880s. Cast as Hichcock's unfortunate second wife was Barbara Steele, a British starlet who had become an Italian horror icon in **La Maschera del Demonio** (*Mask of Satan*/*Black Sunday*, 1960), a vampire film directed by Freda's former cinematographer and uncredited co-director Mario Bava. Looking east to Russian literature and Moldavian lore rather than to Bray Studios, **La Maschera** is a dreamlike, intricate, unconventional gothic, and was the foundation for Bava's subsequent, incredibly inventive genre work. He moved from Expressionist black-and-white to delirious colour for the three-story gothic **I Tre Volti della Paura** (*Black Sabbath*, 1963), the sado-romantic *La Frusta e il Corpo* (*The Whip and the Flesh*, 1963) and the first of many masked slasher pictures, **Sei Donne per l'Assassino** (*Blood and Black Lace*, 1964). Steele also worked with Antonio Margheriti (**La Danza Macabra**, 1964), a prolific player in whatever genre was temporarily hot around Cinecittà. Margheriti's *La Vergine di Norimberga* (*The Virgin of Nuremberg*, 1964) is one of several "masked gimmick criminal" films (the wildest of which is Massimo Pupillo's *Il Boia Scarlatto*/*Bloody Pit of Horror*, 1965) inspired equally by German Edgar Wallace *krimis* and the post-007 revival of franchises like Dr Mabuse and Fantomas (this trend would culminate in Bava's *Diabolik*, 1968).

From Spain crept Jesus Franco, combining the plot of **Les Yeux sans Visage** with the look of early Freda in **Gritos en la Noche** (*The Awful Dr Orloff*, 1962), first of many, many titles from this prolific director, who obsessively reshuffles the few cards (and character names) in his deck and has occasionally turned out pop-surreal masterpieces like **Necronomicon** (*Succubus*, 1967) amid acres of dullness. The country-hopping Franco would be the whole Spanish horror show until screenwriter Jacinto Molina wrote and starred (under the name Paul Naschy) in a homage to *Frankenstein Meets the Wolf Man* (1943) – *La Marca del Hombre Lobo* (*Hell's Creatures*, 1968). Naschy reprised his Waldemar Daninsky medallion-man werewolf role often and beefed up his star status by playing as many famous monsters as Karloff, Lugosi and both Chaneys rolled together. Like Franco and Naschy, France's Jean Rollin has a tendency to mix the inspired with the makeshift and weaves together pulp influences into serial-style pictures, often with a nudie-cutie or nudie-roughie element, from *Le Viol du Vampire* (*Rape of the Vampire*, 1967) onwards. An American equivalent, lacking even the brief flashes of inspiration found in Rollin and Franco, are the films of the producer Sam Sherman

ABOVE: Lizzie Borden took an axe…. Joan Crawford in *Strait-Jacket* (1964).

---

and director Al Adamson (*Blood of Dracula's Castle*, 1969, *Dracula vs Frankenstein*, 1970, etc.). The Sherman-Adamson efforts use relics of Universal (old lab equipment, aged Chaney Junior and Carradine) alongside Hell's Angels and dolphinarium footage and are often cobbled together from two or more stalled projects, existing in manifold versions with a multiplicity of titles (*Fiend With the Electronic Brain*, *Psycho a Go-Go* and *Blood of Ghastly Horror* are all the same film).

It is said that Federico Fellini spent his whole life and career trying to reimagine the film that first excited him as a child – *Maciste all'Inferno* (*Maciste in Hell*, 1927), which Freda actually did remake as a crossbreed film in 1962. Franco, Naschy, Rollin and Adamson-Sherman seem to work the same vein (Dr Orloff, Franco's recurrent baddie, is the Bela Lugosi character from *Dark Eyes of London*, 1939), adding dollops of gore and sex (for which only Rollin shows much enthusiasm) to up the commercial appeal of what would otherwise be filmed fan fiction. These auteurs show more enthusiasm than aptitude: at their best, they play with monsters in a childish, amusing, endearing manner; at their worst, they make films even enthusiasts find difficult to sit through.

One of the great achievements of **Psycho** was to make horror usefully disreputable again. However, there was a minor revival of the stately, tasteful school of shudders: Jack Clayton's **The Innocents** (1961), from Henry James's *The Turn of the Screw*, and Robert Wise's **The Haunting** (1963), from Shirley Jackson's *The Haunting of Hill House*, are careful, creepy ghost stories, impressively shot in widescreen black-and-white, with

BELOW: A subdued and scary Bette Davis terrorizes Jill Bennett in *The Nanny* (1964).

just a touch too much psychology for purist tastes but still capable of harbouring real chills. James is among the classic canon, but Jackson's 1959 novel was new to the horror library – it was only in the '60s that filmmakers started paying attention to the wealth of fine horror material written since the Edwardian era. **Psycho** also made Robert Bloch a name worth evoking, and indeed won him eternal billing as "Robert **Psycho** Bloch". A loose group of slick writers who came to the fore in the '50s started getting attention, working on television for *Alfred Hitchcock*

ABOVE: Faded screen icons Bette Davis and Joan Crawford in a publicity shot from *What Ever Happened to Baby Jane?* (1962).

Presents, *The Twilight Zone* and other anthology shows, doing script work, and having their novels and stories filmed. Richard Matheson, Jack Finney, Stanley Ellin, Charles Beaumont, Harlan Ellison, Ray Russell and Ray Bradbury all grew up in the genre, but had ambitions for it. Well-read in what had come before, they also scripted adaptations of writers who'd yet to achieve the acclaim they deserved: Matheson and Beaumont turned Fritz Leiber's *Conjure Wife* (which had been botched as an Inner Sanctum, *Weird Woman*, 1944) into **Night of the Eagle** (*Burn, Witch, Burn*, 1961); Beaumont did the first screen adaptation of H.P. Lovecraft, though AIP turned "The Case of Charles Dexter Ward" into a supposed Poe/Price/Corman movie, **The Haunted Palace** (1963).

The horror best-seller of the '60s was Ira Levin's **Rosemary's Baby**, filmed in 1968 for Paramount, William Castle and Robert Evans by Roman Polanski, who had already made an important psycho/horror picture in **Repulsion** (1965) and the charming Hammer spoof **Dance of the Vampires** (*The Fearless Vampire Killers*, 1967). **Rosemary's Baby** was the first "event" horror film since **Psycho**. Though its vision of a Manhattan coven isn't far removed from Lewton's **The Seventh Victim** (1943) or even Dennis Wheatley, **Rosemary's Baby** works as much on its pregnant heroine's **Repulsion**-style nervous breakdown as it does the coming of the Antichrist. This was the sort of horror film that could get serious Oscar buzz – Ruth Gordon took home the best supporting actress statuette – and was embraced by audiences who wouldn't have been found at an AIP double bill or an all-night Jesus Franco marathon. Its influence wouldn't truly be felt until the '70s, when writers like Stephen King and Peter Straub became established and films like **The Exorcist** (1973) and **The Omen** (1976) got back in bed with the Devil.

At the other end of the budget range was a very different approach to horror. After running out of ways to film topless women for nudie-cuties, Herschell Gordon Lewis turned out **Blood Feast** (1963). This has been labelled the first "splatter" movie, though the term wasn't coined until Lewis's career was long over, and strings together ketchupy atrocities with a minimal plot about a mad caterer preparing an Ancient Egyptian cannibal feast. Lewis followed up with the *slightly* more professional *Two Thousand Maniacs!* (1964), in which Confederate ghosts dismember Yankee tourists, and other efforts. Important but not actually very good, Lewis has his place in horror history – and even made room for other auteurs of dementia like Andy Milligan (*The Ghastly Ones*, 1968, *Torture Dungeon*, 1969) and Ted V. Mikels (*The Corpse Grinders*, 1971). This is off-off-Hollywood cinema, thrown together in unfashionable parts of the USA in the certain knowledge that *anything* can scrape a few grindhouse playdates. Other efforts from far outside the system popped up, sought out by the curious who'd seen mentions in magazines: Curtis Harrington's up-from-the-underground Lewton homage *Night Tide* (1961), Herk Harvey's Bergman-comes-to-Kansas art chiller **Carnival of Souls** (1962), Ray Dennis Steckler's carnival gimmick musical *The Incredibly Strange Creatures Who Stopped Living and Became Mixed-Up Zombies!!?* (1963), Jack Curtis's gruesome *The Flesh Eaters* (1964), Jack Hill's endearingly demented **Spider Baby** (1964) and William Grefé's dull *Death Curse of Tartu* (1966). The important aspect of these films is that you weren't safe with them: there were no studio executives intent on securing a uniformity of product, no unkillable stars, no submission to the industry's codes and practices.

The true breakthrough, commercially *and* artistically, was George A. Romero's Pittsburgh-shot **Night of the Living Dead** (1968), assembled by filmmakers who had worked in advertising and industrial movies. Inspired by Richard Matheson's novel *I Am Legend*, **Night** depicts modern America overrun by the newly risen dead, who have an insatiable hunger for human flesh. A group of fractious, panicky survivors hole up in an isolated farmhouse, besieged by the living dead, while a posse of tooled-up sheriff's deputies comb the countryside in a Vietnam-style search-and-destroy mission. Besides inventing a new monster – combining zombie, vampire, cannibal and pod person – **Night** strikes a new set of 1968 attitudes: suspicious of authority, disenchanted with regular folk, willing to break taboos (the little girl ghoul killing her mother with a trowel), slyly satirical between suspense scenes, terrified as much by the fact that nobody knows what's going on as by the ramapaging monsters, and ultimately pessimistic. Ambiguous (**The Birds**) or "unhappy" (**Dance of the Vampires**) endings had started creeping into horror in the '60s, but **Night** goes for the throat. The hero, a black man (Duane Jones), fails to save any of the others and only survives by hiding in the cellar, a strategy he has argued against, and shows himself in the morning as the monster-killing posse turn up. Mistaken for one of the living dead, Jones is shot in the head ("kill the brain and you kill the ghoul") and hauled out by men with meathooks to be tossed onto a bonfire of corpses. After that **Night**, things *really* changed.

THE CURSE OF THE WEREWOLF
AKA THE WOLFMAN

1960, UK, dir Terence Fisher, scr Anthony Hinds, starring Oliver Reed, Yvonne Romain, Catherine Feller, Clifford Evans

A marquis in 18th-century Spain has a beggar who approaches him on his wedding day locked in a dungeon, where he is forgotten. Years later, a mute serving girl who resists the marquis's advances is also sent there and is raped by the feral beggar. She escapes and is taken in by a couple, who raise her child Leon, product of the rape, after she dies in childbirth. Leon grows up to be a werewolf, transformed by lust and other vices; as an adult he finds work in a vineyard, where he falls in love with the owner's daughter Christina. He fears transforming before her, but her love is in fact the only thing that can save him. The poor box office of Hammer's loose adaptation of Guy Endore's 1933 novel *The Werewolf of Paris* meant that it was regrettably their only werewolf film. The 23-year-old Reed is magnificent as the brooding adult Leon, whose monstrous poignancy is all the more compelling because his condition is beyond his control; we see him growing up with it, revealing to his foster father that he has dreams of drinking blood; and the bars that keep his father in wretchedness and allow his mother to be raped also keep him from salvation in Christina's arms. This symmetry is repeated in the tolling of bells

ABOVE: "A wild animal, that's all I am – an animal!" Oliver Reed broods in **The Curse of the Werewolf**.

that opens and closes the film, and the exploration of a series of diametrical oppositions throughout (man/beast, love/sex, etc.); mocking parallels are also drawn with the life of Christ. Fisher's concentration on the social origins of Leon's condition – the true villains here are the marquis and Leon's employer, both loveless aristocrats – means that a full half hour passes before his birth. But if the narrative drive is less forceful here than in Fisher's other work, it is amply compensated for by the richness of the imagery and ideas.

HOUSE OF USHER
AKA THE FALL OF THE HOUSE OF USHER

1960, US, dir Roger Corman, scr Richard Matheson, starring Vincent Price, Myrna Fahey, Mark Damon, Harry Ellerbe

Philip Winthrop visits his fiancée Madeline Usher at her family home. Madeline is ill, and her brother Roderick resists their engagement, explaining that the Usher line is tainted, but Winthrop refuses to leave without her. Surprisingly slow-paced and action-

ABOVE: The relentlessly morbid Roderick Usher (Vincent Price),
House of Usher.

free for a drive-in success, Corman's first Poe adaptation stays
fairly faithful to its source but makes Winthrop a suitor whose
sexual interest in Madeline threatens to usurp Roderick's desires. If
Price's Usher carries the film, his arch knowingness staying on the
right side of outright humour even as he plays a grim dirge on the
lute for his guest – "Remarkable! And you composed it yourself?"
Philip asks – Winthrop's obtuse insensitivity provides the film's
best moments, as he suggests without a trace of irony, "Don't
you think that crack in the wall should be replaced?" Winthrop
seeks to control Madeline no less than Roderick does, insisting
when she refuses to eat that, "I'll have no scrawny women in
my house!" Marriage to him hardly presents an attractive escape
and finally his incomprehension of the events unfolding around
him seems more monstrous than the House of Usher itself. For
all Roderick's relentless morbidity and the stifling atmosphere of
the house, from the marvellously gloomy family portraits to the
coffin-lined crypt, Roderick understands his environment as we
sense Winthrop never will, providing a template for the clash
between fevered sensitivity and obstinate rationality that would
inform all of Corman's subsequent Poe films.

JIGOKU
AKA HELL; THE SINNERS TO HELL

*1960, Jap, dir/co-scr Nobuo Nakagawa, co-scr Ichiro Miyagawa, starring
Shigeru Amachi, Yoichi Numata, Torahiko Nakamura, Fumiko Miyata*

Shiro, celebrating his engagement to Yukiko, is involved in a
hit-and-run incident that kills a gangster. When Yukiko dies in
another car crash, Shiro hides in his father's sanatorium, where
he meets Yukiko's double and finds the karma of his past actions
catching up with him. The plot of Nakagawa's ecstatically
morbid morality play is so convoluted and filled with such absurd
contrivances that a potted synopsis cannot do it justice. Virtually
every character Shiro meets dies, each of the hapless protagonist's
resolutions hampered by yet another fatality, while the malevolent
Tamura literally pops up throughout the film as Shiro's omniscient,
malign double, serving the functions of both Greek chorus and
embodiment of Shiro's frustrated desires. Nakagawa's dizzying
story of displaced doublings and pervasive corruption hints at the
malign influence of Western culture – Tokyo is a neon-lit suburb
of hell filled with English-language signs, junkie prostitutes and hot
jazz – but is finally sourly critical of the human condition itself.
Virtually every character we meet ends up in an explicitly Buddhist
hell, their crimes ranging from the monstrous (Shiro's adulterous
father feeds his sanatorium patients rotting fish to save money) to

the mundane (Yukiko is punished simply, it seems, for pre-marital sex with Shiro, whose sins in any case seem to be driven by destiny rather than volition). The entire film is visually stunning with dazzling camera pyrotechnics, gorgeous scope compositions and involved colour schemes giving a **Suspiria**-style sense of heightened artifice occasionally punctuated by flashes of stark realism. But the imagery moves into delirious territory for the final reel, in which Nakagawa dispenses with the intricacies of plot to show each character in turn judged and tortured in the pits of hell, in hallucinatory images of flayed bodies and infernal landscapes whose imaginative use of limited resources ranks with the best of Jodorowsky. The film was remade in 1981 with even more luridly hellish imagery.

LA MASCHERA DEL DEMONIO
AKA BLACK SUNDAY; THE MASK OF SATAN

1960, It, dir Mario Bava, scr Ennio de Concini, Mario Serandrei, starring Barbara Steele, John Richardson, Andrea Checchi, Ivo Garrani

In 17th-century Moldavia, Princess Asa is ritually executed by her inquisitor brother for witchcraft, and curses their family. Two hundred years later, the doctors Kruvejan and Gorovek are en route to Moscow when their carriage breaks down near Asa's crypt. Kruvejan unwittingly reanimates Asa with his blood and she in turn resurrects her lover, Javutich. Prince Vajda's worries about the inauspicious date prove justified when Asa attempts to take over his daughter Katia's life. Bava's directorial debut, a loose adaptation of Gogol's "Vij" (more faithfully adapted in **Viy**), is the crowning achievement of Italian gothic horror and also marks the beginning of Italian cinema's love affair with Barbara Steele. The story is actually closer to Poe than Gogol – an aristocratic family decays under the curse of the past; a beautiful woman, whose portrait hangs on the castle walls, possesses her descendant; the castle is riddled with hidden passageways and trapdoors, one of which leads to a pit lined with spears – but Bava doesn't seem greatly interested in exploring its potential. Indeed, there is much that is not adequately explained: why, for instance, is Asa able to animate Javutich but not herself? Such plot gaps aren't crucial: narrative and characterization (perfunctory at best here) take second place to the magnificently atmospheric visuals. Whether his camera is prowling around the opulently dressed interiors or the swirling mists and ominously looming trees of the cemetery, Bava maximizes the sense of pervasive menace through chiaroscuro lighting and a bag of surprisingly assured tricks, from tilted angles

to slow motion and camera spins. Unlike many of the Italian gothic chillers that followed, some sequences here, such as the peasant girl's walk to the barn, are genuinely creepy; and the film's violence – a spiked mask is hammered into a face, a head melts on a fire – is strong enough to have delayed its UK release until 1968.

IL MULINO DELLE DONNE DI PIETRA
AKA MILL OF THE STONE WOMEN; HORROR OF THE STONE WOMEN; THE HORRIBLE MILL WOMEN; MILL OF THE STONE MAIDENS; DROPS OF BLOOD; ICON

1960, It/Fr, dir/co-scr Giorgio Ferroni, co-scr Remigio del Grosso, Ugo Liberatore, Giorgio Stegani, starring Pierre Brice, Wolfgang Preiss, Scilla Gabel, Dany Carrel

Holland, early 1900s. Hans visits Professor Wahl to write about his carousel, a mechanized display of villainous or victimized women. He meets the professor's daughter, Elphie, and is warned that she suffers from a rare disease: the slightest emotional crisis might kill her. But Elphie has already set her sights on the young journalist, precipitating a chain of events that reveals the mill's ugly secret. Ferroni's film takes elements from its gothic forebears both at home (**I Vampiri**) and abroad (**The Curse of Frankenstein**), and emerges as a unique cross-breed of the two styles, like a Hammer film directed by Mario Bava. Shot in a muted Technicolor that occasionally flares into washes of saturated colour, *Il Mulino*'s setting – the professor's mill is reached by canal, the empty flatlands and wide skies receding endlessly into the distance – gives the exterior scenes a tangibly damp, misty quality contrasting with the artifice of the mill itself, in which nothing is quite what it seems. Everyone in the mill has a secret to hide, the trapdoors and dummies making even the inanimate environment untrustworthy, and the normal rules of time and space do not seem to apply: after accepting sedation from the doctor, Hans has a hallucinatory experience in which the dead come to life, a giddily macabre sequence marking one of the wilder moments of Italian gothic. As with **I Vampiri**, a reflexive strain runs through this story of a doctor's experiments in maintaining female youth and beauty: the **House of Wax**-style carousel is essentially an early analogue of horror cinema itself, its grim displays drawing screams and fainting fits from its audience. Ferroni, better known as a director of spaghetti Westerns, returned to the genre with the lesser *La Notte dei Diavoli/Night of the Devils* (1972).

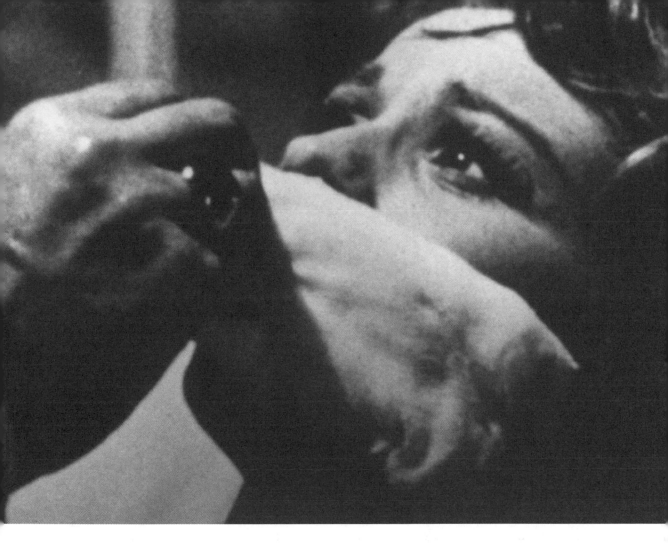

ABOVE: A grisly fate awaits a new victim in **Il Mulino delle Donne di Pietra**.

PEEPING TOM

1960, UK, dir Michael Powell, scr Leo Marks, starring Carl (Karlheinz) Boehm, Anna Massey, Maxine Audley, Moira Shearer

This fascinating and influential film was attacked by an outraged press on its release and quickly taken out of circulation, effectively ending Powell's career. It has since been recognized as a high point in British cinema. Part of the reason for such attacks is the way the film implicates the viewer in a series of voyeuristic murders (in a similar but more sophisticated way to the shower scene in **Psycho**), and exploits the uneasy and hitherto unexplored relationship between scopophilia and cinema, with an explicit focus on the sexual pleasures of

watching. The narrative concerns a professional photographer and cameraman, Mark, who kills women with a camera tripod while filming their deaths: a mirror is fixed to the tripod, so that the women can view their own faces as they die, a conceit that also forces the viewer to identify with killer and victim simultaneously. Mark's father, a psychologist played by Powell himself, had experimented on the boy as part of his research into fear and voyeurism, and Mark ends by "becoming" his father, torn between his growing love for a girlfriend and the urge to continue his experiments. *Peeping Tom*'s complex exploration of the mechanics of viewing and making films is not its only innovation, as the film also marked a turning point in portrayals of madness – Mark may be psychotic but he is still a sympathetic character who can hold down a job. It further represents an early attempt to explore the roots of psychosis, by focusing on Mark's dysfunctional family background, with an absent mother and domineering father. The parallels with **Psycho** are clear,

ABOVE: "Imagine someone coming towards you, who wants to kill you.…" Carl Boehm is armed and dangerous in **Peeping Tom**.

but *Peeping Tom* is a more even, consistent and shocking film, its lurid Eastmancolor giving it an air of seedy grubbiness that won it few fans in early '60s Britain.

PSYCHO

1960, US, dir Alfred Hitchcock, scr Joseph Stefano, starring Anthony Perkins, Vera Miles, John Gavin, Martin Balsam

Over-familiarity and minute critical dissection have dulled its sting so much that it is easy to forget how shocking *Psycho* must have been on its release. *Psycho* simultaneously conferred respectability on the horror film, attracting audiences who would never have gone to see a Hammer release, and gave it a darker edge, providing a grimly realistic take on sexual pathology that mixed urbanoia themes – the Bates Motel has

been empty since the new highway was built – with a brightly lit reimagining of American gothic, transplanting its familial terrors from the Old World dark house to the antiseptic surrounds of a motel bathroom. This event film's marketing strategy – Hitchcock insisted that nobody be allowed to enter cinemas after the film had started – also went a long way towards establishing contemporary audience behaviour. Critics have often interpreted *Psycho* as a reactionary attack on female independence – Marion has stolen money from the patriarchal Cassidy; the Bates home has a domineering mother and an absent father; and Norman's cross-dressing can be seen as parodic of Dr Spock's ideal of the sensitive man, in touch with his feminine side – but Marion has only taken the money so she can marry (hardly an expression of female independence), and Mrs Bates is only seen through Norman's psychosis, rather than existing as a character in her own right. *Psycho* is far more an attack on audience expectations: the putative heroine is killed halfway through (although this innovation is down to Robert Bloch's source novel rather than Hitchcock); the detective also

ABOVE: "A boy's best friend is his mother." **Psycho**.

---

dies without solving the case; the knife in the justly celebrated shower scene slashes at the screen; and Norman's voyeurism implicates the audience in his actions. Even the unevenness of the film, which loses momentum after the death of Marion Crane, forces us to identify further with Norman rather than the drab Sam and Lila. Perkins's portrayal of Norman as the dutiful, likable hobbyist son, kindly preparing sandwiches and milk for the latest guest, is less a sympathetic portrayal of madness *à la* **Peeping Tom** (in which we know Mark is the killer from the start) than another way for Hitchcock to pull the rug from under our feet, and the psychiatrist's glib analysis at the end implicitly suggests its own redundancy – madness cannot be reduced to such pat explanations. Psycho was followed by a rash of psycho-thrillers trading on sexual perversion and twist endings, as well as two surprisingly effective sequels (1983, 1986), a cable-movie prequel (1991) and a virtually shot-by-shot remake (1998).

THE INNOCENTS

1961, UK, dir Jack Clayton, scr William Archibald, Truman Capote, starring Deborah Kerr, Peter Wyngarde, Megs Jenkins, Michael Redgrave

Jack Clayton's adaptation of Henry James's *The Turn of the Screw* remains the definitive period ghost film, superbly directed and rich in atmosphere and detail. James's story of an inexperienced governess who believes that two children may be possessed by the ghosts of dead servants may seem over-familiar now (**The Others** is a deliberate variation on the theme), but Clayton's authority with the material dispels any danger of falling into cliché.

The screenplay notoriously gives James's story a Freudian reading, with moments that still startle today, such as the deliberate lingering over the kisses between the governess, Miss Giddens, and her young charge, Miles. Clayton's direction is full of careful touches, from the child's voice singing a song to a dead lover in darkness before the opening titles, to the brief

ABOVE: "It was only the wind, my dear." Deborah Kerr receives an unwelcome visit in **The Innocents**.

close-ups of wilting flowers, dead birds and guttering candles that connect individual scenes.

Deborah Kerr's career spent playing nuns and uptight English women makes her perfect for the role of the neurotic governess, her cut-glass accent and serious demeanour lending her a gravitas that hints at sexual repression. The child actors Martin Stephens and Pamela Franklin are similarly excellent as Miles and Flora, managing to be at once innocent and knowing beyond their years. Stephens gives Miles the same devious and preternatural intelligence he showed as leader of the alien children in *Village of the Damned* a year before. Freddie Francis was one of the great black-and-white cinematographers and his work here is among his best, with deep-focus used throughout, interior shots shaded at the edges like Victorian vignettes and some quite stunning lighting in the numerous scenes shot in candlelit rooms and corridors. Francis succeeds in realizing the ambiguity at the heart of the story, making the ghosts seem sufficiently tangible without destroying their uncanny presence. The scene of the dead governess manifesting in the middle of the lake during a

rainstorm is one of the outstanding moments of supernatural cinema. [JC]

NIGHT OF THE EAGLE
AKA BURN, WITCH, BURN

1961, UK, dir Sidney Hayers, scr Charles Beaumont, Richard Matheson, George Baxt, starring Peter Wyngarde, Janet Blair, Margaret Johnston, Anthony Nicholls

Norman Taylor is a bright young academic whose arrival at Hempnell Medical College is met with trepidation by the faculty wives, who fear that he will be promoted ahead of their husbands. Norman's wife Tansy believes him to be under magical attack but, when he discovers one of her charms, he insists that all her protective objects be burned – a decision he soon regrets. Beaumont and Matheson met working together on *The Twilight Zone* and were unsuccessful in their US pitches for this second adaptation of Fritz Leiber's *Conjure Wife*, prompting its production in England. This may account for the film's lack of authentic British flavour, which is, along with a double climax and perfunctory final scene, its only substantial shortcoming. Its

RIGHT: "I *do* believe!" Peter Wyngarde in **Night of the Eagle**.

treatment of the supernatural is notable in its credible ambiguity – even by the end nothing is seen as directly caused by supernatural means, which instead rely on natural correspondences for their effect – and its exaggeration of non-supernatural hostilities and gender differences. The witchcraft at Hempnell has petty motivations, centring on displaced ambition and a dislike of outsiders. The boisterously rational men arrogantly believe their success to be all their own work, oblivious to the unspoken communication between their wives, who weave spells behind their backs. This verges on witchcraft as a metaphor for gender relations, and the way in which Norman reacts to Tansy's beliefs – as if she were having an affair – maintains the domestic focus. In this the film anticipates **Rosemary's Baby**, with the roles reversed and Guy unaware of Rosemary's occult plans to further his career. Here, unlike Leiber's novel, not all women are witches, but there's still a whiff of misogyny – Tansy's possession suggests that women are naturally not only agents but subjects of supernatural forces, and implicit parallels are also drawn between Margaret's hysterical fantasies and Tansy's beliefs, at least for Norman – dispelled only by Norman's acceptance that women are the true source of power in the film. Wyngarde and Blair excel as the Taylors, a modern couple whose spotless home hides atavistic secrets, but the film's real star is its villain, Johnston, whose slyly knowing tone gives it a sinister edge it might otherwise lack. Beautifully shot in black-and-white, with a fluid camera and engaging rhythm entirely absent from Hayers's other work, *Night* remains one of the finest British supernatural horror films.

CARNIVAL OF SOULS

1962, US, dir Herk Harvey, scr John Clifford, starring
Candace Hilligoss, Sidney Berger, Frances Feist, Stanley Leavitt

When her car plunges into a river during a drag race, Mary Henry is the sole survivor, emerging from the water hours after the accident. She takes a new job in Utah as a church organist, but finds herself haunted by a strange man and drawn to a derelict pavilion by a lake. A marvellously eerie entry in the run of early '60s American independent, near-experimental horror features, *Carnival* is a meditation on the popular folklore belief that the dead do not know they are dead, its cryptic dialogue anticipating studio treatments of the theme in **Jacob's Ladder** and **The Sixth Sense**. But *Carnival* is both stranger and more effective than these later efforts, as well as inviting other interpretations. After her accident, Mary's world seems flat and lifeless, split into exaggerated caricatures of the spiritual (in the homely, pious intolerance of the church) and the carnal (in Mr Linden's sleazy advances). Alternately catatonic and panic-stricken, and occasionally lapsing into fugues of acute impotence in which nobody can see or hear her, Mary is finally drawn away from the reality of others to confront her fantasies in the derelict carnival. Her activities bear all the hallmarks of a schizophrenic episode, her bewildered tours of the town aligning the film with a cut-rate **Repulsion**. Harvey's crude but effective visual poetry is anchored not only by the carnival location, its empty funhouses unearthly even without the white-faced ghouls, but also by the organ-based soundtrack, shifting from religious solidity to space-age serpentine meanderings, and Hilligoss herself, a refugee from the future lost in a backwards world. The ghouls are an acknowledged influence on **Night of the Living Dead**, but

the film seems closest to David Lynch, especially **Eraserhead** and **Mulholland Drive**.

EL ANGEL EXTERMINADOR
AKA THE EXTERMINATING ANGEL

1962, Mex, dir/co-scr Luis Buñuel, co-scr Luis Alcoriza, starring Silvia Pinal, Augusto Benedico, Lucy Gallardo, Enrique Rambal

Buñuel had flirted with horror before, in his early Poe adaptation with Jean Epstein, **La Chute de la Maison Usher**, the eyeball-slicing *Un Chien Andalou* (1928) and the foiled serial killer of *Ensayo de un Crimen* (*The Criminal Life of Archibaldo de la Cruz*, 1955), but *El Angel* is as close as he came to a genre

---

BELOW: The sacrificial lamb, **El Angel Exterminador**.

movie, although ultimately it's as impossible to categorize as the director's other work. The plot – guests at a bourgeois dinner party find themselves unaccountably unable to leave, the stripping away of the veneer of civilization revealing atavistic superstitions and sacrificial bloodlusts – bears comparison with *Lord of the Flies*; the guests' discovery that hell is other people recalls Sartre's *No Exit*; and Buñuel drew the economic justification for his freest film since *L'Age d'Or* (1930) from the relative success of *L'Année Dernière à Marienbad* (*Last Year at Marienbad*, 1961), a widely distributed feature which had unmoored its fantastic imagery from any narrative safety net. Yet while no explicit reason is given for the trapping of Buñuel's guests, the strain of absurdist humour that runs through the film is specifically targeted at bourgeois conformity, represented by characteristically audacious repetitions (the guests arrive twice, the host repeats a toast, and they are finally freed by repeating their earlier actions, if only to fall into a wider trap) and the final, devastating shot of sheep fleeing a riot by running into a church. After days with minimal food and water, several guests begin to hallucinate: one sees a saw grinding through the strings of a cello that becomes a hand, then a forehead; another watches a severed hand run along the floor, in a nod to Buñuel's contribution to **The Beast with Five Fingers**, an image so trite it offers the supreme horror that the guests' nightmares are as facile and derivative as their waking lives. Buñuel, delighting in bewildering his audience, refused reductive interpretations of his rich imagery and declared that "Perhaps the best explanation for *El Angel* is that, rationally, there is none".

GRITOS EN LA NOCHE
AKA THE AWFUL DR ORLOFF; CRIES IN THE NIGHT

1962, Sp, dir/scr Jesus Franco, starring Howard Vernon, Conrado San Martin, Perla Cristal, Diana Lorys

Inspector Tanner is charged with solving the disappearances of five women. His ballerina girlfriend Wanda is keen to help and sets herself up as bait for the kidnapper. But to Dr Orloff, who has been taking skin from the abducted women to graft a new face for his disfigured daughter, Wanda's face provides too good an opportunity to pass up. Franco's first film for the Continental market launched the Spanish horror industry, its transplant of **Les Yeux sans Visage** into a sexually feverish world of showgirls and surgery providing the impetus for the sex/horror explosion that would dominate Continental genre cinema for the next two

decades. The actual nudity in Franco's film is restricted to one topless shot, but the erotically charged atmosphere extends to the nightclub scenes in which Orloff chooses his victims, the *Belle de Jour* relish with which Wanda explores his demi-monde and the dominatrix trappings of his protégée Anna, while the nightclub's parade of voluptuous female beauty to a jazz score that at its wildest recalls Sun Ra marks out the territory to which Franco would obsessively return over his career of more than 150 films. The director's pillaging of Franju never extends beyond the surface details and much of the film has a slapdash ineptitude – the villainous Morpho's eyes appear to be painted onto his face, the exposition-heavy dialogue never escapes comic-book villainy and the ludicrous props include a "blown-up print" of fingerprints that are clearly drawn on paper – further marred by a pedestrian focus on the police investigation. But the crudeness of the film occasionally works in its favour, the odd mismatch in period details giving it a sense of spatial and temporal dislocation, while the occasional flourish, ranging from the camera tilts that greet one victim's arrival to the cross-cutting parallels drawn between Tanner and Orloff, give it a raw verve that makes up for its lack of technical polish.

L'ORRIBILE SEGRETO DEL DR HICHCOCK
AKA THE TERRIBLE SECRET OF DR HICHCOCK; THE HORRIBLE DR HICHCOCK; THE TERROR OF DR HICHCOCK; RAPTUS

1962, It, dir Riccardo Freda, scr Ernesto Gastaldi, starring Robert Flemyng, Barbara Steele, Maria Teresa Vianello, Silvano Tranquili

London, 1885. The celebrated surgeon Dr Hichcock accidentally kills his wife, Margaret, while preparing to satisfy his necrophile urges on her anaesthetized body. Some 12 years later he returns to his old house with a new bride, Cynthia, who is soon convinced that Margaret's spirit lives on. Sharing the best (fluid camerawork, gorgeous photography, opulent sets, Barbara Steele) and worst (thematic pillaging of Corman's Poe films, dull, jumbled narrative) of the Italian gothic cycle, Freda's lushly atmospheric paean to love and death is notable principally for its unusually explicit tone of sexual perversion. Margaret is an entirely willing subject for the doctor's advances, smiling in bed as he advances with a syringe. He never attempts to fulfil the same fantasies with his current wife Cynthia, but is repeatedly drawn to the morgue's collection of female corpses – red lights signpost his deviant urges, matching Mario Bava's use of coloured lights for psychic states – although colleagues interrupt any mishandling. Sadly, the film never makes enough of these scenes, remaining instead with Steele for endless shots of Cynthia walking down corridors, ubiquitous candelabra in hand, and the film's ending, while approaching the high weirdness of **Il Mulino delle Donne di Pietra**, leaves the true identity of the culprit – Margaret or Martha the maid? – curiously unconfirmed.

THE BIRDS

1963, US, dir Alfred Hitchcock, scr Evan Hunter, starring Tippi Hedren, Rod Taylor, Jessica Tandy, Suzanne Pleshette

Hitchcock's follow-up to **Psycho** came after a three-year hiatus, the longest in the director's career. Technical difficulties were the official line for the delay, but uncertainty over how to top an unrepeatable success is evident in *The Birds'* scrambled themes, as contradictory and confused as man's own relationship to birds. Both masculine (piercing, stabbing beaks) and feminine (soft feathered breasts), birds are simultaneously symbols of freedom and creatures to be caged and eaten, a point made with typically mordant humour when a tweedy ornithologist's explanations are interrupted by a waitress calling an order for fried chicken. Given the British slang of the "stone the crows" visual gag towards the end of the film, it is no surprise that *The Birds* is at least in part about another kind of "bird", the dynamics between its women – particularly the central characters of Melanie, Annie, Lydia and Cathy – taking centre stage, especially in their competition for the attentions of Mitch Brenner, the only effective male character in the film. The bird attacks – flustered, hysterical – are mirrored by the response of Melanie, Lydia and the women of the restaurant; the attacks also, at least early on, illustrate the mounting tensions between Mitch and the women. The first, a superbly choreographed swoop by a gull onto Melanie's immaculately coiffed head, follows her first meeting with Mitch after their initial encounter; in the second, as Annie jealously listens to Melanie's telephone conversation with Mitch, a gull flies into the door. Women are also, crucially, the foundations of family, the film beginning with an asymmetry – Mitch is smothered by a domineering mother, whose influence he must escape before he ends up running the Brenner Motel, while Melanie, with a distant father and absent mother, yearns for the security of the family – that must finally be resolved.

RIGHT: Jessica Tandy regrets signing up for **The Birds**.

EDGAR ALLAN POE

Edgar Allan Poe's stories have provided material for cinema from its very earliest days, a surprising fact given that so many of his tales are deeply introspective and lack the kind of action that Hollywood prefers. From Henri Desfontaines' adaptation of *The Pit and the Pendulum* in 1909, Poe's morbid visions have been mined repeatedly for their themes or images, often as a means of providing cheap films with a royalty-free storyline. Among a host of dreadful B-movies, there have been occasional gems, such as a wonderfully stylish and faithful animated rendering of *The Tell-Tale Heart* in 1953, directed by Art Babbitt and Ted Parmelee. James Mason is the unseen narrator and the film skillfully blends scenes of Expressionist drama with tableaux of Daliesque Surrealism. But the cinema of Poe really comes down to two names, Roger Corman and Vincent Price.

The enormous success of the first Hammer horrors galvanized Corman into convincing AIP's producers to come up with the costs of making a period film with colour stock. Vincent Price was cast as the lugubrious patriarch in **The House of Usher** (1960) and this set the template for nearly all the subsequent adaptations, with Price giving the central performance, an isolated house or castle as the sole location, and at least one extended scene with a minor character wandering down gloomy passages before encountering a shocking revelation. Rich colour photography and lurid lighting was used to disguise sets that were left over from other productions. In *The Pit and the Pendulum* (1961), writer Richard Matheson reworked a slight tale into an extended drama of sadistic madness. *The Premature Burial* (1962) featured Ray Milland in the lead but struggled without Price's histrionics. Corman soon solved the problem of how to develop the stories by making three of them into a single film. *Tales of Terror* (1962) collected "Morella", a humorous take on "The Black Cat" with Peter Lorre, and "The Case of M. Valdemar" with Basil Rathbone and Vincent Price. The last of these superbly captures Poe's morbidity as Rathbone hypnotizes Price, keeping him conscious past the point of death. After the comic fantasy of *The Raven* (1963), Corman reached a peak with the delirious and decadent **The Masque of the Red Death** (1964), overcoming the slightness of the tale by adding "Hop Frog" as a sub-plot. Nicolas Roeg's photography gives Juliana's Satanic dream and the final journey through the coloured rooms a hallucinogenic

ABOVE: Barbara Steele, '60s gothic icon, in *Pit and the Pendulum* (1961).

intensity. Corman finished the series with **The Tomb of Ligeia** (1964), filmed at outdoor locations in England and using a script padded out by *Chinatown* writer Robert Towne.

As with the Hammer films, this kind of period drama has become impossible to produce on a budget, meaning that the gothic dramas of the '60s remain largely untouched by later filmmakers. Subsequent attempts have either been minor updatings of Poe's themes or misguided travesties like Stuart Gordon's *The Pit and the Pendulum* (1990). Until Hollywood is ready for full-blooded gothic melodrama again, Corman has the final word. [JC]

Yet the film is also about the revolt of nature, informing every muddled eco-horror statement to follow, a revolt as unexplained as the lulls between the attacks themselves. If Hitchcock pulls his punches with the gore – only the first fatality is shown with his eyes gouged out and the birds are never elsewhere seen going for this most obvious and disquieting target – the set pieces are marvellously effective, Melanie's caging in a phone booth is the equal of **Psycho**'s shower scene and the impeccably timed siege sequence a key influence on **Night of the Living Dead**, while the score, electronic avian tweets and whirrs, admirably creates a mounting sense of implacably alien menace.

BLOOD FEAST

1963, US, dir Herschell Gordon Lewis, scr Allison Louise Downe, starring Thomas Wood, Mal Arnold, Connie Mason, Scott H. Hall

Mrs Fremont arranges an Egyptian feast for her daughter's party. But she hires Fuad Ramses, an exotic caterer who wants the party to mark an offering to the ancient Egyptian deity Ishtar, so that he can finally use the body parts he's been lopping from Florida's young women. The world's first gore film saw Lewis trading in his trademark "nudie-cutie" sex for eye-popping violence – one woman has her tongue ripped out; another has her leg hacked off – while still retaining enough of the former to add an extra edge of sleaze to the proceedings. One victim's nipples are visible in a bath as her leg is removed; another is whipped until her back is a bloodied mess; the sparsely furnished rooms all look like porno sets; and even the camerawork leaves the flat, medium-shot set-ups of the rest of the film for spastic close-ups as Ramses drools over intestines, a new kind of money shot. All this would probably be offensive if it weren't so sloppily put together – day and night switch back and forth; the actors struggle with their stilted lines, only Ramses, slug eyebrows wriggling wildly as he hypnotizes another victim, bringing any energy to his role – and so tongue in cheek. When the dense cops take time out from their inane banter to warn Mrs Fremont that her feast is crime evidence, she laments, "Oh dear, the guests will have to eat hamburger tonight!" while her daughter only escapes decapitation through her ditzy inability to remember the lines Ramses wants her to say – "Hey! You wouldn't sacrifice me on this altar, would you?" Blessed with Lewis's space-jazz organ noodlings, this drive-in triumph sparked a run of similar but less commercially successful films from Lewis, including *2000 Maniacs* (1964), *Color Me Blood Red* (1965), *A Taste of Blood*, *The Gruesome Twosome* (both 1967), **The Wizard of Gore** and *The Gore-Gore Girls*

(1972), effectively carving out a new sub-genre that also includes **The Incredible Torture Show**, although Lewis's films are (perhaps fortunately) in a class of their own.

THE GORGON

1963, UK, dir Terence Fisher, scr John Gilling, starring Peter Cushing, Christopher Lee, Richard Pasco, Barbara Shelley

Professor Heitz is convinced that his dead son Bruno is innocent of his girlfriend's murder and intends to clear his name. There have been other murders in Vandorf and the victims have been turned to stone, although Namaroff, the village doctor, is covering up the evidence. When Heitz realizes that he is to be the next victim, he calls on his other son Paul to help. One of Fisher's personal favourites, this uneven but fascinating attempt to create a new Hammer monster draws explicitly on Greek mythology, giving it an eerie fairy-tale quality. The screenplay attempts to explore the fear of women underlying the gorgon myth: Bruno's panic on hearing of his girlfriend's pregnancy, and the "obligations" he feels he must fulfil, lead to both of their deaths; Namaroff's hospital contains a mad woman, who routinely attacks the male orderlies; the gorgon appears at the full moon, following a lunar/menstrual cycle; and the image of the snake-wigged head clearly recalls Freud's phallic mother. But, although the later victims (all bar one are male) know what their fate will be if they do so, each turns to stare at the gorgon's face, unable to resist the allure of this archetypal *femme fatale*. Still, the film's imagery, rather than its confused storyline, is its principal draw: the deserted Castle Borski is one of Hammer's finest gothic creations, its dead, grey grandeur recalling the chalky luminosity of the gorgon's victims, each subtly marked with a snake bite, although they have not actually been touched. If the final close-ups of the gorgon herself, snakes clacking from her head, fail to convince, her previous appearances, in the shadows or reflected in water, have a genuinely haunting quality.

THE HAUNTED PALACE

1963, US, dir Roger Corman, scr Charles Beaumont, starring Vincent Price, Debra Paget, Lon Chaney Jr, John Dierkes

When Charles Dexter Ward arrives in Arkham with his wife to take possession of his inheritance, the Curwen palace, he soon regrets ignoring the warnings of the unfriendly descendants of villagers who put his great-grandfather Joseph Curwen to the stake over a hundred years before. It is ironic that what remains one of the most faithful adaptations of an H.P. Lovecraft story (the novella *The Case of Charles Dexter Ward*) was attributed to "Edgar Allen Poe" by AIP, but the film's themes – tainted blood, ancestral curses, possession by the dead – keep it squarely in Corman's Poe tradition. Lovecraft's gross physicality is restricted to the mutant villagers and views of the hideous creatures in the pit and attic kept so murkily distorted that they might easily be taken for Poe's psychic terrors. Yet the depiction of Arkham, a fog-bound village of eternal twilight, has an authentically Lovecraftian dankness; the unlovable villagers display the Puritan meanness characteristic of the author's dour New Englanders; and it's gratifying to hear dialogue about mating humans with the Elder Gods, even if such lurid promise remains unfulfilled while Curwen, who has possessed Ward (Price, in a subtly effective double role), seeks to fulfil his own mating needs by resurrecting the startlingly buxom Hester Tillinghast. "Dreadful rubbish", as the film's slavishly rational doctor puts it, but an atmospheric and intriguing conflation of America's two horror masters nonetheless.

THE HAUNTING

1963, US, dir Robert Wise, scr Nelson Gidding, Michael Austin, starring Julie Harris, Claire Bloom, Richard Johnson, Russ Tamblyn
Shirley Jackson's *The Haunting of Hill House* is one of the classic works of horror fiction and the definitive haunted-house novel. Given that great books rarely make great films it could easily have been spoiled by a screen adaptation but Robert Wise treats the story with care (unlike Jan de Bont). The bones of the narrative are so familiar as to be almost reassuring: the "insane" house with its legacy of suicide and misfortune, and the four

BELOW: "The dead are not quiet in Hill House." **The Haunting**.

disparate individuals drawn there with the intention of exploring its mysteries. But the soul of the story is the tragic figure of the friendless and isolated Eleanor Lance, a woman whose life is so circumscribed that her journey to a place that other people deliberately avoid is revealed to be a kind of homecoming. A fine group of actors, especially Julie Harris as Eleanor and Claire Bloom as the clairvoyant lesbian Theo, immediately lift the film away from William Castle-style histrionics. The production design is exceptional, all misshapen rooms, flock wallpaper, sinister cherubs and Victorian clutter, with mirrors hanging on nearly every wall.

Wise began his career at RKO and directed two low-budget horrors there for Val Lewton; by the '60s he had directed enough serious drama to give Jackson's tale the gravity it deserved. None of the RKO films were as frighteningly intense as *The Haunting*, however. The unseen presences that pound their way down the corridors of Hill House are among the most chilling creations in cinema. In one extraordinary scene Eleanor listens to whisperings and watches as patterns of light and shade shift on the wallpaper (Wise used infra-red film for some of the night scenes) until they resolve into a grimacing face, a manifestation of the house's evil patriarch. As with **The Shining**, the tension comes as much from the hothouse dynamics of strangers locked together in a stressful environment as from any actions of the house itself. The climax has the inevitability of genuine tragedy. A masterpiece. [JC]

I TRE VOLTI DELLA PAURA
AKA BLACK SABBATH

1963, It/Fr/US, dir Mario Bava, scr Marcello Fondato, starring Boris Karloff, Michèle Mercier, Mark Damon, Jacqueline Pierreux

Often cited by Bava as a personal favourite of his films, this portmanteau film of three stories by Chekhov, Tolstoy and Maupassant illustrates the director's three different approaches to horror, and while it may not be as substantial as some of Bava's other features, it works as a taster for his more mature work. The first and weakest episode, "*Il Telephono*", anticipates the *giallo* fusion of sexual sleaze and violent murder explored in more detail in **Sei Donne per l'Assassino** in its tale of a prostitute whose pimp, newly released from the jail she sent him to, menaces her by phone. The second, "*I Wurdulak*", returns to the overwrought gothic of **La Maschera del Demonio** for the best tale of the trilogy, in which Karloff (who also introduces the film) provides a career highlight as the Russian patriarch who

returns to the family home after despatching a vampire – but he has been gone too long and the family suspects that he too may be infected. Notable for being the first triumph of evil over good in horror cinema, "*I Wurdulak*" also draws on the vampire's Eastern European origins for a tale that, like **Viy**, is rich in local colour and boasts a highly atmospheric wintry Russian setting alongside some of Bava's most resplendent gothic imagery. Its vampire is also a trusted member of the family, rather than Stoker's foreign invader, and Bava paints a grimly tragic picture of a supernatural being driven, by love as much as hunger, to infect those he loves the most and reconstruct a family of the undead. The third story, "*La Goccia d'Acqua*", foreshadows the psychological horror of *Shock* (1977) in its expertly crafted tale of a nurse haunted by guilt after stealing a ring from a corpse: the apparition's death rictus is grotesquely chilling, but Bava milks more tension from the sounds – the buzzing of a fly, a dripping tap – that plague the nurse for a simple yet effective exercise in suspense. Bava's American distributors AIP reshuffled the stories and re-edited "*Il Telephono*" to remove a lesbian sub-plot, but they also removed the misplaced humour of Karloff's closing comments, riding a mechanical horse in the studio, regrettably still extant in the original version.

LA DANZA MACABRA
AKA TERRORE; LA DANSE MACABRE; LA LUNGA NOTTE DEL TERRORE; CASTLE OF BLOOD; CASTLE OF TERROR; THE LONG NIGHT OF TERROR; TOMBS OF HORROR; COFFIN OF TERROR; DIMENSIONS IN DEATH

1964, It/Fr, dir Antonio Margheriti, scr Sergio Corbucci, Giovanni Grimaldi, starring Barbara Steele, George Rivière, Margaret Robsahn, Sylvia Sorente

Journalist Alan Foster has tracked Poe down to a London inn. He accepts the wager of Poe's companion, Blackwood, that he will not be able to survive a night in Blackwood's castle, ignoring Poe's warnings, but soon comes to regret the wager. Inspired by the success of the Italian version of *Pit and the Pendulum* (1961), which also features Steele as a character named Elisabeth, *La Danza* purports to be based on a Poe story, but bears only a scant relation to "Never Bet the Devil Your Head"; Poe himself appears in the framing narrative, to finish the film with "When I finally write this story, I'm afraid they'll say it's unbelievable", a line characteristic of the script's inanity. Rivière's Foster is unsympathetic as the bluff cynic and unconvincing as a victim of terror; Ortolani's lumbering score overplays and thus dissipates any tension; the status of the ghosts is confusing, with Elisabeth's lover apparently the only character to attack Foster's predecessors; and the endless shots of people walking down corridors clutching candelabra quickly grow tiresome. Yet the exquisite lighting and delicate black-and-white photography give the whole an ethereal, ghostly quality that glosses over the film's many flaws. If some scenes are dull, others, such as the ball that descends into multiple murder, and the final shots of bodies dangling from the trees, have a delirious intensity, while Steele, shot from every conceivable angle and contrasted with Nordic beauty Robsahn, has never looked more iconic. The film's ghosts are moreover unusually corporeal, Margheriti exploring the sexuality implicit in earlier gothic efforts: Foster has sex with Elisabeth, and the homoerotic beefcake imagery of the gardener, a shirtless, musclebound vampire, is balanced out by a lesbian clinch between Julia and Elisabeth and an unexpected topless scene, both excised from the original American print. Better than Margheriti's other gothic efforts, *La Vergina di Norimberga/The Virgin of Nuremberg* (1963) and *Il Lunghi Capelli della Morte/The Long Hair of Death* (1964); 1971's *Nellostretta Morsa del Ragno* was an ill-advised colour remake.

KWAIDAN
AKA GHOST STORIES; WEIRD TALES
Jap, 1964, dir Masaki Kobayashi, scr Yoko Mizuki, starring Rentaro Mikuni, Ganemon Nakamura, Katsuo Nakamura, Tetsuro Tamba

This portmanteau film's four episodes are drawn from the Orientalist

BELOW: The patriarch returns. Boris Karloff in **I Tre Volti della Paura**.

Lacfadio Hearn's retellings of Japanese ghost stories. In "Black Hair", a samurai regrets leaving his wife for social advancement and decides to track her down; in "Snow Woman" a man's life is spared by a snow demon on condition that he never speak of her to anyone; in "Hachi the Earless" Hachi's skill as a musician leads to his preferment by the dead; and "In a Cup of Tea" recounts the misadventures of a man whose tea is possessed. Released initially in the West without the "Snow Woman" episode, *Kwaidan* was a huge success overseas, winning the Special Jury Prize at Cannes, although it was less popular domestically. The film is shot entirely on theatrical sets, which Kobayashi insisted on painting himself, giving the film a shooting time of over a year but also ensuring a dreamlike quality of unreality that recalls German Expressionism and pushes the film into the first rank of fantasy cinema. There's little in the way of true horror here: even the climaxes of each episode draw attention to their origins in traditional Japanese art and theatre, the characters' movements being stylized and balletic, their rhythms punctuated by the minimal, evocative soundtrack. Each tale has a moral, each encounter presenting a set of conventions for dealing with the inexplicable – truth, honour, honesty – and yet *Kwaidan*'s prestigious production values and stately pace finally prevent the film from carrying an emotional charge. Unlike, for instance, **Ugetsu Monogatari**, the viewer is not invited to identify with the characters so much as admire the *mise en scène*, the set design, the parade of saturated colours and the flawless camerawork with the result that, while *Kwaidan* looks exquisite, at heart it's as flimsy as one of Kobayashi's meticulously painted set walls.

THE MASQUE OF THE RED DEATH

1964, UK, dir Roger Corman, scr Charles Beaumont,
R. Wright Campbell, starring Vincent Price, Hazel Court,
Jane Asher, David Weston

Prince Prospero leaves his villagers to die of the Red Death while he and his cronies feast in his castle. But his adoption of the Christian villager Francesca as his new favourite offends his former partner Juliana, who begins to plot against him. The penultimate entry in Corman's Poe cycle was shot in England, freeing the director from the cramped confines of sound stages to use opulent sets left over from *Becket* (1964) and a predominantly British cast and crew, including the cinematographer and future director Nicolas Roeg (**Don't Look**

BELOW: Prospero (Vincent Price) enjoys the entertainment, **The Masque of the Red Death**.

Now). Taking Poe's story as its starting point, Beaumont's script is unusually literate and intelligent in its depiction of Prospero as a Satanist: his pragmatic beliefs are founded on philosophical enquiry, and his cruelty, monstrous though it may be, has a refined elegance to match his fiery rhetoric. Unlike Corman's other Poe films, here religion is a key theme: Prospero is keen to test Francesca's faith, regarding her corruption as a greater delight than courting Juliana, who has already embraced Satan. Yet Prospero is not punished for his diabolism: his fatal flaw is to believe in religious frameworks, mistaking the essentially arbitrary nature of death, which recognizes no order or system. Price's committed performance as Prospero has none of his usual camp excesses and the supporting cast is also superb, particularly Patrick Magee's gleefully sadistic Alfredo, although Asher's dull, wide-eyed Francesca is no match for Court's lasciviously proud Juliana. But *Masque*'s most memorable quality is its visuals: Roeg's relentlessly prowling camera whirls around the decadent aristocrats as they debase themselves for Prospero's pleasure, while the rooms in his castle are colour-coded, and close attention is paid to rich, saturated colour compositions throughout the film. These features, along with Juliana's distorted dream sequence of surviving her own sacrifice and the choreographed dance of death closing the film, give it a sense of oneiric fable, a gaudy carnival version of Bergman's *Det Sjunde Inseglet/The Seventh Seal* (1956).

ONIBABA
AKA THE HOLE; THE DEMON; DEVIL WOMAN

1964, Jap, dir/scr Kaneto Shindo, starring Nobuko Otowa, Jitsuko Yoshimura, Kei Sato, Jukichi Uno

The first full-bore Japanese horror film to be widely distributed in the West, this 16th-century period tale follows a peasant mother and daughter as they kill samurai fleeing battle, dispose of their bodies in a deep pit and sell their armour. When the daughter strikes up a relationship with a neighbour, the jealous mother, fearing an end to their partnership, dons the demonic mask she has stolen from one of her victims in order to terrify her, only to find afterwards that it won't come off. Shindo's film is intensely atmospheric; long shots of the waving reeds covering the women's swamp dwelling provide the perfect backdrop to the erotic tension that led *Variety* to dub the film "the most nude, sexiest pic to be unveiled in New York so far", a reputation that, probably more than the film's horrific elements, contributed to

its success. Indeed, the film only flirts with horror properly in the final scenes, as the mother attempts to remove the mask with repeated hammer blows, but this devastating sequence puts the film firmly in the Japanese horror tradition of vengeful ghosts from the past. It was followed by a companion piece, **Yabu no Naka Kuroneko**.

SEI DONNE PER L'ASSASSINO
AKA BLOOD AND BLACK LACE; FASHION HOUSE OF DEATH; SIX WOMEN FOR THE MURDERER

1964, It/Fr/W Ger, dir/co-scr Mario Bava, co-scr Marcello Fondato, Joe (Giuseppe) Barilla, starring Eva Bartok, Cameron Mitchell, Thomas Reiner, Ariana Gorini

Isabelle, a model at a fashion house owned by Countess Como, is brutally murdered. The subsequent police investigation uncovers drug running and intrigue, detailed in Isabelle's diary, which the killer will stop at nothing to retrieve. Bava's lurid psycho-thriller moves away from the conventional stylings of his earlier *La Ragazza Che Sapeva Troppo* (*The Girl Who Knew Too Much*, 1963) to provide the first full-blooded *giallo*. Dispensing with pretensions to realism by bathing most scenes in unnaturally vivid colours, Bava introduces the conventions that would come to characterize the sub-genre: the black-gloved, masked killer; the elaborately coiffed and made-up female victims; the explicitly sexualized set-piece murders; the cynical, callous characters, none of whom can be trusted; and the Hitchcockian implication of the viewer in the murderer's acts. The fashion house is devoted to making women beautiful, but beneath the surface lies corruption; Bava inverts the dynamic for the murders, exaggeratedly violent but staged and presented as beautiful spectacles. The degree of eroticized violence – the first victim is strangled then has her head smashed against a tree, her breast and underwear left exposed – is disturbing and has led to accusations of misogyny, but the presentation of killer and victim (masked and characterless, respectively) strips away the hypocritical conventions surrounding the perennial "women in peril" theme to explore its pathological underpinnings with a lurid intensity new to the genre. Fascinating and flamboyantly stylish, Bava's film is also hugely influential, its sleaze jazz score, exhilaratingly staged killings and lighting schemes informing not only the *gialli* to follow, particularly Argento's work, but also the slashers that would dominate the genre 20 years later.

ABOVE: The mask stays on. **Onibaba.**

SPIDER BABY
AKA SPIDER BABY, OR, THE MADDEST STORY EVER TOLD; THE LIVER EATERS; CANNIBAL ORGY

1964, US, dir/scr Jack Hill, starring Lon Chaney Jr, Carol Ohmart, Mantan Moreland, Sid Haig

The Merrye family suffers from a rare degenerative disease whose victims finally regress to a pre-natal condition. Bruno the chauffeur swore to their father before the latter's death that he would look after them, but distant cousins Peter and Emily come to stay, keen to sell the house and have the Merryes put in care. A better Addams Family film than *The Addams Family* (1991), Hill's debut cheapie broadly follows the structure of **The Old Dark House** in its wildly perverse take on inbred cannibal family life. Elizabeth and Virginia are spider-obsessed teenage girls, alternately homicidal and seductive; their brother Ralph (future trash star Haig) does an infantile impression of one of the pinheads from **Freaks**; Uncle Ned and Aunt Martha, refugees from Moreau's island, are confined to the cellar; and the withered corpse of their father lolls in bed awaiting a goodnight kiss. Presiding over them all is a very tired-looking Lon Chaney Jr, – but when he goes away the cousins and their lawyer, Mr Schlocker, realize they should have heeded his warnings. Hill's film sides with its freaks, portraying Schlocker as an officious jobsworth who cries, "This isn't right! There are proper procedures!" as the girls close in, knives at the ready, while Peter and Emily, a vampish blonde purely interested in the value of the property, discover that beneath the Merryes' childlike demeanours lie adult needs that build up to an impressively sick finale.

THE TOMB OF LIGEIA

*1964, UK, dir Roger Corman, scr Robert Towne, starring
Vincent Price, Elizabeth Shepherd, John Westbrook, Oliver Johnston*

Verdon Fell marries Lady Rowena in an effort to escape his obsession with his dead wife Ligeia, but her influence proves too strong. Corman's final Poe film, the second shot in the UK, retreads familiar territory both visually (the usual gothic trappings of cobwebs, candelabra, billowing nighties and four-poster beds) and thematically, but manages by virtue of a subtle, intelligent screenplay by *Chinatown*'s Towne to transcend its conventional set-up for a powerful exploration of romantic obsession that fuses Poe with *Vertigo* (1958). Ligeia (both female roles are played by Shepherd) dominates both Verdon and Rowena, even though she is only seen as a corpse. The building itself seems to personify her presence, the location shooting in a ruined Norfolk abbey anchoring the camera's restless exploration of the spatial relationships between both the characters and the rooms of the abbey in an authentic sense of place. The film's preoccupation with collapsed boundaries, both life and death (it ends with an apposite Poe quote on "the boundaries which divide life from death") and identity, as Verdon and Rowena (an independent, boisterous woman) are possessed and subsumed, finally falters under its own weight. But the leisurely, beautifully photographed visuals and the richly saturated colour schemes result in some of Corman's most delirious dream imagery.

REKOPIS ZNALEZINY W SARAGOSSIE
AKA THE SARAGOSSA MANUSCRIPT

*1965, Poland, dir Wojciech Has, scr Tadeusz Kwiatkowski, starring
Zbigniew Cybulski, Iga Cembrzynska, Elzbieta Czyzewska,
Gustaw Holoubek*

Jan Potocki's rambling picaresque novel began as a serial in 1797 and only came to an end with the intervention of the author's suicide in 1815. Somehow Wojciech Has and Tadeusz Kwiatkowski managed to condense a substantial portion of its Chinese box structure into three hours to create this bizarre and rather unique film, which jumps wildly backwards and forwards in time across a range of genres from erotic comedy to hallucinatory conspiracy to macabre fantasy. Luis Buñuel, who

rarely had a good word for other people's films, proclaimed it as one of his special favourites.

The manuscript of the title is found by a soldier during the Napoleonic Wars and concerns the adventures of Alphonse van Worden in the Sierra Morena mountains of Spain, recounting his travails among bandits, hanged men, seductive Moorish princesses, aged anchorites and the Spanish Inquisition. Eventually, he encounters a gypsy chief, Don Avadoro, whose own narration leads to a series of further tall tales until, by the middle of the film, the narrative layers are five or six deep. Has and Kwiatkowski manage to avoid the novel's confusions partly through the visual nature of the medium which assists the viewer in keeping track of the numerous characters, although the actual motives behind much of the action remain obscure. Has keeps the widescreen frame crammed with incident and Roger Corman would have admired the way he made use of the same sets for different scenes, years or countries apart. Along with its Baron Munchhausen-style shenanigans, mounds of skulls and a surprising amount of female nudity, the film is distinguished by an original score of sparse and eerie dissonances by the avant-garde composer Krzysztof Penderecki. As the multiple stories come to an end, the film keeps the secret of Alphonse's adventures to itself, despite attempting a final glib explanation. Drug hallucination or incomprehensible conspiracy? It's for the viewer to decide. [JC]

REPULSION

*1965, UK, dir Roman Polanski, scr Gérard Brach, David Stone,
starring Catherine Deneuve, Ian Hendry, John Fraser,
Yvonne Furneaux*

The optimism and sexual freedom found in films depicting Swinging London was bracketed by two works from Polish directors with a darker take on that heady period. In Jerzy Skolimowski's *Deep End* (1970), Jane Asher is pursued and then murdered by an obsessive teenage boy and in *Repulsion* Catherine Deneuve plays Carole Ledoux, a sexually repressed beautician slowly succumbing to psychosis before committing murder herself.

After a smart debut with *Nóz w Wodzie* (*Knife in the Water*, 1962) *Repulsion* announced Polanski as a world-class talent. With writer Gérard Brach he takes a simple premise – woman goes insane in a London apartment – and pushes the scenario for all it's worth, combining scenes of a documentary veracity in the South Kensington streets with eruptions of shocking

OPPOSITE: "A rather morbid reaction to the sunlight."
Vincent Price in **The Tomb of Ligeia.**

OCCULT CINEMA

inema, according to the filmmaker and occultist Kenneth Anger, is a black art: "I've always considered movies evil; the day that cinema was invented was a black day for mankind." Whatever the value of this assertion, cinema has certainly concerned itself with the occult from its earliest days, although here "occult" generally manifests as various forms of diabolism, from Faustian pacts to witch cults and tales of demonic possession. Mephistopheles appeared as early as 1896 in *Le Manoir du Diable* by Georges Méliès, and the most notorious occultist of the twentieth century, Aleister Crowley, was interested enough in film to write "What's Wrong with the Movies?" for *Vanity Fair* in 1917. (Bad taste, he decided, and too many uncreative people.)

Crowley never appeared before the cameras but his influence permeates horror cinema, whether as direct inspiration or as a model for the stereotypical magus of ill repute. The first example of this came in 1926 with Rex Ingram's *The Magician*, based on the novel by Somerset Maugham and starring Paul Wegener as the Crowley-styled Oliver Haddo. Ingram cast Wegener after seeing his portrayals as the Golem and decided to bring some of the popular German taste for shadows and sinister themes to American cinema. Germany during the silent era produced more eldritch and occult-inflected films than any other country, with Wegener's Golem being a lumbering man of clay given life by a Rabbi who summons the demon Astaroth. Occultists were even making films themselves: Albin Grau formed Prana-Film in 1921 to produce Murnau's **Nosferatu**. Grau, who argued vociferously against Crowley's entry into the German Ordo Templi Orientis, brought his specialized knowledge to bear on the *Nosferatu* designs, covering the documents that Hutter presents to Count Orlok with sigils and ancient script. Meanwhile, the former Theosophist Gustav Meyrink watched the Golem series spin out from his best-selling novel while providing stories for *Der Mann auf der Flasche* (1920) and *Dr Sacrobosco, der grosse Unheimliche* (1923). Murnau's own intoxicating version of Faust summoned Mephistopheles again for an eager new audience in 1926.

The powerful visions of the German directors were transported to Hollywood when the Nazis took power, bringing a Teutonic gloom to sunny California. Edgar G. Ulmer's **The Black Cat** (1934) borrowed wholesale from earlier European films, with Boris

Karloff as a Crowley-styled devil cultist in a story that owed much to Ingram's *Magician*. Bela Lugosi was Karloff's adversary in **The Black Cat** and it was Lugosi who had earlier introduced the film-going public to the world of Haitian voodoo in **White Zombie** (1932). While the animated corpses staggered off to become a horror staple, voodoo-themed films have been less common. Jacques Tourneur's RKO chiller, **I Walked with a Zombie** (1943), has always been the most substantial of these, presenting voodoo as a valid comparative religion rather than the source of menace it represents in *Angel Heart* (1987) and *The Serpent and the Rainbow* (1988). Another production from the Val Lewton period at RKO, **The Seventh Victim** (1943), posited a cult of Manhattan diabolists 20 years before **Rosemary's Baby**.

Kenneth Anger began his career making Cocteau-inspired shorts during the '40s but by 1954 his occult interests were centre stage in the hallucinogenic Inauguration of the Pleasure Dome. Anger's Magick Lantern Cycle collects nine of his works from 1947–1980 (*Fireworks, Puce Moment, Rabbit's Moon, Eaux d'Artifice, Inauguration of the Pleasure Dome, Scorpio Rising, Kustom Kar Kommandos, Invocation of My Demon Brother, Lucifer Rising*), with *Inauguration* and *Lucifer Rising* as his fullest statements. Anger defines occult cinema in a way that no director had done before and few have managed since, claiming that his films go beyond mere entertainments, being occult workings in themselves. The shade of Crowley presides over the cycle like a watchful deity. Anger's work is decadent, erotic and frequently difficult, yielding little to the uninitiated, but as a major achievement of avant-garde cinema it repays repeated viewing.

Away from the experimental margins, Crowley's influence returned to the screen with the malevolent Karswell in **Night of the Demon** (1957), based on an M.R. James story that took Crowley as its model. Karswell's ease with magical forces would no doubt have provoked the envy of a magus who spent much of his life chasing money. **Night of the Demon** was filmed in Britain, and it was Britain that helped maintain the quality of horror cinema through much of the '60s while America was in the grip of William Castle and hordes of drive-in spooks. **Night of the Eagle** (1961) was an excellent adaptation of Fritz Leiber's *Conjure Wife*, with a college professor discovering that his wife has been using witchcraft to advance his career, while *Eye of the*

Devil (1967) concerned pastoral paganism and ritual sacrifice, with vineyard owner David Niven being prepared by his own workers to feed the crops in a prefiguring of **The Wicker Man** (1973). The Hammer Dracula series had plenty of impromptu mumbo-jumbo devoted to vampire resurrection but it was only with **The Devil Rides Out** (1968) that the censors allowed the company to grasp the Satanic nettle, unleashing yet another Crowley facsimile in Charles Gray's impressively sinister Mocata. Hammer returned to this theme, and to Dennis Wheatley's slanderous take on Crowley, with *To the Devil a Daughter* (1976), where poor Christopher Lee plays a defrocked priest summoning a ridiculous, Muppet-like Astaroth.

To the Devil a Daughter was Hammer's belated attempt to catch the post-Exorcist wave that began with **Rosemary's Baby** in 1968. One of the innovations of Polanski's film that Hammer missed was the everyday banality of its metropolitan devil worshippers, equally at home swapping recipes as discussing the finer points of Satanic lore. **The Wicker Man** showed an even greater ambivalence towards its pagan cultists, offering the audience the choice of siding with a belligerent, prudish policeman, or with an island of cheerful, sexually fulfilled farmers who nonetheless are happy to murder a stranger without compunction. The genuine folk mythology at the heart of the story showed a growing sensitivity among filmmakers to different forms of occult practice beyond the clichéd signifiers of "black magic".

Derek Jarman was the filmmaker most inspired by Kenneth Anger, not only by his zero-budget aesthetic but also by his experimental example, acknowledgement of gay sexuality and thaumaturgic intelligence. While working as a set designer for Ken Russell during the '70s, Jarman was making short films in his spare time, mostly evocative mood pieces such as *A Journey to Avebury* (1971) and *Garden of Luxor* (1972) that almost function as moving Tarot cards. His subsequent progression into feature films enabled him to make a succession of more sustained and consistently inventive occult-themed works including *The Tempest* (1979), *In the Shadow of the Sun* (1980) and *The Angelic Conversation* (1985), the latter a lyrical blending of Shakespeare's sonnets with the ethos of Shakespeare's magical contemporary, Dr John Dee.

Old-fashioned witchcraft still had an audience, however, and it found an ideal director in Dario Argento, whose tales of deathless *strega* (witches), **Suspiria** (1977) and **Inferno** (1980), were so wonderfully excessive as to almost qualify as new forms of cinema. Argento's literate borrowings were emblematic of a growing sophistication in horror cinema, a sophistication that

continued with Clive Barker's arrival and the first film of the *Hellraiser* series. **Hellraiser** (1987) suffered from a low budget and lack of drama but the occult iconography of the Lament Configuration was something genuinely new, a shame then that Barker's innovations had to be buried under a pile of increasingly ludicrous sequels. *Lord of Illusions* (1995) featured another crowd of urban diabolists but ham-fisted presentation managed to spoil one of his better stories. The Cenobites' nightmare puzzle box did have one further use, being part inspiration for the blood-sucking clockwork insect in Guillermo del Toro's **Cronos** (1993). Del Toro seems to be one of the few directors remaining who are capable and determined enough to make these themes work and, like Argento, he is able to draw from a wide range of reference.

If **The Ninth Gate** (1999) represents a backward step to the Dennis Wheatley days, it does so knowingly. It might have seemed at one time that the 21st century would have little place for dusty grimoires and ancient rituals, but the success of *Buffy the Vampire Slayer* and the Harry Potter stories will ensure that interest among a newer generation remains potent for some time yet. [JC]

BELOW: A nasty shock in the cane fields, **I Walked with a Zombie**.

hallucination when Carole is left alone in her flat. Walls crack without warning, an imagined rapist attacks her in one of the director's trademark silent sequences and, in one unforgettable moment, she is seized by hands that spring from the walls. Catherine Deneuve is suitably affectless as Carole, with so little to say that the role is almost a mime performance. Polanski directs with a Hitchcock-like attention to detail, marking the passage of time in the airless rooms – and Carole's growing dissociation – by the uncooked rabbit left rotting on a plate in the kitchen. Hitchcock comes to mind again in the escalating tension when the landlord calls after Carole has killed for the first time.

Despite its William Castle-like title and a rather dated score, *Repulsion* still seems fresh today, its almost clinical dissection of Carole's mania making it one of the most disturbing psychological horror films of the period. As with so many Polanski films, the ending is bleak and unforgiving. He further explored the

claustrophobia of city life in **Rosemary's Baby** and **Le Locataire**. [JC]

DRACULA, PRINCE OF DARKNESS
AKA DISCIPLE OF DRACULA; REVENGE OF DRACULA; THE BLOODY SCREAM OF DRACULA

1966, UK, dir Terence Fisher, scr John Samson, Anthony Hinds, starring Christopher Lee, Andrew Keir, Barbara Shelley, Francis Matthews

Ten years after the events of **Dracula**, four English tourists in the Carpathian Mountains ignore the warnings of Father Sandor and spend a night in a castle near Carlsbad, to which they have been lured for their blood to reanimate Count Dracula. Hammer's fourth vampire film, one of the studio's better entries in the Dracula cycle, is still a disappointment. Lee returns to the titular role after a seven-year hiatus but is given little to do save snarl and look commanding. Although the fairy-tale script treats

BELOW: Catherine Deneuve's sexually repressed beautician, **Repulsion**.

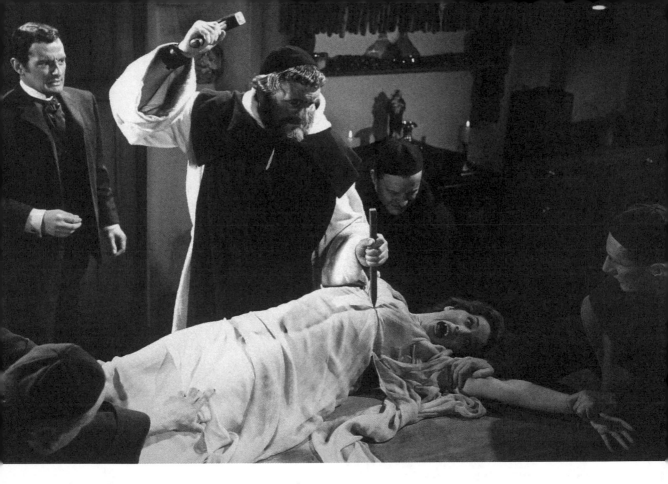

Klove, a Gormenghast-style caricature of a gloomy butler, to lines like "My master died without issue, sir – in the accepted sense of the term", any detailed characterization is restricted to Helen and Charles, the other tourists being barely fleshed out and the gun-toting Father Sandor a poor substitute for Cushing's Van Helsing. The tension between repression and liberation that is central to Hammer's better films is both encapsulated in, and restricted to, Helen, her transformation from prim Victorian maid to flesh-baring voluptuary the film's most memorable feature, if given tantalizingly brief screen time. Sandor's interest in her brutal staking while ignoring Ludwig's activities hints at the dangers of the monastery's sexual repression and, while the film fails to explore the subtext, for all his bearded bluster Sandor is a fallible savant, leaving Diana to hit upon a scheme for the Count's destruction. Fisher's assured direction and the lush Technicolor visuals can't quite gloss over the script's shortcomings as it pillages Stoker for a displaced Renfield character and the opening of Dracula's chest. The glacial travelling shots in the castle, intended to build tension in anticipation of the Count's appearance, ensure that an hour has passed before anything really happens and, once the admittedly impressive resurrection sequence is over, the monastery scenes and subsequent chase have a perfunctory, listless quality, although the icy finale is climactic. This was Fisher's last Dracula film.

FRANKENSTEIN CREATED WOMAN

1966, UK, dir Terence Fisher, scr Anthony Hinds, starring Peter Cushing, Susan Denberg, Thorley Walters, Robert Morris

When Hans is executed for a murder he did not commit, Frankenstein transplants his soul into the body of his lover Christina, who has committed suicide from grief. But Hans seeks revenge on the men who framed him, and in Christina's body he finds just the opportunity. Hammer's fourth Frankenstein film ignores the dismal *The Evil of Frankenstein* (1963), and continues where **The Revenge of Frankenstein** left off, wisely returning Fisher to the series for what would be one of his most poignant and poetic films. The first half, bracketed by the execution of first Hans's father then Hans himself, is principally a love story: Christina is crippled and scarred on one side of her face and body but Hans loves her nonetheless and fights the caddish aristocrats who mock her appearance and eventually frame him for murder. The second half, bracketed by Christina's repeated suicide by drowning, details the revenge taken by the thwarted lovers. Frankenstein has abandoned the impractical patchwork bodies littering previous films and is interested now in soul transplants, although he is as dismissive of Christianity as ever; he has also been obliged to take another assistant, this time the local doctor, his crippled hands no longer able to operate. He speaks up for Hans in court, although he is ruthless enough to recognize his execution as a prime opportunity; but he has also tested his theory on himself, with a mock suicide that leaves him clinically dead for an hour – he does not expect his subjects to do anything he would not. Cushing is as lively as ever and for once the supporting cast excels too, from the snide aristocrats to the suspicious police chief, whose marvellously expressive faces mark them out from Hammer's usual roster; even Walters's buffoon is less irritating than usual, and only Playboy model Denberg seems flat, her incarnation as *femme fatale* curiously less convincing than her crippled Christina. Fisher's direction is unusually dynamic, marked by a fluid, occasionally hand-held camera and a series of exquisitely framed images; and the film transcends the transparent absurdity of its title and premise with a dreamlike power that only intensifies as the imagery grows more bizarre, making this perhaps the best of Hammer's Frankenstein series.

OPERAZIONE PAURA
AKA KILL, BABY ... KILL!; CURSE OF THE DEAD; CURSE OF THE LIVING DEAD

1966, It, dir Mario Bava, scr Romano Migliorini, Roberto Natale, Mario Bava, starring Giacomo Rossi-Stuart, Erica Blanc, Fabienne Dali, Piero Lulli

A return to form for Bava after the misfire of *Le Spie Vengono dal Semifreddo* (*Dr Goldfoot and the Girl Bombs*, 1966), this low-budget gothic masterpiece is an exercise in sustained atmospherics that results in one of the most oppressive yet subtle supernatural horror films ever released. The young coroner Dr Eswai has been called to a remote Transylvanian village to perform an autopsy on a young girl employed as a

maid at Villa Graps. Assisted by Monica, a locally born nurse who has recently returned to her hometown, he finds a gold coin embedded in the girl's heart. Eswai is attacked by villagers for "profaning" the young girl's body, and his questions for the baroness at Villa Graps are similarly unwelcome, although he does discover that the villagers' callous irresponsibility led to the death of the Baroness's daughter, who is now said to haunt the village. Bava cranks up the gothic intensity of **La Maschera del Demonio**, with the camera roving restlessly around fog-shrouded cemeteries and half-lit alleyways, and mixes it with experimental narrative techniques that give the whole an authentic nightmare feel. The final half-hour features such vertiginous effects as a seemingly endless spiral staircase, and a superb sequence in which Eswai finds himself trapped running through the same set of rooms. Bava also manages to invest unlikely images with dread: the ghost of the Baroness's daughter appears, chillingly, as a young girl rolling a pale ball down corridors as she drives those around her to their deaths. Hailed with a standing ovation from Luchino Visconti at its Italian premiere, and acknowledged as an influence on films by David Lynch (**Twin Peaks: Fire Walk with Me**), Fellini (the *Toby Dammit* episode of **Histoires Extraordinaires**) and Martin Scorsese (*The Last Temptation of Christ*, 1988), this is one of Bava's most successful exercises in style.

THE PLAGUE OF THE ZOMBIES
AKA THE ZOMBIE; THE ZOMBIES

1966, UK, dir John Gilling, scr Peter Bryan, starring André Morrell, Diane Clare, Jacqueline Pearce, John Carson, Brook Williams

Gilling was already a veteran director when Hammer hired him, on the strength of *The Flesh and the Fiends* (1959), to work on a number of projects. He would do his finest work for the studio, shooting *Plague* and **The Reptile** (also set in Cornwall) back to back, as well as writing the script for **The Gorgon**. Professor Sir James Forbes travels to Cornwall with his daughter Sylvia to help a former student, now the local doctor, investigate a series of mysterious deaths. The doctor is, as an outsider, unwelcome in the village and is prevented by the local squire, Hamilton, from performing autopsies on the recently deceased. Forbes decides to dig a body up, only to find that the coffin is empty. It transpires that Hamilton, a suave and commanding aristocrat, has visited Haiti and learned the secrets of voodoo in order to provide a

OPPOSITE: Peter Cushing unveils his most attractive creation yet, **Frankenstein Created Woman**.

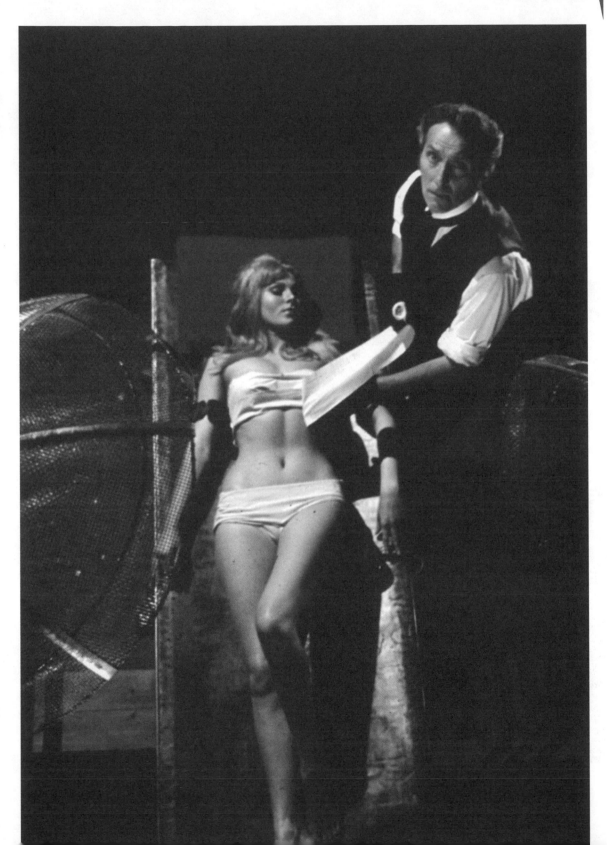

workforce for his otherwise defunct tin mine. The theme of the exploitation of poor labour (already a staple in previous zombie films) gives *Plague* a more sophisticated class consciousness than earlier Hammer films, even if it is still mired in the studio's innate conservatism, and Gilling sets the scene for class tension early on, as Hamilton's band of young bloods, in full foxhunting gear, race past a carriage on its way to a funeral and dislodge the coffin within. The voodoo iconography is predictably wide of the mark, with a few cardboard masks and black drummers obscuring a supernatural framework that veers from European witchcraft (Latinate chants, sympathetic magic) to the studio's own vampire lore (the female victims are in sexual thrall to the squire, and cannot be trusted), but the richness and energy of its rituals are contrasted favourably with the drabness of English Protestantism, as Gilling intercuts a grey funeral with the colourful preparations for a voodoo sacrifice.

Among *Plague*'s firsts are: a clarification of the status of zombies, hitherto riddled with ambiguity – here they are visibly rotting and clearly dead; an explicitly sadomasochistic tone provided by scenes such as the abduction of Sylvia by crop-wielding foxhunters; and a startling dream sequence of corpses rising from their graves that was to provide an inspiration for Romero's zombie films.

THE REPTILE

1966, UK, dir John Gilling, scr Anthony Hinds, starring Jacqueline Pearce, Noel Willman, Jennifer Daniel, Ray Barrett

When his brother dies in mysterious circumstances, Harry Spalding and his wife Valerie travel to Cornwall to live in the cottage they inherit. The plague that killed his brother has taken other lives too and Harry finds bite marks on their necks. Could the strange activities of Dr Franklyn in the big house across the moor be related to the deaths? Slow and talky but fascinating, Gilling's companion piece to **The Plague of the Zombies** is one of Hammer's most spectacularly xenophobic films. Spalding and Tom Bailey, the pub landlord, have travelled widely for the army and navy, respectively, but have brought back little but blustery courage (Spalding) and open-mindedness (Bailey). Franklyn, as a student of "primitive religions of the East", has engaged more directly with "fascinating, horrifying" alien cultures, and has been punished for seeking forbidden knowledge by a curse placed on his daughter Anna. A local man tells the Spaldings that the village was a good place until the Franklyns arrived, "bringing their vileness with them", and the villagers now distrust incomers, associated in their minds with difference (the Franklyns have a Malayan "servant") and disease (the victims of the curse are thought to have died of the "black death"). Yet the Franklyns are also exotic and sensuous, bringing life as well as death to the moribund community. For all his doughty reliability, Spalding is a small, provincial man: in one of the film's best scenes, the Franklyns treat the Spaldings to Oriental food and Anna's sitar recital, leaving Harry, who likes "a good tune", shaking his head in bewilderment. Valerie is moreover no match for Anna's languorous sensuality, and the snake-woman's attacks are implicitly sexual, preceded by letters inviting foolhardy men to save her from her father's tyranny. Other scenes are among Hammer's most striking – the Malay ululates as the snake-woman writhes in her bed and

LEFT: "In England? It's impossible!" A new monster for Hammer in **The Reptile**.

Dr Franklyn finds the reptile skin sloughed off in Anna's bed. If the film fails entirely as a chiller (the monster is more pathetic than threatening and the purported shocks inane rather than frightening), as an adult fairy tale it works wonderfully.

SECONDS

1966, US, dir John Frankenheimer, scr Lewis John Carlino, starring Rock Hudson, Salome Jens, John Randolph, Will Geer

Arthur Hamilton is jolted out of a life of middle-aged drudgery by a phone call from a friend he thought dead, offering the chance of a new life. Hamilton reluctantly agrees, only to find that he has exchanged one trap for another. Reviled by critics at its Cannes premiere, effectively dumped by Paramount and regarded as a failure by its director, *Seconds* is nevertheless a Kafkaesque nightmare of the first order, ranking with **Deliverance** as a study of the dreams and frustrations of American masculinity. Hamilton is cursed because he believes that one dream (happiness lies in eternal youth) can replace another (happiness lies in material wealth and status). Both are empty fantasies sold to him by the world of commerce, distilled in the company arranging his "rebirth", whose fronts are a dry cleaners and a meat packers, vaguely disturbing environments whose sinister import only becomes apparent later. Their approach is mechanized – the "CPS", or Cadaver Procurement Section, will find a body to replace Hamilton's; corrupt – they overcome Hamilton's reluctance by drugging him into taking part in a simulated rape; and folksy, as the Colonel Sanders-style director of the company takes him aside for homely chats. Commerce sells dreams through advertising and part of *Seconds*'s genius is to use grubbily paranoiac visuals that represent the exact opposite of aspirational media, its monochrome study of desperate, haunted faces presented in rapid edits between extreme close-ups and long shots, giving it an intensely claustrophobic atmosphere heightened still further by the use of distorting fisheye lenses. Hamilton, as painter Tony Wilson, has "what every middle-aged man in America would like to have – freedom", but his new life is mapped out so far that this is exactly what he lacks; even the love interest – acting as midwife for his rebirth in an exceptionally powerful scene of Bacchanalian revelry – is finally exposed as an agent of control. She, at least, is not a "reborn": they all appear to be male, and for all horror's traditional focus on a female obsession with youth (**I Vampiri**; *Countess Dracula*, 1970), *Seconds* suggests that it is men who have trouble growing old gracefully.

DANCE OF THE VAMPIRES
AKA THE FEARLESS VAMPIRE KILLERS; THE FEARLESS VAMPIRE KILLERS, OR, PARDON ME BUT YOUR TEETH ARE IN MY NECK; THE VAMPIRE KILLERS; YOUR TEETH IN MY NECK

1967, UK, dir/co-scr Roman Polanski, co-scr Gerard Brach, starring Jack MacGowran, Roman Polanski, Sharon Tate, Alfie Bass

Professor Abronsius and his assistant Alfred track the vampire legend to a small mountain village; when the innkeeper's daughter is taken by the vampiric Count von Krolock they must draw on all their vampire-hunting knowledge to save her. Polanski's affectionate Hammer spoof, a reworking of *The Brides of Dracula* (1960) and *Kiss of the Vampire* (1962) as bawdy slapstick, proves that the director's talents do not lie in comedy: much of the humour is laboured, with the relentless mugging and pratfalling from the comic cast soon difficult to stomach. Yet the high budget, excellent cinematography and richly gothic art direction make this visually highly impressive, with its cobwebbed castle interiors lined with grotesque portraits that come to life for the midnight ball while the snowbound mountain setting lends a wintry enchantment to the exterior shots; and the film does boast two gags – a Jewish vampire who laughs when presented with a crucifix, and the count's homosexual vampire son, who falls for Polanski's Alfred – which work as inspired commentary on the pious conservatism of the Hammer originals. A critical and commercial disaster for Polanski, this was retitled and re-edited for the US market with a cartoon prologue added, whereupon the director tried unsuccessfully to have his name removed from the credits.

ESTA NOITE ENCARNAREI NO TEU CADÁVER
AKA THIS NIGHT I WILL POSSESS YOUR CORPSE

1967, Brazil, dir/co-scr José Mojica Marins, co-scr Aldenora De Sa Porto, starring José Mojica Marins, Tina Wohlers, Nadia Freitas, Antonio Fracari

Marins's alter-ego Zé do Caixão, aka Coffin Joe, is Brazil's most famous movie character, a Nietzschean gravedigger with trademark top hat and curling nails who made his debut in *A Meia-Noite Levarei Sua Alma* (*At Midnight I Will Take Your Soul,*

1963). This startling slab of monochrome madness saw Caixão murder his barren wife and his best friend in order to impregnate the latter's wife, while ridiculing his community's religious beliefs in confrontationally blasphemous sequences that would ensure his films suffered badly at the hands of Brazilian censors. *Esta Noite* picks up where *A Meia-Noite* left off and, while it doesn't contain his wildest imagery (a treat reserved for the LSD visions of 1970's *O Despertar da Bestia/Awakening of the Beast*), its relatively high budget, use of professional actors and flashes of lurid Eastmancolor make this perhaps the best introduction to Marins's bizarre world. Caixão, having picked up a disfigured assistant and mad-scientist lab since the depredations of *A Meia-Noite*, continues his quest for the perfect woman by kidnapping a bevy of local beauties and subjecting them to tests in which tarantulas crawl over their naked skin and snakes (all real, of course) wrap themselves around their necks. As if that weren't enough, Caixão's harem must also listen to his interminable ramblings on the nature of existence; yet some, drawn by his magnetic gaze and irresistible seduction techniques — one has a straight razor put to her throat — still wish to please him. Thus far the film plays like a nakedly psychotic power fantasy,

unabashed outsider vengeance with a powerful streak of eroticized misogyny, but Marins brings genuine flair to Caixão's punishment, an eye-popping nightmare trip to an infernal netherworld of body parts protruding from wall and ceiling and awaiting punishment with lash and trident, all bathed in saturated pink and green light. Disappointingly Marins's original ending, which had Caixão screaming "God doesn't exist!", was changed by censors who ensured that the demented gravedigger's final words are "God is the truth!"

HISTOIRES EXTRAORDINAIRES
AKA TALES OF MYSTERY; SPIRITS OF THE DEAD

1967, Fr/It, dir Roger Vadim, Louis Malle, Federico Fellini, co-scr Pascal Cousin, Daniel Boulanger, Bernardino Zapponi, starring Jane Fonda, Alain Delon, Brigitte Bardot, Terence Stamp

Three Continental directors tackle Poe, with mixed results. The Vadim adaptation of "Metzengerstein" is the weakest, a good-looking but vapid showcase for Fonda in a series of fetishized

mediaeval outfits: even the inclusion of an incest subplot featuring Fonda's brother Peter can't energize its empty gloss. Malle's "William Wilson" is better, featuring Delon as the debauched womanizer and gambler whose conscience is embodied as a spectral doppelgänger: Malle also draws on fashionable SM stylings, with Delon indulging in surgical sex games and whipping Brigitte Bardot, but they make sense in the context of the neatly circular story, although Malle's interpretation elsewhere is disappointingly literal. The real reason to track this down is Fellini's "Toby Dammit", a magnificently atmospheric adaptation of Poe's "Never Bet the Devil your Head" that injects the director's characteristic themes of decadence and artifice with compressed Bava visuals. Dammit is the British actor recruited by Italian producers to star in a Catholic Western, haunted by images of the devil as a young girl bouncing a white ball. Although the originally envisioned casting of Clint Eastwood in the title role would have worked well as an in-joke, Stamp's pallid sensitivity makes him a better Poe protagonist, a tortured aesthete whose ideals – represented, perhaps, by the apparent youth and purity of the girl – have long since been corrupted by immersion in an empty world of wealth and pleasure. Religion, art, love, are all subsumed to commerce, their decadence illustrated in a series of stylized encounters that begin when Dammit, only interested in the Ferrari he has been promised, ignores the Barthes-quoting priest who waxes lyrical about the Bible as commercial film proposition, in ironic counterpoint to Fellini's baroque travelogue of the outskirts of Rome. The actor's yearning for speed can only lead to its own dead end.

NECRONOMICON
AKA GETRAEUMTE STUNDEN; SUCCUBUS

1967, W Ger, dir Jesus Franco, scr Pier A. Caminnecci, starring Janine Reynaud, Jack Taylor, Howard Vernon, Michel Lemoine

Lorna Green's dreams threaten to derail her relationship with the show producer Bill Mulway, and her routine of SM theatre and LSD parties does nothing to preserve her fragile mental health. *Necronomicon* is a genuine curio, a semi-improvisatory riff on female madness and violence that is impossible to synopsize. Lorna's dream sequences are initially presented with a soft-focus, bleached-out veneer, the surreal chintz of her dreamscapes,

---

OPPOSITE: Jane Fonda shows off one of her fetish outfits, **Histoires Extraordinaires**

de Chirico gorged on Ferrero Rocher, accompanied by disembodied voices telling her that "The men with the swords have just beheaded that lovely young mermaid who swam into the harbour!" or an analyst quizzing her about pachyderms. But the dream logic of mannequins being substituted for humans and clothes that change colour with every shot soon bleeds into her waking world, as the men in her life hatch an obscure plot against her and the blood-stained knife she holds in her dreams stays with her as she wakes. Maddeningly arbitrary in its range of imagery and technique, its structure recalling the characters' word games, jumbling high and low culture, trash aesthetics and experimental cinema, *Necronomicon*'s patchwork unevenness, resulting from its lack of a working script (Franco would jot down script ideas each night and give them to the cast the following day), gives the film a hallucinatory, psychedelic quality, most obviously displayed in an acid-minced party sequence featuring a midget dressed as a dog and a man portentously intoning lines like "a spider's foot, a toad's belly, a fox's brain". Financed by a millionaire who had an affair with Reynaud during shooting and ensured that the film was shown at the Berlin Film Festival, where it was reportedly received rapturously by Fritz Lang, *Necronomicon* proved a success in the US and UK, whose hunger for Continental art sleaze was amply satisfied by Franco's generous displays of female flesh. The director had to wait until 1988's *Faceless* to work with a similar budget.

THE SORCERERS

1967, UK, dir/co-scr Michael Reeves, co-scr Tom Baker, starring Boris Karloff, Catherine Lacey, Ian Ogilvy, Susan George

Jaded thrill-seeker Michael Roscoe meets his match in Marcus Montserrat and his wife Estelle, an elderly couple who use him as a subject for their experiments in mind control. Montserrat is keen for his invention, which allows another person's sensations to be experienced remotely, to be used for the benefit of all, but his wife Estelle, intrigued by its deviant potential, has more sinister ideas. Michael Reeves's second feature is a cynical take on the dangers of youthful hedonism: Michael Roscoe's bored search for new experiences allows him to be exploited by an elderly couple whose vicarious desires lean to the delinquent. Rather than enjoying his experiences during sex or trying to wean him off his diet of fast food in favour of something more palatable, they use him first as a tool in a robbery then, hooked on the adrenalin rush of his near-capture, quickly progress to violence. Reeves's theme of youthful desire perverted by an old order is more successfully explored in

H. P. LOVECRAFT

H.P. Lovecraft was famously intolerant of Hollywood's treatment of horror themes, so it is perhaps fortunate that he died nearly thirty years before the first screen adaptation of his work. Lovecraftian cinema can be divided into two camps: films based on actual stories and those that are "Lovecraftesque" in the sense of borrowing Lovecraft's characters, themes or names but little else. The former group is the smaller of the two, partly because putting the grander visions on the screen has required resources that, until recently, have been the preserve of major studios, most of whom have shown little interest in his work.

AIP set things rolling in 1963 when Roger Corman seized on *The Case of Charles Dexter Ward* as a title to add to his collection of Vincent Price Poe films. Despite masquerading under the title of **The Haunted Palace**, this was for years the closest anyone came to an authentic adaptation of Lovecraft's work, reasonably faithful to the novella and as atmospheric as the best of the Poe movies. The plundering continued with the ludicrously titled *Die, Monster, Die!* (1965, based on "The Colour out of Space"), and a psychedelic update of The Dunwich Horror (1969) with Dean Stockwell as a teen Wilbur Whateley a long way removed from Lovecraft's hideous original. Themes and names survived but, as with many later manglings, little of Lovecraft's actual horror remains.

The Lovecraftesque camp received a considerable boost at the start of the '80s from Ridley Scott's **Alien**, with its creature lifted from Giger's *Necronomicon*, and John Carpenter's **The Thing**, based on a story that borrowed it's Antarctic setting from "At the Mountains of Madness". Unfortunately for aficionados, things have been going to Yuggoth in a handcart ever since. Stuart Gordon's **Re-Animator** was trashy fun but its minor success encouraged the director to make a career of treating further stories the way Herbert West treats corpses. **From Beyond**, *Castle Freak* (1995) and *Dagon* (2001) all show little aptitude for creating any atmosphere, relying instead on the rubbery effects, loud shocks and lashings of gore that signify "horror" in a manner usually only impressive to teenage boys. Lovecraft's cosmic grandeur is completely absent. Other film-makers spent the '90s racing Gordon to the bottom of the barrel with *The Unnamable I & II* (1988, 1993), *Necronomicon* (1994) and *Lurking Fear* (1994)

ABOVE: H.R. Giger's Lovecraftian design for the **Alien**.

among a host of vague adaptations or, in the case of *La Mansión de los Cthulhu/Cthulhu Mansion* (1994), works that had no connection to Lovecraft at all.

Such dismal treatment has encouraged the writer's fans to found a cottage industry of low-budget film productions in an attempt to redress the balance. The best of these to date is ironically one of the simplest in cinematic terms. Andrew Leman's "silent" version of *The Call of Cthulhu* (2005) was shot on video and amended by computer effects but manages to be more faithful to the Providence master than those delivered by hacks with more money. Until Guillermo Del Toro makes his version of "At the Mountains of Madness" we should be grateful for small mercies. [JC]

Matthew Hopkins: Witchfinder General. Here the concept is muddled by the poverty of the Montserrats' lives, which initially makes them far more sympathetic than the flippant, selfish Michael, and later by the couple's struggle to control their charge, which finally dissipates any interest in the characters' fates. Reeves's directorial talents are well in evidence, however, whether exploring the contrast between the Montserrats' drab lives and Michael's tours of London in full swing or the implicit parallels between the Montserrats' scheme and cinema itself. But the film's greatest attraction, Karloff's late starring role aside, is as a time capsule with mini-skirted dolly-birds shimmying to groovy club sounds while Michael freaks out with an oil show projected on his face.

VIY

1967, Rus, dir/co-scr Georgi Kropachyov, Konstantin Yershov, co-scr Aleksandr Ptushko, starring Leonid Kuravlyov, Natalya Varley, Aleksei Glazyrin, Vadim Zakharchenko

Three seminarians on holiday spend a night in a remote farmhouse. One is afflicted by a haglike witch and beats her with a stick until she turns into a beautiful girl. He flees, only to be ordered by the deacon to pray over the body of a rich landowner's daughter for three nights – a girl he recognizes as the witch. Bava's **La Maschera del Demonio** takes the same Gogol story as its starting point, but *Viy* sticks more faithfully to its source, with a semi-comic period portrait of a rural Russia fuelled by vodka, borscht and wild Cossack dancing. Closer in tone to European fairy tales like *Das Singende, Klingende Bäumchen/ The Singing Ringing Tree* (1957) or *Der kom en Soldat/Tinderbox* (1969) than Bava's monochrome gothic, *Viy* only really strays into horror territory for the witch's attacks on the hapless seminarian, marvellously atmospheric sequences that escalate in fury and visual spectacle until the third night, a riot of goblins, vampires and Muppet-like oddities spilling over from a grey Morph realm into the cobwebbed wooden church. The crude animation only helps the fairy-tale feel, while the other effects are simple but effective – vodka-enhanced triple vision, superimposed flying sequences – and the look of the film recalls a bucolic **Il Mulino delle Donne di Pietra**, the ubiquitous goats, sheep and cows never out of shot for long. A Russian remake was scheduled for release in 2010.

RIGHT: The Duc gathers his friends into a magic circle, **The Devil Rides Out**.

THE DEVIL RIDES OUT

1968, UK, dir Terence Fisher, scr Richard Matheson, Carl Meyer, starring Christopher Lee, Charles Gray, Nike Arrighi, Leon Greene

Up to his death in 1977, Dennis Wheatley was one of the world's bestselling authors, his historical novels and occult thrillers estimated to have sold up to fifty million copies. *The Devil Rides Out* was one of the most successful, part of a series featuring his hero the Duc de Richleau, a '20s aristocrat who pits himself against the forces of darkness.

Coming at the end of Hammer's golden decade, the film production was delayed until British censors took Satanism off the list of taboo themes. Christopher Lee is excellent as the Duc de Richleau, eager to show his range as an actor and a hero for once. Lee's naturally aristocratic presence lends him authority, especially when faced with the always-welcome Charles Gray, here playing the Satanic cult leader Mocata (supposedly modelled on the occultist Aleister Crowley, whom Wheatley claimed to have met). Mocata lures a friend of Richleau's into his "religious order"; Richleau not only recognizes diabolism when he sees it but knows enough to combat it. When he intervenes, an occult battle for the souls of his weak-willed friends ensues.

Wheatley's world in the Richleau stories is Agatha Christie with an inverted pentagram, all rambling estates and open-topped cars speeding down country lanes. Terence Fisher directs with his customary enthusiasm and manages to pull off a great set piece when the Duc gathers his friends into a magic circle and they await the arrival of evil forces. Absurdity is kept at bay by a resolutely serious cast and the sheer conviction of all involved. James Bernard's score thunders along and Fisher sustains the menace throughout, only allowing things to lapse with the appearance of a distinctly underwhelming Angel of Death. The curious strain of

religiosity that runs through Hammer's vampire films reaches a peak in the climax, a fitting end to a drama so Manichean it could almost be used by present-day fundamentalists as a piece of propaganda. [JC]

MATTHEW HOPKINS: WITCHFINDER GENERAL
AKA WITCHFINDER GENERAL; THE CONQUEROR WORM

1968, UK, dir/co-scr Michael Reeves, co-scr Tom Baker, starring Vincent Price, Ian Ogilvy, Hilary Dwyer, Rupert Davies

1645. England is in the throes of civil war. Law and order have broken down, allowing witch-hunters like Matthew Hopkins to take money for torturing and killing alleged witches. Richard Marshall, a Roundhead soldier, plans to marry his sweetheart Sara – but will Hopkins find her first? Reeves's third feature and undoubted masterpiece, a fictionalized account of the real-life Hopkins's activities, benefits enormously from location photography in Suffolk and Buckinghamshire, where many of the events depicted actually took place, and a meticulous attention to period detail, whether in the absurdity of the witch accusations (one is allegedly guilty of consorting with a black cat and a stoat) or mundane practicalities (children bake potatoes in the embers of a witch blaze). But Reeves's real coups are to use pastoral landscapes to evoke nostalgia for a pre-industrial England even as he depicts the age as one of Hobbesian anarchy, and to populate the film with psychologically complex characters that give the narrative a compelling emotional intensity. While Hopkins's assistant Sterne takes the greater delight in torture, he is at least honest. Hopkins, driven by similar sexual urges, is unable to acknowledge them, and leaves his sole ally to the mercy of the military simply to save his horse. Marshall grows closer to Hopkins throughout the film, similarly using the name of God to vow a revenge driven less by love for Sara (he pushes her away when she throws herself in his arms) than by hatred; by the end he has adopted, and been polluted by, Hopkins's violence, presented with a visceral brutality that appalled many critics on the film's release. AIP's retitling of the film as *The Conqueror Worm* was a spurious attempt to tie it in with the studio's ongoing Poe/Price cycle: Price represents the only anomaly in an otherwise superlative cast, although the actor at least delivers a leaner version of his characteristic ham. This was Reeves's final film; he died of a barbiturate overdose shortly after its release.

NIGHT OF THE LIVING DEAD

1968, US, dir/co-scr George A Romero, co-scr John A. Russo, starring Duane Jones, Judith O'Dea, Karl Hardman, Marilyn Eastman

When John and Barbara visit their father's grave, John is attacked and killed. Barbara takes refuge in a nearby house, which is then besieged by ghouls who can only be stopped by being shot in the head. Other people are hiding there too and the group squabble about how to protect themselves, their plans for escape ending in disaster. Coming from the opposite end of the budgetary scale from **Rosemary's Baby**, Romero's debut does not so much rework gothic convention as entirely dispense with it. If the genre had hitherto been characterized by

a stable order able to deal with irruptions of the chaotic, *Night* offers no such cosy resolutions, its characters' situation growing steadily more nightmarish until the genuinely shocking end. The film subverts audience expectations from the start, explicitly referring to the Universal conventions it is about to turn on their heads and effectively disabling the characters we'd assumed to be the hero and heroine within the first few minutes, while the standard defences – religion, family, authority, love, science – all prove worthless, and Ben's heroic posturing ends with him cowering in the basement he'd previously described as a "death trap". The zombies (never referred to as such here) are freed from the slave-labour associations of the past – they are under nobody's control – and given a new set of conventions: they are cannibals (explicitly shown slobbering over human meat, establishing one of the key images of modern horror) and can only be stopped by a shot in the head. *Night* was savaged by critics on its release, partly because of distributors' decisions to show it on double bills at children's matinees, but was soon accepted as a modern classic. It was also an extremely lucrative film, although not for the filmmakers, hampered by a poor distribution deal and a copyright technicality waiving their rights: Russo and Romero's battle over ownership of the concept led to the former's **Return of the Living Dead** series and the

---

BELOW: The dead walk. **Night of the Living Dead**.

latter's *Dead* films. The film has been colourized, re-released in Russo's "director's cut" and remade by Tom Savini in 1993, an unusual spin on the original.

ROSEMARY'S BABY

1968, US, dir/scr Roman Polanski, starring Mia Farrow, John Cassavetes, Ruth Gordon, Sidney Blackmer

When Rosemary and her struggling actor husband Guy move into a new apartment, he befriends their elderly neighbours Minnie and Roman Castevet. Rosemary becomes pregnant after dreaming of being raped by the Devil and Minnie takes a strong interest in the baby's welfare. Rosemary becomes convinced that the Castevets are Satanists who want to sacrifice her baby, but nobody will believe her story. Polanski's adaptation of Ira Levin's bestselling novel was one of horror's first blockbuster films, grossing over $30 million and reaching number seven on *Variety*'s list of 1968's top films. It also provided a thoroughly modern take on several hoary gothic themes and remains an extraordinarily rich film that can be read on a number of levels. Rosemary is the film's sole viewpoint character and her perception of events can be read equally as trustworthy or the imaginings of a disordered mind: her actions (leaving home, infanticidal urges) correspond to prepartum psychosis, a temporary psychosis associated with pregnancy. Yet there *is* a conspiracy against Rosemary, even if not Satanic: her control over her life is taken away as soon as she becomes pregnant. She is an independent, intelligent woman (she initiates sex with Guy and reads voraciously), but Guy plans out her pregnancy to the last detail, throws away her books and controls her diet, the film thereby tapping into contemporary fears of male control over female reproduction. It also works as a delicious parody of TV culture and the attendant cult of celebrity: Guy will stop at nothing to further his career as a TV actor, while Rosemary dreams of sharing a yacht with archetypal celebrities John F. Kennedy and Jacqueline Kennedy Onassis. The Satanic infant even has its own paparazzo in a snap-happy Japanese photographer. Farrow was the star of *Peyton Place*, while Mrs Gilmore, who raises a glass of wine to hail Satan, is played by Hope Summers, familiar to '60s audiences from *The Andy Griffith Show*. The look of the Satanists, all decked out in

---

ABOVE: "What have you done to his eyes?" Mia Farrow sees **Rosemary's Baby**.

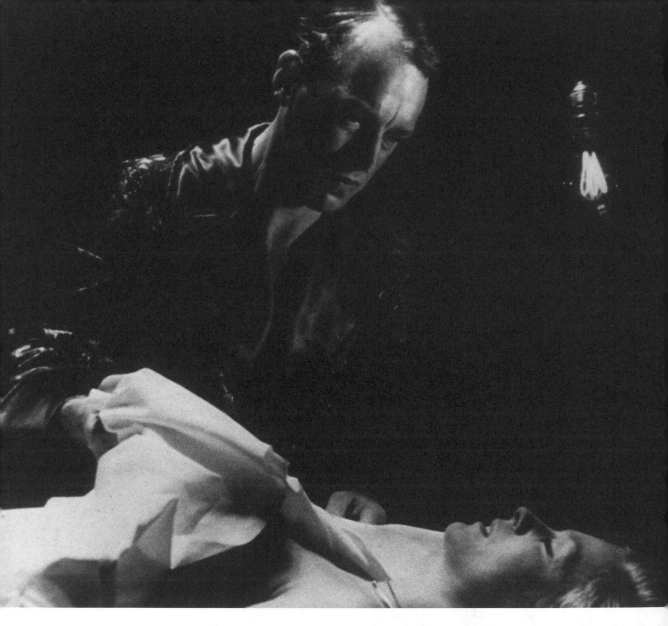

ABOVE: Max Von Sydow gazes at a former lover, **Vargtimmen.**

hideous leisurewear, immersed in *Reader's Digest* and drinking endless cups of Lipton's tea, also sets the film less in a world of realism than the exaggeratedly normal environment of '50s and '60s sitcoms. Yet the absurdity of the Satanists (the hapless Roman, leader of the coven, cannot even mix a cocktail without spilling it) only makes them all the more menacing, lending the film a nightmarish cartoon tone whose only close relation is the director's **Le Locataire**.

VARGTIMMEN
AKA HOUR OF THE WOLF

1968, Swe, dir/scr Ingmar Bergman, starring Max von Sydow, Liv Ullmann, Gertrud Fridh, Georg Rydeberg

The painter Johan Borg stays on an isolated island with his wife Alma, but falls prey to paranoid hallucinations and eventually vanishes without trace. Bergman's "terribly personal" display of "the sore on my soul" is both an ironic commentary on Mozart's *The Magic Flute* (which the director would film for television in 1975) and a tribute to E.T.A. Hoffmann, whose stories provide many of the characters' names. But the feel is closer to Polanski, recalling the isolationist absurdity of *Cul-de-Sac* (1966) and the pervasive sexual disgust of **Repulsion** and **Le Locataire**, although without Polanski's humour and visual verve this account of an artist's descent into madness makes for an oppressively grim, claustrophobic film. Johan is haunted from the outset by feelings of artistic inadequacy, making Alma the sole source of narrative tension – she appears to see some of Johan's demons and wonders what she could have done to help him. But, although the film is bracketed by Alma speaking directly to camera, Bergman keeps us squarely in Johan's mind, whether during the long tales he tells of childhood guilt in the darkest hours of night, his flashbacks and diary entries (hallucinatory, high-contrast sequences whose saturated whites contrast with the gloom of the Borgs' cottage) or, in the second half of the film, an extended psychotic episode in which Johan is lured to a castle to meet a former lover. Bergman drew on recurring nightmares for certain scenes here – an old woman threatens to remove her face; a man walks on the ceiling – yet while the latter is an effectively disquieting image, *Vargtimmen*'s most powerful moments come in inexplicable events whose content is close enough to the everyday to terrify. Alma's encounter with the old woman who seems to have sprung fully formed from Johan's sketchbook, or the dinner party at the castle with Johan growing increasingly unsettled by the babble of sexual perversion and disease surrounding him, approach the dislocated strangeness of Robert Aickman and prove finally more memorable than Johan's more explicitly terrifying hallucinations. However, the current of sexual loathing driving the film – Johan's visions draw on transvestite, masochistic, homosexual, gerontophile and necrophile themes – also packs a powerfully depressing charge.

WHISTLE AND I'LL COME TO YOU

1968, UK, dir/scr Jonathan Miller, starring Michael Hordern, Ambrose Coghill, George Woodbridge, Nora Gordon

The ghost-story master M.R. James might seem an odd choice for such a vocally materialist director as Jonathan Miller, especially when the protagonist of this celebrated tale finds his own dismissal of the supernatural being so severely rebuked. Presumably it was what Miller calls "the atmosphere of cranky scholarship" that attracted him to James, a quality wonderfully conveyed by Michael Hordern as the scatty Professor Parkin, a portrayal seeming to stand for all of James's solitary, haunted characters. James's story is a study in academic hubris, showing how the certainties of a cloistered life can be overturned by unexplained events. When the professor takes a holiday at a windswept coastal resort, his discovery of an old whistle in a nearby graveyard shakes his scepticism and academic complacency to the core.

The BBC adaptations of M.R. James took the same trouble over period detail as Miller but very often seemed to lack a feel for the uncanny. Miller accumulates a sense of unease that shades into unavoidable dread through his carefully composed black-and-white shots. The professor is continually caught in angles of architecture or seen in the reflection of mirrors or wet beaches, implying that the spectral figure coming for him may be as much a product of his own diffuse psychology as any revenant spirit. The nightmare following his blowing of the whistle is a tour-de-force and one of the great screen depictions of the supernatural, one that happily avoids the lazy Hollywood convention of a dreamer waking bolt upright and screaming. After this, Miller's climax can't quite match the rush of terror that James achieves but by this point we've seen enough to be convinced that, as the professor is cautioned, "there are more things in heaven and earth than are dreamt of in your philosophy". [JC]

THE WIZARD OF GORE

1968, US, dir Herschell Gordon Lewis, scr Allen Kahn, starring Ray Sager, Judy Cler, Wayne Ratay, Phil Laurensen

Montag the Magnificent has a stage show with a difference: when he saws women in half on-stage, they appear to be unharmed afterwards and only display their wounds an hour later. Lewis's *Grand Guignol* tribute is perhaps the most luridly stylish of his films, boasting higher production values than its predecessors, likable leads (a sports journalist and the presenter of *Housewife Coffee Break*, keen to have Montag on her show) and a demented performance from Sager as Montag, ranting gleefully about "human butchery". The plot is as flimsy as ever, concocted to string together sequences of unconvincing yet disgusting gore – one woman has a spike nailed through her head; another is subjected to a "punch press"; and two women have swords thrust down their throats – presented in a striptease fashion recalling Lewis's background in nudie-cuties, down to the wonderful sleaze jazz score. The otherwise leaden, uninspired camerawork goes into dizzy hand-held overdrive for these viscerally messy sequences, the camera homing in on blood-matted hair, gore-soaked carpets or Montag's hands as he lovingly fondles slippery intestines while the soundtrack, haphazardly splicing its way through eerie atmospherics and overheated burlesque, goes into spasms of dissonance as the journalist reads about the latest victims in the newspaper. The laughably inept reality slips and trite circular narrative only add to a pervasive sense of psychedelic excess, the film's showcase of hip late-'60s fashions and crazily busy home furnishings making you wonder why anyone *needed* LSD with jaw-droppers like this playing at the drive-in.

YABU NO NAKA KURONEKO
AKA KURONEKO

1968, Jap, dir/scr Kaneto Shindo, starring Nobuko Otowa, Kiwako Taichi, Kichiemon Nakamura, Kei Sato

A mother and her daughter-in-law are raped and killed by marauding samurai in war-torn feudal Japan. They return as vengeful feline spirits to kill samurai, only to find that the mother's son, a successful warrior, is charged with their elimination. Shindo's companion piece to **Onibaba** replays many of its elements – the wartime setting, with its anti-militarist depiction of ruthless samurai exploiting poor peasants; the mother and daughter-in-law luring samurai to their death; the atmospheric rustling of reeds and bamboo; the percussion-heavy soundtrack – but frames them in a supernatural story, resulting in a film that is both more stylized and less substantial than its predecessor. The languid, hypnotic pace is punctuated by bursts of violence, from the cat-women's attacks to the acrobatic wire work, and the style switches between theatricality – the mother's dances are lit and choreographed like a stage performance – and more explicitly cinematic swoops and pans. The results are impressive but uneven: while *Kuroneko* contains some exquisitely framed scenes and startling images – the ghosts' slow-motion jumps and the haunting finale are particularly memorable – the whole is less than the sum of its parts. The faintly ludicrous cat-woman fails to achieve the necessary resonance to unite the film's disparate tones of horror, eroticism and mawkish sentimentality.

KYÔFU KIKEI NINGEN:
EDOGAWA RAMPO ZENSHÛ
AKA HORRORS OF MALFORMED MEN

1969, Jap, dir/co-scr Teruo Ishii, co-scr Masahiro Kakefuda, starring Teruo Yoshida, Teruko Yumi, Tatsumi Hijikata, Minoru Oki

Hirosuke finds himself in an asylum but with no idea how he got there. When he hears a woman singing a lullaby that reminds him of his past he escapes and joins her, only to be framed for her murder. On the run, he discovers that Genzaburo Komoda, a wealthy man looking exactly like him, has recently died. So he fakes his own suicide and assumes the identity of the miraculously revived corpse, only to find his new home besieged by malformed men.

Adaptations of the stories of Edogawa Rampo (real name Taro Hirai, 1894–1965) have produced some of the most outlandish Japanese movies, including *Môjû/Blind Beast* (1969), *Edogawa Rampo Ryôki-kan: Yaneura no Sanposha/The Watcher in the Attic* (1976) and this film, one of eight "ero-guro" (a Japanese-English amalgam of the erotic and grotesque) films Ishii made for the Japanese studio Toei. It's certainly the prolific Ishii's most notorious project, although it is unavailable in Japan for home viewing because, according to Toei, certain groups object to its depiction of disabled people. This is no Japanese **Freaks**, though, and it ends up closer to H.G. Wells than Rampo's spiritual father Poe in its depiction of a remote island populated by a mad doctor and his bizarre creations.

The tone of the film is throwaway and comic in its early stages, but all that changes when we get to the island, where the horror content grows progressively stronger until it peaks with the luridly gothic backstory narrated by Komoda's father. Instead of opting for a gruelling sequence of medical atrocities, as the film's title might suggest, Ishii focuses on wildly imaginative tableaux that recall the best of "Coffin Joe" Marins or Jodorowsky. Sadly, Hirosuke balks at Komoda's father's plan to build a statue of a three-headed, 11-tailed horse god out of "living human flesh" to protect the island, but we are still graced with the sight of several goat-women, beauty and the beast Siamese twins and Komoda's father, who makes up for his lack of substantial deformation (all he can boast is webbed hands) by dancing across the screen like a crab.

The casting of Hijikata in this role, a pioneer of the Butoh school of dance, highlights a theatricality that runs through the film, and many scenes have a staged, choreographed quality in which characters often seem as though they're about to burst into song. But the staginess can't quite contain the dementia, especially on the island itself, and the human firework sequence provides a fittingly cinematic climax. Ishii returned to the world of Rampo with *Môjû tai Issunbôshi/Blind Beast v Dwarf* (2001).

SCREAM AND SCREAM AGAIN

1969, UK, dir Gordon Hessler, scr Christopher Wicking, starring Vincent Price, Christopher Lee, Peter Cushing, Alfred Marks

A killer is stalking women in London nightclubs and drinking their blood; a jogger wakes up in a hospital bed to find his limbs amputated one by one; and a ruthless psychopath seizes power in a totalitarian Eastern European state. Bewildering and exhilarating by turns, Hessler's adaptation of Peter Saxon's novel *The Disorientated Man* is an ambitious attempt to drag classic horror stars (Price, Lee, Cushing) and themes (Frankenstein, vampires) into a modern Swinging London of grooving dolly-birds, mauve silk shirts and political paranoia. It's not entirely successful: the film's obsession with human partition, seen in the limb-lopped jogger, the vampiric Keith's torn-off hand and a freezer full of body parts, has its parallels in a narrative that is so fragmented as to be a near-incoherent patchwork of scenes that fail to make the most of their horror stars (Cushing's role is a cameo, and Lee and Price only meet for a brief confrontation at the climax) or the collision of styles ranging from generation-gap movie through mad science to '60s super-sleuth – as though John le Carré, his mind buzzing with topical events (Gary Powers's spy plane) and ambient fears (organ transplants, cyborg technology), had rewritten *Frankenstein* as a tribute to Bava's *Diabolik* (1968). But, as Hessler avoids static camera set-ups in favour of hand-held cameras and rapid edits, even if the film is finally little more than a collection of dissociated set pieces, they're so bizarre and adrenalin-charged that *Scream* remains enormously entertaining, trading on such extraordinary sequences as cyborg vampire Keith (Michael Gothard in a wonderful Austin Powers turn – "lovely mover", one of the habitués of the Busted Pot observes as Gothard shimmies to the sound of the Amen Corner) being chased around south London by police and tearing off his hand to escape, all fuelled by a jazz score that kicks into high gear at the slightest provocation.

BELOW: "A super race." "Yes, but not an evil super race."
Peter Cushing's cameo in **Scream and Scream Again**.

CHAPTER

7

1970s

In terms of output, the horror film was at its zenith in the '70s. Arguably, it also reached an artistic peak unscaled since the early '30s. Though there were still any number of formula genre pieces and each tentpole film would inspire a flurry of similar efforts, the '70s horror film attracted ambitious and interesting filmmakers as well as play-it-safe schlockmeisters. It was possible for work as unusual and diverse as, say, Harry Kümel's **La Rouge aux Lèvres** (*Daughters of Darkness*, 1971), John Hancock's **Let's Scare Jessica to Death** (1971), Gary Sherman's **Death Line** (*Raw Meat*, 1972), Nicolas Roeg's **Don't Look Now** (1973) and Robin Hardy's **The Wicker Man** (1973) to find their places in cinemas, exciting critics and fans, perplexing and perhaps shocking those who'd turned up expecting something more conventional.

Night of the Living Dead had a slow-burning influence, which would become all-pervasive. AIP passed on distributing Romero's film, but made a hit of another indie pick-up, Robert Kelljan's *Count Yorga – Vampire* (1970). Originally planned as a skinflick (there were a great many horror/porno crossovers in the '70s), *Count Yorga* was the first of a cycle of films which reintroduced classic monsters in contemporary settings. The Count (Robert Quarry), a waspish Dracula imitator, is air-freighted into California in his coffin and preys on hippie students. The film draws on the edgy, up-to-the-moment feel of Romero, with sudden bursts of shocking gore and a downbeat, ironic ending. There would be a sequel, and variations. The weirdly feminist *The Velvet Vampire* (1971), the blaxploitation *Blacula* (1972), Hammer's desperately trendy *Dracula AD 1972* (1972), the gritty *Grave of the Vampire* (1972), television's *The Night Stalker* (1972), the Stephen King-derived mini-series *Salem's Lot* (1979) and the comedy *Love at First Bite* (1979) all follow Count Yorga to some extent, finding a way of fitting the first – and perhaps most overfamiliar – horror-movie icon into a recognizable world nearer our own than Hammer's peculiarly British Transylvania.

Traditional monsters were busy, often in self-aware efforts like Mel Brooks's *Young Frankenstein* (1974) or Paul Morrissey's two films **Flesh for Frankenstein** (*Il Mostro è in Tavola ... Barone Frankenstein*, 1973) and **Blood for Dracula** (*Dracula*

Cerca Sangue di Vergine ... e Morì di Sete,1974). There were already competing attempts to "go back to the original book" such as Jesus Franco's *Count Dracula* (1970), the one where Christopher Lee wears a Stokerian white moustache, and the TV epic *Frankenstein: The True Story* (1974), plus a slew of "Masterpiece Theatre" takes on Stoker, Shelley, Wilde and James from the TV producer Dan Curtis. John Badham's *Dracula* (1979), a lush, romantic film with Frank Langella, is torn between revisionary and classicist impulses and now seems like an expensive Hammer film, down to an eccentric Donald Pleasence performance, and far less interested in Stoker than BBC-TV's outstanding *Count Dracula* (1977), with Louis Jourdan.

There were many direct imitations of **Night of the Living Dead** – some with meat of their own, like Jorge Grau's **No Profanar el Sueño de los Muertos** (*The Living Dead at the Manchester Morgue*, 1974) – but **Night**'s most lasting influence was in encouraging other distinctive filmmakers to make horror films that were at once unprecedentedly gruesome and ferociously intelligent. George Romero, who eventually followed up with his own vampire variant **Martin** (1977) and a Living Dead sequel which restarted the cycle, **Dawn of the Dead** (1979), was the first of the genre auteurs. James Whale, Terence Fisher, Mario Bava and even Val Lewton had worked within a studio system, lobbying for assignments or just taking what came their way. After Romero, there would be many more writer-directors and director-producers in the field. Among the names to make first impressions in the '70s were Dario Argento (**L'Uccello dalle Piume di Cristallo**/*The Bird With the Crystal Plumage*, 1970, **Suspiria**, 1977), Wes Craven (**The Last House on the Left**, 1972, **The Hills Have Eyes**, 1977), John Waters (*Pink Flamingoes*, 1973, *Female Trouble*, 1974), Paul Bartel (*Private Parts*, 1972, *Death Race 2000*, 1974), Tobe Hooper (**The Texas Chain Saw Massacre**, 1974, *Death Trap*, 1976), Bob Clark (**Deathdream**/*Dead of Night*, 1974, **Black Christmas**, 1974, *Murder By Decree*, 1979), David Cronenberg (**Shivers**, 1975, **Rabid**, 1976, **The Brood**, 1979), Peter Weir (*The Cars That Ate Paris*, 1974, **Picnic at Hanging Rock**, 1975), Brian De Palma (**Sisters**, 1973, **Carrie**, 1976), Larry Cohen (**It's Alive**, 1974, **God Told Me To**, 1976), David Lynch (**Eraserhead**, 1977) and John Carpenter (*Assault on Precinct 13*, 1976, **Halloween**, 1978).

OPPOSITE: Blacula (1972) bares his fangs.

ABOVE: British gothic's last gasp. Dave Prowse as the Monster, *Frankenstein and the Monster from Hell* (1973).

Not all these filmmakers have stayed in horror for the long haul and most have had dry spells or drastic career slides but back in the '70s they made the genre exciting, overlaying familiar stories with their own personalities and interests. An astonishingly high proportion of these films and directors founded their own franchises, sub-genres and cycles. The ultimate accolade came, sadly, when many were treated to inferior remakes after the turn of the century.

The message of **Night of the Living Dead**, and most of the auteur films, was that there was something very wrong with America. Earlier horror movies tended to be normative, with monsters who represented an alien threat and would be banished (until the sequel) by a happy ending. **Psycho** cracked this convention – a psychiatrist "explains" Norman Bates but the film has no idea what to do with him. The bullet in Duane Jones's brain suggested that in an era of Mayor Daley, Attica and Kent State, we should worry more about Dr Van Helsing than Dracula. America was eaten away from within – Canada, in the case of **Shivers**, aka *They Came From Within* – and monstrousness tended to rise from strife in the family (evil children, murderous parents, monster babies), society (lingering injustices, economically dispossessed backwoods, mutagenic plagues, bigotries, war-mongering) or a world of the familiar turned threatening (suddenly sentient and malign wildlife, possessed motor vehicles). While Romero, Hooper and Craven explored the rusting, bone-littered, overlooked corners of America, there were films from John Boorman, an Englishman in America, (**Deliverance**, 1972) and Sam Peckinpah, an American in England, (**Straw Dogs**, 1971) with much to say about inbred, strife-ridden communities, murderous families and heroes who find in themselves a disturbing capacity for violence. Neither the Boorman nor Peckinpah movies were perceived as horror films at the time (they owe as much to the Western), but both show an awareness of what was going on in horror and have had a lasting influence.

In this period, there were interesting horror films from all around the world. Italy had a mini-boom with Argento, late Bava masterworks (**Lisa e il Diavolo**/*Lisa and the Devil*, 1973, *Shock*, 1978) and gory, disreputable crazes for cannibal, Nazi or zombie pictures. A few British pictures, like the grim *Guignols* of Pete Walker (**House of Whipcord**, 1974, **Frightmare**, 1974), go as far as the American nightmares, though even Hammer Films turned out despairing, end-of-the-cycle downers like Seth Holt's *Blood From the Mummy's Tomb* (1970), Peter Sykes's **Demons of the Mind** (1972) and Terence Fisher's *Frankenstein and the Monster From Hell* (1973). Meanwhile, the collapse of the small-scale British horror industry didn't immediately stamp out frankly astonishing productions like Freddie Francis's **Mumsy, Nanny, Sonny and Girly** (1970) and *The Creeping Flesh* (1972), Don Sharp's *Psychomania* (1971), in which Nicky Henson leads an undead bike gang, *The Corpse* (1971), a **Les Diaboliques** riff with Michael Gough's nastiest performance, and Norman J. Warren's **Prey** (1978), a disguised redo of D.H. Lawrence's *The Fox* in which a lesbian couple take in and play with a stray man who turns out to be a werewolf from outer space here to see if humans have enough protein to be a suitable food source. The **Wicker Man** is the best-known product of this British collapse, but there are still gems to be mined by the adventurous viewer.

William Friedkin's **The Exorcist** (1973), from the based-on-fact novel by William Peter Blatty, got Hollywood back in the horror game, with Warner Brothers managing as many taboo-breaking shock moments as, say, early Wes Craven in the framework of a supernatural drama whose morality (listen to priests, not doctors) is essentially that of any given Hammer film. Like **Rosemary's Baby**, **The Exorcist** is "New Hollywood", with a grit and realism that owes as much to the French New Wave of the '60s as classical American cinema, nuanced performances from non-star players who seemed more "real" at the time than, say, Robert Redford and Shirley MacLaine

(though the heroine of **The Exorcist** is based on MacLaine, Ellen Burstyn got the role) and a willingness to play fast and low without bothering overmuch about explaining every story point. It may be the film that most straddles competing styles of horror; it is no wonder that none of its sequels in any of their versions have really worked, which probably also goes for the re-edited *Version You Never Saw*. **The Exorcist** kick-started a wave of imitations, including a black version (*Abby*, 1974) and a clutch of Italian efforts, and probably killed off demand for period-set, relatively genteel, low-budget Cushing-Lee-Price-type horror. Its most notable successor was Richard Donner's solemnly silly **The Omen** (1976), which takes the bizarre body-count format of Price vehicles like **The Abominable Dr Phibes** (1971) and the wonderful **Theater of Blood** (1973) and links its decapitations and impalements with a post-Watergate big-politics rerun of **Rosemary's Baby**, bringing the Antichrist into the corridors of power rather than a cosy coven.

The Exorcist was the first horror film to make it to the upper levels of *Variety*'s box-office champ charts, hitherto reserved for the likes of *Gone With the Wind* (1939) and *The Sound of Music* (1965) and soon to be the province of *Star Wars* (1977) and *E.T.: The Extra-Terrestrial* (1981). It was followed by another throwback dressed in contemporary gear, Steven Spielberg's runaway hit **Jaws** (1975), based on Peter Benchley's best-seller about a shark terrorizing a coastal community. Spielberg had done well with the TV movie **Duel** (1972), written by Richard Matheson, in which a lone motorist (Dennis Weaver) is persecuted by a grimy truck, and turned **Jaws** into a pared-to-the-bone monster movie. If **Nosferatu** is subtitled "a symphony of shadows", then **Jaws** is "a concerto for shocks", keyed to its memorable musical theme (like Carpenter's **Halloween**) and intent on pruning away any significance that might distract from the suspense. Earlier terror-by-animal films, from **The Birds** through the rat/revenge gothic *Willard* (1970) to the outrageous *Frogs* (1972), suggest the attacks are our fault, for being complacent, twisted, cruel or ecologically unsound; in **Jaws**, the shark bites because that's just what sharks do – and the plot of the film revolves around what the heroes can and can't do about it. The **Jaws** shark is the Creature From the Black Lagoon without libidinal urges – it chews a naked swimmer without lingering to leer as the Gill-Man did – or Godzilla stripped of any stature as a punishment for man's hubris. This would carry on to **Halloween**, another masterpiece of William Castle-style "pure" horror, in which a masked, mad killer *isn't* the product of a family or a society that has warped him like Norman Bates or the Chain Saw clan but a shark who happens to have been born into a human skin.

The re-emergence of horror into the mainstream was perhaps inevitable. In the early '70s, there was a surprising amount of horror on television on both sides of the Atlantic: in one-offs like *The Night Stalker* and the BBC's Nigel Kneale play **The Stone Tape** (1972) and anthology series like *Night Gallery*, Brian Clemens's *Thriller*, the British *Dead of Night* (whose scariest episode, "The Exorcism", remains a high-point in socially committed terror) and *Ghost Story*. An astonishingly large percentage of "what was the one where...?" queries submitted to movie magazines turn out to refer to '70s TV movies – "the one where Karen Black is terrorized by the fetish doll" (*Trilogy of Terror*, 1975), "the one where the imps are in Kim Darby's basement" (*Don't Be Afraid of the Dark*, 1973), "the one where the crashed air crew turn out to be ghosts" (*Sole Survivor*, 1970), "the one with the crying child" (*Crowhaven Farm*, 1970), and "the one with Salem witches out West sacrificing preacher Roy Thinnes" (*Black Noon*, 1971). Regular shows took note. Starsky and Hutch tracked a real vampire (John Saxon), in an episode directed by Robert Kelljan of the *Yorga* films. Ironside investigated a 12-year-old witch (Jodie Foster). *Doctor Who* "did" Frankenstein ("The Brain of Morbius"), Dracula ("State of Decay"), the mummy's curse ("The Pyramids of Mars") and the Victorian-set weird masterpiece "The Talons of Weng-Chiang". *McMillan and Wife* tangled with a Devil cult. *The Snoop Sisters* solved mysteries involving a horror-movie star (Vincent Price) and another coven (with Alice Cooper). And Rockford faked a mummy's curse. McCloud met Dracula.

Following Ira Levin and William Peter Blatty, more horror novelists joined the ranks of brand-name authors. The former actor Thomas Tryon wrote *The Other* and *Harvest Home*, adapted for film and TV, which were early instances of the latterly popular "imaginary friend" and "sinister community" sub-genres. The Englishman James Herbert turned out a run of paperback nasties (*The Rats*, *The Fog*, etc.) which were passed around '70s playgrounds as the literary equivalent of films like *Night of the Lepus* (1972) or *The Giant Spider Invasion* (1974). The most important new writer, however, was Stephen King, whose debut novel *Carrie* became an instant best-seller and invented an entire genre of high-school horror (though it's also a "turning worm" story on the model of *Willard*). It was spectacularly filmed by Brian De Palma in his own breakthrough film.

Carrie (1976) was a mainstream hit, but still seems like a spiky, all-over-the-place horror show, capable of eliciting a delicate, heartbreaking performance from Sissy Spacek as the abused, telekinetic teen but also of sending audiences out of the theatre with a wholly gratuitous, hand-out-of-the-ground shock. De Palma tries so many things that nothing is really out of place: unjustified as it might be, that punchline scare is perhaps the single greatest jump in the movies. There were more thrillers with psychic or telekinetic hooks – De Palma's follow-up *The Fury* (1978), the Carpenter-scripted *The Eyes of Laura Mars* (1978), *Patrick* (1978), Cronenberg's **Scanners** (1981), **The Sender** (1982), and the King-derived *Firestarter* (1984). With **Halloween** following **Carrie**, American teenagers increasingly became lead characters in horror pictures, often marked for death. De Palma's catch-all approach, typical of the "movie brat" generation, was more often used on the sci-fi rollercoaster rides of George Lucas and Steven Spielberg than in horror, but something of the dream logic of **Carrie** recurs in Dario Argento's masterworks, **Suspiria** (1977) and **Inferno** (1980). Like De Palma, Argento had previously made "Hitchcockian" suspense pictures, with supernatural overtones but basically dependent on knife-wielding mad persons, but was liberated in the late '70s by the fully fantastical. Argento's "Three Mothers" films make no narrative sense, and indeed make a point of it – but deliver an overwhelming effect, through imagery, music, editing, high style, beautiful people, surreal lighting, monumental architecture and elegant nastiness. The director has never matched the potency of these films, and no one else has come close or even really tried to.

King followed **Carrie** with *Salem's Lot*, a vampire novel, and *The Shining*, a ghost story. Both were quickly adapted: *Salem's Lot* (1979) was the first King project mounted for television (where, latterly, he has been better-served than in the movies) in an attempt to "go straight" for **Texas Chain Saw** man Tobe Hooper, whereas **The Shining** (1980) was made by a controversial visitor to the genre, Stanley Kubrick. King had many more books in the pipeline; before the '80s were through, seemingly everyone with any kind of a track record in horror would get to film one of his stories. In the meantime, there were other literary fish worth frying: Richard Matheson's *Hell House* became John Hough's *Legend of Hell House* (1973), Robert Marasco's *Burnt Offerings* (a key, acknowledged influence on *The Shining*) was directed by Dan Curtis in 1976, Peter Straub's *Julia* became Richard Loncraine's *Full Circle* (1976), Dean R. Koontz's *Demon Seed* was overhauled by Donald Cammell in 1977 (a rare adaptation that improves on its schlocky source), Frank DeFelitta's *Audrey Rose* became Robert Wise's horror swansong in 1977, Jeffrey Konvitz's *The Sentinel* got what it deserved in Michael Winner's 1977 film (nevertheless, a model for the supernatural gothics Lucio Fulco turned out in the early '80s) and Martin Cruz Smith's killer-bat novel *Nightwing* was coarsened by Arthur Hiller in a 1979 film. **The Amityville Horror**, a supposedly true account of haunting ascribed to Jay Anson (who may not have written it), became a middling but commercially successful 1979 film and launched its own mini-franchise of wholly made-up sequels.

Just as the '70s began with a boom triggered by **Night of the Living Dead**, so it ended with a boom triggered by **Dawn of the Dead**. Lucio Fulci's **Zombi 2** (*Zombie Flesh Eaters*, 1979) cheekily positioned itself as a sequel to **Dawn** (released in Italy as *Zombi*) but unrolled as a mélange of '30s-style voodoo-island shenanigans and splatter (a zombie vs shark fight, a major eyeball-spearing). If **Night** was informed by Vietnam and the counterculture, **Dawn** is about conformism, consumerism, and American selfishness. Even major studio films in the era of President Carter were worried: Philip Kaufman's remake of *Invasion of the Body Snatchers* (1978) is all about disenchantment with urban life, where a rat-turd in the soup at an expensive restaurant betokens a world where inhuman duplicates point and shriek at the few surviving normals, while *Coma* (1978), directed by paid-up medical/technological paranoid Michael Crichton, was Frankensteinian mad science in an era of corporate profit and the health-care industry. The last big horror hit of the decade was symptomatic of the co-option of B-movie ideas by the A-movie makers: initially scripted in the spirit of *It! The Terror From Beyond Space* (1958) as something which might do for Roger Corman, **Alien** (1979) became much more in the telling, thanks to director Ridley Scott, a cannily assembled cast of British and American semi-names and the fully-realized designs of artist H.R. Giger. **Alien** is just the story of astronauts killed one by one by a constantly evolving creature but, like **Jaws** and **Halloween**, it's a relentless suspense machine with a high degree of visual sophistication. It also benefited, as would more successful Hollywood horrors, from an outsanding ad campaign, making the watch-phrase of the turn of the decade "in space, no one can hear you scream!".

BELOW: Harvest time. *Coma* (1978).

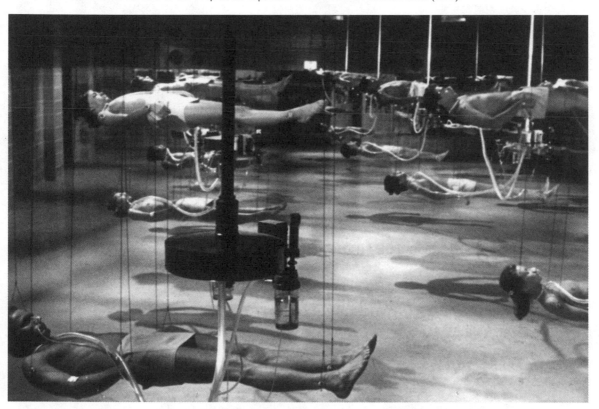

BLOOD ON SATAN'S CLAW
AKA SATAN'S SKIN; SATAN'S CLAW

1970, UK, dir/co-scr Piers Haggard, co-scr Robert Wynne-Simmons,
starring Patrick Wymark, Linda Hayden, Barry Andrews, Michele Dotrice

A farm labourer, Ralph Gower, discovers the remains of a creature in a field. When he returns with a judge to inspect the find, it has gone, but the nubile local temptress Angel Blake finds part of it and leads some of the other youths into pagan rituals as they attempt to raise a demon. Tigon's follow-up to **Matthew Hopkins: Witchfinder General** shares little with Reeves's film except a superbly realized period setting and a distrust of authority. Supernatural forces are at work here and the film correspondingly explores its world with an earthy lyricism far

removed from Reeves's rage. Wynne-Simmons's debut script had to be altered from its original conception of three interlinked tales to one story at the last minute, accounting for some of the film's uneven, confused narrative – characters occasionally seem

---

BELOW: New Friend takes his medicine like a good boy in **Mumsy, Nanny, Sonny and Girly**.

magically transported from one place to the next, and one simply disappears altogether – and some scenes, particularly those involving the titular claw, are simply too ludicrous to work. Yet the film is still powerfully effective, ranking with Reeves's film and **The Wicker Man** in the pagan horror stakes. Wymark's judge is far from a simple force for good, being a prim, self-righteous man whose tyrannical conception of the world demands the unleashing of the "evil". The youths' pagan revels are by contrast energetic, openly sexual and shot through with a pastoral beauty, the characters crowning each other with hawthorn blossoms; yet they are also unambiguously evil, the children's games chillingly transforming into ritual murder and rape. Hayden's diabolic nymphet steals the show with a striptease before a bemused clergyman, but even the smallest supporting characters heighten the sense of time and place. The folk-inflected soundtrack repeats a haunting central theme, although its stings occasionally lapse into horror cliché, and Haggard's direction anchors the film's metaphysical concerns in a palpable rural reality, interspersing ground-level outdoor shots with dizzying hand-held sequences conveying the delirious energy of the pagan rituals.

MUMSY, NANNY, SONNY AND GIRLY
AKA GIRLY

1970, UK, dir Freddie Francis, scr Brian Comport, starring Michael Bryant, Ursula Howells, Howard Trevor, Vanessa Howard

When a drunken partygoer is tricked into thinking he has murdered his girlfriend by Girly and Sonny – adolescents who dress and act like children – he becomes the latest New Friend to join Mumsy and Nanny in their rundown Victorian mansion. But he soon finds out what happened to the last New Friend, and hatches a scheme to escape. *Girly* is an extraordinary blend of comedy and horror that creates a unique atmosphere of diseased infantilism, *Our Mother's House* (1967) as rewritten by Lewis Carroll in particularly demented Mad Hatter mood. The screenplay, based on the Maisie Mosco play *Happy Family*, sticks rigidly to its world of sinister children's games: even the house, a giddy confection of overwrought Victorian tat, recalls the ramshackle mansions common to children's fiction. The guests are fed "soldiers" and told off by Mumsy in a nightmare of child rearing, and the "children" have a lullaby or playground taunt for every occasion, menacing new arrivals with childish pranks or the dreaded "Humpty Dumpty" game. The film takes an infantile relish in subverting expectations, equally likely to present an innocuous gag or something far more sinister, and draws for horrific effect on the dimly remembered but real sexual and violent subtexts of children's games, an unexpectedly literal take on Victorian child iconography and inappropriate age behaviour. Girly, although obviously at least adolescent, acts like a child, apparently oblivious to the display of her pants beneath her short school skirt but she's clearly aware of her sexual allure, using it to recruit new arrivals. New Friend is evidently the first guest to respond directly to her sexual promise, and uses it, *Teorema*-style, to exploit the tensions within the family and provide a sexualized father figure, although Girly's new-found maturity doesn't stop her reciting increasingly malevolent lullabies as she seeks to protect her new partner. A cult gem, ripe for rediscovery.

TASTE THE BLOOD OF DRACULA

1970, UK, dir Peter Sasdy, scr Anthony Hinds, starring Christopher Lee, Geoffrey Keen, Linda Hayden, Peter Sallis

The Count finally arrives in his spiritual home of Victorian London. One of Hammer's best Dracula films, Sasdy's debut feature boasts a marvellous first half, in which three pillars of the community, Hargood, Paxton and Secker, are surprised during an evening's entertainment in a brothel by Courtly (Ralph Bates), an imperious hedonist kept by the brothel's girls. The patriarchal roués approach Courtly for tips on sophisticated debauchery and he arranges for them to buy Dracula's blood, found by a London trader (Roy Kinnear) following the staking of *Dracula Has Risen From the Grave* (1968). A ceremony to sell their souls to the devil goes badly wrong, with Courtly kicked to death by the thrill-seekers he has mocked viciously throughout, but Dracula has returned and vows to take vengeance. Up to this point *Taste the Blood* ranks with the best of Hammer's early '70s entries, sharing with **Dr Jekyll and Sister Hyde** a modern, sophisticated tone of playful self-mockery entirely lacking in the studio's later contemporary Dracula films. The script by Hinds subsequently taps contemporary generation-gap concerns for a tale of oppressed Victorian youths turning on their hypocritical parents, but doesn't really do much with the idea once it's been set in motion. Lee's Count has little to do but look imposing and intone "one … two … three" as his victims are dispatched, an unfortunate reminder of his *Sesame Street* cousin. Hayden, as Hargood's daughter Alice, continues the puppet theme with her best Miss Piggy impression, feebly turning away from Dracula only when he has no further use for her; and the script also is riddled with inconsistencies, from Courtly's death (surely Dracula needs a sacrifice to be resurrected?) through Lucy's fate (a vampire already, she appears to be killed by a particularly savage nibble from the Count) to the bizarre time-slip ending. The real stars of the film are Keen as Hargood, convincingly tyrannical and clearly suspect in his drunken desire to whip his daughter, and the marvellously sneering Bates, soon to be Hammer's leading man, but as neither makes it much past halfway, the task of carrying the film falls to the modestly likable, but not terribly engaging, Paul (Anthony Higgins).

L'UCCELLO DALLE PIUME DI CRISTALLO
AKA THE BIRD WITH THE CRYSTAL PLUMAGE; THE GALLERY MURDERS

1970, Italy/W Ger, dir/co-scr Dario Argento, co-scr George Kemp, starring Tony Musante, Suzy Kendall, Enrico Maria Salerno, Eva Renzi

Sam Dalmas, an American writer living in Rome, witnesses an attempted murder taking place in an art gallery. When he tries to help, he finds himself trapped between two plate-glass doors. Later, increasingly obsessed by what he saw, Dalmas begins to fret that he's missed some vital but maddeningly elusive clue.

This is where the journey starts for fans of Dario Argento. Seen today, *L'Uccello* is still an astonishingly mature and accomplished debut, trailing none of the shortcomings one associates with early work. Indeed, Argento himself must wish that he could match its cold, malicious clarity today.

Unlike the less-evolved brand of Italian murder-mystery (or later Argento clunkers like *Il Cartaio/The Card Player*, 2004), the police investigation in *L'Uccello* is marginalized, with a writer chosen as the focus of the story. Creativity, and its relation to disturbed states of mind, is central to the film: Dalmas's investigation borders on free association, hinging on such details as the disquieting atmosphere evoked by a painting; the sound of an exotic bird (hence the title); and questions of interpretation during the gallery attack that cleverly mirror the discourse around interpretation of art. Meanwhile, Dalmas's frustration at being unable to interpret what he has seen is visualized through images of impotence and entrapment – such as the glass-door sequence and a scene which has him pinned helplessly under a Modernist sculpture.

Much of what is taken for granted in the *giallo* originates here, with motifs that even Argento went on to overuse appearing in their first bloom: the vital clue that eludes the protagonist; a nervous, sweet-and-savage Morricone score; a plot whose

ABOVE: Tony Musante is trapped by art, **L'Uccello dalle Piume di Cristallo**

complexities are almost too much to swallow; and a nakedly voyeuristic camera daring you to share the killer's perspective. Argento's famed technical experimentation is already in evidence too, in scenes such as one in which he uses a specialized camera to peer down the throat of a screaming victim. Stylish and exhilarating, *L'Uccello* is the perfect introduction to Argento's unique body of work. [ST]

VALERIE A TYDEN DIVU
AKA VALERIE AND HER WEEK OF WONDERS

1970, Czech, dir/co-scr Jaromil Jires, co-scr Ester Krumbachová, starring Jaroslava Schallerová, Jan Klusák, Helena Any'zová, Karel Engel

Jires's allegorical vision of a pubescent girl's sexual awakening opens an ornate, gothic toybox of *Mittel*-European fantasy and folkcraft that is visually stunning. Valerie's sensual innocence draws us in as her world becomes a place of wonder, filmed in a rich, soft focus similar to that of the European soft-core of the period. Yet, like all European fairy tales, terrifying anxieties lurk at close range – and within the family. There are strong subtexts of taboo and transgression lurking in Valerie's imagination and the mutable narrative is driven by her untrustworthy subjectivity. All we know for sure is that Valerie is at a liminal point where the mystery of adult sexuality conjures up a treasure trove of erotic reveries and the "return of the repressed". Valerie's "dream" (the film's central narrative) centres round the search for the true identity of her parents, who may or may not be incestuous, shape-shifting vampires. On the night of her first menstruation, her magical silver earrings are stolen by a young man ("Eagle") who may or may not be her brother, and with whom she falls in love. The next day, symbolically, a carnival comes to town and a repulsive dark-cloaked, priest/vampire figure – later revealed to be her handsome father – emerges. He leads a band of undead that operate from a cobwebbed dungeon of smoking alchemical brews where Valerie becomes, in turn, a voyeur to the Sadean spectacle of her grandmother being sexually tormented, complicit in the priest/father's vampirism, and tied up by her dominatrix-styled cousin. In the dream parts of the film the identity of all the protagonists shifts, except Valerie's. We know from the thematically similar **Company of Wolves** that first menstruation is a threshold where strange and beautiful things happen and girls realize men are "hairy on the inside". Here, it is also family members and those who purport to be pious – there are echoes here of Surrealism's anti-religious stance, not surprising as the source novel's author Vitezslav Nezval founded the Czech Surrealist Group in 1934. The dingy, colourless creatures of the half-light are contrasted with the "healthy" earthy sexuality of the local peasants, rejoicing in their natural idyll as women erotically caress trees and bosoms overflow from gypsy bodices. [KS]

BELOW: Ingrid Pitt leads the pack in this publicity shot for **The Vampire Lovers**.

THE VAMPIRE LOVERS

1970, UK/US, dir Roy Ward Baker, scr Tudor Gates, starring Ingrid Pitt, Pippa Steele, Madeline Smith, Peter Cushing, George Cole

Hammer's adaptation of J. Sheridan LeFanu's novella *Carmilla* is relatively faithful to the story – the Countess plants her "daughter" in a succession of households, where she befriends and feeds on the daughters of the family – but never matches its dreamlike intensity, concentrating instead on presenting a reactionary sexual agenda masked by plunging necklines and heaving bosoms. The viewer is invited both to lust over the acres of naked female flesh, unsullied by male interference, and to exult as sexually predatory women with no use for men are decapitated: a woman with a head is a dangerous thing, and one without a man to keep her in check worse still. The film doesn't even have the courage to present its female vampires as entirely autonomous: instead, they are in the thrall of a mysterious male vampire whose appearance, punctuating the plot at critical points, seems needlessly confusing. Yet if Smith's Emma is a ludicrously wholesome portrait of innocence, Pitt brings a tragic sensuality to her role as Carmilla, as well as fulfilling her skin-baring obligations with aplomb: the characters' readiness to fall under her spell is, for

once, entirely credible. The film also approaches visual poetry at times, as Carmilla and her shrouded peers float through the mist-wreathed grounds of the ruined castle, or as Carmilla stares out into the sunset. Hammer's follow-up, *Lust for a Vampire* (1970), would ramp up the billowing nightgowns, soft-core silliness and delirious visuals, reaching a dizzy pitch this only hints at, although it's more squarely aimed at the raincoat brigade than horror fans. However, *The Vampire Lovers*' inauguration of the lesbian vampire boom of the '70s makes it a key entry in the genre.

THE ABOMINABLE DR PHIBES

1971, UK, dir Robert Fuest, scr James Witon, William Goldstein, starring Vincent Price, Joseph Cotten, Virginia North, Peter Jeffrey, Terry-Thomas

London, the '20s. Police are bewildered by the deaths of a series of leading doctors, all of which appear to relate to Old Testament curses. The murdered physicians had only the case of Victoria Phibes, who died during surgery, in common, and a revenge motive seems obvious – but surely Phibes's husband died in a car crash shortly after his wife? Fuest's insubstantial horror comedy was described by *Variety* as an "anachronistic period horror musical camp fantasy" and plays like an amalgam of *The Avengers* and *Batman*, providing a pop showcase for a string of set-piece murders of varying degrees of ingenuity: the plague of locusts is impressively baroque, and the plague of frogs, in which a man wearing a frog's head at a masked party finds his skull crushed by the tightening mask, provides the film's most memorable image. Most of the other murders pale by comparison, but the art direction is spectacular throughout, Phibes's lair a riot of garish automata and Art Deco styling, and a guest appearance by Terry-Thomas as a raffish physician whose home-movie entertainment is spoiled by Phibes's beautiful assistant helps to make up for the throwaway humour elsewhere. It was followed by a flimsier sequel, *Dr Phibes Rises Again* (1972), and a more worthy successor with the superior **Theater of Blood**.

LA CORTA NOTTE DELLE BAMBOLE DI VETRO
AKA SHORT NIGHT OF GLASS DOLLS; MALASTRANA

1971, It/W Ger/Yug, dir/scr Aldo Lado, starring Jean Sorel, Ingrid Thulin, Mario Adorf, Barbara Bach

Gregory Moore, an American journalist working in Prague, wakes up to find himself paralysed, unable to speak or even blink, and about to be committed to the morgue by doctors who can find no vital signs. In flashback, we see the events that have led to his dilemma, from the mysterious disappearance of his Czech girlfriend to his discovery of a sinister establishment conspiracy.

The first film by Aldo Lado (best known for the nasty 1976 shocker *L'Ultimo Treno della Notte/The Night Train Murders*), *La Corta Notte* is a sombre, slow-paced *giallo* that can seem overly talky at first. However, it's worth holding on, because Lado repays your patience with a gradually enveloping aura of doom, some stunning cinematography and a powerful dénouement. The political theme, simple but well handled, is unusual for the *giallo* genre, and the point it makes about state exploitation of the young is as true now as ever. It's just a shame that Lado didn't set the film in Italy – apparently it was the Italian government's banishment of a rebellious, system-bucking judge to a backwater post in Sicily that inspired his script in the first place.

The cinematographer, Giuseppe Ruzzolini, who shot *Teorema/Theorem* (1968) and *Porcile* (1969) for Pasolini, was (according to Lado) a nightmare to work with, showing no respect for what he seems to have regarded as a lowbrow assignment. Despite such snobbery, however, Ruzzolini lends the film the undeniable benefit of his talents. The early scenes of grim, oppressive streets give way to sumptuous, decadent interiors and a stylish use of shadows to heighten key scenes. Highlights include an atmospheric railway murder and a recurrent fascination with oppressively looming chandeliers, which peaks when Sorel suffers a fever and gazes up at one while hallucinating. Lado's ability to attract top talent is also apparent in the casting of Ingrid Thulin, star of Ingmar Bergman's *Nattvardsgästerna/Winter Light* (1962) and *Tystnaden/The Silence* (1963). As Sorel's old flame, Thulin adds emotional weight to the usually shallow role of *giallo* murder suspect, emphasizing the jealousy, spite and suppressed yearning of her character. Topped off with an eerie score by Ennio Morricone, *La Corta Notte* is a highly individual *giallo* that's well worth checking out. [ST]

DR JEKYLL AND SISTER HYDE

1971, UK, dir Roy Ward Baker, scr Brian Clemens, starring Ralph Bates, Martine Beswick, Gerald Sim, Lewis Flander

Dr Jekyll has discovered an elixir of life; unfortunately, its high dose of female hormones leads him to switch gender and he quickly runs out of source material for his research. But there is no shortage of women on the streets of London.

Hammer's last stab at Victorian gothic is one of its best,

The Avengers' Brian Clemens delivering a witty and literate script that explores all the byways of its deliciously perverse concept and points in an intriguingly irreverent direction that the studio would have done well to follow. Conflating Stevenson's story with Jack the Ripper and Burke and Hare, the film makes the most of its milieu of fog-shrouded London streets by peopling them with likable doxies and their roué admirers, as well as providing one of the most ingeniously convoluted explanations for the Whitechapel murders. Hyde greets her first transformation as any man would, by toying with her breasts and admiring herself in the mirror, then wraps herself in a scarlet curtain, establishing her preferred colour from the outset. She is sexually attracted to Howard, her upstairs neighbour, whose virginal, submissive sister Susan has a crush on Jekyll. Both Jekyll and Hyde draw energy from their admirers in the fight for possession of their body, but consummation of their trysts is always interrupted by a further (if only partial) transformation: Hyde is horrified to see a male hand creeping over her lover, while Susan nearly always visits Jekyll when his elixir is about to take effect. As ever, Hyde's character proves strong enough eventually not to need the elixir, and in one of the film's most perverse scenes Jekyll caresses Howard's cheek, possessed by the spirit of his "sister": for him it is less Hyde's existence than her autonomy that is a threat. This playful theme of sexual deviance runs throughout the film, whether in the character of the necrophiliac morgue attendant, Jekyll's cross-dressing or the "sophisticated" tastes one of the prostitutes attributes to him, although Clemens's script doesn't really explore why Jekyll's repressed "other" should be not only a woman but a knife-toting *femme fatale*, sharing nothing but physiology with the meek, prim Susan. Instead, its scenario is presented in simple "what if?" terms, with the focus squarely on the action and characterization – Bates and ex-Bond girl Beswick are superb, but Sim's goatish professor almost steals the show – resulting in one of the studio's most exciting and enjoyable films.

LET'S SCARE JESSICA TO DEATH

1971, US, dir John Hancock, scr Norman Jonas, Ralph Rose, starring Zohra Lampert, Barton Heyman, Kevin O'Connor, Mariclare Costello

Jessica, recently released from a mental institution, arrives at the farm her husband Duncan has bought as a rural retreat. They find a girl, Emily, squatting there, and Jessica invites her to stay. But, when Duncan and his friend Woody take a sexual interest in Emily,

RIGHT: Jessica (Zohra Lampert) fishes a friend from a watery grave. **Let's Scare Jessica to Death**.

Jessica's condition deteriorates; or is Emily *really* the vampiric ghost of a former tenant? Hancock's elegy for the bitter disappointments of the Love Generation is an unjustly neglected masterpiece. In a genre rife with misogynistic portrayals of female insanity, *Jessica* stands out as a sympathetic, sensitive portrait of psychic collapse, underpinned by a devastatingly credible performance from Lampert. Jessica's vulnerability is evident from the start, her stick-thin frame and high-waisted skirts recalling a shy, gawky girl as she tries to follow her friends' cues in acting normally; voiceovers give us privileged access to her mind as she tries to distinguish between hallucination and reality – Jessica must be one of the only characters in horror to be relieved when *someone else* sees the "ghost" – and multilayered voices whisper to her, harbingers of the breakdown to come. But, just because Jessica is paranoid, it doesn't mean they aren't out to get her: the hostile oldtimers of the town all wear strange bandages marking them as victims of the vampire's bite, and the behaviour of Emily, a creepy refugee from the Spahn Ranch, seems calculated to upset Jessica's fragile mental balance, whether suggesting a séance or flirting with Jessica's friends. For all their hippy rhetoric Woody and Duncan are finally more motivated by their libido than any desire to protect Jessica, and her abandonment gives the film a pervasive sense of lysergic loss and despair, aided by the acutely melancholic score, mixing solo piano and guitar with distorted electronic lullabies.

LA NOCHE DEL TERROR CIEGO
AKA TOMBS OF THE BLIND DEAD;
LA NOCHE DE LA MUERTA CIEGA;
CRYPT OF THE BLIND DEAD;
NIGHT OF THE BLIND DEAD

1971, Sp/Port, dir/scr Amando de Ossorio, starring Oscar Burner, Lone Fleming, Maria Silva, José Telman

Old schoolfriends Elizabeth and Virginia meet by chance in Lisbon. Elizabeth's friend Roger invites the girls for a weekend in the countryside, but Elizabeth, irritated by her friends' flirting, jumps off the train to spend the night in a ruined monastery, where she is attacked by zombies. De Ossorio's film provides an original spin on the zombie myth, his undead the impressively dessicated remains of the Knights Templar who have conquered the secrets of death, although not before being hanged and having their eyes plucked out by birds as punishment for their crimes. They can sense their prey only by sound and appear in response to sexual arousal – Elizabeth strips before she is attacked – mirroring the sexual torments they meted out to objects of desire (a graphic

reconstruction shows a woman's breasts being slashed by swords, the Templars drinking from the wounds) while alive. In this sense the film dramatizes the conflict between Franco's old guard and the sexual permissiveness sweeping the Continent: one morgue attendant, looking at Elizabeth's body, makes the tension clear by opining that "They are all asking for it. The way they dress, it's as if they want to be bitten." But the film's principal virtues are visual, whether inspired touches such as a frog landing in a pool of blood or the zombies riding slow-motion horses through the ruined village in pursuit of their prey, images memorable enough to transcend the limitations of a script in which Roger, seeing the crosses of the ruined graveyard, recognizes them instinctively as "Egyptian crosses aflame. Witchcraft states that they come from hell itself and signify Satanic rituals." It was followed by three sequels, *El Ataque de los Muertos Sin Ojos*, *El Buque Maldito* (both 1973) and *La Noche de los Gaviotas* (1975).

MAIS NE NOUS DÉLIVREZ PAS DU MAL
AKA DON'T DELIVER US FROM EVIL

1971, Fr, dir/scr Joël Séria, starring Jeanne Goupil, Catherine Wagener, Bernard Dhéeran, Gérard Darrieu

Teenage convent girls Anne and Lore are inseparable friends who have made a pact dedicating themselves to Satan and the pursuit of evil. Bored to distraction and alienated from their parents' bourgeois lives, the girls spend their spare time reading aloud from Lautreamont's *Maldoror*, teasing the local farmer to the point of near-rape, setting fire to crops and killing their neighbour's songbirds. One summer night they hold an amateur black mass, using a local simpleton gardener in the priest role, before tormenting him with their nubile beauty wearing diaphanous communion dresses. On an inexorable slide into more serious transgressions, they offer shelter to a stranded motorist. After boldly stripping off and inviting adult attention, the girls are unwilling – or too immature – to allow him sexual satisfaction and Anne beats the stranger to death with a log. Fearing that they'll be discovered when the authorities drag the lake for the body, the girls plan an uncompromising exit during a packed attendance of the school play.

This astonishing but little-known film beautifully understates the Satanic theme. There's an absence of any knowing, high-camp occultism and instead we have lush cinematography, a haunting score, an unforgettable ending and two stunning actresses who, although 19 and 20 when the film was made, are utterly convincing as 14-year-old schoolgirls.

DR JEKYLL AND MR HYDE

The publication in 1886 of Robert Louis Stevenson's novel provided a fresh template for horror, ushering in the coming century's obsession with introspection and morbid self-analysis. If tales by Poe and E.T.A. Hoffmann had touched on Stevenson's theme, their use of doppelgängers and automata ensured that the horror had hitherto remained strictly external. By the time Jekyll drank his bubbling potion, the monster was within.

Most adaptations dispense with the structure and carefully concealed mystery of the novel (which contains several viewpoints, and saves the revelation of Hyde's identity for Jekyll's closing first-person chapter) to focus exclusively on Jekyll's perspective. Many also follow Thomas Russell Sullivan's 1887 play in lending Jekyll a girlfriend (thus introducing a sexual angle that was not Stevenson's primary concern) and having the same actor play both Jekyll and Hyde, impossible in Stevenson's original conception as Hyde is markedly smaller than the doctor.

BELOW: *Hulk* smash puny humans!

The conflation in the public's mind of Stevenson's story with Jack the Ripper – Sullivan's play was still running at the time of the first Ripper murder, and the killer was widely suspected to be a surgeon – added another twist to the tale, introducing the character of the lovable tart and relocating the action from London's Soho to the East End.

The theme was popular with early cinema: John Barrymore's 1920 portrayal was the seventh, but the first to become internationally successful in its warnings of the perils of selfless philanthropy. Barrymore's performance, using minimal trick photography and make-up, is extraordinary, even if he looks surprisingly like *Oliver Twist*'s Fagin (and behaves like Bill Sikes), his lank hair, spidery gait and grasping claws unsettlingly close to anti-Semitic caricature. In one astonishing sequence he is seen transformed into a giant arachnid crawling onto Jekyll's bed.

Rouben Mamoulian's 1931 film still stands as the most impressive adaptation. The 1941 version adds little, despite being even more lavishly mounted, reducing Ivy (clearly a prostitute in 1931) to a champagne-guzzling good-time girl, while Spencer Tracy looks too lumpen (and, perhaps, old) to be convincing as Jekyll and too buffoonish for Hyde.

Hammer provided typically idiosyncratic takes on the theme with *The Two Faces of Dr Jekyll* (1960), in which Hyde becomes another kind of ladykiller altogether, an urbane charmer who discovers that Jekyll is being cuckolded by his wife, and **Dr Jekyll and Sister Hyde**, which manages to rope in Burke and Hare along with the now-hoary Jack the Ripper clichés.

The tale has attracted directors as diverse as Jean Renoir (*Le Testament du Dr Cordelier/Experiment in Evil*, 1959) and Walerian Borowcyzk (*Dr Jekyll et les Femmes/Blood of Dr Jekyll*, 1981), while later adaptations have tended to stress the narcotic angle as the cause for Jekyll's personality change – more credible today, perhaps, than in the 1880s. The related rash of imaginary-friend films that flooded cinemas after *Fight Club* (1999) follow Stevenson's lead in saving their revelations for the end, but fall short of being adaptations in a strict sense. Unlike their uncomprehending split-personality protagonists, Jekyll knows exactly who Hyde is and what he does, however much he might like finally to stop him – making Ang Lee's 2003 take on *Hulk* more striking as a modern rendering of the beast within.

Director Séria has always been fiercely anti-establishment and there is much sacrilegious lampooning of the clergy and authority in the spirit of Buñuel. Furthermore, the girls exude a radiantly perverse authority, even when stripped to their bra and pants. Importantly, the actresses never seem exploited and the director has more serious intentions for their erotic power than mere titillation. He uses it to dismantle the very fabric of the bourgeois order.

Banned on release but finally available uncut on DVD, *Mais ne Nous Délivrez pas du Mal* will appeal to fans of master European aestheticians Borowczyk and Metzger, yet there is an extra intellectual dimension to Séria's work that makes this essential viewing. His subversive and gleeful exploration of Sadean philosophy is unique in the cinema, and one can imagine Séria proudly celebrating the charge that his film "depraves and corrupts". Bataille and Baudelaire would have loved it. [KS]

REAZIONE A CATENA
AKA ECOLOGIA DEL DELITTO; A BAY OF BLOOD; TWITCH OF THE DEATH NERVE; BLOODBATH; CARNAGE; LAST HOUSE – PART II

1971, It, dir/co-scr Mario Bava, co-scr Joseph McLee (Giuseppe Zaccariello), Filippo Ottoni, starring Claudine Auger, Luigi Pistilli, Claudio Volonté, Anna M.

A bay is marked for future development, but a string of murders mean that neither the planners nor their opponents are likely to see their dreams come true. By the '70s Bava was in a difficult position: the gothic fantasies with which he'd made his name were out of vogue, and the *giallo* cycle he'd launched with **Sei Donne per l'Assassino** going into overdrive with the bravura stylistic excesses of Dario Argento. Bava's response was to land a machete in a naked woman's neck, laying down the rules for the slasher cycle that would dominate American genre cinema a decade later. All the elements are here: extended killer POV shots; witless, oversexed teens serving only as fodder for gory killings, with a shish-kebab skewering quoted in several later slashers; and the 13 killings even begin on the 13th! Unlike later slashers, though, *Reazione* works best as comedy – murder is, here, not only likely but the inevitable result of human relations, the ludicrous ending highlighting Bava's flippant treatment of his theme – or a jaundiced epitaph for a bygone gothic era, the drunken, hiccupping fortune-teller a sorry shadow of the director's former supernatural extravaganzas. Unfortunately, aside from a number of signature travelling shots and characteristically crisp photography, there's little to mark the film out as the work

of a horror master as Bava lazily relies on heavy-handed zooms, with fuzzed focus replacing standard dissolves. The film's principal pleasure is ultimately kitsch, from the '70s stylings of Ventura's beach apartment to the alarming poodle hair and high boots of slasher victim Bobby, jigging a painful dance before taking a well-deserved axe in the face.

LES LÈVRES ROUGES
AKA DAUGHTERS OF DARKNESS; THE RED LIPS

1971, Bel/Fr/W Ger, dir/co-scr Harry Kümel, co-scr Pierre Drouot, Jean Ferry, Manfred R. Köhler, starring John Karlen, Delphine Seyrig, Danielle Ouimet, Andrea Rau

Harry Kümel is probably best known for the eccentric fantasy *Malpertuis* (1972), and for this elegant vampire film which dispenses with the fangs in favour of something more dreamlike and erotic. Delphine Seyrig is the ageless Countess Bathory, arriving at an out-of-season Ostend hotel at the same time as a young, newly-married couple. The Countess immediately courts, then actively pursues the pair, having decided that Valerie, the wife, needs to be her new companion.

Although produced in the same year as *Lust for a Vampire*, Kümel's film is a world away from late period Hammer melodrama in both style and content. The setting may be contemporary but the atmosphere is redolent of an earlier era, with the Countess arriving in a period automobile accompanied by a young and luscious secretary styled like Louise Brooks. Pouting Ilona is dangled as bait for the brutal husband Stefan while the Countess spins her web around Valerie. The massive, empty hotel and the bleak vistas of a rain-swept resort create a perfect backdrop for this elaborate game of human chess, conjuring the same sense of the lassitude of an immortal amid luxury that Anne Rice would later explore in her Vampire Chronicles. Delphine Seyrig was always suited to aristocratic roles and is perfect here as the sinister, whispering Countess, alluring yet with cruelty enough to kill without compunction. Kümel's treatment of sexuality is far more even-handed than the often prissy or misogynist Hammer school; along with the overt lesbianism, it transpires that Stefan's "Mother" is really an aged man, and that Stefan has married Valerie without telling him. A silly sub-plot concerning a nosey policeman detracts from the mood at times but, with its red/black/white colour scheme and chiming score, *Les Lèvres Rouges* often seems like a cinematic transcription of a Paul Delvaux painting, and a worthwhile addition to the pantheon of Belgian Surrealism. [JC]

ABOVE: Delphine Seyrig as the ageless Countess Bathory, **Les Lèvres Rouges**.

STRAW DOGS

1971, UK, dir/co-scr Sam Peckinpah, co-scr David Zelag Goodman, starring Dustin Hoffman, Susan George, David Warner, Peter Vaughan

An American mathematician, David Sumner, has rented a farmhouse in the Cornish village of Wakley to work on a book. Tensions between David and his English wife Amy are exacerbated by his refusal to respond to the ridicule of locals he has hired to build a garage, one of whom had once been his wife's lover. When he finally takes a stand, protecting a man he has knocked down with his car, the locals aren't about to back down. Ironically, it took an American director to make the finest British rural horror film, Peckinpah's tale of a mild-mannered man driven to violence grafts Western themes onto a contemporary setting and provides, along with **Deliverance** (itself set in the US and shot by a Brit), the template for virtually every other urbanoia/revenge film to follow. In his adaptation of Gordon M. Williams's nondescript novel *The Siege of Trencher's Farm*, Peckinpah paints a portrait of rural Cornwall populated by educationally subnormal adults, sexually precocious teens and hard-drinking labourers but adds, in his depiction of the Sumners, levels of complexity that Williams never approaches. David, a passionless intellectual, has left the US because of his reluctance to "take a stand" – although what on is never clearly expressed – and remains resolutely non-committal in his approach to his wife and the locals, with whom he tries to curry favour even as they openly mock him. His relationship with Amy is strained from the start, but her behaviour, openly displaying herself to the men, mocking David's cowardice, petulantly changing an equation on his blackboard and finally siding with her rapist over her husband in a fight, allows Peckinpah to wind the tension to breaking point for the devastating siege sequence. Amy is an unattractive but credible figure, and the censor-baiting rape sequence an unattractive but credible scene, queasily staged to worry the fine line of consent. When David finally turns on his tormentors, the exhilaration comes partly through Hoffman's exceptional performance, perhaps his finest, but also through the film's parallels with playground dynamics. The hostility masked as politeness, the cruel mock-friendly tricks, and the perpetual escalation of harassment, recall school bullying, with David as the put-upon geek reluctant to put up a fight. But Peckinpah avoids easy triumphalism in favour of a darker ambivalence over David's actions, mixing the film's grindhouse manipulations with arthouse techniques of non-linear editing and tightly controlled bursts of handheld camera energy for a brutally effective shocker.

VIERGES ET VAMPIRES
AKA REQUIEM POUR UN VAMPIRE; REQUIEM FOR A VAMPIRE

1971, Fr, dir/scr Jean Rollin, starring Marie-Pierre Castel, Mireille Dargent, Louise Dhour, Dominique

Two young girls dressed in clown costumes escape from a reformatory. Chased by police, they abandon and burn their getaway car and head across country. Soon they are lost. They seek refuge in an old chateau where they become prisoners of a weary vampire. He is the last of his line and is looking for new blood to propagate his race. But first both girls must be initiated by losing their virginity.

Although the plot of Rollin's third commercial feature sounds like another piece of Gallic sexploitation, the execution is anything but. His approach was to film as much of the story as possible without dialogue, keeping the narrative on the boil by constantly moving his characters through the beautiful French countryside. The result is a lyrical and perverse fairy tale and one of his most perfectly realized films. For commercial reasons a scene where the vampire's assistants molest some chained, naked women was shoe-horned into the film. Rollin's preferred version removes these shots, and with them goes much of the "sex" for which his name has unfortunately become a byword in horror circles.

Plot is not Rollin's strongest point. His films are at their most enjoyable when his visual imagination is allowed free rein to conjure an ambience of wonder and mystery. Here he makes a film that very nearly manages to avoid "plot" entirely. Its pleasures are purely cinematic: the beautiful summer countryside; the garish colours of the clown costumes; a piano played at night in a graveyard; a strange ceremony conducted by cloaked skeletons; and, of course, the coquettish charm of the two girls (female duos being a staple of Rollin's imaginative universe). The playfully lyrical score by Pierre Raph aids immeasurably in the creation of a melancholic atmosphere of languid beauty, against which the tired old world of the dying vampire confronts youth, joy and eroticism. [PT]

DEATH LINE
AKA RAW MEAT

1972, UK, dir Gary Sherman, scr Ceri Jones, starring Donald Pleasence, Norman Rossington, David Ladd, Sharon Gurney, Christopher Lee

American director and story originator Sherman had worked in Britain for a while during the early '70s shooting advertisements, and translated his experiences of getting the last tube home into this gem. The story centres around a feral cannibal, listed as the "Man" in the credits, who preys on late stragglers on the tube. He is the descendant of workers – men and women – who were trapped when a railway tunnel collapsed in the 19th century. The company employing them couldn't afford to dig them out and abandoned the project, leaving them to die. The viewer thus has

---

LEFT: "I will not allow violence against this house." Dustin Hoffman in **Straw Dogs**.

OPPOSITE: The Man mourns. **Death Line**.

some sympathy for his plight, and still more when his pregnant partner dies, leaving him alone. When he abducts the heroine towards the end, he is looking less for meat than love, although to her boyfriend the distinction probably doesn't matter. Despite his prodigious strength, his meat-heavy diet has taken its toll and he suffers from severe vitamin deficiency and a range of other ailments, his body covered in festering sores. His appearance is more convincingly feral than that of the mutant family of **The Hills Have Eyes**, his speech reduced to a plaintive or angry "Mind the doors!", and his cannibal lair, hung with bodies in varying states of decay, seems bizarrely more realistic than the location shots of Russell Square station surrounding it. Pleasence's tea-addicted Inspector Calhoun brings a welcome tone of humour to an otherwise oppressive film, which deserves credit not least for a realistically shocking take on urban alienation in an industry still floundering in gothic melodrama.

DEATHDREAM
AKA DEAD OF NIGHT; THE NIGHT WALK; THE NIGHT ANDY CAME HOME

1972, Can, dir Bob Clark, scr Alan Ormsby, starring Lynn Carlin, John Marley, Richard Backus, Henderson Forsythe, Anya Ormsby

This is an effective reworking of the W.W. Jacobs tale "The Monkey's Paw" (also adapted in **Tales from the Crypt**), in which a woman wishes her soldier son Andy back from Vietnam. He's dead, but no one notices, even his girlfriend putting his strange behaviour down to combat shock. Still, even that can't explain his thirst for blood (he needs a constant supply to maintain his appearance) or erratic acts such as killing the family dog. In an oddly poignant ending, the mother, who won't stop loving him even though he's dead, drives him to the cemetery; he has already dug himself a grave, and frantically tries to pull the earth over himself as the police close in. Tom Savini worked on the special effects with the scenarist Ormsby and the director, Bob Clark, went on to helm the proto-slasher **Black Christmas**.

DELIVERANCE

1972, US, dir John Boorman, scr James Dickey, starring Burt Reynolds, Jon Voigt, Ned Beatty, Ronny Cox

Not widely considered a horror film, due in part to its prestigious production values, *Deliverance* set the scene for virtually every urbanoia film to follow – city slickers insult country folk on a trip to the boondocks, then have to tap into their inner savage to survive the rural vengeance – while putting its characters through an ordeal as nasty as any of its more baldly exploitative imitators. *Deliverance* presents four clearly delineated male types – Lewis the survivalist, waiting for the system to collapse so he can show off his archery skills; Drew the intellectual, bespectacled, guitar-toting and insistent on obeying the law; Bobby the insurance salesman, fat on expense-account lunches and uncomfortable in the wilds; Ed the everyman, a pipe-smoking family man who is still keen to hunt, clearly the central identification figure (and the first-person narrator of scriptwriter James Dickey's excellent source novel) – canoeing down a river that is about to be dammed to feed Atlanta's power needs. (For a broader discussion of *Deliverance*'s themes see the **Urbanoia** box on p.148.) The film's subtler touches are easy to overlook in its visceral impact: several key plot points are deliberately ambiguous, such as Drew's fate and the identity of Ed's victim. Although the character types are stylized, they still have depth, even Lewis's rants about the failing system ironically illustrated by his use of such highly industrialized products as a compound bow. The understated injury effects make their journey gruellingly painful. Essential viewing.

DEMONS OF THE MIND
AKA BLOOD WILL HAVE BLOOD

1972, UK, dir Peter Sykes, scr Christopher Wicking, starring Paul Jones, Gillian Hills, Robert Hardy, Michael Hordern, Patrick Magee

In a remote unnamed European village in the 19th century, a drugged girl, Elizabeth, is returned to the care of her father Baron Zorn and aunt Hilda after enjoying a few days of freedom in the arms of her lover Carl. Zorn believes that Elizabeth and Emile, his children, are infected by a strain of madness that runs in the family, and keeps them locked away, calling on the services of disgraced Doctor Falkenberg to cure them. Falkenberg is far more interested in Zorn, however, and uses his radical techniques – a mixture of prototypical psychiatry and mesmerism – to establish that Zorn's children are extensions of the Baron's will, and that the Baron himself is ultimately responsible for a series of murders in the area. While the dominant theme – the sins of the father visited on his offspring – informs a number of British genre films of the period, Sykes and Wicking bring something altogether new to British gothic, with an elliptical narrative structure, a fluid, roving camera and a focus on atmosphere over story that recalls Italian gothic rather than the traditionally staid British form. The rich colour schemes and saturated reds and blues recall Mario

ABOVE: Lewis won't waste an arrow. **Deliverance.**

Bava's experiments with colour and lend the film a dreamlike intensity, aided by a subtle score a world away from Hammer's usual bombast. One of the last great films from Hammer, even if the studio buried it on a double bill with the deservedly obscure *Tower of Evil.*

DUEL

1972, US, dir Stephen Spielberg, scr Richard Matheson, starring Dennis Weaver, Jacqueline Scott, Eddie Firestone, Lou Frizzell

David Mann's routine business trip turns to nightmare when the driver of a rusting, smoke-belching oil tanker resents being overtaken and hounds him mercilessly. The 23-year-old Spielberg's TV movie was released theatrically in Europe, where it proved especially popular with French critics. The symbolically titled Mann's masculinity is under fire from the start, a radio story about a house-husband playing in the background, and we understand from a strained phone call to his wife that she is disappointed by his lack of assertiveness. He is uncomfortable out of his urban environment, a white-collar worker in a blue-collar world, and his battle with the driver of the tanker draws on all of his insecurities to provoke him to crisis point. The arena in which he must prove his masculinity is the road, his weapon the car and, although the conflict is an ancient one, what better contemporary stage for the car-dependent US than the open road? *Duel* shares many themes with urbanoia movies — city to country, the testing of civilized man — but its stripped-down simplicity gives it a unique feel. With hardly any dialogue, and a villain who remains unseen throughout, Spielberg manages to milk an astonishing pitch of tension from a film whose running time is principally spent with one man driving silently in his car. The duel has a purity, divorced from any other concerns, that makes the few scenes in which Mann interacts with other people reminders of a reality that seems less and less convincing as the film progresses. This showcase for Spielberg's skill in taut minimalism launched his career, although of his later work only **Jaws** comes close to its pared-down tension.

THE LAST HOUSE ON THE LEFT
1972, US, dir/scr Wes Craven, starring Sandra Cassel, Lucy Grantham, David Hess, Fred J. Lincoln

The Collinwoods reluctantly let their teenage daughter Mari go to a rock concert with a friend, only for the two girls to be raped and killed by a gang of hoodlums who end up spending the night at the Collinwoods' house. The parents enact a terrible revenge. Purportedly inspired by Bergman's *Jungfrukällan/The Virgin Spring* (1960), Craven's first feature sets up the themes to which he would

return throughout his career: two contrasting families in conflict, the violence beneath the veneer of civilization, and its corrupting power. The film's reputation as a confrontational horror classic rests on a long sequence in which the girls are humiliated, raped and finally killed. While parts of this are genuinely shocking – chief thug Krug's order for one of the girls to wet themselves, and the protracted mutilation of their corpses – the rank ineptitude of much of the rest of the film detracts from their power. Krug is a comedy villain, his rap sheet of having killed two nuns and a priest before hooking his son Junior on heroin straight out of an early John Waters movie, and Junior's frog impression and the hapless cops are misguidedly played for straight comic relief. When the thugs decide to stay at the Collinwoods', Junior going into a comedy cold-turkey routine, any remaining shred of credibility is left behind. The Collinwoods, distraught over their missing daughter, are nevertheless happy to house the appallingly behaved thugs; after spotting Mari's necklace on Junior's neck, the parents find her body in the woods. Rather than simply shoot them with the gun they have appropriated from Krug, the Collinwoods hatch an elaborate plan for revenge so implausible that the film finally fails to live up to its considerable reputation.

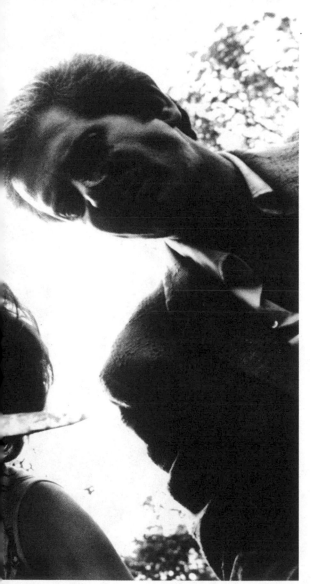

LA MANSION DE LA LOCURA
AKA DR TARR'S TORTURE DUNGEON; HOUSE OF MADNESS; THE MANSION OF MADNESS; THE SYSTEM OF DR TARR AND PROFESSOR FEATHER

1972, Mex, dir/scr Juan Lopez Moctezuma, starring Claudio Brook, Arthur Hansel, Ellen Sherman, Martin LaSalle

The first film from a former theatre and radio producer, this is a surreal *tour de force*. Using a Poe story as its basis, it depicts a world gone mad. The inhabitants of an asylum have imprisoned the former director and staff, and taken over under the fascistic regime of a notorious escaped murderer. A visiting journalist uncovers the deception and attempts to regain control with the help of the director's daughter.

Moctezuma's startling eye for visual composition, aided by Jodorowsky's cinematographer, Rafael Corkidi, makes for a fresh and multi-layered viewing experience. He packs the frame with rich and surprising tableaux, notably the final trial by madmen. His background, working with the Panic Theatre happenings of the mid-'60s, gives events a distinctly psychedelic and ritualistic aspect: the film is very much a product of its time, with hippy dance sequences and drug-tinged dream trips amusingly anachronistic in its nominal 19th-century setting. Claudio Brook, as the murderer, serves as a kind of master of ceremonies, guiding us ever onwards into the increasingly bizarre world of the madhouse. His performance is a constant delight, teetering on the verge of parody but never losing its dark edge.

The film has no connection whatsoever with the commercial world of Mexican horror movies, as represented by the likes

LEFT: Krug and co. in a nasty moment from **The Last House on the Left**.

of Santo and his gang. Moctezuma's approach is much more European. In US drive-ins, the film was promoted as a straight horror film full of sex and violence; disappointed viewers, misled by the garish posters, unfairly gave it a bad name. Now, with pitch-black comedy a familiar TV staple, it may finally be able to find an audience. It was awarded a gold medal at the Paris International Festival of Science Fiction and Fantasy in 1974 and was distributed in a number of European countries. [PT]

LA NOVIA ENSANGRETADA
AKA THE BLOOD SPATTERED BRIDE; TIL DEATH DO US PART

1972, Sp, dir/scr Vicente Aranda, starring Simon Andreu, Maribel Martin, Alexandra Bastedo, Dean Selmier

After Susan's wedding night, she begins to resent her husband's advances and dreams of a female lover, who eventually comes to stay with the couple. Aranda was an established director long before *La Novia*, the first film made by his own production company, Morgana. This adaptation of LeFanu's *Carmilla* shares with its rivals (the Hammer Karnstein trilogy, *Et Mourir de Plaisir*, 1960, **Vampyres, les Lèvres Rouges**) a mixture of soft-core lesbian fumblings and hard-core violence leavened by a slow pace and peppered with dreamlike visuals, but distinguishes itself with an explicitly feminist slant that shades into a political subtext. Like Guerín Hill with **La Campana del Infierno**, Aranda turned to horror to make comments about the Franco regime that would have proved problematic otherwise: Susan's husband, who remains nameless throughout the film, represents Francoist values through his enjoyment of hunting (he kills a vixen caught in a trap), macho chauvinism and insensitive brutality. Yet Aranda's approach adds psychological richness to what might otherwise be dry polemic: Susan's fears of sex exaggerate the cruelty of her husband, who often seems genuinely loving; many of the tensions between them are displaced onto the figure of the 12-year-old Carol, who brings Susan Carmilla's knife, a symbol of sexual aggression that the husband is unable to hide; and Carmilla's Dworkin rhetoric – "He has spat inside your body to enslave you" – is grotesquely parodic of Susan's authentic grounds for complaint. *La Novia* plays like a fairy tale with its schematic colour scheme and flashes of marvellously gothic and Surreal imagery – the husband first meets Carmilla as a

RIGHT: Carmilla (Alexandra Bastedo) offers Susan (Maribel Martin) the knife her husband cannot hide, **La Novia Ensangretada**.

hand and snorkel emerging from a beach – but roots its parable in exceptional location photography that gives a powerful sense of place, building up to a grisly reassertion of male dominance.

NON SI SEVIZIA UN PAPERINO
DON'T TORTURE A DUCKLING

1972, It, dir/co-scr Lucio Fulci, co-scr Gianfranco Clerici, starring Florinda Bolkan, Barbara Bouchet, Tomas Milian, Irene Papas

Young boys are being murdered in Accendura, rural Italy. The police are summoned from Milan to help the local force, while journalists descend on the town. Could the killer be Giuseppe, the village idiot? Or Patrizia, the rich kid hiding in the provinces after a drugs scandal, who likes to flaunt her body to the boys? Or Maciara, the local witch?

Although saddled with perhaps the most risible title in *giallo*-land, Fulci's third horror-inflected thriller is his best, and reportedly his personal favourite of his own films. While it eschews the *giallo*'s traditional urban focus and replaces the standard parade of beautifully dressed and coiffed women with a bunch of unwashed boys, other *giallo* themes and motifs are present and correct, from the credibility-stretching misdirection to the ubiquitous bottle of J&B whisky and the general atmosphere of perverse desire, all shot with precise, crisp photography and widescreen compositions that might have made Argento jealous.

The subject matter of child murder is unpalatable enough to be tackled only rarely in the cinema, and here it has an unhealthy gloss in the theme of child interest in adult sexuality, and vice versa. The boys like to watch men having sex with prostitutes and boast of their experience although they are clearly pre-teen, and though the priest is keen to maintain their innocence he has his work cut out with flame-haired temptresses like Patrizia around.

That said, Patrizia mellows through the film as she joins journalist Martelli, a man who seems incapable of doing up more than half the buttons on his shirt, in the hunt for the killer. But elements of her behaviour and character remain inconsistent because on several occasions she appears to lure the boys to their deaths, while Maciara claims to have killed the boys through witchcraft. The film leaves this possibility open, anticipating **Profondo Rosso**, and the witchcraft scenes themselves, outstanding sequences of scrabbling hands manipulating wax dummies, serve as potent reminders of the gulf between urbane, sophisticated Milan and the credulous superstitions of the surrounding rural communities.

Maciara's death by chain whipping is a justly infamous sequence, although Fulci's insistence on showing wounds in close-up – both here and in the finale – seems crass and clunky in the context of the stylishness displayed elsewhere. Still, it's this focus, rather than any amount of roving camerawork, that made his name among horror fans and few will be disappointed by the skull-crushing climax.

THE POSSESSION OF JOEL DELANEY

1972, US, dir Waris Hussein, scr Matt Robinson, Grimes Grice, starring Shirley MacLaine, Perry King, Lovelady Powell, Barbara Trentham

When Nora Benson's brother Joel is committed after attempting to kill a man, her investigations reveal that he may have been possessed by the spirit of a Puerto Rican friend. But can Mrs Benson bring herself to entrust Joel's life to a Puerto Rican *brujo*? This uneven but intriguing precursor to **The Exorcist** in the big-budget possession stakes is less concerned with Delaney's predicament than that of his sister (MacLaine, herself incidentally the inspiration for the Chris MacNeil character in Friedkin's film), an arrogant, obnoxiously wealthy Manhattan socialite whose money and position can no longer buffer her from the realities of urban poverty. The treatment is at times cringingly heavy-handed: Nora tells her Puerto Rican maid that "the people in my world can't get into your world". Her experience of ethnic communities shifts from one form of cultural and economic distance (a friend's apartment is decorated with tribal artefacts, while her maid is kept in place by Nora's imperious tone) to another, characterized by urban blight, insanity (Bellevue's inhabitants are, here, almost all black or Hispanic) and florid superstition; while Joel's possession amounts to little more than a taste for dark glasses, leather jackets, flick-knives and calling women "*puta*". Nora doesn't appear to grow or learn from her experiences, simply flustered by a *santeria* ritual, and the film never adequately explores her bizarrely incestuous relationship with her brother, whom she treats more as lover than family member. Yet, for all its flaws, the film's never dull, boasting superb location photography in Spanish Harlem, the obligatory hippy party scene and a surprisingly nasty climax in which Joel torments his niece and nephew by making them eat dog food and dance naked for him. The possession theme is also more credible if less viscerally effective than **The Exorcist**, and the *santeria* iconography is colourful and distinctive even if the showcase ritual feels like a vaguely embarrassing tourist display.

THE STONE TAPE

1972, UK, dir Peter Sasdy, scr Nigel Kneale, starring Michael Bryant, Jane Asher, Iain Cuthbertson, Michael Bates

There's an argument to be made for Nigel Kneale being considered a British equivalent to H.P. Lovecraft, although Kneale would undoubtedly dismiss such an assertion. Both employed a similar brand of speculative fiction that mixes SF and horror; and both have a similar concern with ancient or alien forces imposing themselves on the present day, often to ruinous effect.

The Stone Tape was made for a BBC Christmas screening and concerns a technology company taking over an old manor house in order to research new audio recording techniques for commercial development. When it transpires that the oldest part of the building is haunted by a screaming Victorian chambermaid we immediately enter Kneale territory. Lesser writers would make this a great revelation and a shock for the characters; here the engineers immediately set to work intent on finding a scientific basis for the haunting, even hoping that it may provide a breakthrough for their researches. Jane Asher's Jill is the sensitive computer programmer who seems more aware

ABOVE: Shirley MacLaine pulls rank, **The Possession of Joel Delaney**.

than her colleagues of the forces at work in the room's ancient stones, and consequently becomes increasingly worried that the engineers are blithely preparing to dispel a minor supernatural phenomenon that serves as a warning for a far greater horror lurking just out of sight. As in *Quatermass and the Pit* (1967), Kneale's script carefully peels away layers of history, playing with a host of apparent explanations until the real menace locked in the heart of the building is unveiled.

Despite the limitations of the production (shooting interiors on video was common practice in the '70s), and an inevitably dated quality to the technological discussions, *The Stone Tape* still packs a considerable punch. Kneale was always careful to leave gaps in his stories for the audience's imagination; what might easily have been a routine drama about a haunted room takes an increasingly unpredictable course, and the gaps that are left are filled by something truly terrifying. [JC]

TALES FROM THE CRYPT

1972, UK, dir Freddie Francis, scr Milton Subotsky, starring Ralph Richardson, Joan Collins, Ian Hendry, Peter Cushing

Five strangers are separated from their group on a cemetery tour and find themselves in a room with a hooded man who prompts visions of what the future has in store. Ironically, it took a British company, albeit one with strong American connections, to successfully transplant EC Comics' blend of hardboiled *noir* and ghoulish morality tale to the silver screen; American attempts such as *Creepshow* (1982) suffered from overly literal interpretations. Amicus had tried their hand at anthology films before, the series beginning with *Dr Terror's House of Horrors* (1964), but they only escaped the patchiness common to the form with this EC adaptation, drawn from stories in the original comics but retold with a keen eye for British class tensions and a gleeful relish far preferable to the jokiness of earlier entries. The cast reads like a roll-call of British exploitation talent: the first story shows a homicidal Joan Collins being menaced in turn by a madman dressed as Santa Claus; the second has Ian Hendry surviving a car crash to return to a world very different from the one he left; the third delivers the best punchline of the film with the revenge of Grimsdyke, Cushing delivering a career highlight as the dustman whose meagre pleasures are snatched away one by one by his sniffy neighbours; and the fourth retells W.W. Jacobs's "The Monkey's Paw", with an unexpectedly gory finale. But the best is saved for last, with Nigel Patrick as the new superintendent of a home for the blind, a nightmare harbinger of Thatcherite free enterprise who feeds his dog the meat he denies his charges while spending the heating budget on paintings to adorn his office: inevitably he suffers an inventive and satisfyingly grisly fate.

BLOOD FOR DRACULA
AKA DRACULA CERCA SANGUE DI VERGINE E ... MORI DI SETE; DRACULA VUOLE VIVERE: CERCA SANGUE DI VERGINA; ANDY WARHOL'S YOUNG DRACULA; ANDY WARHOL'S DRACULA

1973, It/Fr, dir/scr Paul Morrissey, starring Udo Kier, Vittorio de Sica, Joe Dallesandro, Maxime McKendry

Forced to leave Romania due to the lack of virgin blood, Dracula travels to Italy where he is told that unmarried Catholic women are virgins. Presented as an aristocrat seeking a bride, he is invited to stay with the di Fiore family, who have four unmarried daughters, but soon finds that Mario the handyman has got there first. Shot back to back with **Flesh for Frankenstein**, another Warhol co-production, this lacks the earlier film's 3-D gimmick but benefits from sumptuous visuals, splendidly decayed locations, more mature characterization and a wonderful cameo from an uncredited Roman Polanski. Both Dracula and the di Fiores are decadent aristocrats who need fresh blood in order to survive the revolution Mario dreams of (the surly handyman has painted a hammer and sickle on his wall). Dracula, the putative villain of the piece, is in fact its most sympathetic character, retaining a dignity even through his pallid bouts of vomiting and terminal listlessness. Two of the sisters are portrayed as vacuously oversexed, toying with each other when Mario is spent; their mother's only concern is to preserve their class status – when she finds Mario deflowering the youngest daughter, Perla, she cries, "My God! You're just an employee!"; and their father, a poet without an audience, has ruined the family with his gambling debts. Dracula's assistant is no better, a ruthless but ineffectual pander who offers to betray the Count when caught; and Mario's selfless plan to save Perla is as unconvincing as his political slogans, as he never approaches Esmeralda, the virginal eldest daughter, with a similar offer. She offers herself to Dracula, and the consummation takes place off-screen, their relationship too dignified for the other sisters' soft-core posings.

LA CAMPANA DEL INFIERNO
AKA THE BELL FROM HELL; A BELL FROM HELL; THE BELLS

1973, Sp, dir Claudio Guerín Hill, scr Santiago Moncada, starring Renaud Verley, Viveca Lindfors, Alfredo Mayo, Maribel Martín

Guerín Hill had already established a reputation as an arthouse director before making the marvellously assured *La Campana*, choosing, like Vicente Aranda with **La Novia Ensagrateda**, to mask politically subversive intentions in a genre production. The film opens with John's release from a mental institution and his return home to confront the aunt who had him committed. John is an archetypal disaffected youth, whose activities – running away from home to travel around Europe, riding a motorbike, playing practical jokes, enjoying casual sex – represent a youthful freedom that must be punished through cynical incarceration, as his aunt pays the director of a psychiatric institute to keep him committed while she spends his inheritance. Madness is here explicitly a form of social

---

*OPPOSITE: A spectacular limb-lopping from **Blood for Dracula**.*

control, the institute a prison for those who refuse to adhere to the Francoist code of family, nation and church, here represented by a group of hunters, clearly pillars of their community, who are on the verge of raping a mute girl before John interrupts them. Yet, while John is the central identification figure, he remains ambiguous and at least partly monstrous, his elaborate plans for revenge hinting that he is indeed psychotic. An angry energy informs both his practical jokes, edgily anarchic pranks and Guerín Hill's exquisite visual style, marrying jarring juxtapositions (a white flower by the carnage of a slaughterhouse; the languid movements of a goldfish as a man is drowned in its tank) and rich symbolism with a barrage of unusual camera angles and compositions. Guerín Hill fell to his death from the bell tower featured in the film on the final day of shooting; the film was completed by the star of the "New Spanish Cinema", Juan Antonio Bardem.

DON'T LOOK IN THE BASEMENT
AKA THE FORGOTTEN

1973, US, dir S.F. Brownrigg, scr Tim Pope, starring Gene Ross, Anne MacAdams, Rosie Holotik, William Bill McGhee

Nurse Beale gains employment at a private mental home run by the progressive Dr Stephens, who "doesn't believe in the doctor-patient relationship". It's not long before the patients are expressing the same view, and Nurse Beale must struggle to keep her own sanity as the asylum rings to the sounds of screaming, and chopping, and tearing, and stabbing.

Despite having made four great horror films in the early-to-mid-'70s, Texas-based S.F. Brownrigg, who died in 1996, has never really received the sort of cult adulation extended to other US horror specialists. This, his first film, is admittedly the only one to rival, say, H.G. Lewis's level of gore, but even here Brownrigg's downbeat approach, and his commitment to quality acting from a skilful repertory cast, bar him from the more popular regions of "camp" or "trash".

Initially known as *The Forgotten* (you can see why *that* title had to go), *Don't Look in the Basement* parades a procession of grotesques. Although relatively straight-faced, the film is nevertheless great fun: there's a sinister crone who recites creepy poetry and issues warnings to get out before it's too late – that is, until her tongue is removed. There's a paranoid soldier awaiting attack; a hulking Lenny-ish child-man; a deranged woman mothering a doll; and a guilt-ridden ex-judge obsessed with his past, who's a little *too* fond of Dr Stephens's axe. Key among the staff is Dr Masters (MacAdams), a matriarch with a rather inflexible view of her position. MacAdams not only acted in Brownrigg's films but also worked extensively behind the camera, often directing the actors herself and providing the technically oriented Brownrigg with creative support.

Wildly gory though the latter stages are, it's typical of the Brownrigg experience that we should be left at the end with feelings more of sadness than of horror. Compassionate without being sentimental, his concern for the emotional life of his characters is idiosyncratic in a field more frequently dominated by *Grand-Guignol* humour or seething nihilism. [ST]

GIALLO

The *giallo* is an Italian film genre in which the murder-mystery format pioneered by Hitchcock is taken to baroque extremes, verging on, and sometimes overlapping with, horror. Violent death is fetishized and plotting so convoluted that it borders on the ridiculous. The overall tone is cynical, with Janus-faced characters exhibiting a staggering array of moral shortcomings, sexual perversions and multiple identities. Suspicion is ubiquitous because *everyone* is hiding something; a male in a *giallo* film can't so much as shave without suggestively fondling his straight razor and staring ambiguously in the mirror. Females are either duplicitous harridans or cowering unfortunates having their happy thoughts bashed from their heads with a blunt instrument. The use of subjective camera allows the killer – whose identity the *giallo* filmmaker will do *anything* to obscure – to flit with credulity-straining ease from crime scene to blood-caked crime scene. Reliable plot information is deferred so that the films never "play fair" and the killer's motives are usually as absurd as his methods are elaborate. That's if he *is* a "he".

The word *giallo* – meaning "yellow" in Italian – first cropped up as a genre term via pulp literature: between the '30s and the '60s, vast numbers of mystery-thrillers were published in Italy with distinctive bright yellow covers. The literary *giallo* is a wider genre but the Italian film is generally considered a *giallo* if it features a series of sadistic murders performed by a mystery killer: with various details – the killer's garb of mask, black coat and gloves, for instance, or a decorative and largely meaningless title – as optional extras. Sex is also omni-present, often outrageously entangled with the killings.

The first real *giallo* film was directed by the great Mario Bava: *La Ragazza che Sapeva Troppo/The Evil Eye* (1962) tells of a young woman arriving in Rome to visit her sick aunt, only to find herself embroiled in mysterious intrigue. It's a fun romp, filmed in cool black and white: but its importance is eclipsed by Bava's next *giallo*, **Sei Donne per l'Assassino**, a magnificent achievement in colour-drenched delirium. Bava goes mad with his pulsing colours, prowling camera, ornamentally outrageous décor and brutal scenes of violence. Someone is killing off the models at a *haute couture* fashion house, using methods as nasty as the models are desirable. There's a slightly old-Hollywood feel to the fashion-house setting, but Bava directs with a distinctly modern taste for

excess and the six killings are masterpieces of stylish cruelty. Bava went on to direct two more *gialli*: *5 Bambole per la Luna d'Agosto/Five Dolls for an August Moon* (1969) is an essentially frivolous piece, an orgy of zoom lenses, sexy nonsense and bad décor. Better by far is **Ecologia del Delitto**, which took the genre by the throat, upping the murders in both frequency and severity and amplifying the director's underlying cynicism into genuine black irony.

Dario Argento arrived on the international film scene in 1970 with his stunning debut, **L'Uccello dalle Piume di Cristallo**. This inventive, remorseless *giallo*, about an alienated artist who witnesses a murder in a chic art gallery and becomes obsessed with solving the crime, adds a cold, crisp energy to Bava's template and a powerful sense of paranoia and malice. Argento followed it with the rather dull *Il Gatto a Nove Code/The Cat o'Nine Tails* (1971) and *4 Mosche di Velluto Grigio/Four Flies on Grey Velvet* (1971), which struggles to connect some outstanding *giallo* set-pieces with misguided attempts at humour and terrible scripting. It was only with **Profondo Rosso** that Argento made a quantum leap forward, taking graphic murders to grandiose heights, and letting his imagination for the camera run riot. **Profondo Rosso** is an unfettered *giallo*, a wild, echoing labyrinth of rhymes, precognitions and quasi-supernatural eeriness. Argento returned to the *giallo* in 1983 with **Tenebrae**, a self-reflexive tale about a writer of murder mysteries who arrives in Rome to find that a serial killer is murdering women in homage to his books. Another triumph, **Tenebrae** transcends the *giallo*'s limitations, rewrites its sexual politics and comments on its roots. However, there are only traces of *giallo* in the woefully wonky *Phenomena* (1985) and the excellent **Opera**; *Trauma* (1993) marks the beginning of Argento's decadent, self-referential phase while *Nonhosonno/Sleepless* (2000) plays like a *giallo* greatest-hits compendium.

Lucio Fulci entered the field at the periphery, with *Una sull'Altra/One on Top of the Other* (1969). This characteristically morbid and melancholic thriller lacks the usual emphasis on the body count, instead taking its cue from Hitchcock's *Vertigo* (1958) and Romolo Guerrieri's proto-*giallo Il Dolce Corpo di Deborah/The Sweet Body of Deborah* (1968). Fulci scored a direct hit with *Una Lucertola con la Pelle di Donna/A Lizard in a Woman's Skin* (1971), which demonstrates both his pessimism and his developing sense of style. Starring the icy, aristocratic Florinda Bolkan as a woman accused of real-life murders that we've already seen her committing in a dream, it ropes in all manner of psychedelic visual tricks and convolutions, as well as straying into out-and-out horror, in scenes such as one in which Bolkan enters an off-limits hospital laboratory and sees horrific experiments carried out on flayed, whimpering dogs. With its ravishing score by Morricone and haunting imagery, it shows Fulci – later known as a master of the *irrational* – at his most impressively coherent. **Non Si Sevezia un Paperino**/*Don't Torture a Duckling* (1972) was another triumph: Fulci stretches the definition of the *giallo* by setting the film in a poor peasant region of Italy and making the murder victims young boys rather than chic urban beauties. His digs at contemporary Italian society are a mile away from the frequently trite motivations of the genre. *Sette Note in Nero*/*The Psychic* (1977) is a woefully underrated work, a paranormal *giallo* based around precognition and destiny, and *Lo Squartatore di New York*/*The New York Ripper* (1982) takes the format's sex-and-violence into orbit.

So much for high class. If it's exuberance you're looking for, Sergio Martino is your man. His quintet of gialli – *Lo Strano Vizio della Signora Wardh*/*Next!* (1970); *La Coda dello Scorpione*/*The Case of the Scorpion's Tail* (1970); *Tutti i Colori del Buio*/*They're Coming To Get You* (1972); *Il Tuo Vizio e' Una Stanza Chiusa e' Solo Io ne ho la Chiave*/*Gently Before She Dies* (1972); and *I Corpo Presentano Trace di Violenza Carnale*/*Torso* (1973) – all have their shocking and stylish moments and are efficient, if ultimately glib. Umberto

Lenzi's *giallo* offerings are light years ahead of his infamous cannibal movies: *Il Coltello di Ghiaccio*/*Knife of Ice* (1972) and *Sette Orchidee Macchiate di Rosso*/*Seven Bloodstained Orchids* (1972) are great fun and even the nonsensical *Spasmo* (1974) and hilarious *Gatti Rossi in un Labirinto di Vetro*/*Eyeball* (1974) have their charms.

The great unwashed of the genre include trashy treats like *Perché Quelle Strane Gocce di Sangue sul Corpo di Jennifer?*/*The Case of the Bloody Iris* (Giuliano Carmineo, 1972); *7 Scialli di Seta Gialla*/*Crimes of the Black Cat* (Sergio Pastore, 1972); *La Bestia Uccide a Sangue Freddo*/*Slaughter Hotel* (Fernando Di Leo, 1971); *Alla Ricera del Piacere*/*Amuck!* (Silvio Amadio, 1971); and the title that tells you all you need to know about the scuzzier denizens of *giallo*-land, *Nude per l'Assassino*/*Strip Nude for Your Killer* (Andrea Bianchi, 1975). There are over two hundred *gialli* lurking in the nether regions of Italian cinema, waiting to be explored.

It is probably a mistake to talk of "American *giallos*" or "British *giallos*". With a form already so loosely defined, the Italian flavour is pivotal. Italian co-productions with Spain, like the deliriously camp *La Volpe dalla Coda di Velluto*/*In the Eye of the Hurricane* (1972), occasionally blur the boundaries, but if you can tick off "Italian", "Murders", "Sex", "Sleaze" and "Style" you're probably on the right track! [ST]

BELOW: Marc (David Hemmings) arrives too late to save Helga (Macha Meril) in Argento's exemplary **Profondo Rosso**.

DON'T LOOK NOW

*1973, UK/It, dir Nicolas Roeg, scr Allan Scott, Chris Bryant, starring
Donald Sutherland, Julie Christie, Celia Matania, Hilary Mason*

After the death by drowning of their young daughter Christine, John and Laura Baxter travel to Venice. There they encounter an elderly psychic who claims she can see Christine's spirit. Initially, only Laura believes, but gradually John's angry scepticism gives

way as he experiences visions of his own, including a tiny figure in a red raincoat flitting through the Venice streets.

A jewel in the crown of British cinema, this masterpiece by one of our greatest living directors cannot be overpraised: it's food for the heart, the mind and the eye. Nicolas Roeg, working from Daphne du Maurier's short story, delivers not only his most commercial film of the '70s but also a benchmark by which the genre can measure its ambition. By using primarily visual means to create a complex lattice of information (Roeg is an outstanding cinematographer who also excels at non-linear editing), he proves that wider audiences will accept avant-garde techniques

BELOW: Donald Sutherland is sceptical of Julie Christie's psychic beliefs, **Don't Look Now**.

if they're supported by an emotionally accessible human drama. Parapsychology gives Roeg a perfect opportunity to play with form (since what is at stake here is the "form" of reality itself), yet he never overbalances into experimentation for its own sake. Instead, intricate reflections on precognition and fate are allied to a heartbreaking study of loss. Only the stoniest viewer could fail to empathize, for instance, during the scene in which John tries to rescue his daughter, and yet Roeg shoots the scene as an associative whorl of impressions – "Beyond the Fragile Geometry of Space", as a briefly glimpsed book cover suggests. And so it goes, as the grief-embittered John discovers there's more to reality than meets the sceptic's eye, leading to a mind-blowing finale that redeems one of the hoariest clichés in the book – a scene even more powerful and moving than the frank, explicit sex scene between Sutherland and Christie, which attracted all the press at the time. Still devastating today, *Don't Look Now* is as good as the genre gets. [ST]

THE EXORCIST

1973, US, dir William Friedkin, scr William Peter Blatty, starring Ellen Burstyn, Max von Sydow, Jason Miller, Linda Blair

Chris MacNeil's daughter Regan undergoes a series of medical tests after displaying a range of bizarre behaviour. When the medical tests reveal nothing, an exorcism is suggested – Regan is convinced she is possessed – and MacNeil approaches Father Karras, a local priest whose faith is in crisis.

Rather than choosing an investment banker or politician, the demon opts for the body of a 12-year-old girl, whose possession is couched in almost entirely sexual terms. Friedkin's ecstatically vulgar take on teen rebellion sees Regan rejecting her mother's preferred state of exaggerated infantilism for a lewd line in fruity insults, grabbing a doctor's balls and masturbating with a crucifix before literally rubbing her mother's face in her newfound sexuality. The systems used to nip this worm in the bud range from medicine, as Regan is subjected to a barrage of tests recalling mediaeval tortures, to Catholicism, the film unwittingly exposing patriarchal religion's obsession with the control of female bodies. The torments Regan is put through are so brutish that it's hard not to sympathize with her as she vomits on a priest. The film's conservatism goes further: MacNeil, a single mother whose marital status is hinted at as being responsible for Regan's condition, is acting in a film about student revolt that exhorts radicals to work within the system; and the poverty and insanity glimpsed in Washington's slums are explained less as the product of social factors than as the work of the Devil. The message is clear: be ashamed of your body, fear sexuality, trust priests and avoid change. Yet, subtexts aside, the film is not ineffective: the interplay of light and dark, noise and silence, builds up to a ferocious intensity for the later scenes

---

BELOW: Linda Blair turns heads in **The Exorcist**.

with Regan, and the visual effects – many of which look faintly ludicrous today – are underpinned by a devastating sound design, from Mercedes McCambridge's multi-tracked demon voices to the subtle creaking of Regan's head turning 180 degrees. Tapping into a countercultural burnout and consequent return to establishment values, the film was, of course, a horror phenomenon, quoted as being responsible for everything from miscarriages to suicides, and alternately celebrated and vilified by religious groups that took its purported conviction entirely seriously. It also remains the highest-grossing horror film ever, drawing audiences who would never have stooped to watching a genre product, kickstarting horror industries around the globe and marking a new era in effects-heavy horror that privileged disgust over fear. The film was re-released and re-edited on its 25th anniversary as "the version you've never seen", featuring previously excised footage including the "spider walk" scene.

FLESH FOR FRANKENSTEIN
AKA IL MOSTRO È IN TAVOLA
... BARONE FRANKENSTEIN;
CARNE PER FRANKENSTEIN;
ANDY WARHOL'S FRANKENSTEIN;
FRANKENSTEIN;
THE FRANKENSTEIN EXPERIMENT;
WARHOL'S FRANKENSTEIN;
UP FRANKENSTEIN;
THE DEVIL AND DR FRANKENSTEIN
1973, It/Fr, dir/scr Paul Morrissey, starring Udo Kier, Monique Von Vooren, Joe Dallesandro, Carlo Mancini

The first of two "Andy Warhol Presents" gothic features co-produced by Warhol, this was released in 3D and has the usual tiresome set pieces of bats, intestines and spears flying towards the camera. Morrissey's strategy is to strip previous takes on Frankenstein and Dracula down to their bare bones, expose their sexual and political subtexts, and inflate them as lurid farce. Frankenstein is characteristically more interested in science than sex: here Kier's Baron, a skinny Peter Lorre with a weakness for hair oil, recounts his sexual disgust on visiting a brothel, and lies on top of his female creation, his fist inside her abdomen, in a grotesque parody of intercourse – "To know death, Otto, you have to fuck life in the gall bladder!" Frankenstein is typically an aristocrat who conducts experiments on peasants, the creature's mutiny emblematic of class revolt; here he is decadent enough to have actually married and fathered children with his own sister,

and his plans are only thwarted when Nicholas, the priapic peasant played by Dallesandro, discovers that his friend Sasha has been the subject of the Baron's experiments. As ever, Frankenstein is dogged by bad luck, first when he mistakenly perceives the homosexual Sasha as a suitable mate for his female creation, then with his bumbling assistant Otto's disastrous aping of his sexual practices. Ludicrous, gory and boasting a stately, reserved score that is completely at odds with the excesses on screen, *Flesh's* lavish presentation and splendid locations make it easy to watch, although the luscious visuals can't quite disguise Morrissey's pervasive disgust with his characters, and the throwaway feel stops this film from being as successful as **Blood for Dracula**.

HORROR HOSPITAL
AKA COMPUTER KILLERS
1973, UK, dir/co-scr Anthony Balch, co-scr Alan Watson, starring Michael Gough, Robin Askwith, Vanessa Shaw, Ellen Pollock

Jason, sacked from his job as band manager, goes on a "hairy holiday" to a health farm, where he meets the co-owner's niece, Julie. Together they discover that the health farm is a front for experiments in mind control, and that the doctor in charge hides a terrible secret. Balch had previously directed the experimental Burroughs films *Towers Open Fire* (1963) and *The Cut Ups* (1966), and brings a skewed take on youth culture to this supremely silly outing. Absurdly overplayed countercultural types are enticed to Dr Storm's health farm by the promise of "sex and fun for the under-30s" but once there find themselves battling the forces of control in their purest form, the establishment (represented by the old, crippled and disfigured Storm) feeding off the bodies of the young and beautiful for sexual ends. One freak arrives to "find my chick" and fights the cop-like biker guards, while the heroes' only hope of salvation lies with Storm's "freaky little dwarf" who is tired of being punished for his laziness. If Askwith, a familiar face in his day from appearances in endless British sex comedies, cannot help but irritate, the hamminess of the rest of the cast suits the story, Gough providing a career high as the evil megalomaniac. The film shares with **Scream and Scream Again** a super-spy feel – Storm's car is equipped with spinning blades; a room fills with poison gas – although, unlike Hessler's film, this is played strictly for laughs. With an engagingly bad monster, some off-colour dwarf humour and a hilarious brothel flashback, all in all *Horror Hospital* successfully offers perfect trash entertainment for undemanding moods.

LEMORA – A CHILD'S TALE OF THE SUPERNATURAL
AKA THE LEGENDARY CURSE OF LEMORA; LEMORA – LADY DRACULA

1973, US, dir/co-scr Richard Blackburn, co-scr Robert Fern, starring Lesley Gilb, Cheryl Smith, William Whitton, Richard Blackburn

A gangster shoots his wife and her lover, then flees. Years later, his daughter Lila receives a letter from Lemora asking her to visit her father, who is dying. She leaves the care of a clergyman to accept the invitation, only to find the land decimated by a mysterious plague that has left its inhabitants ravening beast people or white-faced ghouls.

Blackburn's only feature is a fable of budding female sexuality in the vein of **Valerie a Tyden Divu** and **The Company of Wolves**, and while it never approaches the richness of these films it has an eerie charm of its own. Although set in the '20s, Lemora's Southern gothic draws cinematic influences from '30s films such as **Island of Lost Souls** and **White Zombie**, seen through the prism of a peculiarly European sensibility, its natty gangsters, aristocratic vampires and furry werefolk all embodying the sexual hostility both feared and welcomed by the pious young teenager. The film's dream logic and reality slips give it a powerful sense of

oneiric fable: once Lila leaves the church, whose congregation is made solely of grim-faced matrons, she finds that everyone has a sexual interest in her, whether tinged by a desire to corrupt her youthful innocence (the bus attendant offers her sweets) or violence. Even the clergyman (Blackburn himself) struggles with his desire for her, and while the beast people and vampires in pitched battle may represent the forces of instinct and control, both are sexually interested in Lila – for the wide-eyed girl there is no escape. Overt horror content is thin on the ground, for all the nods to genre classics, but *Lemora*'s low-budget fairy tale, while hampered by poor make-up and uneven acting, still presents an imaginative, erotically charged account of sexual awakening that makes it well worth a look.

LISA E IL DIAVOLO
AKA LISA AND THE DEVIL

1973, It/Sp/W Ger, dir/co-scr Mario Bava, co-scr Roberto Natale, Giorgio Monlini, Leonardo Martin, José G Maesso, starring Telly Savalas, Elke Sommer, Alessio Orano, Alida Valli

Lisa Reiner is separated from her tour group in a Spanish village and hitches a lift with a couple whose car breaks down near a mansion. Its inhabitants seem to know Lisa, although she has met only Leandro, the butler, before; but why do they call her Elena, and who is the strange man who keeps following her

BELOW: Elke Sommer visits the mannequin workshop in **Lisa e il Diavolo**.

around? Bava's last great film is a fascinating but incoherent curio, **Carnival of Souls** retold as a '70s soap. The casting of a lollipop-sucking Savalas as the Devil, moaning bitterly about how much work he has to do while munching on a meringue and gargling spirits, is just one of the more bizarre flourishes in a film that roots its *Wizard of Oz* metaphysics in a tacky Spain of canapés and forbidden affairs, shot with a Vaseline smear that gives much of the running time the feel of a shampoo ad. The mansion itself is an Art Nouveau nightmare, its overwrought furnishings decked in hideous colour schemes, with only its ruined rooms and the chapel achieving any sense of gothic splendour; and the acting ranges from Orano's sub-Peter Lorre theatrics to Sommer's curiously flat Lisa, with only Valli escaping with her dignity intact. Yet the elliptical plot, in which characters shift to dummies and back again and Lisa seems condemned to repeat the same actions, gives the film a dislocated quality that recalls the irreducible strangeness of ghost-story masters Robert Aickman or Walter de la Mare, and the visuals and soundtrack occasionally gel for moments of astonishing beauty that rank with the best of Bava's work. After its reception to standing-room-only crowds at the 1973 Cannes Film Festival, the film vanished for several years, no international buyers being interested in its distribution. The producers called Bava back to shoot new scenes tapping into **The Exorcist**'s popularity, resulting in the appalling mess of *La Casa dell'Esorcismo/The House of Exorcism* (1975).

SISTERS

1973, US, dir/co-scr Brian De Palma, co-scr Louisa Rose, starring Margot Kidder, Jennifer Salt, Charles Durning, William Finley

A journalist, Grace Collier, witnesses a murder in a neighbouring flat. The police find no evidence, but Grace discovers that the owner of the flat, Danielle, was separated from her Siamese twin, Dominique, as an adult, and becomes convinced that Dominique is the murderer she saw. Brian De Palma's breakthrough film is a hugely entertaining psycho-thriller whose robust treatment of themes of castration, doubling and voyeurism have made it a popular playground for film theorists. Danielle is "so sweet, so responsive, so normal" in comparison to her sister's sullen, violent resentment while their doctor, Emile, falls in love with Danielle, but is sexually aroused by the danger Dominique represents and is finally as little able to suppress his masochistic desires as he is Dominique's rage. Dominique is punished for refusing to adhere to the "sweet ... responsive ... normal" model of femininity, De Palma drawing parallels with Grace's behaviour in an extraordinary hallucination sequence in which Grace identifies completely with Dominique. Like the "mad" sister, Grace too refuses to conform to stereotypes of femininity and suffers for it, her mother referring

BELOW: Butch (Vincent Price) gives a critic an electrifying hairdo, **Theater of Blood**. .

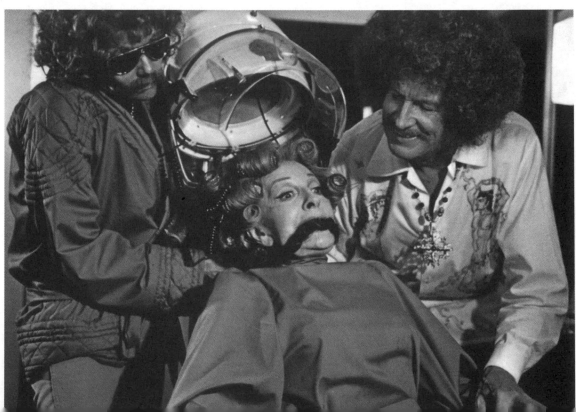

disparagingly to her job as a hobby to occupy her until she finds a husband, the police and private eye rejecting her ideas outright and her newspaper offering her only trivial assignments. De Palma keeps the pace cracking with his trademark Hitchcock nods and tense split-screen sequences, while a deliciously black humour is evident from the opening wink at Michael Powell's most notorious film, as the first victim meets Danielle on a TV show called *Peeping Toms*.

THEATER OF BLOOD

1973, UK, dir Douglas Hickox, scr Anthony Greville-Bell, starring Vincent Price, Diana Rigg, Ian Hendry, Harry Andrews

London theatre critics are being murdered in a variety of gruesome ways. Police are baffled until one critic notices that the deaths correspond to the last repertory season of Shakespearean actor Edward Lionheart, believed to have committed suicide in the Thames. A third Dr Phibes film in all but name, *Theater* improves on its forebears by being both gorier and funnier, and it underpins its gimmicky deaths with a genuine concern for its material, in a welcome change from the earlier films' flippancy. Lionheart is driven to suicide by rich, parasitic critics whose arrogance is matched only by their lack of creativity, and the film reclaims Shakespeare as being less for their cynical circles than for everyman, whether represented by the alcoholic street audience Lionheart now commands or the viewers of degraded pulp-like horror films, playfully worrying boundaries of high and low art

through a focus on the grisliness of the Bard's set-piece murders. Alternating derelict and opulent urban locations, filled with Dickensian street people with the anarchic energy of an early punk crowd, *Theater* also ranks as one of the best London horror films, particularly in the seedy metropolitan menace of the earlier scenes. Later, the comedy takes centre stage, although scenes such as Robert Morley being fed his two poodles in a pie or Price as afroed hairdresser Butch are audacious enough to maintain the momentum, and the jokes are backed up by a genuine sense of pathos, Price's readings of Shakespeare a fitting elegy to a bygone era of repertory theatre whose death is symbolized in the final inferno. One of Lionheart's reviews describes him as a "ham sandwich", recalling some of Price's own notices, but the actor's performance is superlative here, perhaps his best, while the familiar faces of the rest of the cast (including Michael Hordern, Arthur Lowe and Dennis Price) clearly relish their turns as pompous critics fully deserving their grisly fates.

THE WICKER MAN

1973, UK, dir Robert Hardy, scr Anthony Shaffer, starring Christopher Lee, Edward Woodward, Britt Ekland, Ingrid Pitt

Perfectly realized, flawlessly acted, and brilliantly scored, this exceptional contribution to maverick British cinema very nearly

BELOW: The fool reveals his true nature, **The Wicker Man**.

didn't get a release at all. British horror movies of the preceding decade had mostly been gothic or Wheatley-esque in flavour, whereas *The Wicker Man*, like **Blood on Satan's Claw**, used the old religions and calendar customs of the British Isles for inspiration – the *mise en scène* being rural/outdoorsy rather than funereal/camp. The bedrock idea is that of a clash of faiths – between Woodward's uptight Calvinist policeman (Sergeant Howie) and the blatantly sexual, heathen practices of the inhabitants of Summerisle, where he is lured to investigate the disappearance of a young girl. After a meeting with the titular lord and magus Summerisle – played with relish by Lee – Howie swiftly concludes that the girl has been "murdered under circumstances of pagan barbarity". His investigations are thwarted at every turn by a conspiratorial series of red herrings as he binds himself ever tighter in the islanders' trap, culminating in one of the most chilling dénouements in cinema. The production company British Lion changed management during shooting; its new bosses were arrogantly dismissive of the film and primed it to sink into obscurity, although it eventually got a release as the warm-up to **Don't Look Now**. A number of versions exist, the most-often watched being the "short version" of 87 minutes, while the "director's cut" at 99 minutes includes scenes that thematically top and tail the movie and better explain the pagan practices. Most notably absent from the short version is a sequence where Lee, quoting poetry by Walt Whitman, brings the handsome teenager Ash Buchanan to Ekland for ritual deflowering. The film's survival is due in large part to Lee, who galvanized deserved critical acclaim on its release. The haunting soundtrack, conceived by Phillip Giovanni, is based on original British folk music. Remade in 2006 as a Nicolas Cage vehicle by a slumming Neil LaBute.[KS]

DIE ZÄRTLICHKEIT DER WÖLFE
AKA TENDERNESS OF THE WOLVES
1973, W Ger, dir Ulli Lommel, scr Kurt Raab, starring Kurt Raab, Jeff Roden, Margit Carstensen, Wolfgang Schenk

Post-war Germany. Creepy, ingratiating police informant Fritz Haarman rapes and kills young boys, drinking their blood and then selling their flesh on the black market. His sick desire is made easier to indulge by a corrupt police force and the war-weary lack of interest of the townspeople.

Basing his directing debut on the real-life case of Fritz Haarman, who was executed in 1925, Fassbinder protégé Ulli Lommel relocated the story to the shattered Germany of the late '40s (a cost-cutting suggestion from Fassbinder himself,

who produced and acted in the film). Featuring the Fassbinder repertory stars Carstensen, Schenk and El Hedi Ben Salem, *Die Zärtlichkeit* has some alarming moments of visceral horror, but its greatest strength is Kurt Raab, whose multi-shaded portrayal of Haarman ranks with the best work in the genre.

The killings are alluded to more often than they're shown; apart from one sequence in the middle, and another at the end, Lommel measures the escalating body-count in melancholy fashion, by observing details such as the disposal of victims' clothes. A concern with social relationships of a frequently hypocritical nature permeates the film and provides some of the most insidious chills. Of course, everyone has their reasons; poverty is rife, an air of shell-shocked defeat hangs over the assorted store-owners, the *hausfraus*, hookers and spivs, and no one seems inclined to judge others, for to do so might liberate a whole barrel of worms. It was some time before ordinary Germans could absorb the enormity of the Holocaust and the tacit freedom allowed to Haarman implies the wider denial of unpalatable truths.

Technically, *Die Zärtlichkeit* is confident, if emotionally a little cool. The photography of grey-blue rainy streets and misty industrial environs is frequently compelling. Lommel's camera eschews flashiness in favour of unobtrusive set-ups, with just a few carefully controlled tracking shots to propel the ambience. And in Raab's smirking, bald-headed fiend, so wily, obsequious and pitiful, yet so terrifying and gluttonous when sucking blood from his victims, we see one of the most convincing human monstrosities of the cinema. [ST]

ALUCARDA
1974, Mex, dir Juan Lopez Moctezuma, scr Alexis T. Arroyo, starring Claudio Brook, Tina Romero, Susana Kamini, David Silva

Two girls, Justine and Alucarda, meet in a 19th-century convent. Alucarda shows the innocent Justine the delights of the outside world of sensual pleasure. In their wanderings, they fall under the influence of a strange gypsy man. This unleashes something evil in Alucarda and the two girls begin to indulge in Satanic practices. The Mother Superior calls in an exorcist. Blood, death and damnation ensue.

Although part of the "naughty nun" genre that began with Ken Russell's *The Devils* (1971), *Alucarda* is unique – much more theatrical even than Moctezuma's earlier **La Mansion de la Locura**. The film establishes a dark and oppressive atmosphere from the outset, with Alucarda's birth in a strange abandoned chapel decorated with demonic symbols. The later convent scenes have a musty, cavern-like appearance and the nuns seem to be cocooned in bloodstained bandages. The two girls' paganistic nature worship and discovery of dark forces outside the convent parallels their growing emotional and physical closeness. The final conflict, when the authorities try to separate them, is prolonged and bloody. The intensity of this last third of the film is almost overwhelming at times, the soundtrack filled to bursting with female shrieks and the screen consumed by blood and fire.

Brook, who plays three roles here, is more restrained than in **La Mansion de la Locura**, but Tina Romero as Alucarda is a revelation. Her performance is truly demented and genuinely

scary. Susana Kamini's Justine is more conventional, but she has one of the most memorable scenes in all horror cinema when she rises, naked, from a blood-filled coffin and attacks the nun who is praying for her. A sequel, *Alucarda Rises From the Tomb*, was scripted and planned, but Moctezuma was unable to raise finance for it. [PT]

BLACK CHRISTMAS

1974, Can, dir Bob Clark, scr Roy Moore, starring Olivia Hussey, Keir Dullea, Margot Kidder, John Saxon

A sorority house is plagued by obscene phone calls. One student's father arrives to pick her up, but she is missing; a

---

BELOW: Peter (Keir Dullea) takes Jessica's (Olivia Hussey) news badly, **Black Christmas**.

younger girl is found murdered. And Jess has some bad news to break to her boyfriend Pete.

Clark's effective proto-slasher set many of the genre's rules a few years early – the killer's identity is hidden through POV shots; victims are dispatched in various grisly ways using everyday objects; the killings take place around a particular calendar date; the killer has quasi-supernatural powers; and characters speak with Canadian accents (this is set in Canada, but many later US-set slashers were recognizably shot in Canada to cut costs) – yet, as with the early entries in any cycle, it proves more interesting than many of the films that followed. Rather than a gimmick to hang the film on, the Christmas setting is both an important plot detail (nobody notices that characters have gone missing, because it's assumed they've gone home for the holiday) and an ironic commentary on Jess's condition (she is pregnant, but does not want the child). These students are realistic individuals with credible student problems (pregnancy, abusive boyfriends, parents), and are not forced to take witless decisions to meet the killer. There's no correlation between characters' sexual behaviour and their fate and, in contrast to later slashers' focus on explicit display, Clark cuts away before most of the killings, concentrating instead on the disturbing sounds of the obscene phone calls. Also a key influence on any number of babysitter-in-peril TV movies, *Black Christmas* cheats a little in its POV misdirection and suffers from murkily brown visuals but it's the best of Clark's (*Children Shouldn't Play with Dead Things* ,1973; **Deathdream**) impressive genre efforts.

DERANGED

1974, US, dir/scr Alan Ormsby, Jeff Gillen, starring Roberts Blossom, Cosette Lee, Robert Warner, Marcia Diamond

Rural loner Ezra Cobb, unable to cope after his mother's death, digs up her corpse for company. Realizing that it needs patching up, he turns to grave-robbing then living people in his search for raw materials. Although it changes the names and several details, *Deranged* sticks far closer to the true story of Wisconsin maniac Ed Gein than other films purportedly based on his exploits (**The Texas Chain Saw Massacre**, **Psycho**, **The Silence of the Lambs**), and does so with far more verve than the recent biopic *Gein* (2000). Blossom's birdlike, sunken features and protuberant lower lip help make his committed performance utterly credible, and the film draws the viewer so far into his world of isolated rural madness that intrusions of

"normality" seem out of place. The journalist's commentary has a luridly sensationalist true-crime gloss at odds with the subtlety of Blossom's performance, and the first victim, an obese medium keen to pop Ezra's cherry, keeps our sympathies on his side. The true extent of his squalid bachelor derangement is only apparent when Mary, the second victim, stumbles across his collection of corpses and recycling efforts – "Hear this?" he asks, twanging a fiddle, "That ain't cat gut". As his victims grow more sympathetic, Ezra's actions become increasingly horrific, culminating in a shockingly grisly finale. Ezra never lies about his activities and is positively encouraged by his environment: a barfly, looking at Mary, asks him, "Wouldn't you like to tear off a piece of that? If I had the chance I'd bang her brains out," and Ezra promptly does both. Although the cast gleefully relish their cracker dialogue – "Maureen's the only woman I ever did trust. She's fat, that's why – a big heifer" – the acting is convincingly naturalistic throughout, and the dilapidated farmhouse locations and deerhunter milieu give the film an air of grubby authenticity that makes the shift from tongue-in-cheek humour to full-blown horror powerfully effective. The excellent effects are special-effects maestro Tom Savini's first feature work.

FRIGHTMARE
AKA FRIGHTMARE II

1974, UK, dir Pete Walker, scr David McGillivray, starring Rupert Davies, Sheila Keith, Deborah Fairfax, Paul Greenwood

Jackie's father Edmund and stepmother Dorothy have recently been released from an asylum and, in a bid to avoid Dorothy slipping back into the cannibal ways that had her committed, Jackie and Edmund have been feeding her animal brains. But it's soon clear that Dorothy has had a very serious relapse and that her daughter Debbie is following in her footsteps. Walker followed **House of Whipcord**'s attack on law-and-order fanatics with this broadside against the leniency and ineptitude of mental health authorities, but rather than a simple switch from liberal to conservative perspectives, *Frightmare*'s key theme – the inadequacy of overly rational systems in a chaotic universe – puts it squarely in a broader horror tradition. While the asylum authorities are implicitly attacked for having released Dorothy, the film's chief spokesman for the psychiatric viewpoint is Graham, an earnest and breathtakingly arrogant young man who hides his shyness behind thick glasses and psychiatric jargon. His interpretation of events is hilariously inept, and he soon discovers that in this world his reductive brain is only good for eating. The tone is bloody – characters are variously pitchforked, run through with red-hot pokers and have their brains drilled out – and grim, portraying an England of seedy industrial estates, car-park brawls and isolated rural dementia. But a marvellously ghoulish script and period detail (including the inevitable disco scene) give this a cracking pace and a great line in gallows humour, while Sheila Keith's performance as Dorothy, rambling about "the little animals" as she gives another gleefully deranged tarot reading, is a career high.

GHOST STORY

1974, UK, dir Stephen Weeks, scr Philip Norman and Rosemary Sutcliffe, starring Larry Dann, Murray Melvin, Vivian MacKerrell, Anthony Bate

Affable chump Talbot is reunited at a country mansion in '30s England with former university acquaintances McFayden and Duller, who is played with caddish flair by Vivian MacKerrell, the real-life inspiration for Withnail in *Withnail & I* (1997). Having lured Talbot there as bait for the Gothic pile's suspected ghosts, mannered McFayden and suave Duller bond in their upper-class disdain for his erotic postcards and pilchard suppers, while the sensitive Talbot is subjected to a full volley of supernatural terrors as the veil lifts on the unpleasantness that occurred in the house 40 years before.

The background story is approached through that stalwart of the uncanny, a Victorian child's doll, found in Talbot's room. It has been possessed by the spirit of its former mistress, Sophie, played by a woozy, beguiling Marianne Faithfull, who has been banished by her incestuously minded brother to a nearby insane asylum. Talbot then sees a sequence of time-slip scenes conveying the full cruelty and corruption of the Victorian asylum. So while McFayden practises the Charleston and Duller tires of the charade and leaves the party early, poor Talbot is dragged deeper into the psychological trauma of the past.

Weeks' film has echoes of other sinister house movies, especially **The Innocents** and **The Haunting**, but a low budget and simplistic use of the doll as a malevolent force undermine any sense of real terror. Instead, what shines through are the performances – the mesmerising Murray Melvin, in particular, seems to have stepped out of a Saki story. Equally noteworthy is the creepy sound design by Ron Geesin.

Ghost Story resonates with the familiar unease found in the English fictions of the 20th century's finest supernatural writers. With its tea gardens, summer houses, '30s fashions and a house riddled with evil intent, the overall sense is that of M.R. James colliding with P.G. Wodehouse: a disquieting yet cosy nostalgia piece perfect for a wet afternoon. [KS]

HOUSE OF WHIPCORD

1974, UK, dir Peter Walker, scr David McGillivray, starring Barbara Markham, Patrick Barr, Sheila Keith, Penny Irving

Model Ann-Marie accepts an invitation to spend a weekend at writer Mark's house, only to find herself imprisoned by former prison staff who, dismayed by the courts' perceived leniency (Ann-Marie has recently been fined for stripping in public), have decided to take matters into their own hands. This is the first of Walker's grimly effective horror gems (followed by **Frightmare** and *House of Mortal Sin*, 1975). Working with screenwriter David McGillivray and conceiving roles for the marvellously dour Sheila Keith seems to have galvanized Walker away from the tawdry sexploitation (*Cool it, Carol*, 1970) and bloodless thrillers (*Die Screaming, Marianne*, 1971) with which he'd made his name. Walker's sleaze background is evident here, the film playing like corporal-punishment porn with climaxes replaced by hangings – one contemporary reviewer dubbed it a "feeble fladge fantasy" – and no opportunity spared to display the more nubile characters' bare breasts. More unexpectedly problematic is the histrionic treatment of mental illness, here encapsulated in Mrs Wakehurst's demented ramblings, that plagues most of the Walker-McGillivray films: the even less flattering *Schizo* (1976) was met with protests from MIND about equating schizophrenia with violence. Yet there's much to enjoy here: the grimy atmosphere of the prison, with its petty guard rivalries, arbitrary rules and trestle-table mealtimes, is horribly evocative of an English boarding school; Keith is magnificent in her first major role, all mannered delivery and twitchy gaze subtly conveying the sadism fuelled by self-loathing and lust that drives the female jailers; and the film's surprisingly brutal tone, offset by the gaudy fashion crimes of its party scenes, sets it apart from similar women-in-prison scenarios as a genuinely unsettling experience. Only Irving disappoints as the irritatingly vacuous Ann-Marie, so self-obsessed that she fails to notice the danger signs in Mark's seductive spiel about steak knives ripping through skin.

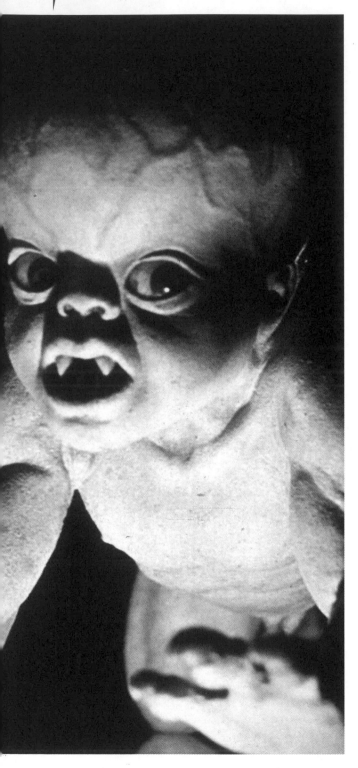

IT'S ALIVE

1974, US, dir/scr Larry Cohen, starring John Ryan, Sharon Farrell, Andrew Duggan, Guy Stockwell

When Lenore Davies's newborn baby decimates the staff of a delivery room before embarking on a city-wide killing spree, her husband Frank refuses to accept the child as his and insists on dispatching it himself. *It's Alive* plays its ludicrous fanged-baby premise entirely straight, focusing less on the mutant tyke's murderous rage than the effect of its birth on its father. Early on, Frank tells the police that as a child he'd confused Frankenstein with his creation – "Sometimes the identities get all mixed up". The baby may be doing the killing, but Frank's refusal to accept it as any relation makes him the true monster, a domestic liar and bully whose insistence that "I'm no different from anyone else" falls on deaf ears at his workplace. Whale's Frankenstein films also provide a title and general framework for understanding Cohen's genre work, Praetorius's "world of gods and monsters" where the director's interests lie. The baby is a powerful mutant, part superhuman and part monster, vanguard of a new breed explored, *X-Men*-style, in two sequels. Chemical contamination is implicated as responsible, a pharmaceuticals businessman bribing the hospital's doctor to destroy the baby's body and avoid potential lawsuits; but the film's cynical distrust of authority never obscures its metaphorical concerns, the baby embodying the difference Frank refuses to accept in himself. Cohen's style rarely draws attention to itself, the sole flourish the use of double vision for baby POV shots, but the handheld cameras and great location work, particularly the storm drains that close the film, anchor its absurd premise in a realistic setting. The subtly humorous touches of Lenore's milk-packed fridge and the baby's dissatisfaction with infant roles draw the film's exploration of collapsed family dynamics away from the grimness of the superficially similar **The Brood**.

RIGHT: A face only a mother could love. **It's Alive**.

NO PROFANAR EL SUEÑO DE LOS MUERTOS
AKA FIN DE SEMANA PARA LOS MUERTOS; NON SI DEVE PROFANARE IL SONNO DEI MORTI; THE LIVING DEAD AT THE MANCHESTER MORGUE; BREAKFAST AT THE MANCHESTER MORGUE; DON'T OPEN THE WINDOW

1974, Sp/It, dir Jorge Grau, scr Sandro Continenza, Muncello Coscia, Juan Cobos, Miguel Rubio, starring Cristina Galbó, Raymond Lovelock, Arthur Kennedy, Jeannine Mestre

When Edna knocks George's motorbike over at a garage, he insists that she takes him to the Peak District. They visit Edna's sister, whose husband has been killed by a zombie. George discovers that a government experiment in ultrasonic pest control is responsible for raising the dead, but the police won't believe his story. This multicultural film – shot in English, with principally Italian money and crew, location photography in the Peak District and interiors in Madrid and Rome – taps into the popular contemporary themes of pollution and establishment stupidity. A bravura opening sequence shows the vagaries of industrial Britain (intercut with a streaker, whose splash of colour goes unnoticed by the suited 'drones), and the Agriculture Agency witlessly tampers with nature. The police refuse to believe George's account of events, principally because of his long hair and beard, and hound him to the end: their blindness to the events around them, as with the zombified commuters shown earlier, draws the usual laboured parallels with the undead. The treatment of these themes is heavy-handed and inconsistent, but the claustrophobic intensity of the zombie attacks, using their shambling slowness to devastating effect, has rarely been bettered. Bucking Romero's rules, these zombies don't die when shot in the head, but are strong, intelligent enough to work together, capable of driving cars (even with broken legs) and very hungry. Benefiting from exceptional photography, great locations (the Peaks, shot with outmoded film stock for saturated red blood spilling on bright green grass, and the hospital used at the end) and impeccable sound design (it was promoted as the first stereo horror film), this transcends its political shortcomings for one of the finest zombie films outside of Romero.

PENDA'S FEN
1974, UK, dir Alan Clarke, scr David Rudkin, starring Spencer Banks, John Atkinson, Georgine Anderson, Ian Hogg

David Rudkin made his name in the '60s as a playwright, moving in the '70s into television, where he produced two outstanding films for the BBC, *Penda's Fen* and the bizarre fantasy drama *Artemis 81* (1981). All of Rudkin's work is distinguished by a powerful imagination and by juxtapositions of malevolent forces with scenes of physical and spiritual transcendence.

Penda's Fen explores Rudkin's familiar conflicts between the sacred and the profane, the torments of sexuality and freedom versus authority. Spencer Banks plays Stephen Franklin, a priggish teenager in his final school year whose view of himself and the world is turned around during the course of a summer. The story leads Steven through a series of confrontations – with his adopted parents, his neighbours and schoolteachers – and also with himself and his own inner demons, which literally manifest in one startling scene borrowed from Fuseli's painting "The Nightmare". Rudkin's technique of staging what amounts to a Manichean psychodrama in concrete terms gives us a series of striking and memorable images, with angels reflected in pools of water, a church floor split in two as a metaphor of spiritual crisis, and encounters with the ghosts of Edward Elgar and Penda, the last pagan king of England. These shade into outright horror with the appearance of the "sick mother and father", a couple modelled on Mary Whitehouse and her cohorts, who set fire to young, rebellious men and – in a nightmare sequence – chop the hands off children.

A powerful dramatist needs a powerful director and Rudkin received the most powerful of them in Alan Clarke, then polishing the style that would later give the BBC landmark television plays such as *Scum* (1977), *The Firm* (1988) and *Elephant* (1989). Clark's direction is typically visceral and direct, giving the supernatural a physical equivalence to the material world. *Penda's Fen* is one of the peaks of the BBC's *Play For Today* series and a highpoint of television drama, made at a time when the corporation dared to screen challenging material during primetime. [JC]

THE TEXAS CHAIN SAW MASSACRE

1974, US, dir/co-scr Tobe Hooper, co-scr Kim Henkel, starring Marilyn Burns, Jim Siedow, Edwin Neal, Gunnar Hansen

Hooper's peerless debut has yet to be bested as an evocation of the universal nightmare. The plot – four city folk come to a sticky end in the Texas boondocks – is the classic urbanoia set-up, down to the cannibal family (named the Sawyers, naturally, in the first sequel) having been mechanized out of their slaughterhouse work, but here Hooper leaves convention behind. Robert Burns's superlative art direction presents a dessicated, dusty aesthetic rare in this characteristically soggy genre, the house filled with feathers and bone sculptures and barely any gore shown on-screen despite the lurid promise of the title. No explanation is offered for the condition of the family, a funhouse reflection of both their victims and the nuclear family of TV sitcoms, but their grotesque habits and appearance – from Leatherface's mask of human skin to Grandpa's parchment features – are somehow utterly credible. Their attitude towards their victims – they have no interest in sex, simply laughing when Sally offers to "do anything" for them – shows that for them humans are merely things, bones to sit on or meat to eat: the true horror of Sally's experience is her reduction in status from a person to an object, and her consequent loss of control. The shots of sunspots opening the film and the woefully gloomy horoscopes read out by Pam suggest that the events are fated to happen, an inevitability mirrored in Hooper's use of a nightmare logic that sees time and space looping back on themselves, Leatherface eternally at Sally's heels as she flees but never quite catching up with her, and Sally escaping only to be dragged back to her captors. Yet for all its inverted fairy-tale mechanics it still looks realistic, the filmmakers' use of found locations and *Texas*'s graininess (it was shot on 16mm then blown up to 35mm) lending the film a sense of grim verisimilitude punctuated by the occasional startling composition and camera flourish. The humour of the film – the cook berates Leatherface for his chainsaw vandalism, and a long-suffering elder brother is vexed by the impish naughtiness of his charge – only adds to its horror, particularly in the appalling dinner sequence. The percussive score and ever-present chainsaw growl keep things cooking until Leatherface's final dance. A masterpiece, regrettably shadowed by a disposable franchise.

VAMPYRES
AKA BLOOD HUNGER; DAUGHTERS OF DARKNESS; DAUGHTERS OF DRACULA; MIDNIGHT SLAUGHTER; SATAN'S DAUGHTERS; THE VAMPIRE ORGY

1974, UK, dir/scr José Larraz, starring Marianne Morris, Anulka, Murray Brown, Brian Deacon

Fran and Miriam are bisexual vampires who lure passing motorists to their ramshackle mansion for sex and blood. But Fran keeps one of their victims, Ted, alive, and a couple caravanning nearby grow suspicious of their nocturnal activities. Shot entirely on location for just £42,000, Larraz's brazenly erotic entry in the lesbian vampire stakes has a very British focus on sexual guilt, curtain-twitching suspicion, large breasts and bad weather, betraying its director's Continental origins only through a sexual lyricism far removed from the contemporary nudge-nudge British attitude to sex. Morris and Anulka, clearly cast for looks rather than acting ability, struggle gamely through their portentous dialogue, but their transformation from sly voluptuaries to bestial feeders, mirrored in slow build-ups of tension that climax in increasingly disturbing bouts of blood lust, makes them more credible figures than their victims, weighed down by '70s hair and grotesque plaid jackets, and the stock innocents, happy campers John and Harriet. Their vampirism is presented as an extension of deviant sex play, the girls using knives rather than fangs to draw blood and Ted's listlessness presented as partly the effect of sexual draining. The sex and violence are both graphic and inextricably linked, repeated shots of blood on bare breasts and the eroticized frenzy of the attacks raising the hackles of censors worldwide, and the atmosphere in the mansion is one of cloying eroticism, the hand-held camera, lurking behind railings or plants, giving much of the film a sense of voyeuristic display. Even the frumpy Harriet is transformed through contact with the girls, ditching her homely woolly hat for a fetish outfit of high boots and raincoat for her trip to the house. Superlative cinematography – the woodland grounds of the mansion have a tangible dampness – and a distinctive, prog-inflected score help make this required viewing.

OPPOSITE: "My family's always been in meat." Gunnar Hansen in **The Texas Chain Saw Massacre**.

LA BÊTE
AKA THE BEAST

1975, Fr, dir/co-scr Walerian Borowczyk, co-scr Dominique Duvergné, starring Lisbeth Hummel, Sirpa Lane, Pierre Benedetti, Elisabeth Kaza

The Marquis de l'Esperance is keen to point out how humankind differs from the beasts. "Intelligence is what enables us to control our instincts," he declares somewhat hopelessly as, all around him, uncontrolled lust thrives. His family mansion and its inhabitants are relics of French aristocracy gone to seed, their survival dependent on the Marquis's impossibly hirsute son, Mathurin, marrying the wealthy young heiress Lucy Broadhurst. A simple-minded pagan, Mathurin harbours a dreadful physical secret that will inevitably throw the wedding plans into chaos. The Cardinal will not give the marriage his blessing, although the local pederast priest performs a baptism after Mathurin has been shaved. The pretence of his suitability as a husband must be maintained at all costs, as the Marquis dispatches *billets doux* and roses to Lucy's bedchamber in his son's name. Lucy is somewhat preoccupied by self-pleasure, however, dreaming of the 18th-century ancestor Marquise Romilda de L'Esperance being pursued, stripped and ravished by a hairy creature of the woods. This sequence, set to Scarlatti's harpsichord music, was originally filmed as an 18-minute short, *La Veritable Histoire de la Bête du Gevaudan*, devoid of any framing story. The creature is obviously a man

in an ungainly, unclassifiable "beast" costume, whose comically huge genitals ooze for the attentions of the svelte Marquise, and is almost endearing in his desperate attempts to find satisfaction. Lucy's masturbation is blatant and shot in close-up, earning the film the "slur" of pornography, although the erotic sequences are richly picaresque – rose petals are mashed into Lucy's sex and a snail inches stickily along Romilda's decorative shoe as she gives herself over to the beast. Short on terror, long on explicit sexual content, *La Bête* was banned from commercial screenings in the UK for 25 years. The movie's central themes are common to contemporary French cinema of the period: the corrupt decadence of the ruling class; a clergy fit for lampooning; and bourgeois panic at the liberation of the natural urges – yet, shot through Borowczyk's central-European fairy-tale lens, it remains a uniquely magical adult fable. [KS]

JAWS

1975, US, dir Stephen Spielberg, scr Peter Benchley, Carl Gottlieb, starring Roy Scheider, Robert Shaw, Richard Dreyfuss, Lorraine Gary

After a suspected shark attack off Amity Island, Chief Brody wants to close the beach, but the mayor worries that the bad publicity will ruin the 4 July celebrations. Two more people are eaten before a bounty hunter, Quint, is hired to kill the shark, taking Brody and Hooper, a scientist, with him. Although its key themes – fear of being eaten, fear of the water – mark this out as horror territory, the soundtrack (away from the shark attacks themselves) and general tone give *Jaws* a *Boy's Own* adventure feel, aligning it more with Spielberg's Indiana Jones movies than **Piranha**. Lacking the subtext of its ecologically aware creature-feature peers, or indeed any subtext at all apart from an anti-establishment sheen, finally displaced onto the shark, *Jaws* presents a pared-down narrative whose simplicity and drive resemble the shark itself. "All this machine does is swim, and eat, and make little sharks," but the film's most enduring legacy is less the rash of toothy rip-offs that followed than the way its blockbuster success helped to reshape the movie industry.

LEFT: "Come on into the water!" **Jaws**.

PICNIC AT HANGING ROCK

1975, Aust, dir Peter Weir, scr Cliff Green, starring Rachel Roberts,
Dominic Guard, Anne Lambert, Jane Vallis

On St Valentine's Day 1900 a party of schoolgirls from Appleyard College picnic at Hanging Rock. Four of them explore the rock, later followed by a schoolteacher, Miss McCraw. Only one, Edith, returns, although a young man, Michael, also picnicking at the Rock that day, finds a survivor, Irma, a week later. Weir's oneiric adaptation of Joan Lindsay's novel must have looked on paper like commercial suicide – a period mystery which is left unresolved – yet it proved an enormous critical and commercial success both at home and overseas. The film's aesthetic qualities aside, it's easy to see why it struck a chord in Australia: European mannerisms and dress are presented as dangerously inappropriate responses to the bush and the more "Australian" characters (principally servants and workers) are liberated and earthy compared to their stuffy, repressed Old World counterparts. The Rock itself is the touchstone for the conflict between the two mentalities, a million-year-old volcanic excrescence where the rules of time and space do not apply:

ABOVE: "Waiting a million years, just for us." **Picnic at Hanging Rock**.

the girls' response is either to strip off their stockings and shoes and mount the stones (presented variously as phallic peaks or vaginal crevices) or run away screaming. As a character study the film fails dismally – perhaps the most interesting character, Miss McCraw, vanishes early on, leaving the viewer to identify with the relatively dull Michael – save for Weir's treatment of the landscape itself as a character, the soundtrack's subdued groans at Irma's rescue hinting that the Rock is somehow alive. Once Irma returns, the film loses pace and direction, failing to marry the theme of the end of innocence (encapsulated in the survivor, now wearing a red cloak in contrast to the ethereal white dresses of the other girls) with the collapse of Appleyard College, and some of its imagery (Michael equates the girls with swans) plays to the European sensibilities the film purports to comment upon. But in its haunting evocation of the end of innocence, its undertones of sexuality repressed by moribund convention and its resistance to closure it remains an intriguing and often startlingly beautiful film.

PROFONDO ROSSO
AKA DEEP RED;
THE HATCHET MURDERS

1975, It, dir/co-scr Dario Argento, co-scr Bernardino Zapponi, starring David Hemmings, Daria Nicolodi, Gabriele Lavia, Macha Meril

When the English jazz pianist Marc Daly witnesses a murder in Rome, he becomes obsessed by the idea that something he has seen provides an essential clue to the case. A journalist, Gianna Brezzi, takes him at his word but, as Marc's investigation brings him to the heart of the mystery, the killer closes in. Argento's exemplary *giallo* follows the model of his debut **L'Uccello dalle Piume di Cristallo** but cranks the intensity up beyond anything the genre had previously offered, unmooring his camera from standard cinema grammar for disembodied POV swoops and pans of pure visual pleasure, presenting a series of luridly flamboyant set-piece murders that invite us to celebrate the killer's deft control of an insane world, and shattering narrative convention for a plot driven by absurdly contrived coincidences and incursions of the supernatural foreshadowing **Suspiria** and **Inferno**. Hemmings, cast for his role in the paradigmatic unsolvable mystery *Blow-Up* (1966), makes Marc one of Argento's most credible protagonists, his outmoded ideas about gender roles (put into sharp focus when Gianna beats him at arm-wrestling) matched only by his bumbling investigation, closer to Watson than Holmes. The crack on a wall revealing a painting hidden underneath represents the chaos about to flood Marc's securely ordered world, and Argento inverts standard models of detection to ensure that, while Marc's investigation appears to draw closer to the truth, finally he learns only about himself, the killer's identity eluding him to the end. But it's the bravura murders that cemented Argento's reputation among genre fans: just as the killer needs to play a lullaby before setting to work, Goblin's exhilarating jazz-rock score introduces each murder, all keyed for maximum visceral effect through the exaggeration of everyday, familiar injuries – scalding water, glass cuts, teeth rapped against hard surfaces – mixed with nonsensical flourishes (Giordani's dummy) and camera tricks whose only purpose is to confound and delight. Of the director's other *gialli*, only **Tenebrae** comes close to *Profondo Rosso*'s giddy richness.

SALÒ O LE 120 GIORNATE DI SODOMA
AKA SALO, OR THE 120 DAYS OF SODOM

1975, It, dir/scr Pier Paolo Pasolini, starring Paolo Bonacelli, Giorgio Cataldi, Umberto Paolo Quintavalle, Aldo Valletti

Pasolini's final film belongs to that select group of works for which issues of entertainment fall into irrelevance, and viewing becomes a question of endurance. Based on the Marquis de Sade's *120 Days of Sodom*, *Salò* pushed Pasolini's confrontational politics to an extreme and to similarly moral ends as the notorious Marquis and, like de

BELOW: Pasolini's bottom inspectors, **Salò**.

ECO-HORROR

The catastrophic consequences of man's witless tampering with nature underpin everything from mad science (though Frankenstein, at least, shows some interest in recycling) to zombies (the pesticides of **No Profanar el Sueño de los Muertos** and *Les Raisins de la Mort/The Grapes of Death*, 1978), mutants (**It's Alive**, **Scanners**) and creature features – whether in their '50s (*Attack of the Crab Monsters*, 1957) or '70s (*Kingdom of the Spiders*, 1977) incarnations. Many of these use a pollution theme as a hook to hang their plots on, their true interests lying elsewhere. More explicit environmental concerns are tackled by Colin Eggleston's *Long Weekend* (1977), a chilling blend of outback mysticism and revolt of nature in which the laws of time and space finally turn against a boorish litterbug; *Prophecy* (1979), John Frankenheimer's disastrous mercury-poisoned monster movie; **Reazione a Catena**, whose multiple murders begin when an unscrupulous developer targets a pristine bay; and *Clearcut* (1992), a politically correct cousin to *Cape Fear* (1991) in which a native American swears vengeance on the owner of a timber company logging in his Canadian homeland.

The theme also informs urbanoia films: **Deliverance**'s grizzled rapists may be responsible for Bobby's pig impersonation, but it's the river itself that breaks Lewis's leg and – perhaps – takes Drew's life. The mutant family of **The Hills Have Eyes** grew up on a nuclear test site and Leatherface in **The Texas Chain Saw Massacre** is intent on returning his urban victims to the food chain.

If **The Birds**, the paradigmatic revolt of nature movie, shows little interest in having our feathered friends eat anything except bits of scalp and a pair of eyes, other animals were quick to realize, like Leatherface, that the rending and tearing of human flesh for food meant big box office. **Jaws** provided a back-to-basics riff on the fear of being eaten, throwing out the eco-sensitivity retained by its aquatic spawn **Piranha**, and was matched in the human-dinner stakes by the self-explanatory *Bug* (1975), *Grizzly* (1976), *Barracuda* (1978), *Alligator* (1980) and *Orca the Killer Whale* (1977), the toothy worms of *Squirm* (1976), the intelligent ants of Saul Bass's hallucinatory *Phase IV* (1974) – and the giant carnivorous rabbits of *Night of the Lepus* (1972).

Occasionally, animal species teamed up to take vengeance on their smug oppressors, as in the imaginatively titled *Day of the*

ABOVE: The fearsome Great White.

Animals (1977), *Frogs* (1972) – "Millions of slimy bodies squirming everywhere – millions of gaping mouths!" promised the ads – the giant-chicken flick *Food of the Gods* (1976) and numerous zoo escapee movies. More specialist tastes were catered for by the crowded field of bee movies (*The Deadly Bees* (1967), *The Swarm* (1978), TV films *Killer Bees* (1974) and *The Savage Bees* (1976)).

Eco-horror has lost momentum since its '70s heyday, although animal attack films are still being made (*Bats*, 1999, *Eight Legged Freaks*, 2002, *Komodo*, 2003), alongside more idiosyncratic entries (Todd Haynes' *Safe*, 1995, Danny Boyle's *28 Days Later*, 2002). But the defining feature of most of these films is their comic ineptitude: it's anyone's guess whether the overwhelming hokiness of US eco-horror has kept the environment from being a salient political issue for the American electorate – but it certainly won't have helped.

Sade, Pasolini was vilified. Rather than make a historical drama rendered safe by distance, Pasolini updated de Sade and moved the location of the story to the final outpost of Italian Fascism in the province of Salò during the last days of the Second World War. Sade's spare tale of four thoroughly depraved leaders of society is easily transposed to Fascist Italy, with their modern counterparts of the Duke, Bishop, Magistrate and President retiring to a villa with their favourite prostitutes, a complement of handsome armed guards and a collection of young men and women whom they can systematically humiliate, rape, torture and murder. Pasolini borrows some of de Sade's rigorous structure while adding his own gloss of Marxist dialectic that seeks to condemn the hypocritical viewer as much as contemporary society.

In a world where killings appear live on websites, *Salò*'s impact may have diminished somewhat, but the mere fact that comparisons are routinely drawn between a work of fiction and documentary hell only points to its substantial and lasting power. Pasolini's minimal style offers no escape, with spartan sets, *verité* camera work and an unrelenting march towards inevitable butchery. In the process it steers possibly closer than the director intended to a kind of vicarious pornography that at least ensures that viewers ask themselves why they're watching this parade of atrocities. De Sade's lengthy philosophizings are replaced by various signifying texts but one has to wonder how much of Pasolini's moral flourishes survive the continual rapes and scenes of people being force-fed excrement. The final act of wholesale slaughter is a *tour de force* of grisly terror; what any viewer takes away from it all remains debatable. [JC]

SHIVERS
AKA THEY CAME FROM WITHIN; THE PARASITE MURDERS

1975, Can, dir/scr David Cronenberg, starring Paul Hampton, Joe Silver, Lynn Lowry, Allan Migicovsky

Dr Emil Hobbes, working on a project to develop parasites to act as organ replacements, has discovered that the parasites induce a sexual frenzy in their hosts. Believing that "man is an animal that thinks too much", he experiments with them on a teenager, only to kill her when he sees the results. But she has already spread the parasites around her other partners in the luxurious confines of Starliner Towers.

Cronenberg's first commercial feature remains his most viscerally shocking film, reflecting his desire to "show the unshowable, speak the unspeakable". The parasites themselves seem designed to look and behave in the most offensive manner possible, in appearance halfway between a turd and a phallus and variously leaping onto faces with wet squelching sounds, writhing around under characters' skins, passing from mouth to mouth or invading Barbara Steele's vagina; and the sexual acts they inspire are similarly grotesque, running the gamut of deviant practices from incest to gerontophilia and brutal rape. But anyone might agree with Hobbes after spending a few hours in Starliner Towers, a clinically sterile environment sold to prospective tenants with lines like "Sail through life in quiet and comfort". The film exaggerates the Cartesian mind/body split and displays both in their most horrific forms, the sex-crazed hosts representing the body run amok while the apartment complex is its equally unpleasant opposite, a pure, emotionless mind. The film's protagonist, Dr St Luc, is a doggedly rational figure more aligned with the latter, resisting not only the attacks of the infected but also his girlfriend's earlier come-ons: he inspires no audience sympathy, and his final relinquishing of control seems if anything a positive act. The audience is more likely to identify with tenant Janine Tudor, whose marriage is collapsing even before the film starts: her naturalistic portrayal anticipates the exquisite melancholia of Cronenberg's later work. Although *Shivers* draws on other films (**Invasion of the Body Snatchers**, **Night of the Living Dead**) and has parallels with J.G. Ballard's novel *High Rise*, the sensibility is uniquely Cronenberg's, a disgusted fascination with its mind/body, control/chaos dialectics tempered by a playful, ironic humour. As a pure expression of "body horror", a term essentially coined to describe Cronenberg's early features, it has yet to be topped.

CARRIE

1976, US, dir Brian De Palma, scr Lawrence D Cohen, starring Sissy Spacek, Piper Laurie, Amy Irving, William Katt

Carrie is the school misfit, mocked in the film's opening for her naïve horror when she begins to menstruate in the communal showers and receiving no comfort at home from her sin-obsessed mother. She's frail and seemingly powerless but her budding sexuality is accompanied by growing telekinetic powers and, when she's set up for a cruel practical joke at her senior prom, her repressed anger is given free rein. The film, which by allowing the audience to share the other characters' disdain for the genuinely odd Carrie makes them complicit in her torment, was followed in the '80s by a spate of misfit-as-heroine teen movies in which the audience was asked to see the swan inside the duckling. But in a post-Columbine age, it is *Carrie*'s insistence that the misfit should be feared as well as pitied which has the greater resonance.

Carrie was De Palma's first big hit, as well as the first novel by Stephen King to be adapted into a movie, but it remains one of the most successful big-screen transitions of the writer's work, perhaps because a relatively limited budget forced the film to find its shocks in something other than spectacular effects. It picked up two Oscar nominations, best actress for Spacek as the eponymous teen and best supporting actress for Laurie, returning to the screen after a long absence, as the ultra-religious mother. The performances certainly contribute to the film's success, with Spacek's peculiar Carrie never begging for the audience's sympathy or love. They're aided by a thoughtful screenplay from Cohen (not to be confused with the director of **It's Alive**), who would later script a well-regarded TV adaptation of King's It. Credit too must go to de Palma's imaginative camera work, including a trailblazing six-minute slow-motion scene and a memorable sequence in which the camera circles a dancing Carrie. The 1999 sequel has virtually nothing to recommend it. [RL]

LA CASA DALLE FINESTRE CHE RIDONO
AKA THE HOUSE WITH THE LAUGHING WINDOWS

1976, It, dir/co-scr Pupi Avati, co-scr Antonio Avati, Gianni Cavina, Maurizio Costanzo, starring Lino Capolicchio, Francesca Marciano, Gianni Cavuna, Giulio Pizzirani

Northern Italy, in the '50s. Stefano is hired to restore a fresco of St Sebastian in a remote village church. Its painter, Ligniani, had died before finishing it and, as Stefano hears stories of the painter's obsession with death, he is warned to leave town. But when Antonio, a friend who promised to reveal the village's secrets, dies unexpectedly, he vows to solve the mystery.

Ligniani's desire to capture the authentic flavour of death in his art serves both to apparently isolate him in his madness and to provide an ironic commentary on the aims of the film; but as the story unfolds we learn that he is simply the most visible manifestation of an entire community's perverted interpretation of Christian ideas of sacrifice and resurrection. Avati's focus is less on providing a tight narrative than slowly building an atmosphere of dread that seems to come from the landscape itself: set in the director's native Emilia Romagna, *La Casa* makes much of its marshland setting, the crumbling paintwork and riotous

RIGHT: "They laughed at me!" Sissy Spacek is **Carrie**.

vegetation adding to a pervasive sense of decay and madness. If Capolicchio's Stefano is slightly flat, a cipher whose principal trait is a desire to know (which, typically, endangers his girlfriend), Avati populates the village with a gallery of more memorable grotesques, from Stefano's dwarfish employer to the village idiot, Lidio. The cumulative eeriness of shots such as the night-time discovery of a body in the green water and the titular house itself builds up to a genuinely shocking and violent conclusion, although the presentation of the final turn of the screw – based, according to Avati, on a true story – strains credibility.

COMMUNION
AKA ALICE, SWEET ALICE; HOLY TERROR
1976, US, dir/co-scr Alfred Sole, co-scr Rosemary Ritvo, starring Linda Miller, Mildred Clinton, Paula Sheppard, Niles McMaster

When Mrs Spages's daughter Karen is murdered just before her first communion, the chief suspect is her older sister Alice. But could a 12-year-old girl really be responsible for the series of brutal murders plaguing Patterson, New Jersey? Sole conceived *Communion* as a response to the Catholic Church's successful pursuit of an obscenity charge for his debut feature, *Deep Sleep* (1972), a satire on pornography. The film is set in 1961, year of the first Catholic presidency, and Sole effectively skewers the Church by contrasting its aura of sanctimonious innocence with the perversions harboured by its subjects, from Father Tom's housekeeper to the senile priest in her charge, whose childlike babblings point to the old/young dynamic at the heart of the film. In this *Communion* resembles **Don't Look Now**: the killer also wears a bright yellow raincoat, and Karen's father, seeking to understand her death, unwisely follows a childlike figure into a derelict building. The film's visual gloss, set-piece murders and soundtrack (featuring a child's lullaby) also recall **Profondo Rosso**, with a focus on necks, shins and teeth as sites of assault giving the violence a nastily Argento-ish physicality. The film's broadsides at organized religion are underpinned by the aura of perverse eroticism surrounding Alice. Virtually all the male characters, from the police to the grotesquely obese landlord and principal priest, take a sexual interest in the girl, whose confused response meshes with the film's inspired misdirection – for Sole the Church's pious obsession with female purity masks a morbidly unhealthy sexuality. Brooke Shields's performance as Karen ensured the film's re-release through the late '70s, although it never received its due attention in the proto-slasher

stakes: perhaps its tone of autumnal melancholia and edgy subject matter were too much.

GOD TOLD ME TO
AKA DEMON
1976, US, dir/scr Larry Cohen, starring Tony Lo Bianco, Deborah Raffin, Sandy Dennis, Sylvia Sidney

NYC is besieged by a series of random murders in which killers remorselessly pick off their families or strangers before explaining that "God told me to". The Catholic detective Peter Nicholas attempts to track down a young man, Bernard Phillips, implicated in the murders, but the more he learns about Phillips' background, the closer he comes to understanding the role he himself has to play. Cohen's bizarre conflation of alien abduction fantasies and Erich von Daniken's *Chariots of the Gods* results in one of the most fascinating entries in the '70s cycle of religious horror: here God is a bisexual alien hermaphrodite who invites his brother to mate with him and spawn a new race of hermaphrodite deities, thus ending an era of patriarchal control. Resembling J.G. Ballard's story "The Life and Death of God" in its apocalyptic depiction of the advent of God, greeted with added religious riots and a collapsing economy, the film pays more attention to the human impact on its key players, particularly Nicholas himself, peppering its confusing storyline with emotionally overwrought encounters between the detective and his wife and lovers and sepia-tinted flashbacks explaining the virgin births at the core of the tale. Phillips has gathered a group of bureaucrats to do his bidding, proving his existence to them by orchestrating the murders, explained by analogy to Old Testament plagues as the most effective demonstration of a deity's powers. However, Cohen seems less interested in implicit digs at organized religion than an exploration of religious conviction itself, the film's ending resisting the pious closure of the decade's other religious genre films. Cohen throws so many ideas at the screen that the narrative occasionally lapses into incoherence, but the hand-held camerawork, location shooting (depicting a Manhattan of seedy peepshows and, most impressively, a St Patrick's Day parade interrupted by a homicidal cop) and allusions to the Kennedy assassination and Charles Whitman case give the film's wild speculations a semi-documentary feel, with a sop to grindhouse patrons in a blaxploitation subplot recalling the director's work on *Black Caesar* (1973).

THE INCREDIBLE TORTURE SHOW

1976, US, dir/scr Joel M. Reed, starring Seamus O'Brien, Louie de Jesus, Niles McMaster, Viju Krim

Sardu's Theatre of the Macabre, in which women appear to be tortured and killed, is a hit with New York City audiences, but the critics are unimpressed. Yet Sardu, who runs a lucrative sideline selling slave women to a Middle Eastern dealer, craves critical acceptance and will stop at nothing to be accepted as an artist. Reed's zero-budget sleazefest, combining plot ideas from **A Bucket of Blood** and **The Wizard of Gore** with a sawn-off-shotgun offensiveness recalling early John Waters, is so absurdly tasteless that it's impossible, finally, to be offended by it – although that didn't stop Women Against Pornography shutting down theatrical showings in the US. Any film that involves a woman's head being shaved before her brains are sucked out through a straw is a lost cause against accusations of misogyny, although to be fair the perpetrator has his heart torn out in turn. The structure of the film brings it close to SM pornography, for all Sardu's conviction that "It's not SM! This is *art*!": the flimsy plot is little more than an excuse to parade scene after scene of naked women being tortured in inventively nasty ways. One is killed with an iron tourniquet around the head; another has her teeth pulled out; a ballerina's feet are sawn off with a chainsaw; and in the most authentically Sadean scene, a girl holding the rope of a guillotine in her mouth is caned, and decapitated when she screams. Sardu's dwarf sidekick Ralphus then uses the head for a blow job. Sardu's treatment of his slave girls is subtler and more realistic, and hence more disturbing: women are "trained" with electrodes to the nipples, and kept in a basement where they are fed raw meat and driven insane by captivity. This sounds rougher than it actually plays: the impact of the violence is invariably lessened by the strain of sick humour running through the film and the effects are so unconvincing that their cumulative impact is one of absurdity. Still, not for the easily offended.

LE LOCATAIRE
AKA THE TENANT

1976, Fr/US, dir/co-scr Roman Polanski, co-scr Gérard Brach, starring Roman Polanski, Isabelle Adjani, Melvyn Douglas, Jo Van Fleet

Polanski's third exploration of urban paranoia (after **Repulsion** and **Rosemary's Baby**) is based on a short novel by the French Surrealist Roland Topor, a writer and artist with a view of the world that manages to be even more pessimistic than that of the director. Having fled America after his statutory-rape arrest, Polanski found himself a Polish immigrant in Paris, a position that would have made him sympathetic to the character of Trelkovsky, an immigrant in the same city. This identification is sealed by Polanski playing the central role himself, a remarkable move considering how well he acquits himself in front of, as well as behind, the camera.

Topor's work presents the world as a place subject to sudden eruptions of cruelty and motiveless violence. *Le Locataire* offers a typically French take on his concerns with the violence emanating from the ritual humiliations of petit bourgeois society and a city that looks upon immigrants with suspicion or even contempt. Yet the title of the piece also refers to the previous tenant of Trelkovsky's cramped apartment, a young woman, Simone Shule, who went insane and leapt to her death from the window. The real horror unfolds by degrees as Trelkovsky comes to suspect first that the other tenants drove the woman to her death, then that they want him to become her and repeat the process. As with **Repulsion**, a simple idea becomes a brilliant study of progressive degeneration into madness, this time with an unwilling victim, certain of what is happening to him yet unable to resist. Subtle and disturbingly unexplained touches recur throughout, like the toilet wall covered in Egyptian hieroglyphics, and the posters of leering grotesque faces glimpsed in the streets. The film deviates from Topor only at the end with the implication that Trelkovsky is hallucinating his persecution. Topor had a more shocking suggestion, that the house and its aged tenants exist solely to process new tenants into paranoid, cross-dressing suicides. [JC]

NGAU WAN GONG TAU
AKA BLACK MAGIC 2

1976, HK, dir Ho Meng Hua, scr Ni Kuang, starring Lo Lieh, Ti Lung, Tanny Tien Ni, Lilly Lee

A doctor calls in two Hong Kong colleagues to help him investigate what he believes is an outbreak of black-magic-related sicknesses. At first the newcomers, a husband and wife, are unconvinced. The woman doctor volunteers herself as the subject for a magic spell. Soon the small group find themselves in the power of an evil sorcerer. He is creating an army of undead female zombies and keeps himself young by drinking human milk.

Like many of their black-magic movies, this Shaw Brothers production is set outside Hong Kong, in this case in Singapore, where the recent economic explosion, with its international hotels and high-rise office blocks, has not completely wiped out the old ways and traditions. We are treated to a whole ward full of cases of mysterious boils or attacks by vicious worms, all of which, we are told, must be the result of black magic. The film is trashier, faster paced and more full-blooded than its companion title, with barely a pause for breath between set pieces. The energetic direction from Ho Meng Hua even finds time for some martial-arts action between humans and zombies as well as a heart-stopping fight on a cable car high above the bay.

But what really makes the film work is the matter-of-fact way it presents its seemingly endless catalogue of the bizarre. At one point a "good magician" turns up to save the day. He beats the possessed Tanny about the face with a dead mongoose, cuts open her back to allow a horde of wriggly black worms to escape, then tears out his eyes and gives them to Ti Lung to eat. The director was a specialist in the more exotic Shaws titles, with *Xuedizi/Flying Guillotine* (1974), *You Gui Zi/Oily Maniac* (1976) and *Xing Xing Wang/The Mighty Peking Man* (1977) also to his name. [PT]

THE OMEN

1976, US, dir Richard Donner, scr David Seltzer, starring Gregory Peck, Lee Remick, David Warner, Billie Whitelaw

Director Richard Donner began his career working on scores of TV shows ranging from *The Twilight Zone* to *Kojak* and would later become best known for helming the mismatched-cop-template *Lethal Weapon* movies, but *The Omen* is perhaps his most iconic work. As much thriller as horror movie, the story follows the fateful adoption of a baby boy by the American ambassador to the UK to replace the newborn lost in childbirth by his wife. The baby, Damien, is gradually revealed to be the Antichrist, whose supernatural powers cause the grisly deaths of all who oppose him.

The film came late in the cycle of supernatural horror that includes **The Exorcist** and **Rosemary's Baby**, and adopted the most literal interpretation of its Christian source material, in this case the Book of Revelation. The religious iconography is effectively used, the uncovering of Damien's 666 birthmark being perhaps the most chilling moment in the film, and is unusual in its reliance on fundamentalist Protestant tropes in contrast to the ritualistic Catholicism of most Devil horror. The centrepiece death scenes, on the other hand, teeter precariously between the shocking and the risible, with Patrick Troughton's church-spire impaling the worst offender. Nevertheless, they are undoubtedly the moments for which the movie is best remembered and the forerunner of many subsequent staged slaughters.

The bombastic but effective choral score earned composer Jerry Goldsmith the only Oscar of a long career. Peck, who hadn't worked for five years before the film, delivers the material with complete conviction, and his quiet authority makes the improbable seem plausible. Rumours of a curse afflicting the movie, trading on stories of rottweilers attacking their trainers and the cast's plane being struck by lightning, added to the film's reputation as being far more frightening than it actually is. More dated now than the earlier occult horror films, it is best viewed as a sometimes creepy and occasionally absurd period piece. [RL]

¿QUIEN PUEDO MATAR A UN NIÑO?
AKA WHO CAN KILL A CHILD?; WOULD YOU KILL A CHILD?; DEATH IS CHILD'S PLAY; ISLAND OF DEATH; ISLAND OF THE DAMNED

1976, Sp, dir Narcisco Ibañez Sarrador, scr Luis Peñafiel, starring Lewis Fiander, Prunella Ransome, Antonio Iranzo, Miguel Narros

A young Englishman and his pregnant wife come to the coastal town of Benavis, en route to the remote island of Almanzora. When they reach the island, they find the place apparently deserted. Gradually, after the discovery of a body or two, they begin to guess the awful truth. The island's children have risen up against their elders and slaughtered them. And they are to be the next victims.

One of the more fondly regarded products of Spain's horror boom of the '70s, the film is successful for several reasons, but largely due to the believability of its location. There is something about southern European towns, deserted during the quiet mid-afternoon siesta, that gives them a decidedly unsettling air. The film exploits this very effectively, with the bright sun shining back off the bleached white walls of the houses, creating deep shadows within, where lurk vaguely glimpsed flashes of ... something.

The film moves at a measured pace, its shocks coming through the slow accumulation of detail and effective juxtaposition of mood. The first 25 minutes are set on the crowded mainland: these scenes, with the lively fiesta and fireworks, the crowded

---

OPPOSITE: "What could be wrong with our child?" Harvey Stephens and Lee Remick, **The Omen**.

bars full of revellers, are eerily contrasted with the near-total silence in the streets of Almanzora. The film then jumps into horror territory with the sight of a small girl giggling to herself as she beats an old man to death with his walking stick.

Very much a product of its time, the film cleverly plays on late '60s generational fears that the old world was about to be radically altered and that "the kids" were going to take over. The Spanish version opens with a lengthy documentary-style look at the way the adult world has mistreated children over the years, from the Nazi death camps down through the partitioning of India and on to Vietnam. [PT]

RABID

1976, Can, dir/scr David Cronenberg, starring Marilyn Chambers, Frank Moore, Joe Silver, Howard Ryshpan

Hart crashes his motorbike near the Keloid Clinic of Cosmetic Surgery. He is relatively unharmed, but his girlfriend Rose is operated on at the surgery, using an experimental skin-graft technique that leaves her unable to digest any food except blood, which she extracts from her victims using a dart in her armpit, unwittingly spreading a particularly virulent form of rabies. A key entry in the apocalyptic horror cycle kicked off by **Night of the Living Dead,** *Rabid* improves on the weak leads of **Shivers**, Cronenberg's first feature, by casting Marilyn Chambers in the central role. Chambers, whose media career began as a child in soap advertisements, had since become a successful porn star, combining the twin US obsessions of cleanliness and sex, and *Rabid* capitalizes on her notoriety by presenting her attacks like porn scenarios – Rose approaches a girl in a Jacuzzi, is hit on by a farmer in a barn, gets picked up hitch-hiking and meets a man in an adult cinema – with penetration by the predatory Rose's disease-carrying dart replacing sex in each case. A sense of antisocial glee is evident from the start, when a character in the clinic complains that Rose's damaged body hasn't been covered by a sheet, but the tone only escalates into joyful mayhem when the victims begin to spread the disease, an infected doctor at the clinic slicing off the end of a nurse's finger while mumbling, "I need something to cut with", in one of the neatest expressions of surgical horror on film. Cronenberg's playful sense of humour wouldn't receive another workout until **Scanners**, but *Rabid* remains its most engaging outlet, even given the downbeat ending in keeping with the fashion of the period.

THE SIGNALMAN

1976, UK, dir Lawrence Gordon Clark, scr Andrew Davies, starring Denholm Elliott, Bernard Lloyd, Reginald Jessup, Carina Wyeth

The BBC had an excellent run of supernatural dramas throughout the '70s, with original works like Nigel Kneale's now-classic **The Stone Tape** and adaptations such as Leslie Megahey's *Schalcken the Painter* (1979), from a story by Sheridan LeFanu. With "A Ghost Story for Christmas", begun in 1971, the corporation produced a new period chiller to be shown during each festive season. The first five of these were taken from the stories of M.R. James. *The Signalman* broke the trend by looking to Charles Dickens for inspiration, with an excellent adaptation by Andrew Davies of Dickens's other famous ghost story. The choice is fitting considering that Dickens wrote a number of Christmas ghost stories for magazines and encouraged other writers to do the same.

At their worst, the M.R. James films come off as typical staid BBC costume dramas with the novel addition of a cowled figure or some other representation of the supernatural: well acted and directed, laden with period detail but at times lacking in atmosphere. *The Signalman*, like Jonathan Miller's **Whistle and I'll Come to You**, is stark by comparison and conjures a palpable quality of dread from a few simple ingredients – a dismal railway cutting with its baleful warning light, the black mouth of a railway tunnel and Denholm Elliot's haunted features.

When an unnamed stranger comes to visit Elliot's lonely signalman a series of fireside talks lay bare the workman's recurrent premonitions of disaster haunting his stretch of the line. The unpredictability of this setting works in its favour. Where James's stories often telegraph a spectre's appearance through the usual curses and visitations, *The Signalman* summons new fears for an industrial age, of sudden calamity and death delivered by an alliance of thundering steam engines and an implacable fate. The scenes in the dank railway cutting have an authentic, visceral chill and Davies successfully withholds the tragic secret at the heart of the tale right up to the moment of its shattering climax. [JC]

ERASERHEAD

1977, US, dir/scr David Lynch, starring Jack Nance, Charlotte Stewart, Allen Joseph, Jeanne Bates

David Lynch has never made a generic horror film but the fact remains that a large proportion of his work is more intense, visceral, horrific and disturbing than many of the tepid pantomimes masquerading under the horror label.

"A dream of dark and troubling things" is the director's description of this remarkable debut feature. Few films are truly original yet *Eraserhead* fulfils all the claims made for its uniqueness as well as defying easy summary. Lynch, like Tarkovsky, has always refused simplistic interpretation of his dark visions, both insisting that audiences find their own meaning in what appears on the screen. *Eraserhead* has a narrative of sorts but remains open-ended, the vague story of Henry Spencer, his wife Mary X and their bizarre baby serving to connect scenes of nightmare comedy and grotesque tableaux that even have room for song-and-dance routines courtesy of Peter Ivers and the Lady in the Radiator. Familiar elements of Lynch's later work are seen here

BELOW: In heaven everything is fine. The titular **Eraserhead**.

for the first time: banal and uncomfortable domestic scenarios, industrial clamour, spurting body fluids, a preoccupation with texture and the creation of mood almost for its own sake.

Eraserhead was the product of a brief flourishing of the American Film Institute in the '70s and the film's strangeness effectively conceals its minuscule budget and the years Lynch spent working on it. Henry's mewling, bandaged baby is one of the most memorable and disturbing creations in cinema, the foetal culmination of the many umbilical and spermatazoid creatures that splash and crawl throughout the film, and all the more horrific for being at once so ordinary and so inexplicably repellent.

Any discussion of the film has to note the landmark contribution of Alan Splet, a sound designer of genius whose rumbling pipes and hissing radiators launched an entire sub-genre of sinister ambient music. Splet went on to win an Academy Award for other sound work but died too young in 1995. *Eraserhead* is as much his masterpiece as Lynch's. [JC]

THE HILLS HAVE EYES

1977, US, dir/scr Wes Craven, starring Russ Grieve, Virginia Vincent, Susan Lanier, Dee Wallace

The Carter family make a detour from their trip to California to visit an old silver mine. Their car goes off the road and they are attacked by a group of cannibals, who crucify and burn their father, kill two of the women and steal a baby, leaving the others to fight for their lives. Craven's follow-up to **The Last House on the Left** is a far more successful film, even if it draws on the superior **Texas Chain Saw Massacre** for much of its imagery (Robert Burns worked as art director on both films). The motif of two contrasting families, weakly executed in Craven's debut through unconvincing characterization, is more credible here, mixed with an urbanoia theme: the area has been used as a nuclear test site, and Jupiter, the clan's patriarch, was born an oversized mutant. As in **Deliverance**, the city's need for energy may have ruined a rural area, but its inhabitants are so degenerate – unemployed, with bad teeth, matted hair and a taste for human flesh – that urban exploitation seems completely justified. Jupiter resents the incursion of others onto his territory – "You come out here and stick your life in my face!" he roars at Bob Carter's corpse – even as he relies for food on unwary travellers passing through. This time the family is delighted to find a baby and Mercury, the simpleton of the pack, offers to "make joke like last time and eat toes". They dress in animal skins and bone jewellery, but although Pluto looks genuinely alien (the film made a trash star out of Michael Berryman), as a whole the family is hardly convincingly feral, particularly the daughter, Ruby, who has clean skin and social-climber aspirations that prompt her to see babies as more than just food. When first attacked, the Carters are entirely unprepared: Bob, for all his blustery cop history, is no match for Jupiter, his savage counterpart; Brenda goes into shock; and Bobby frantically wails "What are we going to do?" Naturally they must imitate their assailants' savagery, initiative and self-reliance if they are to survive; until then only their dog Beast (Beauty, his partner, is of course the first to die) fights against the cannibals, and is awarded a long flashback in the execrable sequel for his pains. The film uses static long and medium shots (some explicitly POV) to give a menacing sense of the Carters being watched, while some of the night scenes picture lone figures in long shot, surrounded by darkness, highlighting their isolation. But Craven mixes these with hand-held close-ups for the two most gruelling sequences, the genuinely shocking assault on the camper and the grimly effective climax. The 2006 remake is entertaining enough but replaces its mutants' personalities with rubber masks and ends in a gore-soaked triumphalism that finally shades over into comedy.

BELOW: "We're gonna be French fries! Human French fries!" Michael Berryman (centre) menaces an unwary tourist in **The Hills Have Eyes**.

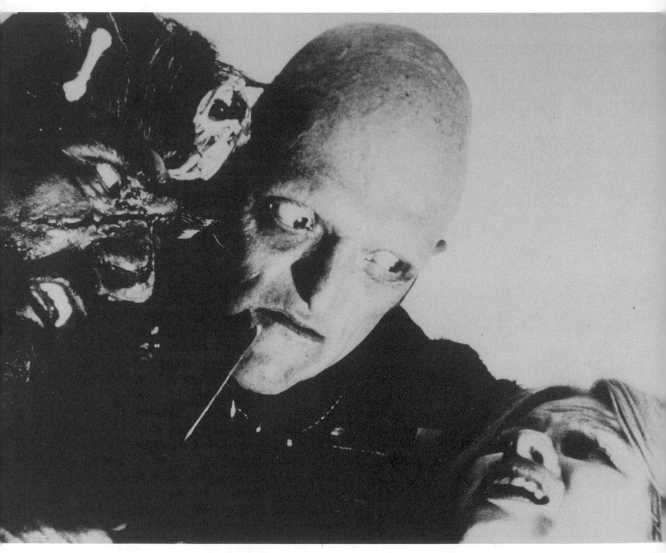

IE
HOUSE

1977, Jap, dir Nobuhiko Obayashi, scr Chiho Katsura, starring Kimiko Ikegami, Kumiko Ohba, Yôko Minamida, Ai Matsubara

Seven schoolgirls decide to spend the school holidays with Oshare's aunt. Their visit appears to revive the old lady, but the rural idyll is interrupted when they find a severed head in a well. Is auntie really a vampiric ghost intent on devouring them whole? Why do strange things happen when the cat's eyes flash? And what's going on with the hungry furniture?

Long available in the West in bootlegged form with no subtitles, but now officially distributed, Obayashi's debut feature has been described as resembling *Beetle Juice* (1988) as directed by Dario Argento. It could also be **Suspiria** remade by the Monkees or an episode of *Rentaghost* directed by Takashi Miike, whose *Katakuri-ke no Kôfuku / Happiness of the Katakuris* (2001) boasts a similarly unholy collision of styles and genres.

If this makes the film sound silly, it is, and early scenes of Benny Hill-style farce and syrupy schoolgirl cutesiness may well try the viewers' patience. It's worth persevering with, however, because when the girls arrive at the titular mansion Obayashi pulls out all the stops for the most endearingly demented haunting ever. Much of the supernatural activity is strictly of the "Sorcerer's Apprentice" variety, with inanimate objects whizzing around rooms to be stopped by karate chops from a character called "Kung Fu" as the soundtrack lurches from chipmunk voices to a full-on prog rock assault. But some of this reaches a pitch of such exhilarating craziness that it has to be seen to be believed.

A first viewing of *Ie* is likely to floor audiences with its form-destroying audacity, though if seen too many times the schmaltz may well grate. Still, the animated sequences remain extraordinary no matter many times they're seen and, as possessed cats go, Snowflake, a fluffy refugee from Blofeld's lap, certainly beats the meat-happy moggies of *The Uncanny* (1977). Just remember: "All cats can open doors. Only ghost cats can close them." So if *your* cat starts closing doors, fling a severed leg at it before you're eaten by the soft furnishings. Who says horror can't be educational?

MARTIN

1977, US, dir/scr George A. Romero, starring John Amplas, Lincoln Maazel, Christine Forrest, Elyane Nadeau

Martin, a teenager who believes himself to be a vampire, moves to Pittsburgh to stay with his cousin Cuda. Cuda also believes in Martin's vampirism, but in the context of a vampire lore – garlic and crucifixes – that Martin has discarded long ago in favour of straight razors and hypodermic syringes. Martin's work delivering groceries for Cuda introduces him to people who may "cure" his vampirism, but they have their own problems to cope with. Romero's most accomplished and moving film, the best of the rash of '70s revisionist vampires, is also an extended riff on one of the director's key themes: the social construction of fantasy. If Martin's vampirism is a perverted expression of his sexual needs, "curable" through normal sexual relations with a woman, his family seems to have pushed him into this position. Cuda confirms Martin's belief that he was born in 1896 and even hires an exorcist to deal with him, but the backdrop of a decaying Pittsburgh, whose inhabitants are depicted as variously alcoholic, out of work, adulterous or homeless, hints at the harsh material realities of urban life that superstition and adherence to custom serve to obscure. Martin's memories are inextricably linked to Universal-style gothic fantasies of vampirism, but he at least has learned that the fantasy is vastly different from the reality: to his dismay women are less in thrall to the vampire than confused and terrified by his attacks, and as he points out to Cuda's granddaughter, "Things only seem to be magic". Ironically, his need to share his ideas about vampire lore leads to him becoming a talk radio star; tragically, full and satisfying adult relationships elude him to the end. Greatly aided by convincing naturalistic playing from the cast, particularly Amplas as Martin, superbly choreographed action scenes, innovative editing techniques and Donald Rubinstein's exceptional score, *Martin* remains one of the finest American horrors of the '70s.

SHOCK WAVES

1977, US, dir Ken Wiederhorn, scr John Harrison, Ken Pare, starring Peter Cushing, John Carradine, Brooke Adams, Fred Buch

A group of tourists out on a pleasure cruise take refuge on a nearby island when their boat is damaged in a collision. They are warned by the island's sole inhabitant to leave, but remain to be menaced by the Nazi zombies the island's owner thought he'd disposed of forever. This American forerunner of the Italian zombie aesthetic plays its absurd premise straight-faced, and contains enough interesting scenes to lift it periodically from the zombie mire. The zombies themselves mark a break with tradition, being highly skilled in holding their breath and lurking, throttling rather than eating their victims, and deriving from Nazi

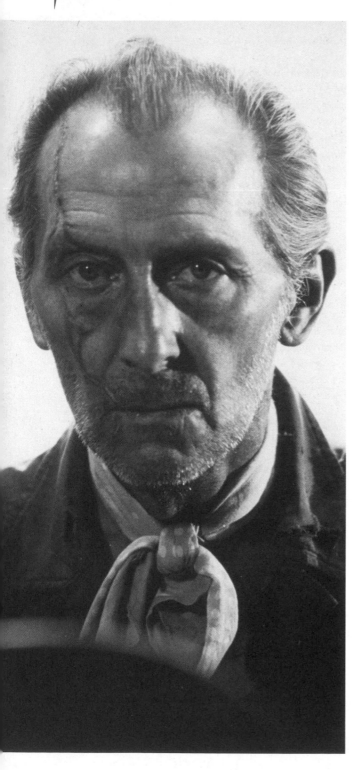

occultism rather than Haitian iconography or Romero-style apocalypticism. The underwater photography is surprisingly effective and features such startling images as a zombie walking along the ocean bed; other evocative images include the zombies lying in rock pools and the discovery of a gramophone in an apparently deserted hotel. The setting is used to impressive effect, conveying a palpable sense of tropical decay, particularly in low camera swoops over the water that make full use of the reflective surface. Apart from the overheated imagery and a bizarre electronic soundtrack, however, the film has little to offer. Cushing, professional to the end, stands out among a forgettable cast that boasts an incoherently raddled John Carradine. The zombies act inconsistently, some "dying" when their goggles are ripped off while others remain unfazed, and the plot quickly degenerates into standard stalk'n'slash territory, without even bothering to explain why the final female survivor escapes attack.

SUSPIRIA

1977, It, dir/co-scr Dario Argento, co-scr Daria Nicolodi, starring Jessica Harper, Stefania Casini, Flavio Bucci, Miguel Bosé

"Magic is everywhere," declares the occult expert Professor Milius in one of *Suspiria*'s fleeting attempts to explain its excesses. The magic proves to be of a particularly dark and violent kind, as the American student Suzy Bannion discovers when she arrives at a dancing school in Freiburg, Germany, home to a coven of malevolent witches with no qualms about murdering anyone who stumbles upon their secrets. *Suspiria* borrows its theme from De Quincey's "Levana and Our Ladies" who rule the world from different cities with sighs, tears and darkness. **Inferno** is the second part, with an as yet unfilmed final chapter still to come.

So much for the story. Most horror films prior to *Suspiria* consist of set pieces separated by chunks of exposition. Argento took the bold step of reducing exposition to a bare minimum in order to expand his set pieces as much as possible, in the process creating a film so deliriously excessive that it genuinely qualifies for the term "symphony of horror". *Suspiria* may be a long series of graphic executions but the bravura staging, the elegance of its production design and the extraordinary photography (the negative was printed using an old Technicolor process) lift the film into a sphere of its own. A quite incredible score by Goblin

LEFT: A late starring role for Peter Cushing, professional to the end. **Shock Waves**.

is as essential to the melodramatic atmosphere as are Bernard Herrmann's shrieking violins in **Psycho**, and if Jessica Harper has little to do as Suzy aside from looking bewildered (she certainly doesn't do much dancing), then this is understandable in a film that dispenses with plot in order to assault the audience's senses. The film starts with a climax and builds from there so it's no surprise that the ending comes as something of a disappointment, but after 90 minutes of mounting hysteria even the most jaded viewer should feel sated. [JC]

DAMIEN: OMEN 2

1978, US, dir Don Taylor, scr Harvey Bernhard, Stanley Mann, Mike Hodges, starring William Holden, Lee Grant, Jonathan Scott-Taylor, Robert Foxworth

Executives at 20th Century Fox gave the green light to two sequels to **The Omen** as soon as they'd seen a rough cut of the first movie, but the first sequel experienced a difficult birth, with the original director Mike Hodges replaced early in filming by Don Taylor, and perhaps as a consequence it lacked the ambition to enrich its parent film's legacy. The second story is little different from the first: people around a 12-year-old Damien gradually come to suspect that he is the Antichrist, only for improbable accidents to remove them from the story. The most interesting new idea is also the least fully realized: Damien's discovery of his demonic nature. There are moments that deliver on this dramatic promise, as when the teenage boy confirms his worst fears about himself with the discovery of the 666 tattoo on his head, the mirror of a scene in the original movie in which Damien's father makes this discovery. Likewise, the scene in which he pleads with his cousin to join rather than oppose him hints at the tragic potential of the story, but Damien's character is so underdeveloped that we can't truly empathize with his dilemma.

Overall, *Damien* is little more than an unsatisfactory retread of the original. The dialogue is strained and the acting drifts into melodrama as a consequence so that we never really believe that what we see on screen is real. The death scenes themselves often feel perfunctory, as if the film knows that a dramatic high is required at that point in the narrative but isn't quite sure how to deliver it. Only two invite re-watching: the doctor's elaborate lift-cable dispatching, an antecedent of the **Final Destination** franchise's set-piece accidents, and the frozen lake drowning, an eerily

RIGHT: "You're going to meet death now … the living dead!" **Suspiria**.

beautiful sequence heightened by its victim's complete silence. Neither, however, is enough to rescue the film from mediocrity. *The Final Conflict* wound up the trilogy in 1981 but added nothing to its reputation. [RL]

BELOW: **Damien** (Jonathan Scott-Taylor) on the brink of puberty.

HALLOWEEN

1978, US, dir/co-scr John Carpenter, co-scr Debra Hill, starring Donald Pleasence, Jamie Lee Curtis, Nancy Loomis (Nancy Kyes), P.J. Soles

Halloween, 1963, Haddonfield, Illinois. A six-year-old Michael Myers watches his sister having sex, then kills her and her lover. Fifteen years on, he escapes from an asylum and is tracked by Dr Loomis back to Haddonfield. Police ignore Loomis's warnings and Myers stalks a number of babysitters, one of whom – Laurie Strode – is resourceful enough to fight back. *Halloween*'s success as one of the most profitable horror films ever made kicked off the regrettable slasher boom of the late '70s and early '80s, although it's a far more skilful and inoffensive film than its successors. As a scare machine it's virtually flawless, Carpenter's memorable score and a series of impeccably timed buses keeping the tension high; the Panavision format, a rare indulgence in a low-budget exploitation quickie, is milked for all it's worth, with pantomime scares that gloss over the holes in the plot (How can Myers drive? Why does Laurie keep dropping the knife?); and the set pieces, whether the bravura opening shot (inspired by *Touch of Evil*, 1958) or the subtler chills of Laurie running from house to house, her neighbours pulling down the blinds, showcase Carpenter's technical and visual flair. *Halloween* has come under fire for its purported equation of sex with death, a formula adopted wholesale by later slashers: Myers kills his sister after watching her having sex, and later characters are killed either after sex or preparing to have sex, while the virginal Laurie survives. Carpenter's defence is that that's what teenagers do – get drunk, have sex. Laurie survives less because she's a virgin than because she has less to distract her. In fact, *Halloween*'s teenagers are well drawn and sympathetic, far from the witless drones of films like **Friday 13th**: we care about these characters and have some insight into their lives. Yet for all its putatively realistic setting the film takes place in a neverland of eerily empty streets and glowing pumpkins, with Myers less an escaped lunatic than the archetypal boogeyman, endowed with supernatural powers and apparently indestructible. Loomis's ludicrously portentous dialogue, delivered by Pleasence with admirable sangfroid, describes him as "purely and simply evil" and this scare show's complexity doesn't go much further than that.

PIRANHA

1978, US, dir Joe Dante, scr John Sayles, starring Bradford Dillman, Heather Menzies, Kevin McCarthy, Barbara Steele

People-tracker Maggie McKeown recruits the alcoholic recluse

ABOVE: "Purely and simply … evil." **Halloween**.

Paul Grogan to help her track down two campers. They trace them to a secret military installation and drain a tank into the river, unwittingly unleashing a school of mutant piranha. Dante's crowd-pleasing **Jaws** rip-off is unabashed exploitation fare, showcasing New World's usual mix of bare breasts, fast cars, gore and Dick Miller, but proves itself a cut above the rest of Spielberg's toothy progeny with a witty, subversive script by Sayles, later to carve out his own directorial career, and a B-star cast including McCarthy from **Invasion of the Body Snatchers**, the horror icon Barbara Steele, in one of her final American roles, and *Eating Raoul*'s director Paul Bartel, as a bullish camp counsellor: "Handicraft doesn't take any nerve, any intestinal fortitude!" The piranha had been developed (and forgotten) as a military weapon for use against the North Vietnamese. When alerted to the fishes' escape, the military refuse to warn the community,

"national security" concealing a colonel's fears of jeopardizing his investment in Aquarena, a new lake development, and instead the river is filled with poison – "sometimes it's necessary to destroy in order to save". Grogan and McKeown escape from the military only to be arrested by a cracker policeman and after plenty of footage of sharp teeth nibbling at bare flesh, the media pile in to get full milage out of the carnage: "Lost River Lake. Terror, horror, death. Film at eleven". Full of sly digs at Spielberg's film – Maggie is first seen playing a **Jaws** videogame – *Piranha* also owes a debt to the '50s creature features with which executive producer Corman made his name, particularly the non-Corman **Creature from the Black Lagoon** in its use of underwater photography and its ending.

HORROR ON TELEVISION

ollowing the Second World War, television began to replace the cinema as the new entertainment medium for the public. But with programmes now being beamed directly into people's homes for the first time, networks realized that the type of horror they produced would have to be subtly different to what could be found on the big screen.

Therefore such early live shows as NBC's *Lights Out* (1946-52) and *Inner Sanctum* (1954) were based on well-established radio programmes that would already be familiar to the new small-screen viewer, while perennially favourite stories such as "The Monkey's Paw" and "Dr Jekyll and Mr Hyde" were adapted more than once for CBS' *Suspense* (1949-54).

In fact, Robert Louis Stevenson's story proved popular with early television producers, also being adapted for CBS' live *Climax!* in 1955 and again just two years later for NBC's *Matinee*

Theatre. The latter show also broadcast versions of *Dracula* (1956) and *Frankenstein* (1957).

However, because budgets could not cope with expensive make-up effects or multiple camera set-ups, most early anthology shows replaced the more traditional monsters with psychological plots and character-driven narratives.

American television's first successful adult fantasy series was *Tales of Tomorrow* (1951-53), a half-hour anthology show on ABC. A memorable 1952 episode featured a reputedly drunk Lon Chaney Jr as a mute Frankenstein Monster blundering through the entire live transmission thinking it was a rehearsal!

Boris Karloff had embraced the new medium early on with such series as *Mystery Playhouse Starring Boris Karloff* (1949). In

BELOW: Scooby Doo Where Are You! The original '70s TV series.

1958, he hosted and starred in *The Veil* (1958-59), an unsold 10-episode anthology series that presented supposedly "documented" stories with a mildly supernatural slant.

ABC's *One Step Beyond* (1959-61), hosted by John Newland, covered similarly "true" themes, and years later inspired a brief revival as *The Next Step Beyond* (1978-79).

Hollywood's undisputed "Master of Suspense" jovially hosted *Alfred Hitchcock Presents* (1955-62), which comprised 268 half-hour episodes. The format was expanded for *The Alfred Hitchcock Hour* (1962-65) and, five years after his death, a computer-colourised Hitchcock presented a revived series of *Alfred Hitchcock Presents* (1985-89) from beyond the grave.

Meanwhile, in Britain, writer Nigel Kneale was changing the face of televison drama with his Quatermass trilogy for the BBC – *The Quatermass Experiment* (1953), *Quatermass II* (1955) and *Quatermass and the Pit* (1958-59) expertly mixed science fiction with adult horror and political invective. Kneale also managed to cause an outcry with his adaptation of George Orwell's *Nineteen Eighty-Four* (1954) and he explored the Abominable Snowman myth in *The Creature* (1955), both starring Peter Cushing. It was not long before other programme-makers were jumping on the same bandwagon with lesser serials such as *The Strange World of Planet X* (1956) and *The Trollenberg Terror* (1956-57).

Kneale's American counterpart, scriptwriter Rod Serling, created, co-produced and urbanely hosted *The Twilight Zone* (1959-64) for CBS. One of the most intelligent and influential genre series ever broadcast, attempts to revive the show in the '80s and early 2000s failed to match up to Serling's original vision.

13 Demon Street (1960) was a 13-episode anthology series created and often directed by Curt Siodmak that was hosted by an unkempt Lon Chaney Jr. Filmed in Stockholm, it failed to sell to America.

Unjustly overlooked when first broadcast by NBC, *Thriller* (1960-62) is now considered possibly the finest horror series ever created for television. Boris Karloff hosted with a twinkle in his eye and occasionally starred in several of the 67 episodes.

During the early '60s the airwaves were awash with short-lived anthology series such as *Moment of Fear* (1960), *The Mystery Show* (1960), *Dow Hour of Great Mysteries* (1960), *Great*

ABOVE: Lurch (Ted Cassidy), *The Addams Family* (1964).

Ghost Tales (1961) and *Tales of Mystery* (1961-63). *Witchcraft* (1961) and *Famous Ghost Stories* were pilots for two more, hosted by Franchot Tone and Vincent Price, respectively.

Inspired by the classic Universal Monsters, comedy sitcom *The Munsters* debuted on CBS in 1964 and ran for two years, exactly the same time as ABC's slightly better *The Addams Family*, which was inspired by the macabre cartoons of Charles Addams. Both spooky families enjoyed various spin-off movies, cartoon adaptations and ill-conceived remakes.

The British-made *Mystery and Imagination* (1966-70) featured hour-long adaptations of classic horror stories, including those reliable old standbys *Dracula* and *Frankenstein* (both 1968).

Jonathan Frid portrayed 175-year-old vampire Barnabas Collins in ABC's daily supernatural soap opera *Dark Shadows* (1966-71), which clocked up an incredible 1,225 episodes. An attempt to revive the series in 1990-91 with Ben Cross as the reluctant bloodsucker was cancelled after just 12 shows. The Canadian-made *Strange Paradise* (1969-70) tried to emulate the same format.

Having previously attempted to launch a television series back in 1958 with Curt Siodmak's unsold pilot for *Tales of Frankenstein*, Hammer Films had more success with *Journey to the Unknown* (1968-69), an hour-long anthology show that lasted 17 episodes.

Among countless cartoons aimed at children, *Scooby Doo Where Are You!* (1969-72) spawned numerous spin-off shows and movies, along with a successful commercial franchise that is still going strong today.

Rod Serling's swan-song, *Night Gallery* (1970-73), never managed to reach the heights of his *Twilight Zone*, but it was still able to outshine such rivals as *Sixth Sense* (1972), *Ghost Story* (1972)/*Circle of Fear* (1973), *The Evil Touch* (1973-74) and *Orson Welles' Great Mysteries* (1973-74).

Having played investigative reporter Carl Kolchak in the TV movies *The Night Stalker* (1971) and *The Night Strangler* (1972), Darren McGavin recreated the role for 20 episodes of ABC's disappointing *Kolchak: The Night Stalker* (1974-75). An ill-advised attempt to revive the show (2005-06) was thankfully cancelled after just one season.

Forrest Tucker and Larry Storch teamed up with a beanie-wearing gorilla to become *The Ghost Busters* (1975-76), and the classic monsters were reunited for *The Monster Squad* (1976-77). Both shows had their titles subsequently appropriated for unconnected movies.

Storytellers desired entry into the Club of the Damned in the BBC's *Supernatural* (1977), which only lasted eight episodes. More successful was Roald Dahl's *Tales of the Unexpected* (1979-88), a popular anthology series initially hosted by the respected British author who had performed the same duty on *Way Out* back in 1961.

Nigel Kneale proved he had lost none of his edge with the haunting one-off drama **The Stone Tape**. The six-episode series *Beasts* (1975) failed to pack the same punch, but the writer was back on form with *Quatermass* (1978), the four-part conclusion to his quartet about the eponymous scientist.

Michael Nouri portrayed an urbane Dracula in *The Curse of Dracula*, which was serialized as part of NBC's weekly *Cliffhangers* (1979), while veteran character actor Jack Elam was an ageing Frankenstein Monster in *Struck by Lightning* (1979), which was cancelled by CBS after just three episodes.

Hammer Films made another stab at television with *Hammer House of Horror* (1980), an hour-long anthology show, then reworked the format into a series of made-for-TV movies under the title *Hammer House of Mystery and Suspense* (1984). However, both attempts failed to capture the studio's past glory.

Patrick Macnee hosted a pilot for *Comedy of Horrors* in 1981, Christopher Lee performed the same duty for *Tales of the Haunted* (1981), and an unlikely James Coburn introduced the short-lived *Darkroom* (1981-82).

After the first season, Nicholas Campbell was replaced by Page Fletcher as the enigmatic traveller in *The Hitchhiker* (1983-86). Shot on video, *Tales from the Darkside* (1984-88) and *Monsters* (1988-91) were a pair of cheap-looking anthology series.

Dennis Dugan and Trevor Eve teamed up to investigate the paranormal in ABC's *Shadow Chasers* (1985-86), and the owners of an antique store attempted to recover a number of cursed objects in *Friday the 13th The Series* (1987-90), which had nothing in common with the movie franchise.

A good lycanthrope went looking for the creature that bit him in *Werewolf* (1987-88), a hirsute variation on *The Fugitive*. The razor-gloved Freddy Krueger, as played by Robert Englund, introduced the anthology show *Freddy's Nightmares* (1988-90), but the actor fared less well as the mysterious proprietor of the short-lived *Nightmare Cafe* (1992).

Nightmare Classics (1989) was a four-part cable series introduced and executive produced by Shelley Duvall. At least HBO's *Tales from the Crypt* (1989-96) was based on the infamous EC horror comics of the '50s, while *Tales from the Cryptkeeper* (1993-95) was a children's cartoon spin-off introduced by the ghoulish horror host.

A group of teens opposed a blond-haired Count in the Luxembourg-produced *Dracula The Series* (1990-91). Kate Hodge turned into a female werewolf in *She-Wolf of London* (1990-91) before the show changed its title to *Love and Curses* and relocated to California for the final six episodes.

Location was also everything in *Shades of LA* (1990-91), **Twin Peaks** and the quirky *Eerie Indiana* (1991-92), which was the centre of weirdness for the entire planet. *Eerie Indiana 'The Other Dimension'* was an attempt to revive the show in 1998.

Geraint Wyn Davies played an undead cop in the Canadian series *Forever Knight* (1992-96), but the most influential vampire show on television was *Buffy the Vampire Slayer* (1996-2003), starring Sarah Michelle Gellar and inspired by the 1992 movie. David Boreanaz played a vampire with a soul in the spin-off series *Angel* (1999-2004).

In *Poltergeist The Legacy* (1996-99) a secret society investigated the supernatural, and equally dedicated groups battled evil in *The Burning Zone* (1996-97), *Psi Factor Chronicles of the Paranormal* (1996-99), *Sleepwalkers* (1997), *GvsE* (1999), *The Others* (1999-2000), *Freakylinks* (2000-01), *The Chronicle:*

News from the Edge (2001-02) and Special Unit 2 (2001-02). Meanwhile, the stand-alone horror episodes of The X Files (1994-2002) were invariably superior to the alien conspiracies, and influenced companion series Millennium (1996-99).

Anthology shows such as Are You Afraid of the Dark (1992-96), Goosebumps (1995-98) and Bone Chillers (1996) were based on popular young adult book series. Canada's The Hunger (1997-99) was definitely more adult fare, hosted by Terence Stamp and David Bowie over two seasons.

Two series that deserved to survive beyond their single seasons were American Gothic (1995-96), set in the strange southern town of Trinity, and Brimstone (1998-99), in which Peter Horton's damned detective had to recapture 113 escaped souls from Hell.

A trio of witchy sisters cast their spell over The WB's Charmed (1998-2006), and Channel Four's six-part Ultraviolet (1998) was a modern take on vampires.

By now, the airwaves were awash with genre shows, each vying for a slice of an ever-decreasing audience share.

Cheap-looking British series such as Shockers (1999-2001), Urban Gothic (2000), Dr Terrible's House of Horrible (2001), The Fear (2001), Spine Chillers (2001-02), Garth Maranghi's Darkplace (2004) and Twisted Tales (2005) did nothing to boost viewing figures.

Lou Diamond Phillips' Seattle detective found himself amongst a community of shape-shifters in Wolf Lake (2001), which was cancelled by CBS after just eight episodes. At least HBO's magical Carnivále (2003-2005), set during the '30s Depression, managed to survive for two seasons.

Stephen King's ambitious Kingdom Hospital (2004) for ABC TV was a reworking of Lars von Trier's Danish 1994 mini-series Riget/The Kingdom. It was a ratings disaster, unlike The Dead Zone (2001-2007), which was inspired by the 1983 movie version of King's novel.

Richard Coyle played a de-ordained occult investigator in the BBC's underrated Strange (2003), which ran for six episodes. More successful, the dull Sea of Souls (2004-2007) was about a Glasgow-based parapsychology research team which investigated the unusual. At the other end of the spectrum, fallen angels, lesbian ghosts and sexy demon-hunters populated the increasingly ludicrous Hex (2004-2005).

Another former priest investigated apocalyptic Miracles (2003), and two brothers hunted down urban legends in Supernatural (2005-). Meanwhile, the female protagonists of Medium (2005-), Afterlife (2005-2006) and Ghost Whisperer (2005-2010) could all communicate with dead people.

ABOVE: Sarah Michelle Gellar is Buffy the Vampire Slayer.

Showtime's Masters of Horror (2005-2007) not only revived the moribund anthology format, but also pushed the envelope for horror on the small screen as major movie directors, such as Dario Argento, John Carpenter, Joe Dante, Stuart Gordon, Tobe Hooper and John Landis now began filming= their favourite short stories.

For the first time in decades, horror on television actually rivalled its big screen counterpart and proved that the genre could still find an audience in the home. [SJ]

ABOVE: "Science in the service of the military." **Piranha**.

PREY
AKA ALIEN PREY

1978, UK, dir Norman J. Warren, scr Max Cuff, starring Barry Stokes, Sally Faulkner, Glory Annen, Sandy Chinney

The alien werething Kator arrives on Earth in search of food sources for his people. Assuming the form and name of Anderson, the first human he meets, he is taken in by lesbian couple Jo and Jessica, and proceeds to watch their relationship unravel as he scours the grounds for wildlife. Warren's spins on popular horror themes are always bizarre enough to be interesting, from **Alien** knock-off *Inseminoid* (1981) to time-travel zombie movie *Bloody New Year* (1987), but *Prey* really is in a class of its own. Like any tabloid illegal immigrant, Kator has peculiar food tastes, eyeing the swans in a pond and fascinated by Jess's parrot – in one hilarious sequence he even pounces on a fox – but in other respects he's done his homework before arrival, quickly picking up the important things (opening champagne bottles, resisting advances from psychotic separatist lesbians) and learning from his hosts' response that it just isn't polite to vomit at the dinner table. Jess tells Jo that "You taught me so many beautiful things," but what Kator picks up from watching their extended bouts of fondling and nipple-sucking is a muddled interpretation of their sexually playful biting that leads to an alarmingly strong climax.

Still, with teachers like these he can't be blamed for not picking everything up straight away. Jo, with an institutional background, homicidal tendencies and a great line in ripe dialogue – "Ours is a pure love, not a foul animal function" – insists on putting Kator in drag to celebrate the death of the fox; and the thematic high weirdness is matched by incomprehensible stylistic flourishes like an interminable slow-motion drowning scene underlined by spastic synth stabs. Not really like anything else at all, *Prey* also boasts surprisingly good turns from the three leads, particularly Stokes's alien incomprehension and Faulkner's simmering rage.

THE SHOUT

1978, US, dir/co-scr Jerzy Skolimowsky, co-scr Michael Austin, starring Alan Bates, Susannah York, John Hurt, Robert Stephens

An underrated chamber piece, Skolimowsky's adaptation of a short story by Robert Graves comes across like an English take on Pasolini's *Teorema/Theorem* (1968) blended with the strain of Australian mysticism that was running through cinema during the '70s. Alan Bates is Crossley, a charismatic drifter who inveigles himself into the Fielding household, exacerbating the tensions in a marriage nearing the point of collapse. John Hurt's Anthony is at first fascinated, then repelled, by Crossley's energy and physical presence, a presence that contrasts with Anthony's passionless anaemia (conveyed by the electro-acoustic music he produces in his spare time). Rachel, his wife, takes an opposite view of their interloper, first annoyed at the way he forces his attentions on the couple then succumbing to his sexual interest until their cuckolding of Anthony is quite blatant.

The domestic drama would be fairly mundane were it not for Crossley's bizarre tales of being married by a witch-doctor in the Australian outback and having learned there the secret of killing a man with an Aboriginal "terror shout". In the climactic scene, Crossley leads Anthony out to the beach one morning and shows him the truth of his stories, inadvertently killing a shepherd that they fail to see behind the dunes. Skolimowsky maintains a subtle balance throughout as further supernatural resonances are revealed. Crossley seems a boastful charlatan one minute and a terrifying shamanistic figure the next, able to penetrate a person's secrets at a glance. When the latter part of the film also shows him to be a murderous madman, we can't dismiss what we've seen of his powers already.

Skolimowsky's film is haunting and memorable, with the implications found in the work of Alan Garner or David Rudkin, that ancient, supernatural forces are present still in the modern world but one needs a special insight (or madness) to find and channel them. Bates's charisma and mercurial demeanour are the cold heart of the piece, giving this sinister film the aura of a contemporary fable. [JC]

BELOW: Alan Bates demonstrates his "terror shout", **The Shout**.

ALIEN

1979, UK/US, dir Ridley Scott, scr Dan O'Bannon, starring Tom Skerritt, Sigourney Weaver, Veronica Cartwright, Harry Dean Stanton

The crew of the *Nostromo* are awoken by an apparent distress signal. When they investigate the planet it comes from, a creature attacks Kane. When he is returned to the *Nostromo*, he is incubating an alien, which soon escapes. While *Alien* represents a missed opportunity in reducing its tale of inter-species encounters to a space slasher, instead of the intriguing Lovecraftian conception originally scripted, it remains the most effective modern SF/horror crossover, its effects and visuals still convincing today. If the plot is weak – as with any other slasher, the characters lurch from one dumb move to the next – the imagery is magnificent, particularly the alien's many guises, designed by H.R. Giger, and the *Derelict* spacecraft. The film's outlandish expressions of birth anxiety also pack a primal punch, even if they represent a misogynist strain, or at least a profound ambivalence about the reproductive process. The film begins with an antiseptic scene of birth through technology, as "Mother", the ship's computer, awakens the crew, a calm, clean scene contrasted with the

spectacularly messy chest-bursting alien "birth". Parts of both the *Nostromo* and the *Derelict* resemble wombs and claustrophobic uterine passages, the latter full of threatening cervical hatches. Ripley, moreover, is a sexless heroine whose cold, "masculine" lack of emotion enables her to survive while her female peer, Lambert, dissolves into a tearful mess. Yet, if the immediate threat to the crew is couched in broadly feminine terms, its origins are coded as masculine: science may provide a clean birth, but it is also responsible for Ash, the android carrying out the Company's orders, with the crew entirely expendable. The film's three sequels have tended to stress SF over horror elements, and bring little new to the original concept except for Ripley's increasingly eroticized relationship with the aliens.

THE AMITYVILLE HORROR

1979, US, dir Stuart Rosenberg, scr Sandor Stern, starring James Brolin, Margot Kidder, Rod Steiger, Don Stroud

Amityville stripped the bare bones from Jay Anson's purportedly true story of a Long Island haunting – the Lutzes move into a house where a multiple murder took place a year before – and added an **Exorcist**-style subplot about a hip young priest and an older

BELOW: Baby's first breath. **Alien.**

partner injured while battling against the forces of evil, making the film about as "based on a true story" as **The Texas Chain Saw Massacre**. For all the importance of subtlety in other ghost films, part of *Amityville*'s problem is that not much happens: a window won't open, or won't close; flies gather out of season; a cross is inverted; and two lights appear at a window. These effects aren't very special, nothing that a few black metallers couldn't conjure up, and the back story too suffers from a lack of visual interest – for a horror film, having a family shot in their beds as they sleep betrays an imaginative failure regarding the many means for mass murder. When *Amityville* finally rises from its torpor, its most effective scenes – an enraged father using an axe to batter down a door behind which his children cower; blood weeping from walls and stairs – seem uncanny premonitions of the vastly superior **The Shining**. Finally, the film only works as unintentional comedy: Kidder's Cathy Lutz awakens in bed to scream "Waauggh! She was shot in the head!"; Brolin's deterioration as George is marked by his refusal to change his T-shirt, his insistence on keeping a sharp axe and readiness to thieve from a public library; Steiger's priest shouts and burps a lot (the house tends to give uniformed Christians terrible indigestion) and just can't get a good signal on his phone; and a tacky cop muses, "Maybe I *am* just chasing shadows". The real horror of *Amityville* is its appalling script and the only intelligent thing about the movie is the ghost, which steals $1500, presumably to reinvest in the many sequels and remakes following *Amityville*'s unaccountable success. The prequel, *Amityville II: the Possession* (1982), improves on the original by treating its tale (the events leading up to the mass murder) with pulp verve; the other sequels continue *Amityville*'s strain of interminable drivel, as does the inevitable 2005 remake.

THE BROOD

1979, Can, dir/scr David Cronenberg, starring Oliver Reed, Samantha Eggar, Art Hindle, Henry Beckman

Frank Carveth has split up from his wife Nola, and both want custody of their daughter Candace. Nola attends the SomaFree Institute of Psychoplasmics, where Dr Raglan encourages patients to manifest their psychic traumas physically. Nola's mother, who beat her as a child, is killed by mysterious figures in anoraks, who go on to attack Nola's other enemies. When Raglan realizes that his method is yielding unusual results,

RIGHT: "Waauggh!" Margot Kidder flees **The Amityville Horror**.

he shuts the institute down, ready for a showdown between Nola and Frank. *The Brood*, written during Cronenberg's own painful divorce, is often regarded as his first mature work. It's certainly far grimmer than **Shivers** or **Rabid**, lacking their anarchic playfulness and featuring near-unwatchable scenes such as the battering of a teacher in a room full of children. It's also as concise an exploration of key Cronenberg themes as any: Raglan is the mad scientist in '70s self-help clothes, whose well-meaning exhortation to "go all the way through it" ends typically disastrously; and the director's characteristic theme of bodily revolt receives its first full workout, with one disgruntled ex-patient making the body politic analogy clear – "I have a small revolution on my hands, and I'm not putting it down very successfully." Several critics have complained that the film is misogynistic: the cycle of physical abuse from Nola's mother to Nola is repeated with her own daughter and the final scenes of Nola's external womb express a specific horror of woman's generative function. Yet Cronenberg's sympathy lies in many ways with Nola. As with all his early films, the casting of the agent of order betrays a lack of interest in his function, Eggar towering over Hindle; and it is, after all, a man (Reed's Raglan) who encourages the formation of the brood, by far Cronenberg's scariest monsters. Finally, this idiosyncratic entry in the lucrative evil-child stakes of '70s horror tells the truth about dysfunctional relationships where straightforward drama might struggle: sometimes, painful stories demand painful metaphors.

DAWN OF THE DEAD

1979, US, dir/scr George A. Romero, starring David Emge, Ken Foree, Scott H. Reiniger, Gaylen Ross

The second part of Romero's zombie saga was in its own way as influential as **Night of the Living Dead**, heralding a golden age of effects-heavy Italian zombie films, and remains one of the most intelligent genre works of the period. The story follows two zombie-shooting National Guardsmen, Roger and Peter (later joined by television technician Steve and his girlfriend Fran), as they travel from an apartment block in a Hispanic ghetto to a brightly lit mall full of shambling ghouls. The situation has deteriorated since the end of **Night** – zombies clearly have the upper hand now – and Romero's focus too has shifted, from Vietnam and the family unit to consumerism and adult relationships (both heterosexual couples and male "buddies"). The parallels between the zombies and their living counterparts are expertly built up: both are creatures of instinct, the zombies returning to the mall to satisfy dimly remembered cravings for luxury goods while the humans run around taking photos that can never be processed and cash that can buy nothing. Their ennui is finally broken by a raid on the mall by a marauding gang of bikers, whose attacks on the zombies are so grotesque that the viewer actually feels sorry for them. Romero's film plays against Hollywood convention at every turn, being shot in Pittsburgh,

BELOW: "Shoot it in the head!" **Dawn of the Dead**.

RIGHT: "Midnight to one belongs to the dead" in **The Fog**.

released unrated and featuring, with no self-conscious fanfare, a black male lead. Its female character, Fran, moreover proves far more sensible than her male counterparts, growing plants and learning how to fly a helicopter while her friends gorge themselves on caviar. *Dawn* even goes against the grain of the bleak horror endings that had become a '70s cliché, with some hope of redemption held out at the end. Parts of the film are closer to the action genre than horror, and the music foregrounds the comic elements of scenes that could be played for straight tension, anticipating the "splatstick" of films like **Braindead**. Still, horror fans had little reason to be disappointed, especially with Tom Savini's lurid effects – limbs are ripped off, machetes buried in heads, and bikers torn apart in what was probably the grisliest finale of any film to date. *Dawn* was remade surprisingly well in 2003 and the remake even spawned a British spoof, *Shaun of the Dead* (2004).

THE DRILLER KILLER

1979, US, dir Abel Ferrara, scr Nicholas St John, starring Jimmy Laine (Abel Ferrara), Carolyn Marz, Harry Schultz, Baybi Day

A struggling artist, Reno, faces eviction from his NYC apartment if he can't pay the rent. He has high hopes for the success of his buffalo painting, but when a punk band move in next door he starts to eye the derelicts lining the streets as potential drilling victims. The title of Ferrara's ballsy debut was enough to ensure its notoriety as one of the principal titles in the UK's "video nasty" furore, but it's hardly an exceptionally gory film. Only one drilling is shown in any detail and rather than a splatter movie Ferrara presents a **Repulsion**-style descent into madness (complete with skinned rabbit) with a punk-rock sensibility whose welcome rawness is soon offset by interminable footage of The Roosters playing the same chord over and over again. Semi-experimental montage dream sequences, untutored acting, bad music and guerrilla NYC location work make this the forerunner of Richard Kern films like *Submit to Me* and *The Right Side of My Brain* (both 1985), and the narrative isn't much stronger. Reno may attack the Bowery bums because he fears becoming one of them, but his inability to face up to financial realities, abuse of his live-in girlfriend and reluctance to take a power tool to the punks next door mean our sympathy soon dries up. Ferrara handled similar themes with far more skill in the rape-revenge drama *Ms 45* (1980).

THE FOG

1979, US, dir/co-scr John Carpenter, co-scr Debra Hill, starring Adrienne Barbeau, Hal Holbrook, Janet Leigh, Jamie Lee Curtis

Antonio Bay's centenary celebrations are marred by a series of bizarre events, including an attack on a boat that leaves the crew

URBANOIA

LEFT: "You sure do got a purty mouth."
Jon Voight in **Deliverance**.

exploitation is finally implicitly justified with the rural landscape becoming little more than an arena for the testing of urban man, an ordeal that reveals, in a manner simultaneously horrific and reassuring, that the modern city dweller can still kill.

The otherness of **Deliverance**'s hillbillies is demonstrated by poor dental hygiene and a readiness to rape the soft, fat Bobby, a sexual deviance shared by the rednecks of *I Spit on Your Grave* (1978). Country folk are also frequently seen breaking the dietary taboo of cannibalism, practised by the families of **The Texas Chain Saw Massacre** and **The Hills Have Eyes**, both similarly displaying a displaced guilt over what the city has done to the country. The theme was a box-office favourite in the late '70s and early '80s, the better entries including **Straw Dogs**, which stands virtually alone as an evocation of British rural savagery, the paradigmatically titled *Tourist Trap* (1979), the demented **Deliverance** inversion of *Mother's Day* (1980) and Walter Hill's Cajun swamp classic *Southern Comfort* (1981).

Travel from town to country has always involved danger, as seen in travel narratives from the myths and fairy tales underpinning Western culture (Hansel and Gretel, Theseus) to accounts of *banditti* waylaying adventurers on the Grand Tour, and it is significant that the protagonists in urbanoia films tend to be tourists, displaying the flagrantly non-essential use of income in deprived areas that marks them as potential if not justified victims. Yet tourism trades on authenticity, which for many sectors of the industry means at least a flirtation with danger: **Deliverance** and **The Descent** take adventure tourism as their starting point, same-sex groups pitting themselves against hostile environments that prove to hold nasty surprises. Recent US genre efforts like **Jeepers Creepers** and **Dead End** also provide new spins on the theme but the wilderness of the Australian outback has inspired the most interesting contemporary urbanoia films, from the kangaroo-hunting horrors of **Razorback** to **Wolf Creek**'s blend of exquisite location photography and brutal backpacker torture, inspired by the real-life tourist killer Ivan Milat, suggesting that the European dark forest may now have been replaced even at home by its Antipodean mirror image.

I f **Psycho** hinted at the horrors to come in its tale of madness in a rural America forgotten since the highway was built, **Deliverance** stands as the urbanoia ur-text, setting the template for virtually all city-country genre films to follow. The canoeists' journey is simultaneously a stylized rite of passage — a journey into the unknown in which they must brave terrors, lose something but emerge wiser — and a complex, ambivalent meditation on the relationship between city and country. Rather than protest against the damming of a river, which involves the uprooting of rural communities and the devastation of the landscape to feed the city's power needs, the canoeists exploit it in a different way, using their city money to humiliate the locals, already impoverished by urban exploitation. Yet the rural community has degenerated so far — whether through inbreeding and disease or unconventional sexual tastes — that such

missing or dead. The town's minister discovers that a hundred years ago his grandfather tricked the rich leader of a leper colony into paying for the privilege of moving the colony near Antonio Bay; instead the colony's boat was lured onto the rocks, and the money used to found the township. A hundred years on, the ghosts of the colony are out for revenge. Carpenter's follow-up to **Halloween** takes an entirely different approach to its predecessor. Where **Halloween**'s influences were visual and cinematic, *The Fog*'s are literary – the film begins with a Mr Machen telling a ghost story, many of the place names are taken from Lovecraft and the plot hinges on the discovery of a book. Moreover, where **Halloween** tells Laurie Strode's story, *The Fog* has no single central character, relying instead on a perfectly played ensemble cast that seems closer at times to Robert Altman than an exploitation film, particularly in its broad range of female characters; and where **Halloween** is tightly plotted and energetically paced, *The Fog* is leisurely, short on plot and heavy on atmosphere. Carpenter's determination to try something different – even if it is an old-fashioned ghost story – deserves credit, and the film makes superb use of its coastal locations and Panavision format, even managing occasionally to attain a genuinely dreamlike feel, aided by the **Suspiria**-style saturated red and blue lights and the look of the shambling ghosts, which are rarely clearly seen. But, while the disparate elements work well enough, they don't quite gel and the film lacks the cohesion of **Halloween** and **The Thing**, with the mystical ending in particular hurried and unconvincing.

NOSFERATU: PHANTOM DER NACHT
AKA NOSFERATU THE VAMPYRE

1979, W Ger/Fr, dir/scr Werner Herzog, starring Klaus Kinski, Isabelle Adjani, Bruno Ganz, Roland Topor

At first glance Werner Herzog's remake of Murnau's original might seem as pointless as Gus van Sant's *Psycho* (1998), but all worries are dispelled immediately by the opening shots. Herzog's passion for realism over fakery gives us a parade of mummified corpses screaming silently at the camera as the haunting theme plays on the soundtrack, followed by a real bat flying in slow motion, an image so simple and striking one wonders why no one had thought of it before.

The other revelation of the film is Klaus Kinski's reinvention of the Dracula role (Herzog restored the Stoker nomenclature concealed by Murnau's screenplay). Kinski's usual manic emoting

is completely absent here, showing a depth and subtlety to his acting he was rarely given credit for. His appearance – modelled on Max Shreck's original – is shockingly bloodless and inhuman, an alien presence that seems especially startling when juxtaposed against the human characters, his voice laden with a weariness that conveys the ennui of a degraded and repetitive immortality. In a somewhat passionless film (despite the lust for life and blood at the centre of the story), Kinski's Dracula is the passionless heart of the piece, like a black hole draining the emotion from his surroundings, as he delivers the people of Wismar into the hands of the plague. Only the giggling Renfield, played by the French Surrealist Roland Topor, displays any signs of animation.

Despite pitting himself against a great predecessor, Herzog manages to produce some memorable flourishes of his own, especially in the scenes of the town being overrun by rats and the plague-infected townspeople dancing as bodies are carried through the streets. With its excellent score (Wagner, Gounod and Herzog's beloved Popol Vuh), its Symbolist beachscapes and mountain ranges reminiscent of the paintings of Caspar Friedrich, Herzog's *Nosferatu* is less a Murnau copy than a harking back to the Teutonic Romantic tradition, thoroughly German and gothic in the best sense of the word. [JC]

PHANTASM

1979, US, dir/scr Don Coscarelli, starring Michael Baldwin, Bill Thornbury, Reggie Bannister, Angus Scrimm

When his brother Tommy dies, Jody returns to his hometown for the funeral at Morningside cemetery. His younger brother Michael sees strange things happening there and is attacked by the undertaker when he visits the mortuary at night. Jody visits in turn and is chased by a dwarf with Tommy's face. What is happening to the dead at Morningside? Trashy and nonsensical fun, *Phantasm* anticipates the teen-horror pictures of the '80s by having a precocious (drinking, driving, bomb-making) 13-year-old as its hero. Its use of dream imagery – the sleeping characters see themselves being attacked at Morningside – also makes it the forerunner of the **Nightmare on Elm Street** series. While it is often supremely silly – at one point the brothers struggle with a demonic insect bound up in a denim jacket – and its standard response to an encounter with the unexplained is to shoot at it with a big gun, *Phantasm* also tackles more serious issues, presenting its narrative as a set of oblique responses to Michael's fear of abandonment. Some of the ideas are outlandishly compelling – the dead are being put

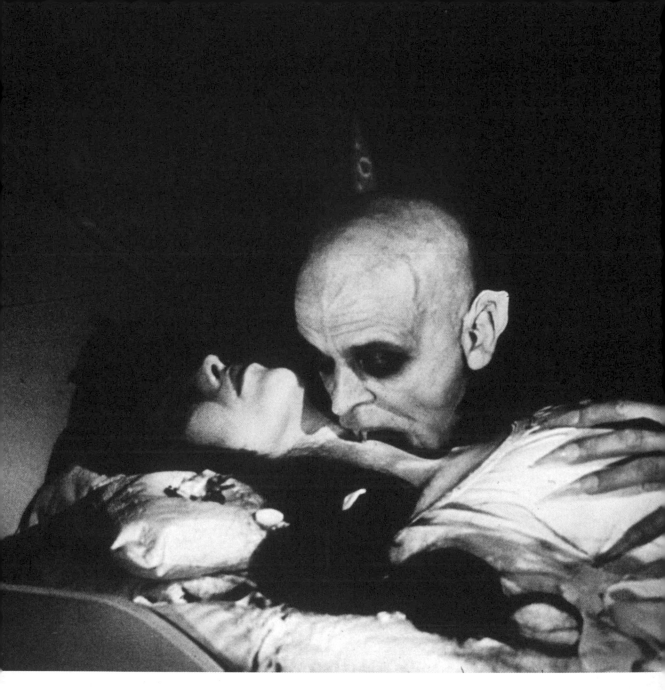

to work as dwarf slaves in another dimension – and while not everything Coscarelli throws at the screen sticks, the imagery, in particular Scrimm's gender-shifting Tall Man and the skull-drilling silver sphere, is compelling enough for the film to have sparked three lesser sequels.

ABOVE: Klaus Kinski feeds, **Nosferatu: Phantom der Nacht**

ZOMBI 2
AKA ZOMBIE FLESH-EATERS; ZOMBIE

1979, It, dir Lucio Fulci, scr Dardano Sacchetti, starring Ian McCullogh, Richard Johnson, Tisa Farrow, Auretta Gay

A journalist and a young woman seeking her missing father travel with a young couple to a Caribbean island, only to discover that the dead have begun to walk.

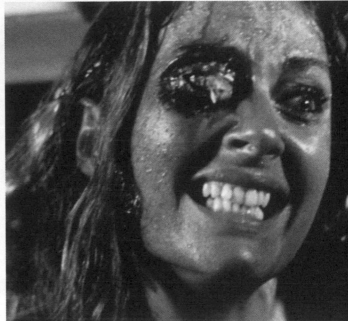

ABOVE: Fulci delivers, **Zombi 2**.

of place and, apart from a tense prologue on an apparently deserted schooner, the horror stems largely from gross images aggressively displayed.

The film contains the signature moment of Fulci's career: a woman pulled by the hair through a shattered door-frame, until her eye is impaled, in tight close-up, on an extruded splinter. It's suspenseful, but not because we doubt the outcome – Fulci makes it grindingly obvious what's going to happen. Instead, the suspense comes from wondering if the director will really go all the way. When the scene climaxes, in the most gruesome fashion, horror fans around the world took Fulci to their hearts – here was a filmmaker who *really* delivered!

In other respects, *Zombi 2* is an imperfect creation. The business of getting the principal cast out of New York to the Caribbean takes too long and, apart from a breathtakingly weird underwater scene in which a zombie fights a shark, the film only really kicks into gear at the halfway mark. The result is a film that's spectacular without being complex, lacking the visual poetry of Fulci's next few horror films or the cunning plotting of his previous thrillers. That said, its charm is irresistible: like a favourite pop song, its superficiality is entirely redeemed by its ability to delight. [ST]

Lucio Fulci burst onto the international horror scene in 1979 with this classic zombie film, which amplifies the brutality of his earlier *giallo* films and adds the magic ingredient of fantasy. Initially set up to exploit the success of George Romero's **Dawn of the Dead** (a huge hit in Italy the year before), *Zombi 2* lacks the social commentary of Romero's more cerebral film, but Fulci quickly establishes his own credentials. The emphasis is firmly on decay and disgust; corporeal revulsion takes pride

CHAPTER

8

1980s

The first thing to say about horror cinema in the '80s is that, on the whole, it was dumber than it had been in the preceding decade. This is not to say that the intelligent, innovative creators of the '70s fell silent, though most of them did struggle, but horror *audiences* changed. In 1985, fans preferred Dan O'Bannon's aggressive, comical, trivial semi-parody **Return of the Living Dead** to George A. Romero's thoughtful, disturbing, serious third Living Dead movie, **Day of the Dead**. This shift was evident in the popular success of the decade's first horror hit, Sean S. Cunningham's **Friday the 13th** (1980). Cunningham had produced Wes Craven's **Last House on the Left** (1972) – in turn Craven did uncredited editing assistance on **Friday**, specifically the **Carrie**-style last-second nightmare shock with Jason rising from the lake. But the models for **Friday** are **Halloween** (1978) and Mario Bava's *La Ronde*-with-murders **Reazione a Catena** (*Bay of Blood*, 1971), mixed with campfire tales of murdered camp counsellors and the sort of "body-count" plotting made popular by **Alien** (1979). One ingredient in the commercial success of the crude, only intermittently effective shocker was the gory effects of Tom Savini, who arrived at Crystal Lake fresh from the Monroeville Mall where he had worked on **Dawn of the Dead**. If anyone became a star on the strength of **Friday the 13th**, it was Savini. Horror-themed publications furthered a trend by becoming far more interested in special effects make-up than writing or direction – which led to a genre bled dry of its content but overflowing with effects.

For the first time since the initial burst of "monster kid" activity around *Famous Monsters of Filmland* in the early '60s, there was a loosely organized community of horror fans intent on arguing about the way their favourite movies were going. They read the growing shelfload of books on the genre (publication of these mushroomed in the '80s) and magazines (*Cinefantastique*, *Fangoria*, *Starburst*), published their own fanzines (*Sleazoid Express*, *Gore Gazette*, *Shock Xpress*,

OPPOSITE: A teen-horror showdown in *The Lost Boys* (1986).

RIGHT: Michael Berryman in Wes Craven's rural slasher/demon film *Deadly Blessing* (1981).

Samhain) and attended horror-film festivals (Shock Around the Clock, Dead By Dawn, Black Sunday). This fandom was born of adversity, especially in the United Kingdom, where horror movies came under concerted attack. The so-called "video nasties" tabloid kerfuffle in the wake of the widespread introduction of the video player – which itself effected changes in the production and consumption of horror films – led to massively increased censorship which people who were disposed to watch **The Driller Killer** (1979), *Cannibal Ferox* (1980) or **The Evil Dead** (1981) perceived as an injustice. People went to jail for owning or selling horror films, or had their video collections seized by the police. Compared to, say, the Chinese Cultural Revolution, in which *fiction* was banned (let alone fantasy or horror), or the reign of the Khmer Rouge, who killed every Cambodian who wore glasses on the suspicion that they read too much, this was a minor oppression, but it was a symptom of the way things were going. Horror comics had suffered similar attacks in the '50s, similarly taking the blame for real-life violence, and were essentially wiped out by the industry. Horror films carried on, but their response was to become more lightweight, not necessarily in terms of reducing levels of gore and violence but in becoming more disposable, less personal work.

Friday the 13th outgrossed **Halloween** in every way, and suddenly cinemas were packed with psychopaths murdering teenagers. Well over a hundred of these things were rushed out, including the inevitable **Friday** and **Halloween** sequels, which further formularized already formulaic conventions. In 1980 alone, there appeared *Bloody Birthday*, **The Boogeyman**, *The Burning*, *Don't Answer the Phone*, **Don't Go in the House**, **Dressed to Kill**, *Fade to Black*, *Happy Birthday to Me*, *He Knows You're Alone*, *Home Sweet Home*, *Just Before Dawn*, *Madman*, **Maniac**, *Motel Hell*, *Night School* (*Terror Eyes*), *New Year's Evil*, *Phobia*, *Prom Night*, *Silent Scream* and *You Better Watch Out* (*Christmas Evil*). Anyone paying close attention could sub-divide the psycho plague into streams: psychos in high school or on college campuses (this is where the horny teenagers most associated with the form tend to fall under the axe or the machete), psychos in the woods (lingering there to crossbreed with the redneck massacres of the '70s), holiday-themed psychos (after **Halloween** and **Friday the 13th**, killers often struck on particular calendar dates), psychos in attics (*Silent Scream* is an "old dark house" gothic about a nasty family secret who turns out to be Barbara Steele), comedy

BELOW: Old monsters won't stay dead, *Fright Night* (1986).

cannibal psychos, supernatural psychos (even before Elm Street there was **The Boogeyman**'s possessed mirror), psychos with gimmicks (the film-fan fancy-dress killer of *Fade to Black* and the murders-keyed-to-particular-neuroses of *Phobia*), masked but identified psychos (like Michael of **Halloween** and Jason of the **Friday** follow-ups), classy psychos (Brian De Palma's **Dressed to Kill** is the most stylish of this batch and more interested in homaging Hitchcock and Antonioni than recycling Carpenter and Cunningham), whodunit psychos (usually easily identifiable from the range of suspects – for example, *Happy Birthday* and *Prom Night* – neither of which are quite as casual as **Friday the 13th**, which introduces its culprit all of five minutes before revealing her surprise guilt) and depraved slob psychos (yes, I know … but the madmen in *Don't Answer the Phone* and **Maniac** are *significantly* more repulsive than, say, Rachel Ward in *Night School*). Despite this range of approaches, the upshot was that at last horror-movie production achieved the levels of conveyor-belt, cookie-cutter sameness hitherto achieved only by series-B Westerns of the '30s and '40s. If anything, traces of originality – as shown by *When a Stranger Calls* (1979), a psycho picture produced *before* **Friday the 13th** – were stamped out as the cycle continued, with any new wrinkles likely to be novelty weapons (the miner's pick of **My Bloody Valentine**, 1981) or gimmicks like *Friday the 13th Part III in 3-D* (1983).

For a while, it seemed that auteur-driven horror would survive, with efforts like John Carpenter's **The Fog** (1979), Romero's *Creepshow* (1982), Larry Cohen's **Q – the Winged Serpent** (1982) and David Cronenberg's **Videodrome** (1983) standing out among all the identikit slashers. However, these filmmakers began their see-sawing careers: all would, at some point, "play safe" with Stephen King adaptations, be torn between independence and major studio work (Carpenter and Cronenberg directed remakes of '50s properties, **The Thing**, 1982, and **The Fly**, 1986), have important films prove less popular at the box office than mindless schlock from lesser lights, and fall silent for periods of years or have creative slides. Tobe Hooper made one freak psycho movie, *The Funhouse* (1981), and was credited director of the hit **Poltergeist** (1982), though the producer Steven Spielberg was widely seen to be that film's true auteur, then fell in with Cannon Films for the botched *The Texas Chainsaw Massacre 2* (1986) and a pair of big-budget sci-fi flops (he did a lot less with *Invaders From Mars*, 1986, than Carpenter and Cronenberg with their '50s-redux projects) before sliding back into a swamp of TV pilots and direct-to-video schlock. Carpenter would never quite join Hooper among the untouchables, but after dissatisfaction with

major studio politics (**The Thing** was not the success it ought to have been) tended to work on a smaller scale, with modestly likable results for the rest of the '80s (*Prince of Darkness*, 1987, *They Live*, 1988) and modestly unlikable ones ever since (the more stress on Carpenter's credit, the less likely the film is to have much going for it). After **The Fly**, Cronenberg made a niche for himself – delivering *Dead Ringers* (1989), one of his most disturbing films but a fringe genre production, then becoming more interested in adaptations of unusual literary source material than in working from his own scripts. Cohen was prolific in the '80s, being among the first real filmmakers to see that straight-to-video could be the new B picture. His scrappy, lively output includes gems (*Special Effects*, 1986), dogs (*Wicked Stepmother*, 1989) and many films where messiness is the price you have to pay for touches of brilliance (*The Stuff*, 1986, *A Return to Salem's Lot*, 1987). Romero, criminally, had trouble getting anything made.

Although Wes Craven began the decade shakily with the okay rural slasher/demon film *Deadly Blessing* (1981) and the comic-book monster mash *Swamp Thing* (1982), before sinking in desperation to *The Hills Have Eyes, Part 2* (1984), he fared the best of the horror directors who had emerged during the '70s. His career has had major downs, from *Deadly Friend* (1986) to *Cursed* (2004), but he has *twice* revived the played-out slasher-film formula with franchise-founding, genuinely revisionary break-out hits. **A Nightmare on Elm Street** (1984), like **Scream** (1996) a decade on, arrived when folk were tired of formula sequels, and welded an original idea (a ghost psycho who stalks his victims' dreams) to an American small-town milieu out of Stephen King (alone of his generation, Craven has never made a King movie), with a cartoonish but effective depiction of American ills writ large. In contrast to the dumb teenagers of most slashers, the Elm Street kids are smart and catch on early, while their parents and other authority figures are drunken, foolish, arrogant and dangerous, and it turns out that Fred Krueger wants to punish them for killing him by lashing out at their innocent kids. Sequels were inevitable, and diminishing returns set in – though Robert Englund's Freddy, a shadowy and perverse spectre in the first film, became a monster icon with his own hobby kits, merchandise and semi-comic schtick, which in turn encouraged attempts to market the likes of Leatherface, Michael Myers and Jason as the Universal monsters of the '80s.

Old monsters stayed in the game, thanks to a fortuitous collison of interests and aptitudes. Directors like Joe Dante (**The Howling**, 1980), John Landis (**An American Werewolf in London**, 1981), Neil Jordan (**The Company** of Wolves, 1984), Tom Holland (*Fright Night*, 1986) and Fred Dekker (*The Monster Squad*, 1987) hooked up with special make-up effects artists (yes, them again) Rob Bottin, Rick Baker, Christopher Tucker, Steve Johnson and Stan Winston. New technologies in make-up could be used for more than gore – and in the early '80s, the screens were awash with shapeshifters, from werewolves and cat-people (in Paul Schrader's 1982 remake) to unclassifiables like the morphing, tentacle-sprouting Thing ("you gotta be fuckin' kidding!") and the video-signal-altered mind-mutants of **Videodrome**. The best of these films were more than effects showreels: Dante, in particular, weaves his *Famous Monsters* enthusiasms (he had written for the magazine) into a 1980 rethink of the werewolf myth (his lycanthropes are riven by internal dissent between factions, headed by a pop psychologist who wants to integrate with regular humans and wilder things who want to prey on us) and makes the show-stopper transformations *scary* as well as amazing. Dante went on to *Gremlins* (1984), a toothy, satirical monster picture with a small-town setting, which was perfectly matched as a Christmas release by Ivan Reitman's *Ghostbusters* (1984), a parapsychological effects comedy which offered supernatural activity "on a Biblical scale". Vampire variants continued, keyed to passing trends, mostly stressing Anne Rice's vision of vampirism as a lifestyle choice rather than a plague or a curse, often played by pop singers like David Bowie and Grace Jones: hence the gloomy New Romantics of Tony Scott's **The Hunger** (1983), the teenage party animals of Joel Schumacher's *The Lost Boys* (1986), the voracious strippers of Richard Wenk's *Vamp* (1986) and the grungy Western drifters of Kathryn Bigelow's **Near Dark** (1987).

Bustling new creatives popped up in odd corners, beginning in the indies but fast-tracked for Hollywood, where their careers would be chequered: Sam Raimi (**The Evil Dead**, 1981), Stuart Gordon (**Re-Animator**, 1985), Clive Barker (**Hellraiser**, 1987). All these debuts showed a black sense of humour, which would mushroom in their sequels, but have a commitment to physical shock which makes them apt stablemates with the (mostly humourless) Italian and American video nasties and a tendency to use sexual situations as a trigger for the gross-out (tree rape, cunnilingus delivered by a living severed head, a skinless kiss). This is risky material, and it takes a master to carry it off: Raimi admits the tree scene in **The Evil Dead** works less well than the film's other assaults.

Barker, the most extreme of these filmmakers, shows the most delicacy, preferring odd physical juxtapositions (a demon's face studded with hardware-store nails, a skinless man smoking a cigarette) rather than go-for-gore violence. There were few masters in this field. In his best work, Lucio Fulci, of the vomited intestines (**Paura nella Città dei Morti Viventi**/*City of the Living Dead*, 1980) and hole-through-a-child's-head (**L'Aldilà**/*The Beyond*, 1981), seems an idiot savant, whipping gore and the gothic into shambling, strained, suspenseful pictures that retain their fascination – though his golden period was brief, and his subsequent attempts to recapture it unendurable. A lot of filmmakers tried to pull off transgressive gore-comedy (Frank Henenlotter in **Basket Case**, 1982, Jim Muro in *Street Trash*, 1986), but it wasn't as easy as it looks. If anything killed off this field it was the concerted efforts of Lloyd Kaufman's Troma to make films which didn't even try to be good on any level – *The Toxic Avenger* (1985), *Class of Nuke 'Em High* (1986) and sequels. Contempt for the audience is the covert Troma slogan, and seamy, juvenile, misogynist, homophobic smugness makes their product easy to dislike. Even the best gore films had a limited audience – while the Evil Dead, the Re-Animated and the Cenobites were big at festivals and on video, cinemas earned more with forgettable, family-friendly, play-it-safe films like *Witchboard* (1985), *House* (1986), *The Gate* (1986) and *Child's Play* (1988).

On the home front, things really were changing. The "video nasties" brouhaha drew attention to the fact that films which would not have made it to British cinemas were easily available for home viewing. For every title hitherto kept off our screens by a BBFC ban (like **Blood Feast**, **Last House on the Left** or **The Texas Chain Saw Massacre**) there were dozens which had previously not showed up in the UK on the grounds of sheer obscurity. Now any horror film could get a video release – and, within months, the back catalogues were scoured dry. In 1985–86, Christopher Lewis, son of the '40s screen siren Loretta Young, directed three films which seem to be the first horror movies intended from the outset to bypass theatrical release and be distributed solely on video – *The Ripper*, with a cameo by Tom Savini as Jack the Ripper, *Blood Cult* and *Blood Cult 2: Revenge*. After that, the deluge – which continues unabated into the new millennium, especially as digi-beta, filmlook video, Hi-Def and even plain old camcorder become acceptable formats for a straight-to-tape or disc release. Long-time production outfits like Troma, Charles Band's Empire/Full Moon or Roger Corman's various companies stepped up to supply the video Moloch with product, and many small groups of people got together and did it in the barn (the Texan *Through the Fire*, 1987, the Oklahoman *Terror at Tenkiller*, 1987, the Michiganese *The Changer*/*The Nostril*

ABOVE: No way out for John Travolta in De Palma's *Blow Out* (1981).

outstanding **Henry … Portrait of a Serial Killer** was made in 1986, but didn't get shown until well into the '90s.

The art-horror interface in America and Europe produced resonant, memorable work: Michael Mann's **The Keep** (1983) and *Manhunter* (1986) flopped at the box office and wouldn't become influential for some years; Pedro Almodovar's *Matador* (1986) opens with an obsessive masturbating to Mario Bava and Jesus Franco films; Peter Greenaway's *The Cook The Thief His Wife & Her Lover* (1989) is a charade mingling Jacobean revenge tragedy and Poe's *Masque of the Red Death*; and David Lynch's **Blue Velvet** (1986) is a surreal, terrifying small-town film which became an instant, much-imitated classic. Meanwhile, big-studio horror still tended to mean Stephen King adaptations. Brian De Palma continued to work his own vein in *Blow Out* (1981) and *Body Double* (1984), but increasingly moved out of self-penned psycho-horror into crime projects scripted by other people.

Still, above-ground horror sometimes worried at America's sensitive throat: Robert Harmon's **The Hitcher** (1986) is a stripped-down road movie about a teenage driver (C. Thomas Howell) and his inexplicable, mass-murdering doppelgänger (Rutger Hauer); and Joseph Ruben's **The Stepfather** (1986) is a meditation on "family values", making a big return in the era of Reagan and Thatcher, with Terry O'Quinn as the decade's most resonant psycho, a troubled middle-class husband and father who snaps when his new families can't live up to an impossible Norman Rockwell ideal. Tim Burton's *Beetlejuice* (1988) is a reverse ghost story in which nice spooks employ a "bio-exorcist" (Michael Keaton) to drive nasty living folk out of their haunted house; Joe Dante's *The 'burbs* (1988) suggests that suburbanites are scarier than outright gothic maniacs; Bob Balaban's **Parents** (1988) reveals that '50s parents who conform to the stepfather's idea of how family life should be are secretly cannibals; Michael Lehmann's *Heathers* (1988) is about a murder spree triggered by class divisions in high school; and Brian Yuzna's **Society** (1989) alleges that rich people aren't even human. There were clutches of films about voodoo (*The Serpent and the Rainbow*, 1987, *The Believers*, 1987) and the Devil (*The Unholy*, 1987, *The Seventh Sign*, 1988) suggesting that evil was "out there" and "other", and the most commercially successful horror picture of the late '80s was a conservative tract disguised as a talking-point social drama, Adrian Lyne's *Fatal Attraction* (1987). If the best horror films were still committed and oppositional, Lyne's Psycho Bitch From Hell effort – progenitor of a whole sub-genre of paranoid male woman-hating – was the most in tune with the fraying, desperate mood of society.

Picker, 1988, etc.) and then sold their amateur endeavours to real distributors. There have been entertaining, interesting and even important direct-to-video horror films, but there have also been enough dreadful bores to satiate even the most committed completist. With all the jostling schlock, it had also been harder for the new Herk Harveys and George Romeros to get noticed alongside the far greater number of new Jim Wynorskis and Fred Olen Rays. John McNaughton's

THE BOOGEYMAN
AKA THE BOGEY MAN

1980, US, dir/co-scr Ulli Lommel, co-scr David Herschel, Suzanna Love, starring Suzanna Love, Ron James, John Carradine, Nicholas Love

Two young children, Lacey and Willy, witness their mother having kinky sex with her lover. Willy is tied to his bed as punishment for spying, but Lacey frees him and Willy stabs the man to death. Twenty years later, Lacey is taking care of Willy, now a mute, with the help of an aunt and her boyfriend Jake. A letter from their mother leads Lacey to revisit the old family home, where she sees the man Willy murdered reflected in a mirror. Smashing it, she liberates an evil force – and those who come into contact with the shards die in a variety of horrible ways.

The Boogeyman is hard to synopsize, thanks to its frequently senseless story. Much is left unexplained (although a Lacanian would have a field day with the relentless use of mirrors). We never find out how the mirror became "possessed" but the fact that a boy sees a man indulge in kinky sex with mommy seems to want to "out" the psychological undercurrents of **Halloween**, which displaced the Oedipal implications onto an older female sibling. The whole thing is further confused by the ungainly collision of movies from which Lommel borrows, chiefly **Halloween**, **The Amityville Horror** and **The Exorcist**. However, if you just "go with the flow" it's an enormously entertaining supernatural slasher. Thanks to a lovely score that effectively mimics John Carpenter and some simple but attractive location photography, what it lacks in coherence is made up for in mood, and it is not unlike the films which Lucio Fulci was making at the time (although Lommel lacks Fulci's extremes).

Once the film has settled down to tell the tale of a haunted mirror, things begin to cook, and the scenes involving mirror shards that compel people to suicide have a real charge – although what ultimately drives the force is left unclear by a less-than-impressive exorcism finale. Still, German emigré Lommel throws his American horror motifs in the blender with enough spice to make you forgive the inconsistencies. [ST]

CANNIBAL HOLOCAUST

1980, It, dir Ruggero Deodato, scr Gianfranco Clerici, starring Robert Kerman, Francesca Ciardi, Perry Pirkanen, Luca Giorgio Barbareschi

When Alan Yates's team of American documentary filmmakers go missing in the Amazon basin, a rescue team are sent to find out what happened to them. They return with a set of film cans, the contents of which prove too grisly for their proposed TV screening. Deodato's notorious film has lost little of its power to shock since its release, and remains the only essential release from the Italian cannibal cycle of the early '80s. Structurally a major influence on the "mockumentary" strand of horror filmmaking that includes *The Last Broadcast* (1998) and **The Blair Witch Project**, *Cannibal Holocaust* is a far more involving film, the shoddiness of its effects and the way the documentary footage conveniently hiccups just as each new atrocity is staged detracting little from the film's confrontational power. According to Deodato the film was made in response to the exploitative Italian press coverage of real-life violence in the '70s and the then-popular cycle of "mondo" films, but the director's justification, and the explicit message of the film – that the savagery of the developed world is more pernicious than that of tribal "savages", as it relies on no code of conduct – cannot be taken at face value. Although the rescue team's dealings with the Amazonian tribes seek to heal the wounds left by the Yates team, there's no doubt that Deodato's crew come uncomfortably close to Yates in revelling in the display of atrocities, including several indefensible on-screen animal killings, and treating the Amazonian cast with racist contempt.

Still, although Deodato's position may be untenable, and he tackles his theme with a bludgeoning lack of subtlety, the Yates footage remains devastatingly effective, and a handful of scenes – the Yamamomo emerging from the trees, the bone-sculpture remains of the Yates team and the apocalyptic ending – have an iconic power that ranks with the best of the decade's other genre offerings. *Cannibal Holocaust* was also one of the most profitable Italian films of the '80s, grossing $20 million worldwide according to its director. However, it was banned in Italy for three years under an ancient law forbidding the torture and killing of animals for entertainment, although lesser copies such as Umberto Lenzi's *Cannibal Ferox* (1981) escaped prosecution.

DON'T GO IN THE HOUSE

1980, US, dir/co-scr Joseph Ellison, co-scr Ellen Hammill, Joseph R. Masefield, starring Dan Grimaldi, Charlie Bonet, Bill Ricci, Robert Osth

After the death of his domineering mother, Donny takes revenge on women by burning them alive. A jaw-dropping mix of reprehensible misogyny and unintentional mirth, *Don't Go in the House* is defensible only as pure trash sleaze. On his mother's death, voices tell Donny that "You can do anything you want to". His first response is to play a disco record and jump on a chair, but he soon takes inspiration from his job at an incinerator and converts a room into a metal-lined firebug paradise. A woman is lured to the house, stripped and torched with a flamethrower, the only murder shown in detail, but it's so gruellingly realistic that it sits uncomfortably with the throwaway feel of the rest of the film. The most spectacularly outré sequence has Donny being kitted out in the finest disco gear by a camp salesman who recommends an elasticated suit – "Unless you're into the more wild look, which is really passé?" Predictably enough, Donny's attempt at mingling with coke-snorting disco bunnies ends in flames, and he goes home to berate the charred corpses he's kept for company – "A fine lot of thanks I get. I bring you into my home. I give you love, and shelter!" – in preparation for the **Maniac**-style finale. Grimaldi's scenery-chewing as Donny does even more damage than his flamethrower and the film's attempt to contextualize his madness – flashbacks show him being tortured by his mother – only highlight its irredeemable cynicism, but its ineptitude means it's never as grimly offensive as the similarly grotty **Maniac,** while

the disco barbecue theme gives the whole enterprise a distinctly wrong-headed charm.

DRESSED TO KILL

1980, US, dir/scr Brian De Palma, starring Michael Caine, Angie Dickinson, Nancy Allen, Keith Gordon

When a sexually frustrated housewife, Kate Miller, is murdered after a one-night stand, Liz, a prostitute, is the prime suspect. But the real killer is after Liz and only Kate's son Peter believes her story. De Palma's Hitchcock homage plays like a blackly comic updating of **Psycho**, complete with two shock endings, two eroticized shower scenes and a psychiatrist's ridiculous summing-up, but the director's real interests seem to be in

---

BELOW: Michael Caine and Angie Dickinson in **Dressed to Kill**.

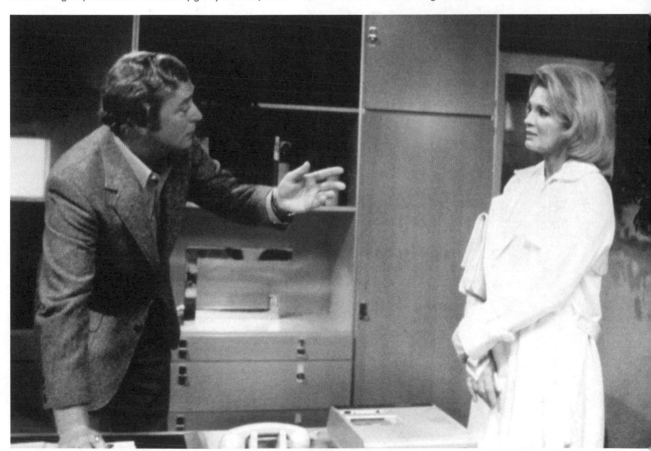

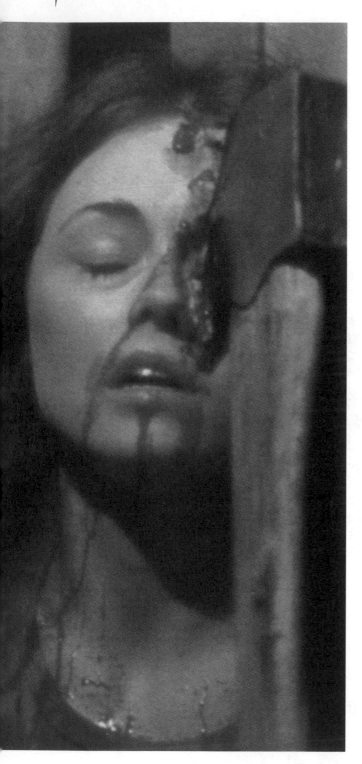

parodying gender roles in horror. Mrs Miller's fling, a near-dialogue-free set piece that presents its technically brilliant game of cat-and-mouse in tawdry soft-core visuals, is also a ludicrously overblown warning of the perils of adultery or ditziness, as its plot is advanced solely through Mrs Miller's forgetful shedding of personal items in the heat of the moment. The bluff cop, a macho stereotype who misses key events by taking his kids to "the game", blames her sexual availability for her death and it is up to Peter, an asexual boffin who boasts, mad-scientist-style, that "instead of making a computer, I can make a woman – out of meat!", to help the sexually predatory Liz solve the case. The identity of the killer provides another spin on gender issues, which along with the perverse edginess of some scenes – Kate's rape dream, or Liz's staged but similar fantasies – and the murder iconography (black leather gloves, straight razor) give the film a *giallo* flavour. However, the overwrought soundtrack and absurd plot contrivances make it difficult to take seriously, for all De Palma's assured handling of suspense techniques and signature split-screen cut-ups.

FRIDAY THE 13TH

1980, US, dir Sean S. Cunningham, scr Victor Miller, starring Betsy Palmer, Adrienne King, Jeannine Taylor, Robbi Morgan

Camp Crystal Lake, 1958. A pair of camp counsellors are killed while "making out". Twenty-two years later, a new group of camp counsellors arrive to prepare for the camp's reopening and discover that Crazy Ralph wasn't kidding when he told them they wouldn't come back. If **Halloween** started the slasher boom, *Friday the 13th* provided the template most of its successors slavishly followed, with its succession of witless teens (featuring at least one future star, here Kevin Bacon) wandering off alone at night to be graphically skewered by farm tools and sporting goods. To its credit, the film looks relatively glossy, makes at least some use of its backwoods locations and boasts grisly murders (courtesy of Tom Savini) and a Herrmann-pillaging string score rather than the synthesizer noodlings plaguing other low-budget contemporary American product. However, the direction is inept, providing no suspense for the murders that pad out its running time, and the revelation of the killer, who has hairy hands and large work boots and is strong enough to heft a corpse through a window, is a con trumped only by Jason's purported survival in the lake for 22 years to

LEFT: Tom Savini's crowd-pleasing effects in **Friday the 13th**.

emerge as a homicidal aquatic ape. But *Friday the 13th* is less interesting as a film than as a brand: distributed by a major studio, it proved a major success, its highly profitable franchise making Jason Vorhees (not, incidentally, the killer here, let alone in his hockey-masked incarnation) a hugely popular teen-horror icon. One of the more bizarre scenes has a cop warning the campers that he won't stand for any "weirdness": this surface jibe at authority, with the teens giggling behind his back, masks a conservatism that sees the virginal Alice as the sole survivor and the killer's motivation revolving around punishment for sex. The theme, relied upon more heavily in later slashers, betrays horror's subversive potential for an implicit affirmation of moral-majority values, an egregious de-clawing that carried over into the vacuous '90s teen-horror boom.

THE HOWLING

1980, US, dir Joe Dante, scr John Sayles, Terence H. Winkless, starring Dee Wallace, Patrick Macnee, Dennis Dugan, Belinda Balaski

Newsreader Karen is sent to the Colony, a self-help institute run by talkshow psychologist Dr Waggner, to recuperate after being used as bait to trap a suspected serial killer. But when her husband Bill is bitten by a wolf, she soon learns the Colony's dark secret.... More successful as sly monster-movie tribute than werewolf film, *The Howling* not only admits the existence of other cinema lycanthropes but revels in its knowledge of them, naming its characters after their directors (Fred Francis, Terry Fisher, George Waggner), letting its newsmen learn werewolf lore from watching **The Wolf Man** on TV and realizing that its principal *raison d'être* is Rob Bottin's transformation sequence, showcasing the graphic snout extrusion that virtually all subsequent werewolf movies would feel obliged to follow. The in-jokes extend to the casting, John Carradine playing a whiskery old-timer at the Colony who argues that "You can't tame what's meant to be wild", Dick Miller as the owner of an occult bookshop who complains of werewolves, "They're worse than cockroaches!" and cameos from Roger Corman and Forrest J. Ackerman – but although these prove entertaining enough for genre buffs, they highlight a throwaway tone in the film's treatment of both characters and ideas. Despite the gruelling ordeal that opens Karen's story, we're never really invited to sympathize with her, whether during her love-rat husband's slavering-beast sex or her hairball demise, a shallow,

RIGHT: Bizarrely hairless poster art for **The Howling**.

emotional involvement that extends to the other characters. The admittedly impressive transformation sequence occurs halfway through the film, leaving its structure uneven, while some of the earlier scrabbling wolf claws look surprisingly hokey and the marvellous concept of warring werewolf factions (the separatist "old ways" vs Waggner's liberal integration) hiding behind an Esalen-style consciousness-raising front hardly gets the room it deserves. Still, this led the pack in werewolf transformations and spawned a furry franchise of its own with five increasingly risible sequels.

INFERNO

1980, It, dir/co-scr Dario Argento, co-scr Daria Nicolodi, starring Leigh McCloskey, Irene Miracle, Eleonora Giorgi, Daria Nicolodi

In the sequel to **Suspiria**, Dario Argento puts some flesh on the bare bones of his "Three Mothers" trilogy, revealing that the Freiburg dance school of the first film is one of three dwelling places for evil witches built by an alchemist/architect named Varelli. **Suspiria** showed how these malevolent females kill anyone who stumbles across their secrets and this pattern continues in *Inferno* with a young woman in New York being murdered after reading Varelli's journal. Her death brings her brother, Mark, to New York from Rome, unaware that before he left he encountered one of the Three Mothers himself, the young and pouting Mater Lachrymarum.

Leigh McCloskey's Mark is another of Argento's innocents adrift in a nightmare world where any object, from a simple window to a work of art, can be transformed into an instrument of death. Mark comes to discover that the New York building is home to Mater Tenebrarum, the Mother of Darkness, who eventually reveals an even more sinister face. Unfortunately, McCloskey's presence is even more limp than Jessica Harper's was in **Suspiria**, which is a shame since Argento's trademark set pieces are just as inventive, especially in the scenes of a flooded room filled with floating corpses and a death during a lunar eclipse. The story is slightly more coherent this time round, although with Argento it's debatable how much story he actually needs as connecting tissue between his scenes of exquisite mayhem. Argento's elegance puts the fumblings of lesser directors to shame, and the lighting, photography and design are just as luscious as in **Suspiria**. Keith Emerson provides a decent score, although his florid keyboards are a poor substitute for the insane clatterings of Goblin in the earlier film. A quarter of a century on Argento completed the trilogy with the critically snubbed *La Terza Madre/Mother of Tears* (2007). [JC]

BELOW: Rose (Irene Miracle) finds her keys in a puddle, **Inferno**.

MANIAC

1980, US, dir William Lustig, scr C.A. Rosenberg, Joe Spinell, starring Joe Spinell, Caroline Munro, Gail Lawrence, Kelly Piper

Although the field is increasingly crowded by nasty, depressing SOV efforts like Eric Stanze's *Scrapbook* (1999), *Maniac* still has the dubious distinction of boasting cinema's sleaziest, scummiest serial killer – and this is a part Spinell wrote for himself. The minimal plot follows Frank Zito (Spinell) around NYC as he stalks, kills and scalps a series of women, then nails the scalps to the mannequins littering his apartment. The scenes of a sweating, overweight Spinell in his apartment, alternately sobbing and sweet-talking his mannequins, beggar belief, although the apartment itself is an inventively decorated psycho retreat. But the film's real jaw-dropper comes when he starts dating an enthusiastic fashion photographer (Munro), the most unlikely romantic entanglement in the movies since Kong tried to undress Fay Wray. This brings it close to **Don't Go in the House**'s mixture of unintentional laughs and grim sleaze, but *Maniac* keeps the edge in the latter stakes, with grisly don't-look-now scalpings, the best exploding head outside **Scanners** (the head in question belonging to effects maestro Tom Savini) and a genuinely horrific finale. The film also benefits from convincingly grimy urban locations and a great early '80s synth score, and manages to milk its stalk 'n' slash scenes for genuine tension (particularly the subway sequence) and, at times, an unexpected subtlety (one victim's face changes to Zito's mother as he strangles her). Reprehensible and horrific but never dull, *Maniac* also boasts one of the nastiest posters ever to grace a horror movie.

LE NOTTI DEL TERRORE
AKA BURIAL GROUND; THE ZOMBIE DEAD; ZOMBIE 3; ZOMBIE HORROR

1980, It, dir Andrea Bianchi, scr Piero Regnoli, starring Karin Weil, Maria Angela Giordan, Gian Luigi Chrizzi, Peter Bark

An archaeologist studying the magical practices of the ancient Etruscans succeeds in raising the dead. A group arrive to stay at a villa near the dig and check on his progress, but find themselves besieged by the undead. Virtually plotless, with the most perfunctorily sketched characters, Bianchi's film distils the Italian zombie cycle to its barest essentials, presenting a series of gory attacks from slow-moving ghouls with a pornographic repetitiveness while leaping jackdaw-style from **Zombi 2** to de Ossorio's Blind Dead series for inspiration. The inventively

decayed dead appear to have regressed to primordial clay, their dull mud colourings, flaking surfaces and greyish fluids contrasting with the clean skin, scarlet blood and sexual vitality of the living. To assuage their entrail envy, the dead open their victims to pull out their intestines, the camera lavishing the same lingering care on the crude dissections as it does on the attacks on the zombies themselves. Bianchi achieves a certain claustrophobic panic in the later attacks, making the most of the zombies' glacial pace, and while the sexual enthusiasm of the living can be put down to exploitation values rather than any profound commentary on sex and death, the Oedipal sub-plot concerning Michael, a late breastfeeder who looks like the product of an unholy union between Michael Berryman and Dario Argento, adds a dollop of genuine perversity to the gory mix.

PAURA NELLA CITTÀ DEI MORTI VIVENTI
AKA CITY OF THE LIVING DEAD; THE GATES OF HELL

1980, It, dir Lucio Fulci, scr Dardano Sacchetti, starring Katherine (Catriona) McColl, Christopher George, Janet Agren, Carlo De Mejo

A priest commits suicide in the town of Dunwich: the event is witnessed by Mary, a psychic, during a seance. An ancient *grimoire* reveals that the priest's actions presage the opening of a gateway to Hell, through which the living dead will emerge to destroy the Earth. Can Mary prevent it happening?

After the grisly hit **Zombi 2**, *Paura nella* shows Lucio Fulci adopting a gothic approach that would stand him in good stead for **L'Aldilà** and *Quella Villa Accanto al Cimitero/House by the Cemetery* (1981). But beware if you demand coherence from your horror films, because *Paura nella* devoutly embraces the irrational. It's a seething brew of sub-plots and digressions, interrupting the adventures of its likable leads (Catriona McColl's psychic and Christopher George's reporter) with so many sideways lurches that conventional storytelling values are left in the dust. In this it recalls the early novels of James Herbert (*The Fog*, for example, in which a lead plotline is interpolated with grisly vignettes). Traditional horror fans may find the result irritating but, for those with a love of the gruesome and bizarre, *Paura nella* is a carnival of horrors, juxtaposing marvellous painterly images, electrifying set pieces (including an outstanding "buried alive" sequence quoted in Tarantino's *Kill Bill: Vol. 2*, 2004) with scenes of horrific violence. Alongside Fulci's trademark zombies (as wonderfully vile as ever), the film boasts a horde of oddball minor characters:

a querulous medium, a sleazy undertaker and, most memorably, a hapless dropout called Bob, whose death by drilling lathe outdoes even Abel Ferrara's **Driller Killer** (although it's a tad less plausible as social commentary).

Fulci is notorious for screen violence and, with repulsive images here such as a woman throwing up her internal organs, he lives up to his reputation to the hilt. But, for all the maggots and gore, it's the misty, shadowy, wind-ravaged town of Dunwich, stylishly explored by a prowling camera, that beguiles most: that, and the way Fulci is forever willing to sacrifice credibility for an extraordinary image. [ST]

LA REGINA DEI CANNIBALI
AKA ZOMBIE HOLOCAUST; DR BUTCHER MD; QUEEN OF THE CANNIBALS; THE ISLAND OF THE LAST ZOMBIES

1980, It, dir/co-scr Frank Martin (Marino Girolami), co-scr Fabrizio de Angelis, starring Ian McCullough, Sherry Buchanan, Alexander Cole (Alexandra dei Colli), Peter O'Neal

In a Manhattan hospital an orderly is caught stealing body parts and commits suicide. The tattoo on his chest and his final words refer to the religion of a SE Asian island; a team of anthropologists and journalists is sent to stay with world-famous surgeon Dr Abrera on a nearby island to solve the mystery. This cheap and tacky

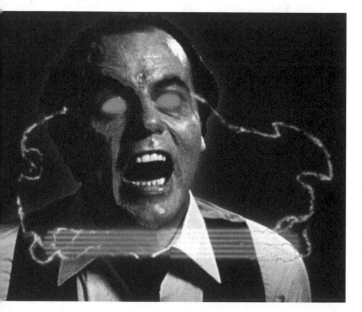

Zombi 2 rip-off repeats Fulci's Manhattan-to-tropics trajectory as well as sharing its ineptly gory special effects, but adds to the mix by making the island's natives slobbering cannibals who have not yet learned to cook. Abrera's sweatily mad surgeon has relocated to practise brain transplants without interference from do-gooders. Zombies result from his experiments: they take orders and speed up when told to, although without Abrera to instruct them they're too slow to avoid audacious ends like a propeller in the head. Unlike the zombies, the cannibals' presence is never adequately explained: their adoption of Lori, one of the female characters, as a deity is bewildering and their attack on Abrera's jungle surgery a hypocritical dénouement given their thoroughly racist depiction. While never escaping the tawdriness of its exploitation values – the females parade around in states of undress or, if they're unlucky, end up scalped and put under the cranial saw – the film is pulpy fun and uses its jungle locations surprisingly well.

SCANNERS

1980, Can, dir/scr David Cronenberg, starring Stephen Lack, Jennifer O'Neill, Patrick McGoohan, Michael Ironside

Homeless Cameron Vale is recruited by ConSec's Dr Ruth to infiltrate an underground scanner group run by Darryl Revok. Scanners like Vale and Revok can read and control minds, and Vale becomes involved in a battle between ConSec, which wants to control scanners through addiction to Ephemerol, a drug that helps them to function normally, and Revok, who resists ConSec's efforts. Essentially a commercial reworking of Cronenberg's early experimental work *Stereo* (1969), *Scanners* is the most SF-tinged of Cronenberg's early films, although a graphic exploding head ensured its distribution as a horror film.

Lack's blandness as Vale makes him plausible only as a credulous flunky, eagerly believing everything he is told by the sinister Dr Ruth while allowing himself to become addicted to Ephemerol. Ironside's intensity as Revok makes him a far more engaging character, as his band reject ConSec's control and deal with their telepathic abilities through sheer force of will. Another scanner develops a third way of coping, through art, by living inside a giant sculpture of his own head in one of Cronenberg's most audaciously literal metaphors. As with the director's previous films, *Scanners* comments on radical '60s social experiments and psychology: Vale falls in with a benign hippy group, enjoying group

LEFT: Michael Ironside is about to melt, **Scanners**.

ABOVE: "Here's Johnny!" A terrified Shelley Duvall in **The Shining**.

mind experiences that are blissful enough but fail to challenge the existing order, until they are disrupted by Revok's gun-toting direct-action radicals. The scanners' back-story both redraws the conflict as one of family, Dr Ruth's authoritarian patriarch obeyed by "good" son Vale and rejected by "bad' son Revok, and draws uncomfortable parallels with the Thalidomide scandal, with ConSec's conscious use of medical "accidents" to produce weapons. If the ending lacks conviction, the commercial appeal of its relatively conventional scenario and iconic head explosions paved the way for a franchise of more SF-oriented sequels.

THE SHINING

1980, US, dir/co-scr Stanley Kubrick, co-scr Diane Johnson, starring Jack Nicholson, Shelley Duvall, Danny Lloyd, Scatman Crothers

The lukewarm response that greeted *The Shining* on its initial release seemed to be prompted by expectations that Kubrick was intending to deliver some ultimate statement *à la 2001: A Space Odyssey* (he wasn't) and disappointment from fans of the novel that key scenes had been altered. Stephen King's book laid out in detail the troubled history of the Overlook Hotel but Kubrick threw most of this away in order to focus on the central story of the family left alone in malign surroundings. The original complaints seem irrelevant now that Jack Nicholson's leering visage and his manic cry of "Here's Johnny!' are universally recognized as tokens of one of the major films of the period. The limp television remake from a disgruntled King only served to make Kubrick's film seem all the more powerful, remote and truly chilling.

With a minimal cast, vast sets, impeccable photography from John Alcott and a dissonant score from Bartók and Penderecki which matches the shots so well that it seems to have been written especially for the film, Kubrick conjures an atmosphere of epic claustrophobia. The hotel may be huge and empty but the air becomes increasingly poisonous with unspoken resentment and, eventually, murderous hatred. In Kubrick's hands *The Shining* is less a haunted-house story than a meditation on the potentially destructive power of close relationships – lock a dysfunctional family away for a whole winter and watch them tear themselves apart. For all the apparitions and visions of blood-soaked corridors, this remains the film's true source of horror, a horror given a tragic dimension as the caretaker Jack Torrance recognizes too late that the influence of the hotel is driving him to destroy his family. Kubrick's elisions leave an ambiguity that King's original story avoids. How much does Torrance imagine of the hotel's hauntings? And how much is his young son Danny controlling or even causing the events that drive his father insane? Kubrick refuses to explain; he leads us into the maze and abandons us there. [JC]

BELOW: Change doesn't come easy for David Naughton, **An American Werewolf in London**.

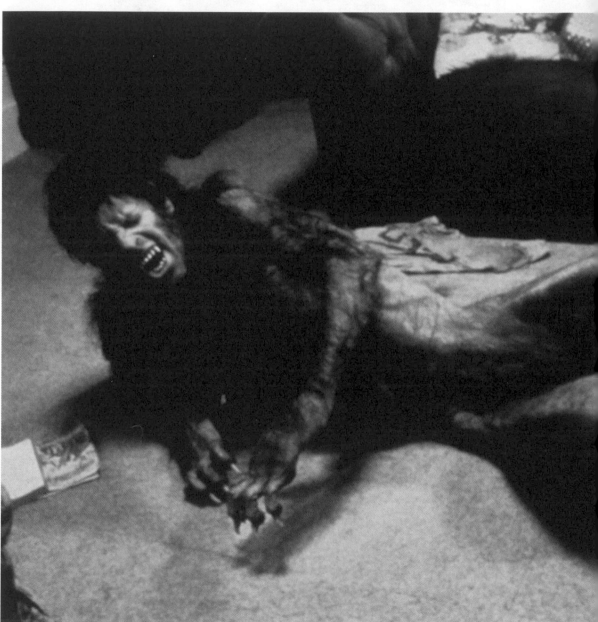

L'ALDILÀ AKA THE BEYOND; SEVEN DOORS OF DEATH

1981, It, dir Lucio Fulci, scr Dardano Sacchetti, starring Katherine (Catriona) McColl, David Warbeck, Al Cliver, Sarah Keller

When Liza Merrill inherits a rundown Louisiana hotel, she imagines her luck is improving. Not so: the hotel is built over one

of the Seven Gateways to Hell and Liza must eventually confront "The Sea of Darkness", with only handsome Doctor McCabe and blind, ethereal Emily to help her.

If you only see one Lucio Fulci film, make it *L'Aldilà*. Poetic and brutal, like a dream about a nightmare, it gathers a fistful of influences (**The Shining**, *The Sentinel,* 1976, **Inferno**), turns the gore up to 11, and delivers something utterly unique. This is Fulci in full flight, creating violent set pieces which float, unmoored, in a plot devoid of rationality. Be careful if you're squeamish because the human head comes in for special attention: whether slathered in quicklime, poked in the eye by undead fingers, ripped at by a dog, chewed up by flesh-eating spiders, drenched in acid, quilled with shards of glass or, in one unforgettable scene involving a child, radically ventilated by a .44 Magnum. All of which could have been unbearably grim except that Fulci's sense of elegance amid the offal lifts *L'Aldilà* towards beauty. With cinematographer Sergio Salvati, Fulci makes even the grisliest of scenes ravishing to look at. The dominant imagery is of decay: the hotel is falling apart, the cellar crumbling and waterlogged and Fulci's zombies are putrescent and distorted. But this is set against the stylishness of New Orleans, Emily's house, and the antiseptic modernity of the hospital where John works. For sure, this has some of the most horrific imagery in Fulci's career, and some of the silliest (like the spiders), but it's the dream-narrative structure and sumptuously decayed art design that guide you through the gore. *L'Aldilà* is steeped to the splattered eyeballs in melancholy, amplified by Fabio Frizzi's marvellous score and, thanks to the instantly adorable McColl and Warbeck, there's even some human warmth in there. The result is Fulci's masterpiece, and one of the peak achievements of Italian horror. [ST]

AN AMERICAN WEREWOLF IN LONDON

1981, US, dir/scr John Landis, starring David Naughton, Jenny Agutter, Griffin Dunne, John Woodvine

Landis is predominantly known as a comedy director, with *National Lampoon's Animal House* (1978) and *The Blues Brothers* (1980) probably his best-loved works. Here he manages the difficult feat of combining humour and horror into an amalgam that loses nothing of the essence of both, a particularly remarkable accomplishment considering he wrote the screenplay aged just 19. He's aided immeasurably in this by effects supremo Rick Baker, whose werewolf transformation effects remained unbeaten in the pre-CGI era and retain a gruesomely tactile

SLASHERS

Bastard cousin of the *giallo*, serial killer film and psycho-thriller, the slasher is generally considered close to the nadir of the already disreputable horror genre, trumped only by the Italian cannibal cycle and the mock snuff of Japan's infamous *Guinea Pig* series. Early prototypes like **Communion** and **Black Christmas** showed verve and originality, but the films that followed the monumental success of **Halloween** displayed neither, reverting to the formulaic nature of the slasher's other forebear, the babysitter-in-peril TV movie.

While **Halloween** boasted textbook scares, likeable teens, visual flair to burn and surprisingly bloodless killings, its pared-down, easily imitated narrative and immense profitability drew film producers like flies to a rotting carcass and, with its first major imitator, **Friday the 13th**, the die was cast. If **Halloween** was a well-deserved but surprise success, the early '80s slasher boom unfortunately took more cues from **Friday the 13th**, not least its cynicism and ineptitude. Subsequent films followed the "rules" established by **Halloween** and enshrined by **Friday the 13th** with religious fanaticism – a killer, created by a traumatic past event, returns to its location, often on a specific date featured in the title, to stalk and murder odious, inane teens with sporting or farming implements; a virginal "final girl" survives to vanquish the killer, although loopholes are usually left for his return should the film prove a success.

Audiences enjoyed the predictability of such formula fare, shunning originality except in settings (**My Bloody Valentine**, 1981 and *Tourist Trap*, 1978, at least have the wit to stay away from the usual student dorms and summer camps) and innovative murders, which tended to be quoted by other slashers in such a baldly imitative manner that the films are beyond the parody of contemporary spoof *Pandemonium* (1982).

The explosive growth of home video in the early '80s ensured that the original slashers had a longer shelf life than originally anticipated, with viewers selecting rentals on the basis of their effects work (Tom Savini, who provided graphic slayings in **Friday the 13th**, *The Burning*, 1981 and *The Prowler*, 1981, as well, more fruitfully, as Romero's **Dawn** and **Day of the Dead**, proving particularly popular) rather than their directors.

The cycle appeared to have played itself out by the mid '80s, hammered into the ground by genuinely nasty entries like Lucio Fulci's *Lo Squartatore di New York/The New York Ripper* (1982), only for Wes Craven to foreground the supernatural element implicit in the lazy plotting of many slashers and crossbreed it with the subjective fantasy worlds of effects' showcases *Brainstorm* (1983) and *Dreamscape* (1984) in **A Nightmare on Elm Street**. The fact that he repeated the trick a decade later with **Scream**, again infusing the frayed sub-genre with new life, prompted some to wonder why he couldn't let the slasher die a dignified death. While Craven's technical skill is undeniable, **Scream**'s real horror comes principally from its vacuous, mean-spirited teens, a different breed from the *Porkys* (1981) clones of the original slashers. A slew of slashers followed, some of which dispensed with Craven's genre familiarity for extraordinarily witless fare (*Valentine*, 2001), leaving the field open for the impressively grim **My Little Eye** as a rare stylish effort in the post-**Scream** slasher boom.

BELOW: "You can't kill the bogeyman!" **Halloween**.

ABOVE: "We're going to get you!" Something in the cellar in **The Evil Dead**.

quality that is scarcely matched by computer effects. The final transformation and chase through central London's landmarks look their age but don't feel dated.

The story concerns two young American students who are backpacking through Britain and wander into the wrong pub on the wrong moor. When they are later attacked by a ravening wolf one dies and one lives, but the latter has not escaped unscathed. As he recovers in a London hospital, a series of terrifying nightmares featuring his slaughtered friend inform him that he too will change into a werewolf with the next full moon if he does not kill himself first.

Other films that revel so heartily in their gore tend to encourage the audience to eagerly anticipate the slaughter. Landis's movie is unusual in that we are fully invested in the survival of the hero and the doomed love affair on which he embarks with a British nurse and, while the final werewolf transformation is thrilling, we watch it with some regret because of what it means for our hero. This was the third entry in the '80s cycle of relatively high-budget werewolf movies, following **The Howling**

and *Wolfen* (1981), and perhaps the most fondly remembered; if there's been a better werewolf movie since, it certainly isn't its dismal CGI-dependent sequel, 1997's *An American Werewolf in Paris*. [RL]

THE EVIL DEAD

1981, US, dir/scr Sam Raimi, starring Bruce Campbell, Ellen Sandweiss, Betsy Baker, Hal Delrich

When Ash and four friends spend a night in a woodland cabin, they find a book and a tape-recording detailing the successful invocation of demons. One girl is raped by trees, becomes possessed and attacks her friends; who will survive until morning? Despite being described as "ferociously original" by Stephen King on its release, *The Evil Dead* borrows magpie-fashion from a range of sources: the Book of the Dead and language used in the tape recording recall Lovecraft, and the film's unity of time and space (the events take place over one night in the cabin) align it with the archetypal nightmares of **Night of the Living Dead** and **The Texas Chain Saw Massacre**. The rural Tennessee location and glimpses of the poster for **The Hills Have Eyes** in the basement suggest an urbanoia trajectory the film never really follows, while the demons' multi-tracked voices and pasty green faces draw on **The Exorcist**, and Ash's trajectory from naïve coward to blood-smeared demon slayer is squarely in the Wes Craven tradition of civilized men tapping into their inner savage. Not that it matters: Raimi's micro-budgeted debut is astonishingly assured and inventive, infusing hackneyed horror tropes with cartoon energy drawn from the director's love of the Three Stooges and a virtuoso technical flair showcasing inventions like the "Ram-o-Cam" (a camera attached to the centre of a long plank, the weight of which would even out bumps in motion), imaginative touches such as a mirror of water and an inspired claymation finale, and some extremely splashy gore effects. The effect is finally so over-the-top that it shades over into comedy – some investors were even upset at the comic tone – but when distributed in the UK, the film was caught up in the "video nasties" furore and even listed among the films for prosecution. Understandably upset, Raimi toned down the violence and amped up the explicit humour for the sequel, **Evil Dead II**.

MY BLOODY VALENTINE

1981, Can, dir George Mihalka, scr John Beaird, starring Paul Kelman, Lori Hallier, Neil Affleck, Keith Knight

As the residents of Valentine's Bluff gear up for their first Valentine's Day party for 20 years, the mayor starts receiving grisly packages. Has Harry Warden, the mining town's legendary killer, escaped from the asylum? Can anything stop the youth of Valentine's Bluff in their hunt for a good party?

My Bloody Valentine ticks all the slasher boxes – a calendar killer with a signature weapon (a miner's pick), killer POV shots with mandatory heavy breathing, obnoxious youths crying out to be sliced and diced, and it's even Canadian – but remains a cut above its peers. This is partly due to its surprisingly high production values and partly to its EC Comics feel. It comes with its own crypt-keeper, the gloriously doom-ridden bartender who tells one of his clients to "Beware what you make fun of, you little asshole!", and owes a nod to the "Poetic Justice" segment of **Tales from the Crypt**, although British horror has rarely approached this film's delight in gleeful mayhem.

The slasher was always a magpie sub-genre, but My Bloody Valentine selects only the choicest cuts for its "greatest hits" murder scenes and serves them up with a proud flourish. A skewered couple, a boiled face and a nailgun to the head on full-frontal display

---

BELOW: "We were having a party and Harry Warden started killing everybody!" **My Bloody Valentine**

along with the fatal pickaxe injuries, and the film even adds some killings it can happily call its own, including an impalement on a shower faucet and a body found in a tumble-dryer. Meanwhile the location shooting at the mine and the town gives a grubby reminder of dead-end industry that strikes a minor chord offset by the film's exuberant ghoulishness, while the setting offers a welcome break from the slasher's usual stamping ground of campsite, suburb and high school. Atmospheric cinematography, imaginative camera angles and art-film lighting might seem excessively precious for a film that boasts lines like "We were having a party and Harry Warden started killing everybody!", but the cornball dialogue only adds to the fun. *My Bloody Valentine* shows a refreshing lack of cynicism by acknowledging that we are in on the joke, but the same cannot be said for the 2009 3D remake. As the mayor of Valentine's Bluff says, "It can't be happening again!"

ABOVE: Isabelle Adjani, **Possession**.

POSSESSION

1981, W Ger/Fr, dir/scr Andrzej Zulawski, starring Isabel Adjani, Sam Neill, Heinz Bennent, Margit Carstensen

When Anna walks out on her husband Marc, he traces her to a lover called Heinrich. However, this is more than a mere love triangle: Anna has another apartment downtown and has given birth to a tentacled monster – with whom she makes love. Can Marc learn to live with the competition?

There's really nothing like *Possession*. Its whirl of ideas, restless and frenetic, has often been derided as hysterical, but that's scarcely the half of it. *Possession* is paradoxically both exhausting and invigorating: you're left feeling a bit like the characters, struggling with an experience beyond the power of language to exorcize. Zulawski's art-horror mélange engages with one of the principal Decadent projects, the seeking of states akin to madness. It succeeds in getting pretty close, especially during a standout scene in which Adjani has a violent fit in a subway tunnel (having entered a trance state at Zulawski's encouragement). With its gelatinous, phallus-headed monster, *Possession* enters uncharted territory for the art-house. The creature is an impossibility (Anna's possibility that "pierces reality"), which in a less ambitious film would have remained a metaphor or simply a delusion. Zulawski makes it real, visible to all who encounter it.

Possession is clangorous and discordant, full of wild verbal excesses and wrenching changes of pace. However, it's also a very beautiful film, with Zulawski's audacious creativity making each scene resonate. There are literally no boring shots, no wasted spaces. While the actors create maximum tension with the

extraordinary script, Zulawski's camera seduces and transforms. Never again would Sam Neill look so strange and tormented – and Adjani is so mercurial you need frame-advance to keep up with the expressions coursing through her features. *Possession* riles many people: its resistance to conclusive interpretation can be frustrating, especially since part of the film's appeal is its embarrassment of symbolic riches. The film seems to invite the viewer to advance theories yet, once you start, horizons recede and structures slyly disassemble. However, its ability to pose relentlessly unanswerable questions may be its greatest strength. [ST]

BASKET CASE

1982, US, dir/scr Frank Henenlotter, starring Kevin van Hentenryck, Terri Susan Smith, Beverly Bonner, Robert Vogel

Duane Bradley travels to New York to take revenge on the doctors who separated him from his Siamese-twin brother Belial, a homicidal lump he keeps in a wicker basket. But when Duane starts spending time with a female receptionist, Belial is reminded of his own adult needs. Zero-budget filmmaking with trash verve to spare, Henenlotter's debut feature provides the missing link between H. G. Lewis's comedy gore epics and the "splatstick" of **Evil Dead II** and **Braindead**. Boasting great location shots of 42nd Street, then wall-to-wall peepshow parlours and triple-bill grindhouses, *Basket Case* populates its world of cheap NYC sleaze with the kind of oddballs and misfits who keep Travis Bickle in business, none odder than Duane himself, who laughs hilariously as he drunkenly tells a neighbour that his brother's "deformed, a freak!" Strong gore effects, audacious stop-motion animation and the irreverent glee with which Henenlotter mounts scenes like Belial sniffing a woman's underwear gloss over the inept acting, while the distributor's decision to give surgical masks out at screenings – "to keep the blood off your face!" – recognized the film's rightful place in the carny freakshow tradition. Five years passed before Henenlotter's second feature, **Brain Damage**, another bona fide trash classic, but the director's talents were wasted on the rubber-monster hell of *Basket Case*'s two sequels and the unworkable crack-whore farce of *Frankenhooker* (1990).

THE BEAST WITHIN

1982, US, dir Philippe Mora, scr Tom Holland, starring Ronny Cox, Bibi Besch, Paul Clemens, Don Gordon

Nioba, Mississippi, 1964. When Eli MacCleary leaves his new wife Caroline in their broken-down car while he looks for a garage, she is raped by a creature from the swamp. Seventeen years later their son Michael is dying from an unknown illness and the couple return to Nioba hoping the identity of the rapist will help them find a cure. This is a Lovecraft adaptation in all but name, sharing themes (a remote rural town haunted by the sins of the past), character names (Dexter Ward, the Curwens) and high weirdness (Michael transforms into a giant cicada) with the Providence writer. But perhaps the closest Lovecraftian link is a rich sense of place, albeit small-town Dixieland rather than New England, that sees the only crimes committed in Nioba as "the occasional barn burning" while the dialogue is peppered with references to "salteens" and "coondogs". Nioba's townspeople are surprisingly credible given the wildness of the plot, from the impressively flinty-eyed sheriff to the psychotic hillbilly father of Michael's sweetheart Amanda, and if the MacClearys are less convincing, with Michael's battle between fawning affection and insectoid vengeance in Amanda's presence particularly ripe, scenes such as a dog dropping a severed hand on Amanda's face as the young lovers smooch serve as welcome distractions. This relatively late entry in the transformation stakes is also easily the strangest: there's no explanation of why Michael should turn into a cicada, although it does leave him displaying a touching species affinity by snapping "No they're not!" when Amanda complains of the swamp's "horrible" bugs. His final transformation, a riot of protracted bladder effects and hydrocephalic queasiness, is a real show-stopper.

BOARDINGHOUSE

1982, US, dir/scr John Wintergate, starring Hawk Adley (John Wintergate), Kalassu Kay, Alexandra Day, Joel McGinnis Riordan

When Jim Royce inherits a large house with a pool, he turns it into a boarding house for attractive young women. But the house has killed off all its previous occupants. Can Jim's powers of telekinesis prevent tragedy striking again?

A cult classic exemplar of the strain of '80s video psychosis, highlighted by Stephen Thrower in *Nightmare USA*, *BoardingHouse* goes beyond "so bad it's good" into the realms of extreme dislocation. Scenes start and stop abruptly, as though cut halfway through, characters either have arbitrary quirks or prove chronically indistinguishable from each other, corpses vanish or manage not to be found and pointless zooms are intercut with pregnant pauses, which lead nowhere except to the next witless line. This might seem merely encouraging – you too can make a movie! Anyone can! – if it weren't for the high weirdness saturating the film, from the extraordinary fly-buzzing soundtrack to the cheap video effects and bizarre visitations of the supernatural.

While taking a shower, one woman's face turns into a rubbery mask and when another character flees the house she has a bloody pig's head brandished at her from an open doorway. By the end of the film it's difficult to tell just what the characters are screaming at, but *BoardingHouse*, a horror film made in a parallel universe, has the cardinal virtue of never being dull. If you enjoy this there's plenty more on offer, although perhaps nothing quite so florid: try *Cataclysm* (1980), *Evilspeak* (1981) and *Mausoleum* (1983) for starters.

POLTERGEIST

1982, US, dir Tobe Hooper, scr Steven Spielberg, starring Craig T. Nelson, JoBeth Williams, Beatrice Straight, Dominique Dunne

A strange blending of talents, *Poltergeist* uneasily combines the take-no-prisoners nihilist aesthetic of director Hooper, infamous for helming **The Texas Chain Saw Massacre**, with screenwriter/co-producer Spielberg's sentimental celebration of American family life. Spielberg is generally considered the uncredited co-director of the movie, unable to officially step behind the camera because of a contract with Universal, and he was certainly the creative force with greater power, leading to a work which explores his concerns and largely ignores Hooper's: it's significant in this respect that the film does not feature a single fatality. Spielberg, master of the safe scare, carries mainstream

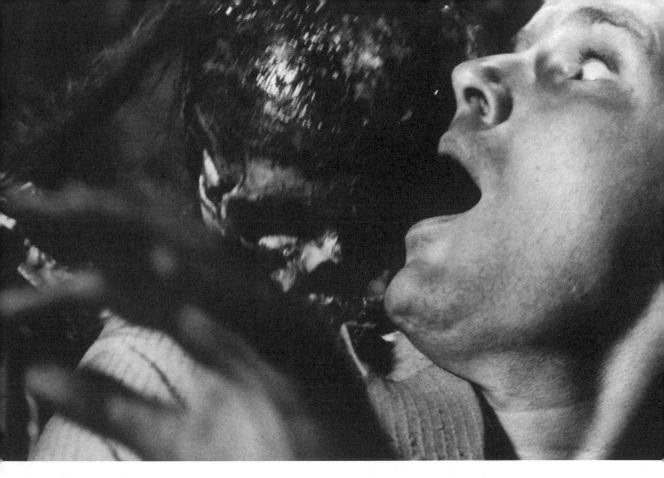

audiences with him because he never threatens to take them too far: his are the horror movies parents feel it safe for children to watch but, perhaps thanks to Hooper, *Poltergeist* at least hints at a darker reality than Spielberg is generally willing to acknowledge.

The narrative follows a happy, everyday family who soon discover that their new house is home to an evil force which preys on their individual fears. The performances are excellent and Spielberg's decision to cast unknowns as the family was inspired, helping to maintain the illusion that these are real people suffering real problems. His obsession with the relationship between kids and adults hadn't yet become tiresome and the children are endearing without being winsome. The real problem, though, is that the film can't decide whether it wants to be a slow-burning chiller or an outright shocker and in the end decides to be both. The first half, though a little sedate, cleverly utilizes everyday objects – the static of an untuned television, a misshapen tree – to build the atmosphere of dread.

In the second half atmosphere is sacrificed for in-your-face effects, including a swimming pool filled with the undead and a closet leading to another dimension and, though there are some genuinely shocking moments, the real terror is lost. [RL]

Q – THE WINGED SERPENT
AKA THE WINGED SERPENT
1982, US, dir/scr Larry Cohen, starring David Carradine, Michael Moriarty, Candy Clark, Richard Roundtree

NYC police are baffled by a series of ritual murders and airborne attacks, but a small-time crook's discovery of a giant egg in the steeple of the Chrysler Building may give them the break they've been looking for. *Q* is pure '50s monster-movie hokum, spiced up with '70s exploitation values and the cut-price metaphysics explored in Cohen's earlier **God Told Me To**. As ever, the director's focus is less on his gods and monsters than the human element, the film closely following Quinn, a hapless career criminal who tries to hold the city to ransom, and Shepard, a cop whose conviction that the bird is an ancient

Aztec deity resurrected through blood sacrifice receives no blessing from his elders. The film's unapologetic trash treats, comprising *Shaft*'s Roundtree, two Carradine brothers, audacious sub-Harryhausen animation, gory beheadings and a topless sunbather armed with a tube of suncream, mean the pace never flags. In fact, it moves too fast, the patchy structure and throwaway one-liners depriving some intriguing ideas of the space they need to breathe. But the great NYC locations, unusual aerial photography and Cohen's characteristically sly wit make this never less than entertaining, and it's fun to see Aztec iconography getting a workout rather than the usual Christian paraphernalia.

THE SENDER

1982, US, dir Roger Christian, scr Thomas Baum, starring Shirley Knight, Kathryn Harrold, Zeljko Ivanek, Paul Freeman

A young man attempts suicide by walking into a lake, his pockets filled with rocks. He is taken to a state mental hospital, where he is treated by psychiatrist Dr Gail Farmer – but Farmer soon finds that the amnesiac dreams of "John Doe #83" are entering her mind. Christian's debut feature is a subtly effective entry in the run of "psicopath" films sparked off by **Carrie**, though it feels closer to the psychic slashers of *In Dreams* and *The Ugly* (both 1997) while anticipating the "dreams can kill" theme of **A Nightmare on Elm Street**. Christian makes much of the contrast between the cold, clinical surrounds of the hospital and the violent chaos of Doe's visions, uncontrolled irruptions of energy whose apparently arbitrary content gradually reveals more and more of Doe's story. The *Cuckoo's Nest* collection of institutional oddballs is too theatrical to convince, but Ivanek's haunted features and ghastly pallor, just a shade off the hospital sheets, give him a credibly disturbed air, while Harrold's well-meaning bewilderment as Farmer makes her a sympathetic protagonist and Knight gives a chilling performance as Doe's **Carrie**-style religious-fanatic mother, convinced that she has given birth to Jesus. Predictably the hospital contains another Christ, but Doe's "miracle" visions sway the balance in his favour as the true Messiah, as the pretender's head is knocked from his shoulders, blood runs from cracked mirrors and, in one gratuitously nasty scene, a rat crawls from Doe's mouth. If the sentimental score, incoherent dénouement and cheesy shock ending prevent *The Sender* from being a true genre classic, its intelligent script, original concept and understated performances keep it a cut above most of its peers.

TENEBRAE
AKA TENEBRE; UNSANE

1982, It, dir/scr Dario Argento, starring Anthony Franciosa, Daria Nicolodi, John Saxon, John Steiner

Peter Neal, a writer of murder thrillers, arrives in Rome for a press junket, only to find that his work is rather *too* popular with a serial killer who's currently murdering young women and stuffing their mouths with pages from his latest novel, *Tenebrae*. After receiving a death-threat, Neal decides to try and track down the killer himself.

Emerging from the supernatural fug permeating Argento's previous two films (**Suspiria** and **Inferno**), *Tenebrae* is so acute, so sly and so wonderfully violent that it's virtually the last word on the *giallo* format. The murders are extremely graphic and yet achingly stylish (even when the weapon of choice shifts from razor to axe), taking place for the most part in fabulous modernist interiors, and lit with a baleful glare that's almost radioactive. Matching the visual intensity, there's a brittle, edgy feel to the acting – *Tenebrae*'s parade of sleek, heavily made-up women and clothes-horse males exude a jittery, coked-up neurosis, making even relatively straightforward scenes vibrate with weird, almost comic tension.

Argento was *not* the topic of intellectual discussion in Great Britain when *Tenebrae* was released, although since then he has attracted many academic analyses of his work, something that *Tenebrae* did much to provoke. It's a film in which Argento addresses head-on the complaints of his critics: first during an afternoon TV interview in which a startled Neal is challenged about his "sexist novel", and later during a scene in which a member of the "gentler sex" orally rapes a man with her high heels. Demonstrating in no uncertain terms that Argento's opinion of women takes full account of their power, this rape scene is pivotal to the plot, and (as has often been pointed out) gains even more resonance when you learn that the actress who plays the scene is actually a hermaphrodite. Such self-conscious game-playing is of course further bait for critics, but Argento anticipates this too with a book critic who gets to offer some very skewed interpretations of Neal's work. Playful, technically astonishing and unrepentantly nasty, *Tenebrae* is Argento's densest film text, and remains essential viewing for anyone seeking more from their sex and violence. [ST]

OPPOSITE: A dead end for **Christine**'s latest victim.

THE THING

*1982, US, dir John Carpenter, scr Bill Lancaster, starring Kurt Russell,
A. Wilford Brimley, T. K. Carter, David Clennon*

A Norwegian helicopter chases a dog into an American research
station. While trying to shoot the dog, a Norwegian hits
one of the Americans, and is shot dead in turn. A visit to the
Norwegians' camp reveals their discovery of a spacecraft and its
alien inhabitant, a capable and hostile mimic that works its way
through the Americans' dog pound then turns its attention to
larger prey.

Carpenter's take on John Campbell's short story "Who Goes
There?" sticks closer to its source than 1951's **The Thing**, and
looks and sounds like a Cronenberg film – wintry body-morphing
with a Shore-style soundtrack – with all the ideas leached out. The
characterization is perfunctory and the concept equal parts **Alien**
("Man is the Warmest Place to Hide" … again) and **Invasion of
the Body Snatchers**, but taken as a comic-book adventure it
works admirably. Carpenter uses the spectacular Antarctic setting
to contrast icy form with the Thing's slithering formlessness: it
may be able to take any shape, but fortunately for the viewer it
specializes in fantastically fleshy distortions, and the sheer novelty
of Bottin's effects, augmented by a rich sound design, has yet to
be matched by CGI, even if by the end overexposure diminishes
their impact. A couple of plot holes – the men understand that
the Thing's infection may be contagious, but use the same scalpel
to draw blood from each person; how does Blair expect his ship
to leave its underground cavern? – don't detract from the pace,
and Carpenter misdirects the viewer at every turn. But for all its
outlandish displays, the film won few fans on its release. SF purists
objected to Carpenter's novel take on an acknowledged classic,
while for others the melancholy tone and unresolved ending
proved altogether too bleak.

CHRISTINE

*1983, US, dir John Carpenter, scr Bill Phillips, starring Keith Gordon,
John Stockwell, Alexandra Paul, Robert Prosky*

When bullied geek Arnie restores a 1958 Plymouth Fury
automobile to its original glory, his personality changes too. But
his friends resent his new love, dubbed Christine, and when
Arnie is implicated in a series of murders the police start to close
in. This is a flawed but fascinating addition to the long run of

ABOVE: Christopher Walken and Brooke Adams in **The Dead Zone**.

Stephen King adaptations. The first 45 minutes of the film are narrated from the point of view of Arnie's jock friend Dennis, whose resentment at being replaced in Arnie's life by the car packs a mild homoerotic charge, but if his sports injury is on one level a bid to win Arnie's attention it fails dismally. The film's most compelling scenes come after Dennis's accident: it is 50 minutes before we see Arnie alone with Christine and the sudden revelation of the depth and strangeness of their relationship comes as a genuine shock. By the time bullies smash up the car, we have grown so used to her personification that it disturbs almost as much as if she *were* human. The transformation scene that follows is among the finest in a decade of eye-popping mutations, as Christine creaks and groans her way back to a pristine condition; but everything that follows is a disappointment, Carpenter's characteristically crisp Panavision compositions notwithstanding. The sight of Christine chasing her victims lamentably reminds us of the film's absurd premise and the ending is particularly disappointing, the film's two blandest characters – the jock and Arnie's unlikely girlfriend – scheming to outwit Arnie and Christine. Despite a solid supporting cast, including Harry Dean Stanton as a world-weary cop, *Christine* suffers from the insubstantiality of its putative heroes, while Gordon's Arnie is more convincing as geek than dude, his egotistical strutting ringing particularly false, although of course Christine herself is the real star of the show. The film's horror imagery is probably its least successful element: *Christine* works best as a tale of forbidden love, of automobile fetishism that approaches Cronenberg's *Crash* (1996) in its loving embrace of machine curves.

THE DEAD ZONE

1983, US, dir David Cronenberg, scr Jeffrey Boam, starring Christopher Walken, Brooke Adams, Martin Sheen, Sean Sullivan

Schoolteacher Johnny Smith awakens from a five-year coma to find his job gone and his girlfriend married to another man. A chance encounter with a nurse proves that he has precognitive abilities, but these come at a heavy price. Cronenberg's perceived shift to the mainstream after the personal vision of **Videodrome** dismayed many fans. This adaptation of a best-selling Stephen King novel was his first film (bar 1979's negligible *Fast Company*) directed from another writer's script, and bore all the hallmarks of a mainstream production, from the Hollywood star cast to the studio distribution. Yet it's a pivotal work in Cronenberg's career, thawing the cerebral coldness of his earlier work with intense emotional involvement, while its tear-jerking accent on sorrow and suffering anticipates the melancholia of his later films, and in its origins (a literary adaptation) and content (a criminally unbalanced president citing divine inspiration for his actions) *The Dead Zone* has precognitive abilities of its own. But its central subject is less precognition than repression, the mirror image of **Videodrome**'s nightmare of untrammelled instinct. Even before his accident John is self-effacing and melancholy, turning down an offer of sex from his girlfriend, and his near-vision on a rollercoaster demonstrates that his accident simply accelerates a process that had already begun. His visions, shot in a kinetic, colourfully dramatic style at odds with the wintry drabness of the

rest of the film, represent explosive incursions of everything he has sought to repress – his fearful yearnings for family, sexuality, impetuous action – and are brought on by the physical contact he otherwise denies himself. While his visions help others, they only serve to distance him still further from his peers, his batwing coat, pronounced limp and pallid features (it's impossible to imagine the film without its lingering focus on Walken's physiognomy) marking him out as irretrievably other; but the reluctant seer's masochistic devotion to his own suffering finally finds its own justification in a Christ-like martyrdom. Cronenberg's approach is far subtler here than the luridly visceral focus of his earlier films: both John (who is doubled in the sex killer) and Stillson (a politician) are driven by their own visions and present monstrous exaggerations of the masculine energies John has repressed in himself. His final actions, riding a Greyhound bus with a rifle on his lap, give the merest hint of "God told me to" lone-nut justification and the devout religious beliefs of the community, rarely commented upon but providing a metaphysical backdrop to the action, have led the director to comment that God might be seen as the absent mad scientist of the film, putting John through a Job-like wringer in the "controlled environment" of a never-ending winter.

THE HUNGER

1983, UK, dir Tony Scott, scr James Costigan, Ivan Davis, Michael Thomas, starring Catherine Deneuve, David Bowie, Susan Sarandon, Cliff De Young

Miriam Blaylock, a millennia-old vampire, promised John eternal life when she seduced him two centuries earlier. When he abruptly begins to age at an accelerated pace, he seeks the help of Dr Sarah Roberts, whose clinic specializes in longevity issues. But Miriam has her own interest in Dr Roberts.

It's easy to see why Scott's debut feature, an adaptation of Whitley Strieber's novel, is widely dismissed as an empty exercise in style: the music (from Bauhaus to bite-size classical quotations) and the look of the film, all billowing white drapes and languorously lit cigarettes, betray the director's advertising background; the performances are so opaque that it's easy to be indifferent to the characters' fates; and the reliance on spatially disorienting close-ups and jittery editing further obscure an already confusing narrative. Bowie and Deneuve look coldly selfish enough to be credible as the vampire lovers, but the film sorely misses Bowie in the second half, the ending sporting two twists that make little sense in the context of what has already happened, and the frenzied attacks come as a welcome respite from the inert stateliness of the other scenes. Yet beyond the yuppie-goth lifestyles and music-video visuals lie the germs of an intriguing idea: an immortal being so lonely that she must trick lovers into staying with her, condemning them ultimately to a horrific half-life as withered corpses. Miriam watches aghast as John crumbles in superbly realized Dick Smith "illusions", but she already has her eyes on his successor, seduced, after a big-hair struggle, in a painfully tacky lesbian clinch. *The Hunger* draws parallels between vampirism, addiction and blood disease, anticipating the spectre of AIDS and '90s efforts like *The Addiction* (1994), but its most intriguing feature is its presentation of vampirism as fashionable lifestyle, influencing a generation of goths to follow. Sarah Roberts takes on some of Miriam's effortless cool and taste in interior furnishings following her welcome to the fold – and what's a little selfish bloodletting against the prize of eternally smooth skin?

ABOVE: "You will be young forever." Susan Sarandon falls for Catherine Deneuve's con in **The Hunger**.

THE KEEP

1983, US, dir/scr Michael Mann, starring Scott Glenn, Jürgen Prochnow, Gabriel Byrne, Ian McKellen

Romania, the Carpathian Mountains, 1941. A detachment of German soldiers guard a keep at a mountain pass; when they begin to be killed off by a mysterious force, an SS force is sent to deal with the presumed partisan activity. Mann's second feature, an adaptation of F. Paul Wilson's novel, is a fascinating but flawed Second World War supernatural thriller that filters vampire conventions through the prism of Nazi occultism. The Carpathians are **Nosferatu** territory, the keep's demon feeding on soldiers to regenerate itself while its opponent, Glaeken, carries what looks like a vampire-hunter's kit. But the demon promises to crush the Nazis if it is released, while Glaeken himself casts no reflection and uses his psychic abilities for seduction: for all the obvious black and white symbolism this is no simple battle between good and evil. Yet the muddled metaphysics finally

devolve into laser pyrotechnics and the film's moral complexity works best on a human level: the keep exaggerates its inhabitants' qualities, accelerating a conflict between an SS major and an army captain, and draws on a crippled professor's hatred of the Nazis to unleash a far greater evil. Hampered by a cramped visual style that gives much of the film the feel of an episode of *Dr Who*, with the inevitable '80s backlighting and swirling mists and some extraordinarily wayward accents from the main players, *The Keep* at least attempts uncharted territory: a tantalizing glimpse of the interior of the keep suggests some kind of temple, with the implicit suggestion that the demon is being harnessed for military use – why else should the soldiers be there? But the film never follows up its most interesting ideas, any *Quatermass*-style exploration of military occultism dropped in favour of zapping eyes and portentous heroics, although various plot lacunae suggest that at least some of the incoherence is due to studio meddling.

VIDEODROME

1983, Can/US, dir/scr David Cronenberg, starring James Woods,
Sonja Smits, Deborah Harry, Peter Dvorsky

"Television is reality, and reality is less than television," says David Cronenberg's doomed TV-prophet Brian O'Blivion in this remarkably prescient work of horror/SF. Other films, such as Bertrand Tavernier's *La Mort en Direct/Deathwatch* (1980) and Michael Crichton's *Looker* (1981), had played with ideas of how television might develop in the near future but only Cronenberg tackled the subject directly and in his typically forthright and gore-splattered fashion. Cronenberg always casts his films well and James Woods is excellent as seedy porn-channel operator Max Renn, seaching for something tougher to serve his jaded audience. He finds more than he expects when Deborah Harry's Nicki Brand leads him to Videodrome. What seems at first to be an illegal snuff-TV channel is revealed to be a tumour-inducing weapon designed by neo-Fascists intent on punishing a "sick society". Renn is drawn into their conspiracy and then joins forces against them with a band of visionary rebels in pursuit of "the new flesh".

Bald descriptions of Cronenberg's films do little to convey the visceral impact of his metaphoric images. Amid the pulpy (and at times rather confused) plot we're witness to Renn pushing his face into a palpitating television set, living videocassettes inserted into a vaginal slot in his abdomen and a flesh gun that shoots cancer at its victims. Despite its speculative theme, *Videodrome*'s deep-red décor and run-down locations and Howard Shore's

ABOVE: James Woods is in for a nasty surprise when he scratches that itch. **Videodrome**.

doomy synth chords give the film a relentlessly oppressive and morbid atmosphere. Cronenberg has shown himself many times to be the cinema equivalent of Philip K. Dick (he was first in line to direct *Total Recall*) but his visions are full-blown Dickian nightmares without Dick's leavening flashes of desperate humour.

In an age of multi-channel porn, 24-hour television wars and non-stop reality TV, *Videodrome* might run the risk of seeming quaint, but a powerful imagination and multi-levelled script brimming with ideas wins through. Cronenberg leaves us to speculate what the "new flesh" might be; that question is still open. Watch it on TV. [JC]

ZEDER
AKA ZEDER: VOICES FROM THE BEYOND; REVENGE OF THE DEAD

1983, It, dir/co-scr Pupi Avati, co-scr Antonio Avati, Maurizio Costanzo,
starring Gabriele Lavia, Anne Canovas, Cesare Barbetti, Paola Tanziani

A struggling writer (Lavia) discovers mysterious phrases imprinted on a second-hand typewriter ribbon. They lead him to a derelict holiday camp in the Italian countryside, where sinister priests and unscrupulous scientists are trying to raise the dead....

Zeder is a curious creation from Pupi Avati, the celebrated director of **La Casa dalle Finestre che Ridono**. It lacks tension, strolls far too slowly through page after page of dialogue and has little of the violence one expects from Italian horror in the early '80s. However, its measured pace and restraint do eventually make their mark. The plot strains credulity (especially during the confusing climax), but all is redeemed with a terrifically chilling coda, bearing an uncanny similarity to Stephen King's *Pet Sematery*, written the following year. There's a touch of **Rosemary's Baby** to the story too, with corrupt Christianity and a veritable deluge of "nice guys who turn out to be nasty". The egomaniacal Lavia (given to strolling around in his underpants at the slightest opportunity) has few opportunities to grandstand, thanks to the subtle script, but he's a credible enough focus. Although the film lacks momentum, there are numerous pleasures along the way: the prologue, for instance, in which callous scientists expose a teenage medium to appalling occult danger; the supremely creepy disused holiday camp; the priest who abandons his faith after discovering an alternative means of resurrection; and the central conceit of the used typewriter ribbon, a *giallo*-esque notion that Argento himself would envy.

Avati is more highly regarded for **La Casa dalle Finestre che Ridono** than *Zeder*, but the earlier film is, if anything, even slower to marshall its good ideas. For some, Avati is a fine wine of Italian cinema, requiring a sensitive palate; for others, especially those taken in by *Zeder's* misleading American title, *Revenge of the Dead*, he's all talk and no bottle. The truth, as ever, lies somewhere in between. *Zeder* is a film I often revisit, despite its failings; it's beautifully photographed, artfully composed and boasts a staggeringly good if slightly out-of-place Riz Ortolani score. Quality fare, then, and rewarding as long as you don't judge it by Italian zombie-movie standards. [ST]

ZHONG GUI
AKA SEEDING OF A GHOST

1983, HK, dir Yueng Kuen, scr Lam Yee Hung, starring Norman Chu, Philip Ko, Maria Yuen, Wong Yung

Late one night, a taxi driver inadvertently saves the life of a grave-robbing wizard. A short while later, the taxi driver's cheating wife is abandoned by her playboy lover, raped by some opportunist thugs and then falls to her death while trying to escape. The taxi driver seeks the aid of the wizard to get his revenge. This involves digging up her dead body and turning it, by magic, into a *plazawa* – a type of zombie succubus that uses sexuality to seduce and kill its victims.

This was one of the last Shaw Brothers productions before they abandoned cinema for TV. It's a relentlessly grim piece, dark in every sense. Much of it takes place at night and there are no

real heroes. Typically, the taxi driver's "good deed" that opens the film is seen as the piece of bad luck from which all his subsequent miseries derive. Hong Kong is pictured as a dark, urban jungle where everyone is out to screw (literally as well as figuratively) everyone else, a place where those at the bottom of the heap are being crushed to death by the weight of those above them. No wonder the powerless have to turn to magic to even the odds. The authorities are no help. Rather than sympathize with the taxi driver over his wife's murder, the police hold him as the chief suspect. As with other Shaw Brothers horrors, the catalogue of bizarre events

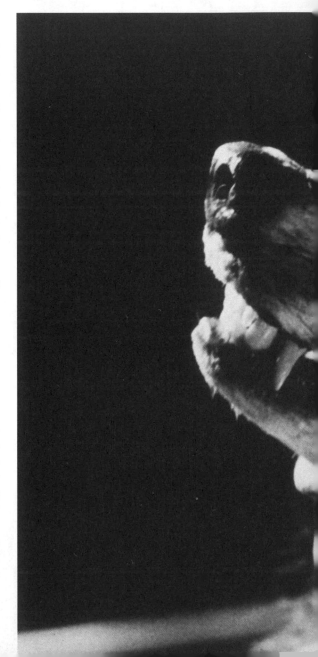

and strange lore provides much of the entertainment, not only the *plazawa* itself but also the cruel and inventive ways in which victims are killed. One man is drowned in a stream of excrement from his toilet and another vomits gallons of live worms. The climactic monster-birth scene is particularly spectacular, as the demon foetus mutates into a tentacled, snapping-jawed monster from which emerges the head of the dead wife's lover. [PT]

BELOW: "Hairy on the inside." A spectacular transformation in **The Company of Wolves**.

THE COMPANY OF WOLVES

1984, UK, dir/co-scr Neil Jordan, co-scr Angela Carter, starring Angela Lansbury, David Warner, Sarah Patterson, Stephen Rea

Jordan's adaptation of several Angela Carter stories from her 1979 collection *The Bloody Chamber* makes explicit the educational dramatization of sexual crises coded in many fairy tales, but in its self-conscious awareness loses some of the stories' raw immediacy. Rosaleen, on the cusp of puberty, dreams of a fairy-tale village beset by wolves that kill her elder sister; her

STEPHEN KING

Born in 1947, King began his writing career penning horror stories for men's magazines, but success came with the 1974 paperback publication of his first novel, *Carrie*. His importance as the late twentieth-century's pre-eminent horror writer is hard to overstate and it seems indisputable that he has done more than any other author to bring the genre to a mass audience. His film legacy, however, has been far more mixed.

King's writing has a strong thematic unity. He returns, again and again, to stories of ordinary people confronting the uncanny in everyday life, and many other motifs recur throughout his books: the author overpowered by his creations; the childhood secret that lies buried but not fully forgotten; and the metaphysical struggle between good and evil. King's body of work forms a coherent oeuvre in terms of narrative as well as theme – throughout his career he has tried to place all his books within the same universe, with characters from one being name-checked in others and the origins of the universe itself laid out in his magnum opus, the decades-spanning *Dark Tower*.

Perhaps this is why so many King films have failed: as soon as they become vehicles for competing voices, King's own unique tone is drowned out. **Carrie** was the first and still one of the best movies based on his work, directed by De Palma with a sympathy for the source material that would not be shown by later directors more determined to swap King's vision for their own. When an auteur such as Kubrick approached King's work, the result was less a King adaptation than a Kubrick movie: **The Shining** is well regarded by critics but disliked by many fans and by King himself, who felt it strayed too far from his original conception and later attempted an unsatisfactory mini-series adaptation of his own to set this right. When less talented directors worked with King, the films generally lacked even the unifying vision that Kubrick brought. It could be argued that only one director has ever succeeded in bringing King's work to the screen with its unique essence intact, one whose icy Canadian sensibility would seem entirely at odds with King's own down-home style. Yet somehow David Cronenberg's **The Dead Zone** alchemically mixed these two opposing elements to produce a work which remained faithful to both.

TV mini series such as *The Stand* (1994) and *Salem's Lot* (1979) have been better received than many of the movies, perhaps because the extended running times allow more of King's narrative to make it onto the screen. They are all, however, profoundly flawed, suffering from the medium's tendency to soften horror and sentimentalize emotions. King's books are very dark and occasionally bleak, surprising enough in best-selling novels but an impossible proposition for a mass-appeal medium like television, and adaptors have tended to respond by rewriting his work as little more than supernatural soap operas.

The books take place deep within their characters' heads, but movies and TV can only do so much to convey thought and, without the richness and breadth of characterization that King provides, the adaptations are often reduced to a sequence of set pieces. King, who believes in writing without pre-planning, has never been known for the elegance or conciseness of his plots. Stripped of the complex character development of his novels, many movie adaptations of his work have been nothing more than retellings of not exceptionally interesting tales, from the government-conspiracy mundanity of *Firestarter* (1984) to the unintentionally hilarious aliens of *Dreamcatcher* (2003).

Perhaps this is why the best-loved adaptation of King's work is a film outside the horror genre. With no set-piece gore to fall back on, *The Shawkshank Redemption* (1994) can mine the rich seam of humanity which lies, sometimes deeply buried, inside all King's work. [RL]

BELOW: "Thou shalt not suffer a witch to live." Sissy Spacek cowers in *Carrie*.

grandmother (a marvellously creepy turn from Lansbury) tells her horrific tales of men who are "hairy on the inside", while her mother attempts to reassure her that "If there's a beast in man, it's as much in women too", as the women attempt to map out the route Rosaleen's sexuality should take. Jordan's decision to construct the village and surrounding woods on set adds to the film's fairy-tale feel – this is a land as dreamlike as Oz, the woods filled with snakes and lizards even in winter – but it loses the earthiness and sense of place essential to tangentially related films like **Blood on Satan's Claw**, a loss only partially redeemed by the use of real wolves. The artificiality becomes cloying at times and the symbolism of the undeniably beautiful imagery heavy-handed, so that a bird's egg cracking open to reveal a homunculus is over-egged by the faltering touch of a tear rolling from the homunculus's eye, and the film's sumptuous gloss and arch knowingness finally detract from its poetic intensity. Yet, while *Company*'s structure of tales nested within dreams means that it eludes true emotional involvement, it boasts a succession of startling images – a decapitated wolf's head lands in a pail of milk to become the head of a man; and the grandmother's head, similarly knocked off, unexpectedly shatters into porcelain shards – and magnificently evocative set pieces (Terence Stamp's suited devil is a highlight) that climax in an extraordinary transformation sequence of a wolf's snout pushing through the mouth of a man, perhaps cinema's greatest single werewolf image.

A NIGHTMARE ON ELM STREET

1984, US, dir/scr Wes Craven, starring John Saxon, Ronee Blakley, Heather Langenkamp, Robert Englund

A killer with razors on his fingers is pursuing you through your dreams; you can no longer tell those dreams from reality; and your parents know what is happening but refuse to reveal the truth. *Nightmare*'s three key concepts carry enough atavistic terror for it to have survived the dating of its special effects and remain one of the scariest horror movies of the '80s. Unlike many of the decade's other high-concept movies, *Nightmare* wrings every ounce of fear out of its central premise. Every nightmare a child has ever experienced is here, from stairs that sink beneath your feet as you try to escape to everyday objects that suddenly become menacing and strange, and a pursuer who will always confront you, no matter how fast you run. Craven's direction

RIGHT: "One, two, Freddy's coming for you...."
A Nightmare on Elm Street.

ABOVE: Deader than ever. **Day of the Dead.**

ensures that the audience experience the same uncertainty as the characters, with scenes that appear to be set in reality turning out to be dreams and vice versa.

Englund – previously best known for his part in kitsch SF mini-series *V* – delivers a Freddy Krueger who is far more of a character in his own right than the man-in-a-mask likes of Jason and Mike Myers, though in this first film he is not yet the wise-cracking antihero he would later become. The terrorized teens – including Johnny Depp's debut and rather inadequate performance – are at times in danger of falling into *Breakfast Club*-style stereotypes, but Langenkamp's Nancy is ballsy enough to provide an adequate identification point for the audience. Seven sequels followed, as well as crossover *Freddy Vs Jason* (2003), with some – such as the slasher-standard *Freddy's Revenge* (1985) – being barely worthy of the title, and only *Dream Warriors* (1987) and the post-modern *New Nightmare* (1994) possessing any real originality or artistic merit. None, though, can compete with the impact of the original. [RL]

PURANA MANDIR

1984, India, dir Tulsi & Shyam Ramsay, scr Kumar Ramsay, starring Aarti Gupta, Mohnish Bahl, Ajay Agarwal, Jagdeep

Although there had been Indian horror films before, this was the first to break through into the commercial mainstream. Its success sired a wave of imitations and helped to establish horror as a viable genre within Indian cinema. The prologue, set in the distant past, shows a raja's caravan delayed while a carriage wheel is repaired. The Raja's wife wanders off into an abandoned temple, where she falls victim to the evil wizard Saamri. Caught and punished, he is cut up into pieces and burned. Before dying he curses the Raja and his family. Back in present-day India, the Raja's descendant is worried. His daughter is of an age when she is becoming interested in boys. A flashback shows what happened to her mother: she died in childbirth, after turning into a hideous scaly monster, a victim of Saamri's curse – as are all women of their family. The girl decides to put an end to such nonsense and, with her boyfriend, she sets off for the old temple to sort things out.

The Hindi horror film is a startling mixture of elements. Scenes of terror, sex and suspense are juxtaposed with comedy and lengthy musical numbers. When it works it can be exhilarating. The Ramsay family were experienced producers by this time and knew how to pack the screen with production value. The comedy sub-plot, a kind of parody of *Sholay* (1975), is less successful, but the rousing climax and terrific set pieces more than compensate. The real star of the show – and the reason it works so well – is Saamri. As incarnated by Ajay Agarwal, he is one of the best monsters ever to grace a Hindi horror. He appeared again in a loose sequel – *Saamri* (1985) – and Agarwal turned up later in *Bandh Darwaza* (1990), the Ramsays' take on the Dracula legend. [PT]

RAZORBACK

1984, Aust, dir Russell Mulcahy, scr Everett De Roche, starring Gregory Harrison, Arkie Whiteley, Bill Kerr, Chris Haywood

Beth Winters, an American reporter specializing in animal-rights issues, visits Australia for a TV special on kangaroo slaughter. When she goes missing, her husband Carl searches for her: did she fall foul of the Pet Pack cannery boys or the giant razorback terrorizing the area? Mulcahy's debut feature, an adaptation of a novel by Peter Brennan, draws on a wide range of outback iconography, referencing both true crime (particularly the "dingo baby" case, although tales of missing tourists and beer-guzzling rapists with poor dentistry also get a look-in) and other films (*The Cars That Ate Paris*, 1974, *Mad Max*, 1979, **Jaws**), for a highly evocative urbanoia film shot through with extraordinary imagery. The outback here becomes a magical yet terrifying arena for the testing of man, a dusty, sunbaked desert bristling with murderous pigs. The sense of a fantasy setting is helped by Mulcahy's hallucinatory visuals, loading Carl's walkabout with vivid purple skies and skeletons erupting from the parched earth.

But the outback location is also recognizably a real place, the ground pockmarked by opal mines and the township of Gamulla populated by scuzzy kangaroo hunters portrayed with a brash earthiness that only occasionally slips into caricature. If Mulcahy's background in pop promos prompts him to light the cannery at the end like an industrial set for a goth video, all rattling chains and dry ice, a keen sense of visual flair elsewhere ensures the film always looks interesting, with the giant razorback wisely kept out of clear view. Its use of the very real horrors of the meat industry is also notable, but Mulcahy's real coup is in presenting a peculiarly Australian take on weathered urbanoia and eco-horror themes.

DAY OF THE DEAD

1985, US, dir/scr George A. Romero, starring Lori Cardille, Terry Alexander, Joseph Pilato, Jarlath Conroy

The third instalment of Romero's zombie saga is a step back from his original conception of a world in which trained zombie armies fought wars for human masters: the $6.5 million anticipated budget and Romero's refusal to tone down the gore for an R-rated domestic release proved incompatible, leading the director to retreat to an earlier period in the zombie mythos. The tone of *Day* is more apocalyptic and darker than its forebears: the human community, holed up in a missile silo in Florida, know of no other survivors, the zombies' decay is more impressively advanced (representing the pinnacle of Savini's effects work), while the jokiness of **Dawn ...** is entirely absent. If the earlier film's shopping mall represented a temple to consumer society, *Day*'s silo is that society's tomb. Romero's sense of social satire is as acute as ever, the conservative retirement communities of Florida providing the perfect backdrop to the victory of the living dead, while the humans' response – Romero's real interest – is to bicker between factions (Sarah, the protagonist, is trapped between the military, scientists and pilots) while maintaining a store of redundant tax and immigration records. Yet *Day*, more than Romero's previous work, provides cultural as well as social commentary, glossing not only its prequels – Logan's use of child-rearing techniques on zombies provides a perverse replacement for the family unit comprehensively destroyed in **Night** – but also Universal horrors (the presentation of Bub, a zombie with vestigial speech and half-remembered manual skills, recalls **Frankenstein**), the archetypal '50s conflict between science and the military, and the zombie's Caribbean origins. Romero attempts to invert the racial hysteria implicit in the latter as John, the film's Caribbean character, espouses a utopian alternative to the defunct society represented by the silo, while the Caribbean finally becomes a safe haven from the primitive savagery of the USA. This is hampered by the film's own racial stereotyping (the shiftless John smokes weed, listens to calypso music and peppers his speech with craven slave imagery), but *Day*'s Reaganomics-inspired critique of military-industrial insanity makes it one of the most subversive American genre films of the period, even if audiences preferred the buffoonery of **Return of the Living Dead**.

BELOW: "West, you bastard!" A headless David Gale berates Jeffrey Combs in **Re- Animator**.

RE-ANIMATOR

1985, US, dir/co-scr Stuart Gordon, co-scr Dennis Paoli, William J. Norris, starring Jeffrey Combs, Bruce Abbott, Barbara Crampton, David Gale

Medical student Dan Cain's academic prospects are ruined when he tries to tell the Dean about the success of his new roommate Herbert West in re-animating dead tissue. Cain's girlfriend Megan, the Dean's daughter, is none too impressed either and Cain's troubles go from bad to worse when he smuggles West into the morgue. Gordon's early, irreverent entry in the "splatstick" stakes takes little from Lovecraft but names and a whiff of respectability, soon quashed by scenes of severed heads giving oral sex and intestines snaking round unwilling victims,

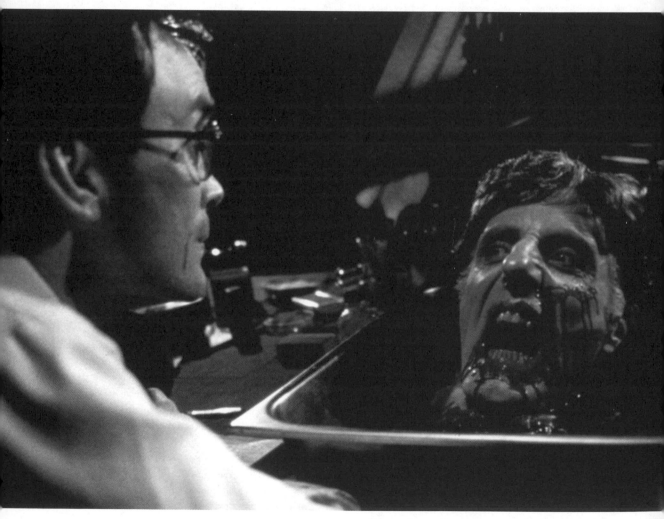

but still proves more entertaining and less braindead than its many imitators. West resembles Pretorius from **Bride of Frankenstein**, driving a wedge between Dan and Megan with his magnificent nerdish derision, while Dr Hill, the shamelessly plagiaristic grant engine for Miskatonic Medical School, joins the dots between mad science and commerce while sporting a bad rug and worse line in seduction techniques, creepily reminding Megan that "you're all by yourself now" after booking her father into the rubber motel. He won't let being dead and headless quench his thirst for power either, bumping his way blindly around morgue and lab while developing a new use for West's luminous reagent that drives the film into full-bore zombie mayhem. While *Re-Animator*'s success was principally down to its nifty effects and anything-goes tone, its subtler touches, such as the tussles between Megan and West, jockeying for Cain's attention, keep the pitch deliciously black even away from the gruesome excesses. It was followed by two lesser sequels, *Bride of Re-Animator* (1990) and *Beyond Re-Animator* (2003), as well as a raft of similar Gordon-Yuzna productions.

RETURN OF THE LIVING DEAD

1985, US, dir/scr Dan O'Bannon, starring Clu Gulager, James Karen, Don Calfa, Thom Matthews

Following the genre-defining **Night of the Living Dead**, creators John Russo and George Romero failed to agree an artistic direction for the sequels and eventually compromised by bifurcating the franchise. Russo sold the rights to the title *Return* in the late '70s, and O'Bannon's film finally took the opposite route from Romero, gaining some cheap laughs and a manic energy at the expense of almost everything that made the original great. The connection to the earlier film is made apparent in a pre-title sequence set in a medical cadaver store, in which a new worker is informed that the events of **Night** really occurred and that its zombies are stored in the basement below. The sequence itself is a masterful blend of humour and a growing realization that something nasty is soon to happen, but the rest of the movie fails to live up to its promise. The remaining action is far more predictable, as twin narratives slowly converge: the discovery by the men who freed the zombies – in one of the film's comedic highlights – that they are not merely unwell but already dead; and the ill-advised decision by a band of punky teens to party in a nearby graveyard.

Performances range from the eccentric to the outright terrible and many are conducted at a pitch of permanent hysteria

ABOVE: "It hurts ... to be dead." **Return of the Living Dead**.

that quickly becomes wearing. Scream queen Linnea Quigley, fresh from 1984's *Silent Night, Deadly Night*, spends almost the entire movie naked for no other reason than adolescent titillation, and the work is clearly aimed at this age group. The zombies are naturally the highlight but, apart from one badly decomposed specimen whose gleeful cries of "Brains! Live brains!" are strangely endearing, they are given little personality. Nonetheless, the film is not without its pleasures, chiefly the moments when its humour is sufficiently dark to underline rather than undermine the horror. Four sequels followed along very much the same lines. [RL]

BLUE VELVET

1986, US, dir/scr David Lynch, starring Kyle MacLachlan,
Dennis Hopper, Isabella Rossellini, Laura Dern

Out of darkness comes ... darkness. After the commercial failure of *Dune* (1984), the de Laurentiis organization took a gamble bankrolling another Lynch movie. Incredibly, they didn't interfere in production, leaving the auteur director to realize a meticulously stylized exploration of favoured themes: repressed desires and the fatal allure of hidden knowledge, shot through with Surrealist humour. At its heart lies a story of criminal detection, but no less of a mystery are the random, unpalatable triggers to erotic arousal that lie within us all. Clean-cut Jeffrey Beaumont (MacLachlan) is recalled home from college after his father suffers a bizarre gardening accident. After visiting him in hospital the listless Jeffrey finds a severed ear on waste ground. So begins a descent into an ugly and unfathomable world operating just outside the candy-

ABOVE: "You put your disease in me." Isabella Rossellini sweet-talks Kyle MacLachlan, **Blue Velvet**.

sweet yet fragile comforts of small-town America.

Jeffrey's covert mission to unravel the story behind the ear finds him turning voyeur, hiding in the wardrobe of magnetic but troubled chanteuse Dorothy Vallens (Rossellini) as she engages in extreme masochistic sex with unforgettable "rom-psycho" Frank Booth (Hopper). Psychoanalytic theory favours Oedipal readings of the claustrophobic dynamic between these three characters. Frank demands to be called "Daddy", yet calls himself "Baby" during his penis-absent sexual frenzy, his obsession with Dorothy's robe that of an infant inseparable from its transitional object. The weirdness escalates, with Jeffrey catapulted into nightmarish scenarios, most memorably the "joyride" with Frank and his psycho pals, where homosexual brutality is hinted at and '50s pop tunes – brilliant in their incongruity – are employed against the ultra-violence.

ABOVE: "A disease with a purpose." A barely recognizable Jeff Goldblum, **The Fly**.

J.G. Ballard accurately described *Blue Velvet* as *The Wizard of Oz* re-shot as scripted by Kafka with décor by Francis Bacon, and there is much in the neo-*noir* collision of '50s and '80s styling to delight the knowing viewer. Sound design by Alan Splet perfects the experience of being taken further into the unconscious desires of maniacs than you ever wanted to go. A masterpiece. [KS]

THE FLY

1986, US, dir/scr David Cronenberg, starring Jeff Goldblum, Geena Davis, John Getz, Joy Boushel

A scientist, Seth Brundle, demonstrates his new matter-transporters to reporter Veronica Quaife and they become lovers. While drunk, Brundle transports himself, unwittingly fusing with a fly. The only way to arrest his transformation is to fuse with another human and he kidnaps Veronica, who is intent on aborting their unborn child.

Cronenberg's most lucrative release to date, grossing more than all of his previous films combined, may hide its more interesting ideas under a barrage of crowd-pleasing Chris Walas transformation effects, but it remains a fascinating, quintessentially Cronenbergian take on Kurt Neumann's 1958 original. Goldblum's Brundle is both apotheosis of, and comment on, the classic mad scientist, owning five sets of the same clothes, playing melodramatic chords on his piano to impress his female guest and ranting passionately about his experiments. But, rather than any grand altruistic gestures, Brundle wants to use the transporters for personal development, bringing the film closer to a superhero-origins story than its source. Rather than worry that there are some things that man should never know, Brundle shows off his new powers, snapping a man's arm in a bar and indulging in marathon sex sessions. When his transformation begins to go wrong – self-development in Cronenberg films always ends badly – it is only Brundle whose life is ravaged, unlike the broader

ABOVE: "It's always the same ... always different."
Michael Rooker, **Henry ... Portrait of a Serial Killer**

communities of the director's earlier films: he has referred to *The Fly* as "three people in a room". Yet Brundle remains articulate and humorous throughout, keeping a museum of vestigial body parts – ears, teeth, penis – and remaining a mouthpiece for Cronenberg's Burroughsian ideas, ranting about "a disease with a purpose" and "society's sick, grey fear of the flesh". Many critics interpreted Brundle's transformation as a comment on AIDS but, according to the director, the film is about ageing, with Brundle's transformation a particularly accelerated ageing process, and the tragedy of love affairs in which one person dies. Cronenberg's triumph is to make the film work as tragic romance as much as effects extravaganza, a spectacularly messy tale of poignant monster love whose impact is finally and unexpectedly more emotional than visceral.

FROM BEYOND

1986, US, dir Stuart Gordon, scr Dennis Paoli, starring Jeffrey Combs, Barbara Crampton, Ken Foree, Ted Sorel

Dr Pretorius believes the pineal gland to be a dormant sensory organ, and develops a resonator to stimulate the gland and allow users to experience another realm. But, after an experiment that ends with Pretorius's head bitten off, his assistant Crawford Tillinghast is arrested for his murder, only for psychiatrist Dr McMichael to re-create the experiment in a bid to establish Tillinghast's fitness to stand trial. The Yuzna-Gordon follow-up to **Re-Animator** is even trashier and sillier than its predecessor but, while it falls flat as a Lovecraft adaptation, it's not without a crazed charm of its own. Pretorius's skills as an SM dom – as Tillinghast remembers, "He used to bring beautiful women here. They'd eat fine meals, drink fine wine, listen to music – but it always ended with screaming!" –

allow him to control the gloopy submarine creatures from beyond as well as his own molecular structure, with predictably rubbery effects. The others fare less well: Crampton's McMichael ditches the glasses, prim blouse and skirt for Pretorius's fetish gear in a bid to have sex with someone … anyone … ; Foree's cop is attacked by flesh-eating insects; and Tillinghast, his head denuded after an encounter with a giant lamprey, finds his waggling stalk-like pineal extension comes at the cost of an irrepressible craving for brains. Tillinghast's pineal visions of cheap solarized video effects rank this alongside **Brain Damage** in the small field of '80s US psychedelic horror, with Richard Band's sparkling score adding to the cut-rate hallucinogenic feel, and if Pretorius's body mutations quickly descend into farce, the lower orders emerging from the **Phantasm**-style tuning forks are eerily effective.

HENRY … PORTRAIT OF A SERIAL KILLER

1986, US, dir/co-scr John McNaughton, co-scr Richard Fire, starring Michael Rooker, Tom Towles, Tracy Arnold, David Katz

Henry stays with his ex-con friend Ottis on his release from prison. He soon involves Ottis in his killing sprees, although Ottis's sister Becky seems to offer the possibility of a new direction in his life. But Henry disapproves of Ottis's sexual peccadilloes and before long he returns to solo killing.

McNaughton's debut feature remains the last word in serial-killer cinema. Part of its power is tied to its low budget: the impeccable cast is made up of amateur theatre actors, denying audiences the comfortable distance that comes with star vehicles, although for Rooker at least *Henry* provided a springboard to Hollywood success. The film is also shot on location, partly because sets were beyond its budget, and the characters' grubby, dead-end boarding rooms provide a far more convincing setting than, for example, the mocked-up motel sleaze of the Eileen Wuornos biopic *Monster* (2003). The murders are structured for maximum effect, too, with the first on-screen killing occurring 40 minutes into the film and presented largely as entertainment. It is followed shortly afterwards by the devastating "home invasion" sequence, which Henry and Ottis watch on video, implicating the viewer in their consumption of screen violence.

But the film's principal virtue is its scrupulously realistic depiction of a serial killer. A disclaimer at the start avers that "Henry is not intended to be an accurate portrayal of a true story", similarities between the narrative and the real-life story of serial-killer Henry Lee Lucas notwithstanding, but its vision is authentic in a way that any number of "real-life" serial-killer films – *Ed Gein* (2000), *Ted Bundy* (2002), *Gacy* (2003) – are not. Henry, Ottis and Becky all belong to the low socio-economic group that produces most serial killers, and all have been shaped by their environment: Henry is the illegitimate product of a prostitute mother and crippled father, while Becky was abused by her father and is escaping a failed marriage. There is no pop-psychology explanation for Henry's crimes, nor any retribution: the police are conspicuous by their absence. Henry is a consummate liar and fantasist, recounting three different versions of his mother's murder, and while he picks his victims from a range of backgrounds, all are white, in line with characteristic serial killers' avoidance of crossing racial boundaries. Finally, it is Henry's blankness that is most convincing and shocking: the film was released just before the glut of big-budget '90s serial-killer films exemplified by **The Silence of the Lambs**, but while Hannibal Lecter is presented as a kind of epicene superhero, *Henry* by contrast emphasizes the banality of evil, Henry's offer of some chips easily quashing Ottis's misgivings about murder.

THE HITCHER

1986, US, dir Robert Harmon, scr Eric Red, starring Rutger Hauer, C. Thomas Howell, Jennifer Jason Leigh, Jeffrey DeMunn

Jim Halsey, driving through Texas on his way to California, regrets picking up psychotic hitchhiker John Ryder when he is implicated in Ryder's crimes. Harmon's debut feature boasts art direction from **The Texas Chain Saw Massacre**'s Robert Burns, but the film feels closer to **Duel**, another road movie in which a benign man is menaced by an implacable force he cannot begin to understand. *The Hitcher* opens superbly, with a marvellously creepy encounter between Hauer's laconic, world-weary madman and Howell's callow youth, polite enough to say "bless you" when Ryder sneezes and joke that "My mother told me never to do this" as he stops for the hitcher. Halsey's baptism of blood – he manages to kick Ryder out of the car, only for the hitcher to haunt him like a ghost for the rest of the film – soon sees him ditching the nice-guy approach for a delinquent greaser look and deft gun-handling skills, while the film shifts gear away from Ryder's shadowy horrors into faintly ludicrous action mode, focusing on big guns, the damage they cause and a satisfyingly overblown series of police-car pile-ups. There's never any explanation for the hitcher's obsession with Halsey, although in a diner Ryder places coins on Halsey's eyes and tells him, "You're a smart kid, you figure it out," a Classical allusion to the preparation of the dead for the underworld that offers the merest hint that Halsey may not have survived the near-collision with a lorry that prompted him to pick up the hitcher in the first place. But the film shies away from glib explanations to rely instead on evocative photography of the Texas badlands and superb performances from its leads for a superior psycho-thriller, another nail in the coffin of the fine art of hitchhiking.

THE STEPFATHER

1986, US, dir Joseph Ruben, scr Donald E. Westlake, starring Terry O'Quinn, Jill Schoelen, Shelley Hack, Charles Lanyer

A man kills his family, changes his appearance and starts a new life in a new town as real-estate salesman Jerry Blake. Obsessed with traditional family values, he is dismayed to find that his new stepdaughter, Stephanie, distrusts him, and begins to plan another change of life. Although hampered by a TV-movie soundtrack and the John Hughes-style depiction of school life characteristic of mid-'80s American films, *The Stepfather*'s unusually subversive take on family life presents inflexible patriarchy as innately psychotic. Blake is so obsessed by the idea of a sitcom-perfect happy family that the slightest hint of rebellion or difference drives him to violence. His idealized vision of the American dream soured once more, he puts the tools he used to build a model house to work killing another family. The film is at its best exploring the technicalities of Blake's con: the preparations for a new life, and his confusion as he occasionally forgets which role he is playing – challenged by his wife, he openly wonders "Who am I here?" His shifts from over-friendliness to murderous rage are also impressively played, the bouts of violence unexpectedly brutal and his conservative outbursts hilariously overboiled – on finding his daughter being kissed goodnight by a suitor, he explodes, "You could go to jail! This girl is only 16 years old!" "So am I!" the boy protests – although the black quips that punctuate the mayhem eventually turn him into a cartoonish Freddy Krueger figure and dissipate much of his menace. The film's focus on Blake and Stephanie means that the appeal he holds for his wife is never properly explored – are widows necessarily so vulnerable? – and the teenager's position as the only character who distrusts her stepfather has a Spielberg sickliness, but O'Quinn's performance as the oily real-estate salesman with a murderous tic holds the film together. It was followed by a less successful sequel in 1989.

RIGHT: "I cut off his legs. And his arms." **The Hitcher**.

STREET OF CROCODILES

1986, UK, dir/scr Stephen & Timothy Quay, starring Feliks Stawinski

Many of the best fictions are resistant to the crude reductions of visual adaptation and the oneiric fables of Bruno Schulz seem more resistant than most. It is fitting then that Schulz finds an ideal interpreter in the hermetic Brothers Quay whose short animated films are often equally dreamlike signifiers of private mythology.

Despite the use of dolls and puppets as characters in their tableaux, the Quays' films are consistently adult in tone and frequently avant-garde in presentation, with endless shifts of focus, brief cuts to images that the viewer barely has time to

take in, and the whole presented by mute or miming figures. This technique can often create a sense of dizzying incoherence but in *Street of Crocodiles* all aspects of their direction come together with considerable power, turning Schulz's tales of shadowy half-lives in a Polish town into a haunting and disturbing vision of a lost *Mittel*-Europe buried under layers of rust and grime.

Street of Crocodiles is full of striking and memorable images: the pocket watch filled with raw meat, the provocatively leering dummy in a shop window, incomprehensible contraptions, the doll child playing with light bulbs and animated screws. The stalking, angular figure that explores the filthy streets and dimly-lit shopfronts seems to have stepped from Schulz's illustrations, while the striped box it carries is an obvious nod to *Un Chien Andalou* (1928). The Quays create their most memorably sinister characters in the erotically menacing tailors, a tribe of doll-headed mannikins with glowing eyes. Much of the atmosphere is sustained by careful sound design – all reverberant creaks and muted radio voices – and a distinctly Bartókesque score. As with many of their films, multiple viewings are necessary to tease out the subtleties of their fleeting images. The viewer is the final collaborator in a Quay Brothers film, piecing together the narrative just as they have pieced together their mannikins from antique remains. [JC]

WHITE OF THE EYE

1986, US, dir/co-scr Donald Cammell, co-scr China Cammell, starring David Keith, Cathy Moriarty, Art Evans, Alan Rosenberg

Tucson, Arizona. Police investigating a series of ritual murders are sure they've found their man in hi-fi technician Paul White, but Paul's wife Joanie provides the perfect alibi: hadn't she caught him having sex with another woman? This is Cammell's third feature, following a nine-year hiatus after the machine-rape SF entry *Demon Seed* (1977), recut by the studio against Cammell's wishes. The director's appalling fortune (he completed only one more feature, 1996's *Wild Side*, again released in truncated form, before committing suicide) extended to this exemplary psycho-thriller's poor distribution and critical neglect, although it remains, alongside *Performance* (1970, co-directed with Nicolas Roeg) his most coherent and satisfying film. In some respects, this resembles his seminal identity-switch debut: non-linear editing and contrasting film textures are used to tell the tale of an ex-hippy as concerned with performance as Turner – the killer is a sexual athlete whose murders are staged as works of art, the hallucinatory visuals and immaculate surrounds recalling Argento, black leather replaced by rawhide gloves – and as troubled by gender as Chas, convinced that at the centre of the universe lies a black hole that sucks all life into it: "If that isn't female, I don't know what is!" But the Cammells' principal concern (and the central theme taken from Margaret Tracy's disposable source novel *Mr White*) is the killer's relationships: he is a family man, with wife and daughter, and the film's exploration of the cosy domesticity of a serial killer focuses on the effect his outlandish revelations have on his wife. Beautifully shot and acted, and languidly paced, filled with asides that do nothing to drive the narrative (repeated pans over the desert; a cameo from China Cammell visiting Joanie's ex-boyfriend Mike), *White of the Eye* finally avoids the gruelling tone the story could easily have taken – the murders may be nasty, but the portrayal of the vain, smug victims removes much of their sting, while Joanie ends the film smiling – for a measured, sympathetic character study and a paean to the desert landscape itself.

BRAIN DAMAGE

1987, US, dir/scr Frank Henenlotter, starring Rick Herbst, Gordon MacDonald, Jennifer Lowry, Theo Barnes

Elmer, a brain-eating parasite, escapes captivity and targets

Brian as its new host. Happy at first to get high on the parasite's euphoric injections, Brian battles to regain control of his life after becoming suspicious of Elmer's activities during his drug fugues. Henenlotter's second feature plays like **Shivers** reimagined as a cautionary tale of narcotic excess. Elmer, the turd-like parasite whose history can be traced back to the Crusades, enthusiastically promises "a life filled with colours, music and euphoria", like some shrivelled Tim Leary, but the price is high, blood-caked underwear after a brain-sucking binge and an addiction that's impossible to kick. Brian goes cold turkey in a fleabitten hotel straight out of **Basket Case**, hallucinating pulling his brains out through his ear in between bouts of vomiting, and finally snaps when Elmer croons "Elmer's tune" in the filthy sink. The director's evident familiarity with psychedelics makes for some intriguing visuals: Brian, leaping up and down like a demented rave casualty, stares at a shattered windscreen in a car junkyard, then watches his meatballs turn into throbbing, moaning brains and finally sees his body covered by purple discs, in a bizarre sub-**Videodrome** vision telegraphed by strobe lighting. The cheap effects and painful New Wave music give this the indelible stamp of '80s video trash, but Henenlotter's ballsy invention never falters and it's hard not to admire the director's stated aim of combining an LSD comedy with a gore film.

EVIL DEAD 2
AKA EVIL DEAD 2: DEAD BY DAWN

1987, US, dir/co-scr Sam Raimi, co-scr Scott Spiegel, starring Bruce Campbell, Sarah Berry, Dan Hicks, Kassie Wesley

Ash and his girlfriend Linda spend a night at a woodland cabin. They find a recording by Professor Knowby describing the discovery of the Book of the Dead and are both possessed by demons. Knowby's daughter arrives and is convinced that Ash has murdered her parents, but the appearance of her possessed mother clears the air and the spirit of Professor Knowby helps them combat the demons. Essentially a remake of **The Evil Dead**, Raimi's third feature dispenses with many of the first film's scares in favour of cartoonish humour, bringing the film closer to the "splatstick" of Peter Jackson's early films than the '70s shocker spirit of **The Evil Dead**. Some of the humour is a little laboured – a severed hand in a bucket is weighed down by a copy of *A Farewell to Arms* – and the final reel descends into rubber-monster nonsense, but much of the film retains the whiff of nightmare, distorting time and space to present a series of sleep-paralysis loops, and the film's most effective moments come when Ash's manic laughter shades into

LEFT: "Who's laughing now?" **Evil Dead 2**.

screams. The first half of the film is a *tour de force* of compacted storytelling, melding *Roadrunner* sound effects, kung-fu camerawork and crazy camera tilts to climax with Ash's edgy descent into madness. Raimi's handling of the reality slips is easily overlooked in the amphetamine pacing of the rest of the film, but the quieter scenes retain a deranged menace that confirms the film's status as essential viewing. The sequel, *Army of Darkness* (1993), is far less effective.

HELLRAISER
AKA CLIVE BARKER'S HELLRAISER

1987, UK, dir/scr Clive Barker, starring Andrew Robinson, Clare Higgins, Ashley Laurence, Sean Chapman

Frank Cotton's desire for new experiences leads him into the clutches of the Cenobites, SM demons who tear him apart. But when his brother Larry and Larry's wife Julia move into Frank's old house, Frank realizes he can escape his fate. Barker's debut feature, an adaptation of his own *The Hellbound Heart*, is a bold attempt to reinvigorate the defunct British horror film with a new iconography of horror that draws on SM/fetish imagery. The imaginatively designed Cenobites only embody a theme that runs throughout the film, the proximity of pleasure and pain, sex and death. After Frank cuts Julia's blouse with a knife, sex with the pedestrian Larry holds limited appeal, especially while Frank is slicing a rat in half at the foot of the bed; even one of Julia's pick-ups growls at her menacingly when she seems reluctant to fulfil her promise, as though her haughtily dominant poses, bouffant hair and dark glasses didn't mark her out as trouble, the twin of **Les Diaboliques**' icily homicidal Simone Signoret. For all the Cenobites' fanboy-pleasing designs, *Hellraiser*'s best moments are subtler: the clash of textures, raw flayed flesh against white cotton and the sordid pick-ups, the shade of Dennis Nielsen hanging over the murders. The peculiar grubbiness of English crime, only tapped cinematically elsewhere in films like *The Black Panther* (1977), provides a stark contrast to Larry's cosy domesticity.

Regrettably, these elements are ditched as the focus shifts to Larry's daughter Kirsty, the kind of teen savant endemic in '80s horror, who knows exactly how to battle Cenobites and fends off the increasingly ludicrous rubber monsters and lamely villainous catchphrases by running around screaming and flapping her hands. Worse still, almost the entire cast speak in irritatingly transatlantic accents, forgivable enough for the explicitly American Larry and Kirsty but senseless in the Budweiser-guzzling removal men and Kirsty's English boyfriend Steve. The film is finally reduced to relying on gratuitously weird figures like the Alan Moore-lookalike derelict for impact and even the effects, impressive enough as Frank reconstitutes himself into an educational écorché, descend into farce for the final half-hour which, with its bad sets and worse wisecracks, provides a portent of the many sequels to follow.

RIGHT: "We'll tear your soul apart." Doug Bradley's Pinhead looks forward to the **Hellraiser** franchise.

NEAR DARK

1987, US, dir/co-scr Kathryn Bigelow, co-scr Eric Red, starring Adrian Pasdar, Jenny Wright, Lance Henriksen, Bill Paxton

When Midwest farmboy Caleb meets Mae, she seems responsive to his advances until she notices the sun coming up. He refuses to drive her home until she kisses him and, after her subsequent bite, he is picked up by Mae's family but they won't accept him as one of their own until he kills for them. Bigelow's directing debut crossbreeds cast (Henriksen, Paxton, Jenette Goldstein), macho bluster and gun fetishism from *Aliens* (1986, shown playing at a cinema as Caleb stumbles past) with the desert psychosis, halogen-lit roads and laconically menacing asides of co-screenwriter Eric Red's previous **The Hitcher** for a seminal vampire Western. Dispensing with the traditional vampire iconography of crosses, fangs and coffins (though motel

CANNIBALISM

Early horror cinema, when it dealt with cannibalism at all (*Dr X*, 1932; *Sweeney Todd, Demon Barber of Fleet Street*, 1936) was discreet enough not to show the consumption of human flesh on screen. Even **Blood Feast**, no slouch when it came to explicit gore, never quite got around to the titular feast itself, leaving its eyebrow-wriggling Egyptian caterer the only character eaten, and then only by a garbage truck. **Night of the Living Dead** was the first film to revel in the giddy sight of human flesh gnawed to the bone: after that the gloves were off and the dentures on, although the '70s most fruitful area of anthropophagic activity, the cannibal family, was still reluctant to follow **Night**'s lead. **The Texas Chain Saw Massacre**, **The Hills Have Eyes** and **Death Line** all share not only urbanoia themes of economic guilt displaced onto dietary taboos but also a surprising coyness in what they put on screen. For all **Texas**'s imagery of girls hung on meat hooks, **Hills**' rousing battle cry of "Tenderloin baby!" and the Man's racks of well-hung meat, nobody actually got to chow down.

Again, it took Romero to raise the bar. **Dawn of the Dead**'s displays of gut-munching had a visceral intensity that sent talent scouts scouring the world looking for actors prepared to stuff raw intestines into their mouths, most of them evidently being found in Italy and the Amazon basin. **Dawn** kicked off not only a wave of ultra-gory Italian zombie pictures and freakshows like Joe d'Amato's *Anthropophagus* (1980) – whose killer ends the film by chewing on his own intestines – but also the Italian Third World cannibal cycle. If it took **Dawn** to prove that audiences would pay to see explicit, full-colour footage of people eating each other, the roots of the Italian cannibal cycle go further back, to horror-tinged jungle adventures like **The Most Dangerous Game** and the dubiously "authentic" displays of the "mondo" genre, and have the distinction of being a native cycle in a national industry typified by rip-offs of foreign successes.

The earlier entries, Umberto Lenzi's *Il Paese del Sesso Selvagio/Deep River Savages* (1972), Ruggero Deodato's *L'Ultimo Mundo Cannibale/Last Cannibal World* (1976) and Sergio Martino's relatively high-budget *La Montagna del Dio Cannibale/ Prisoner of the Cannibal God* (1978), share with their urbanoia cousins a displacement of developed-world guilt over cultural and economic exploitation of the Third World into the rawer,

more immediate image of barely-clothed "savages" not even bothering to cook their human victims. Deodato's fascinating Cannibal Holocaust and Lenzi's inferior *Cannibal Ferox* (1981), compromised the tradition by keeping their peers' racist disdain for tribal communities but presenting their coke-snorting rapist Westerners in an even worse light. These films are characterized by inept gore effects, interminable travelogue footage and real animal killings that keep them from critical rehabilitation or easy cult recuperation, but they at least take their taboo subject seriously, lending them a confrontational impact missing in the comedic trend of later cannibal movies in everything from *Parents to Ravenous* (1999). Only modern entries from Hong Kong (*Gou Yeung Yi Sang/Dr Lamb*, 1992) and Japan (*Taiji No Yume/Dream of an Embryo*, 1990) keep the bleak spirit of the Italian cycle alive.

BELOW: Cannibalism proved to be a box-office draw in **Dawn of the Dead**.

ABOVE: "I sure haven't met any girls like you." **Near Dark.**

rooms make an adequate stand-in) – vampires themselves are never mentioned – *Near Dark*'s best moments come less from the tiresome sub-*Mad Max* posturings of Mae's clan and her romantic canoodlings with dull ingénu Caleb than the subtle touches of the vampires' hunting procedures and a handful of explosive set pieces. The family's child, Homer, originally tricked Mae into the clan in high school by telling her he was in the fifth grade and needed help with his homework; Caleb struggles to show such panache, jittery and sweating as Mae tries to goad him into feeding from a friendly truck driver, and only shows any propensity for violence in the superb honky-tonk sequence, when the family's resident psycho greaser Severen (Paxton, in the film's most colourful performance) picks a fight with a "meatball" barfly. The scenes that follow are the film's highlight, marked by a surprising nastiness and welcome shift away from the guitar heroics of the Tangerine Dream soundtrack into more palatable fare. Only the ensuing motel shootout, the shafts of sunlight left by police bullets proving far more dangerous than the bullets themselves, can compare. Although the plot occasionally strains credulity – these vampires have survived for a long time considering how often they're almost caught out by the sun; exactly why they pick Caleb up is never adequately explained and the final blood transfusion details are sketchy at best – Bigelow directs with a verve and conviction lacking in 1987's other vampire-family offering, *The Lost Boys*, and later, messier entries in the vampire Western stakes like *From Dusk til Dawn* (1996) and *The Forsaken* (2001).

OPERA
AKA TERROR AT THE OPERA

1987, It, dir/co-scr Dario Argento, co-scr Franco Ferrini, starring Cristina Marsillach, Ian Charleson, Daria Nicolodi, Urbano Barberini

Betty, an opera-singer's understudy, gets her big shot at stardom when the lead diva is hit by a car. It's a classic showbiz fairy-tale but lurking in the wings is an admirer who's waited for this

OPPOSITE: Argento's painful literalized metaphor, **Opera**.

moment as much as she has; and his "congratulations" plunge her life into nightmare.

Opera is the last truly great Argento film and, although its final reel pulls a few too many desperate twists, overall it ranks with his best work. The central image of the film is of Betty bound and gagged, with needles taped beneath her eyes to prevent her from blinking, thus forcing her to watch the killer's twisted "homages" – brutal acts of murder the equal of any in Argento's repertoire. As a visualization of the director's sado-masochistic relationship with his audience, it's so intimate and honest it hurts.

Opera boasts some truly audacious imagery: the spiralling bird's-eye camera swooping over a terrorized opera-house audience (another great literalization of Argento's relationship to his viewers); the shots of the killer's throbbing brain; the supremely nasty stabbing of Betty's cute boyfriend; and the ultimate in bullet-to-the-eye encounters, to name but a few. Argento even turns the last minute walk-out of Vanessa Redgrave (scheduled to play the diva) to his advantage, replacing her with a breathtaking set-piece for subjective camera that thrills far more than a glimpse of the faded British theatre icon ever could. Although the story is *giallo*-esque, Argento uses the camera and his elliptical way with narrative to concoct scenes that feel as dreamily disassociated from reality as his supernatural-themed **Suspiria** and **Inferno**, with a recurring visit to a tightly coiled spiral staircase presaging sequences that float somewhere between flashback and fantasy.

On the downside, several killings are scored to the same sort of inappropriate heavy-metal music that marred *Phenomena* (1985) and the English dubbing is occasionally lamentable. Similarities to *Phenomena* are also emphasized by a last act that's set in that film's Swiss tourist-brochure locations and the final shot of Betty "at one" with nature is frankly risible – but *Opera* easily transcends its failings, standing as the climax and farewell to Argento's classic period. [ST]

GHOSTS ... OF THE CIVIL DEAD

1988, Aust, dir/co-scr John Hillcoat, co-scr Nick Cave, Gene Conkie, Evan English, Hugo Race, starring David Field, Mike Bishop, Chris DeRose, Kevin Mackey

Hillcoat's debut feature out-brutalizes competitors like *Midnight Express* (1978) and *Scum* (1979) to exploit the fertile arthouse/grindhouse territory of shockers like **Cannibal Holocaust** and **Irreversible** in its presentation of prison life as a harrowing

portrait of hell. The film is loosely based on the testimony of David Hale, a warder turned whistleblower at an Illinois jail who complained of management tactics in the months leading up to a prison lockdown, but relocates the action to a vaguely futuristic outback prison populated principally by real ex-cons and guards (there are only six professional actors in the film). It presents its tale of escalating mayhem in a semi-documentary style that uses voiceovers from two prisoners and a guard, and quotes from a report into the prison lockdown that are presented in ironic counterpoint to the visuals. The film follows the misadventures of a new inmate, Wenzil, whose attempts at self-assertion quickly result in his being raped and graced with a facial tattoo, as the administration manipulate tensions in the prison to their own ends by removing personal property, barring outdoor recreation and finally bringing in Nick Cave (the Bad Seeds also provide the soundtrack) as a psychopath whose howled insults push events over the edge for the bloodcurdling finale. Hillcoat presents his entirely convincing prison milieu with a security camera's unblinking eye, his grim austerity recalling Michael Haneke as he refuses to glamorize or condemn either guards or prisoners but instead casts a jaundiced eye over a system whose interest in self-perpetuation foments brutality. Gruelling violence aside, *Ghosts* also shades into horror territory through its distillation of the order/chaos dynamic central to many genre films: the return of the repressed never looked so apocalyptic. From the country that gave the world *Prisoner Cell Block H*.

PARENTS

1988, US, dir Bob Balaban, scr Christopher Hawthorne, with Randy Quaid, Mary Beth Hurt, Sandy Dennis, Bryan Madorsky

1954. The Laemles are a model American couple, but Michael's behaviour at his new school makes his teachers suspicious of his home life. And Michael has his own suspicions: why does his family eat leftovers every night? Using a similar satirical re-creation of '50s American suburbia to *Hairspray* (also 1988), *Parents* switches uneasily between an evocation of childhood anxieties about the adult world and a black comedy about a cannibal family. The former is the more successful strand, making much of its central theme of food as a tool for parental control and conformity. Michael is a morbidly imaginative boy who tells stories about boiling cats in class and is credulous enough to believe a schoolmate's story that she comes from the moon. He also distrusts his parents, and adults in general, and with a father like Randy Quaid's Nick Laemle, who, when he's not working at

ABOVE: Leftovers again…. **Parents**.

Toxico developing defoliants, terrifies his son with edgy displays of paternal reassurance, who can blame him? Most of the film retains enough ambiguity over the Laemles' activities to suggest that Michael's idea that his parents might be cannibals stems from an inability to understand the adult world. Early on, he sees them in a passionate clinch, later reinterpreted in a fantasy sequence as an orgy of flesh-eating, and he consistently puts a negative interpretation on their adult euphemisms. But perhaps he's not so wrong: the golf-playing, barbecue-crazed Nick, only able to speak to his son in catchphrases, is a seething ball of repressed hostilities, and Michael's sensitive response is deliciously played, if marred by several overblown dream sequences. Later, the film loses much of its ambiguity and moves into more standard horror territory, although even here the identity of the aggressor in the **Halloween**-inspired attack sequence is unclear: does Michael have more in common with his parents than he cares to admit? *Parents*' comedy and horror elements never quite gel, but its wonderful performances (particularly Quaid), inspired art direction and a handful of startling set pieces still make it worth seeking out.

SPOORLOSS
AKA THE VANISHING

1988, Neth/Fr, dir/co-scr George Sluizer, co-scr Tim Krabbé, starring Bernard-Pierre Donnadieu, Gene Bervoets, Johanna Ter Steege, Gwen Eckhaus

When Rex Hofman's girlfriend Saskia goes missing at a French service station, he becomes obsessed with her disappearance and devotes his life to finding out what happened to her. When her kidnapper finally contacts him, he offers to explain her fate – at a price. Sluizer has suggested that his superior psycho-thriller is about "the banality of greatness, and the greatness of banality", and the theme is key to the film's success: shot almost entirely in drab, mundane settings – service stations, motorway rest stops, featureless apartment blocks – with a flat visual style that never draws attention to itself yet maintains a subtly rich symbolism, *Spoorloss* forces the viewer into the characters' psyches partly because there is nowhere else to go. Hofman, a magnificently haunted Bervoets, should be an easy identification figure, yet even from the outset he is compromised, launching into crazed schemes for catching Saskia's kidnapper as soon as she vanishes. This is excusable at the time, but three years on our sympathies are firmly with his new girlfriend as she is forced to sit through another re-run of his TV appeal. Donnadieu's sociopath Lemorne, a successful family man whose skewed logic is far scarier than the grubby sexual transgressions of Hollywood psychos, is perversely almost a more appealing figure, his botched attempts to kidnap women played for laughs, although he is not above mining their angered ripostes for sensible advice or using his family to check the soundproofing of his country retreat. His readiness to pick up on subtle suggestions is mirrored in the film's understated use of banal events to reveal key plot details – we learn that Lemorne is claustrophobic when he is pulled over for not wearing a seatbelt – that fall into place only with the deliciously grim climax, while the film's structure plays on a powerful sense of fate, apparently random events building mercilessly to the inexorable conclusion. Sluizer's sixth feature catapulted the director to international fame and the dubious pleasures of Hollywood, where he was invited to remake the film, only to have his ending changed by the studio.

CLOWNHOUSE

1989, dir/scr Victor Salva, starring Nathan Forrest Winters, Brian McHugh, Sam Rockwell, Michael Jerome West

On being told they can't visit the travelling circus, three lunatics kill a guard, break out of the asylum and make their way to the big top. Meanwhile, Casey's morbid fear of clowns makes him the butt of his brothers' jokes, especially after he freaks out in the circus having been selected for audience participation by Cheezo the Clown. But when the lunatics put on the greasepaint, red noses and comedy shoes, all Casey's worst fears start to come true.

Pennywise in Stephen King's *It* (1990) was perhaps horror's first on-screen clown, but he was a malevolent alien entity masquerading as a clown, making *Clownhouse* the point zero of what would become the surprisingly crowded field of clown horror movies. Salva's film establishes some of the conventions that later films – including the *Carnival of Souls* (1998) remake, *Fear of Clowns* (2004) and *The Fun Park* (2007) – would rely on: an association of clowning with insanity, an exploration of childhood fears and a stress on inappropriate sexuality, here thankfully confined to the opening shots of three boys wandering around in their underwear, awkward viewing in the light of Salva's well-publicised abuse of Winters. But the film distinguishes itself from its horn-honking progeny by making the clowns behave like clowns, rather than psychopaths who simply happen to like painting smiles on their faces. Inspired by the sight of a balloon dog they try twisting their victims into novel shapes, specialize in "Behind you!" panto scares

and run around with their big shoes and oversize white gloves flapping goofily. The response of the boys they target is quite naturally to thwack them on the head with a frying pan. Yet the cartoon violence only serves to make the film more disturbing, its candy colours and garishly plastic props are grotesque incursions into the real world of a cartoon dementia in which injury is comic and pain inevitable. The hallucinatory unreality of the film makes it authentically nightmarish, and Casey's final response to the clown attacks – he sits, hiding, with his back to the clowns and his hands over his eyes – is a monstrously convincing evocation of childhood terror. *Clownhouse* may lack sophistication but, in the absence of a screen adaptation of Ramsey Campbell's extraordinary *Grin of the Dark*, it has the last word in fright-wigged fear.

SANTA SANGRE

1989, It/Mex, dir/co-scr Alexandro Jodorowsky, co-scr Roberto Leoni, Claudio Argento, starring Axel Jodorowsky, Blanca Guerra, Guy Stockwell, Sabrina Dennison

Fenix escapes a Mexican mental hospital to provide arms for his armless mother, who is intent on transforming her son's sexual desires into violence. Jodorowsky's most coherent and accessible film, loosely based on the exploits of the Mexican serial killer Goyo Cardenas, unavoidably recalls Tod Browning (**The Unknown**, **Freaks**) in its circus milieu and fascination with human deformity, whether accidental (the mother's arms are amputated by her lover) or innate (midgets, an acromegalic soldier and coke-snorting Down's-syndrome sufferers dance across the screen). But, rather than Browning's EC-style morality tales, Jodorowsky's riff on classic horror (quoting everything from **The Invisible Man** to **Psycho**) is simultaneously an account of a psychosis caused and conquered, and a paean to the transformative powers of the psychotic imagination. The distillation and reworking of generic images provides a parallel between the jigs and props of Fenix's madness and Mexico's cultural assimilation and reconstitution of European and American tropes, the film's Universal horrors being worked through a gaudily red and green, tequila-soaked haze. But if Jodorowsky's is a Mexico of the mind, it still has an authentic local flavour lacking in more realistic portrayals, the film's spectacular imagery underpinned by subtly faithful touches like the transsexual wrestler's insistence on shaking Fenix's hand every time he gives her a new bottle, or the animals emerging from the shadows to lap up each fresh spill of blood. Similarly, Jodorowsky's audaciously literal metaphors, whether describing

parental control or Alma's muteness, often tell their story better than more sensitive renditions. *Santa Sangre*'s principal flaw is that Jodorowsky's fondness for set pieces leaves little room for anything else: characterization is minimal and there's a flippancy to some of the scenes, while the travelling shot and stylized violence of the first murder, like a pastiche of Argento (the film was produced and co-scripted by Dario's brother Claudio), reduce the film's emotional impact. But the set pieces are so spectacular (the elephant funeral is among Jodorowsky's finest) that to complain seems churlish.

SOCIETY

1989, US, dir Brian Yuzna, scr Rick Fry, Woody Keith, starring Billy Warlock, Patrice Jennings, Devin DeVasquez, Charles Lucia

Billy Whitney's worst suspicions about his family are confirmed when a friend plays him a tape recording of them having sex together. His psychiatrist thinks he's just being paranoid, but Bill is convinced he's being prepared for a grand entrance into society. Yuzna, who produced **Re-Animator** and **From Beyond**, made his directorial debut with this gloopy parody of Beverly Hills elitism. If the social satire is laboured and unsubtle, it still provides a neat riposte to popular TV's celebration of body-beautiful mediocrity, particularly in its casting of *Baywatch*'s Warlock in the lead role. The film works best as a sickly study of family paranoia lensed as a parody of '80s teen movies. Billy isn't like the rest of his family: he looks different, has different interests and feels like an outsider, even though he drives a jeep and dresses in the same marblewashed denim as his peers. So far, so John Hughes, but the family's over-tactile caresses feed a sexual disgust that takes the film into darker territory. Billy hallucinates several times and his evidence of a conspiracy routinely vanishes

ABOVE: Shadows close in on Saskia (Johanna Ter Steege), **Spoorloss**.

before anyone else can see it: he watches his sister in the shower, seeing her breasts and bottom on the same side of her body (an exploitation filmmaker's dream of condensed T&A), and beats up her ex-boyfriend, suggesting that his incest suspicions are the product of his own sublimated desires. He is sexually inexperienced – his lover Clarissa wonders when he lost his virginity, and on her offering to urinate in his tea he can only call her "a class act", foreshadowing the final nightmare vision of collapsed boundaries and anal trauma, the slimiest perversion of the ruling class yet committed to film. Yuzna can't quite maintain a **Rosemary's Baby** ambiguity and the film's queasily paranoid atmosphere is spoiled by Screaming Mad George's comic effects and the arbitrary grotesquerie of Clarissa's hair-eating mother, but in its note-perfect acting and refitting of **Invasion of the Body Snatchers** paranoia into a modern world of bland consumerist aspirations, *Society* remains essential viewing.

TETSUO
AKA TETSUO: THE IRON MAN

1989, Jap, dir/scr Shinya Tsukamoto, starring Tomorowo Taguchi, Kei Fujiwara, Nobu Kanaoka, Renji Ishibashi

In the six years after Shôhei Imamura's *Narayama Bushiko/The Ballad of Narayama* won the Palme d'Or at Cannes, Japanese cinema had all but vanished from the international stage: the release of Tsukamoto's electrifying 16mm debut, which won first prize at 1989's Fantastic Film Festival in Rome, paved the way for the resurgent interest that would make directors like Takeshi

Kitano festival favourites. Self-financed from Tsukamoto's day job in advertising, *Tetsuo*'s abrasive mixture of clunky stop-motion animation and Sellotaped transformations opens as it means to go on, with a man (Tsukamoto himself, also responsible for the art direction, lighting, editing and effects) gouging a wound in his leg then filling it with a length of ribbed metal tubing. The man is then hit by a car driven by a couple who ignore their victim, only for the driver to later find himself transforming into a pile of scrap. Crossbreeding the grimy industrial decay and Expressionist nightmare feel of **Eraserhead** with the body-popping mutations of **Videodrome**, *Tetsuo*'s eroticized fusion of man and machine – the hit-and-run couple engage in messy sex involving an oversized metal drill-bit penis – seems like a psychotic response to the trauma of road accidents, Ballard's *Crash* filtered through the *kaijû* (monster) movies Tsukamoto grew up with. The collision also feels like the inevitable result of urban stress, the protagonist's encounter with a berserk semi-transformed woman on the subway a paranoid commuter fantasy of unwelcome rush-hour encounters, while the characters' blood spurts in jets of intense pressure: everything here is at bursting point. While the soundtrack's collage of screams and deafening industrial percussion becomes wearing on repeat viewings, for all *Tetsuo*'s baldly displayed influences it's a unique, remarkable achievement. What Tsukamoto's later films gain in budget and gloss they lose in raw immediacy, only *Tokyo Fist* (1995) approaching *Tetsuo*'s visceral impact.

THE WOMAN IN BLACK

1989, UK, dir Herbert Wise, scr Nigel Kneale, starring Adrian Rawlins, Bernard Hepton, David Daker, Pauline Moran

The solicitor Arthur Kidd is sent to the coastal village of Crythin Gifford to arrange the affairs of a recently deceased client. But, when he saves the life of a gypsy child, he finds himself targeted by the spectre that haunted his client to her grave. This TV adaptation of Susan Hill's novel followed a successful stage play and in its stripped-down narrative, mist-wreathed coastal locations and meticulous '20s period trappings remains an extraordinarily effective ghost story. Lacking the psychological ambiguities of **The Innocents** or **The Haunting** – everyone is able to see the titular spook, even if they won't admit it – Wise employs a Lewtonesque approach, focusing on sound (drawing parallels between the recording device through which Kidd discovers the occasionally confusing back story and the looped causeway haunting at the heart of the tale) and suggestion. The bleached-out visuals are

impressive enough and the ghost's gaze is terrifyingly malevolent while Eelmarsh House, where Kidd foolhardily decides to spend a night, is a sinister, ramshackle warren of maze-like passages and haunted playrooms. But the film's potency derives mainly from its structure, its most hair-raising scenes – a manifestation at the inn stands as perhaps the movies' most appalling spectral visitation – appearing at unexpected junctures that, if anything, recall the "just when you thought it was over" double climaxes beloved of slasher movies, although their payoff is far more impressive. The judicious use of Rachel Portman's eerie, melancholic score adds to the tone of grim foreboding, while the film's trajectory of innocent enthusiasm to shocking tragedy is surprisingly bleak for TV fare. Highly recommended.

BELOW: Tsukamoto's nightmare collision of flesh and metal, **Tetsuo**.

CHAPTER

9

1990s

The beginning of the '90s was not a good time for horror. The most interesting high-profile filmmaker in the shudder business was Tim Burton. He didn't manage an out-and-out horror picture until the exuberant **Sleepy Hollow** (1999), though the fairy-tale *Edward Scissorhands* (1990), the Expressionist-look *Batman Returns* (1992) and the sincere biopic *Ed Wood* (1994) say all sorts of interesting things about freakish outsiders with bizarre hairstyles and fetish clothing. The genre was more typified by dead losses like William Friedkin's *The Guardian* (1990), in which a nanny (Jenny Seagrove) worships a killer tree. Series horrors were flagging, as demonstrated by *The Exorcist III* (1990), *Leatherface: Texas Chainsaw 3* (1990), *Bride of Re-Animator* (1991), *Amityville 1992: It's About Time* (1992) and soulless returns to *Elm Street*, *Friday the 13th* and *Halloween*. All these franchises petered out in the '90s, only to be revived or remade in the new century. Indeed, the first sign of the apocalypse might have been the (fairly decent in itself) Tom Savini-directed remake of *Night of the Living Dead* (1990).

In 1991, horror returned in style with Jonathan Demme's **The Silence of the Lambs**, adapted from the best-seller by Thomas Harris. The book is a sequel to *Red Dragon*, which Michael Mann had filmed as *Manhunter* (1986) without anyone much taking notice, but the film seemed a standalone. It became the first horror movie to sweep the Academy Awards – indeed, it is probably the only film in history to score double-wins at the Oscars and *Fangoria*'s Chainsaw Awards. The topic of serial killing had been around forever – characters like Dracula and Mr Hyde qualify as serial killers, and non-supernatural menaces like the villains of *The Lodger* (1944) and *The Spiral Staircase* (1946) were well within the Jack the Ripper tradition, not to mention Norman Bates, Michael Myers and the black-gloved slashers of Dario Argento. Throughout the '80s, when the term became current, films tackled the subject, notably John McNaughton's **Henry … Portrait of a Serial Killer** (1986), which wasn't widely seen

until the '90s. **Silence** co-opted the serial killer, as found in police procedurals (*The Boston Strangler*, 1967) and inside-the-mind-of-a-madman street dramas (**The Driller Killer**, 1979), into the horror film. In the process, Demme proved the horror movie could be a matter of treatment as much as subject: Hannibal Lecktor (Brian Cox) in *Manhunter* is imprisoned in a white, striplit, credible mental institution; Hannibal Lecter (Anthony Hopkins) in **Silence** is kept in what looks like the dungeon of Castle Dracula.

Lecter, who combines elements of Dracula and Renfield, became *the* bogeyman of the '90s. A cultured cannibal epicure, worlds away from any real-life serial killer, he is witty, sensitive, charismatic and dangerous. Hopkins reprised the role in Ridley Scott's *Hannibal* (2001), from Harris's sequel novel (which seems to follow up the film of *Silence* rather than his earlier books), and Brett Ratner's *Red Dragon* (2002), a remake of *Manhunter* done

---

OPPOSITE: Sibling rivalry in *Halloween H20: Twenty Years Later* (1998).

RIGHT: Harry Connick Jr misses that big-band sound, *Copycat* (1995).

ABOVE: A louche, hissing Tom Cruise in *Interview with the Vampire* (1994).

in imitation of Demme's style. As the cycle progressed, Lecter became less an uncontrollable psychotic and more a refined vigilante, dining on "the free-range rude". There were, inevitably, imitations with ever-more-bizarre genius murderers and neurotic profilers, from the aptly named *Copycat* (1995) through *Kiss the Girls* (1997) and *The Bone Collector* (1999) to *Taking Lives* (2004). David Fincher's **Seven** (1995) is obviously in the **Silence** tradition, but it displaced some cultural water on its own strengths: its killer's gimmick – bizarre deaths themed to the seven deadly sins – would have done for Vincent Price in Dr Phibes mode, but the film has a distinctively *noir*ish, rainy, twisted intensity that others have tried to copy (the UK TV series *Messiah*, most blatantly). The most influential five minutes of horror film in the '90s are the credits of **Seven**, directed by Kyle Cooper – a montage of micro-script diary entries, classical paintings, crime-scene photos and other artefacts, cleverly edited together. Cooper did other, similar credits, and almost every subsequent genre TV series (for example, *Buffy the Vampire Slayer*) imitated his style.

Hopkins stepped from the Lecter role into Dr Van Helsing in Francis Ford Coppola's **Bram Stoker's Dracula** (1992), another significant gothic revival. This at once trumpeted its faithfulness to Stoker's text in the title and reworked the story in ways its author would have found ridiculous. Here the slogan is "Love Never Dies" and the Count (a ratty Gary Oldman), like Jack Palance in the 1974 TV movie, is out not to bring a vampire plague to Victorian Britain but to reunite with the reincarnation of his lost love (Winona Ryder). Though it didn't quite satisfy anyone, the film opened the way for a trickle of subsequent big-budget gothic-horror romances: Anne Rice's long-in-development *Interview with the Vampire* finally made it to the screen in 1994, with Neil Jordan directing a pouty Brad Pitt and a hissing Tom Cruise as louche vampires; Kenneth Branagh tried to wrestle *Mary Shelley's Frankenstein* (1994) into a tale of passion, rather than rejection – with Robert De Niro giving an especially disappointing performance as the craggy Creature (some comic potential is missed in that this monster is supposed to have John Cleese's brain); Mike Nichols's *Wolf* (1994) had Jack Nicholson as a meek publisher who becomes an alpha-male werewolf with a Henry Hull knock-off make-up job and pursues Michelle Pfeiffer; and Stephen Frears ended the cycle with the much-disliked Jekyll and Hyde variant *Mary Reilly* (1996), from Valerie Martin's novel in which Stevenson's story is seen from the below-stairs point of view of a maid (Julia Roberts) in the household of Dr Jekyll (John Malkovich). As is often the case, the most reviled of the cycle is also the most interesting – Frears engages with his subject matter on a deeper level than any of his distinguished colleagues, actually taking Stevenson (and Martin) seriously rather than paying lip-service to fidelity while turning out goth date movies.

Auteurs with a commitment to the genre were having a hard time. George Romero and Dario Argento collaborated on a Poe picture, *Two Evil Eyes* (1990), then slipped: Romero made an okay Stephen King film, *The Dark Half* (1992), and fell silent for over a decade, while Argento was responsible for a run of disappointments, mostly starring his daughter Asia (best of the batch is *La Sindrome di Stendhal/The Stendhal Syndrome*, 1996). Larry Cohen directed a Hitchcockian thriller, *The Ambulance* (1990), and reverted to peddling spec scripts – one of which became *Phone Booth* (2002). Sam Raimi managed *Darkman* (1990), a superhero-monster movie that suggested how his big-budget career might eventually turn out, and *Army of Darkness* (1992), a lightweight third *Evil Dead* movie, before tackling a Western (*The Quick and the Dead*, 1995), a sports movie (*For the Love of the Game*, 1999) and (most successfully) a small-scale thriller (*A Simple Plan*, 1998). David Cronenberg adapted William Burroughs (*Naked Lunch*, 1991) and J. G. Ballard (*Crash*, 1996) – and made the what-was-he-*thinking?* M. *Butterfly* (1993). Clive Barker let the *Hellraiser* franchise slip away from him, but his interesting follow-up *Nightbreed* (1990) was botched on several levels, and *Lord of Illusions* (1995) is at best makeshift; his presence in genre cinema was mostly as the original author of Bernard Rose's **Candyman** (1992), which became a minor franchise of its own. John Carpenter turned out *In the Mouth of Madness* (1994), *Village of the Damned* (1995) and *Vampires* (1998); about the best to be said for Carpenter's later work is that at least it's better than Tobe Hooper's *Spontaneous Combustion* (1990), *Night Terrors* (1993) and *The Mangler* (1995). Brian De Palma fitted one underrated, personal film (*Raising Cain*, 1992) into a schedule of mainstream assignments either disastrous (*The Bonfire of the Vanities*, 1990, *Mission to Mars*, 2000) or acceptable (*Carlito's Way*, 1993, *Mission: Impossible*, 1995).

David Lynch had an iffy decade commercially, but continued to maintain a reputation at the cutting edge. **Twin Peaks** (1990–92), an ambitious TV series which he co-created (with Mark Frost) and supervised throughout its up-and-down run, began as a mix of small-town melodrama, quirky comedy, murder mystery and psycho-horror, but opened up realms of Lovecraftian terror with its bogeyman "Bob" and the constant impingement of the supernatural into the lives of a peculiar community. **Twin Peaks** drew on Stephen King, **A Nightmare on Elm Street** and Thomas Harris, and itself fed into *The X-Files* (another FBI-based drama of the paranormal), Lars von Trier's Danish haunted-hospital TV soap *Riget* (*The Kingdom*) and a surprising number of mainstream fright films (note how many **Twin Peaks** cast members landed gigs in horror pictures). Lynch's big-screen prequel **Twin Peaks: Fire Walk With Me** (1992) prunes much that is endearing about the show, *doesn't* pick up from an unresolved cliffhanger and wasn't accepted by fans – but, at a stretch, it's the scariest movie of the decade. Lynch continued with **Lost Highway** (1997), another unclassifiable effort with much truly terrifying material, and the aptly titled *The Straight Story* (1999), which showed he could do gentler though still-barbed Americana. He is unlikely to become prolific, but each of his pictures has proved more rewarding with multiple viewings: **Mulholland Drive** (2001) is another touchstone, a film that horror movies look to for ideas in casting, tone and subject matter.

It is rarely noted that Lynch enjoys a back-and-forth relationship with Wes Craven: the monster father of Laura Palmer in *Twin Peaks* is played by Ray Wise, the human shape of Craven's *Swamp Thing* (1982), and "Bob" is essentially Fred Krueger taken to an existential extreme. In *The People Under the Stairs* (1991), Craven uses a couple tipped in from **Twin Peaks** (Everett McGill and Wendy Robie) as monster landlords. It seemed for a while that the '90s would be as troubled for Craven as for his peers. *People* is an underrated social cartoon, mixing Scooby-Doo chase/horror with ruminations on class and race in contemporary America, and *Wes Craven's New Nightmare* (1992), a meditation on the *Elm Street* films which takes place in

BELOW: "When you leave a man for dead...." *I Know What You Did Last Summer* (1997).

"the real world", is an ingenious, post-modern think piece which still remembers to be scary. Neither worked with audiences who unaccountably preferred more generic material, and *Vampire in Brooklyn* (1995), the first Eddie Murphy vehicle that required someone else to be comic relief, was *Blacula* reborn and severely bereft of soul. Then Craven signed with Dimension (Miramax's genre boutique) to direct a script called *Scary Movie*, written by genre enthusiast Kevin Williamson. Retitled **Scream** (1996), this clicked in a way Craven's other '90s films hadn't and revived not only the director's career but the slasher genre. **Scream** is post-modern, but more approachable than *New Nightmare*, and has a feel for the callous hipness of '90s American kids that gives it an uneasy undercurrent. Craven stayed on for sequels *Scream 2* (1997) and *3* (2000), making sure that Williamson's clever-clever concepts and dialogue went with perfectly judged stalk-and-scare sequences. Craven, a former editor, has the best timing of any horror director and a knack for making potentially hackneyed scenes in which people are menaced by killers into textbook exercises in shock and shiver.

Williamson went on to script *I Know What You Did Last Summer* (1997), a modest thriller that did well enough to earn a disappointing sequel, and *The Faculty* (1998), a high-school take on the *Body Snatchers* sub-genre, then directed the under-performing *Teaching Mrs Tingle* (1999). **Scream** encouraged a trickle of other gimmick slashers (the *Urban Legends* films) and *Halloween H20: Twenty Years Later* (1998), which Williamson contributed to, achieved a higher profile (with Jamie Lee Curtis returning to the franchise) than the sequels cranked out between *Halloween II* (1981) and *Halloween: The Curse of Michael Myers* (1996). Williamson's writing style has much in common with that of Joss Whedon, who had written the frankly limp *Buffy the Vampire Slayer* (1992), a lost-in-the-shuffle teen horror comedy, but still managed to have the format relaunched as a long-running, successful TV series, casting Sarah Michelle Gellar – a victim in *Scream 2* and *I Know What You Did Last Summer* – as the Californian airhead who accepts her destiny as a monster-fighter. *Buffy* spun off a vampire private-eye series (*Angel*) and encouraged a slew of similar shows, like the surprisingly durable *Charmed* and even the *Superboy* rethink *Smallville*. It says as much about a small casting pool as it does the boundaries of genre that faces from these shows soon started popping up in quickie, teen-themed horror movies, and **Scream** had itself drawn on on-camera talent from hot TV shows. It's easy to take against the buffed, coiffed and smart-mouthed kids who posed on Dimension posters in the late '90s, but it is worth remembering that they replaced the sort of knocked-around B-picture Z-listers found

in *Scream Queen Hot Tub Party* (1991). The TV kids are mostly at least competent actors and, seriously, Eliza Dushku is a better bet to build your film around than, say, Julie Strain.

The Faculty was directed by Robert Rodriguez, who'd handled another script from a '90s hot name in *From Dusk Till Dawn* (1996), a messy road/vampire story from Quentin Tarantino, once planned (like Peter Jackson's *The Frighteners*, 1996) as an entry in the *Tales From the Crypt* film franchise. Though there wasn't a flow of ambitious genre directors on the '70s pattern, the '90s saw an influx of Tarantino-like video-store-clerk horrormakers, mostly kids who'd grown up in an era when the exploitation films of the past were easily available on cassette and who wanted to get into the game. The New Zealander Jackson, active as early as *Bad Taste* (1987), showed how far the *Evil Dead* splatter style could be taken in **Braindead** (*Dead-Alive*, 1992), a zombie comedy with a sweet streak (which distinguishes it from, say, Troma's output) and a willingness to go for the extreme (a lawnmower massacre) which seems odd in the light of Jackson's Tolkien-powered enthronement as an Oscar-winning A-lister. The Mexican Guillermo del Toro went from **Cronos** (1993), an unusual Spanish-language vampire film, to *Mimic* (1997), a New York-set giant-insect picture for Dimension. As with Sam Raimi, there's a sense that these filmmakers want to see-saw between big pictures and down-and-dirty projects, but are capable of making a hundred-million-dollar spectacular with an eye on the box-office records or the Academy Awards into a bizarrely personal project.

The countdown to the millennium brought thoughts of the end of things and, eventually, religion. The inevitable apocalypses included a revival of the alien invasion/disaster format in Roland Emmerich's big '70s TV movie *Independence Day* (1996) and Tim Burton's retro-look sick joke *Mars Attacks!* (1996). A quieter, creepier vision is Michael Tolkin's *The Rapture* (1992), which at once depicts and criticizes the fundamentalist Christian vision of the End Times. Later in the decade, the fundies got to make their own movies, often with direct-to-video talent like Mr T, Caspar Van Dien and Gary Busey earnestly struggling with the Antichrist in bloodless rethinks of *The Omen*: witness *Apocalypse* (1998) and sequels, *The Omega Code* (1999) and sequel, and *Left Behind* (2000) and sequels. The tone of these Protestant films isn't all that different from the run of **Exorcist**-style Catholic Devil movies that flopped around the turn of the century: *Stigmata* (1999), *End of Days* (1999), *Bless the Child* (2000), *Lost Souls* (2000). The Devil might be back in business, courtesy of the Conservative "demon eyes" poster that failed to defeat Tony Blair at the 1997 election, but doubting audiences were more scared by less tangible menaces. A more sustained, unusual apocalypse – keyed to a prescient finale in which skyscrapers are brought down by a terror campaign – is David Fincher's *Fight Club* (1999), from Chuck Palahniuk's novel, which is also a canny rethink of Jekyll and Hyde for changing times, meditating on masculinity, identity and unrestrained impulses in a darkly satirical fashion.

At the end of the century, three horror films became cultural phenomena. From Japan, Hideo Nakata's **Ringu** (*Ring*, 1998) – based on a novel by Koji Suzuki which had already been done as a TV series – was the break-out entry in a run of Asian ghost stories arguably begun with the Korean haunted-school effort *Yeogo Goedam* (*Whispering Corridors*, 1998) but which had roots in the classical ghost tales of the Far East with their melancholy, lank-haired, waiflike girl spectres. **Ringu** welded this convention, epitomized by the spooky Sadako, to an urban legend about a cursed videotape that brings doom within a week to anyone who watches it. A box-office hit, with competing sequels and an instant Korean remake, **Ringu** took a while to connect internationally but became hugely influential. M. Night Shyamalan's **The Sixth Sense** (1999) is another ghost story, with a twist guessable by anyone who watched a TV movie in the '70s (though it still took many audiences by surprise), but also a

subtle, affecting, genuinely scary sense of things beyond the veil. Along with *Fight Club*, **The Sixth Sense** made an instant cliché out of hardly unprecedented twist endings involving apparently solid characters who turn out to be ghosts or imaginary friends. Shyamalan made films on the same pattern in the new century, tackling superheroes (*Unbreakable*, 2000), aliens (*Signs*, 2002) and a fear-haunted community (*The Village*, 2004). All are interesting, though high seriousness of style is sometimes applied to frankly silly ideas (lazy plotting is taken as proof of divine intervention in *Signs*) and none have resonated with filmgoers the way **The Sixth Sense** did. The third 1999 hit was even more unexpected: Edward Myrick and Daniel Sanchez's micro-budgeted, ingeniously marketed **The Blair Witch Project**, a *mondo*-look mock documentary with a sense of the unappealing way people actually behave in bad situations and a feel for the haunted landscape, which evokes genre precedents from innumerable walking-around-in-the-woods Bigfoot efforts of the '70s to the ghost stories of M. R. James and Algernon Blackwood.

BELOW: A CGI spook in *The Frighteners* (1996).

BRAIN DEAD

1990, US, dir Adam Simon, scr Charles Beaumont, Adam Simon, starring Bill Pullman, Bill Paxton, Bud Cort, Patricia Charboneau

One of the wilder (and gorier) entries in the '90s spate of reality-slip films, this starts like a **Re-Animator**-era splatter comedy, with neurologist Rex Martin blackmailed into operating on a paranoid murderer, Jack Halsey, by Jim Reston, a business friend, whose employers have an interest in the contents of Halsey's mind. The operation – to remove the part of Halsey's brain apparently making him paranoid – is a success, but from then on the themes of ethical guilt and corporate paranoia are ditched and it's **Lost Highway**-lite, as Martin appears to have undergone an identity switch with Halsey … or is the latter just a figment of his own paranoid mind? The story involves so many shifting levels of reality that it's difficult to follow, but the gleeful energy with which the hapless Martin is put through the wringer means that the plot holes don't really matter, and the imagery's shift from surgical anxiety to the transcendent weirdness of the final half-hour is so deftly handled that most viewers won't even notice. More effective than the bargain-basement metaphysics are the sleep paralysis scenes, in which Martin keeps appearing to wake up from the same sequence of events, and his unsettling encounters with the inmates of a mental hospital.

JACOB'S LADDER

1990, US, dir Adrian Lyne, scr Bruce Joel Rubin, starring Tim Robbins, Elizabeth Pena, Danny Aiello, Matt Craven

NYC, the early '70s. Jacob Singer is plagued by flashbacks from Vietnam and begins to hallucinate that demons are surrounding him. But the funeral of a fellow veteran reveals that he is not alone and he soon suspects that his battalion was subjected to military testing. Lyne's messy tale of psychedelic paranoia

BELOW: Trapped between worlds. Tim Robbins wakes up in **Jacob's Ladder**.

plays at first like an updated version of *Blue Sunshine* (1978), in which former LSD acolytes find their bid for the straight world foiled when, 10 years on, their hair falls out and they fall prey to murderous rages. But it soon develops into something far closer to Philip K. Dick's *Ubik*, anticipating the gimmick twist endings that would clutter cinemas later in the decade. Although Lyne tries to maintain both strands they are mutually exclusive readings, leading to a muddled narrative kept afloat by high production values, superlative cinematography, naturalistic acting from likable principals, a consistently creepy atmosphere and a series of brilliantly executed hallucinations. The latter are the film's strongest point, as Jacob reconfigures subtly disquieting elements in his environment, a dank and grimy Manhattan shot in washed-out colours, into visions that range from the suggestive (a nurse's cap falls off, revealing a hideously warty scalp) to the horrifically explicit (hospital corridors devolve into a descent into

Hell, complete with Victorian bedlamites and a floor slick with the blood of amputated limbs). The trajectory and tone of the hallucinations has a credibly psychedelic quality and it's ironic that such a nightmarish take on the entheogen experience should contain worthwhile psychedelic advice, dispensed by Aiello's angelic chiropractor and regrettably sugared by the saccharine sentimentality of the appalling Macaulay Culkin.

MISERY

1990, US, dir Rob Reiner, scr William Goldman, starring James Caan, Kathy Bates, Richard Farnsworth, Frances Sternhagen

Misery opens with the car crash of the successful but unfulfilled historical-romance writer Paul Sheldon just as he has killed off his titular heroine and embarked on his first "proper" novel. Everyone believes him to be dead, but he's rescued from the snow by a nurse, Annie Wilkes, who claims to be his biggest fan. Soon, Sheldon discovers that he is Wilkes's prisoner rather

BELOW: "You dirty birdy!" Kathy Bates is James Caan's number-one fan, **Misery**.

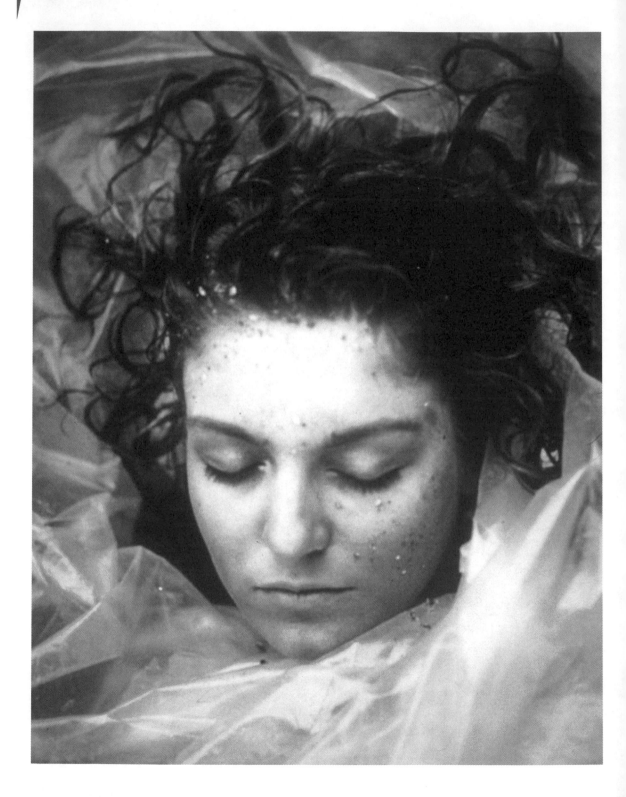

than her patient and that she is far from happy at the fate he has meted out to her beloved Misery. The film is the archetypal chamber-piece horror, tightly constraining its location and cast. Trapping the audience in a room with the two leads was a risky proposition, potentially a recipe for boredom rather than terror, but solid if unflashy direction and finely judged acting ensure that the film achieves the desired effect. Bates's performance in particular is inspired and well deserved its Oscar. It is a part that could easily have tipped over into camp – as the performances in the film's thematic precursor, *What Ever Happened to Baby Jane* (1962), sometimes do – but she succeeds in making Wilkes's unpredictability truly frightening.

This was the second Stephen King adaptation by director Rob Reiner, following 1986's coming-of-age drama *Stand By Me*. Screenwriter Goldman was not known for his work in the genre but claims that he was attracted to the book by its most shocking and memorable scene, in which Wilkes cuts off Sheldon's foot to prevent him from escaping. The scene, however, was later rewritten on Reiner's instructions so that Sheldon's feet are merely broken rather than amputated, as the director believed the audience would cease rooting for the hero if he suffered an injury from which there could be no recovery. In film terms, it was undoubtedly the right decision – as Goldman later recognized – but it signifies the way in which King's original claustrophobic horror story was softened to buy commercial success, and is an ironic mirror of the book's exploration of an author's sacrifice of integrity for recognition. [RL]

TWIN PEAKS

1990, US, dir/co-scr David Lynch, co-scr Mark Frost, starring Kyle MacLachlan, Michael Ontkean, Mädchen Amick, Dana Ashbrook

This brooding murder mystery from David Lynch and Mark Frost was a surprise success when its pilot aired in 1990, not least because of the way it tore up the rule-book of staid television drama. Hitherto frequently bored viewers were presented with a cast of 40 unusual and interesting characters, film-quality production values, scripts laden with in-jokes, catchphrases and arcane cultural reference, with the whole wrapped in Angelo Badalamenti's highly influential soporific score.

Frost was an ex-*Hill Street Blues* writer and Sherlock Holmes fan who managed to dilute some of Lynch's intensity to serve up a kind of **Blue Velvet**-lite for an audience who wouldn't have

been able to stomach Lynch in the raw. So Kyle MacLachan's investigative youth becomes the eccentric FBI agent Dale Cooper, a character of excessive charm and some of the preternatural deductive powers of the world's greatest detective. The small town with a heart of darkness expanded into a whole community shot through with various shades of corruption, and with something truly evil at its core.

Frank Booth in **Blue Velvet** was terrifying enough but at least he remained human and mortal. *Twin Peaks* presents a very different face of horror amid the good humour and endless cups of coffee. The emissaries of the supernatural Black Lodge, the "darkness in the woods", are all the more disturbing because their motives and true nature remain opaque, despite attempts later in the series to connect them to Native American lore or even (four years before *The X-Files*) UFOs. Lynch's monsters are strikingly original, surreal and banal in equal measure; only he would name a force of inhuman malevolence "Bob" and only he would give him a companion like the red-suited dwarf that talks backwards in Cooper's dreams. Whatever the errors of a series that eventually lost its way after network pressure, without *Twin Peaks* blazing its trail through the woods there would be no *X-Files* or *Lost*, and the landscape of American television would be a poorer place today. [JC]

C'EST ARRIVÉ PRÈS DE CHEZ VOUS
AKA MAN BITES DOG

1991, Bel, dir/co-scr Andre Bonzel, Rémy Belvaux, Benoît Poelvoorde, co-scr Vincent Tavier, starring Benoît Poelvoorde, Jacqueline Poelvoorde-Pappaert, Nelly Pappaert, Jenny Drye

A documentary team follows serial killer Benoît around Belgium as he kills for the camera. But as they spend more time socially with their subject, they find themselves increasingly involved in his crimes.

C'est Arrivé had its debut at Cannes in the same year as *Reservoir Dogs*, (which won the Critics' Week award) and was another controversial success that galvanized the ongoing debate over screen violence. While it follows the mock documentary format meticulously, using one hand-held camera (shooting in high-contrast black-and-white), lacking unified sound and vision if the sound man wanders away and boasting all the hallmarks of TV documentary – "day in the life" banalities, interviews with the subject's family (actually Poelvoorde's own, who reportedly believed that a documentary was being made about their son) – it has little more to say than **Cannibal Holocaust** on

documentary complicity and involvement in film violence, and works better as a parody of the drive to authenticity behind such purportedly objective portraits of serial murder as **Maniac** and **Henry ... Portrait of a Serial Killer**. The filmmakers' moral justification for the film is as disingenuous as Deodato's, or that of the documentary team for continuing after their sound man is killed. *C'est Arrivé* is both industry calling card (a film student debut shot over two and a half years and financed by family and friends) and edgy serial killer comedy, the film's occasional shift into queasy horror (the aftermath of a rape murder, the killing of a child) clashing with the broadly comedic tone elsewhere, as though to remind the viewer that serial killing *isn't funny*. Thanks, boys.

The film's main draw, then, is the character of Benoît himself, an amateur ornithologist and professional bore who shares some of the preening absurdity of his favoured pigeons, even appearing in his lean, gangly frame like some oversized flightless bird. Keen to share his inane tabloid views on everything from architecture to race, Benoît is clearly delighted to have others join him in the lonely art of serial murder; desperate to impress, even financing the film himself as a vanity project, he offers us one privileged glimpse into his self-image – a naked child of nature, running floppily around the dunes to the sound of witless marine doggerel – before vomiting spectacularly over the seafood dinner he has bought to win the filmmakers' approval.

THE SILENCE OF THE LAMBS

1991, US, dir Jonathan Demme, scr Thomas Harris, Ted Tally, starring Jodie Foster, Anthony Hopkins, Scott Glenn, Anthony Heald

The second adaptation of a novel by Thomas Harris featuring Hannibal Lecter following 1986's Michael Mann-directed *Manhunter*, *The Silence of the Lambs* replaced clinical coldness with visceral excess. The story follows woman-in-a-man's-world FBI agent Clarice Starling as she enlists the help of one monstrous but imprisoned serial killer – the notorious Hannibal the Cannibal – to catch another who is still on the loose. The film earned a brace of Oscars, including best picture and best actor for Anthony Hopkins, whose performance was, at 16 minutes, the shortest ever to secure a leading acting gong. There's nothing subtle about his mannered portrayal of the cultured serial killer – he himself described his voice as a combination of Truman Capote and

LEFT: Dining on the "free-range rude". Anthony Hopkins as Hannibal Lecter, **The Silence of the Lambs**.

Katharine Hepburn – but with so little screen time it dominates the movie and plays perfectly off Jodie Foster's more restrained take on her role. The audience's fear of Hannibal is cleverly amped by the writing and direction: the extreme security arrangements around him and the wariness of his gaolers all combine to tell us that this is a man to be feared above all others.

This was the film that made serial killers the must-have accessory for mainstream-crossover horror movies, but the relationship between Lecter and Starling is more complex than any of its many imitators. Of all the men in the movie, Hannibal is the only one who treats Starling with genuine respect or sees her as more than a means to an end. They touch just once, his finger brushing hers when she hands him a report, and the moment has a disturbing sexual charge. The Ed Gein-inspired Buffalo Bill, the real villain of the movie, is by contrast presented as a sexual freak who yearns to become a woman rather than relate to one. At its twisted heart, *The Silence of the Lambs* can be read as a love story, but when this subtext became text in the subsequent *Hannibal* (2000) it was drained of its power. [RL]

BRAINDEAD
AKA DEAD-ALIVE

1992, Aust, dir Peter Jackson, scr Stephen Sinclair, starring Timothy Balme, Diana Peñalver, Elizabeth Moody, Ian Watkin, Brenda Kendall

Peter Jackson's third feature after *Bad Taste* (1987) and *Meet the Feebles* (1989) is still perhaps the soggiest gore film ever made. A young man, Lionel, finds his potential for a love life severely curtailed when his tyrannical mother is bitten by a sutran rat monkey and becomes a zombie. Soon she has spread the plague around the neighbourhood and Lionel struggles to keep up appearances with a basement full of flesh-eating ghouls. Taking its cues from any number of other horror films (Lionel's mother is a Mrs Bates-style domineering matriarch, with Lionel a more functional Norman), *Braindead*'s entertainment value comes largely from its invigorating taboo-busting, with extended mockeries of religion, child-rearing, the Second World War ... and *The Archers*. The film's blood-drenched effects – at one point Lionel uses a lawnmower to dispose of wave after wave of undead – were amazingly passed uncut by the British censors at a time when they were still making heavy cuts to horror material; perhaps they respected the hero's decision to turn a picture of the Queen to the wall before the carnage ensues.

RIGHT: "They're not dead exactly, they're just sort of ... rotting." **Braindead**.

Sadly, the film gets sillier and sillier as it goes on and suffers from a bad case of rubber-monster overload by the end. Jackson, who probably felt he'd taken his brand of comedy horror as far as it could go with this film, eventually hit A-list territory with the *Lord of the Rings* trilogy.

BRAM STOKER'S DRACULA

1992, US, dir Francis Ford Coppola, scr James V. Hart, starring Gary Oldman, Winona Ryder, Anthony Hopkins, Keanu Reeves

Since renouncing God in 1462 when his beloved Elisabeta committed suicide, the Romanian Count Dracula has lived in a state of immortal desperation, waiting to be reunited with his true love. Now that she has been reincarnated as Mina Murray, a middle-class London schoolmistress, he sets about an elaborate courtship, arranging his sea-borne emigration to London and luring her betrothed, Jonathan Harker, to confinement in his Transylvanian castle. Despite its title, this lavish, romantic interpretation of the Dracula story deviates significantly from

LEFT: "... much to be learned from the beasts." Gary Oldman and Winona Ryder, **Bram Stoker's Dracula**.

RIGHT: "They will all abandon you." Virginia Madsen finds that Tony Todd isn't joking in **Candyman**.

the original text and was targeted at a generation used to high-production-value music videos. It is drenched in opulent detail and, with his florid Eastern European accent, affected aristocratic demeanour and Shakespearean sense of tragedy, Oldman's seductive, mournful goth makes a far more tantalizing count than Christopher Lee's largely silent, leaden vampire.

In a London thrilled by new inventions Dracula cuts a dapper dash and his first meeting with Mina is both erotically potent and tragic, as she recognizes his voice from "across the oceans of time". There's a heady swirl of absinthe-soaked delirium about the production. Costumes and sets are sumptuous, from the Gustave Moreau-inspired *femmes fatales* who hold the laughably wooden Keanu Reeves captive in Castle Dracula to Lucy's bestial couplings in her moonlit fairy-tale garden. Hopkins makes a lion-hearted, maverick Van Helsing but the chase and action sequences seem out of kilter with the film's dreamy poignancy. Overall, it is a deeply sensual film, informed by a uniquely feminine eroticism, and one wonders if the action was put in to save male interest in the light of the woeful miscasting of Reeves as the "hero". Certainly, the audience's sympathies are guided to the sexually anarchic vampires over the God-fearing stuffed shirts who intend to behead them. Sadie Frost makes a magnetic, beguiling Lucy and Tom Waits is a grimy delight as lunatic Renfield, but gore fans will be disappointed and overall it's one for the ladies. [KS]

CANDYMAN

1992, US, dir/scr Bernard Rose, starring Virginia Madsen, Tony Todd, Xander Berkeley, Kasi Lemmons

Helen, an anthropologist, researches the urban legend of Candyman or "the hook" in the Chicago housing projects. She is beaten by a man with a hook during her research and the police arrest the assailant, who is blamed for a series of recent murders. But when Helen subsequently meets Candyman himself, her life is turned on its head as she is framed for a new set of killings. Rose's follow-up to the intermittently interesting *Paperhouse* (1988) is drawn from Clive Barker's story "The Forbidden" and proves to be the best Barker adaptation to date, as well as the most interesting treatment of the urban-

legend theme informing genre entries from the **Nightmare on Elm Street** series to *I Know What You Did Last Summer* (1997). Helen's apartment block has the same layout as the projects; it was built for the same purpose but was then developed into luxury flats. This doubling runs throughout the film, which draws much of its power from the tension between a series of antonyms: black/white, rich/poor, sane/insane, reality/fantasy. Helen's willingness to cross boundaries – she summons Candyman, saying his name three times before a mirror to see if it will work, and is the only white face when she visits the projects – demonstrates an arrogance that is punished severely.

She is accused of murdering a friend's child, her husband starts an affair with a student and her talk of Candyman is dismissed as the ravings of a lunatic. Rose retains enough ambiguity to suggest that perhaps Helen *is* insane, Candyman's startling appearances having a hallucinatory quality, but as the entire film is narrated from her viewpoint, we are never quite sure. It's refreshing to see a dream demon put in a realistic environment a world away from the usual preppy suburbs, and Rose boldly draws on the true horrors of social exclusion and poverty to tell his intelligent and compelling story. A 1995 sequel dispensed with Rose's approach for standard slasher fare.

DUST DEVIL

1992, UK/SA, dir/scr Richard Stanley, starring Robert Burke, Chelsea Field, Zakes Mokae, John Matshikiza

Wendy runs from her abusive husband to drive through the Namibian desert towards the sea. En route she falls into the clutches of a hitch-hiking demon, the Dust Devil, who is attracted by her despair. If the shadow of British SF comic *2000AD* looms over Stanley's debut feature *Hardware* (1990), *Dust Devil* is haunted by the spectre of London's Scala. A repertory cinema specializing in arcane double bills and trash all-nighters, the Scala

provided Stanley's film education and financing, its owners running Palace, a successful distribution and production company finally run into the ground by repeated censorship scares and increasing industry corporatism. *Dust Devil* was left in post-production limbo when Palace went into receivership, forcing Stanley to finish the film with his own funds. Its savant is a projectionist, screening a typical Scala double bill of **L'Uccello dalle Piume di Cristallo** and *The Legend of the Seven Golden Vampires* (1974) to an unlikely Namibian audience. The film ends in a deserted cinema, harbinger of the death of British repertory cinema, and its feel, jumping from psychedelic Western (*El Topo*, 1970) to mystical slasher (**White of the Eye**) while quoting Fulci's tears of blood and Peter Weir's outback mysticism, is a distilled tribute to coffee-fuelled all-nighters in King's Cross. Yet London is far from the Namib desert and one of *Dust Devil*'s greatest assets is its setting, the arid locations used to spectacular effect and the *muti* limb-lopping tapping into African witchcraft's fertile store of imagery, effectively ignored by other genre filmmakers despite the continent's rich supernatural traditions. Stanley's lavish visuals pile on the heavy symbolism, particularly for a laboured theme of spirals and circularity, and occasionally fluoresce into breathtaking set-pieces – the camera's pull away from the "other side of the mirror" and the Dust Devil's gaze into night are astonishing. But the showboating finally fails to gloss over either a plot that gets more confused the more Stanley throws at it or the stilted, unconvincing acting, Burke (the Dust Devil) in particular dissipating any real menace every time he comes out with more macho traveller drivel. Still, Stanley's gorgeous imagery and some genuinely unsettling sequences keep the film afloat and, for all its pillaging of Scala favourites, it's certainly different.

TWIN PEAKS: FIRE WALK WITH ME

1992, US, dir/co-scr David Lynch, co-scr Robert Engels, starring Sheryl Lee, Ray Wise, Mädchen Amick, Dana Ashbrook

Subtitled "The Last Seven Days of Laura Palma", *Fire Walk With Me* opens with screams and shots of a television being smashed to pieces, a pungent comment on the watering down and cancellation of the **Twin Peaks** TV series. *Fire Walk With Me* attempts to explain some of the mysteries of that series by showing us the events leading to the pivotal death of Laura Palma. Despite its origins in the compromised world of network

LEFT: David Lynch's unique supernatural realm, **Twin Peaks: Fire Walk with Me**.

television, this is a particularly dark and disturbing film, even set beside Lynch's other dark and disturbing works.

Two of the partially buried themes of the series are here brought to the surface: Leland Palmer's incestuous relationship with his daughter and the inexplicable activities of The Lodge (or the Black Lodge) and its inhabitants, especially the thing known as "Bob", which has possessed Laura's father and which acts as a conduit between the everyday world and another dimension. Lynch's unique supernatural realm is presented here at its most explicit, conveyed in stray flickers of sound, backward speech and momentary glimpses of utterly bewildering scenes and images. The cumulative effect is deeply unnerving, not least because so much remains unresolved, from Laura's intermittent possession by the same malign forces that are consuming her father to the bizarre disappearance of at least two FBI agents investigating The Lodge. Mix this with tragic, violent family drama that omits the humour of the TV series and you have a story that makes the pleasant streets of Twin Peaks seem like an annexe of Hell. It is unfortunate that much of the appreciation of *Fire Walk With Me* relies on knowledge of the TV series: the numerous characters and their complex relationships are barely explained as Laura moves towards her demise. Yet Lynch's ability to summon horror from the most mundane circumstances while avoiding clichés remains unparalleled. *Fire Walk With Me* hints at a new mythos of nightmare that demands exploration. [JC]

BENNY'S VIDEO

1993, Aus/Swi, dir/scr Michael Haneke, starring Arno Frisch, Angela Winkler, Ulrich Mühe, Ingrid Stassner

Fourteen-year-old Benny is a video obsessive, alternately renting films and filming his own experiences then playing back the tapes. He invites a girl back to his parents' house and kills her with a farm tool, then tells his parents, whose response is unexpected. The second film in Haneke's "bourgeois trilogy", sandwiched between *Der Siebente Kontinent /The Seventh Continent* (1989) and *71 Fragmente einer Chronologie des Zufalls/71 Fragments of a Chronology of Chance* (1994), *Benny's Video* shares cast (Frisch, Mühe) and themes with the director's better-known **Funny Games**. For Benny, mediated images have come to replace reality – his bedroom blinds are drawn and a video camera trained on the street outside displays the view on a monitor – and he watches certain sequences over and over again, in an apparent bid to decipher their meaning. Although Haneke refuses to provide psychological explanations for his behaviour, it is contextualized

by background detail – the ubiquitous TV shows news footage from Bosnia, scenes of chaotic violence neatly packaged, with all emotional affect drained away; his status-obsessed parents have bought Benny his video equipment, showering their son with gifts if not attention; and his sister throws parties to interest her peers in pyramid schemes, reducing human contact to financial transactions. In this context Benny's fascination with death might be less morbid curiosity than a desire to confront the natural processes invisible in his urban environment and to provide an emotional intensity lacking in his human contact. He hardly speaks to his parents, most of his relationships again reduced to simple transactions (buying a McDonalds, renting a video, borrowing homework from a schoolfriend). Perversely, his murder allows him to engage emotionally with his surroundings for the first time. Haneke matches the cold austerity of the tale with a glacial visual style, using a muted palette and static camera set-ups in which the action often occurs off-screen. For the director, visual depictions of violence are compromised by their widespread use as entertainment. Instead, he focuses on sound, letting the viewers generate their own harrowing images, and the emotional aftermath of violence which is superbly conveyed by Frisch's emotionally stunted teen and the grief displayed by his mother.

BODY MELT

1993, Aust, dir/co-scr Philip Brophy, co-scr Rod Bishop, starring Gerard Kennedy, Andrew Daddo, Ian Smith, Vincent Gil, Regina Gaigalas

A pharmaceutical company tests its products on an unwitting group of Melbourne suburbanites, with predictably splashy results. Brophy's horror comedy, an Australian *Street Trash* (1987), has the bolshy, irreverent feel common to antipodean genre material and brings an adolescent gross-out mentality (surprising considering Brophy's mannered, erudite film criticism) to its body-horror themes. Only one body "melts", but others are variously drowned in mucus, attacked by flying placentas or simply explode, with most of the horror effects bookended by visual or verbal gags. Brophy's satire on fitness fanaticism gets lost somewhere in the soup of bodily fluids, but other ideas are more effective, such as the **Hills Have Eyes**-style cannibal outback family, whose children hunt kangaroos for their adrenal glands while their elderly mother sits glued to hard-core porn, and the hallucinations suffered by one victim, which have a subtly disquieting quality at odds with the rubbery gore effects. Fans of early '90s Australian soap will be amused to recognize three faces from *Neighbours*.

CRONOS

1993, Mex, dir/scr Guillermo Del Toro, starring Federico Luppi,
Ron Perlman, Claudio Brook, Margarita Isabel

An antiques dealer, Jesus Gris, discovers a clockwork device, the Cronos, hidden in the base of a statue. The Cronos, which he takes at first to be a toy, cuts his hand: he feels rejuvenated, but is now addicted to its bite. A local businessman, de la Guardia, owns the 16th-century alchemist's notebooks giving strict instructions on the use of the device, which confers immortality through a bloodsucking insect, and will stop at nothing to secure the Cronos for himself.

Del Toro's debut feature is a marvellously imaginative reinvention of the vampire legend, explicitly linked to Christian ideas of resurrection – the protagonist's name is Jesus, and de la Guardia

---

BELOW: The vampire sheds his rotting skin, **Cronos**.

points out that "Christ walks on water; so does a mosquito" – and, bizarrely, insects. What may at first seem a crazed preoccupation *à la* Argento's *Phenomena* (1985) becomes more credible when de la Guardia explains that ants and spiders occasionally resurrect themselves. Insects are, after all, the most common bloodsuckers and Del Toro milks the concept for inventive, outlandish imagery, from Gris shedding his rotting skin to reveal a shiny white carapace beneath to the design of the Cronos itself, a wonderful conflation of Fabergé egg and Lament Configuration. Gris is perhaps the screen's most sympathetic vampire, using his rejuvenation to reassert his love for his wife and hiding his undead body in his granddaughter's toy box; Luppi strikes the perfect pitch of dignity and befuddled pathos, his degradation complete when, in one astonishing sequence, he is reduced to licking a drop of blood from a public toilet floor. But Del Toro's idiosyncratic approach filters down through all the characters, from Aurora, the silent

SERIAL KILLERS

The serial killer is the movies' favourite monster, appearing in everything from vigilante cop thriller (*Dirty Harry*, 1971) to Charlie Chaplin comedy (*Monsieur Verdoux*, 1947), supernatural horror (*The Exorcist 3*, 1990), film noir (*Born to Kill*, 1947), psychic-link movie (*Eyes of Laura Mars*, 1978), SF extravaganza (*Virtuosity*, 1995), giallo (**Tenebrae**), slasher (**Friday the 13ᵗʰ**) and case studies that themselves range from real-life police procedurals to fictional character studies and all points between.

Early serial-killer films set the template, 40 years before the FBI agent Robert Ressler coined the term to describe killers following a pattern of murdering strangers that were increasingly common in '70s America. Films depicted the real-life serial killer as fantasy bogeyman (*Jack the Ripper in Das Wachsfigurenkabinett/Waxworks*, 1924); and semi-documentary police procedural, introducing the debate over madness – can a serial killer be held responsible for his actions? – while highlighting the inadequacy of standard detection models in catching a killer (**M**).

If **M** is the first great serial-killer film, it still portrays its murderer as physically different (Lorre's bald, pop-eyed baby face). By the '40s serial killers might look like anyone else and, while **M**'s Hans Beckert murdered from compulsion, the psychotics of the *noir* entries *Kiss of Death* (1947), *Shadow of a Doubt* (1945) and the Leopold and Loeb inspired *Rope* (1948) essentially killed for kicks.

Many serial-killer films of the period bridged the gap between horror and *noir* (Jacques Tourneur's 1943 *The Leopard Man* was a Val Lewton production in the same series as **Cat People, I Walked with a Zombie** and the Burke and Hare-related **The Body Snatcher**) but the Lewtonesque *The Spiral Staircase* (1947) is the decade's most influential film in the development of horror visuals, with its pervasive theme of voyeurism, repeated close-ups of its killer's eyes (quoted in many Argento films) and murderous POV shots, including a startling hallucinatory image that forces the viewer into the killer's mind.

A flurry of semi-documentary *noir* manhunts (*Boomerang*, 1947; *Naked City*, 1948; *Panic in the Streets*, 1950) drew the focus away from the victim to concentrate on the killer and the investigator. In the wake of noir a growing number of true-crime case studies attempted to contextualize and explain repeat murder (Leopold and Loeb proved especially attractive, inspiring not only *Rope* but also *Compulsion*, 1959).

The '60s opened with **Psycho** and **Peeping Tom**, enormously influential not only in their depiction of killers as gainfully employed, sympathetically portrayed young men troubled by mental illnesses explicitly caused by their histories – soon to become shorthand for a propensity to kill, as shown in titles like *Schizo* (1977), **Maniac** and *Madman* (1981) – but also the set-piece killings, which led to an increased (and, after **Blood Feast**, increasingly explicit) focus on letting audiences share the killer's experiences.

Ironically, considering that **Psycho** was conceived partly in response to the success of low-budget shockers from William Castle and Hammer, the gimmicky showman director and Bray's finest led the pack when it came to **Psycho** imitations. Castle's *Homicidal* (1961), *Strait-Jacket* (1964) and *I Saw What You Did* (1965) stuck close to Hitchcock, even parroting the director's marketing tactics, while Hammer's "mini-Hitchcocks" *Paranoiac* (1963), *Maniac* (1963), *Hysteria* (1965) and *Fanatic* (1965) tended to rely on **Les Diaboliques**-style twist endings.

Other serial-killer films after **Psycho** tried to stand out from the pack by focusing on the killer's preferred MO (perhaps inspired by the innovative spiked tripod of **Peeping Tom**), with axes and blowtorches replacing the more mundane gun, rope and knife. The trend continued into the '70s, with *The Toolbox Murders* (1979), *The Axe* (1977) and **The Driller Killer** about as far from the coyness of earlier titles (*Night Must Fall*, 1937, *The Lodger*, 1926) as possible.

Albert de Salvo's 1962–64 reign of terror was filmed by Richard Fleischer in 1968's *The Boston Strangler*, which merged the police procedural with the case study and introduced the profiler, a figure of paramount importance in serial-killer cinema from the mid '80s onwards, even if the film's casting (Tony Curtis plays de Salvo) works against its impact. Real-life cases continued to inspire filmmakers through the '70s, with entries based on the 1937 serial killer Joe Ball (Tobe Hooper's *Eaten Alive*, 1976), '40s "Lonely Hearts" killers Beck and Fernandez (*The Honeymoon Killers*, 1970), Ed Gein (*Deranged*, 1974), Fritz Haarmann (**Die Zärtlichkeit der Wölfe**), John Christie (*10 Rillington Place*, 1970) and Donald Nielson (*The Black Panther*, 1977).

The Christie and Nielson films are rare examples of British case studies that tackle contemporary crimes rather than Jack the Ripper. In '80s America portrayal of the serial killer moved away from sensationalist true-crime monster to nihilistic apocalypse-culture antihero, enshrined in trash-culture artefacts like trading cards, board games and comics, but British serial murder has an air of grubbily mundane tragedy. The British true crime industry has tended to prefer gangster stories to serial killers and its cinema leavens even these with a "cheeky chappie" humour that avoids confronting brutality (Paul McGuigan's *Gangster No 1*, 2000, being a notable exception). This means that although the US director Matthew Bright can apply the cynical grotesquerie of serial-killer comedy *Freeway* (1998) and its 1999 sequel to the astonishingly tasteless real-life story of *Ted Bundy* (2002), in the UK funds for "The Ballad of Fred and Rose" remain unforthcoming.

If *The Boston Strangler* introduced the profiler, *Manhunter* (1986) emphasized his importance and focused on the interdependence of the profiler and killer, a theme lent an extra sexual frisson in the Starling-Lecter relationship of **The Silence of the Lambs**. The success of **Silence** led to a glut of big-budget serial-killer films throughout the '90s, many following its lead by having a quasi-superhuman killer with a special relationship to his profiler.

By the time **Seven** was released, this relationship had shifted to complicity, as John Doe involves a detective in his cycle of murders. The theme quickly became clichéd, with the killer in *Kiss the Girls* (1998, also starring Morgan Freeman), convinced that he is only carrying out the profiler's repressed desires. A more interesting angle on complicity is offered by **C'est Arrivé Près de Chez Vous**, in which the documentary team following a serial killer eventually lends a hand in his work, and the home invasion sequence of **Henry ... Portrait of a Serial Killer**, a devastating assault on the viewer's complacency in consuming violence. A more tiresome

strand is exemplified by *Copycat* (1995), whose killer is aware of his murderous heritage, refers to previous killers and boasts of his ambition to ape their accomplishments.

Other '90s serial killers share with many slashers a supernatural gloss: the psychic-link movies *Hideaway* (1996) and *In Dreams* (1997), the demonic slayer of **Dust Devil** and the computer-generated psychotics of *Ghost in the Machine* (1993) and *Virtuosity* (1995) may represent attempts to inject new life into an increasingly moribund sub-genre, but they also run the risk of celebrating the serial killer as Nietzschean superman, either literally superhuman or at least intelligent enough to mount such ludicrously intricate killing campaigns as **Seven**'s deadly sins or the twist-too-far absurdities of **Saw** (2004).

The nastier '80s entries like **Maniac** and **Don't Go in the House** seem initially more reprehensible than glossy '90s fare like *The Bone Collector* (1999), but they at least portray serial killing as a grubby human failing rather than superhuman achievement. This makes them in some ways more palatable than their '90s counterparts and the celebratory tone of early 21st-century case studies *The Manson Family* (2003) and Ted Bundy – although with a poster as grisly as **Maniac**'s, **The Silence of the Lambs** probably makes a better date movie – while the banality of serial murder, and its resistance to the glib explanations offered by many other films, are best explored in **Henry ... Portrait of a Serial Killer** and the extraordinary Italian character study *Roberto Succo* (2001).

BELOW: Michael Rooker's Method acting pays off on the set of **Henry ... Portrait of a Serial Killer**.

granddaughter who hides the Cronos in a teddy bear in a nod to *The Night of the Hunter* (1955), through de la Guardia, living in antiseptic Howard Hughes-style seclusion, to his nephew Angel, who listens to "Plastic Surgery and You" as he tries out models for a new nose and can't understand why his uncle, a cancerous wreck who "does nothing but shit and piss all day", would want to live forever. As a horror film *Cronos* finally lacks any real menace, but as an innovative fantasy it marks the debut of one of the genre's most impressive new talents.

DELLAMORTE DELLAMORE
AKA CEMETERY MAN

1993, It/Fr, dir Michele Soavi, scr Gianni Romoli, starring Rupert Everett, François Hadji-Lazaro, Anna Falchi, Mickey Knox

The dead are returning to life at Buffalora cemetery and it's up to the watchman, Francesco Dellamorte, to ensure that they don't leave the cemetery gates. But, when Dellamorte shoots a grieving widow he mistakes for a "returner", a visit from death prompts him to turn his attentions to the living.

A belated final flowering for Italian gothic, *Dellamorte* adapts Ticiano Sclavi's popular *fumetto* (adult-oriented comic) *Dylan Dog*

ABOVE: "The most beautiful living woman I have ever seen."
Dellamorte Dellamore.

for perhaps the most flamboyantly stylish (and bizarrely cast) zombie film ever made. Returning obsessively to the theme of sex and death – a woman is aroused by an ossuary, the grasping fingers of a skeleton peeling off her clothes, only for a rotting corpse to bite her naked flesh; Francesco seems condemned to eternally murder or lose the woman he loves – *Dellamorte*'s concern is, according to the director, the "fear of living". Both Francesco and his grunting assistant Gnaghi find it easier to deal with the dead than with the living, Gnaghi losing his customary shyness after severing his amour's head from her shoulders, and Francesco is keen to maintain the situation at the cemetery, the only place where his actions appear to have any effect. Playing like *Brazil* (1985) re-imagined as necrophile fantasy, Soavi's "fable about today's Blank Generation" teeters on the verge of terminal silliness and utter incoherence, frustratingly resistant to interpretation – what are we to make of scenes such as Gnaghi expressing interest in the mayor's daughter by vomiting on her, or the identity-shift ending? – but transcends its messy storyline with a delirious visual inventiveness that showcases some of the most richly gothic imagery ever committed to film.

CLEAN, SHAVEN

1994, US, dir/scr Lodge Kerrigan, starring Peter Greene,
Megan Owen, Jennifer MacDonald, Robert Albert

Matched only by David Cronenberg's *Spider* (2002) as a clinically accurate portrait of schizophrenia, Kerrigan's debut slips into horror territory through a child-murder sub-plot and the inclusion of several unwatchably harrowing scenes. Peter Winter is a paranoid schizophrenic who, on his release from a mental institution, attempts to track down his daughter, Nicole, who was put up for adoption by his mother. The film's claustrophobically unsettling sound design, mixing scrambled voices and radio whine to explore Winter's world of tortured isolation, builds tension to a near-unbearable pitch that makes even the spreading of mustard on a slice of bread gruelling to watch. Winter's actions themselves are similarly disturbing, whether taping over or shattering any reflective surfaces, receiving arcane messages from his environment or, most viscerally, indulging in personal grooming, rubbing himself with steel wool, shaving ineptly and digging under his fingernails with a penknife, his eyes emotionless and dull. Kerrigan's unflinching camera captures every nuance of Greene's committed performance, adding to the sense of paranoid isolation by framing him in tight close-ups in his car and fleabitten hotel rooms, claustrophobic spaces that contrast with the desolate beauty of the film's island setting. Winter's schizophrenia is also seen in the context of the behaviour of his mother, whose treatment of him recalls the schizophrenogenic, or the schizophrenia-inducing behaviour outlined by R.D. Laing. If the concept is unfashionable today, at least Kerrigan attempts to explain Winter's madness; less successful are the ambiguous child-killing sub-plot and the characterization of a detective on Winter's trail, although to be fair almost any performance would pale beside Green's hollow-cheeked ravings.

EL DIA DE LA BESTIA
AKA THE DAY OF THE BEAST

1995, Sp/It, dir/co-scr Alex de la Iglesia, co-scr Jorge
Guerricaechevaria, starring Alex Angulo, Armando de Razza,
Santiago Segura, Terele Pavez

The priest Angel Berriartura has deciphered a code in the Book of Revelation revealing that the date for the Apocalypse is Christmas Day 1995. Reasoning that he must contact Satan to discover where the Antichrist will be born, he goes to Madrid and enlists the help of a heavy-metal fan, José Maria, and the TV occultist Professor Cavan in raising the Devil.

Iglesia's only full-blown horror outing ranks with **The Ninth Gate** in the millennial apocalypse stakes, effectively parodying a range of popular belief systems (Catholicism, New Age occultism, consumer Satanism) while still packing a supernatural punch. Madrid is apocalyptic enough even without Berriartura's rantings, filled with prophets, roaming street gangs and overloaded symbolic imagery onto which the priest can map any crazy scheme he chooses. His attempts to embrace evil are hilariously petty, whether scratching cars or stealing from beggars, and his faith in Cavan's powers is apparent evidence of his insanity – until their invocation, with LSD and processed white bread standing in for *amanita muscaria* and communion wafers, reveals a goat standing on its hind legs. The perfectly realized blend of horror and comedy then takes a darker turn, although the tripping José Maria's giggling fit on being faced with a demonic assault is one of the film's funniest scenes, and once Iglesia has set up the scenario, the film takes an inordinate time to reach its *Ghostbusters*-style climax. But he keeps the film moving with stylistic flourishes recalling Jeunet and Caro (*Delicatessen*, 1990), combining slapstick humour and a drily witty script with flashes of real menace. The mixture occasionally shades into uneasily cartoonish violence and the film's portrayal of women smacks of misogyny, but Iglesia's blasphemously irreverent inverted nativity never fails to entertain.

SEVEN

1995, US, dir David Fincher, scr Andrew Kevin Walker, starring
Brad Pitt, Morgan Freeman, Gwyneth Paltrow, Kevin Spacey

In an unspecified US city, Detective Somerset (Freeman) has one last case to crack before retirement. His new partner, Mills (Pitt), is more enthusiastic about investigating the case, a series of murders based on the seven deadly sins, but even Somerset's inspired detective work can't stop the killer from drawing them into his crimes.

Walker's script feeds every mismatched cop cliché in the book through a **Theater of Blood**-style run of gimmicky killings – one murder even features a pound of flesh – for a surprisingly dark entry in the post-**Silence of the Lambs** serial-killer stakes. It is dark in every sense: the killer leaves a Milton quotation, "Long is the way and hard / That out of hell leads up to light", at the scene of the first crime, and the earlier victims are found in rooms so murky that the wall lights cannot penetrate the gloom – even Mills's torch gives out – while the colour scheme's muddy reds and browns contribute to an oppressively grimy atmosphere of urban hell.

Fincher delivers some exhilarating set pieces amid the intricacies of the plot, including a spectacular chase scene, although an earlier police raid seems ludicrously overblown. His visual flair, aided by a superb Howard Shore score that perpetually builds to an ever-receding crescendo, smoothes over the occasional absurdity – why should Somerset need backup in a closed library to read Dante and Chaucer? – while Walker's script intrigues in its serial killer whose portrayal not only mocks criminological commonplaces but also, far from presenting him as an insane outsider, aligns him with the police characters, his targets drawing on their (and the audience's) prejudices against obesity, legal finagling, prostitution, paedophilia and drug dealing.

Seven's trajectory of darkness to light climaxes in the open desert, an ironic escape from the earlier enclosures given the impressively bleak, unexpected twist. Pitt, convincing enough elsewhere, can't quite carry the scene, although it's forgivable in light of his insistence on retaining the ending against studio wishes. As for Paltrow, no fate could be worse than joining the Coldplay entourage.

AFTERMATH

1996, Sp, dir/scr Nacho Cerdá, starring Pep Tosar, Ángel Tarris, Jordi Tarrida, Xevi Collellmir

Two morticians perform autopsies on the victims of a car crash. When one mortician leaves, the other selects a female body to satisfy his necrophiliac lusts. Cinema at its most psychotically confrontational, Cerdá's 30-minute short puts the amateurish fumblings of peers like hobbyist Jorg Buttgereit to shame. Only the films of Gaspar Noé (*Seul Contre Tous*, 1998, **Irreversible**) compare to its presentation of extreme content with high production values and technical flair. The central part of a loose trilogy about death, flanked by *The Awakening* (1990) and *Genesis* (1998), *Aftermath* asks what happens to the physical body after death and provides the vilest response imaginable. Both *Kissed*'s (1996) romanticizing of necrophilia and the weird beauty of Stan Brakhage's *The Act of Seeing with One's Own Eyes* (1971), which transforms real autopsy footage into a surreal travelogue of colourful alien landscapes, are entirely absent here. Cerdá

BELOW: "What's your favourite scary movie?" **Scream**.

focuses instead on the ugly physicality of death and the visceral messiness of corpse love through gruesome sound design (all snapping sounds and wet squelches) and lighting schemes that let the camera linger on everything from congealed blood on cold skin to the gleaming metal of the autopsy room, echoed in the furnishings of the mortician's house. Tosar's performance is terrifyingly committed, conveying diseased desire through a wild gaze and obsessive handling of the mortician's tools (the film was shot in an actual morgue, and reportedly used only tools found there), and the meticulously edited montages and languid pans build up to the transgressive displays with expert precision. Yet the effect is finally more depressing than cathartic: the viewer is shown the girl's grieving parents and obituary notice, positioning her as more than just a body and making the mortician's treatment of her heart, the ultimate indignity, evoke an uneasy sorrow rather than the grim humour apparently intended. Approach with caution.

SCREAM

1996, US, dir Wes Craven, scr Kevin Williamson, starring David Arquette, Neve Campbell, Courteney Cox, Skeet Ulrich

Post-modern examplar *Scream* may not be the first film to mock the conventions of horror while its characters openly discuss them – the slasher boom had contemporary parodies in films like *Pandemonium* (1982), and a recursive strain can be seen in the genre as early as *Mark of the Vampire* (1935) – but it *is* the first that remembers to be scary. The central story itself is standard slasher fare, which is of course the point: high-schoolers are stalked by a masked maniac who is one of their own, and it is up to Neve Campbell's virginal heroine to expose and stop the culprit. The self-knowing devil is in the details, with characters ironically advising each other on what it takes to survive in a film like this, and a pivotal sequence centring on a viewing of generic godfather **Halloween**. It's undeniably witty stuff from the screenwriter who would later create the teen-angst drama *Dawson's Creek*, but it's easy to forget that, before the movie descends into an enjoyable but ultimately empty inter-textual romp, it opens with 12 of the most terrifying minutes in horror cinema, as Drew Barrymore is mocked and menaced in her own home by a caller who may or may not be a maniac but who is very definitely watching her.

It's also easy to forget, while enjoying the many horror in-jokes – Wes Craven's own cameo as a janitor dressed as Freddy Krueger from **Nightmare on Elm Street** is a typical example – that this is also a very bloody movie. It's unusual, though, in growing less frightening as it heads to its climax when the jokes begin to undermine the suspense, and seems destined to be best remembered as the moment when slasher movies ate themselves. Sequels kept the wit and irony but lost too much of the horror and, despite Wes Craven's competent direction, displayed the usual law of diminishing sequel returns. [RL]

CURE

1997, Jap, dir/scr Kiyoshi Kurosawa, starring Kôji Yakusho, Masato Hagiwara, Tyuyoshi Ujiki, Anna Nakagawa

A series of random murders grips Tokyo: a man bludgeons a prostitute to death, a husband stabs his wife and a policeman shoots his partner. Though they're all apparently motiveless crimes, the victims have been mutilated in precisely the same way. Takabe, the detective assigned to handle the case, suspects that the killers have been hypnotised and, when amnesiac Mamiya's prints are found to match those at the crime scenes, he thinks he has found his man. But can he resist Mamiya's power?

Marketed in the West as a serial killer film in the same vein as **Seven** and **The Silence of the Lambs**, this is a far stranger and more disquieting confection, closer to **God Told Me To** for a technophobe sensibility than anything serial-killer cinema has ever given us. Only David Lynch matches Kurosawa's ability to wring so much menace from so few elements – a stain spreading on a ceiling, a barely perceptible darkening of the light in a room – and Kurosawa shares his American peer's commitment to meticulous sound design and acute awareness of spatial atmosphere.

Cure spends so much time in the antiseptic institutional confines of hospitals, psychiatric wards and police interrogation rooms that Takabe's apartment finally feels like an annex to these lifeless zones, especially given the mental fragility of his

BELOW: The police lose patience in **Cure**.

wife. The film anticipates **Pulse** in its evocation of a Tokyo where technology has become a senseless prop – Takabe's wife repeatedly starts an empty spin-drier, to his eventual exasperation – while madness and magic threaten to spill through the cracks.

Kurosawa's tightly controlled direction, favouring static set-ups in long and medium-shot, makes the incursions of the supernatural devastatingly effective, with occasional sequences of montage or hand-held camera all the more startling for their contrast with the rest of the film. Kurosawa's weirdness is distinctive enough to have carved him a unique niche in Japanese cinema, and Mamiya is one of his weirdest creations – a student of Anton Mesmer whose elliptical conversational style is evidently enough to drive anyone to murder, an amnesiac who is passive, quiet and non-confrontational yet still manages to disrupt social convention, and a hypnotist whose technique is so accomplished it prises open cracks in reality itself. Highlighting the theme of mystical transcendence that permeates the film, the police psychiatrist describes him as "a missionary, sent to propagate the ceremony". You don't get people saying that about Derren Brown.

FUNNY GAMES

1997, Aus, dir/scr Michael Haneke, starring Susanne Lothar, Ulrich Mühe, Arno Frisch, Frank Giering

A family's lakeside holiday is disturbed by two young men who proceed to torment them. Haneke's austerity gets one of its fullest workouts in this gruelling film, which purports to be an attack on violence as entertainment in mainstream cinema. The depiction of violence itself is studiously avoided throughout the film, one key sequence aside, but its aftermath is lingeringly depicted, with particular attention paid to the characters' emotional trauma: in one barely watchable sequence Anna, the mother, retches with grief. If the family seem all too human and vulnerable – the final expression of love between Anna and her husband is particularly moving – their assailants, dressed in white sports shirts, shorts and cartoonish gloves, are anything but. Constantly shifting identities – Peter/Paul, Tom/Jerry, Beavis/Butthead – they also repeatedly turn to camera, to wink, further involving the viewer in the torments being meted out on-screen,

or ask "Is that enough?" The film's only moment of violence as catharsis, when one of the boys is shot, is audaciously reversed by his partner using a remote control, thereby denying the audience even this pleasure while further commenting on the technology of the consumption of violence.

Haneke's film is a devastatingly effective psycho-thriller, aided immeasurably by an extraordinary cast and virtually music-free soundtrack, the sound of Formula 1 racing on the TV providing the only counterpoint to the family's sobs and screams, but its explicit intent makes it stand up less to repeat viewing than some of the director's other films. As a comment

RIGHT: "What do you think will happen now?" Arno Frisch and victim, **Funny Games**.

on action films it falls down by failing to address that audience – few Seagal fans will be tempted by a subtitled Austrian film – and, as a more general comment on the consumption of violence, it underestimates the staying power of its audience. If action films tend to use violence as light-hearted entertainment, many horror films present it as sickening and offensive; the genre's popularity rests in part on masochistic drives well served by Haneke's film, which joins a handful of other art shockers (**Cannibal Holocaust**, **Salò**, **Irreversible**) in providing a genuinely confrontational viewing experience. Remade by Haneke himself in 2007.

LOST HIGHWAY

1997, US, dir/co-scr David Lynch, co-scr Barry Gifford, starring Bill Pullman, Patricia Arquette, Balthazar Getty, Robert Blake

Complaints that *Lost Highway* is confusing assume that David Lynch makes mainstream movies, when his career has really been a series of guerilla raids on the mainstream. It's curious that *Lost Highway* began as an attempt by Lynch and the writer Barry Gifford (whose stories formed the basis for *Wild at Heart*, 1990) to target a youth audience, given that the film's narrative and tone are so antithetical to popular concerns.

COMEDY

Alfred Hitchcock once famously observed that horror and comedy are Siamese twin genres, joined at the nervous laugh. But, while there have been outright parodies of everything from individual films (the **Exorcist** spoof *Repossessed*, 1990) to specific studio cycles (Universal's Frankenstein films in *Young Frankenstein*, 1974; Hammer's vampires in **Dance of the Vampires**) and sub-genres including slashers (**Scream**) and serial killers (*Serial Mom*, 1994), humour and horror complement each other's gleeful irreverence, taboo-busting energy and gross-out mentality best when balanced more evenly.

A blackly comic vein ran through the genre from early entries such as the spook spoof **The Cat and the Canary**, but only reached a sophisticated pitch with James Whale's post-**Frankenstein** Universal films. **The Old Dark House**, **The Invisible Man** and **Bride of Frankenstein** move away from the isolated comic relief of their contemporaries for an edgier blend, the invisible man's grandiose pronouncements – "Even the moon's

---

BELOW: Drew Barrymore in one of **Scream**'s scarier moments.

frightened of me!" – simultaneously funny and scary. The mixture informs even the genre's darker offerings: **Eraserhead** and **The Texas Chain Saw Massacre** are absurd nightmares whose inappropriate flashes of humour only serve to underscore the terror, while David Cronenberg's early films are driven by transgressive displays that prompt nervous laughter as much as disgust.

The gross-out strand of horror comedy has its roots in H. G. Lewis's gore spectaculars, following **Blood Feast**'s model of soggy, queasily explicit violence framed by off-colour humour. John Waters' early films (*Multiple Maniacs*, 1970, *Pink Flamingos*, 1972, *Desperate Living*, 1977) share Lewis's confrontational exuberance but sit on the edge of the genre. **The Incredible Torture Show** and **Basket Case** are more direct descendents, the latter anticipating the "splatstick" of Peter Jackson (*Bad Taste*, 1987, **Braindead**), Stuart Gordon (**Re-Animator**, **From Beyond**), Jim Muro's *Street Trash* (1987) and Sam Raimi's *Three Stooges*-inflected *Evil Dead* series. It's not really so far from these films to Farrelly Brothers comedies like *There's Something about Mary* (1998) or Monty Python's gore skits, although horror fans tended to lose interest after one too many intelligence-insulting Troma release. **Braindead** also proved a tough act to follow, although contemporary audiences still find zombies funny (*Shaun of the Dead*, 2004).

The producer/director Roger Corman managed a gentler strain of horror comedy, albeit less in his superlative spoof quickies *The Little Shop of Horrors* (1960) and **A Bucket of Blood** than the long line of Corman alumni, from the favoured Poe interpreter Vincent Price (later to star in exemplary body-count comedies **The Abominable Dr Phibes**, its 1972 sequel and **Theatre of Blood**). The 1984 hit *Gremlins* from the director Joe Dante (**Piranha**, **The Howling**) joined its contemporary *Ghostbusters* in making horror comedy big box office, paving the way for the egregious *House* series (1986–89) and space-wasters like *Spookies* (1986) and *Ghoulies* (1985).

If the in-jokes that followed **Scream**'s success simply provided another compelling reason for obnoxious teens to die, Ronny Yu's entries (**Bride of Chucky**, *Freddy vs Jason*, 2003) blended self-reference with impressively manic verve, while **Dead End** demonstrated that horror comedies could still deliver without relying on irritating genre familiarity.

The story is a "Moebius strip" according to its creators, and a *noir*-inflected one at that, with Bill Pullman as Fred Madison, a free-jazz sax player who believes his wife is having an affair. An encounter at a party with another of Lynch's extraordinary supernatural creations, Robert Blake's white-faced and eyebrowless Mystery Man, ends with Madison's imprisonment for murder. The first story twist comes when Madison is transmuted with much flashing of electricity into young Pete Dayton, who awakes to finds himself living a kind of mirror existence to Madison's. Dayton's release brings him into the orbit of a gangster, Mr Eddy, and he begins an affair with Eddy's wife, Alice. The *noir* allusions are almost as overt as Lynch's previous quotings from *The Wizard of Oz* (1939), only here the *femme fatale* Alice is an inverse character to Madison's dead wife, with both women played by Patricia Arquette. The Mystery Man hovers at the margins like a baleful spirit, his presence unexplained, his motives obscure.

Lost Highway is occasionally uneven compared to the often similar but superior **Mulholland Drive**. The middle section with Pete and Mr Eddy feels at times like an attempt by a lesser director to ape **Blue Velvet**, with Robert Loggia making a poor substitute for Dennis Hopper. But the opening and closing scenes, and Blake's chilling Mystery Man, show once again that Lynch can conjure an aura of incredible menace from a few simple ingredients in a manner that eludes other directors. A Lynch failure is worth a hundred lesser successes. [JC]

BRIDE OF CHUCKY

1998, US, dir Ronny Yu, scr Don Mancini, starring Jennifer Tilly, Katherine Heigl, Nick Stabile, John Ritter

Tiffany has the Chucky doll retrieved from a police depository and reanimates it using a copy of *Voodoo for Dummies*, planning to transfer its personality, that of her lover Charles "Chucky" Lee Ray, back into his own body. But when Chucky mocks her offer of marriage, Tiffany locks him in a playpen, only for the doll to take revenge by electrocuting her in a bath and transferring her personality into another doll.

An unlikely triumph, *Bride* lifts its scarred plastic head and shoulders above its **Scream**-inspired peers for a genuinely funny

ABOVE: John Ritter's Pinhead tribute, **Bride of Chucky**.

and bizarre horror outing. Mancini, who wrote the scripts for the previous three Chucky films (the *Child's Play* franchise) and went on to direct a further instalment, *Seed of Chucky* (2004) – none of which compare to *Bride*'s demented energetic barrage of one-liners and in-jokes – clearly found inspiration in this sordid tale of puppet love, mocking the patent absurdity of his creation ("Chucky? It's so ... eighties. He's not even scary!" Tiffany's goth boyfriend complains) before going on to pillage, reference and homage everything from **Bride of Frankenstein** to **It's Alive**, **The Hitcher**, and the Zuni doll episode from the TV movie *Trilogy of Terror* (1975). While the film inhabits a colourful cartoon world with no pretensions to realism, it still features audacious, near-libellous contemporary references and credible but inventively drawn secondary characters, like the tourist criminals who rip off newlyweds at a Niagara Falls motel – "I told you we would have seen more action at Club Med!" – and even finds time for a subtle dig at the franchise's chequered censorship history (an earlier film was spuriously implicated in a notorious British child murder), as Chucky disgustedly turns off a radio show blaring "Violence in movies and television is one of the worst problems facing our society" with "What is this shit?" If *Bride* can't quite maintain the momentum to the end, it has a lot of fun getting there, thankfully keeping its slyly knowing tone embedded in the film's universe rather than its likable young lovers. The veteran Hong Kong director Yu went on to bring his blend of camera pyrotechnics and anything-goes verve to *Freddy vs Jason* (2003).

PERFECT BLUE

1998, Jap, dir Satoshi Kon, scr Sadayuki Murai, voice cast Junko Iwao, Rika Matsumoto, Shinpachi Tsuji, Masaaki Ôkura

Mima's managers are keen for her to leave the pop-group Cham and become an actor, but after she agrees to do a rape scene on TV she is haunted by her former pop-idol doppelgänger. An obsessive fan, "Mimaniac", is also stalking her and, when the people surrounding Mima's new career begin to die grisly deaths, she becomes unable to distinguish between fantasy and reality.

Kon's dazzling *anime* takes a handful of elements from Yoshikazu Takeuchi's 1991 source novel but ditches the rest for a spectacularly disorienting exploration of media exploitation and subjective realities. Mima is barely consulted about the direction her career should take, being bullied into agreeing to a rape scene that, tellingly, features her wearing a Cham-style cutesy outfit. Afterwards, she is unnaturally happy in public and tearful in private, anticipating the personality split that forces her to rely on a fan-website's fictional diary to track her actions. The occasional visual flourish – Mima screaming into her bath; and the hallucinatory appearances of her double – serves as a reminder that the flat, repetitive style is a conscious choice that fits the story, particularly during an extraordinary half-hour series of multilayered reality slips in which neither the viewer nor Mima is able to distinguish between her life, the "Mima's Room" diary, the fantasies of "Mimaniac", her own fantasies, hallucinations and dreams and the TV show *Double Bind*, whose plot seems a recursive string of provisional representations of Mima's plight. The film's expert play on the hypnotic repetitiveness of commercial animation makes it difficult to imagine the sequence working so well in a live-action film and its subtle visual sophistication is matched by a rich psychological complexity, looping dirge soundtrack and surprisingly strong adult content, from the gruelling rape scene to the Argento-ish murders. The closing revelations provide an unworkably neat explanation given what has gone before, and finally seem like a terminal rung in Mima's descent into madness, but as an unsettling portrait of the florid psychoses underlying squeaky-clean celebrity culture *Perfect Blue* has few peers.

RINGU
AKA RING

1998, Jap, dir Hideo Nakata, scr Hiroshi Takahashi, starring Nanako Matsushima, Miki Nakatani, Hiroyuki Sanada, Yuko Takeuchi

A TV reporter, Reiko Asakawa, recruits her ex-husband Ryuji to help her investigate an urban legend: anyone who watches a cursed video is later warned by phone that they will die within a week. The enormously successful *Ringu*, based on a bestselling novel by Kôji Suzuki, remains Japan's highest-grossing horror film and spearheaded a renaissance in Japanese horror. Yet this tale of the vengeful past asserting itself through the hi-tech accessories of consumer society has a barely coherent narrative, held together principally by a series of startling images and a pervasive eeriness. Reiko and Ryuji's search for a solution to the mystery of the video is presented as rational detective work, but instead relies on non sequiturs, free association and psychic intuition, and while the story they uncover provides some of the film's most unsettling moments, it actually fails to help them lift the curse at all. That none of this really matters is testament to Nakata's success in creating an atmosphere of oppressive, claustrophobic gloom in which even the loose ends seem less like plot holes than elements designed by their lack of resolution to increase tension. The film's Japanese release was met with near **Exorcist**-style hysteria, following suggestions that Reiko's apartment in the film was actually haunted. *Ringu* also spawned a theme park, along with three sequels, two remakes – one Korean, the other a surprisingly effective American effort – and a host of pan-Asian clones, formula pieces parading an endless succession of wraith-like girls with long black hair and pallid features, occasionally enlivened by scenes such as the exorcism set piece in *Chakushin Ari/One Missed Call* (2003).

THE BLAIR WITCH PROJECT

1999, US, dir/scr Daniel Myrick, Eduardo Sánchez, starring Heather Donahue, Joshua Leonard, Michael C. Williams, Bob Griffin

Reportedly made for around $35,000, *Blair Witch* went on to become one of the highest-grossing films in a summer that included such bloated effects extravaganzas as *The Phantom Menace* and *The Mummy*, proving once again that low-budget horror provides the genre's most effective chills. Its success was partly due to an aggressive marketing campaign that leaked "true" documents such as police reports onto the Internet over a number of months before the film's release, building up a level of hype – especially regarding the supposedly factual content of

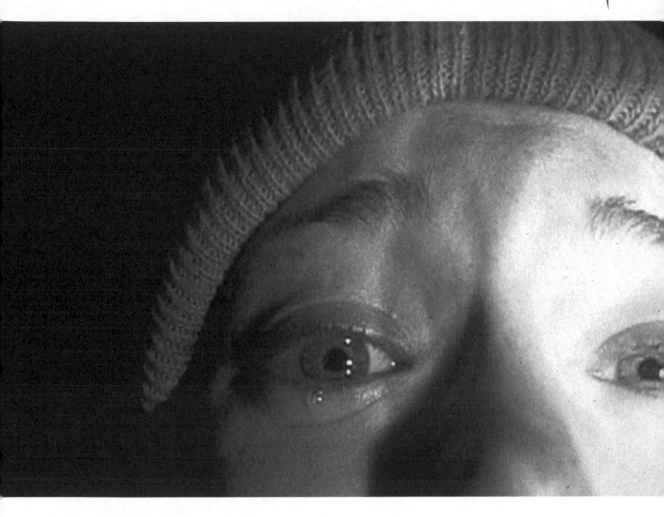

ABOVE: "We are going to die out here!" Heather Donahue, **The Blair Witch Project**.

---

the film – that major studios were unable to emulate. The flimsy story involves three student filmmakers who travel to forests in Maryland to make a documentary about a local legend, the Blair Witch. They never return, but a year later their film and tape materials are found in the woods, ostensibly edited together and released as *The Blair Witch Project*. Although the structure is derivative – *The Last Broadcast* (1998) and **Cannibal Holocaust** used the idea earlier – the film's use of location and sound is highly effective, building up an intangible atmosphere of dread, and it retains a degree of ambiguity (the audience doesn't finally know what has happened to the filmmakers) which is entirely absent

from most contemporary genre cinema. Its use of two cameras (one black-and-white, one colour) aids the documentary feel, but its sustained use of the topical reality-TV conceit only appeared in a handful of subsequent genre films (most notably **My Little Eye**), the studios responding with ever-flashier CGI hauntings like *The Haunting of Hill House* (1999) and *Ghost Ship* (2002). *Blair Witch* has divided horror fans more than most genre films, many viewers complaining of Heather's whininess, of nausea brought on from the constantly moving cameras or simply that the film doesn't live up to its hype. It certainly doesn't hold up to repeated viewings, which are more likely to generate irritation than fear, but the filmmakers' effective torture of their cast, who allegedly didn't know what was going on during filming, is an object lesson for aspiring filmmakers. Followed by a terrible sequel, *Book of Shadows: Blair Witch II* (2000).

LOS SIN NOMBRE
THE NAMELESS

1999, Sp, dir/scr Jaume Balagueró, starring Emma Vilarasau, Karra Elejalde, Tristán Ulloa, Toni Sevilla

The Giffords are told by the police that their missing daughter, Angela, has been found dead. Five years later Claudia Gifford receives a phone call from a woman claiming to be her daughter. When she contacts Massera, the detective who worked on the case, they unearth evidence of a secret society whose aim is the distillation of evil.

Balagueró's first feature to be distributed internationally – one of only two screen adaptations of Ramsey Campbell's novels to date – successfully transplants the author's dank Liverpudlian "miserabilism" to sunny Spain. Sun is in short supply because the film is set in winter, but the near-monochrome palette of silvers, blues and browns is a fitting colour scheme for a narrative revolving around a parent's grief. Massera too is suffering, from the loss of a wife, and the gradual revelation of the hidden community at the heart of the tale puts his and Claudia's isolation into sharp relief: a community is precisely what both of them lack.

Los sin Nombre is heavy on atmosphere (its bleak morbidity is leavened only by the occasional saccharine interlude) and short on action, but the backstory, revealed in fits and starts, holds the viewer's interest throughout. Santini, committed to Dachau for a minor physical abnormality, is inducted into the secrets of Nazi occultism and a world of atrocious medical experiments. After the war he becomes a leading occultist in London, then vanishes from sight, only to reappear in Valencia where he is charged with raping and killing two young girls and sentenced to life imprisonment.

Rumours abound concerning the society which Santini left behind, namely that its members seek to isolate evil and achieve transcendence through horror. The theme aligns the film with **Cure**, but the images of bestial angels and human-headed birds littering the cult's derelict hideouts give it a distinctive iconography. One of the film's flaws is that it doesn't make enough of this, but it suffers from other problems too: some of the subplots (particularly one concerning Tony, Claudia's ex-boyfriend) seem redundant, especially on repeat viewing; the pace flags badly in the middle of the film; and the status of the "nameless" is never clearly established – are they victims or aggressors? But the final scenes, in which Claudia's family reunion takes an unexpected turn, bring the film back on track for an astonishing finale. Balagueró's later films have been more commercially successful, particularly *[Rec]* (2007), but less distinctive.

THE NINTH GATE

1999, US, dir/co-scr Roman Polanski, co-scr John Brownjohn, Enrique Urbizu, starring Johnny Depp, Frank Langella, Lena Olin, Emmanuelle Seigner

Rare books aren't Hollywood's idea of great subject matter but this occult thriller, a welcome return to mainstream cinema by Roman Polanski, manages to keep them compellingly centre stage. Johnny Depp's "book detective" Corso is pursued across Europe by murderous diabolists and a sinister patron, all of them in search of a volume supposedly penned by Lucifer himself. "Some books are dangerous," Corso is told; he discovers just how dangerous as the bodies accumulate around him.

Anthony Shaffer (**The Wicker Man**) had written the initial screen adaptation of Arturo Perez-Revert's *The Dumas Club* shortly before his death. Shaffer isn't credited in Polanski's rewrite, which drops the convoluted Dumas plotline of the novel in favour of the book's other quest, a search for the ultimate edition of a cursed volume, *The Nine Gates of the Kingdom of Shadows*. Polanski relishes the chance to play Hitchcock once again (*Frantic*, 1988, shared a Parisian setting), the Dennis Wheatley-meets-Umberto Eco plot providing him with more than enough chases and narrow escapes from wealthy Satanists among its convincing bibliographic detail.

Darius Khondji's camera follows Corso through doors and gateways into a succession of gloomy interiors, shadowed by his "guardian angel" (Emmanuelle Seigner), a woman with odd socks, glowing eyes and the ability to float in the air at crucial moments. Johnny Depp demonstrates a growing versatility in the role of Corso while Frank Langella is suitably menacing as his obsessive and threatening book-collector client, Balkan. With its Lucifer theme and cast of devil-worshippers being picked off one after the other, *The Ninth Gate* at times seems like a more cerebral updating of *Angel Heart* (1987), witty and ominous but sustained by a serious approach to its subject matter. If the ending doesn't quite live up to its promised revelations, the journey at least is one that manages to entertain without insulting the intelligence. [JC]

RIGHT: Johnny Depp's book detective Corso, **The Ninth Gate**.

ÔDISHON
AKA AUDITION

1999, Jap, dir Takashi Miike, scr Daisuke Tengan, starring
Ryo Ishibashi, Eihi Shiina, Renji Ishibashi, Tetsu Sawaki

Seven years after the death of his wife, TV producer Aoyama, encouraged by his son, decides it is time to find a new bride. A colleague suggests a TV audition as a source of likely candidates, and when Aoyama meets former ballet dancer Asami he is smitten.

The first of the prolific Miike's films to receive wide distribution in the West, *Ôdishon* (adapted from a Ryu Murakami novel of the same name) eschews the berserk flashiness of the director's other films for a saccharine romance that draws the unsuspecting viewer in, only to deliver a devastating sucker punch at the end. The film's reliance on surprise means that a detailed analysis would spoil the fun – suffice to say that Miike's story arcs are like no other.

Although Aoyama's innovative dating technique may be an abuse of his position – he compares choosing a woman to choosing a car – he is riven by sexual guilt in the form of his disapproving spectral wife, and hardly deserves what happens to him. Miike's target seems less his sexism than the inadequacies of his generation's romantic idealism. Asami's seduction takes place in a series of staid, interchangeable bars and restaurants with dinner jazz playing lightly in the background, environments so blandly benign they seem to demand the diseased eroticism that finally breaks through. While the explicit violence of the terminal scenes had festival-goers running for the exits at the film's Western debut, it's this perverse sexuality that stays in the mind. The genuinely sadistic torture scene is inter-cut with footage of an abusive ballet teacher masturbating, and an extraordinary sustained hallucination sequence presents alternative versions of earlier scenes that paint a far darker picture of Asami's past. It is here that Miike's form-destroying glee comes to the fore, the film moving from long, static takes to the rapidly morphing nightmare visions of a collapsed psyche, reality slips so deftly handled that this sequence's relentless non-linearity may have contributed as much as the gruelling violence to *Ôdishon*'s resistance to being given the Hollywood remake treatment.

THE SIXTH SENSE

1999, US, dir/scr M. Night Shyamalan, starring Bruce Willis, Haley Joel Osment, Toni Collette, Olivia Williams

M. Night Shyamalan's first major hit garnered six Oscar nominations, including best supporting actor for 11-year-old Osment's extraordinary performance as Cole Sear, the troubled boy who "sees dead people". At heart it is an old-fashioned ghost story, though some gorier moments reveal a lack of confidence in the ability of mere spirits to frighten a modern audience. Shyamalan's direction is a big asset, eschewing the MTV fast editing of many contemporary horror films in favour of a more measured style that finds the shots it likes and sticks with them. He is aided by his superb cast, including Willis in one of his quieter performances and the versatile Australian Collette, previously best known for her titular part in *Muriel's Wedding* (1994). Perhaps the film's greatest strength, though, is the rich way it explores themes of loneliness, guilt and redemption as Willis's child psychologist, a victim of a shooting by a former patient, attempts to atone for that past failure by curing his new client Cole Sear of his ghostly "hallucinations".

It is possible that the film would have been a success on those terms alone, but word-of-mouth and a strong marketing campaign ensured that it drew an audience primarily because of its shocking final twist. Unusually, there's no cheating involved in this. The audience is supplied with all the information it needs to determine what is really going on and repeat viewing, far from

ABOVE: Haley Joel Osment sees dead people, **The Sixth Sense**.

revealing flaws in the narrative, demonstrates how each scene is cleverly constructed to both hint at and hide the central truth. Nevertheless, this focus on the ending has had the unfortunate effect of obscuring the meatier material making up the bulk of the movie and may fix the work in the public's mind as a big-budget parlour trick. It should instead be treasured for its confident, character-driven storytelling and Osment's preternaturally mature and moving performance. [RL]

SLEEPY HOLLOW

1999, US/Ger, dir Tim Burton, scr Andrew Kevin Walker, starring Johnny Depp, Christina Ricci, Miranda Richardson, Michael Gambon

1799, NYC. Constable Ichabod Crane is sent to the small village of Sleepy Hollow to investigate a series of decapitations. A modernizer, he refuses to believe the local legend of a headless horseman, but the events unfolding around him try even his strict rationalism.

The first outright horror film from Hollywood's favourite fantasist suffers from the same problem as virtually every other live-action Burton feature: exquisite set design and visual flair let down by negligible emotional involvement. The wobbly script is peppered with lame one-liners and non sequiturs (a cut hand provides a particularly arbitrary plot hinge), and seems more interested in bringing Depp's effete Ichabod Crane and Ricci's voluptuous child-woman Kristina together than presenting a coherent narrative. This is surprising given that Walker – who takes little from Washington Irving's original story save names and the horseman (exposed by Irving as a fraud) – scripted **Seven**. More pertinent, perhaps, is the involvement of Francis Ford Coppola as executive producer, evidently hoping to lavish the same revisionist treatment on America's first native horror monster as he had on **Bram Stoker's Dracula** and *Mary Shelley's Frankenstein* (1994). *Sleepy Hollow* falls somewhere between the stylistic excesses of the former and the pompous ambition of the latter, but all three display a chronic lack of scares (even the decapitations here are absurdly bloodless) and pack no real emotional punch.

Burton's films nearly always feel indulgent, like sketches extended to feature length, and *Sleepy Hollow* is no exception, even the fan-pleasing casting (reuniting Christopher Lee and Michael Gough from **Dracula**, among many other cameos) seeming more infantile extravagance than response to the demands of the story. Only Christopher Walken shines as the Berserker horseman, finally reunited with his head in the film's most satisfying sequence. At least *Sleepy Hollow* pillages '60s gothic rather than the '70s grindhouse that Burton's contemporaries find so fascinating, but the occasional flare of genuine invention among the nods to Corman and Hammer can't save this from being insubstantial whimsy.

ABOVE: Christopher Walken enjoys his turn as the soon-to-be Headless Horseman in **Sleepy Hollow**.

YEOGO GOEDAM II
AKA MEMENTO MORI

1999, S Kor, dir/scr Tae-yong Kim, Kyu-dong Min, starring Min-sun Kim, Yeh-jin Park, Young-jin Lee, Jong-hak Baek

Min-ah, a student at a Korean girls' high school, finds a red diary that details the growing affair between two of the more unpopular pupils, Hyo-shin and Shi-eun. As the girl reads the shared diary she comes to empathize with the two outsiders. Flashbacks show how the two diarists met. Then we see the tragedy that ensues after their relationship breaks up and Shi-eun commits suicide. Events come to a head at a school concert, as students and staff find themselves trapped in the building during a torrential rainstorm while the dead girl seems to have reappeared amongst them.

The film was promoted as a sequel to the earlier *Yeogo Goedam/Whispering Corridors*, a horror hit from 1998. In fact, it's less successful as a horror film than as a highly emotional portrait of first love and tears. The early scenes detailing the students' lives, their crushes and conflicts, are beautifully played and very well observed by the film's two male writer/directors. The diary, with its intricately designed pages and hidden secrets, is also a fascinating creation. The film is deftly constructed, with past and present subtly layered together to present a complex portrait of its troubled central relationship, its complexity repaying repeat viewings. Elements such as the telepathic link between the two lovers and the deafness of one of the girls seem at first to be adding to the confusion, but are well-integrated plot points that come into play as the story progresses.

The horror elements are introduced at the beginning of the film via a voiceover, but only really emerge in the film's last third, where we detect strong echoes of other films, notably **Carrie** and **Suspiria**. However, the film rises above its influences to become an original and moving achievement. Its box-office success led to a third girls'-school horror story, *Yeogo Goedam 3: Yeowoo Gyedan/Wishing Stairs*, in 2003. [PT]

CHAPTER

10

2000s

The world did not end with the 20th century. The much-hyped "millennium bug" turned out to be a damp squib – its contribution to genre horror was a hysterical paranoid TV movie, *Y2K* (1999), which doesn't get much airplay in the new century.

The first mini-boom of the 21st century was in **Blair Witch** knock-offs – almost certainly because, of all the horror trends ever to come down the turnpike, this cycle required the least in the way of budget and resources. Though there were no rules to follow, the **Blair Witch** style was something of a parallel with the Dogme95 cycle initiated by Thomas Vinterberg and Lars von Trier – abjuring the expensive gloss of Hollywood to get down and dirty (though Dogme precluded genre movies, so a Dogme horror film would be impossible) and shooting with available resources. First came parodies, like *The Bogus Witch Project* (2000), *The Blair Underwood*

OPPOSITE: "Do it like I showed you, the neck is first." Bill Paxton as the Hand of God Killer, *Frailty* (2002).

BELOW: "What do you see?" Richard Gere sees giant moths, *The Mothman Prophecies* (2001).

Project (2000) and *The Erotic Witch Project* (2000), perhaps the only soft-core porno parody with a higher budget than the film it was imitating, and the foundation of an agonizingly dull empire of lesbian-themed genre-tagalong nudie cuties (often starring Misty Mundae). Then came imitations like *The St Francisville Experiment* (2000), not to mention walking-around-in-the-woods slashers (*Camp Blood*, 1999, *Blood Reaper*, 2003) turned out by amateurs with camcorders who wondered why *their* shaky cinematography, amateur actors and non-existent screenplays didn't add up to a box-office bonanza of **Blair Witch** proportions. An official sequel, *Book of Shadows: Blair Witch 2* (2000), which is more conventionally scripted (and budgeted), made little impression and probably strangled the franchise in infancy. But lessons were learned and a few zero-budgeted, shot-on-digital-video efforts with some imagination eventually turned up, notably the Internet-themed *The Collingswood Story* (2002) and the more mainstream *Session 9* (2002), the zombie movie *[•REC]* (2007), the giant monster picture **Cloverfield** (2008) and the breakout hit **Paranormal Activity** (2009).

Psychopathy continued to be a major theme, with Mary Harron filming Bret Easton Ellis's "unfilmable" novel *American Psycho* (2000).

In Patrick Bateman (Christian Bale), a Wall Street yuppie active in the cruel '80s, obsessed with terrible music (he commits one of his murders while enthusing about Whitney Houston) and pernickety about his clothes and grooming, the film consigned the fearsome figure of the serial murderer to the dead past, equally definitively undoing now-stale sub-genre conventions such as *Abbott and Costello Meet Frankenstein* (1948). However, this time it didn't take, and the serial cycle ground on, taking in lumpen true-crime schlock (*Ed Gein*, 2000, *Ted Bundy*, 2002, *The Manson Family*, 2003) and, unbelievably, a sequel, *American Psycho 2: All American Girl* (2002), which crept out on video without irony despite featuring William Shatner. In that its atrocities might well be taking place inside its protagonist's warped-by-Genesis head, *American Psycho* is also an entry in the surprisingly crowded cycle of "provisional worldview" or "rubber reality" films. Picking up from both **The Sixth Sense** and *Fight Club*, plus the science-fictional rug-pulling of *The Matrix* (1999), these mind-twisting efforts became commonplace in the early years of the 21st century. On some level, this field might have been a reaction to the terrorist attacks of September 11th, 2001: in many films, there is an attempt to turn away from, revoke or rewrite a reality that has become too much to bear. But the cracks were there before 9/11 and widened for many reasons. Into this category fall actual or apparent ghost stories (**The Others**,

ABOVE: One of the "huge fuckin' howlin' things" from *Dog Soldiers* (2002).

2001, *Session 9*, 2002; *El Orfanato/The Orphanage*, 2007), time-or-memory gameplay (*Memento*, 2000, *The Butterfly Effect*, 2004), psychotic subjective realities (*The Cell*, 2000, *The Attic Expeditions*, 2002, *Frailty*, 2002, *Identity*, 2003), more murderous imaginary-friend/doppelgänger tales (*The Machinist*, 2003, *Secret Window*, 2004, *Haut Tension/Switchblade Romance*, 2004, *Hide and Seek*, 2005) and bizarre combinations of several of the above themes (*The I Inside*, 2003, **Janghwa, Hongryeon**/*A Tale of Two Sisters*, 2003, *The Jacket*, 2004, *Trauma*, 2004, *Shutter Island*, 2009).

From Japan, Korea, Thailand and China came a flood of ghost stories on the pattern of **Ringu** (1998), with lank-haired, big-eyed, malevolent girl ghosts, curses spread on a viral pattern, spooks loitering in a terrifying manner in elevators (which seem especially haunted in Asia), investigative female protagonists learning secrets they will eventually wish they didn't know, a mix of Internet-era hi-tech and ancient sorceries, and mostly downbeat endings: **Gin Gwai** (*The Eye*, 2002), *Hayanbang* (*Unborn But Forgotten*, 2002), **Honogurai Mizu no Soko Kara** (*Dark Water*, 2002), **Ju-On** (*The Grudge*, 2004), **Kairo** (*Pulse*, 2001), *Phone* (2002), *Geo-woo Sok-eu-ro* (*Into the Mirror*, 2003). The pattern was paralleled in the

ABOVE: Max Schreck (Willem Dafoe) is unimpressed by Murnau's (John Malkovich) catering arrangements in *Shadow of the Vampire* (2000).

West by *What Lies Beneath* (2000) and *The Mothman Prophecies* (2001), then imitated by *FeardotCom* (2002), *They* (2002) and *Gothika* (2003). Eventually, Hollywood hit on the simple expedient of remaking the originals for audiences that had never seen them. With *The Ring* (2002) and *Dark Water* (2005), remakes of Hideo Nakata films, in cinemas, Hollywood summoned Nakata himself to helm *The Ring Two* (2005), which is confusingly not a remake of his Japanese *Ringu 2* (1999). This Asian activity extended into more bizarre areas, like the puzzlingly obsessive **Uzumaki** (*Spiral*, 2000), the schoolgirl zombie picture *Stacy* (2001), the weird thrillers of Kyoshi Kurosawa (*Korei/Seance*, 2000, *Dopperugenga/ Doppelgänger*, 2004, *Ghost Cop*, 2004), Chan-wook Park's *grand guignol* vengeance trilogy (*Boksuneun Naui Geot/Symapthy for Mr Vengeance*, 2002, *Oldboy*, 2003, *Chinjeolhan Geum-ja/Sympathy for Lady Vengeance*, 2004) and a flood of all-over-the-place multi-genre efforts from Takeshi Miike (sadly, few as strong as the first film of his to get much international play – the uncharacteristically controlled **Ôdishon**/*Audition*, 1999). Symptomatic of the field's health was a run of multi-director, sometimes multi-country anthology pictures:

Bangkok Haunted (2001), *San Geng* (*Three*, 2002), *Saam Gaang Yi* (*Three … Extremes*, 2004) and *Suiyô Puremia: Sekai Saikyô J Horâ SP Nihon no Kowai Yoru* (*Dark Tales of Japan*, 2004).

The early 2000s also saw a modest revival of the British horror film. Rob Green's *The Bunker* (2000), in which Nazis are plagued by guilt-induced phantoms, was at the head of a surprising blip of son-of-**The Keep** horror/monster/ghost stories with wartime settings – arriving well before the First World War movie *Deathwatch* (2002) and Neil Marshall's werewolves-ate-my-platoon picture *Dog Soldiers* (2002), not to mention the Hollywood haunted-submarine film *Below* (2002) and the Korean Vietnam spooker *Arpointeu* (*R-Point*, 2004). There were disposable British body-count pictures trying to ape the murdered pretty faces of the Dimension movies (*Long Time Dead*, 2001, *Nine Lives*, 2002), but more interesting approaches to old themes are taken by *The Hole* (2001), *The Last Horror Movie* (2003), *London Voodoo* (2003), *Creep* (2004) and *Lie Still* (2004), *Severance* (2006), *The Disappeared* (2008), *Wishbaby* (2008) and *Black Death* (2009). Among the breakouts of the new Brit-horror pack were Marc Evans's inventive Internet/reality TV slasher **My Little Eye** (2002), Danny Boyle's '70s-themed but 2000s-styled digital video zombie/ plague/apocalypse shocker *28 Days Later …* (2002), Edgar Wright's surprisingly pertinent Romero skit *Shaun of the Dead* (2004) and Neil Marshall's female-cast caving terror film **The Descent** (2005).

Stephen Sommers's *The Mummy* (1999), a tiresome film without a whiff of terror or magic, initiated a trend for all-action monster movies, which would eventually crossbreed with the comic-book-derived dark superhero films that had been around since *The Crow* (1994). Sommers followed through with *The Mummy Returns* (2001) and the insufferable *Van Helsing* (2004), which resurrected and scuppered the Universal monster franchise by pitting Hugh Jackman against Dracula and involving the Frankenstein Monster and the Wolf Man. Similar headaches could be had by watching *From Hell* (2001), *Queen of the Damned* (2002), *Underworld* (2003), *League of Extraordinary Gentlemen* (2003), *Constantine* (2004), *The Brothers Grimm* (2005), *The Wolf Man* (2010), *Solomon Kane* (2010) and some *Blade* sequels. None of these manage to match the effectiveness of the contemporary *Spider-Man* or *X-Men* films, despite CGI shapeshifting, already-dated techno music, pouting chiselled male and female beauty, gimmick monster-destroying weapons, the faintest traces of some of the genre's most iconic characters and open endings that promise (threaten?) sequels and spin-offs to come. The sole triumph of this black-leather boom was Guillermo del Toro's *Hellboy* (2003) and *Hellboy II: The Golden Army* (2008), and even they weren't as interesting as his more personal ghost story, **El Espinazo del Diablo** (*The Devil's Backbone*, 2001) and *El Laberinto del Fauno/Pan's Labyrinth* (2006). It seemed that the knack of reviving classic creatures was lost in Hollywood, leaving the field open to oddball, self-reflexive efforts like *Shadow of the Vampire* (2000) and Guy Maddin's Expressionist ballet *Dracula: Pages from a Virgin's Diary* (2001), though Tim Burton and Johnny Depp made a fair fist of *Sweeney Todd: The Demon Barber of Fleet Street* (2007). That the comic-book monster/kung fu/fantasy genre could be made to work in an era of the *Lord of the Rings* films

was demonstrated by super-productions from France (*Le Pacte des Loups/Brotherhood of the Wolf*, 2001) and Russia (*Nochnoy Dozor/Night Watch*, 2004). And the best werewolf variant was a cleverly written Canadian teenage chick flick, **Ginger Snaps** (2000) – which even managed interesting sequels.

Mainstream, teen-skewed American horror continued, though minor self-aware variations like *Cherry Falls* (2000) and psycho stalkers like *The Watcher* (2000) were edged out of the business by spoofs like *Shriek If You Know What I Did Last Friday the 13th* (2000), the dreadful *Scary Movie* films (from 2000), a couple of big-screen *Scooby-Doo* outings and *Club Dread* (2004). **Final Destination** (2000) and *Dracula 2000* (2000) founded their own franchises – though the fairly ingenious **Final Destination**, in which contrived death scenes are given metaphysical weight, maintained a theatrical presence, while the follow-ups to *Dracula 2000*, which regenerated the Count as a different actor every time (like Doctor Who), slunk straight to video/DVD. Other franchise wannabes stalled after a single instalment – though as of 2010, sequels to *Bones* (2001), *Soul Survivors* (2001) and *Darkness Falls* (2003) seem unlikely, but *Boogeyman* (2004), *Reeker* (2005) and *Vacancy* (2007) have at least managed direct-to-DVD follow-ups.

The solidly okay 1999 remake of William Castle's *House on Haunted Hill* triggered a vogue for raiding the back catalogue for vaguely remembered titles that were worth another go: *Thir13en Ghosts* (2001), *Ghost Ship* (2002 – not a remake but designed to seem like one), *Willard* (2003), *House of Wax* (2005), *2001 Maniacs* (2005) *The Wizard of Gore* (2008). Perhaps inspired by the surprising

BELOW: Guy Maddin's Expressionist ballet Dracula: Pages from a Virgin's Diary *(2001).*

critical and commercial success of apparent no-hoper **Bride of Chucky** (1998), there were stirrings in thought-dead franchises: *Jason X* (2002), *Freddy vs Jason* (2003), *Beyond Re-Animator* (2003), *AVP: Alien vs Predator* (2004), *The Exorcist: The Beginning* (2004). Someone eventually noticed that remakes of titles that were still having sequels made could be pushed as event movies rather than being sent straight to home video – hence reduxes for *The Texas Chainsaw Massacre* (2003), **Dawn of the Dead** (2004), *Assault on Precinct 13* (2005), *The Amityville Horror* (2005), *The Fog* (2005), *The Hills Have Eyes* (2006), *Prom Night* (2008), *My Bloody Valentine* (2009), *Last House on the Left* (2009) and *A Nightmare on Elm Street* (2010). These are slick, good-looking pictures – with good-looking casts – but tend to strip out much of the material that made the original films interesting: the gore and excitement is still there, but any sense that these films meant anything is left behind. While his own greatest film was being redone as a hot-ticket platform release, Tobe Hooper toiled on a lower-case remake of something hardly anyone remembered, *Toolbox Murders* (2004). At least George Romero used the clout of the **Dawn** remake – and maybe even *Shaun of the Dead* – to get financing for a comeback, **Land of the Dead** (2005), which might not be on the level of the earlier films in the series but still had something to say; he went independent again for *Diary of the Dead* (2007) and *Survival of the Dead* (2009). A zombie apocalypse boom of sorts continued with several *Resident Evil* sequels, *I Am Legend* (2007), *Dance of the Dead* (2008), **Død Snø/Dead Snow** (2009) and *Zombieland* (2009), which also ran to interesting little pictures like *The Signal* (2007), *Pontypool* (2008) and *Dead Set* (2008).

A new generation of horror filmmakers, reared on '70s cinema, moved into the field and essayed their own variations on established themes – though it was often debatable whether the homages were any more soulless than the remakes. This trend began with a little cluster of horror/road movies that rediscovered the unease of the flyover country between America's cities and subjected callous urban teens to ordeals in the sticks: the monster film **Jeepers Creepers** (2001), the psycho stalker *Joy Ride* (*RoadKill*, 2001), the vampire quickie *The Forsaken* (2001), the ghostly **Dead End** (2003) and the pulpy *Monster Man* (2003). There were even bigger-budgeted takes on this theme, with recognizable actors and old '70s TV movie plots in which unwary townies move to creaky old mansions in the backwoods and there become the victims of psychotic or Satanic conspiracies: the dreary *Cold Creek Manor* (2003) and the sprightlier *The Skeleton Key* (2005). Along with official remakes of *The Texas Chainsaw Massacre* and *The Hills Have Eyes*, lookalikes *Wrong Turn* (2004), *Dead & Breakfast* (2004) and Rob Zombie's

ABOVE: The hapless heroes of *The Fog* (2005).

House of 1000 Corpses (2003) were made. Eli Roth's *Cabin Fever* (2002) and **Hostel** (2005), Rob Zombie's *The Devil's Rejects* (2005) and James Wan's **Saw** (2004) – along with Quentin Tarantino's *Kill Bill* films – homaged grindhouse days with more commitment, though many of these films feel more like glosses on older movies than anything like life. The cynical snarkiness (especially in Zombie's *oeuvre*) of these films is as much a turn-off as any number of tied-to-a-chair-and-tortured sequences. **Saw** spawned the most successful horror franchise of the 2000s, with annually-released sequels developing the original idea into an attenuated, serial-like story of labyrinthine complexity, studded with set-piece deaths. More life, more intelligence and more interest can be found in off-Hollywood approaches to similar subject matter like Oliver Hirschbiegel's German *Das Experiment* (*The Experiment*, 2001) and Larry Fessenden's **Wendigo** (2001), among the few 2000s horror films that have obviously been made by grown-ups.

In the second decade of the 21st century, the horror genre is thriving if hardly in one of its most creative spells. Innovation tends to take place far from Hollywood but is almost instantly co-opted: besides Hideo Nakata from Japan and Mexican Guillermo del Toro, other creatives from around the world have been brought aboard the American genre mainstream – Takeshi Shimizu, director of four Japanese *Ju-On* films, stayed with the property for its Sam Raimi-produced remake *The Grudge* – and ideas that surface anywhere in the world are likely to be reused in a conventional American horror film starring someone young and pretty whom you've seen on TV. A vampire movie boom has yielded the outstanding Swedish **Låt den Rätte Komma In/ Let the Right One In** (2008), the book/film *Twilight* franchise and TV shows like *True Blood* (2008-) and *Being Human* (2009-). As the new century wears on, a scarier, more complicated world demands scarier, more complicated horror films.

FINAL DESTINATION

2000, US, dir/co-scr James Wong, co-scr Glen Morgan, James Wong, starring Devon Sawa, Ali Larter, Kerr Smith, Tony Todd

Writer Glen Morgan and novice director James Wong cut their teeth on early seasons of *The X-Files*. Bringing that show's quietly creepy sensibility to the big screen along with not-fit-for-TV levels of violence, they created an unusually melancholy entry in the teen horror canon. As the film opens, a high-school student, Alex, has a premonition of a fatal crash that causes him and a few of his fellow classmates to step off a plane heading for Paris minutes before it takes off to its doom. Soon after, one of the survivors is killed in an improbably convoluted accident, and a wink-wink cameo from **Candyman** star Tony Todd informs us that death itself is out to get the students who have temporarily cheated it.

The film – loosely and rather tastelessly based on the real-life crash of TWA Flight 800, also carrying students to Paris – is interestingly flawed, its narrative and the conventions of its genre pulling in opposite directions. By eschewing the teen horror staple of a Freddy-esque gloating maniac who dispatches the cast and allows the viewer to take vicarious pleasure in their deaths, *Final Destination* leaves audience sympathy squarely with the protagonists. Unusually in this genre, the death of the young is treated as a genuine tragedy and, while the dialogue in which the characters discuss their unavoidable fate is far from sparkling, the performances are just strong enough to make you care. But the deaths themselves are the set-piece highlights of the film, and the lovingly staged Rube Goldberg devices that lead to them encourage an enjoyment of the slaughter at odds with the mournful tone of the rest of the film. Spectacle wins out over contemplation in the reshot finale, which promises us that death hasn't yet finished with the few survivors. Three sequels followed, culminating in 2009's 3D extravaganza *The Final Destination*. [RL]

GINGER SNAPS

2000, Can/US, dir John Fawcett, scr Karen Walton, starring Emily Perkins, Katharine Isabelle, Kris Lemche, Mimi Rogers

Brigitte and Ginger Fitzgerald are inseparable outsiders until Ginger is attacked by a werewolf during her first period. Brigitte, at least as alarmed by Ginger's new sexual confidence as she is by

BELOW: Plane going down…. **Final Destination**'s spectacular opening sequence.

RIGHT: "I can't have a hairy chest, Bea, that's fucked!" **Ginger Snaps**.

her physical changes, must turn to Sam, the school drug-dealer, for help.

Mining a similar vein to **The Company of Wolves** in its equation of lycanthropy and puberty/menstruation, *Ginger Snaps* (for all its realistic high-school setting) is almost as stylized as Jordan's film *The Breakfast Club* (1985) with hairy palms. The sisters are archetypal disaffected teens, taking refuge from adulthood (at the start of the film neither has begun menstruating, although they are 15 and 16) in goth paraphernalia and ghoulish dressing-up. Their peers include the jock, who takes a shine to Ginger; the bitch, who attacks Brigitte on the hockey field; and the druggie, whose pharmaceutical knowledge happily makes him the hero of the piece. So far, so schematic, but the intelligent, amusing script milks the lycanthropy metaphor both for cringing embarrassment – the counsellor proudly proclaims "It's a period!" – and pathos, as Ginger's sexual awakening leaves Brigitte in the cold. If the film's self-conscious sensitivity seems overly didactic at times, the handling of the changing relationships in the Fitzgerald family, showcasing the film's best performances, is funny, touching and subtly played. The horror elements are slightly less successful, although the early stages of Ginger's transformation, her attack and the animation of the werewolves themselves, hairless but convincingly powerful, are impressive enough. But Ginger's shift into a full-blown monster only maintains the puberty theme if considered as a metaphor for a delinquent teen, hellbent on casual sex and mayhem. With it, the film also shifts gear into standard monster-movie fare, distinguished only by a surprising brutality and the startling image of Brigitte attempting to join her sister at the feast.

UZUMAKI
AKA SPIRAL

2000, Jap, dir Akihiro Higuchi (aka Higuchinsky), scr Junji Ito, Kengo Kaji, Takao Nitta, Chika Yasu, starring Eriko Hatsune, Fhi Fan, Hinako Saeki, Shin-eun Kyung

When small towns suffer hostile infestations, they usually come from tangible entities that slither, shuffle or prowl, but the Japanese port of Kurouzucho is cursed by all things spiral. If you become obsessed by the spiral, like the parents of dreamy high-school girl Kirie and her solemn, nerdy boyfriend Shuichi, you will meet a strange and macabre demise. Spirals are everywhere – from the interior of a spin dryer to the cochlea of the inner ear; from a snail shell to a fingerprint – and are all catalysts for gruesome acts of transmogrification and mutilation. You can make the spiral come out of you and it will use you as a host until you no longer function as a human being. If your classmates are coming to school only when it rains, leaving a slimy trail and growing a hump, you can be sure they've turned human/snail.

Based on the popular late '90s *manga* by Junji Ito, *Uzumaki* features a confection of styles, from rapid rostrum edits to subliminal animations and mind-bending special effects. The sickly green filter that overlays much of the film's colour has a dulling, queasy effect, but there are moments of such startling creative originality in this debut feature from former pop-promo director Higuchi that the viewer is left scrabbling for meaning. Could

Higuchi be a Japanese Lynch, pointing at the lurking horror that underpins the seemingly conservative small town? Is the spiral a metaphor for the never-ending cycle of conformity that binds and constricts? There are suicides, loneliness and elemental interference in the form of hurricanes, twisters (of course) and torrential rain, which lend a profound sense of melancholia to the atmosphere. One believes Kirie and Shuichi will escape the irrational, menacing tyranny of the whirly weirdness but, like everything in *Uzumaki*, the ending is neither predictable nor derivative of any cinematic precedent. [KS]

EL ESPINAZO DEL DIABLO
AKA THE DEVIL'S BACKBONE

2001, Sp/Mex, dir/co-scr Guillermo del Toro, co-scr Antonio Trashorras, David Muñoz, starring Marisa Paredes, Eduardo Noriega, Federico Luppi, Fernando Tielve

During the Spanish Civil War, a remote school, a repository for leftist gold and the sons of leftist supporters killed in combat, reluctantly takes on a new boy, Carlos. Carlos's struggle to fit in isn't helped when he sees the ghost of a dead boy, but Jacinto, the janitor, proves far more dangerous.

Presenting its political concerns with a supernatural gloss, although marketed as a ghost story – and boasting one of the period's more unobtrusively impressive CGI hauntings – *El Espinazo*'s ghost is less important to the film than the idea of ghosts, related explicitly through a framing voiceover to cinema itself. The menace of the supernatural cannot compare to the horrors of war, or rather its ambient brutality, as del Toro eschews any display of battlefield heroics for a portrait of the ravages meted out on the film's microcosmic society. Tielve's portrayal of Carlos is indispensable to del Toro's sensitive evocation of a child's world of honour and imagination, never slipping into sentimentality despite its new-boy traumas of bullying, locker pilfering and whispered ghost stories. Luppi (the star of **Cronos**) brings a dignity and pathos to the role of Casares, an impotent schoolmaster, and matinee idol Noriega portrays the hardened Jacinto with a desperately frayed machismo. The elegance of the performances is matched by the film's stately, reserved pace, slow travelling shots gorging themselves on the rich sepia tones of day and glacial blues of night, and its exquisite sound design, boasting a superbly realized sequence of subjective hearing when Casares is deafened by an explosion.

JEEPERS CREEPERS

2001, Ger/US, dir/scr Victor Salva, starring Gina Philips, Justin Long, Jonathan Breck, Patricia Belcher

Trish and Derry Jenner are driving to their parents' house for a spring break when they see a figure throwing what look suspiciously like bodies down a chute. Derry insists on looking down the chute, a decision he will live to regret. The opening to *Jeepers Creepers* is wonderfully creepy, the sight of the ruined church and chute tantalizingly indistinct, and the film's best moments retain this subtlety, with much of the action

taking place either in the background or in darkness. Trish and Derry bicker incessantly but credibly and don't indulge in the stereotypical sex'n'drugs routine of other genre teens. Although they do, predictably, have a working knowledge of horror convention – "Do you think he's dead?" "They never are" – the film never shades into the irritating self-reference of its peers, even the humour staying on the right side of black. On the other hand, the film does lose momentum when the siblings are joined by the police, its supernatural take on rural horror devolving

into a string of **Shining** and *Terminator* clichés, but its biggest nod is to the children's folk story of the Sandman, who harvests children's eyes while they sleep and feeds them to hook-beaked birds, immortalized in E.T.A. Hoffmann's tale of the same name. While the revelation of the creature's true nature is staggered throughout the film, each appearance revealing something new and its final incarnation as a winged demon impressively monstrous, many of the film's other details are needlessly grotesque. The bodies which Derry discovers are stitched together and consequently make no sense in the broader context of the creature's activities, while the cat-lady and Jezelle

BELOW: "Tastes so damn good!" A pair of peepers in **Jeepers Creepers**.

technology – the Internet is here a portal for the dead to invade the world of the living and vice versa – but they also represent the alienation such technology fosters, the difference between life and death in modern Tokyo so negligible that death finally presents a more attractive option. The film's twin storylines – Michi and Junko investigate the suicide of their friend Taguchi while Internet novice Kawashima finds himself haunted by an eerie website that dials itself up even when he has turned his computer off – suffer themselves from its key theme of entropy, winding-down to stasis, as though its energy-sapping ghosts had bled into the narrative. But the plot is secondary here to the atmosphere, ambient computer whirrs and electric hums providing a perpetual backdrop to a Tokyo whose sooty, monochrome pall is barely enlivened by the burning cars and buildings of the astonishing apocalyptic finale. It's telling that the technophobe Kawashima is the film's principal character; his peers tend to interact solely through screens, their Internet use providing information exchange with no emotional content and their human contact devolved to a series of bleak monologues on the futility of friendship. The film's leached atmosphere is matched by the appearance of the blurred, stumbling ghosts themselves, while its repeated images of suicide – one jump, fall and landing is shot in a single startling take – give the whole a tone of listless despair. Remade as the Wes Craven-scripted *Pulse* (2006) in the US.

MULHOLLAND DRIVE

2001, US, dir/scr David Lynch, starring Naomi Watts, Laura Harring, Ann Miller, Dan Hedaya

David Lynch's most satisfying film since **Blue Velvet** began life as a pilot for an ABC TV series that the network rejected, forcing the director to flesh out what had already been shot into a self-contained feature. The result is almost a mirror image of **Lost Highway**, with two women taking the place of the male leads in the earlier film and a similar structure of twinned stories. Lynch has counted *Sunset Boulevard* (1950) among his favourite films and *Mulholland Drive* serves as his own equally dark portrait of Los Angeles and its movie business, with the innocent starlet Betty Elms, played by Naomi Watts, arriving in the city to begin an acting career only to find that Hollywood is another Lynchian world of bright surfaces concealing a nightmarish darkness. The main story thread of her helping Laura

add nothing to the film. In true 21st-century style, Salva also makes his cops friendly, trustworthy figures, perhaps hoping to stay on the right side of the law after the well-publicized arrest that followed his feature debut **Clownhouse** (1989). Salva also directed the serviceable 2003 sequel.

KAIRO
AKA PULSE

2001, Jap, dir/scr Kyoshi Kurosawa, starring Haruhiko Katô, Kumiko Aso, Koyuki, Shun Sugata

Kurosawa's typically idiosyncratic entry in the post-**Ringu** wave of Eastern hauntings also paints the cycle's gloomiest portrait of human endeavour. Its ghosts may spread through modern

Harring's amnesiac Rita to reassemble her past snakes its way through several minor narrative strands like the twisting road of the film's title. There are too many disparate characters and not all the plot lines are properly resolved, but a mosaic portrait of the city gradually emerges, from its street hustlers to the upper echelons of the movie business. Moments of genuine horror come with the women's search for the elusive Diana Selwyn and some increasingly bizarre business involving a terrifying derelict and a mysterious blue box. What might have been an incoherent mess works through Lynch's belief in his material and a perfectly sustained mood. The extraordinary scene in the Club Silencio is inexplicable but could hardly have come from anyone else. If the twist in the final act does little to dispel the accumulated aura of enigma (even as it attempts to explain what has gone before), this should be seen as a strength, not a weakness. Lynch would agree with Borges that the solution to the mystery is always inferior to the mystery itself; the rest is *silencio*. [JC]

THE OTHERS

2001, Sp/Fr/US, dir/scr Alejandro Amenabar, starring Nicole Kidman, Fionnula Flanagan, Christopher Eccleston, Alakina Mann

A Spanish co-production, **The Others** became Spain's highest-grossing domestic film of all time after only two months on release. It is, however, the first movie to have received the Spanish Goya for best film without one word of Spanish being spoken throughout, and its sensibility is almost entirely British, its inspiration clearly drawn from the Henry James adaptation **The Innocents**. The auteur Amenabar, in his first English-language film, not only wrote and directed the film but even composed the score, and his control over every aspect of the movie pays off in a tight, coherent work. Internationally, the film was unfortunate to come out in the wake of the massively successful **The Sixth Sense**, leaving it feeling like a pale imitation of the stylistically and thematically similar movie, when it is if anything a more compelling work.

Set in the aftermath of the Second World War, the story concerns Grace Steward and her sickly, photo-sensitive children Anne and Nicholas, characters who occupy the same archetypal space as **The Innocents**' troubled governess and her charges. They too live in a gloomy and, it soon appears, haunted mansion, awaiting the return of Grace's husband from a war which we realize he has not survived. The sinister new servants know more than they are saying, but it is unclear if they represent a threat to the family or its only hope of salvation. The film very effectively uses the Victorian iconography of death, including eerie posed photos of the recently deceased, to build an atmosphere of uncertainty and dread. Kidman is as usual a rather cold presence, but her depiction of Grace's increasingly neurotic obsession with her children's health gives the story its heart, while the children themselves shine in the grand British horror tradition of otherworldly offspring. The film's twist ending forgoes **The Innocents**' unresolved ambiguity, but the idea that the dead may themselves be haunted by the living has a melancholy force. [RL]

WENDIGO

2001, US, dir/scr Larry Fessenden, starring Patricia Clarkson, Jake Weber, Erik Per Sullivan, John Speredakos

A winter weekend in the country for stressed-out advertising creative George, his wife Kim and their son Miles goes wrong when they hit a deer being stalked by a group of hunters. One of the hunters, Otis, is particularly upset and finds out where they are staying; meanwhile Miles is given a talisman of a *wendigo*, a Native American spirit, by a Native American whom only he can see.

Fessenden's follow-up to the exemplary indie vampire picture *Habit* (1997) puts a novel spin on familiar urbanoia themes with its child's viewpoint, but happily avoids infantile sickliness in favour of an exploration of childhood fears and the function of myth. Miles is traumatized not only by Otis's killing of the deer but also his parents' bickering, and interprets most of what he sees – rural development, the forbidding woods, the menacing hunters – in terms of the *wendigo* legend. George, spending some rare time alone with his son before events take a darker turn, tells him that while myths might help interpret reality, they are no substitute. But Otis also seems to see the creature envisaged by Miles, in its guise both as suggestive bundle of twigs and, less convincingly, a man in a deer suit, although his poor mental health maintains the film's carefully nuanced ambiguity. Much of the film has a Dogme feel, aided by the naturalistic lighting and acting and handheld camera, but the freewheeling rhythm is punctuated by rapid montages covering everything from a game of cards to, most impressively, Miles's vision when unconscious. Although *Wendigo*'s subtlety hampered its commercial prospects, its weakest moments are unsubtle – the appearance of the antlered monster, for instance, or the heavy-handed symbolism of Miles picking up his father's boots. Still, in its haunting evocation of childhood anxieties and the primal fear of the woods, this is one of the most effective and intelligent American chillers of the period.

GIN GWAI
AKA THE EYE

2002, HK/Sing, dir/co-scr Danny & Oxide Pang, co-scr Jojo Hui, starring Lee Sinje, Lawrence Chou, Chutcha Rujinanon, Candy Lo

Blind violinist Wong Ka-man receives a corneal transplant that allows her to see. Her vision is blurred at first, but she soon realizes that she can see ghosts invisible to everyone else, prompting her to travel from Hong Kong to Bangkok to discover the identity of the donor.

The Pang brothers' first horror feature may seem derivative of **The Sixth Sense** to Western viewers, with Ka-man having picked up Cole Sear's morbid curse, but it derives more from local models, particularly the "ghost-seeing eyes" of *Youling Ren Jian/Visible Secret* (2001) and the monochrome back-story of **Ringu**, evidence of a profoundly pan-Asian sensibility that informs everything from the casting (mixing actors from Thailand, Singapore, Hong Kong and Taiwan) to the imagery (the antiseptic modern surrounds of Hong Kong's hospital rooms and apartments are contrasted with a pervasive belief in the supernatural) and pacing (cloyingly sentimental interludes fill the space between scare scenes). The film's treatment of Ka-man's isolation as she attempts to enter the world of the seeing provides its emotional hinge, obscured by a reliance on redundantly flashy visual effects that occasionally provide a genuine frisson – Ka-man's room flips back and forth between two modes and the face of a ghost in a lift is impossibly squashed – and climax in an impeccably choreographed **Final Destination**-style CGI conflagration, seen largely (if improbably) from the viewpoint of a rat.

HONOGURAI MIZU NO SOKO KARA
AKA DARK WATER

2002, Jap, dir/scr Hideo Nakata, starring Hitomi Kuroki, Rio Kanno, Mirei Oguchi, Asami Mizukawa

Yoshimi is fighting her ex-husband for custody of their daughter Ikuko. Mother and child move to a new apartment, but the flat above seems to be haunted. As Yoshimi discovers more about the former tenants of the upstairs flat, she comes dangerously close to repeating the past through neglect of her own child. Nakata made good on the promise of **Ringu** with this more accomplished and coherent chiller, again adapted from a Kôji Suzuki novel. For all the film's visual nods to **Don't Look Now**,

LEFT: Lee Sinje sees too much, **Gin Gwai**.

most notably in the brightly coloured raincoat worn by the child ghost, Nakata here develops a unique style, typified by a sensitive use of space, a talent for finding the sinister in the everyday, a single-minded focus for the imagery that leaves the film feeling chronically waterlogged and a mounting sense of claustrophobic oppression that ends on an unexpectedly downbeat note. Nakata's closest analogue in the West is probably M. Night Shyamalan, whose films have also used ghosts to explore human relationships and are similarly marked by an innate conservatism and occasional plunge into mawkish sentimentality. But Nakata's visuals are far more atmospheric, the doubling of the families here more complex and effective than the twist of The Sixth Sense. The inevitable American remake followed in 2005.

IRREVERSIBLE

2002, Fr, dir/scr Gaspar Noé, starring Monica Bellucci, Vincent Cassel, Albert Dupontel, Joe Prestia

Essentially a rape-revenge film, in which Marcus (Cassel) seeks to avenge the anal rape and severe beating of Alex (Bellucci), ignoring her former lover Pierre's (Dupontel) attempts to restrain him, *Irreversible* turns the conventions of the field on their head by presenting the events in reverse order, *Memento*-style. A series of spastic camera darts, loops and plunges rest only for a discussion of the nature of crime in a boarding room above the Rectum, a gay SM club, then continues through the reddish murk of the interior to present teasing glimpses of depravity before remaining static for a genuinely sickening murder. This brutal, shocking opening not only punishes viewers for their desire to see more clearly (inevitable given the dizzying camerawork) but also denies them the dubious pleasure of closure most rape-revenge films present: even if the identity of the rapist remains unclear, the act of vengeance has clearly destroyed all the participants.

Critics were more exercised by the cinema-clearing rape scene, picking up on issues – Bellucci's nipple-accentuating dress and the sheer length of the sequence – that are key to Noé's confrontational strategy. A victim of anal rape could be male or female, but the act is here contrasted with Alex's healthy, life-giving vaginal sexuality. The rapist's obvious enjoyment of her body and his dialogue during the scene, much of its mixture of abuse, familiarity and wonder unsettlingly close to consensual dirty talk, makes her eroticization still less comfortable. The protracted monotony finally reminds viewers of the relentless anality of hard-core pornography, underscoring the discussion of male sexuality implicit in the disparate approaches of Pierre, Marcus and the "Tenia", and the grotesque physicality is matched by the film's sheer bodily assault on the audience, from the jarring solvent-headache soundtrack to the strobed screen at the end.

While one screening will be enough to flatten most viewers, it takes a second to tease out the subtleties of Noé's treatment

BELOW: Monica Bellucci wishes she'd crossed the road, **Irreversible**.

of time. Alex is reading J.W. Dunne's *An Experiment with Time*, which posits a future already written and accessible through premonitory dreams, and *Irreversible* is filled with echoes and anticipations, from the obvious (Alex's dream, Marcus's dead arm) to the understated (Marcus mimes smashing a bottle against Pierre's face, anticipating his fight in the Rectum). The film ranks with **Funny Games** as a devastating critique of the viewer's complicity in screen violence but, while Haneke refuses to put anything on display, *Irreversible* shows us altogether too much.

JISATSU SAAKURU
AKA SUICIDE CLUB; SUICIDE CIRCLE

2002, Jap, dir/scr Shion Sono, starring Ryo Ishibashi, Akaji Maro, Masatoshi Nagase, Saya Hagiwara

Fifty-four schoolgirls join hands to leap in the path of an oncoming train. A white sports bag is left at the scene of the suicide, later found to contain a large roll of human skin. The suicide epidemic spreads throughout Japan, but police are unsure whether a cult is to blame – until they find a website tracking the suicides before they take place. A child caller seems to know too much about the craze; a group of glam rock'n'roll suicide enthusiasts proudly proclaim themselves responsible; and the videos of pre-teen pop group Desert hypnotize all who see them. So who's to blame for the suicides?

Sono's extravagantly bizarre feature starts like a detective story – albeit one with an astonishingly off-colour opening – then spirals off in a number of unanticipated directions, full of narrative dead ends, red herrings and elaborate set pieces. Although Sono's theme of technological alienation recalls **Kairo**, its story unfolds with a gleeful pop vibrancy that couldn't be further from Kurosawa's mournful tone; even its suicides are presented with an exuberance that is completely at odds with the subject matter, strong gore scenes (a young mother slices into her hand with a kitchen knife, apparently oblivious to the pain) backed up by chirpy pop music.

The seesawing narrative finally approaches the film's desolate heart with the revelation of who is behind the suicides and why, and if Sono leaves many questions unanswered, the actions of a female survivor provide a fitting emotional closure. The film's parade of extraordinary images – the pet-stomping Manson-styled glam rockers at home in their "Pleasure Room"; the claustrophobic cubicle used to remove strips of skin – ensures moreover that while *Jisatsu* may bewilder on an initial viewing, it's certainly never dull.

MY LITTLE EYE

2002, UK, dir Marc Evans, scr David Hilton, starring Sean (C.W.) Johnson, Kris Lemche, Stephen O'Reilly, Laura Regan

Five American contestants take part in a reality webcast in a remote woodland house to win $1 million. They must all stay for six months to collect the money, but when an unexpected visitor fails to recognize them as Internet celebrities, they begin to wonder who's watching them – and why.

Potential viewers could be forgiven, on the basis of the contestants of virtually every *Big Brother* variant, for assuming that the characters in this inevitable fusion of reality TV drama and horror "mockumentary" would be obnoxious enough for their deaths to play as welcome light relief. But Evans takes a decidedly different tack, presenting a grimly claustrophobic atmosphere of desperate emotional bullying that ensures that, while it's difficult to empathize with any of the predictably flawed characters, their deaths are genuinely shocking. Rex, the mouthiest and most cynical of the contestants, gets all the best lines, attempting to seduce the jittery Charlie by suggesting that they're being punished for not having delivered the requisite sexual action – "Maybe we're punishing ourselves, you know?" But quiet, disturbed Danny, seen early on snapping an injured crow's neck, provides more emotional engagement, flinching from the girls' mockery after he presents one of them with an ill-considered gift.

Typically, the longest-surviving character is also the most weakly drawn, and once the film's key revelation is out of the way it has nowhere to go but stalk'n'slash territory. It also suffers from credibility-stretching plot holes – although the contestants appear to make their own way to the house, they later claim not to know where it is, and although the film is set towards the end of the six-month period the characters relate to each other as though they'd been there for six weeks. Yet the reality webcast conceit is well used, the surveillance and infrared cameras underpinned by an oppressive score of ambient noise and bass rumbles; the characters are amusingly more mortified by finding a camera in the "no webcam" area than by realizing their fate, and even the killer wants to put on a good performance.

DEAD END

2003, Fr, dir/scr Jean-Baptiste Andrea, Fabrice Canepa, starring Ray Wise, Alexandra Holden, Lin Shaye, Mick Cain

Frank nearly crashes his car while driving his wife Laura, son Richard, daughter Marion and her boyfriend Brad to Laura's

ABOVE: A Nagoya of the mind, **Gozu.**

family for Christmas. He's taken a short cut off the freeway, but there are no other cars on the road, and when they stop to pick up a young mother it's too late to turn back. *Dead End* opens like a backwoods urbanoia film – the family have entered uncharted terrain that may turn rurally nasty when they stop at a cabin full of hunting trophies and rusty blades – but rapidly takes a detour into refreshingly unexpected territory. If the *Ubik*-style twist is hardly unexpected and the final scenes a betrayal of the intelligence shown by the rest of the film, for most of its running time *Dead End* is a delicious, near-Lynchian blend of dislocated horror and sick humour (an association strengthened by the casting of Ray Wise from **Twin Peaks**). Much of the humour comes from the portrayal of the family themselves, the incessant squabbling familiar to anyone who has suffered long car journeys with close relatives, and each uses the traumas of the journey to bury bad news or raise festering resentments. If Marion is relatively bland, the obnoxious teen Richard, the dorkish jock Brad and the increasingly demented Laura get the fruitiest lines. Richard has his lip bitten off when he kisses the "lady in white" and can only respond, "I love you," and in the film's bad-taste highlight, Laura rubs an open head wound in orgasmic glee while calling out the name of a former

lover. These are the only instances of even mild gore in the film, which relies elsewhere on the expressions of disgust on survivors' faces to convey the mangling of victims' bodies, a minimalist approach that extends to the setting – virtually all of the action takes place either in the car itself or its immediate vicinity, with occasional aerial shots of the car moving through an endless forest only reinforcing the claustrophobic tone – and the supernatural imagery, repeating a handful of ingredients (a black car, a "lady in white") for a circularity that feeds neatly back into the narrative.

GOZU

2003, Jap, dir Takashi Miike, scr Sakichi Satô, starring Hideki Sone, Sho Aikawa, Kimika Oshino, Shohei Hino

Minami, a young and keen *yakuza* (Japanese mafia) member, is charged with the task of snuffing out one of his more senior colleagues, a man who saved his life and has become his mentor. The two set off to drive to Nagoya, where the dirty deed will be done. Uneasy about his mission, the younger man allows his mind to wander and almost drives into a river. Slamming on the brakes, he causes a whiplash that results in the early death of his intended victim. He pulls into the car park of a run-down restaurant to phone his bosses in Tokyo. When he gets back to the car, he discovers the dead body has vanished. His search for it takes him into a bizarre world where dream and reality appear to have merged.

Takashi Miike, the "adult terrible" of new Japanese cinema, is at his genre-hopping peak in this V cinema oddity. In a year in which he made no less than five films, his inventiveness and transgressive energy show no signs of running dry. A particularly memorable creation is the gang boss who can only achieve erection after a soup ladle is inserted into his anus. He has a series of different types of ladle, depending on how firm he wants his penis to become.

What the film means is anybody's guess, but clues are scattered along the way. The title, for instance, refers to the cow-headed god who guards the entrance to the underworld, a creature that we actually meet via one of many dream sequences. Is the river that Minami nearly runs into the border between life and death? Certainly there seems a hellish monotony to the lives he encounters in this Nagoya of the mind. [PT]

BELOW: "There's something strange in this house," **Janghwa, Hongryeon**.

JANGHWA, HONGRYEON
AKA A TALE OF TWO SISTERS

2003, S Kor, dir/scr Ji-woon Kim, starring Jung-ah Yum, Su-jeong Lim, Geun-yeong Mun, Kap-su Kim

Two young sisters return to their father's house after a long absence. It's an uneasy homecoming. The house seems filled with strange sounds and hidden dangers. The girls soon find themselves menaced by their new stepmother. Or are they...? There's also a ghost in the house. Or is there...? Things take a distinct turn for the worse when the stepmother's brother and his wife come to dinner one night.

Taking a well-known and much filmed Korean folk tale, Ji-woon Kim propels it firmly into the post-**Ringu** wave of new Asian horror via a clever mixture of shifting point of view, narrative trickiness and skilful sound design. For most of its first half the film is not so much horror as a gothic-tinged, dysfunctional-family nightmare, a genre that goes back in Korean film at least as far as *The Housemaid* (*Hanyo*, 1960). Then, following a startling revelation from the father, the film's narrative starts to open up like the petals of a flower. One revelation leads to another and soon we begin to realize just how effectively Kim and his team have turned the tables on us. The film holds back on the shock tactics until this last volley, but maintains momentum through its early stages with several well-placed and almost subliminal flashes of startling horror.

WEREWOLVES

If zombie cinema has transcended the limitations of lacking a definitive literary antecedent like *Dracula* or *Frankenstein* by treating **Night of the Living Dead** as its primary text, movie werewolves tend to take the hardly stellar **The Wolf Man** as their starting point and thus fare less well. It's not the first werewolf film, an honour belonging properly to Universal's *The WereWolf of London* (1935), but its tragic portrait of Lon Chaney Jr growing yak hair when he can't have the woman he loves set the tone of romantic doom that informs everything from Hammer's **Curse of the Werewolf** to **An American Werewolf in London**.

Never a hugely popular movie monster, the werewolf's appearances between **The Wolf Man** and the '80s were negligible at best, although a host of cinematic hairballs kept their shaggy heritage alive through these dark decades. The teen-angst entry *I Was a Teenage Werewolf* (1957) was more credible than its peers – doesn't everyone sprout weird hair in their teens? – and Spain's Paul Naschy carved a career of sorts out of his Universal-inspired Count Waldemar Daninsky (or "Wolfenstein" according to his original US distributors), appearing in at least a dozen outings beginning with *La Marca del Hombre Lobo* (1967). Other lycanthropes appeared in political spoofs (*The Werewolf of Washington*, 1973), gimmicky whodunits (*The Beast Must Die*, 1973) and even a biker movie (*Werewolves on Wheels*, 1971).

Advances in special effects technology made the transformation scene the preferred calling card for effects wizards following the startling snout extrusions of **The Howling**. **An American Werewolf in London** and *Wolfen* (1981) followed in quick succession, and Dante's film even gave birth to an increasingly ludicrous franchise. Yet, while both **The Howling** and *Wolfen* suggest the intriguing idea of werewolf societies coexisting with humans, it took **The Company of Wolves** to establish a genuinely new direction for movie werewolves in its equation of lycanthropy with menstruation, both "curses" running on a lunar cycle. **Company** is also one of the few werewolf films to acknowledge forebears beyond **The Wolf Man**, highlighting the legend's links to witchcraft through the use of a salve familiar from recorded werewolf trials.

Ginger Snaps fused the twin strands of romantic tragedy and furry adolescence, and *Dog Soldiers* (2002) provided a novel spin on the theme with its tale of soldiers under attack in the Scottish highlands, but perhaps the most compelling modern werewolf comes in Tim Hope's form-destroying animated short *The Wolfman* (1999), although furry fun was firmly back in the mainstream eye with its big-business 2010 namesake.

Given the limited range of thematic treatments for screen werewolves, it seems fair to turn our attention to other shape-shifters, such as **Cat People** and *Cat Girl* (1957), inspired by the "were-cats" of Algernon Blackwood's "Ancient Sorceries", and the serpentine writhings and colonial guilt of *Heba the Snake Woman* (1915) and *Cult of the Cobra* (1955), reconfigured for a new generation in Hammer's **The Reptile**. The effects showboating of the early '80s subsequently had actors morphing into everything from giant cicadas (**The Beast Within**) to human VCRs (**Videodrome**), although few Western films were prepared to top the wild transformations of Japanese movies like *Matango* (1963), whose characters mutate into mushrooms, and **Uzumaki**'s snail-people.

BELOW: A Chris Tucker écorché, mid-transformation. **The Company of Wolves**.

From its opening scenes, the film works through the slow accumulation of detail, meticulous art direction and rich, chiaroscuro lighting to create a palpable mood of almost languorous melancholy. This painstaking scene-setting is essential in order to sustain the narrative through the turbulent twists that occupy its second half, but did tax the patience of some critics and viewers. Nevertheless, the film was a big box-office hit in South Korea and showed that the newly regenerated national film industry was indeed now able to produce works of world-class cinema. [PT]

CALVAIRE
AKA THE ORDEAL

2004, Bel/Fr/Lux, dir/co-scr Fabrice du Welz, co-scr Romain Protat, starring Laurent Lucas, Jackie Berroyer, Philippe Nahon, Jean-Luc Couchard

A lonely farmhouse should always sound alarm, yet low-budget crooner Marc Stevens heeds no reason when his van conks out on a rain-lashed December night in rural Belgium. So begins his descent into abjection in the freezing rural gloom of a landscape whose inhabitants offer a country welcome straight out of **Deliverance**. The *auberge* he checks into is the B&B of nightmares, where owner Bartel — mentally unhinged since his wife Gloria left him — transfers his feelings of abandonment onto Marc, making him sing, torching his van and stoving his head in. When Marc comes to, he is feminized, brutalized and raped, his head remaining a bloody pulp for the rest of the movie. Attempts at escape are futile, although du Welz take us into the Siberian hostility of the woods, where a Steadicam sequence of spectacularly edited cinematography tracks Marc running through the trees. There is dialogue of darkly ironic humour: "This will be the best Xmas you ever had … now where did I put that axe?" and a dinner scene reminiscent of **The Texas Chain Saw Massacre**, complete with extreme close-up of the victim's terrified eye and cruel imitation of his screaming, before the locals gatecrash for an orgy of rape and murder. Du Welz's direction runs a trajectory of styles — from the flat documentary realism of the beginning to a dénouement situated in a post-apocalyptic swampscape of petrified trees and a crucifixion that is as compelling a representation of Hell on Earth as any ever filmed. The acting is superb, with Lucas's Marc fostering no sympathy as a blank canvas onto whom the locals project sick delusions — although the young du Welz hammers home the point of the locals' "weirdness" with an unnecessary dance sequence. The film is devoid of soundtrack, and is stark, shocking and at times hilariously funny, in the best horror tradition. This director is a rising star with a gleeful sense of the inappropriate. [KS]

DAWN OF THE DEAD

2004, US, dir Zack Snyder, scr James Gunn, starring Sarah Polley, Ving Rhames, Jake Weber, Mekhi Phifer, Ty Burrel

Ana and a handful of other survivors take refuge from the zombie plague that has already decimated her family in a suburban shopping mall. But the mall's security guards have their own ideas about survival, and when it becomes apparent that no rescue is forthcoming, the survivors realize they cannot stay there forever. This "re-envisioning" of Romero's classic, to date the highest-budgeted zombie movie ever made (upwards of $20 million), takes the setting, gore and *A-Team*-style action of the original and dispenses with the rest. The mall here doesn't symbolize anything: it's just a good place to hide from the zombies, and Romero's commentary on vapid consumerism is replaced simply by its display. The characters, led by the feisty nurse Ana and the dutiful black cop Kenneth, are perfunctory stereotypes, who don't seem particularly upset by the death of their loved ones. Intriguing ideas — the zombie baby, the petty tyranny of the security guards — get a brief airing before being dropped in favour of another gory spectacle, and many scenes (for example, the survival of the orphaned girl in Andy's place, surrounded by zombies) strain credibility. Yet, for all its lack of substance, *Dawn* is still one of the best results of Hollywood's recent pillaging of '70s independent horror. The zombies run, fast, and mount claustrophobic attacks on the survivors; the effects are convincing and extravagantly messy; the tone is bleak, with various schemes ending disastrously and nobody's survival guaranteed; and a grim sense of humour enlivens scenes like the one when Andy takes pot shots at the zombies, named for their similarity to celebrities. Empty-headed but exhilarating, and unusually dark for a major studio offering, *Dawn*'s rapid edits and structure are closer to videogames like *Resident Evil* than Romero, reflecting the game's recent influence.

JU-ON
AKA THE GRUDGE

2004, Jap, dir/scr Takashi Shimizu, starring Megumi Okina, Misaki Ito, Misa Uehara, Yui Ichikawa

A nondescript house in the Tokyo suburbs is the scene of a series of macabre events. A vengeful ghost woman and her boy child terrorize and destroy all who live in the house or are connected with it in any way. A female social worker and a policeman are among those who find their lives and those of their families have become entangled with the evil house.

This is the first theatrical version of a saga that began as part of the TV horror anthology *Gakko no Kaidan G* in 1998. Following those fragments came the first *Ju-on* (2000), a TV feature that was successful enough to get some theatrical exposure as, later that same year, did its sequel (*Ju-on 2*). The theatrical version follows the format of these earlier releases. All are episodic narratives that detail how individuals come into contact with the evil house and the fate that befalls them. The TV versions made a virtue of their tiny budgets, limited locations and low-fi effects to create a genuinely unsettling ambience. Some of this is lost in the transition to the big screen, but the soulless gloominess of the haunted house and the claustrophobic intensity of its horrors are still central to the film's effect.

As with several entries in the '90s cycle of Japanese horror films, the ghosts in *Ju-on* use all the paraphernalia of modern technology (mobile phones, TV, photography, etc.) to propagate. Again, as in **Ringu**, the curse in *Ju-on* spreads like a kind of virus, attaching itself to anyone who comes into the house and then being passed on again.

The 2004 US remake (*The Grudge*) retained the original Japanese setting and director, and used episodes drawn from across the series. This version had its own sequel and there has been another theatrical sequel in Japan, with a third announced, making *Ju-on* an even more extensive franchise than **Ringu**. [PT]

WOLF CREEK

2004, Aust, dir/scr Greg McLean, starring John Jarratt, Cassandra Magrath, Kestie Morassi, Nathan Phillips

English backpackers Liz and Kristy team up with Australian Ben to drive across the outback to Cairns. They visit a meteorite crater, Wolf Creek, en route, and accept the offer of help from a local, Mick Taylor, when their car breaks down. It is a decision they will live to regret.

"Based on actual events" but tagged with the standard fiction disclaimer in the end credits, McLean's debut feature borrows piecemeal from Australian true crime. The director has referred to the Falconio case of 2001, in which a British tourist disappeared, presumed murdered, but elsewhere the film recalls the serial killer Ivan Milat, convicted of killing seven people (principally tourists) in the '80s and early '90s, particularly in Taylor's collection of tourist trophies and taste in rifle targets, while the "head on a stick" sequence is lifted verbatim from Milat's trial. Yet Falconio was a man, and Milat an equal-opportunity killer, making *Wolf Creek*'s focus on the suffering and death of two young women problematic, especially considering the survival of Ben, a flat character who effectively vanishes from the film as soon as things get nasty.

Wolf Creek borrows heavily from slashers in its supernatural inflections (tourists' clocks and car engines stop working at the crater), dumb moves (the girls wing Taylor with a bullet, then beat him weakly on the back rather than crushing his skull) and characterization (McGrath's Liz is for much of the film the central viewpoint character, more resourceful, sensitive and sensible than her companions), but denies its audience even the shaky comforts of the "final girl" ending her character implies. This is perhaps McLean's intention – he has described the film as a "cinematic hand grenade" – but it feels like a cheat, especially given the unlikely circumstances of Liz's fate, and Jarratt's cartoon psycho sits uneasily with the depressingly realistic trauma suffered by the girls. Yet the film certainly delivers on its gruelling promise, taking the national sport of pom-bashing to new extremes, and in its first half at least paints a convincingly naturalistic portrait of its three backpackers, all overlapping dialogue and tentative, awkward sexual interest, while McLean mixes Dogme-style hand-held cameras and natural lighting with extended shots of the landscape that keep the film squarely in the established Australian outback horror tradition.

SAW

2004, US, dir James Wan, scr Leigh Whannell, starring Leigh Whannell, Cary Elwes, Danny Glover, Ken Leung

Two men are chained by their ankles to pipes in a derelict bathroom. A body lies between them. Clues as to how they can escape are hidden around the room, and they soon discover they are in the clutches of the infamous "Jigsaw" killer.

The *Saw* franchise has proved the most durable of the new millennium, to date clocking five sequels and a videogame. Wan's film (he directed none of the sequels) takes ideas from David Fincher's **Seven**, namely a "zero-tolerance" killer employing elaborate means for his victims to dispatch themselves and a detective with elements of Morgan Freeman (black, respectable) and Brad Pitt's (obsessive, vengeful) characters. Wan crossbreeds these with the themes of environmental puzzle and gameshow ordeal that underlie everything from *The Crystal Maze* to the various *I'm a Celebrity!* incarnations.

But *Saw* is unable to carry anything like the weight of **Seven**. The budgetary constraints make the principal setting unconvincing, the characters' hysterical acting comes close to parody and the hyperactive death scenes look like something Chris Morris might have dreamt up. A recognition that the killer's Heath Robinson contraptions, ludicrous film-trailer voice and fat-faced dummy align the film more closely with **The Abominable Dr Phibes** than **Seven** would have allowed the film a much-needed wink at the audience. As it is, we are lumbered with comic scenes such as the fake death of Adam and the doctor's hysterical delivery of lines like "There! I've done it! I've killed him with the poison, like you wanted. Now where's my family?"

The game show ordeal theme is more compelling in its stark binary moralism, and has infected films beyond the Saw franchise such as the more interesting WΔZ (2007). It's effective because of its televisual rather than cinematic references: gameshows and celebrity ordeal programmes trade so heavily on audience aspiration that the self-mutilation scenarios at the end of the Saw films pack a peculiarly effective charge – what would you do? If there really was a celebrity show like this it might even be worth watching TV.

SHUTTER

2004, Thai, co-dir Banjong Pisanthanakun, Parkpoom Wongpoom, co-scr Banjong Pisanthanakun, Sopon Sukdapisit, starring Ananda Everingham, Natthaweeranuch Thongmee, Achita Sikamana, Unnop Chanpaibool

Tun and his girlfriend Jane, driving home from a party, hit a woman with their car. Tun persuades Jane to drive on. He finds that any photograph he takes after the accident is marked with a shadow, severely hampering his work as a professional photographer and, to make things worse, his neck hurts, although medical tests reveal no cause for his pain. Jane vows to put whatever is haunting Tun to rest, but discovers more than she bargained for.

While **Gin Gwai**'s characters travel to Bangkok, the Pang brothers' film was financed with Hong Kong/Singapore money, making Shutter the first Thai horror film to be widely shown overseas. There's not much to distinguish it from the horde of Japanese **Ringu** clones, though, apart from a couple of Buddhist monks and a propensity for the characters to wear flip flops: the image of the black-haired vengeful wraith evidently now haunts virtually all of Asia. Shutter isn't afraid to borrow from Euro-horror either. Tun's vision of a woman with bleeding eyes vomiting up her intestines shows he's been watching too many Fulci films, while the spatial loop that sees him forever descending to the fourth floor of his apartment building is lifted straight from Bava's **Operazione Paura**.

From the opening hit and run Tun appears entirely unsympathetic, so we don't much care what happens to him. Any lingering doubts about his self-centredness vanish when we discover that he doesn't even know about the suicides of two close friends, making the story's revelation of his caddish past behaviour something less than a shock. Jane is more sympathetic but is barely characterised, making the ghost the most credible and likeable character in the film – you certainly can't fault its tenacity.

For a 2004 film, Shutter's print shops and darkrooms seem almost nostalgic. The 2008 American remake shifts the focus to digital technology but still fails to make the most of the potentially fruitful idea of spirit photographs. The plot doesn't quite hang together either – later developments suggest that the car accident can't have happened, though this is never followed up, and Tun seems resilient enough to ditch the camera and take up stunt work – but there are a couple of effective scare scenes and the pace is brisk throughout. Highlights include a strobing flash that illuminates an uninvited guest, and the use of Polaroids to detect supernatural activity, although the risible twist means any goodwill soon evaporates. Less disturbing and imaginative than virtually any British road safety advert.

THE DESCENT

2005, UK, dir/scr Neil Marshall, starring Shauna MacDonald, Natalie Mendoza, Alex Reid, Saskia Mulder

Scotland. Sarah's husband and child are killed in a car crash after he picks her up from a white-water-rafting trip. A year later, Sarah rejoins her rafting friends for a caving expedition in the Appalachian Mountains. But the plan of the team leader, Juno, to explore uncharted terrain goes badly wrong when a tunnel collapses – and they find something else down in the caves with them.

Marshall's exemplary follow-up to Dog Soldiers (2002) sustains a pitch of raw terror rare in the genre since its '70s heyday. If its impressive elaborations of the subterranean cannibals of **Death Line** and Creep (2004) seem a superfluous flourish in a film whose iconography of tightly constricted spaces and appalling injury is gruelling enough, there are teasing suggestions that this shift into full-bore monster movie is the result of Sarah's hallucinations. Before the trip begins she takes a handful of pills; a friend warns that "paranoia, panic attacks, hallucinations" are possible consequences of caving; and things take a distinct turn for the worse after she is trapped in a tunnel. We are introduced to her subjective world earlier – a run down a hospital corridor, chased by darkness; a dream at the hut – and her experiences depict abjection and collapsed boundaries so concisely that they take on a hallucinatory quality, a textbook example of what the psychologist Stanislav Grof has termed a "BPM2" bad trip, itself related to negative experiences in the womb.

The Descent is aware of its genre heritage – **Deliverance** (another single-sex group indulging in ill-advised adventure tourism with a nasty leg break); **The Texas Chain Saw Massacre** (the gore-soaked Sarah looks like "final girl" Sally); and **Alien** (the initial descent into the cave recalls the trip to the Derelict) – but reconfigures these elements for an intensely claustrophobic evocation of womb anxiety, a female response to the all-male horrors of Dog Soldiers. "There's only one way

out of this chamber and that's down the pipe," declares Juno; and this is one of the most impressively messy births committed to film.

LAND OF THE DEAD
AKA GEORGE A. ROMERO'S LAND OF THE DEAD

2005, US/Can/Fr, dir/scr George A. Romero, starring Simon Baker, John Leguizamo, Dennis Hopper, Asia Argento

Fortifications have been built around a city to keep the zombie menace at bay, but the wealthier inhabitants choose to live in Kaufman's gated apartment complex, Fiddler's Green. Riley is retiring from his job running Dead Reckoning, an armoured vehicle used for food raids outside the city, but Kaufman hires him to track the vehicle down after it is stolen by Riley's successor, Cholo.

BELOW: Cary Elwes just can't stand that ringtone. **Saw**

Given that financing for the fourth instalment in Romero's zombie saga came only after *28 Days Later* (2002), *Shaun of the Dead* (2004) and the 2004 **Dawn of the Dead**, the most surprising thing about *Land* is how dated it feels. The look recalls *Escape from New York* (1981) or *The Warriors* (1979), down to the design of *Dead Reckoning* and its biker outriders, while the inhabitants of Fiddler's Green have reverted to a '70s vision of modernity. The zombie onslaught may have turned back the clock, but odd anachronisms remain: dollars still have value (an unlikely development in the wake of **Day of the Dead** – even Cholo's demand for $5 million seems old-fashioned), while a **Shivers**-style TV ad (they still have TV?) highlights the benefits of living in Fiddler's Green. The characters, too, seem like stock types from an earlier era, their personalities outlined in comic-book tics: the retiring, world-weary hero, given to flights of pastiche idealism; his scarred, slightly subnormal dependant, redeemed by his skill with a rifle; the tart with a heart (and a large gun), forced into prostitution by Kaufman's two-dimensional villainy; and all lack the conviction necessary to infuse the roles with life.

The trademark gore effects are present and correct, if shot in a murky style to ensure an R rating in the US. Some scenes (particularly the soldiers in the munitions room) approach the visceral impact of the previous films, but they tend to feel like an aside, an obligation Romero simply isn't interested in any more. And while credit is due to the director for his broadsides against the Bush government, his sledgehammer approach hardly presents an incisive critique, leaving *Land* to impress mainly in its incidentals. The zombies' increased intelligence is marked in subtle touches like the hanged businessman who, rather than gorging on entrails, turns to his wife after biting his son, keen perhaps to retain their bodily integrity in death; a club features a "Take your picture with a zombie" concession and an undead paintball target marked "No head shots"; and the casting of a black actor as the lead zombie suggests, after the heroes of **Night**, **Dawn** and **Day**, that Romero's sympathies have finally switched entirely to the world of the dead.

HAZE

2005, Jap, dir/scr Shinya Tsukamoto, starring Shinya Tsukamoto, Takahiro Murase, Takahiro Kandaka, Masato Tsujioka

A wounded man awakens in a network of dark tunnels. He is dragged around by an unseen force and repeatedly assaulted by his environment. After witnessing a roomful of people whose prayers are answered by being torn apart, he meets a woman who insists that they can escape, but only by going into a waterlogged ditch filled with body parts.

Tsukamoto's 50 minutes of claustrophobic hell plays like **Saw** remade by David Lynch. At no point is there any explanation for this bizarre world, and the tunnels are so dark that it's often hard to make out exactly what's going on. We see enough, though, to know that it's very unpleasant: teeth are dragged along pipes and heads whacked repeatedly with hammers. He eventually convinces himself that he has become the plaything of a "rich pervert", a belief confirmed when he finally emerges from the tunnels into a brightly lit living room.

Given what happens next, though, *Haze*'s confined spaces seem less torture chamber than afterlife or purgatory, with scenes of violent dismemberment being balanced by amniotic bliss as soon as he braves the limb-clogged water. Whatever the "really big and dark thing" is that's tearing people apart, it probably isn't human. But even this can't account for the coda, in which a visibly aged Tsukamoto gazes up at a blue sky while drying sheets flap around him in the breeze, making *Haze* a head-scratcher of the first order. Metaphysics aside, the film's industrial nightmare at times approaches **Eraserhead** or the director's earlier **Tetsuo** in its visceral intensity. After this compelling experimental oddity, Tsukamoto returned to commercially viable films with *Akumu Tantei/Nightmare Detective* (2006) and its 2008 sequel.

HOSTEL

2005, US, dir/scr Eli Roth, starring Jay Hernandez, Derek Richardson, Eythor Gudjonsson, Barbara Nedeljakova

Roth does for Slovakia what *Borat* (2006) did for Kazakhstan, with similarly unedifying and laughable results. Two young Americans, Paxton and Josh, are in Amsterdam with their Icelandic friend Oli. They are persuaded to visit Slovakia for its beautiful and available women – "because of the war there are no guys", an acquaintance assures them, before giving them the address of a hostel which they won't find in any guidebook. Keen to avoid other Americans by travelling off the beaten track, the trio descends on the hostel to find their dreams of easy sex come true – at a cost.

Given that the term "torture porn" was coined to describe this and its equally inbred cousin **Saw**, it's surprising how difficult *Hostel* is to take seriously. Indeed with scenes involving a man slipping on a pool of vomit and chainsawing through his leg, and children crushing a skull for bubblegum, *Hostel* plays

ABOVE: The dead bite back, **Land of the Dead**.

best as farce, a live-action *Team America* (2004) or, given the stoned, frat-boy antics of the backpackers, a film better entitled *Dude, Where's My Fingers?* The torture scenes are not especially strong, with the exception of the field medicine sequence that has become *de rigueur* in virtually any new US horror film, and the porn tag only really applies to the ludicrous, unbelievable scenarios.

Hostel is a dumb movie. If someone like Paxton can escape his captors (he's surprisingly handy with a gun, but then he *is* Californian) anyone can. Torture rooms are glimpsed with their doors open, when surely they should follow the "you look, you pay" regime of the brothel visited in an earlier scene. Nubile young women, none of whom seem to be Slovakian, lure the men to their deaths, though what's keeping the Japanese women at the hostel is never explained. And for a film purportedly about American ignorance of Europe (the characters presumably confuse Alex's reference to the war in Slovakia with Slovenia and the bloody break-up of Yugoslavia), it makes some ignorant oversights of its own, not least the fact that while the film is principally set in Slovakia all the street signs are in Czech. *Hostel*'s main point of interest, then, is the killers themselves, particularly Paxton's tormentor, who gapes fishlike with excitement at the sight of his victim, and the "American client", who grins like an animated gopher while trying to bond with Paxton as a fellow torture freak in what's undoubtedly the film's finest scene.

Hostel makes good on *Pulp Fiction*'s (1994) promise to "get medieval on your ass" (Tarantino was one of the film's executive producers), perhaps to distance these torture scenes from any association with Guantanamo Bay or Abu Ghraib. Given that *Hostel* was reportedly the most popular film among US forces during the invasion of Iraq, its extraordinary xenophobia and vengeful triumphalism make it politically suspect to say the least. In an unwitting comment on its characters' desire to exploit cheap bodies in a post-Soviet Eastern Europe, *Hostel* ironically does just that, being shot in the Czech Republic using an almost entirely local – and cheap – crew.

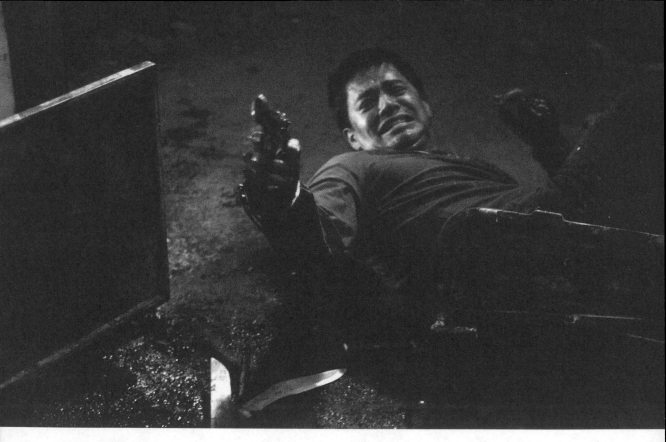

SÍLENÍ
AKA LUNACY

2005, Cz/Slov/Jap, dir/scr Jan Svankmajer, starring Pavel Liska, Jan Triska, Anna Geislerová, Jaroslav Dusek

Svankmajer's fifth feature, an extraordinary blend of meat puppetry and sabre-rattling blasphemy, opens with the director explaining that what we are about to see is a horror film, "with all the degeneracy peculiar to that genre", influenced by Poe and de Sade. Svankmajer has borrowed from Poe before, in the shorts *Kyvadlo, Jáma a Nadeje/The Pit, the Pendulum and Hope* (1983) and *Zánik Domu Usheru/The Fall of the House of Usher* (1981). Here he weaves elements from "The Premature Burial" and "The System of Dr Tarr and Professor Fether", elsewhere adapted as **La Mansion de la Locura**, into a tale of a Sadean yet benevolent Marquis attempting to cure young Jean Berlot's fear of insanity.

Other Svankmajer films such as *Neco z Alenky/Alice* (1988) are perhaps more disturbing than *Sílení*, which tellingly moves into outright horror only when its asylum has returned to its lawful administration, recalling psychiatry's history of aggressive surgical intervention. Elsewhere the horror is strictly of the Gothic variety, with coffins being dragged through moonlit cemeteries and the Marquis presiding over the most authentically blasphemous

ABOVE: "Dude, where's my fingers?" Jay Hernandez doesn't bleed much in **Hostel**

black mass in the movies, hammering nails into a statue of Christ until it resembles a West African fetish while naked women have communion wafers scattered over their upturned rears in preparation for sex. Jean spends an hour of the film's running time in the Marquis' crumbling Gothic pile being introduced to, and utterly confused by, his Sadean philosophy, before witnessing two diametrically opposed ways to run an asylum – total freedom under Dr Murloppe and total control under Dr Coulmiere.

Síleni's schematic structure and ideological debates are enlivened by inserts of jaunty, playful animations that often comment on the narrative. Disembodied tongues slurp at beer, lumps of gleaming meat leap around a birdcage and sheep's skulls come back to clattering life, all in Svankmajer's trademark hallucinatory stop-motion clarity. The events of the film are seen from Jean's perspective, which we are slyly invited to share, but his interpretation of events, however well meaning, is always wrong and finally leads to his incarceration. His behaviour around Charlotte, a woman he naively hopes to rescue from the clutches of the degenerates surrounding her, only illustrates the accuracy of the Marquis' rants about "goodness". In fact she turns out to

be the "devious whore" the Marquis warns him of, an unfortunate turn given that she is the film's only female character.

Ironically, the characters we might expect to be the film's villains, the Marquis and Dr Murloppe, prove far less dangerous than the characters with whom Jean allies himself, Dr Coulmiere and Charlotte. The Marquis' response to Jean trashing one of his rooms in a fit of night terrors is to dismiss the damage with aristocratic largesse, while for the "deeply religious" Coulmiere it is evidence of a mental illness that must be physically punished. For Jean the road to hell really is paved with good intentions, and we are left with the grotesque, unforgettable and typically acerbic image of a shrink-wrapped steak throbbing on a supermarket shelf.

THE LAST WINTER

2006, US/Ice, dir/co-scr Larry Fessenden, co-scr Robert Leaver, starring Ron Perlman, James LeGros, Connie Britton, Zach Gilford

North Industries have been given permission to extract oil from an Alaskan wildlife refuge, on condition that they work with environmental experts on-site. Pollock returns to their Arctic base from a break, only to find environmental observer Hoffman in bed with his ex, and when Hoffman refuses to sign off Pollock's proposals tensions begin to run high. The winter is too warm and the tundra is beginning to melt, releasing something that clouds the judgment of the workers. When disaster strikes, they're a long way from home.

The Last Winter returns to the "nature strikes back" theme of '70s eco-horror with a pertinent contemporary slant. Climate change fatigue may have led to the film's poor distribution and lack of commercial success, but it takes pains not to be preachy and finally focuses on a clash of mentalities – the blinkered, exploitative and bullish against the rational, conservative and humane (and bearded naturally) – that recalls the director's **Wendigo** more than an Al Gore-style science lesson.

For all that, it's refreshing to see a horror film with something to say rather than the usual parade of witless blade fodder and, as a horror film, *The Last Winter* succeeds admirably. Early scenes might recall **The Thing**, another Arctic base under attack from something weird, but the film soon establishes its own identity. Fessenden's characteristically sensitive take on Native American folklore adds a mythic gloss to the compelling idea of ghosts rising from the melting tundra. The characters'

ABOVE: Vincent Cassel prepares to operate in **Sheitan**

Sakebi reshuffles and refines tropes and images from Kurosawa's other horror films, including **Kairo** and **Cure**, to result in their most distilled expression and the director's masterpiece. Slow moving, cerebral and occasionally hard to follow, *Sakebi* repays close attention and multiple viewings to reveal one of the most profoundly downbeat and beautiful films in Japanese genre cinema. The wan face and long black hair of the film's ghost might come from any generic J-horror offering but the similarities end there. *Sakebi* is effects-free, apart from two extraordinary scenes, and its chills are subtly disquieting rather than noisy or brash.

This may disappoint some audiences used to more extravagant hauntings, but receptive viewers will recognize that Kurosawa's grasp of spectral dynamics is second to none. *Sakebi* is not without its flaws, chiefly a slightly overwrought police psychiatrist and a crucial plot gap concerning the revelation of its first killer's identity, but the bleak haunting at the centre of the film has such a grave weight that such criticism seems petty. Kurosawa evidently felt he'd taken his brand of uniquely morbid horror as far as it could go with this film and his next, *Tokyo Sonata* (2008), was an Ozu-style tale of family breakdown. Highly recommended.

erratic behaviour – one wanders naked into the Arctic night while another smothers an injured colleague – is made more credible by a wince-inducing focus on injury and danger. A plane crash and subsequent fire on the ice provides one of the film's most harrowing sequences, but a drop into an icy river and the loss of a shoe during a trek over the icy wastes are equally effective in their visceral impact. After this, the sight of spectral monsters is almost a relief.

SAKEBI
AKA RETRIBUTION

2006, Jap, dir/scr Kiyoshi Kurosawa, starring Kôji Yakusho, Manami Konishi, Tsuyoshi Ihara, Hiroyuki Hirayama

Yoshioka investigates the murder of a young woman. Clues point to his involvement in the crime, but subsequent copycat killings suggest that a serial killer is at work. Yoshioka becomes convinced that he is being haunted for a crime he did not commit and attempts to appease the unquiet spirit that plagues him.

SHEITAN
AKA SATAN

2006, Fr, dir/co-scr Kim Chapiron, co-scr Christian Chapiron, starring Vincent Cassel, Olivier Bartélémy, Roxane Mesquida, Nico Le Phat Tan

Paris, two days before Christmas. Bart is thrown out of a nightclub after starting a fight. His friends, Thai and Ladj, join him with two women, Eve and Yasmine, in tow. Eve invites them all to her country house. When they arrive they are met by Joseph, the housekeeper, who takes them swimming in a hot spring. Bart wants to leave but his friends are keen to stay, having been promised sex. But that's not all that's on the menu.

Sheitan is a colourful entry in the New French Extremism wave of films, which includes the work of **Irreversible**'s Gaspar Noé, **Calvaire** and **Martyrs**. It manages to distinguish itself from its more brutal peers with a twisted fairy-tale sensibility but cannot quite make its disparate parts stick together. The film is shot through with Biblical imagery – Joseph's wife Marie is due to give birth on Christmas Day and Eve eats an apple while the men discover a snake – that doesn't lead anywhere except to a perverse Nativity scene. *Sheitan* also seems

ABOVE: Kôji Yakusho is haunted for a crime he is sure he did not commit. **Sakebi**

perpetually on the verge of doing something interesting with its racial mixture. Joseph casually insults his guests by referring to them as "the Chink" (Thai's parents are Vietnamese), "the little Turk" (Yasmine is French-Algerian) and "the nigger", while the Muslim Yasmine and Ladj are upset by Bart's assertion that "religion's bullshit", yet none of this amounts to anything more than a liberal-baiting tease.

Sheitan's virtues, then, lie elsewhere. Its imagery is extraordinary: maleficent goats are wheeled around on hospital gurneys and a deliciously grotesque doll is used to charm the newborn infant at the finale, a fitting climax to the parade of broken dolls and madly grinning dummies that seem to be the house's principal inhabitants. The film's queasy depiction of rural France is firmly in the **Calvaire** tradition with its imbecile children, rough locals and sluttish women with an inappropriate take on handling pets. But pride of place in the rural madness stakes goes to Cassel's manic Joseph, grinning from ear to ear as he proffers his niece for sex, regales his guests with drunken tales of incest and demonic pacts, and keeps his jumper firmly tucked into his trousers until it's time to pull out his nasty, homemade knife.

TURISTAS
AKA PARADISE LOST

2006, US, dir John Stockwell, scr Michael Ross, starring Josh Duhamel, Melissa George, Olivia Wilde, Desmond Askew

After a lucky escape from a bus crash, a group of backpackers bonds over caipirinha cocktails on a Brazilian beach. Next morning they wake up to find all their belongings gone. An unfortunate incident with one of the local children means that the backpackers have to leave town fast, and Kiko, a young local they'd befriended the night before, offers to take them to his uncle's remote jungle lodge. What he doesn't mention is that his uncle will want their kidneys and livers in payment.

Where **The Ruins** leapfrogs any real exploration of its backpacker milieu in its haste to get to the titular ziggurat, with *Turistas* you can almost taste the banana pancakes. The only thing missing from its ragtag band of international holidaymakers (three Americans, two Swedes, two Brits and an Ozzie) is a support team of Israeli trance fans. *Turistas* has more local colour than its tourist-terror rivals, bases its narrative on a real folk legend circulating in Central and South America of gringo organ-harvesters, and presents its backpackers in all their loudmouthed Anglophone glory – one even plays a recorder, convincingly badly. It is also chock-full of racist stereotypes: when we see the sweaty driver picking his nose in the opening scenes we know trouble is afoot, and other Brazilians

ZOMBIES

Zombies are back, rising up again to wrap their mouldy fingers around cinemagoers' hearts, in hit films like the remake of **Dawn of the Dead** (2004), the comedy *Shaun of the Dead* (2004), the spoof goreflick *House of 1000 Corpses* (2003), and **Land of the Dead**, a comeback by the grand-daddy of the genre, George Romero.

Zombies make unlikely stars, lacking the glamour of other movie monsters. Dracula is an honest-to-goodness Count, The Mummy was once a King; even the Werewolf is Mr Lover-Man. The Phantom of the Opera and the Hunchback of Notre-Dame are poignant reminders that behind a twisted visage noble thoughts and fine feelings can flourish. We even experience a sneaky complicity with Mr Hyde.

Zombies, on the other hand, are rotten. Decaying flesh has no glamour. When it comes to passion, rigor mortis is no substitute for an erection and the zombie is devoid of any hidden depths. Nevertheless, there's something tragic and compelling about these sorry creatures. They frequently herald the end of civilization and the best zombie films show either the real world collapsing (**Dawn of the Dead, Day of the Dead**), or reality itself under siege (**Paura nella Città dei Morti Viventi**; **L'Aldilà**).

Unlike horror's other major players, zombies have no foundation in literature. They began as an anthropological curiosity, drawn from William Seabrook's non-fiction book about Voodoo practices in Haiti, *The Magic Island* (1929). **White Zombie** was the first screen treatment to pick up on Seabrook's research and for many years after the zombie was defined as a slave – maybe dead, maybe not – under the spell of a Voodoo master. The basic assumption continued through a handful of cheapies in the 1940s, until Hammer's **Plague of the Zombies** brought this phase to a close with a tale of a Cornish tin mine staffed by reanimated cadavers, under the rule of a colonial country squire and Voodoo expert.

The second phase began with George A. Romero's **Night of the Living Dead**. For all the charms of the earlier films, this is the Ur-text of the modern zombie film. It tells the story of a small group of people, thrown together by chance, who must barricade themselves in a dismal farmhouse as hordes of the walking dead try to get in. Romero came up with several innovations: the terror comes from a pervading sense of meaninglessness,

the authorities being at a loss to explain what's happening; the surviving humans are a motley bunch, ill-equipped to deal with the situation; while the zombies have simply walked out of local funeral parlours, still dressed in their "day" clothes or toe-tagged for the morgue. But Romero's foremost innovation was to have his ghouls eat the flesh of the living. By tapping into the cannibalism taboo, he unleashed a truly primal fear (and once you're bitten, the wound spawns a terminal infection, so *you* become a zombie too, an idea borrowed from vampire lore).

Romero followed **Night** with four sequels: **Dawn of the Dead**, an action-horror classic that was easily as influential; **Day of the Dead**, a bleak, exhausting film with lots of shouting and some extraordinary effects; **Land of the Dead** and *Diary of the Dead* (2009) – all add conceits about the decadence of consumer capitalism derived from Romero's raging pessimism.

Night was followed by such diverse American oddities as *Messiah of Evil* (Willard Huyck, 1973) – touting a "hippy-dream gone sour" meets "consumer-society gone crazy" theme well before Romero's **Dawn**; **Deathdream** – a *Monkey's Paw* variant in which a Vietnam soldier dies in combat, then returns home to resume his old life; *Children Shouldn't Play with Dead Things* (Alan Ormsby, 1972) – a send-up about grave robbing that turns surprisingly creepy; *Garden of the Dead* (John Hayes, 1972) – with its talking, formaldehyde-addicted chain-gang zombies; and *The Child* (Robert Voskanian, 1977) – in which a nasty little girl uses psychic powers to terrorize her family and tutor, before introducing them to her "friends" from the graveyard.

From Spain, the beguiling **La Noche del Terror Ciego** spawned three sequels, featuring skeletal zombie Knights Templar on horseback; and the marvellous **No Profanar el Sueño de los Muertos** unleashed zombies in the Peak District. However, in Italy the massive commercial success of **Dawn of the Dead** in 1978 inspired directors such as Lucio Fulci, the leader of the Roman pack, with **Zombi 2** making an indelible mark in the genre. Fulci's ghouls were far more disgusting than Romero's and their gory attacks even more shocking. He emphasized putrefaction and corporeality, then, in the wonderful **Paura nella Città dei Morti Viventi** and **L'Aldilà**, added ghostly weirdness to the mix, with cadavers that appear and disappear at will, emerging from the most unlikely places to attack their victims.

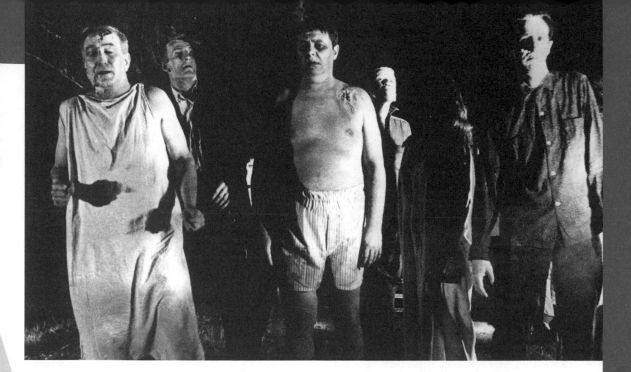

Fulci's success was a green light to the Italians: see **La Regina dei Cannibale**; *Le Notti Erotiche dei Morti Viventi/ Erotic Nights of the Living Dead* (Joe D'Amato, 1980); *Inferno dei Morti-Viventi/Zombie Creeping Flesh* (Bruno Mattei, 1980); and **Le Notte del Terrore**. In Spain, Jesus Franco made *La Tumba de los Muertos Vivientes/Oasis of the Zombies* (1983), having already paid the French horror specialist Jean Rollin to film zombie inserts for his 1971 film, *Christina, Princesse de l'Érotisme*, retitling it *Virgin among the Living Dead* (1980). Rollin himself made the picturesque, moody and sorely underrated *Les Raisins de la Mort/The Grapes of Death* (1978); the slightly overrated *La Morte Vivante/ The Living Dead Girl* (1982); and the charmingly awful *Le Lac des Morts Vivants/Zombie Lake* (1981).

Meanwhile, backyards across America provided locations for a variety of ultra-low budget **Dawn** spin-offs such as Tony Malanowski's *Night of Horror* (1980) and *Curse of the Screaming Dead* (1982) and Fred Olen Ray's inept but amusing *The Alien Dead* (1980). *Fiend* (Don Dohler, 1980) is a rare example of a post-**Dawn** zombie film that owes nothing to Romero, with a reanimated cadaver, possessed by a demon, giving violin tutorials in deepest Baltimore. *The Dark Power* (Phil Smoot, 1985) unleashes zombie Toltec Indians and then shoehorns them into a Sorority slasher film; *Forest of Fear* (Chuck McCrann, 1979) shows that living in Pittsburgh is no guarantee you can direct zombie flicks; *Frozen Scream* (Frank Roach, 1980) has dead people stored in cryogenic suspension ordered to kill by radio control; and *Raw Force* (Edward D. Murphy, 1982) features cannibalistic monks who can raise the dead.

Taking a cue from the intermittent slapstick in Romero's **Dawn**, the 1980s saw several comedy-horror zombie flicks, starting with **Return of the Living Dead**, an unofficial sequel to Romero's **Night** written by John Russo, who co-wrote the original. Along with **Re-Animator**, it combines splashy gore effects and macabre humour – a formula that soon became tiresome. The nadir came with **Return**'s wretched sequels and such dreary teen rubbish as *Night Life* (David Acomba, 1989) and *Chopper Chicks in Zombietown* (Dan Hoskins, 1989), a title that says it all.

The recent zombie revival is a mixed blessing: the **Dawn of the Dead** remake lacks interesting characters and gets by largely on adrenaline. **Land of the Dead** disappoints with a corny supervillain and bland hero and by suggesting that the zombies are now the real locus of sympathy, yet failing to explore them in detail, Romero leaves us with a hollow theoretical abstraction that must have looked good on paper but fails to ignite onscreen. As for *28 Days Later* (2002), the director Danny Boyle took great care to distance his "Eco-Horror" tale from the Zombie sub-genre, even as he milked its style. It's true that his running, screeching "rage" victims aren't zombies, strictly speaking: perhaps a better comparison would be Umberto Lenzi's earnest, daft-as-a-brush runaround *Incubo sulla Citta Contaminata/Nightmare City* (1980). [ST]

ABOVE: Feeding time for the monstrous assailants of **The Mist**

directors the means to put anything they want on screen but you wouldn't know it to watch recent horror cinema, which is why Frank Darabont's third Stephen King adaptation – after *The Shawshank Redemption* (1994) and *The Green Mile* (1999) – seemed surprisingly fresh, arriving at a time when the weirdest creatures were invariably found in fantasy films.

King's best fiction thrives on a simple idea that's pursued relentlessly and *The Mist* is a simple B movie with a premise straight out of William Hope Hodgson – a cloud of mist of unknown origin besieges a group of small-town Americans in the local supermarket. Lurking in the cloud is a host of increasingly lethal and monstrous creatures. The explanation of a military experiment gone awry is perfunctory and redundant; of more concern is how the trapped neighbours will cope with the external menace and with each other once the beasts start breaking in and tempers begin to fray. Throw in another of King's dangerous Bible-thumpers muttering about "end times" while fretting at divided loyalties, and you have a fraught and desperate atmosphere where the monstrous assailants outside are hidden not by shadows but by a sheet of terrifying blankness.

Thomas Jane is the reluctant hero trying to protect his young son from invading creatures and from Marcia Gay Harden's religious mania. One of King's favourite horror artists, Berni Wrightson, designed the creatures which run through a taxonomy of insectoid, tentacled and leather-winged nightmarishness. Darabont cranks the suspense by establishing the uncompromisingly murderous nature of the mist before forcing his survivors to venture into it. The tension remains taut throughout, all the way to a shockingly bleak conclusion, and the glimpse at the end of some colossal abomination stalking the landscape is one of the few moments in recent cinema when Hollywood has dared approach the monstrous imaginings of H.P. Lovecraft. [JC]

are presented as glue huffers, crack smokers, thieves, prostitutes and mad surgeons. The only icon of Brazilian tourist tales missing is the transsexual, leaving clear grounds for a sequel.

The principal friendly Brazilian, Kiko, seems to have learned his English and mannerisms from watching *Borat* (2006), and the evil doctor's attempts to harvest some gringo offal are continually foiled by his underlings' insistence on pausing for sex and drugs. Sadly, the most irritating of the tourists makes it to the end, suggesting that all you need to survive is a chiselled jaw, a plaintive whine and a morbid fear of local ice cubes, and the film's conservatism is highlighted not only by the fact that his fears are justified – they *should* have taken the plane, the bus driver *was* going too fast – but also that those tourists marked for death have had some kind of sexual contact. If you leave the question of how this might play to a Brazilian audience aside, though, *Turistas* is a guilty pleasure, beautifully photographed, fast-paced, engaging and violent. Moral: drink more cachaça and nobody will even *want* your liver and kidneys.

THE MIST

2007, US, dir/scr Frank Darabont, starring Thomas Jane, Marcia Gay Harden, Laurie Holden, Andre Braugher

Monster fans disappointed by the flood of humanoid horrors that proliferated throughout the Noughties would have welcomed *The Mist* as a relief from yet more vampires, zombies, ghosts and torturing psychopaths. Computer graphics have given

PARANORMAL ACTIVITY

2007, US, dir/scr Oren Peli, starring Katie Featherston, Micah Sloat, Mark Friedrichs, Amber Armstrong

Paranormal Activity built up a substantial online reputation after Peli circulated DVD screeners at festivals in 2007, but it was the intervention of Steven Spielberg that led to its official 2009 theatrical release. The story is simple and familiar to anyone who has sat through a "reality" ghost show like *Most Haunted*. Micah buys a video camera to record the supernatural phenomena reported by his live-in girlfriend Katie in their San Diego home.

The film, which reportedly cost just $15,000 to make, is

a producer's wet dream with minimal cast and crew (the film could almost, as it suggests, have been made by two people), no special visual effects, no music track, no sets, no script (the actors improvised their dialogue) and just a sequence of mounting pops, groans and creaks, backed up by the audience's conviction that a lack of technical polish means that what they're seeing is actually real. The idea has potential, especially in response to the CGI heavy hauntings of the '90s, but the film ultimately represents a missed opportunity with any subtle chills being dissipated by a handful of crass scenes.

Katie and Micah are credible enough until the cracks in their characterization begin to show. First she complains about his obsessive camera use and suspects that the filming is antagonising the demon haunting her, but she subsequently uses the camera herself, while his assholish behaviour, convincing in its early stages – he is, after all, a day trader – slips into parody as he bullishly asserts property rights over both Katie and the house. Other elements veer too close to self-parody or a jaw-dropping hokiness to work: a ouija board spontaneously bursts into flame; footage of an exorcism ends with a possessed woman eating her own arm (heavily edited for the theatrical release); and an ineffectual psychic visits for all of five seconds before backing out. Perhaps the most risible scene is when Micah lays powder outside their bedroom and finds what look suspiciously like webbed footprints in the

morning, suggesting that Katie is being stalked by a giant duck and that what they really need is less an exorcist than a Chinese chef. This is a shame, as there are some satisfyingly creepy ingredients in the mix. The theatrical version of the film differs in many respects from the original, not least in its Spielberg-suggested ending which dispenses with the original's trigger-happy police; the unrated DVD/Blu-ray release has yet another ending.

THE CHILDREN

2008, UK, dir/scr Tom Shankland, starring Eva Birthistle, Stephen Campbell Moore, Jeremy Sheffield, Rachel Shelley

Picture this. Your food is mashed up for you and you have to eat with a plastic spoon. Your only reward for good behaviour is a useless gold star. Mealtimes and bedtimes are strictly enforced, and you have to endure a sickly bedtime story before the lights go out. To top it off, all you got for Christmas was a xylophone. You're too small to fight back against the grown-ups, so is there anything you can do besides scream? Oh yes.

Shankland's addition to the distinguished horror tradition of creepy kids is one of the best. The set-up is simple. Elaine and Jonah and their three children – including an older, pre-Jonah daughter, Casey – visit Elaine's sister Chloe and her family for New Year's Eve. Tabloid depictions of uncontrollable children tend to focus on young teens of the "underclass", but the children in

---

BELOW: Timelapse terror. Katie Featherston rocks in **Paranormal Activity**

3:30:00 AM

Shankland's film are younger than this (they look between four and eight, with the exception of Casey) and are resolutely middle-class. This allows Shankland to indulge in some wicked digs at middle-class parenting, making the first half of the film feel like Mike Leigh in a peculiarly aggressive mood.

Chloe's family live in a large country pile and Robbie, her husband, is obviously very successful. Jonah, by contrast, is limping from one harebrained scheme to the next, and tries to sell a Chinese medicine business plan to Robbie at every opportunity. The differences between the two couples are reflected in their parenting styles, and part of the fun comes from the exploration of unspoken rivalry and hostility between the middle-class families. Chloe berates Elaine for bringing an ill child to the house and endangering her children, which seems unreasonable at the time but turns out to be completely justified. In fact both seem untrustworthy and unreasonable at the time, but also turn out to be right. One of Elaine's children has infected all of Chloe's with an unknown virus, although their condition has gone way beyond ginseng treatments. Rather than turning them into slavering crazies or rabid cannibals,

Shankland merely ups the ante on their childish games: lacking the strength to get what they want, the children rely on abuse of trust. The film's violence extrapolates from credible domestic accidents, and is all the more viscerally effective for being seen only in glimpses. As the age of criminal responsibility in the UK inches ever lower, contraception never looked like such a good idea.

CLOVERFIELD

2008, US, dir Matt Reeves, scr Drew Godard, starring Michael Stahl-David, T. J. Miller, Odette Yustman, Lizzy Caplan

The events of 11 September 2001 hang like a toxic cloud over Hollywood's recent apocalypses, and the dust lies heaviest over *Cloverfield* where New York City is comprehensively trashed by ... what, exactly? We're spared the usual reductive explanation

ABOVE: New York City is comprehensively destroyed in
Cloverfield

in J.J. Abrams' production, and the film retains some mystery as a result. Abrams' intention was to create a Toho-like creature for an American city (King Kong and the creature in the *Beast from 20,000 Fathoms* (1953) not being worthy enough, it seemed), and, with director Matt Reeves, gave the idea a novel twist by filming it **Blair Witch**-style from the point-of-view of an amateur cameraman.

The documentary form had already been used to destroy New York in Orson Welles' radio adaptation of *War of the Worlds*, and the monster-in-the-city theme goes back to Harry O. Hoyt's *The Lost World* (1925), with its escaped dinosaur roaming London. *Cloverfield*'s strength is in making a familiar theme seem fresh again, the hand-held camera giving an immediacy lacking in similar works even though it restricts our view of events. For much of the film all that's seen or heard of the monster is its titanic bellowing and brief glimpses of something enormous blundering through the streets. The frantic chase through New York's alleys and subways is presented with a formal rigour of which Hitchcock would have been proud, and while the bland protagonists are given little to do but react to the rampage of the monster and its scuttling parasites, this hardly matters because we're experiencing their trauma in real time.

Reeves turns the entire city into a set where the Statue of Liberty's head comes bouncing down the street and ruined skyscrapers lean at dangerous angles. Verisimilitude is maintained throughout, and there's no musical score to break the spell: everything we see is from a found video recording including occasional glimpses of a lovers' trip to Coney Island – and a clue to the creature's origin – underneath the disaster footage. Perfect viewing for TV or computer screen, in other words, where the viewer can pretend it really happened. [JC]

EDEN LAKE

2008, UK, dir/scr James Watkins, starring Kelly Reilly, Michael Fassbender, Tara Ellis, Jack O'Connell

Steve takes his girlfriend Jenny to a flooded quarry surrounded by woodland for a camping weekend. Their lakeside idyll is disturbed by a group of unruly urchins playing loud grime music and letting their pitbull run loose. The next day the couple's car is stolen. When Steve confronts the gang their dog is killed in a struggle over a knife, prompting Brett, the leader of the pack, to vow revenge.

The leader of a pack of British chav horror films including the intermittently entertaining *Donkey Punch* and the irredeemably nasty *Mum and Dad* (both 2008), *Eden Lake* presses so many tabloid buttons in its depiction of a broken Britain populated by boy racers and proud ASBO-wearers that it could almost be a party-political broadcast, although you wouldn't want to hug *these* hoodies. The first half hour is a superbly realized weekend gone wrong. The all too convincing behaviour of the "little hoods" – when first seen one is gobbing in the lake while their dog shits uncontrollably on the beach – and the brilliant location dressing of one of the youths' homes reveal that Watkins is not about to make specious parallels between poverty, poor parenting and feral kids.

The central sequence slips more into standard stalk'n'slash territory, with scenes of grimy torment that look curiously generic in the context of the decade's other horror outings and an escalation of the youths' criminality that finally nudges farce, like *BMX Bandits* (1983) gone wrong. Inspiration returns for the finale, in which a fleeing Jenny crashes (literally) a party in the nearby town, only to discover that in this community family comes first. *Eden Lake* plays at times like an updated **Straw Dogs**, but with a distinctive English sensibility that would have escaped Peckinpah. Jenny works as a primary-school teacher, highlighting the English obsession with seeing children as little angels or unsocialized demons, a division often made along class lines. Jenny and Steve are solidly middle-class, and the youths accosting them would seem emblematic of the "underclass", except that they aren't poor and they don't live in some rural backwater. Brett's house is large, clean and detached, even if it does have a hole punched through one of its internal doors. Brett, in an extraordinary performance by O'Connell, is simply a psychopath, a point highlighted in the devastating final sequence. For once Steve and Jenny should have listened to their satnav, which advised them: 'At your first opportunity, turn around.' *Not* recommended by the English tourist board.

BELOW: 'You stuck my dog!' Weekend campers suffer the consequences in **Eden Lake**

LÅT DEN RÄTTE KOMMA IN
AKA LET THE RIGHT ONE IN

2008, Swe, dir Tomas Alfredson, scr John Ajvide Lindqvist, starring Kåre Hedebrant, Lina Leandersson, Per Ragnar, Henrik Dahl

'80s Sweden. A man and a child move in next door to 12-year-old Oskar. Oskar lives with his mother and is being bullied at school. A string of local murders keeps him from venturing further than the playground but, when he meets Eli, his new neighbour, he is persuaded to fight back.

At first glance Alfredson's film seems to lack the useful disreputability of the genre's finest offerings, yet while it shares with international arthouse hits such as *El Orfanato / The Orphanage* (2007) and *Bakjwi / Thirst* (2009) a stately, reserved score and an accent on emotional response rather than outright terror, it's also surprisingly subversive for a horror film that your parents might see. The theme of childhood bullying underpins films as various as **Straw Dogs** and **The Texas Chain Saw Massacre**, but is rarely confronted directly. Even here the theme is filtered through genre tropes, but the bullying scenes are played straight in their convincing ugliness, and so is Oskar's response: he fantasizes about stabbing his tormentors and keeps a scrapbook of news reports of violent crimes.

The film's response is stronger and still further off-message, suggesting not only that Oskar should fight back but also that his aggressors deserve to be torn limb from limb. The film's treatment of male bonding is also unusual, although the implications of Oskar's relationship with Eli are subtle enough to pass under many radars. There isn't a single successful heterosexual pairing in the film – Oskar's parents are separated, Lacke prefers the company of his buddy Jocke to his partner Ginia, and Oskar soon discovers that Eli isn't kidding when his new friend says, 'I'm not a girl.' Elsewhere the film fits more squarely in the established vampire tradition: Eli is lonely, and wants to play like any normal (if geeky) 12-year-old, while the vampire recalls Bram Stoker's conception of Dracula as a disease-carrying immigrant.

Slyly humorous touches keep the film from slipping into po-faced seriousness, but what stays with the viewer after the credits roll is the power of individual scenes such as a body in a hospital bed that bursts into flames, Eli demonstrating why a vampire needs to be invited in and bullies getting a righteous comeuppance at the local pool, one of the few scenes of child killing in cinema ever to be greeted with audience applause.

LINKEROEVER / LEFT BANK

2008, Bel, dir/co-scr Pieter Van Hees, co-scr Christophe Dirickx, Dimitri Karakatsanis, starring Eline Kuppens, Matthias Schoenaerts, Sien Eggers, Marilou Mermans

Marie is a moody, cute professional runner whose immune system fails her just before an important tournament. Frustrated, she moves

BELOW: Lina Leandersson shows why vampires need to be invited in. **Låt Den Rätte Komma In**

out of her mother's home and into new boyfriend Bobby's apartment for a change of scene. Sinewy hunk Bobby is the dean of the ancient Flemish archers' guild and has the torso to prove it. Despite Marie's illness, she and Bobby enjoy bouts of raw, uncomplicated sex but when a neighbour tells her that the previous tenant disappeared, tensions emerge. Marie contacts the boyfriend of the missing woman and together they trawl the archives to uncover evidence of human sacrifice, fertility rites and dark mysteries connected to the site of the apartment block and to the distinctly Odinist archers' guild.

Meanwhile, a sinister, cavernous darkness is lurking in the building's basement and Marie's mother – an ageing hippy who senses the bad energy – is anxious for her daughter to move out. As Marie's condition worsens, she tells Bobby she wishes she could start her life all over again. Bobby, along with his archer friends and grandmother, conspires to to make her wish come true.

Van Hees has created a brooding, original film that squeezes the maximum atmosphere from every dank drizzling corner, and people and places are bathed in an infected, silvery grey light that makes you very grateful you don't live in Antwerp. Instead of the conventional horror formula of suspenseful shock edits, we are carried along by a

creeping, malign aesthetic and superb acting that builds to a powerful, bizarre and surprisingly moving climax.

The idea of nature as a voracious regenerative force of death and rebirth, which needs honouring with a sacrifice, has been explored in other films about paganism, such as **The Wicker Man**, but the rites practised in *Linkeroever* are far removed from dancing around the Maypole. Although the epilogue takes some logistical liberties, the overall feel of the film has a huge impact and conveys a deep understanding of what it is to be a doomed outsider yearning to return to the womb of the earth. "Every beginning is a new end." [KS]

MARTYRS

2008, Fr/Can, dir/scr Pascal Laugier, starring Morgana Alaoui, Mylène Jampanoï, Catherine Bégin, Robert Toupin

Lucie tracks down and kills the family she believes was responsible for her being abused as a child. Her friend Anna helps her dispose of the bodies, but Lucie is still tormented by a phantom oppressor. Anna fears that Lucie may have killed the wrong people, until she discovers a secret staircase leading to a basement where she finds another torture victim.

Mercilessly serious in intent and grim enough to carry it off, *Martyrs* is perhaps the most harrowing horror film of

---

BELOW: Morjana Alaoui prepares for another beating in **Martyrs**

the decade. It might bear surface similarities to **Hostel** in its exploration of a secret society dedicated to torture but there's no comic relief or gleeful vengeance here. Child abuse, suicide and the nastiest self-harm scenes since Peter Greene gave himself a manicure in **Clean, Shaven** only make a narrative which already plays like a long scream of rage and despair even more gruelling. It's astonishing that Laugier was able to realize such a relentlessly death-driven vision with such high production values. The violence is neither cathartic nor entertaining, and Anna's aggressors are entirely dispassionate and display no interest in her as a sexual being or individual. Early scenes with Lucie in the house are stomach-churning enough but there's something about the silent, impersonal beatings that makes them virtually unwatchable.

Like many of his Gallic peers, Laugier raises issues of race and fascism in an oblique commentary on the right-wing leanings of the Sarkozy regime. Lucie's ethnicity is Asian and Anna's is Middle Eastern, while their tormentors are upper-middle-class Caucasians who keep both their house and torture chamber spotlessly clean. More unusual is the theme of

transcendence through pain that finally takes centre stage. The group is searching for a martyr who can come into contact with what lies beyond death, and an extraordinary shot that pays homage to Dreyer's *La Passion de Jeanne d'Arc / The Passion of Joan of Arc* (1932) suggests that in Anna they have chosen well. Hardcore horror.

THE RUINS

2008, Aus/US, dir Carter Smith, scr Scott B. Smith, starring Jonathan Tucker, Jena Malone, Laura Ramsey, Shawn Ashmore

Two young American couples are coming to the end of their holiday in Mexico. They meet Mathias, a young German who offers to take them to a remote Mayan ruin, off the beaten track. The allure of seeing the "real" Mexico is too much to resist, but when they arrive at the ruins one of their party is shot and they are soon surrounded by gun-toting Mayans who are not about to let them leave.

The tourist horror films of the decade (see also **Turistas**) recall the Italian jungle cannibal cycle of the '70s in their mixture of tourist-board travelogue and rending of flesh, with the key difference being that where once such exotic locales were the preserve of anthropologists and fortune-hunters, now they are

---

ABOVE: Holidays from hell. Laura Ramsey and Jena Malone in **The Ruins**

more likely to be crawling with holidaymakers. And here they are fairly credible: the Americans speak hardly any Spanish, are inordinately worried about poor Mexican hygiene, are unprepared for an expedition (they have just two small bottles of water and a litre of tequila), they think you can solve any problem by waggling a handfuls of dollars at it and take photos of everything as a reflex response. Even when they realize why they've been corralled in, they're arrogant enough to try to escape.

There's a sense, as with the films' "urbanoia" predecessors, of displaced guilt here: for privilege, for the ability to take advantage of relative poverty abroad, and for the ability, crucially, to be *missed*. The odd behaviour of the vines choking the ziggurat, their red flowers recalling opium poppies while their leaves look suspiciously like the world's favourite weed, suggest another narrative of displacement – that the atrocities visited on indigenous communities and environments through the US-sponsored War on Plants have finally come home to roost.

While *The Ruins* succeeds in turning classic tourist anxieties into horror scenarios – note the linguistic and cultural incomprehension that leads to Dimitri being shot and the wormy, parasitical tendrils snaking under Stacey's skin – it's the presentation of the plants, both visual and auditory, that finally impresses. Not since the seedpods of **Invasion of the Body Snatchers** has chlorophyll been put to such terrifying use.

BELOW: Team-building the hard way in **Splinter**

SPLINTER

2008, US, dir Toby Wilkins, scr Ian Shorr, Kai Barry, starring Jill Wagner, Paulo Costanzo, Shea Whigham, Rachel Kerbs

CGI has been both boon and curse for the fantastic film genre: the freedom to show anything has resulted in largely formulaic creations that lack the weight of the real, while the jaw-dropping transformations of '80s effects extravaganzas like **The Thing** and **Videodrome** are today found only in SF and fantasy cinema. This makes *Splinter*'s back-to-basics mechanical effects a treat for anyone missing the giddy "what the f***" excitement of the '80s' finest moments. Playing like a stripped-down version of **The Mist**, *Splinter* locks three people in a gas station while something nasty tries to get in. As with the earlier film there's a nod to an eco-horror explanation – they are near an "experimental oil extraction" site – but *Splinter* is more concerned with showcasing its bristling human sea-urchin effects and exploring the shifting dynamic between its characters than providing pat explanations for what's going on.

Splinter draws on zombie lore, virus anxiety and monster movies as reanimated corpses shamble around with grotesquely contorted limbs, an infection comes from the titular splinter and spreads fast, and the contagion reassembles its victims' body parts for some misshapen fun. Yet while the spiny effects are impressive enough, the film is carried by Wagner, Costanzo and Whigham in the key roles. Seth (Costanzo), a doctoral student in biology, is on an abortive camping holiday with his girlfriend Polly (Wagner) when their car is stopped by Dennis (Whigham) and Lacy (Kerbs), a white trash couple on the run from the

police. Dennis is astonished by Seth's lack of practical nous: he can't drive or change a tyre, and his theorizing about the "parasitic mould" is dismissed as academic by Polly and Dennis, who bond over a plan to torch the surrounding forest to get help. But Seth's scientific background eventually comes in handy with a deliciously chilling self-sacrifice, and when Dennis needs some emergency medical attention the ice is finally broken. Few films can boast the line "It's OK, we'll cut your arm off!", but as *Splinter*'s characters soon discover it takes more than a Stanley knife to sever a limb.

AMER

2009, Fr/Bel, dir/scr Hélène Cattet, Bruno Forzani, starring Marie Bos, Delphine Brual, Harry Cleven, Bianca Maria D'Amato

Recycling has provided much material for the decade's horror films, from straightforward remakes of anything from the '70s and '80s with a recognizable name to period homages like *Grindhouse* (2007) and the films of Rob Zombie and Eli Roth. Homage has even been paid to early '80s American horror with *House of the Devil* (2009). *Amer* fits into this tradition with its meticulous recreation of the look, feel and sound of classic '70s *giallo* cinema, particularly the work of Dario Argento, but rises above it to create something utterly unique.

In the world of the *giallo* sexuality is aggressive and perverse, nobody can be trusted and a black-gloved killer lurks in the shadows. *Amer* takes the crude pop psychology usually offered as the throwaway motivation for these killers and plays it straight.

For Ana, seen through three sequences featuring key moments in childhood, adolescence and adulthood, the feverishly suspicious, sexually saturated *giallo* represents an accurate reflection of the world. The first sequence depicts the young Ana's response to the death of her grandfather and the sight of her parents having sex, which prompts a **Suspiria**-inflected psychic collapse. The second shows her as an adolescent, growing acutely aware of the interest she provokes in men when she's on holiday with her mother. And in the third she returns "amer" or bitter from a lifetime of intense, yet repressed, sexuality to the **Profondo Rosso**-style derelict home of her childhood.

Virtually dialogue and narrative-free, *Amer* plays like a distillation of the peak moments of surreal beauty from the *giallo* era without the convoluted plotting and kitsch fashions that pad out the original films. In its focus on rhythm rather than narrative, and willingness to blur the line between fantasy and reality, *Amer* also owes a nod to experimental cinema, although Cattet and Forzani's love of the trashy *giallo* aesthetic means that it's never a dry exercise in style.

ANTICHRIST

2009, Den/Ger/Fr/Swe/It/Pol, dir/scr Lars von Trier, starring Willem Dafoe, Charlotte Gainsbourg, Storm Acheche Sahlstrøm

No stranger to controversy, von Trier alienated critics yet again with *Antichrist*'s talking fox, scenes of graphic sexualized violence and a dedication to Tarkovsky that provoked howls of derision at its Cannes première. Distributors made the most of the fuss to rush *Antichrist* into cinemas, where it was promoted as a horror

BELOW: Charlotte Gainsbourg in Eden, **Antichrist**

film on the grounds of its themes of suffering, mutilation, witchcraft and Satan, all played out in a generic woodland setting. Von Trier set himself a high bar with the dedication, and it's tempting to see the film, especially in its later stages, as animated more by the spirit of John Waters in its excessive bad taste. However, the dedication reminds us that the metaphysical themes once explored by Tarkovsky have virtually vanished from art cinema, even if they are alive and well in the debased refuge of the horror film.

Now that the dust has settled, what's surprising about *Antichrist* is how tight and coherent most of it is, and the beauty and strangeness of some of its imagery. *Antichrist* is effectively a two-hander detailing the attempts of a couple (Dafoe and Gainsbourg are never named) to cope with grief after the death of their child. Shades of **Don't Look Now**, then, although von Trier's characters acquit themselves rather less well. The director has often been accused of misogyny and Gainsbourg is yet another of his women put through the wringer, though what's less often noted is the appalling behaviour of the men. Dafoe's therapist treats his partner as a medical subject throughout, his sketchpad diagrams and cheesy New Age slogans evidence of a woefully inadequate response to her grief. He patronisingly dismisses the inexplicable that she has experienced as merely the product of fear, inviting his own hallucination of a gnomic fox as a marker of his collapsing outlook.

Gainsbourg describes nature as "Satan's church", and her alignment with it is what he finally punishes. (Despite her fear of the woods she is actually better able to cope here than Dafoe, who

is troubled by visions that shatter his romanticized conceptions.) Such a schematic alignment of man with logic, rationality and control and woman with emotion, intuition and nature might seem facile, and once the leg-drilling, scissor-snapping violence starts the film dispenses with any pretensions to realism and loses much of its taut control. What we are left with is a set of extraordinary images including bodies draped around a dead tree in a Bosch tableau, hands curling around a massive root system as Dafoe and Gainsbourg desperately couple, the miraculous resurrection of a bird that resists all attempts to silence it and the parade of faceless children surrounding Dafoe as he attempts to leave the woods.

DØD SNØ
DEAD SNOW

2009, Nor, dir/co-scr Tommy Wirkola, co-scr Stig Frode Henriksen, starring Vegar Hoel, Stig Frode Henriksen, Charlotte Frogner, Lasse Valdal

A group of gung-ho medical students travels to a remote mountain hut for Easter. When they arrive their hostess is nowhere to be seen, and an obnoxious visitor reveals that the area was once the site of Nazi atrocities. They find a cache of World War II gold in the cellar, and dream of paying off their student loans – but its owners want it back.

Norway, whose film industry has long been overshadowed by its Scandinavian neighbours and the powerhouse of Denmark to the south, entered the genre fray with this modestly likeable splatstick caper. If you were hoping for dark pagan tales from the land of church burnings and black metal, look elsewhere: this is a fanboy gorefest firmly in the tradition of **The Evil Dead** and *Bad Taste* (1992), and one character even wears a **Braindead** T-shirt. There's not much in the way of a distinctively Norwegian flavour apart from the snowbound landscape and the ruddy-cheeked, absurdly healthy-looking students, probably a safer bet in terms of zombie dietary requirements than their Anglo or Italian peers: no nipping out for a crafty reefer here. But it's probably just this generic flavour that has led to its export success, and the minimal dialogue and comic, splashy effects mean it speaks the international language of limb-lopping. The presence of the Nazi, a perennial favourite in Euro villainy and here displayed in its **Shockwaves** zombie incarnation, doesn't hurt either. These Nazi zombies run (probably a logistical necessity north of the Arctic Circle), talk (although the opportunity for undead banter is missed) and seem more interested in untangling entrails than actually chowing down. There's no attempt to explain their

BELOW: Life in the freezer – after a fashion. **Død Snø**

survival in the Arctic fastness, but the bloody quarterings, head-splittings and eye gougings gloss over any plot holes, and it's refreshing to see zombies rise from the snow rather than their usual habitats – the graveyard and mortuary slab.

DRAG ME TO HELL

2009, US, dir/co-scr Sam Raimi, co-scr Ivan Raimi, starring Alison Lohman, Justin Long, Lorna Raver, Dileep Rao

In line for promotion and keen to impress her boss, Christine rejects an elderly woman's application for a loan extension on her mortgage. The woman later attacks her and rips off a coat button, using it to curse Christine with a demon. As the flies gather and shadowy claws scrabble at her door, Christine seeks professional help from a seer, Rham Jas, only to discover that if she hasn't appeased the demon or sicked it on someone else within three days, her soul is toast.

Raimi's first horror film since hitting A-list territory with the *Spider-Man* films harks back to a pre-**Evil Dead** era, particularly **Night of the Demon**, and plays at times like a live-action Tex Avery cartoon, down to the anvil plunging on an unsuspecting villain's head. This makes a refreshing change from the '70s plunderings and unrepentant brutality of much of the decade's genre output, while there's just about enough grit to keep horror fans amused. That's amused rather than disturbed because the accent is on gross comic horror, with several gummings from a gypsy hag highlighting an ongoing motif of mouths being used in all the wrong ways. The scare scenes are efficient enough if family-friendly, crowned by perhaps the finest séance in cinema, but the film's lasting pleasures are subtler. They include the delicious embarrassments of office politics and the ghastly trauma of meeting the parents, entertaining incidentals like the blackened and uneven hag dentures and sly digs at unscrupulous bankers, which would have struck a chord worldwide at the end of the decade.

Christine's curse comes less from her refusal of a loan extension than her response to being begged, which is to panic and call security. Still, she hardly deserves to be dragged to hell: our sympathies are firmly with her as soon as we see a photo of her chubby former self, Pork Queen at the 1995 Fair. The M.R. James tradition of excessive supernatural vengeance is evidently alive and well, even if it has to be filtered through a *Roadrunner* sensibility to appeal to a contemporary audience.

BELOW: The hag dentures are back in play. **Drag Me to Hell**

THE LOVED ONES

2009, Aust, dir/scr Sean Byrne, starring Xavier Samuel, Robin McLeavy, John Brumpton, Victoria Thaine

Handsome high-schooler Brent turns down a timid invitation from his classmate Lola to accompany her to the prom, but Lola is not as mousy as she pretends. Brent is soon trapped in a nightmare of madness and pain as sick Lola and her insane father extend a forcible invitation to party.

A taut, terrifying, gratifyingly visceral addition to the "tied-up-and-tortured" school of horror, *The Loved Ones* spends a while convincing you that it's a generic high school revenge story before cranking up the gore and putting its male lead through the sort of degrading physical horrors the genre used to reserve for female victims. Wisely, Brent is portrayed as a decent guy (in **Carrie** terms, he's more of a Tommy Ross than a Billy Nolan), which means we do not view Lola's violence with the moral get-out clause that the victim is a brute who deserves what he gets – as if anyone could really deserve what happens here. The focus is upon Robin McLeavy's brilliant performance as Lola, her daddy's little "Princess", who radiates festering spite and gleeful cruelty, served up with a side dish of belittling sarcasm. The nastiness is intense, drawing upon some especially sickening details of the Jeffrey Dahmer case (Dahmer poured drain fluid into a victim's brain to create a 'zombie' sex slave), and when we learn about

the previous victims of this evil "Princess" the film crosses the line between Grand Guignol splatter and the genuinely nightmarish. This is the first feature by Byrne and while it's ultimately just an exercise in terrorizing the audience, with little going on under the surface, it's still a tense and alarming shocker that announces the arrival of a promising new talent. [ST]

OKARUTO
AKA OCCULT

2009, Jap, dir/scr Kôji Shiraishi, starring Kôji Shiraishi, Shôhei Uno, Shinobu Kuribayashi, Yumi Yoshiyuki

After a man goes berserk at a remote Japanese beauty spot, killing two people and carving strange symbols on the flesh of a third, a documentary team led by Kôji Shiraishi decides to research the case in depth. The mutilated survivor, Shôhei Uno, reveals that ever since the attack he sees what he terms "miracles" wherever he goes; intrigued, Shiraishi lends him a camera to film them, with shattering consequences.

This is an engrossing variation on the camcorder documentary format, mixing the set-up of **The Blair Witch Project** with elements of Japanese folk myth and bang up-to-date urban atrocity. The appeal lies in the film's gradual expansion of its subject matter; what begins as a straightforward pseudo-documentary giddily expands to take in science fiction, supernatural weirdness and, in its extended third act, a brilliantly observed confrontation with the 21st century's pre-eminent social horror. Packed with intriguing detail, and acted with immaculate naturalism, *Okaruto* weaves an unpredictable path through topics including urban loneliness, professional insecurity, automatic writing, and the potent mystery of the Japanese landscape. The film takes a cue from the Belgian **C'est Arrivé Près de Chez Vous**, its strongest suit being the gradual corruption of the filmmakers' objectivity, signalled by the way one of them falls into step with the world-view of Shôhei, the disturbed survivor. Signs, symbols and portents coalesce around the documentary crew as their reality is besieged by Lovecraftian entities and the dangerous influence of Shôhei, who steers events towards an astounding and horrific conclusion.

I say "astounding", although some may quibble; *Okaruto* divides audiences with the oddity of its special effects, which are so eccentrically lo-fi they can provoke snorts of laughter. Many of Shôhei's "miracles", as caught on his camcorder, resemble the sort

LEFT: Brent (Xavier Samuel) finds that being the high school dreamboat has a downside in **The Loved Ones**.

of floating abstractions seen in the human eye when peering at a light source, and their incorporation is crude to say the least. You simply have to make a leap with the film and accept these homemade manifestations as real; they're the result of an enthusiastic desire to meld abstract animation concepts with live action. While one can't help but recall similar, better-budgeted films like **From Beyond**, it's really worth accepting these defiantly cut-price trans-dimensional monsters. Even if you can't, make sure you experience the film's dread-soaked final reel, as Shôhei prepares for action, convinced he's under the orders of a higher power. [ST]

THE ROAD

2009, US, dir John Hillcoat, scr Joe Penhall, starring Viggo Mortensen, Kodi Smit-McPhee, Robert Duvall, Charlize Theron

Two nameless survivors of an unexplained catastrophe, a man and his 10-year-old son, trudge through a dust-swathed landscape foraging for food and clothing. They must fight off murderous attacks from other survivors, and resist the twin spiritual threats of cynicism and despair.

While not quite as harrowing as Cormac McCarthy's novel on which it is based, the film is a sensitive, respectful adaptation of a modern masterpiece that retains much of McCarthy's intention without corrupting it with Hollywood sentiment. Although the iron grip of the original is allowed to relax here and there, Mortensen is perfect as the taciturn survivor focused solely upon the future of his son, and Kodi Smit-McPhee is thankfully devoid of the syrupy child-actor sweetness that could have been unbearably mawkish. Hillcoat maintains McCarthy's studied refusal to explain the apocalypse; instead, the absence of information emphasizes the enormity of events. It suggests a fall into the void, as represented by the dead vegetation and collapsing forests; the excellent sound design adds the distant crunch of colossal subsidence in the background of night-time scenes. Faced with this ultimate calamity, we see the human animal reduced to its crudest characteristics, and it's not a pretty sight. Cannibalism, murder, the sacrifice of community in favour of devil-take-the-hindmost survivalism – these are revealed as the bones beneath the decaying flesh of civilization. Yet there burns a tiny flame of resistance: in an otherwise Stygian moral darkness, Mortensen's protection of his son is a radiant statement of love and selflessness. There are certainly flaws, but from the jolting terror of the cannibal cellar scene to the subtle horror of an old man's response to an invitation to eat with the man and his son ("What do I have to do?"), *The Road* is a gruelling exploration of a world in trauma while also offering a passionate affirmation of life. [ST]

22 MEI
AKA 22ND OF MAY

2010, Bel/Neth, dir/scr Koen Mortier, starring Sam Louwyck, Jan Hammenecker, Barbara Callewaert, Titus De Voogdt

After a suicide bomb attack on a shopping centre kills dozens of people, Sam, a security guard, blames himself for not preventing the atrocity. Tormented and lonely, he encounters the spirits of those who were killed in the blast, including the perpetrator.

Koen Mortier's *22 Mei* is an emotionally restrained but cumulatively wrenching study of guilt. The film approaches one of the most appalling phenomena of modern times more in sorrow than in anger, exploring sensational material through a shifting prism of multiple realities and supernatural visions. Various characters caught up in the horror agonize over their failure to stop it, none more so than Sam, whose heroism immediately after the blast (he pulls several mutilated people from the rubble) turns to blind panic when he witnesses a man crushed to death by falling masonry. Running away, he enters a hallucinatory netherworld in which tragic events from his past interweave with visions of the recently dead.

22 Mei's take on "the land beyond" is staunchly matter-of-fact; no twinkling lights, leering demons or angelic choruses. Those killed in the blast react to their deaths by re-visiting the day in question, trying to interrogate or dissuade the killer. The victims include a customer prone to masturbating in changing cubicles, a children's photographer and his rabbit-costumed friend, and an off-duty cop who unwittingly influenced the perpetrator, and all find themselves in an eerily depopulated cityscape, one that is agonizingly close to the real world. The film is ultimately more concerned with the sorrow of death than the trauma; although the grim-faced bomber initially refuses to engage with the fury or puzzlement of his victims, we soon realize that tragedy underpins even his wretched character. A genuinely eerie film, confronting the darkest of contemporary topics, *22 Mei* ends with an astonishing sequence merging beauty and horror to reach a Buddhist acceptance of death's inevitability. [ST]

THE KILLER INSIDE ME

2010, US, dir Michael Winterbottom, scr John Curran , starring Casey Affleck, Kate Hudson, Jessica Alba, Chester Conway

Once the appeal of Jasons and Jigsaws begins to pall, we may ask ourselves what sort of killer is really to be feared in the world. The answer, as delivered in this brutal and affecting adaptation of Jim Thompson's 1952 novel of the same name, is the sort who makes his victims love him. It's a fact that men who abuse women inside relationships are often shielded by the abused; *The Killer Inside Me* dares to portray that ugly, frustrating truth. On its release it attracted angry responses from people who resisted its portrait of female masochism, and it's certainly a film that will have you yelling at the screen for the characters to wake up and realize what they're doing. However, nothing in the characterization of homicidal lawman Lou Ford, or the women he destroys, exceeds the boundaries of truth.

The Killer Inside Me is a near-perfect examination of the detachment of a clinical psychopath. For Lou, other people are just props to be shuffled around to maintain a desirable fiction of which he is both author and star. The fact that he functions perfectly well as a deputy sheriff, only running into difficulties when the complexity of his schemes arouses suspicion, is a vital assertion that not all psychopaths are degenerate loners. He has it all: a prestige role in society, beautiful women who find him desirable, the respect and devotion of his peers. The fact that he has been conning everyone underlines the dangerous plausibility of the psychopath.

There is an alternative reading of the film: Lou himself is reporting the story, and a psychopath is, of course, the ultimate unreliable narrator. So the women in Lou's life, who seem so terribly pliable and forgiving, may simply reflect Lou's self-serving perspective. This is a coherent possibility, but I like it less; it requires so little of us, whereas the notion that some women accept punishment from charismatic boyfriends because of defects in their character is a tougher intellectual burden, with further-reaching social implications. A cautious reading might accept both views.

The skill of the film is misdirection. It sets out as a period noir thriller, somewhere between *L.A. Confidential* and *Blood Simple*, then proceeds to hurtle down a dark highway we could never have anticipated. Affleck is extraordinary, and takes enormous risks: thanks to him, Lou is damnably sexy and charismatic, combining the amoral allure of the baby-faced bad boy and the confident authority of the lawman. Yet in a scene that goes beyond anything served up outside the rarefied world of gore-for-gore's-sake, we see him beat a woman to an unrecognizable pulp, after which we gaze in disgust at that same handsome face as it whispers tissue-thin apologies. *The Killer Inside Me* is one of the most persuasive portraits of human destructiveness in modern cinema. [ST]

ABOVE: Jessica Alba and Casey Affleck exuding neo-noir seductiveness in **The Killer Inside Me**.

RED WHITE & BLUE

2010, US/UK, dir/scr Simon Rumley, starring Amanda Fuller, Noah Taylor, Marc Senter, Jon Michael Davis

Texas: Erica spends her evenings trawling blue-collar bars, picking up men for unsafe sex; Nate, her neighbour, is a sociopath who nurtures a rare emotional attraction to her; Franki is a guitarist in a punk band who discovers he's HIV-positive after casual sex with Erica. When Franki seeks revenge, the three become horribly enmeshed in each other's lives.

Cool where other films of this sort tend towards melodrama, unflinchingly lucid in its depiction of the depths to which people can sink, focusing relentlessly on character while delivering some of the roughest scenes of torture and home invasion in the genre, *Red White & Blue* is a gruelling but intensely moving work of high intelligence and humanity. There are not many films out there that deserve to be held up alongside **Henry: Portrait of a Serial Killer**, but this is one of them. It's unsettling from the very beginning, as we witness Erica seducing a string of one-night stands, then joylessly extricating herself from their arms and moving on; when she deliberately goads a man not to use a condom, we suspect the worst. Her story parallels the 2006 case of Sarah Jane Porter, a London hairdresser who set out to infect a string of men after contracting HIV, but writer-director Rumley deliberately muddies the water by giving everyone emotional complications that resist simple classification. While never descending into apologia, nuanced scripting creates a complex lattice of empathy and revulsion, forcing us to engage with the characters as human beings. Even Nate, whose opening gambit with Erica is to tell her about the animals he tortured as a child, is given subtle and compelling gradations. When he snaps, in the film's terrifying later scenes, we are witnessing the grotesque actions of a damaged human being, not the wickedness of an unknowable demon; it's this that makes the film distressing.

The acting honours go to British actor Noah Taylor as Nate, whose haunting eyes, raddled sense of dignity and laconic self-awareness (plus flawless Texan accent) make him a fascinating, fearsome creation. Amanda Fuller's portrayal of the emotionally dislocated Erica induces a bewildering mixture of loathing and pity; only Marc Senter's Franki is less than convincing. At times heartbreaking (the fate of Franki's mother), or almost unbearably grim (the terrorizing of a child caught in the crossfire is as dark as it gets in the genre), *Red White & Blue* is the work of a major new filmmaking talent. [ST]

SRPSKI FILM
AKA A SERBIAN FILM

2010, Ser, dir/co-scr Srdjan Spasojevic, co-scr Aleksandar Radivojevic, starring Srdjan Todorovic, Sergej Trifunovic, Jelena Gavrilovic, Slobodan Bestic

Milos, a retired porn star, is persuaded by intellectual auteur Vukmir to return to the screen. Agreeing to participate in an experimental art-porn blow-out, Milos is subsequently drugged, abused, and tricked into a series of escalating atrocities.

The cinematic equivalent of a pub drunk trying to punch you in the guts, this simultaneously horrific and absurd film aims to stake out its territory at the furthest edge of what can be shown, but ends up swinging short of the mark. By employing all the gizmos and stylistic quirks of modern horror (pounding techno-industrial music, speeded-up motion, neurotically athletic camerawork), it brandishes a show-off stylishness that unwittingly sabotages the extreme horror; it tries to thrust nightmarishly grubby images into your mind but fumbles like an over-enthusiastic teenager. That's not to say the film is without appeal; just that the achievement is nowhere near as appalling as it would like to be.

It is the story of a legendary porn stud sucked into an escalating nightmare of degradation, but one thing no one can accuse the film of is pandering to misogyny and celebrating the phallus. Male potency is not so much celebrated as forced into grotesque pantomime. Such matters recede in the memory, however, thanks to the inclusion of material depicting the sexual exploitation of children, and, in one especially gross sequence, a

newborn baby. But while the intent is to shock by depicting what has not been shown before, one has to say that British TV comedy got there first (see Chris Morris's *Brass Eye* parody of Eminem's appeal to pre-teen audiences, which not only shocked but had a genuine moral point to make). Far too much of what we see in *A Serbian Film* is conveyed with a head-banging celebration of its own transgressiveness; no one involved seems to have understood that if you try too hard to outrage people, the neediness cushions the impact. What's required is a strategy, if not a philosophy – and no, the nihilistic posturing of Vukmir doesn't count.

What *A Serbian Film* does have to its credit is colossal vitality. It's an "extreme sports" version of horror, pumped up on sweat, steroids and speed. Its bull-in-a-china-shop approach is energizing and amusing, and there's something to be said for its Tasmanian-devil vigour. Kinetic power apart, however, it trips over its feet. Much has been made of the film's national provenance by director Spasojevic, who claims that it's a cry of pain and anger at the parlous state of his country. Well, if you believe that you'll probably believe that Sergio Garrone's *SS Experiment Camp* (1976) is an impassioned attack on the slumbering dragon of European fascism, or Hideshi Hino's *Guinea Pig 2: Flower of Flesh and Blood* (1985) is an exposé of feudal aristocratic values in modern Japanese society. Anyone who makes a film this sensationalistic, so high on its own grotesque shock effects, should take a good long look at Elem Klimov's *Come and See* (1985) and comprehend the difference between horror as political commentary and the mining of one's sordid obsessions for the sake of notoriety. [ST]

SHUTTER ISLAND

2010, US, dir Martin Scorsese, scr Laeta Kalogridis, starring Leonardo DiCaprio, Mark Ruffalo, Ben Kingsley, Max Von Sydow

U.S. Marshal Teddy Daniels finds terrors from his past rising to the surface when he investigates a missing murderess at an asylum for the criminally insane.

Martin Scorsese has hovered at the boundaries of the horror genre before, in *Taxi Driver, After Hours* and *Cape Fear,* but *Shutter Island* is the closest thing yet to an out-and-out horror film from this titan of the cinema. Based on a novel by Denis Lehane, the film takes madness as its topic, here decked out with all of the trappings of the "scary asylum" sub-genre: the threat of wrongful incarceration, the fear that insanity might be contagious, the possibility that those entrusted with caring for the mad might themselves be dangerously unbalanced. Scorsese revels in Expressionist visual touches, leaving us uncertain as to whether the extreme hostility of the weather and the dank cavernous basement of Ward C are truly as appalling as we're seeing or are somehow indicative of the fevered state of mind of the protagonist. DiCaprio is excellent in a role that exploits his persistent aura of "a boy in a man's job" which sometimes compromises him elsewhere, and he's pitted against two of the most imposing presences in the acting profession: Ben Kingsley and Max Von Sydow. Both provide that exquisite brand of polite, modulated menace which suggests danger behind the most seemingly innocuous of comments.

Before we can say anything about *Shutter Island*, it must be noted that we're dealing with an unreliable narrator. Figuring out just how unreliable, and to what extent he's being manipulated by the people around him, is the crux of the film. Paranoia is the dominant psychological motif, embracing CIA mind-control, Nazi medical experiments and secretly administered hallucinogens. There are many powerful and intense sequences, although one may raise an eyebrow at the depiction of concentration camp victims, seen during flashbacks to Daniels' war experience: these are historically accurate and yet, because they're photographed with a patina of artful stylization, somehow rather tasteless. Far better is the gloomy grandeur of the central location itself, as windswept and rain-lashed as the fashion-house in Mario Bava's **Sei Donne per l'Assassino,** and equally filled with duplicity. *Shutter Island* is ultimately a B-movie wearing a heavy overcoat of seriousness, but it's immaculately crafted, beautiful to look at, and signs off with an ending that's open to a discomfiting range of interpretations. [ST]

MICHAEL

2011, Aus, dir/scr Markus Schleinzer, starring Michael Fuith, David Rauchenberger, Christine Kain, Ursula Strauss

Just when you thought Michael Haneke had cornered the market in Austrian bleakness, along comes this painstakingly naturalistic study of a paedophile who keeps a 10-year-old boy locked in his cellar. Drawing upon the nightmarish cases of Josef Fritzl (an Austrian who kept his daughter Elisabeth in a tiny basement for 24 years) and Wolfgang Priklopil (an Austrian who abducted the 10-year-old Natascha Kampusch), *Michael* takes the viewer close to some of the most vile and horrific aspects of human behaviour. That it does so with quiet, calculated detachment serves two purposes: to give the viewer insight into the mind of someone who could do such things, and to ensure that the film does not become exploitative or simply impossible to watch. That said, it comes very close to the latter; scenes in which little Wolfgang

is left imprisoned for an undisclosed amount of time with only candy to eat, whilst his abductor goes off on a skiing holiday with two acquaintances, are ghastly in the subtle pressure they inflict. A television news report features the mother of a missing child stressing to the camera, with grim helplessness, that it's the uncertainty that tortures her most. Schleinzer uses precisely the agony of uncertainty at three pivotal moments in the film, turning the screws on the viewer's already screaming nerves.

It's in the nature of such an appalling story that what goes on when the abductor turns out the lights and climbs into the child's bed should remain unseen. Like Haneke's *Funny Games*, a lot of the horror occurs off-camera, yet the thought of it festers in the audience's mind like a splinter lodged out of reach. There are scenes here that can induce tears of anger, such is the relentless psychological cruelty of the scenario. For instance, the abductor attempts to procure a second boy, ostensibly as a "companion" for the first, and we see Wolfgang waiting on his newly fitted bunk bed, which he has decorated with crêpe-paper stars in anticipation of company in his hellish prison. *Michael* triggers feelings of furious, helpless compassion that many will find hard to process; suffice to say it's probably as challenging an experience as one is ever likely to see on the subject of paedophile abduction. [ST]

THE HUMAN CENTIPEDE 2 (FULL SEQUENCE)

2011, US, dir/scr Tom Six, starring Laurence R. Harvey, Ashlynn Yennie, Vivien Bridson, Bill Hutchens

The first *Human Centipede* (2009) never really left behind a reassuring sense of "normal moviemaking" – and this, despite the repulsive central concept, rendered the horror safely distant. Thankfully, director Tom Six ups his game for the sequel, first of all draining the colour to grubby black and white, then setting the story in the shabbiest backstreets of London, and best of all, replacing the first film's more conventionally camp "mad doctor" with Martin, a grotesque butterball weirdo resembling a Terry Gilliam cartoon of retarded depravity. The masterstroke is to make him an obsessive fan of the first film; we see him masturbating to it on his laptop at the desk of the multi-storey car park where he works. Filled with slobbering admiration, and deranged enough to want to imitate his favourite movie, Martin embarks on one of the most hilariously impractical homages in movie history; indeed, with its sarcastic digs at the notion of copycat violence *The Human Centipede 2* plays like a sustained raspberry in the face of censorship, which makes its current heavily cut DVD status all the more bitterly amusing. Six's scabrous comic vision of British life is a scuzzy parade of Monty Python dragon-mothers, sleazy child-molesting doctors and obnoxious fascist fatheads. (Brownie points too for making one of the victims-to-be a viewer of the first film who sobbingly knows what's coming.) Capping it all is the astonishing Laurence R. Harvey, who brings to the screen a character so comically depraved he might have stepped out of a *Viz* cartoon (most likely "The Bottom Inspectors"). The one great pity is that Six abandons the idea of Martin being unable to imitate the first film: for a while, as he tries to patch faces to buttocks with an industrial staple-gun, the likelihood of dismal failure looms; instead of surgical precision just a ragged bloody train-wreck that won't hang together. Perhaps Six was afraid that this would be how reviewers would describe the film, because Martin ultimately succeeds, albeit making rather more of a mess than the original. From its hilariously awful images of London (even the rain is black) to the string of gargoyle victims and disgusting family dynamics, this is a sustained assault on good taste that may be incredibly shallow but has the ability to make you gasp at the sheer comic ugliness of it all. [ST]

SNOWTOWN

2011, Aust, dir/co-scr Justin Kurzel, co-scr Shaun Grant, starring Daniel Henshall, Lucas Pittaway, Louise Harris, Matthew Howard

Sixteen-year-old Jamie and his brothers Alex and Nicholas live with their divorced mother Elizabeth in a run-down Adelaide suburb. Elizabeth begins a relationship with John, a cheerful fellow who initially seems like the answer to the family's prayers. However, John gradually reveals his dark side, stoking and encouraging the resentment, paranoia and homophobia of those around him and encouraging Jamie into progressively more extreme and horrendous acts of violence.

Based on the real-life case of Australian serial killer John Bunting, and filmed on locations near to where the murders took place, *Snowtown* is a dauntingly horrific tour-de-force. It excels as both a portrait of a troubled family unit struggling at the fringes of society and a depiction of the pernicious influence one man can have over the moral choices of others. Central to its power is Daniel Henshall, whose chilling portrayal of John Bunting is utterly naturalistic and devoid of cliché. Instead of explosive rage and beetling brows, he has a smiling but relentless persistence that demands agreement under cover of a "best mate" persona. While the story bears similarities to Joseph Ruben's *The Stepfather* (1986) in its depiction of a psychopathic father figure, *Snowtown*

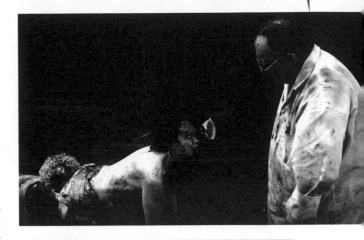

ABOVE: Martin (Laurence R. Harvey) surveys his handiwork in **The Human Centipede 2**.

is no tongue-in-cheek satire but something far more painful and real. This is a killer who draws cynically upon the prejudice and pain of those around him to further his vicious agenda; knowing that Jamie has been the subject of advances from a local pederast, and indeed the victim of sexual abuse within his family, he exploits the situation to entangle the boy in a torture and murder pact that spirals way beyond retribution. Utilizing a semi-improvised approach, halfway between Larry Clark and Mike Leigh, Kurzel reveals Bunting's true colours during chaotic round-table discussions involving Jamie's family and their "white trash" neighbours, with John constantly needling the others to support his aggressive hatred of sex offenders and drug-addicts. What begins as the sort of "sounding off" that many would consider normal is revealed, in gut-churning scenes that test the viewer's ability to keep watching, to be a front for John's sickening lust for violence; moral outrage is merely the licence he gives himself to commit atrocities. The film's significant achievement is to take the viewer from a position of nodding complicity to the realization that here is a vile human being who thrives on the moral acquiescence of others. [ST]

THE WOMAN

2011, US, dir/co-scr Lucky McKee, co-scr Jack Ketchum, starring Pollyanna McIntosh, Sean Bridgers, Angela Bettis, Lauren Ashley Carter

Chris Cleek is a bland fellow on the surface, but in reality he's a psychopathic bully who rules his family with a rod of iron. While on a hunting trip, he finds a feral woman living rough in the woods and decides to capture her, keeping her tied up in an outhouse. Cleek sets about breaking her spirit and training her for sexual and domestic servitude.

On one level this is a splatter film from the "tied-up-and-tortured" school of modern horror. Far more interesting, however, is the underlying theme of family, an arena in which a man can inflict constant pain without the need to tie up his victims. Based on a novel by Jack Ketchum, *The Woman* asks just how far a family will go to accommodate the depravity of its figurehead, and it comes up with some very disturbing answers. While the agent of change is the feral woman, the real focus of the story is the family unit, specifically a family under the rule of an oppressive father. Certainly, when the wife stands up to her husband and receives a devastating punch in the face, we understand that it represents all the force and tyranny exerted on women in abusive marriages, condensed into a single horrific splat. The fearful saucer-eyed daughter is plausibly a child just hanging on in there until she's old enough to get away, and the son's defiantly knuckle-headed mimicry of his father provides another terrible indictment of patriarchal family dynamics. However, the power of the film resides in the way it problematizes our sympathy: the things we learn in the final reel make excuses hard to sustain, as we finally understand just how far down the road to hell the family has allowed itself to wander. Also under the spotlight is the sanctity and privacy of family, a principle so insulated against criticism that parents often express outrage at the idea that a mere teacher (who probably spends more time with their children than they do) might "interfere" and "poke their nose in" to the hallowed halls of home. The scene in which a visiting teacher tries to inform Chris that his daughter is pregnant is a tour-de-force of simmering danger. After watching *The Woman*, one begins to wonder if the Israeli Marxist concept of the kibbutz might not be for the best after all. [ST]

V/H/S

2012, US: "Tape 56" dir Adam Wingard, scr Simon Barrett, starring Calvin Reeder; "Amateur Night" dir/co-scr David Bruckner, co-scr Nicholas Tecosky, starring Hannah Fierman; "Second Honeymoon" dir/scr Ti West, starring Joe Swanberg; "Tuesday the 17th" dir/scr Glenn McQuaid, starring Norma C. Quinones; "The Sick Thing That Happened to Emily When She Was Younger" dir Joe Swanberg, scr Simon Barrett, starring Helen Rogers; "10/31/98" dir/scr Radio Silence, starring Chad Villella

Tired of repetitive camcorder opuses burdening the horror market in the wake of **Paranormal Inactivity**? If so, it's worth making an exception for *V/H/S*, which circumvents the greatest downside of the format (swathes of dead air masquerading as suspense) by offering six short stories in one package. Yes, it's a resurrection of the much-loved portmanteau format; **Tales from the Crypt** and **Creepshow** for the shaky-cam generation. Hustling along so swiftly that you don't

---

BELOW: Girls just wanna have fun; Hannah Fierman in the **V/H/S** segment "Amateur Night".

have time to get sick of one idea before another lurches into view, it's a chance to savour multiple solutions to the genre's limitations. Once Segment I has established the wraparound characters, we're plunged into Segment 2, David Bruckner's "Amateur Night", which homes in on three beer-swilling jocks enjoying a boys' night out, picking up girls in a bar before heading off to a cheap motel for an orgy. Stoned and drunk and hopelessly horny, no one notices that one of the girls is a little too intense, an oversight that leads to a gratifyingly grisly bloodbath and an encounter with a deeply weird vampire, whose feeding habits are so enthusiastically messy she deserves a whole feature. Segment 3 eschews the supernatural for a creepy incursion into a couple's second honeymoon that reveals nastiness closer to home; Segment 4 takes the greatest risks, being an implausible tale of a technological/supernatural serial killer who can only be seen in video drop-out, while Segment 5 gives us respite from queasy camerawork by focusing on a relationship conducted via Skype, in which a lonely woman is talked through spooky visitations by her absent, curiously calm boyfriend. Then it's back to hand-held camera for the 6th segment, a Halloween special that sees a bunch of teenage goofballs stumble into a devilish house of horrors far in excess of their joke-store expectations.

Mercifully quick on its feet, *V/H/S* avoids the claustrophobic experience of being trapped with the same bunch of reality-cam dullards for 90 minutes, and there's enough exuberant invention to make the film admirable for more than just brevity. We're still doomed to spend time with people who screech "Oh my god! Oh my god!" or "What the fuck? What the fuck?" and run from mortal danger with the camera diligently pointed at the stuff we need to see, and the eye grows inevitably weary of the blurry image quality and hectic shaking around. But if the medium insists on screwing with the message, at least the messages are conveyed with wit and concision. Also of note is the persistence of supernatural subject matter in the camcorder sub-genre; the unglamorous glare of videotape is constantly being exhorted to yield metaphysics, the pressure of too much reality creating a (futile?) desire for transcendence. If all we end up seeing is the machine in the ghost, it's nevertheless an indication that "other realms of existence" retain their appeal in a post-technological media age. [ST]

MAMA

2013, Sp/Can, dir/co-scr Andy Muschietti, co-scr Barbara Muschietti, co-scr Neil Cross, starring Jessica Chastain, Nikolaj Coster-Waldau, Megan Charpentier, Isabelle Nélisse

Having shot his ex-wife, a deranged man collects his two baby daughters and drives off with them. After crashing the car, he drags the kids to a dilapidated cabin and prepares to commit that most odious of family bonding rituals, the parental murder-suicide. Just in time, a weird supernatural entity snatches him away. Five years later, the girls are found by a search party, and when they speak, they refer constantly to someone called "Mama". This is the entity who's been looking after them all this time, and she's very possessive.

The latest film to arrive with Guillermo del Toro's name attached as producer is by no means an embarrassment, but its slumberous, tasteful rhythms and thoroughly respectable mainstream stylings are about as gripping as blancmange. The film scores highly with its gangling monster, but since she's the ghost of an unfortunate mad woman who just happened to fall off the ugly tree and (literally) hit a branch on the way down, I don't suppose we should really be calling her a "monster" at all – not if we want to parade the sort of sensitive adult emotions the film so desperately wishes to evoke. Sadly, the closest thing to an adult story here is thrown away at the start with the children's psychotic father. What follows, as two-dimensionally virtuous Uncle Luke and his equally improbable rock chick wife Annabel grow to love and cherish the two semi-feral girls, is almost surreally featureless. He is played by Nikolaj Coster-Waldau with all the charisma of a stainless-steel toast rack, and she's introduced while celebrating a negative pregnancy result, which means, as night follows day, that in a film called *Mama* she's going to end up with her maternal hormones oozing all over the place by the final reel.

The strange, spidery little girls are a different matter; the film could profitably have spent most of its time with them. I would happily let the adults blur into the background so that we might get to know better these odd, animalistic kids who find themselves torn between the blandishments of bourgeois comfort and the strange febrile fairytale they've been living in for five years. Likewise, the eponymous Mama has a backstory that deserves more than the (admittedly well-orchestrated) dream-cum-mental-projection scene it receives. It would also liven the film up no end if it were crossbred with the plot of the disturbing camcorder horror flick *Home Movie* (2008), in which irritating parents are menaced and eventually tortured to death by their progressively creepier and more hostile children. Instead, *Mama* opts for a resolution that's part Disney, part Tim Burton. The madness that exploded the family unit in the early scenes is dismissed, while the rock chick's wings are clipped to ensure another generation of conformity. [ST]

INDEX

Note: page numbers in **bold** refer to main film entries.